UNL🔗CK

Second Edition

1–5

Listening, Speaking & Critical Thinking

Reading, Writing & Critical Thinking

TEACHER'S MANUAL AND DEVELOPMENT PACK

Chris Sowton
with Peter Lucantoni, Jessica Williams,
Kate Adams, Michele Lewis and Sabina Ostrowska

CAMBRIDGE
UNIVERSITY PRESS

CAMBRIDGE
UNIVERSITY PRESS

University Printing House, Cambridge CB2 8BS, United Kingdom

One Liberty Plaza, 20th Floor, New York, NY 10006, USA

477 Williamstown Road, Port Melbourne, VIC 3207, Australia

314–321, 3rd Floor, Plot 3, Splendor Forum, Jasola District Centre, New Delhi – 110025, India

79 Anson Road, 06–04/06, Singapore 079906

Cambridge University Press is part of the University of Cambridge.

It furthers the University's mission by disseminating knowledge in the pursuit of education, learning and research at the highest international levels of excellence.

www.cambridge.org
Information on this title: www.cambridge.org/9781108678728

© Cambridge University Press 2019

First published 2019

20 19 18 17 16 15 14 13 12 11 10 9 8 7 6 5 4

Printed in Italy by Rotolito S.p.A.

A catalogue record for this publication is available from the British Library

ISBN 978-1-108-67872-8 Teacher's Manual and Development Pack

CONTENTS

UNLOCK
TEACHER'S MANUAL AND DEVELOPMENT PACK

Unlock your teaching potential

We've carried out research with teachers across the world to understand their needs and how we can better meet them with *Unlock* Second Edition. The result is an all-new Teacher's Manual and Development Pack.

A single manual for levels 1–5, so that every answer key and additional activity are conveniently in one book.

Better Teaching WITH UNLOCK SECOND EDITION

BE CONFIDENT

Support your teaching with the **flexible lesson plans** with **timings** for every unit.

READING 2

⏱ 60 min

Reading 2 is another reading text on the unit topic, often in a different format to Reading 1. It serves as a model for the Writing task (in terms of style, structure and format, but not length) and gives students additional exposure to, and practice with, language and reading skills, while helping them generate and refine ideas for their Writing Task.

1 PREPARING TO READ

PURPOSE

- To prepare students to understand the content of the text
- To help students anticipate content, using visuals and prior knowledge
- To introduce and build key academic and topical vocabulary for the Reading and for the Writing Task

Encourage students to complete the pre-reading activities in this section in pairs or small groups, to provide support and peer encouragement. Circulate among the students, taking notes of common strengths and areas of difficulty. Once students have completed the activities, check for understanding and offer clarification, paying particular attention to any problem areas you noted. If you wish to extend the vocabulary activity in this section, elicit other word forms of the key vocabulary.

BE FLEXIBLE

Decide when to use the **optional activities** to extend your students' learning and provide **differentiation** to meet individual students' needs.

Be flexible

👥 Ask students to take roles from the script and read it aloud together, using correct sentence stress.

Before they do this, allow **lower-level students** to listen again and mark the script for stress.

BE FOCUSED

Understand the **learning objectives** for every lesson, so you and your students can be clear on what you're achieving.

Learning objectives

- Evaluate the effectiveness of interview questions against a set of criteria
- Create a list of questions for a research interview
- Evaluate and refine your questions for a research interview

BE INFORMED

Refer to **Common student errors** boxes highlighting the challenges your students might meet with the target language, informed by our exclusive Corpus research. This information is downloadable from e-Source for each Student's Book.

⊙ Common student errors

Japanese, Chinese and Spanish L1 students tend to confuse the order of adjectives and nouns. This is because the adjective comes after the noun in their L1.

- *I went to the bank to discuss my plan business.*
- *You need to have a partner business you can trust.*

BE BETTER

Access the broad range of *Unlock*-specific **teacher development material** whenever it suits you.

UNL⌀CK TEACHER DEVELOPMENT

BE INFORMED

→ **Choosing relevant information** is an important skill for students because: (1) It is the next logical stage of the research and writing process (after categorizing information); (2) They might think that all research information has the same value and importance, which is clearly not true; (3) A problem area when writing essays is including irrelevant information which does not answer the question.

BE CONFIDENT

→ Develop this skill for yourself by doing the following activity:

Look at the website for your educational institution. Think about whether there is any information which is not relevant. Why is it not relevant?

INSIGHT

Our research tells us that 93% of teachers believe their students want to develop their critical thinking skills, yet only 18% of teachers have had specific training on how to support their students with this.

CONTENT

Teacher development material, on developing critical thinking skills in your students, available in every unit.

RESULTS

Teachers are more confident and better equipped in supporting students as they develop their critical thinking skills. Students are better prepared for their academic studies.

UNLOCK SECOND EDITION TEACHER DEVELOPMENT

We have reviewed research and reports on teacher development around the world to identify features of teacher development that have been critical for success. There are seven principles which derive from the research, and we've kept these at the heart of *Unlock* Second Edition teacher development.

So that teacher development can be successful, it needs to be:

INSPIRE

IMPACTFUL	Impactful, so that you can see the difference in your teaching and the difference in your students' learning. There is a teacher development objective for every unit of *Unlock* Second Edition, with the opportunity to review it. There are also peer lesson observation templates, so that you can see the impact in your classroom.
NEEDS-BASED	Needs-based, so that it is useful and relevant to you and your students' teaching and learning context. One of the elements of teacher development material in *Unlock* Second Edition is focused on developing critical thinking skills in your students, because we know there is a strong link between critical thinking and academic success.
SUSTAINED	Sustained, so that you can build on your teaching skills in the same way your students build on their language skills. There is teacher development material in every unit of the Teacher's Manual and Development Pack.
PEER-COLLABORATIVE	Peer-collaborative, so that you can share your development with other teachers. There are a range of ideas on how you can achieve this in *Unlock*, including peer-to-peer teacher training material.
IN-PRACTICE	In-practice, so that you can apply your learning immediately in the classroom and foster a deeper understanding of what works for your students. *Unlock* Second Edition teacher development material is directly linked to students' course material.
REFLECTIVE	Reflective, so that you can develop an awareness of your teaching and then make changes. There are self-reflection questions throughout the manual.
EVALUATED	Evaluated, so that change and progress can be tracked and measured. There is Impact Study material to help you consider how your development has impacted on your students' overall learning. There are also mobile quizzes for the peer-to-peer teacher development workshops.

SELF-DEVELOPMENT MATERIAL

- **Teacher development material** in every unit of the Teacher's Manual and Development Pack, focused on developing critical thinking skills in your students, including teacher development objectives, in-practice activities and opportunities for review and self-evaluation.

- **Online teacher training course**, *Teaching with Unlock Second Edition*, in the Cambridge Learning Management System (CLMS). This online training will help you to become more familiar with the content, methodology and components of *Unlock*, so you feel confident working with the books and the digital and online resources.

- **Impact Study material** downloadable from e-Source via the code inside the front cover of the manual.

- **Articles** for teachers on a range of topics specifically selected to extend your knowledge, downloadable from e-Source via the code inside the front cover of the manual.

PEER-COLLABORATIVE MATERIAL

- **Peer-to-peer teacher training materials**, downloadable from e-Source via the code inside the front cover of the manual, so that you and your colleagues can develop together and share ideas.

- **Further ideas to peer-collaborate**.

- **Lesson observation template**, so you can get feedback from your colleagues.

COMPREHENSIVE TESTING PACK

- Unit, mid-course and end-of-course tests

- Available as PDF and editable Word documents

- New for Second Edition – all tests now include key vocabulary sections

UNLOCK
USING THE CLASSROOM APP

As part of our extensive market research, one of the common things we hear from teachers is the need for more practice activities for classroom use. We also hear again and again how much students enjoy using their mobile phones for learning purposes in the classroom.

With the new *Unlock* Classroom App, students are motivated by having relevant extension material on their phones to maximize language learning. Teachers can be reassured that the Classroom App adds real-language value to lessons.

WHAT MAKES THE *UNLOCK* CLASSROOM APP SPECIAL?

- Content is **fully integrated into every unit with *Unlock*-specific content** to extend the lesson.
- Offers extra **motivating practice** in speaking (engaging discussion activities), critical thinking and language to **develop what's been learnt** in the classroom.
- Provides a convenient **bank of language and skills reference material**, informed by our exclusive Corpus research.
- **Easily accessible and navigable** from students' phones.
- Students can **stream the Class Video**.
- Students can **review their answers** to interactive activities.
- **Scores feed into the CLMS gradebook**.
- Extends students' vocabulary by providing quick access to **Cambridge Dictionaries Online**.

All *Unlock* content is integrated with the Cambridge Learning Management System (CLMS), so students only need to be enrolled once to access the Online Workbook, Classroom App and Student Resources.

HOW TO ACCESS THE CLASSROOM APP

1 **Download** the Cambridge Pocket App from the **Apple App Store** or **Google Play**.

2 **Students need to register on the Cambridge Learning Management System (CLMS) before they can log in to the app.** (See full instructions on the inside front cover of their Student's Books on how to get their CLMS access code.) **Once registered on the CLMS, they can log in to the app using the same user name and password.** Students only need to log in to the app once and they are logged-in for one year.

3 **Access the content** in three easy steps:

1. Select the course

2. Select the unit

3. Select the activity

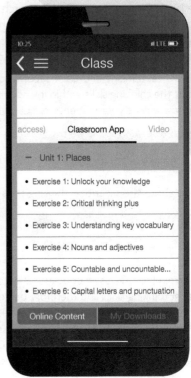

Icons in the margins of the Student's Book pages will indicate when teachers and students can move to the app to complete the additional activities.

For more guidance on using the Classroom app in your lessons, see the **Flexible Lesson Plans** on pages 16 and 24.

For extra guidance on using mobile in the classroom, why not try the **peer-to-peer workshop**, *Using the Unlock classroom app*, with your colleagues? Use the e-Source code inside the front cover of this manual for access. You will also find here *Using mobile devices in the language classroom*, part of the **Cambridge Papers in ELT** series.

UNL🔒CK

TEACHER DEVELOPMENT: INTRODUCTION TO CRITICAL THINKING

Unlock your teaching potential

We know from a wide range of research that critical thinking is becoming increasingly important in English Language Teaching, especially on Academic English courses and as part of 21st Century Skills. We also understand from speaking with teachers that very few have had specific training on how to teach critical thinking, or perhaps even overt teaching of critical thinking skills in their own educational backgrounds.

The critical thinking in *Unlock* Second Edition is informed by Bloom's Taxonomy. Taking some time to inform yourself about the thinking skills within it, and what they mean in your teaching practice, will boost your confidence and prepare you to support your students' critical thinking development.

BE FOCUSED

Learn about the six critical thinking skills and what they mean in the classroom.

BE INFORMED

Benjamin Bloom was an educational psychologist who, in 1956, published a taxonomy allowing us to classify specific critical thinking skills and therefore better understand them. This work has often been described by the educational community as one of the most influential of the 20th Century, and it now finds a place in 21st Century Skills, following revisions by Lorin Anderson and David Krathwohl in 2001. The six discrete skills Bloom identified are divided into Lower Order Thinking Skills (LOTS) and Higher Order Thinking Skills (HOTS) as below, with the higher-order skills being more cognitively challenging and therefore more difficult to develop.

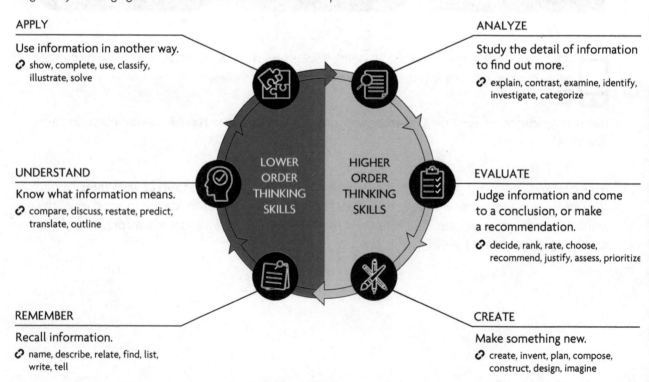

APPLY

Use information in another way.

↻ show, complete, use, classify, illustrate, solve

UNDERSTAND

Know what information means.

↻ compare, discuss, restate, predict, translate, outline

REMEMBER

Recall information.

↻ name, describe, relate, find, list, write, tell

ANALYZE

Study the detail of information to find out more.

↻ explain, contrast, examine, identify, investigate, categorize

EVALUATE

Judge information and come to a conclusion, or make a recommendation.

↻ decide, rank, rate, choose, recommend, justify, assess, prioritize

CREATE

Make something new.

↻ create, invent, plan, compose, construct, design, imagine

LOWER ORDER THINKING SKILLS

HIGHER ORDER THINKING SKILLS

BE CONFIDENT

Match the example activities (1–6) to the critical thinking skills (a–f). Check your answers on page 512.

1 Categorize the features of the two cities.	**a** Remember
2 Complete the table with the information.	**b** Understand
3 List the problems the speaker mentioned.	**c** Apply
4 Rank these items in order of importance.	**d** Analyze
5 Restate it in your own words.	**e** Evaluate
6 Compose a survey to find out more.	**f** Create

BE READY

Insights into classroom practice reveal that most questions teachers ask their students during a lesson require students to use their lower-order critical thinking skills.

Write the questions in the box in the correct column in the table below.

What facts can you find?	Can you identify...?	When?	What alternative ...?
Who?	Name ...	Why?	What?
Do you know ...?	List ...	Why might ...?	Why do you think ...?
Where?	How many?	How would you ...?	What criteria ...?

lower-order thinking skills	higher-order thinking skills

Increase opportunities to develop your students' higher-order critical thinking skills by thinking about which questions you might ask them, ahead of each lesson.

BE REFLECTIVE

Ahead of a lesson, write down three higher-order thinking skills questions you will ask your students. After the lesson, reflect on how your students responded to these, what impact they had on the lesson and what you might do differently in the next lesson.

BE COLLABORATIVE

Ask a colleague to observe one of your lessons and write down the questions you ask your class. After the lesson, classify these questions into lower- and higher-order thinking skills, and consider whether you need to spend more time on the higher-order ones.

BE BETTER

For extra guidance on teaching critical thinking, why not try the **peer-to-peer teacher training workshop**, *A practical approach to critical thinking* with your colleagues? Use the e-Source code inside the front cover of this manual for access.

UNLOCK
INTRODUCTION TO MIXED-ABILITY TEACHING

In an ideal world, every language class would always be filled with students who all operate at a similar level of proficiency, and where 'pre-intermediate means pre-intermediate'. In the real world, teaching groups of mixed-ability students is becoming increasingly common. Effective mixed-ability learning relies heavily on the teacher and on their ability to adapt both their teaching and their use of materials accordingly. You should aim to tailor these demands to – and address the individual needs of – each learner, in each class.

The support provided in *Unlock* Second Edition is informed both by current research into the practical considerations of mixed-ability learning environments, and by experienced mixed-ability teachers. By ensuring that you read and reflect on this, you will be able to enter the mixed-ability classroom with a greater awareness of how differentiation can be delivered.

BE FOCUSED

Consider the key differentiating factors in language learning and how they impact on your teaching.

BE INFORMED

A mixed-ability teaching context is not merely restricted to, for example, an A2 learner being placed in a B2 class. Some key differentiating factors in language learning are:

- **Proficiency:** This is the overarching theme that underpins all other factors. Differences in proficiency can be easily spotted by the alert language teacher, who will be acutely aware that learners will struggle to cope with input for which they have not yet acquired the language awareness.

- **Age:** Different types of activities are better suited to different ages. While it seems obvious that neither an adult group nor an EAP group are the best environments for frequent and regular language play, singing or games, the mixed-ability teacher should be aware of other, less obvious, differences that arise from the age of their class. For example, research has shown that adolescent learners respond better to a teacher providing clear rules and explanations, while adult learners benefit more from being shown multiple examples of the target language and deducing meaning and form, without explicit teacher intervention.

- **Motivation:** This is not simply and always a case of, 'I don't want to be in the class, but somebody or something is forcing me to come'. For example, in a language course, everyone has differing end-goals for what they want to achieve and improve upon. If a new learner joins a group with the explicit aim of improving one particular skill, only to find that the rest of the class is intent on improving other skills (and the teacher focuses more on developing these), motivation levels in that learner will drop.

- **Aptitude:** This can sometimes be mistaken for proficiency, whereas in fact the two factors are entirely different. In learners' aptitudes, there are considerable differences in how efficiently and quickly individuals can process language; this could be related to variations in short-term memory, or in the ability to identify and interpret patterns and sounds (e.g. of grammar or pronunciation). In short, some people simply make quicker and more trouble-free progress than others.

- **Cultural background:** Differences in educational experience can lead to varied expectations of what should happen in the classroom, and you should use this awareness to ask questions of yourself, and adapt to these answers. How much homework are they expecting to be given? Is the learner familiar with a collaborative learning environment? Do they believe pair or group work can actually be beneficial in any way?

BE CONFIDENT

For each statement, choose which of the two differentiating factors seems likely to have produced these common learner concerns. Check your answers on page 512.

1 I want my teacher to explain it, not just show me.
2 I need more time than my classmates to do the exercises in my coursebook.
3 My teacher doesn't give me enough work to do outside of class.
4 I want to be in a class where everyone is better at English than I am.
5 I get confused when the teacher starts talking about verbs and nouns and things like that.
6 I don't like the teaching style, so I don't feel I am making progress.

Age / Cultural background
Aptitude / Proficiency
Cultural background / Motivation
Motivation / Aptitude

Age / Aptitude
Proficiency / Cultural background

BE READY

What could you do to address each of the common learner concerns in *BE CONFIDENT*? Make short notes.

BE REFLECTIVE

Consider each student you teach. Write down a short description of how you see them in terms of each of the key factors described above. Then ask them how they see themselves, in a short needs analysis questionnaire (e.g. *How does your AGE affect your progress? What MOTIVATES you to improve your language skills?*). Use this information to challenge your own preconceptions and then to adapt your lesson planning accordingly.

BE COLLABORATIVE

One of the most time-consuming parts of mixed-ability teaching is actually producing differentiated material and adapting the coursebook to the needs of your learners. Consider forming a 'teaching pool' with your colleagues, where you can share materials and approaches for, and reflections on, lessons you have delivered.

BE BETTER

For extra guidance on adapting materials for mixed-ability students, why not try the **peer-to-peer teacher training workshop**, *Unlocking mixed-ability teaching* with your colleagues? Use the e-Source code inside the front cover of this manual for access.

UNL⌀CK
PEER COLLABORATION IDEAS

The process of teacher learning and development is continuous. Whether you are a seasoned teacher or new to classroom instruction, it is crucial to have regular support and feedback from your colleagues in order to continue growing as a professional. As reflected in the INSPIRE approach to teacher development (see page 6), it is important that any teacher development programme be peer-collaborative, so that you can share your development with other teachers. There are a number of ways you can achieve this, including:

- peer coaching

- joint planning in pairs or small groups of teachers who teach the same level or course

- team-teaching, followed by joint evaluation of the planning, teaching and learning achieved

- focused peer observation, leading to discussion of specific issues or key aspects of implementation

Consider holding **peer observation** sessions as you work through the key skills in the teacher development course in this Teacher's Manual, focused on developing critical thinking skills in your students. Through peer observation, teachers can develop a more reflective approach to their teaching and identify development goals together. The teacher being observed should identify a specific focus for observation. The teacher and the observer should have a pre-observation discussion about the focus and the lesson. During the lesson, the observer should take notes using the **Lesson Observation Template** on the page opposite, focusing on behaviour and actions that occur in the lesson related to the observation focus. We also recommend holding a post-observation discussion, reflecting on the focus, the lesson, learning points and a possible action plan.

You can also use the e-Source code in this book to access our **peer-to-peer workshops** on topics including unlocking critical thinking skills, unlocking academic writing, giving feedback on academic speaking, unlocking mixed-ability teaching and using the *Unlock* classroom app. These workshops are designed to be easily accessible and conducted by teachers with their peers. Peer groups will also have access to pre- and post-workshop quizzes through the Cambridge Pocket App to measure progress. **Contact your local sales representative for access to the *Unlock* peer-to-peer workshop quizzes.**

For extra guidance on peer-collaborative professional development, *see Effective professional development: Principles and best practice: Part of the Cambridge Papers in ELT series* by Silvana Richardson and Gabriel Díaz Maggioli, April 2018, Cambridge University Press.

UNLOCK
LESSON OBSERVATION TEMPLATE

Teacher: _____   Observer: _____

Class: _____   Class size: _____   Date: _____

Observation focus point(s):	Observation notes:

What went well?

What could be improved?

Suggestions for further improvement:

Other comments:

FLEXIBLE LESSON PLAN

> This flexible lesson plan can be used with every unit in *Unlock* Second Edition Listening, Speaking & Critical Thinking Levels 1–5.
>
> Note on timing: we recommend a maximum of **eight** hours per unit. Note that timings are given **for guidance only** and will depend very much on your own particular context; you should adjust timings accordingly. Note also that the sections in different units and levels do not always require the same amount of time to complete.
>
> **For general support on classroom management, see *Classroom Management Techniques* by Jim Scrivener, Cambridge University Press, 2012. For teachers who deal with large classes, see *Teaching Large Multilevel Classes* by Natalie Hess, Cambridge University Press, 2001.**

UNLOCK YOUR KNOWLEDGE

⏱ 15 min

Each unit opens with a striking two-page photo related to the topic, a Learning Objectives box and an Unlock Your Knowledge activity.

PURPOSE

- To set the learning objectives for the unit
- To introduce and generate interest in the unit topic
- To make connections between students' background knowledge and the unit topic

1 LEARNING OBJECTIVES

Draw students' attention to the Learning Objectives (LOs) box on the first page of each unit. Point out that there are six LOs in every unit and that the final one is always the productive task that the students will complete. The other five focus on Watch and listen, Listening skills, Critical thinking, Grammar and Speaking skills. Check comprehension of the six LOs, using the students' first language (L1) with lower levels if appropriate, and encourage students to ask questions about the content of the objectives. Show students that at the end of each unit there is an Objectives Review section where they will evaluate their performance.

2 PHOTO

Lead an open-class discussion on the connection between the unit opener photo and topic. Depending on the level of the class, start off with questions like:

lower levels	higher levels
What is the first thing you notice in the photo?	Imagine you are messaging a friend. How would you describe the photo?
Where do you think the photo was taken? Why?	
What do you think of when you look at the photo?	What do you think happened before/after the photo was taken?
If there is somebody in the photo, what do you think they are saying/thinking?	Why do you think the photographer took this photo?
How is the photo connected to the unit title?	Have you ever seen something like this before? Where might you expect to see this photo? (e.g. a news website, a travel magazine, social media, a personal album, etc.)
What do you like/dislike about the photo? Why?	

Note that not all these questions will work in every unit.

After the open-class discussion (which will be led by you), move on to the Unlock Your Knowledge questions, which should be used in a very student-centred way.

For more about using visuals in the language classroom, see *Visual literacy in English language teaching: Part of the Cambridge Papers in ELT series* by Ben Goldstein, August 2016, Cambridge University Press.

3 UNLOCK YOUR KNOWLEDGE

These questions are designed to unlock students' knowledge. Working in pairs or small groups, students discuss the questions. Then ask each pair/group to share the answer with the class that they think is the most interesting.

You can also use the activity to practise fluency. Instruct students to answer the questions as quickly as possible without worrying about creating grammatically correct sentences. Keep time and do not allow students more than 15–60 seconds per answer, depending on the level and complexity of the question. If there are any major language inaccuracies you can then address these, but remember that the focus here should be to engage and to encourage students.

CLASSROOM APP

The *Unlock* Classroom App provides teachers and students with additional practice activities for specific parts of the Student's Book. The app activities are a combination of open discussion activities and closed practice tasks to boost student engagement and build on important language and skills practice.

The Unlock Your Knowledge activity in the app is an open-ended discussion task that is organized into multiple screens, to allow for multiple discussion options or A/B student debate options. This activity may also include images as discussion prompts, similar to the image in the unit opener.

Navigate students to the relevant screen of the app and instruct them to answer the questions on the first screen on their own. For subsequent screens of the app, students should be paired with other students who gave the same answer to the first screen questions. Allow students five minutes to get into an in-depth discussion about the questions. Then ask each pair to share the answer with the class which they think is the most interesting.

For more about using mobile devices in the classroom, see *Using mobile devices in the language classroom: Part of the Cambridge Papers in ELT series* by Robert Godwin-Jones, January 2018, Cambridge University Press.

WATCH AND LISTEN

⏱ 60 min

Each unit includes a short authentic video that is related to the unit topic, from a range of sources, along with activities for students to do before, during and after watching. The video can be played in the classroom using Presentation Plus or watched outside of class by students by downloading it from e-Source, using the codes inside their books.

Note: A glossary defines the most important above-level or specialized words that appear in the video and that are essential for students to understand it, so that teachers do not have to spend time pre-teaching or explaining this vocabulary while viewing. Students are not required to produce these words in any of the unit activities, nor in the final productive task.

PURPOSE

- To generate further interest in and discussion of the unit topic
- To build background knowledge and ideas on the topic
- To develop and practise key skills in prediction, comprehension and discussion
- To personalize and give opinions on a topic

1 VIDEO STILLS

At the start of each Watch and Listen section there are four stills from the video. Focus on these and ask students to make predictions about the content of the video, and to ask questions if they have any. There may be more focused questions in the Predicting Content Using Visuals activity.

2 PREPARING TO WATCH

Ask students to work in pairs, and then small groups, to answer the Activating Your Knowledge questions. Moving from pairs to groups can help students who are reluctant to speak to build up their confidence and be better prepared for plenary discussions. Then ask volunteers to share their answers with the class. For a livelier class discussion, answer the questions together as a class.

Students can complete the Predicting Content Using Visuals activity on their own, to build their confidence, and then compare answers with a partner. Refer students to the glossary for help with above-level or specialized vocabulary.

3 WHILE WATCHING

Play the video twice, once while students listen for main ideas and once while they listen for key details. After each viewing, facilitate a discussion of students' answers and clarify any confusion. If some students still have trouble with comprehension, suggest that they watch the video again outside of class or during a computer lab session.

If you want to spend more time exploiting the video content, or for some variety in the way you use the video in the classroom, here are some suggestions. All of these can help promote language fluency and increase learner confidence:

- Pause the video at certain points and ask students to predict what they think happens next.
- Play parts of the video without any sound. Students produce their own voiceover.
- Play the sound without the video. Students imagine what is happening in the video.
- Select 6–8 key images from the video and put them into a slide presentation (or print and display) in random order. Then play the sound only while students put the images into the correct order. Students can then reproduce the voiceover.
- Select scenes from the video and encourage students to take written notes as they watch. These could be guided by using prompts supplied by you or be completely free choice.

For more ideas on using video in the classroom, see *Language Learning with Digital Video* by Ben Goldstein and Paul Driver, Cambridge University Press, 2014.

4 DISCUSSION

Have students work in pairs or small groups to answer the discussion questions, and then compare their answers with another pair or group. Volunteers can then share their answers with the class. If possible, expand on students' answers by making connections between their answers and the video content, or simply comment to provide positive feedback. For example:

lower levels	higher levels
That's interesting. Did the speaker in the video say the same thing? Or something different?	That's an interesting perspective. How is it similar to what the speaker in the video mentioned? How is it different?
Can you remember what the speaker(s) said? Give some examples.	Why do you think that? Give reasons.
	Think of two different ways to make the same point.
Does anybody agree with you? Ask and find out how many people agree or disagree with you.	Why did you include/exclude X in your answer?

Note that not all of these questions will work in every unit.

LISTENING

The first half of each unit focuses on the receptive skill of listening. Each unit includes two listening texts that provide different angles, viewpoints and/or genres related to the unit topic. Listening 2 provides a model for the productive Speaking Task. All audio files are available for students to download from e-Source. Audioscripts are provided in the back of the Student's Book, as well as under the Resources tab on the Cambridge Learning Management System (CLMS).

LISTENING 1

 60 min

Listening 1 includes a listening text on an academically related topic. It provides information on the unit topic and gives students exposure to, and practice with, language and listening skills, while helping them begin to generate ideas for their Speaking Task.

1 PREPARING TO LISTEN

PURPOSE

- To prepare students to understand the content of the listening
- To introduce, review and/or practise key pre-listening skills
- To introduce and build key academically related and topical vocabulary for the Listening and for the Speaking Task

Encourage students to complete the pre-listening activities in this section in pairs or small groups; this will promote a high level of engagement. Once students have completed the activities, check for understanding and offer any clarification.

Encourage your students to keep a vocabulary notebook for new words. This should include new key vocabulary words, parts of speech, definitions (in the students' own words) and contextual sentences. To extend the vocabulary activity in this section, ask students to find synonyms, antonyms or related terms for the vocabulary items they just practised. These can then be added to their vocabulary notebooks. If appropriate, students could translate key words into their own first language (L1) and check in pairs or groups for consistency.

For further support on the use of translation and L1 in the classroom, see *Translation and Own-language Activities* by Philip Kerr, Cambridge University Press, 2014.

Key vocabulary exercises can also be assigned ahead of the lesson, so that you can focus on the listening content and skills in class.

2 WHILE LISTENING

PURPOSE

- To introduce, review, and/or practise key academic listening skills
- To practise listening comprehension and note-taking skills
- To hear key vocabulary in a natural, academically related context
- To provide information and stimulate ideas on an academically related topic

Depending on class level, you can break up the audio into more manageable parts as students complete the exercises. For students who need extra support, allow them to read some or all of the audioscript before or after (but not while) they listen. Reading before listening can help learners to get a general understanding, whereas reading after listening can help learners to check their understanding. Because students can access the audio files at any time online, consider asking them to listen to the text before the lesson so that they are familiar with the content. Then, during class, you have a chance to check with your students about the level of difficulty of the text. You can do this by asking if they found any vocabulary particularly challenging and suggest how they can find the meaning of words, e.g. using an online dictionary (such as the Cambridge Dictionary at https://dictionary.cambridge.org). You could also ask a few general listening comprehension questions to check understanding. Students who still struggle with comprehension can listen again for homework.

For more open-ended note-taking practice, have students listen and take notes with books closed. During the first listening, instruct them to take notes on main ideas and general points. Then, with your guidance, have them listen again to take notes on specific details. They can then use their notes to complete the exercises in the section.

3 PRONUNCIATION FOR LISTENING

This section appears in each unit but changes location, based on where it most logically belongs.

PURPOSE

- To help students understand pronunciation in authentic, academically related discourse

Review the Pronunciation for Listening skills box as a class, to ensure that students understand the explanation and examples before doing the exercises.

If possible, assign a podcast, video, Online Workbook listening or other source for students to listen to, and locate instances of the Pronunciation for Listening skill.

4 POST-LISTENING

Note: This section does not appear in level 1.

PURPOSE

- To analyze, expand on and/or practise key pronunciation or listening skills from the previous section
- To introduce, review and/or practise key critical thinking skills applied to content from the listening text

Ask students to complete the activities in pairs or small groups; do not play the audio again at this point. After checking answers, survey students on what they found most challenging in the section. Then have students listen to the audio again for homework and take additional notes on the challenging skills and content, to be shared at the beginning of the next lesson or in an online forum.

5 DISCUSSION

PURPOSE

- To give students the opportunity to discuss what they heard and offer opinions
- To think critically about what they have just heard
- To further personalize the topic and issues in Listening 1

Give students three to five minutes to prepare, discuss and jot down notes for their answers. Then go through the discussion points and have groups volunteer to share their answers. If possible, expand on their answers by making connections between their answers and the listening content, or simply comment to provide positive feedback. For example, you can use similar questions to those listed in the Watch and Listen Discussion section on page 18 in this Flexible Lesson Plan.

You can provide oral or written feedback on common strengths in fluency and language use, as well as on mistakes, at the end of the section. This does not need to be individual feedback but more general, so that no individual student feels singled out. You could start by saying *'I noticed the following very good examples of language ...'* or *'I heard many of you speaking clearly and confidently, saying things like ...'.* Some examples could be put on the board for students to note down. If you noticed any areas for improvement, these can also be highlighted in a similar manner: *'While I was listening, I heard a few of you say …. Who can suggest a better way of saying this?'* or *'Can anybody tell me what's wrong with …? How could we say it more clearly?'.*

CLASSROOM APP

In either Listening 1 or Listening 2 there is a Critical Thinking Plus activity for the discussion questions. This is an extension to the discussion activities; it extends the questions that are in the Student's Book and promotes the use of higher-order thinking skills.

As with Unlock Your Knowledge, this is an open-ended discussion task that is organized into multiple screens to allow for multiple discussion options or A/B student debate options.

Navigate students to the relevant screen of the app and instruct them to answer the questions on the first screen on their own. For subsequent screens of the app, students should be paired with other students who gave the same answer to the first screen questions. Allow students five minutes for an in-depth discussion about the questions. Then ask each pair to share the answer with the class which they think is the most interesting.

LANGUAGE DEVELOPMENT

 45 min

Each unit includes the introduction and practice of academic language which is relevant to the unit topic and listenings and useful for the unit Speaking Task. The focus of this section is on vocabulary and/or grammar.

PURPOSE

- To focus and expand on grammar that may appear in Listening 1 and Listening 2
- To recycle and expand on vocabulary that may appear in Listening 1 and Listening 2
- To expose students to corpus-informed, research-based language for the unit topic and level
- To practise language and structures that will improve student accuracy and fluency in the Speaking Task

For grammar points, review the Grammar box as a class and check students' understanding. Alternatively, have students review it in pairs and allow time for questions. Then have students work in pairs to complete the accompanying activities. Review students' answers and allow time for any clarification.

For vocabulary points, review the Vocabulary box, if there is one, and then have students complete the activities in pairs. Then review answers and allow time for any clarification. To extend this activity, have students create sentences using each term and/or make a list of synonyms, antonyms or related words and phrases for each term. Students should also add relevant language to their vocabulary notebooks. For homework, have students annotate the audioscripts in the back of the book, underlining or highlighting any language covered in this section. If appropriate, students could translate key words into their L1 and check in their pairs or groups for consistency.

Depending on the time available and the level of your students, you can pick and choose the most relevant and useful activities. Stronger students could also assist less able students, taking on the role of 'teachers' and thus reinforcing their own knowledge while teaching their peers.

CLASSROOM APP

The Language Development activities (one or two exercises per unit) in the app are closed activities of five to eight items that practise the grammar/vocabulary from the Language Development section. These activities either build on the Student's Book exercises or bridge between closed and open practice in the book. If the app icon appears at the start of an activity, the app activity should be done before the Student's Book activity. If the app icon appears at the end of an activity, the app activity should be done after the Student's Book activity.

Students should complete the app activities on their own, or for homework. Once students have completed the activity, check for understanding and offer any clarification. If students already have a good understanding of the language point(s) covered in the app activity, ask students to complete the activity in the fastest time possible.

LISTENING 2

 60 min

Listening 2 is another listening text on the unit topic, often in a different format to Listening 1. It serves as a model for the Speaking Task and gives students additional exposure to, and practice with, language and listening skills, while helping them generate and refine ideas for their Speaking Task.

1 PREPARING TO LISTEN

PURPOSE

- To prepare students to understand the content of the listening
- To help students anticipate content, using visuals and prior knowledge
- To introduce and build key academic and topical vocabulary for the Listening and for the Speaking Task

Encourage students to complete the pre-listening activities in this section in pairs or small groups, to promote a high level of engagement. Circulate among the students, taking notes of common areas of difficulty. Once students have completed the activities, check for understanding and offer clarification, paying particular attention to any problem areas you noted. If you wish to extend the vocabulary activity in this section, elicit other word forms of the key vocabulary. Model pronunciation of these word forms, so that students are able to recognize them in context.

CLASSROOM APP

The Understanding Key Vocabulary activity in the app provides an additional practice activity that presents the key vocabulary in new contexts. It is scorable and typically a gap-fill exercise. These activities typically include eight items of vocabulary from both listenings, but the vocabulary is contextualized differently to its contextualization in the Student's Book. Students should complete this activity on their own. Once students have completed the activity, check for understanding and offer any clarification. If students already have a good understanding of the vocabulary covered in the app activity, ask students to complete the activity in the fastest time possible. The Understanding Key Vocabulary exercise can also be assigned ahead of time, or after class, so that you can focus on the reading content and skills in class.

2 WHILE LISTENING

PURPOSE

- To introduce, review and/or practise key academic listening skills
- To practise listening comprehension and note-taking skills
- To hear Key vocabulary and Language development elements in a natural, academic context
- To provide information and stimulate ideas on an academic topic
- To serve as a model for the Speaking Task

As with Listening 1, you can break up the audio into more manageable parts as students complete the exercises. Depending on time and proficiency level, have students listen to the text for homework before class, so that they are familiar with the content. Discuss with them the difficulty level of the text in comparison with Listening 1. Ask students who still struggle with comprehension to listen again for homework, and set specific questions for them to answer or areas for them to take notes on. Again, as with Listening 1, for students who need extra support, allow them to read some or all of the audioscript before or after (but not while) they listen. Reading before listening can help learners to get a general understanding, whereas reading after listening can help learners to check their understanding.

3 POST-LISTENING

PURPOSE

- To analyze, expand on and/or practise key pronunciation or listening skills from the previous section
- To introduce, review and/or practise key critical thinking skills applied to content from the listening text

Note: Post-listening sections do not appear in Level 1, and they are not in every unit in Level 2. In Levels 3–5, they appear in every Listening section.

Ask students to complete the activities in pairs or small groups; do not play the audio again at this point. After checking answers, survey students on what they found most challenging in the section. Then have students listen to the audio again for homework and take additional notes on the challenging skills and content, to be shared at the beginning of the next class or in an online forum.

4 DISCUSSION

PURPOSE

- To personalize and expand on the ideas and content of Listening 2
- To practise synthesizing the content of the unit listening texts
- To transition students from the receptive to the productive half of the unit

Before students discuss the questions in this section for the first time, introduce the key skill of synthesis, i.e. combining and analyzing ideas from multiple sources. Stress its importance in higher education: at university, students will be asked to synthesize ideas from a wide range of sources, to think critically about them, to make connections between them and to add their own ideas. Note that you may need to review this information periodically with your class. The discussion questions will require students to use ideas from both Listening 1 and Listening 2 in order to supply the answers; this is good practice for the key skill of synthesis.

Ask students to answer the questions in pairs or small groups, and then ask for volunteers to share their answers with the class. Facilitate the discussion, encouraging students to make connections between Listening 1 and Listening 2. If applicable, ask students to relate the content of the unit video to this section, or even to previous units. This is also a good context in which to introduce the Speaking Task at the beginning of the next section and for students to consider how the content of the listening texts relates to the task prompt.

SPEAKING

The second half of each unit focuses on the productive skill of speaking. It begins with the prompt for the Speaking Task and systematically equips students with the skills and language to plan for, prepare and execute the task successfully.

CRITICAL THINKING

⏱ 60 min

PURPOSE

- To introduce the Speaking Task
- To help generate, develop and organize ideas for the Speaking Task
- To teach and practise the lower-order critical thinking skills of remembering, understanding and applying knowledge, through practical brainstorming and organizational activities
- To teach and practise the higher-order critical thinking skills of analyzing, evaluating and creating, in order to prepare students for success in the Speaking Task and, more generally, in the university classroom

Encourage students to work through this section collaboratively in pairs or small groups, to support and encourage each other. Facilitate their learning and progress by circulating and checking with students as they work through this section. If time permits, have groups exchange and evaluate one another's work.

PREPARATION FOR SPEAKING

⏱ 45 min

PURPOSE

- To introduce and practise academic speaking skills that can be used in the Speaking Task
- To introduce or recycle language that supports these key skills and the Speaking Task
- To help students ensure correct pronunciation. Note that most units include a Pronunciation for Speaking skills box and practice in this section

Review any skills boxes in this section as a class and clarify points of confusion. Then have students work on the activities in pairs or small groups. After they complete any speaking activities, have some students share their answers with the class.

Since the section focuses on form and function, it is important to offer corrective feedback to your students. You can then focus on fluency in the next section. Here are examples of ways to provide interactive corrective feedback, depending on the level of your class:

A student says, '*It possible to use that technology today.*'

1) The teacher writes the incorrect form on the board and asks the student to come to the board and correct the statement.
2) The teacher repeats the incorrect form with rising intonation: '*It possible ...?*', to see if the student can self-correct. If not, then the teacher prompts the student, for example, '*Are you missing a subject/verb/preposition?*'
3) The teacher supplies the correct form and asks the student to repeat.

In all cases, the correct form should be modelled for the student and for the rest of the class.

For more about giving corrective feedback, see *Giving feedback on speaking: Part of the Cambridge Papers in ELT series* by Philip Kerr, December 2017, Cambridge University Press.

CLASSROOM APP

The Preparation for Speaking activity in the app is an activity with A and B parts. The first exercise or A part is closed, scorable practice, and the second exercise or B part may be more creative, open, static text practice (and therefore not scorable). In some units there may only be a closed activity.

Students should complete the closed activity on their own. Once students have completed the activity, check for understanding and offer any clarification. If students already have a good understanding of the language point(s) covered in the app activity, ask students to complete the activity in the fastest time possible.

The open-ended discussion task is organized into multiple screens to allow for multiple discussion options or A/B student debate options. Navigate students to the relevant screen of the app and instruct them to answer the questions on the first screen on their own. For subsequent screens of the app, students should be paired with other students who gave the same answer to the first screen questions. Allow students five minutes to get into an in-depth discussion about the questions. Then ask each pair to share the answer with the class which they think is the most interesting.

If the app icon appears at the start of an activity, the app activity should be done before the Student's Book activity. If the app icon appears at the end of an activity, the app activity should be done after the Student's Book activity.

SPEAKING TASK

⏱ 60 min

PURPOSE

- To work collaboratively in preparation for the Speaking Task
- To revisit, revise and expand on work done in the Critical Thinking section
- To provide an opportunity for students to synthesize the language, skills and ideas presented and generated in the unit
- To improve oral fluency

Depending on time and class level, students can complete the preparation activities for homework or in class. If conducted in class, work should be done collaboratively. It can be helpful to pair a quieter student with a more outgoing student. It is also important to circulate among students, asking and answering questions as needed.

If students agree, record their Speaking tasks on a phone or video camera. At the same time, take notes on key areas, such as grammar, pronunciation, key word stress, eye contact and pacing. Students can view their performances and receive your oral and written feedback at the same time. If any students lack confidence to present on their own, allow them to present with a partner, turn-taking throughout the presentation.

OBJECTIVES REVIEW

⏱ 15 min

Use the Objectives Review section to help students reflect on what they have done during the unit. Point out that the '*I can ...*' objectives link back to the Learning Objectives on the opening page of the unit. Students should read the '*I can ...*' objectives and self-assess how well they can do each one, referring back to completed work and lessons in the unit if necessary. Ask students to provide evidence for their scores, so that the exercise does not become mechanical, and give feedback to students on this: '*Really? You've given yourself 1? I think you did very well and you deserve to give yourself a 2*'. If any students need more practice with any of the unit's Learning Objectives, they can go to the *Unlock* Online Workbook.

WORDLIST

The Wordlist contains the key words from the unit, which students should be encouraged to use in the final Speaking Task. As a challenge for students, you might suggest that they try to use five or eight words, or whatever you think is a reasonable number; stronger students could be encouraged to use more while less able students could be given a lower target. Note that high-frequency words in the Cambridge Academic Corpus are highlighted in the Wordlist.

READING, WRITING & CRITICAL THINKING

FLEXIBLE LESSON PLAN

This flexible lesson plan can be used with every unit in *Unlock* Second Edition Reading, Writing & Critical Thinking Levels 1–5.

Note on timing: we recommend a maximum of **eight** hours per unit. Note that timings are given **for guidance only** and will depend very much on your own particular context; you should adjust timings accordingly. Note also that the sections in different units and levels do not always require the same amount of time to complete.

For general support on classroom management, see *Classroom Management Techniques* by Jim Scrivener, Cambridge University Press, 2012. For teachers who deal with large classes, see *Teaching Large Multilevel Classes* by Natalie Hess, Cambridge University Press, 2001.

UNLOCK YOUR KNOWLEDGE

 15 min

Each unit opens with a striking two-page photo related to the topic, a Learning Objectives box and an Unlock Your Knowledge activity.

PURPOSE

- To set the learning objectives for the unit
- To introduce and generate interest in the unit topic
- To make connections between students' background knowledge and the unit topic

1 LEARNING OBJECTIVES

Draw students' attention to the Learning Objectives (LOs) box on the first page of each unit. Point out that there are six LOs in every unit and that the final one is always the productive task that the students will complete. The other five focus on Watch and listen, Reading skills, Critical thinking, Grammar and Academic Writing skills. Check comprehension of the six LOs, using the students' first language (L1) with lower levels if appropriate, and encourage students to ask questions about the content of the objectives. Show students that at the end of each unit there is an Objectives Review section where they will evaluate their performance.

2 PHOTO

Lead an open-class discussion on the connection between the unit opener photo and topic. Depending on the level of the class, start off with questions like:

lower levels	higher levels
What is the first thing you notice in the photo?	Imagine you are messaging a friend. How would you describe the photo?
Where do you think the photo was taken? Why?	
What do you think of when you look at the photo?	What do you think happened before/after the photo was taken?
If there is somebody in the photo, what do you think they are saying/thinking?	Why do you think the photographer took this photo?
How is the photo connected to the unit title?	Have you ever seen something like this before? Where might you expect to see this photo? (e.g. a news website, a travel magazine, social media, a personal album, etc.)
What do you like/dislike about the photo? Why?	

Note that not all these questions will work in every unit.

After the open-class discussion (which will be led by you), move on to the Unlock Your Knowledge questions, which should be used in a very student-centred way.

For more about using visuals in the language classroom, see *Visual literacy in English language teaching: Part of the Cambridge Papers in ELT series* by Ben Goldstein, August 2016, Cambridge University Press.

3 UNLOCK YOUR KNOWLEDGE

These questions are designed to unlock students' knowledge. Working in pairs or small groups, students discuss the questions. Then ask each pair/group to share the answer with the class that they think is the most interesting.

You can also use the activity to practise fluency. Instruct students to answer the questions as quickly as possible without worrying about creating grammatically correct sentences. Keep time and do not allow students more than 15–60 seconds per answer, depending on the level and complexity of the question. If there are any major language inaccuracies you can then address these, but remember that the focus here should be to engage and to encourage students.

CLASSROOM APP

The *Unlock* Classroom App provides teachers and students with additional practice activities for specific parts of the Student's Book. The app activities are a combination of open discussion activities and closed practice tasks to boost student engagement and build on important language and skills practice.

The Unlock Your Knowledge activity in the app is an open-ended discussion task that is organized into multiple screens, to allow for multiple discussion options or A/B student debate options. This activity may also include images as discussion prompts, similar to the image in the unit opener.

Navigate students to the relevant screen of the app and instruct them to answer the questions on the first screen on their own. For subsequent screens of the app, students should be paired with other students who gave the same answer to the first screen questions. Allow students five minutes to get into an in-depth discussion about the questions. Then ask each pair to share the answer with the class which they think is the most interesting.

For more about using mobile devices in the classroom, see *Using mobile devices in the language classroom: Part of the Cambridge Papers in ELT series* by Robert Godwin-Jones, January 2018, Cambridge University Press.

WATCH AND LISTEN

⏱ 60 min

Each unit includes a short authentic video that is related to the unit topic, from a range of sources, along with activities for students to do before, during and after watching. The video can be played in the classroom using Presentation Plus or watched outside of class by students by downloading it from e-Source, using the codes inside their books.

Note: A glossary defines the most important above-level or specialized words that appear in the video and that are essential for students to understand it, so that teachers do not have to spend time pre-teaching or explaining this vocabulary while viewing. Students are not required to produce these words in any of the unit activities, nor in the final productive task.

PURPOSE

- To generate further interest in and discussion of the unit topic
- To build background knowledge and ideas on the topic
- To develop and practise key skills in prediction, comprehension and discussion
- To personalize and give opinions on a topic

1 VIDEO STILLS

At the start of each Watch and Listen section there are four stills from the video. Focus on these and ask students to make predictions about the content of the video, and to ask questions if they have any. There may be more focused questions in the Predicting Content Using Visuals activity.

2 PREPARING TO WATCH

Ask students to work in pairs, and then small groups, to answer the Activating Your Knowledge questions. Moving from pairs to groups can help students who are reluctant to speak to build up their confidence and be better prepared for plenary discussions. Then have volunteers share their answers with the class. For a livelier class discussion, answer the questions together as a class.

Students can complete the Predicting Content Using Visuals activity on their own, to build their confidence, and then compare answers with a partner. Refer students to the glossary for help with above-level or specialized vocabulary.

3 WHILE WATCHING

Play the video twice, once while students listen for main ideas and once while they listen for key details. After each viewing, facilitate a discussion of students' answers and clarify any confusion. If some students still have trouble with comprehension, suggest that they watch the video again outside of class or during a computer lab session.

If you want to spend more time exploiting the video content, or for some variety in the way you use the video in the classroom, here are some suggestions. All of these can help promote language fluency and increase learner confidence:

- Pause the video at certain points and ask students to predict what they think happens next.
- Play parts of the video without any sound. Students produce their own voiceover.
- Play the sound without the video. Students imagine what is happening in the video.
- Select 6–8 key images from the video and put them into a slide presentation (or print and display) in random order. Then play the sound only while students put the images into the correct order. Students can then reproduce the voiceover.
- Select scenes from the video and encourage students to take written notes as they watch. These could be guided by using prompts supplied by you or be completely free choice.

For more ideas on using video in the classroom, see *Language Learning with Digital Video* by Ben Goldstein and Paul Driver, Cambridge University Press, 2014.

4 DISCUSSION

Ask students to work in pairs or small groups to answer the discussion questions, and then compare their answers with another pair or group. Volunteers can then share their answers with the class. If possible, expand on students' answers by making connections between their answers and the video content, or simply comment to provide positive feedback. For example:

lower levels	higher levels
That's interesting. Did the speaker in the video say the same thing? Or something different?	That's an interesting perspective. How is it similar to what the speaker in the video mentioned? How is it different?
Can you remember what the speaker(s) said? Give some examples.	Why do you think that? Give reasons.
	Think of two different ways to make the same point.
Does anybody agree with you? Ask and find out how many people agree or disagree with you.	Why did you include/exclude X in your answer?

Note that not all of these questions will work in every unit.

READING

The first half of each unit focuses on the receptive skill of reading. Each unit includes two reading texts that provide different angles, viewpoints and/or genres related to the unit topic. Reading 2 provides a model for the productive Writing Task.

READING 1

⏱ 45 min

Reading 1 includes a reading text on an academically related topic. It provides information on the unit topic and gives students exposure to, and practice with, language and reading skills, while helping them begin to generate ideas for their Writing Task.

1 PREPARING TO READ

PURPOSE

- To prepare students to understand the content of the reading
- To introduce, review and/or practise key pre-reading skills
- To introduce and build key academically related and topical vocabulary for the reading and for the Writing Task

Encourage students to complete the pre-reading activities in this section in pairs or small groups; this will promote a high level of engagement. Once students have completed the activities, check for understanding and offer any clarification. Key vocabulary exercises can also be assigned ahead of time so that you can focus on the reading content and skills in class.

Encourage your students to keep a vocabulary notebook for new words. This should include new key vocabulary words, parts of speech, definitions (in the students' own words) and contextual sentences. To extend the vocabulary activity in this section, ask students to find synonyms, antonyms or related terms for the vocabulary items they just practised. These can then be added to their vocabulary notebooks. If appropriate, students could translate key words into their own first language (L1) and check in their pairs or groups for consistency.

2 WHILE READING

PURPOSE

- To introduce, review and/or practise key academic reading skills
- To practise reading comprehension skills

- To see key vocabulary in a natural, academically related context
- To provide information and stimulate ideas on an academically related topic

Depending on class level, you can break up the text into more manageable parts as students complete the exercises. For example, students in pairs or small groups could read only one paragraph and then share their findings with other pairs and groups, consolidating the main ideas and details in the text. Students who still struggle with comprehension can read the text again for homework.

Make sure students keep any written answers short and to the point, focusing on the key pieces of information that answer the questions. Working in pairs and groups offers students an opportunity to revise their answers and to produce the best ones they can with their partner or partners.

3 READING BETWEEN THE LINES

PURPOSE
- To help students achieve a deeper understanding of the text using a variety of methods, including: working out meanings from context; distinguishing fact from opinion; making inferences; and identifying purpose and audience

Reading between the lines can be challenging, so make sure students have sufficient time to do the exercises. Students should work alone at first, and then work with a partner or partners to share and discuss their answers.

4 DISCUSSION

PURPOSE
- To give students the opportunity to discuss what they read and offer opinions
- To think critically about what they have just read
- To further personalize the topic and issues in Reading 1

Give students three to five minutes to discuss and make notes for their answers. Monitor student groups, taking notes on common strengths and mistakes. Then, have groups volunteer to share their answers. If possible, expand on their answers by making connections between their answers and the text content, or simply comment to provide positive feedback. For example, you can use similar questions to those listed in the Watch and listen Discussion section on page 26. You can provide oral or written feedback on common strengths in fluency and language use, as well as on mistakes, at the end of the section. This does not need to be individual feedback but more general, so that no individual student feels singled out. You could start by saying 'I noticed the following very good examples of language ...' or 'I heard many of you speaking clearly and confidently, saying things like ...'. Some examples could be put on the board for students to note down. If you noticed any areas for improvement, these can also be highlighted in a similar manner: 'While I was listening, I heard a few of you say .... Who can suggest a better way of saying this?' or 'Can anybody tell me what's wrong with ...? How could we say it more clearly?'.

CLASSROOM APP

In either Reading 1 or Reading 2 there is a Critical Thinking Plus activity for the discussion questions. This is an extension to the discussion activities; it extends the questions that are in the Student's Book and promotes the use of higher-order thinking skills. As with Unlock Your Knowledge, this is an open-ended discussion task that is organized into multiple screens to allow for multiple discussion options or A/B student debate options.

Navigate students to the relevant screen of the app and instruct them to answer the questions on the first screen on their own. For subsequent screens of the app students should be paired with other students who gave the same answer to the first screen questions. Allow students five minutes for an in-depth discussion about the questions. Then ask each pair to share the answer with the class which they think is the most interesting.

READING 2

⏱ 60 min

Reading 2 is another reading text on the unit topic, often in a different format to Reading 1. It serves as a model for the Writing Task (in terms of style, structure and format, but not length) and gives students additional exposure to, and practice with, language and reading skills, while helping them generate and refine ideas for their Writing Task.

1 PREPARING TO READ

PURPOSE
- To prepare students to understand the content of the text
- To help students anticipate content, using visuals and prior knowledge
- To introduce and build key academic and topical vocabulary for the Reading and for the Writing Task

Encourage students to complete the pre-reading activities in this section in pairs or small groups, to provide support and peer encouragement. Circulate among the students, taking notes of common strengths and areas of difficulty. Once students have completed the activities, check for understanding and offer clarification, paying particular attention to any problem areas you noted. If you wish to extend the vocabulary activity in this section, elicit other word forms of the key vocabulary.

CLASSROOM APP

The Understanding Key Vocabulary activity in the app provides an additional practice activity that presents the key vocabulary in new contexts. It is scorable and typically a gap-fill exercise. These activities typically include eight items of vocabulary from both readings. The vocabulary is contextualized differently to its contextualization in the Student's Book. Students should complete this activity on their own. Once students have completed the activity, check for understanding and offer any clarification. If students already have a good understanding of the vocabulary covered in the app activity, ask students to complete the activity in the fastest time possible. The Understanding Key Vocabulary exercise can also be assigned ahead of time, or after class, so that you can focus on the reading content and skills in class.

2 WHILE READING

PURPOSE

- To introduce, review and/or practise key academic reading skills
- To practise reading comprehension skills
- To see key vocabulary in a natural academic context
- To provide information and stimulate ideas on an academic topic
- To serve as a model for the Writing Task

As with Reading 1, you can break up the texts into more manageable parts as students complete the exercises. Depending on time and proficiency level, have students read the text for homework before class, so that they are familiar with the content. Discuss with them the difficulty level of the text in comparison with Reading 1. Ask students who still struggle with comprehension to read the text again for homework and set specific questions for them to answer.

3 READING BETWEEN THE LINES

PURPOSE

- To help students achieve a deeper understanding of the text, using a variety of methods, including: working out meaning from context; distinguishing fact from opinion; making inferences; and identifying purpose and audience.

Reading between the lines can be challenging, so make sure students have sufficient time to do the exercises. Students should work alone at first, and then join with a partner or partners to share and discuss their answers.

4 DISCUSSION

PURPOSE

- To personalize and expand on the ideas and content of Reading 2
- To practise synthesizing the content of the unit reading texts
- To transition students from the receptive to the productive half of the unit

Before students discuss the questions in this section for the first time, introduce the key skill of synthesis, i.e. combining and analyzing ideas from multiple sources. Stress its importance in higher education: at university, students will be asked to synthesize ideas from a wide range of sources, to think critically about them, to make connections among them and to add their own ideas. Note that you may need to review this information periodically with your class. The discussion questions will require students to use ideas from both Reading 1 and Reading 2 in order to supply the answers. This is good practice for the key skill of synthesis.

Ask students to answer the questions in pairs or small groups, and then ask for volunteers to share their answers with the class. Facilitate the discussion, encouraging students to make connections between Reading 1 and Reading 2. If applicable, ask students to relate the content of the unit video, or even previous units, to this section. This is also a good context in which to introduce the Writing Task at the beginning of the Critical Thinking section and for students to consider how the content of the reading texts relates to the prompt.

LANGUAGE DEVELOPMENT

⏱ 45 min

Each unit includes the introduction and practice of academic language relevant to the unit topic and readings, and useful for the unit Writing Task. The focus of this section is on vocabulary and/or grammar.

PURPOSE

- To focus and expand on grammar that may appear in Reading 1 and Reading 2
- To recycle and expand on vocabulary that may appear in Reading 1 and Reading 2
- To expose students to corpus-informed, research-based language for the unit topic and level
- To practise language and structures that will improve student accuracy and fluency in the Writing Task

For grammar points, review the Grammar box as a class and check students' understanding. Alternatively, have students review it in pairs and allow time for questions. Then have students work in pairs to complete the accompanying activities. Review students' answers and allow time for any clarification.

For vocabulary points, review the Vocabulary box, if there is one, and then have students complete the activities in pairs. Then review answers and allow time for any clarification. To extend this activity, have students create sentences using each term and/or make a list of synonyms, antonyms or related words and phrases for each term. Students should also add relevant language to their vocabulary notebooks. For homework, have students annotate the readings in the unit, underlining or highlighting any language covered in this section. If appropriate, students could translate key words into their L1 and check in their pairs or groups for consistency.

Depending on the time available and the level of your students, you could pick and choose the most relevant and useful activities. Stronger students could also assist less able students, taking on the role of 'teachers' and thus reinforcing their own knowledge while teaching their peers.

CLASSROOM APP

The Language Development activities (one or two exercises per unit) in the app are closed activities of five to eight items that practise the grammar/vocabulary from the Language Development section. These activities either build on the Student's Book exercise or bridge between closed and open practice in the book. If the app icon appears at the start of an activity, the app activity should be done before the Student's Book activity. If the app icon appears at the end of an activity, the app activity should be done after the Student's Book activity.

Students should complete the app activities on their own or for homework. Once students have completed the activity, check for understanding and offer any clarification. If students already have a good understanding of the language point(s) covered in the app activity, ask students to complete the activity in the fastest time possible.

WRITING

The second half of each unit focuses on the productive skill of writing. It begins with the prompt for the unit Writing Task and systematically equips students with the skills and language to plan for, prepare and execute the task successfully.

CRITICAL THINKING

Ō 60 min

PURPOSE

- To introduce the Writing Task
- To help generate, develop and organize ideas for the Writing Task
- To teach and practise the lower-order critical thinking skills of remembering, understanding and applying knowledge, through practical brainstorming and organizational activities
- To teach and practise the higher-order critical thinking skills of analyzing, evaluating and creating, in order to prepare students for success in the Writing Task and, more generally, in the university classroom

Encourage students to work through this section collaboratively in pairs or small groups, to support and encourage each other. Facilitate their learning and progress by circulating and checking with students as they work through this section. If time permits, have groups exchange and evaluate one another's work.

GRAMMAR FOR WRITING

Ō 30 min

Each unit includes the practice of academic grammatical structures and features relevant to the unit topic and readings, and useful for the unit Writing task. The focus of this section is only on grammar and is designed to help learners become good writers of English. There is a strong focus on sentence structure, word agreement and referencing, which are important for coherent and organized writing.

PURPOSE

- To focus on grammar for the Writing Task
- To practise language and structures that will improve student accuracy and fluency in the Writing Task

Review the grammar boxes as a class and facilitate answers to any unclear sections. Alternatively, have students review the grammar boxes in pairs and allow time for questions. Then have students work in pairs or small groups to complete the accompanying activities. Review students' answers and allow time for any clarification. Depending on time and the level of the class, you could allocate different activities to different students, and then allow time for sharing answers.

ACADEMIC WRITING SKILLS

 30 min

Each unit includes a section on Academic writing skills, which practises all of the writing skills needed for the Writing Task.

PURPOSE

- To focus on and practise academic writing skills required for the Writing Task

Review the skills boxes as a class and facilitate answers to any unclear sections. Alternatively, have students review the skills boxes in pairs and allow time for questions. Then have students work in pairs or small groups to complete the accompanying activities. Review students' answers and allow time for any clarification. Depending on time and the level of the class, you could allocate different activities to different students, and then allow time for sharing answers.

CLASSROOM APP

The Academic Writing Skills activity in the app is a closed activity of five to eight items that practise the skills from this section. For some skills there many only be one or two items, if this is more appropriate. If the app icon appears at the start of an activity, the app activity should be done before the Student's Book activity. If the app icon appears at the end of an activity, the app activity should be done after the Student's Book activity.

Students should complete this app activity on their own or for homework. Once students have completed the activity, check for understanding and offer any clarification. If students already have a good understanding of the language point(s) covered in the app activity, ask them to complete the activity in the fastest time possible.

Note: In Levels 3–5, some units may have a Grammar For Writing activity instead of an Academic Writing Skills activity.

WRITING TASK

⏱ 45 min

PURPOSE

- To prepare for the Writing task
- To revisit, revise and expand on work done in the Critical Thinking section
- To provide an opportunity for students to synthesize the language, skills and ideas presented and generated in the unit
- To develop students' skills in reviewing and rewriting their written work

Students should refer back to the activities they completed in the Critical Thinking section earlier in the unit, as these will support them in completing the Writing Task. Students should work alone, but should be encouraged to share their thoughts and writing with each other, and then to revise and edit their work, using the Revise and Edit checklists towards the end of the unit.

REVISE AND EDIT

⏱ 30 min

There are two checklists after the Writing Task: one for the task and one for the language. These can be used by students to review their written work, and then to make any changes necessary. It is important that the checklists are not omitted, because they act as a reminder to students that written work should always be checked before giving it to the teacher for feedback. For variety, you could ask students to exchange their work with a partner's and review it; alternatively students could work in small groups, reviewing each other's work and giving each other feedback (while referring to the two checklists).

OBJECTIVES REVIEW

⏱ 15 min

Use the Objectives Review section to help students reflect on what they have done during the unit. Point out that the 'I can ...' objectives link back to the Learning Objectives on the opening page of the unit. Students should read the 'I can ...' objectives and self-assess how well they can do each one, referring back to completed work and lessons in the unit if necessary. Ask students to provide evidence for their scores, so that the exercise does not become mechanical, and give feedback to students on this: *'Really? You've given yourself 1? I think you did very well and you deserve to give yourself a 2'*. If any students need more practice with any of the unit's Learning Objectives, they can go to the *Unlock* Online Workbook.

WORDLIST

The Wordlist contains the key words from the unit which students should be encouraged to use in the final Writing Task. As a challenge for students you might suggest that they try to use five or eight words, or whatever you think is a reasonable number; stronger students could be encouraged to use more, while less able students could be given a lower target. Note that high-frequency words in the Cambridge Academic Corpus are highlighted in the Wordlist.

LISTENING, SPEAKING & CRITICAL THINKING 1

PEOPLE UNIT 1

UNIT OBJECTIVES	
Watch and listen	Watch and understand a video about business people in South Africa.
Listening skills	Understand key vocabulary; take notes.
Critical thinking	Choose information for an ideas map.
Grammar	Use subject pronouns and possessive adjectives; use the verb *be*.
Speaking skill	Introduce and start a talk.
Speaking task	Talk about a famous person from your country.
⊘ **Teacher development**	Help your students become better at **choosing information for an ideas map**.

UNL⊘CK YOUR KNOWLEDGE

Background note

The photo shows a celebrity being interviewed by journalists at a red-carpet event. The man in the photo could be a famous actor, musician or sportsman. The journalists are taking photos of the celebrity and asking questions. They could be asking the man questions about his career.

Lead-in

Ask students to name some people they think are interesting. Create a list of five people that most of the class agree are interesting. List the names on the board and elicit short descriptions of who the people are, encouraging topics from the unit, such as *age, job, where the person is from*, etc.). Allow students to use the internet if needed. Further the conversation by analyzing the types of people who were listed as interesting. Questions could include: *What jobs do they have? Why are they interesting? What makes somebody interesting?*

page 15
Possible answers:
1 A crowd of photographers, a celebrity
2 People are taking photos / asking questions / interviewing the celebrity
3 *Answers will vary.*

WATCH AND LISTEN

Learning objectives

- Listen and identify main ideas in a video about small businesses in South Africa
- Listen and identify detailed information
- Complete a set of inferences about the information in the video
- Practise talking about clothing and small businesses

Exercise 1 page 16
Answers will vary.

Exercise 2 page 16
a photo 2 **b** photo 4 **c** photo 1 **d** photo 3

Exercise 3 page 17
1; 3; 4; 6

Exercise 4 page 17
1 sews **2** colourful **3** Four **4** advice **5** United States

Exercise 5 page 17
1 workers **2** difficult **3** business **4** popular

Exercise 6 page 17
Answers will vary.

LISTENING 1

Learning objectives

- Understand key vocabulary for family and jobs – *student, sister, manager*
- Gain awareness of, and identify word stress in, multi-syllable words
- Listen and understand main ideas and detailed information in a conversation about families
- Use a table to organize notes from listening
- Describe personal information in a discussion

Lead-in

Remind students that when you know somebody, and others don't, you should introduce that person. You may want to model by introducing a student to the rest of the class. Then, ask students to name situations where you introduce somebody (e.g. *in class, at a job, hanging out with new friends*, etc.). You may want to categorize these into formal and informal situations.

Exercise 1 page 18
Answers will vary.

Exercise 2 page 18
family: brother, sisters, family, mother, father
jobs: doctor, student, engineer, managers

Exercises 3–4 page 19
1 introduce (3)   **2** please (1)   **3** Peru (2)   **4** Turkey (2)
5 twenty (2)   **6** eighteen (2)   **7** study (2)   **8** business (2)
9 computer (3)   **10** college (2)

Exercise 5 page 19
1 Nehir: Turkey   **2** Carlos: Peru   **3** Koko: Japan

Be flexible

👥 👥👥 With **a stronger group**, ask students to close their books while they listen for the first time. Tell them to take notes about the different speakers and write down details about them. Then students compare their notes with a partner and discuss Exercise 5 in pairs. Students can then use the notes to answer questions in Exercise 6 before listening again to check their answers.

Exercise 6 page 20
1 b   **2** a   **3** c

Exercise 7 page 20
1 T   **2** T   **3** T

4 F; She has a brother.
5 F; His father is an engineer / His mother is a doctor.
6 F; He wants to study Computer Science.

Exercise 8 page 20
student 1: 2 19   **3** Turkey   **4** one brother   **5** study Business

student 2: 1 Carlos   **2** 19   **3** Peru   **4** None mentioned
5 study Computer Science

student 3: 1 Koko   **2** 18   **3** Sapporo, Japan
4 None mentioned   **5** study English

Exercises 9–10 page 21
Answers will vary.

LANGUAGE DEVELOPMENT

Learning objectives

- Use subject pronouns and possessive adjectives to write about people – *This is her book. They're managers. He's from Brazil.*
- Use the verb *be* accurately to talk about yourself – *Is your school in Cairo? No, it isn't. Are your parents in business? Yes, they are.*

Exercise 1 page 22
1 She   **2** They   **3** I   **4** It   **5** They   **6** We

Exercise 2 page 22
2 his   **3** her   **4** their   **5** our

Optional activity

👥👥👥 Divide the class into teams. Play Carlos's part from audio 1.2. (With a more advanced class, play the whole track again.) Ask the teams to write down all the subject pronouns and possessive adjectives they hear on a piece of paper. The team which has all the words from the audio wins. Write the words on the whiteboard as a class and check understanding. Ask students to name the noun that each pronoun or possessive adjective refers back to. Also, review the parts of the contractions, e.g. *I'm = I am*; *She's = She is*, etc.

Exercise 3 page 23
1 Her   **2** your   **3** your   **4** He   **5** Their   **6** Its   **7** I; my
8 We; our

Exercise 4 page 24
1 Who's   **2** name is   **3** old is   **4** isn't   **5** She's   **6** I'm not
7 I'm   **8** 're not   **9** They're   **10** We're

Exercise 5 page 24

2 is not / isn't **3** is / 's **4** Are **5** am **6** Are
7 are not / aren't **8** is / 's **9** is / 's **10** Are **11** are / 're

Exercise 6 page 24
Answers will vary.

LISTENING 2

Learning objectives

- Understand key vocabulary for jobs –
  businessman, teacher, scientist
- Listen to identify syllables and word stress in key
  vocabulary for jobs
- Listen and understand main ideas and detail in
  two student presentations about famous people
- Listen and complete a set of detailed notes
- Synthesize information from two sets of notes in
  a discussion

Lead-in

Help students with the vocabulary necessary to
talk about jobs. For each job listed on page 25, list
a short job description. Use the pictures as needed.
Give students the sentence frame to help them.
For example,

___works with___ (*A teacher works with students.;
A writer works with words.* etc.)

Challenge students to add one or more sentences to
each of the descriptions.

Exercise 1 page 25
Answers will vary.

Exercise 2 page 25
Possible answers:

a writer **b** teacher **c** businessman **d** businesswoman
e scientist **f** chef

Exercise 3 page 26
Answers will vary.

Exercise 4 page 26
1 writer (2) **2** teacher (2) **3** businessman (3)
4 businesswoman (4) **5** chef (1) **6** scientist (3)

Exercise 5 page 26
1 Nadiya Hussain **2** chef; writer; TV presenter
3 Salman Khan **4** scientist; teacher

Exercise 6 page 26
Nadiya Hussain:
family: husband; two sons; daughter
famous for: wonderful desserts
other information: *Answers will vary.*

Salman Khan:
family: father; mother; wife; son; daughter
famous for: his free school, the Khan Academy
other information: *Answers will vary.*

Exercise 7 page 27
1 c **2** d **3** e **4** f **5** g **6** a **7** h **8** b

Exercise 8 page 27
Student A: Ursula Burns; the US; first African-American
female CEO of a large company in the US; mother, Olga Burns

Student B: Larry Page; the US; started Google with a
friend; father, Carl Page / mother, Gloria Page

Optional activity

Prepare ten flashcards with photographs of
famous people and a very brief description of who
they are, where there are from, what they do and
what they are famous for. Choose famous people
who are familiar to students, e.g. currently in the
news or of historical importance. You may want to
use one or two people that students are familiar with
from the Unit Lead-in activity. A volunteer chooses
a flashcard and reads the information about the
famous person. Help the student with any unknown
vocabulary. The rest of the class ask *Yes/No*
questions about the famous person. Model simple
questions, e.g. *Is it a man?*, *Is he an actor?*, *Is he
American?*, etc. The student with the card can only
answer *yes* or *no*. The student who correctly guesses
the identity of the famous person wins. To make it
more competitive, you can put students into teams
and assign points for each correct guess.

CRITICAL THINKING

Learning objectives

- Identify the main ideas in an ideas map
- Apply your understanding of an ideas map to
  organize your notes
- Create an ideas map about a famous person

UNLOCK TEACHER DEVELOPMENT

BE INFORMED

→ **Choosing information for an ideas map** is an important skill for students because: (1) Ideas maps can help students realize what they already know about a subject; (2) They are a useful way of organizing information; (3) They can help students realize they know more than they think they do.

BE CONFIDENT

→ Develop these skills for yourself by doing the following activity:

Create an ideas map with the following question at the centre of the ideas map: 'Why is critical thinking important?'.

Lead-in

Go through the instructions with the class and focus on the speaking task. Explain that the following sections of the unit will help students to prepare to tell their group about a famous person from their country.

UNLOCK TEACHER DEVELOPMENT

BE READY

Look at the Critical Thinking section in the Student's Book on pages 28–29.

→ Which elements of the lesson do you think your students will find easiest / most difficult / most useful? Why?

→ Are your answers true for all students in your class?

→ How can you adapt your teaching or the material to meet your students' needs?

BE FLEXIBLE

An activity that you could do at the end of this lesson is to display all the 'ideas maps' in a class gallery (e.g. by sticking them all on the board). The information at the centre (i.e. the person) should be covered up. Students then look at the other information and guess who the person is.

Exercise 1 page 28
1 Nadiya Hussain   2 Home; Job; Family

Exercises 2–5 page 29
Answers will vary.

UNLOCK TEACHER DEVELOPMENT

BE REFLECTIVE

Think about the following questions:

→ Did you create your own ideas map before the lesson? Was this useful? Did it improve the quality of your teaching in the lesson?

→ Ask colleagues to also create an ideas map for the question in *Be confident*, either on paper or electronically. Compare your answers.

BE COLLABORATIVE

Your development is more meaningful when it is shared. See page 14 for ideas on how to peer-collaborate. Why not share the ideas you generated in the *Be ready* section, and their outcome?

PREPARATION FOR SPEAKING

Learning objectives

* Use adjectives and *from + noun* to describe nationality – *Eunseong Kim is a famous Korean scientist. Ana García is from Mexico. Karim Abdel Aziz is an Egyptian actor.*
* Form job titles from nouns and verbs – *manage > manager, act > actor, art > artist*
* Use phrases for introducing people and starting presentations – *I'm going to tell you about Ana García. Ana García is a famous Mexican chef. This is Haruki Murakami.*
* Use word and sentence stress correctly in sentences about famous people.

Exercise 1 page 30
1 Egyptian   **2** Emirati   **3** Japanese   **4** Turkish
5 American   **6** Omani

Exercise 2 page 30
1 South Korean   **2** Mexico   **3** Egyptian   **4** Japan
5 Chinese   **6** American   **7** Omani   **8** Emirati

Exercise 3 page 31
Verb + -er/-r: dancer, singer, painter, manager, player, presenter, teacher
Verb + -or: director
Noun + -er: gardener, photographer, driver, engineer, designer
Noun + -ist: journalist

Exercise 4 page 31
1 b   **2** b   **3** c   **4** c

Optional activity

👥 👥 Students work in pairs and use the sentence structures from Exercise 4 to make new sentences about famous people they know. Students don't have to write these down. Ask students to make as many sentences as they can in three minutes. As a class, ask each pair to demonstrate their best sentences to the other students.

Exercise 7 page 32

2 <u>Ka</u>rim <u>Ab</u>del <u>Az</u>iz is a <u>fa</u>mous <u>ac</u>tor.

3 <u>Car</u>men Su<u>lei</u>man's a <u>fa</u>mous <u>sing</u>er.

4 <u>Ka</u>rim's <u>fa</u>ther is Mo<u>ham</u>med <u>Ab</u>del A<u>ziz.</u>

5 <u>He</u>'s a <u>film</u> di<u>rec</u>tor.

6 <u>Ka</u>rim's aunt is Sa<u>mi</u>ra <u>Muh</u>sin.

7 <u>She</u>'s an <u>ac</u>tor.

Exercises 8–9 page 32

Answers will vary.

SPEAKING TASK

Learning objectives

- Prepare for a presentation by reviewing and adding to your notes
- Prepare an introduction
- Give a presentation on a famous person
- Listen and take notes on presentations about famous people
- Decide and justify why you would like to meet a famous person

Exercises 1–6 page 33

Answers will vary.

RESEARCH PROJECT

Create a documentary about a famous person.

Divide the class into groups and ask each group to pick a famous person. Tell them that they have to find out about that person's childhood, career and personal life, including video clips and photos. They could search for that person's website or look for information in online newspapers. Social networking sites also often have pages about famous people. Students could use online tools to record and share their research.

Students then use this information to film or record a documentary about that person. To plan the documentary, students will need to create a script or storyboard. They will also have to think about who will direct and record the video, who will do the editing and who will do the presenting.

CLASSROOM APP

Exercises 1–2

Answers will vary.

Exercise 3

1 My mother is a teacher.   2 I like your car.   3 She's my sister.   4 They study with me.   5 Maria lost her book.

Exercise 4

1 is   2 are not   3 is   4 are you   5 what is

Exercise 5

1 businesswoman   2 chef   3 mother   4 businessman   5 family   6 teacher   7 father   8 student

Exercise 6A

1 -or   2 -ist   3 -er   4 -er   5 -tist

Exercise 6B

Answers will vary.

UNIT OBJECTIVES

Watch and listen	Watch and understand a video about deserts.
Listening skill	Use visuals to predict content.
Critical thinking	Use visuals in a talk.
Grammar	Use *there is / there are*; use adjectives.
Speaking skill	Describe visuals.
Speaking task	Describe photos of a place you want to visit.
↻ Teacher development	Help your students become better at **using visuals in a talk**.

UNLOCK YOUR KNOWLEDGE

Background note

The photo shows Exit Glacier, located in Kenai Fjords National Park, Alaska, the USA. It is one of the most popular glaciers that is accessible by road. The photo was taken from one of the trails during spring or autumn. In the photo, we can see the icy glacier in the background, with a grassy field full of wild flowers in front of it.

Lead-in

Write the seasons for your country on the board. Then briefly show a picture to represent each season and give a short weather description. Invite students to name the season.

page 37

1 snow and ice; colourful flowers; grass; trees and shrubs
2 There is snow very close to colourful flowers, grass, trees and shrubs. The two areas are very different but right next to each other.
3 *Answers will vary.*

WATCH AND LISTEN

Learning objectives

- Listen and identify main ideas in a video about desert climates
- Listen and identify facts and figures
- Complete a set of inferences about the information in the video
- Practise talking about deserts

Exercise 1 page 38
Answers will vary.

Exercise 2 page 38
1 T   2 T   3 T   4 F; A desert is not necessarily flat.

Exercise 3 page 38
1 very hot   2 does not have   3 There are   4 the equator

Exercise 4 page 39
1 c   2 a   3 b

Exercise 5 page 39
1 difficult   2 rain   3 fruits and vegetables   4 careful

Exercise 6 page 39
Answers will vary.

LISTENING 1

Learning objectives

- Understand key vocabulary for seasons – *cold, autumn, snow*
- Use visuals to understand a topic before you listen
- Gain awareness of and identify sentence stress
- Listen to and understand main ideas and details in a talk about a country's climate
- Describe weather and places in photographs

Lead-in

Tell students Listening 1 is a classroom conversation that is focused on the photos on page 41. Ask students to look at the photos and describe them in pairs. Elicit ideas as a class.

Exercise 1 page 40

1 hot   **2** cold   **3** snow; weather   **4** spring
5 autumn   **6** temperature

Exercise 2 page 40

Answers will vary.

Exercise 3 page 41

1 *Answers will vary. Note that all of these photos are of Japan.*

2 a   **3** a   **4** b
5 a summer   **b** winter   **c** autumn   **d** spring
6 a hot   **b** cold   **c** cool   **d** cool / warm

Exercise 4 page 42

1 Take a look at the photos.
2 They are all from one place.
3 There's a beautiful beach next to a big lake.
4 It's winter, and there's a mountain.
5 It's hot and there's sand.

Be flexible

👤 👥 To give more practice with sentence stress, ask students to go back to Exercise 1 on page 40 and read the sentences out loud. Students work in pairs and underline the stressed words in each sentence. Challenge them to identify the stressed words as nouns, adjectives or verbs. Then ask students to take turns saying the sentences, stressing the underlined words. Ask **more advanced students** to circle the stressed syllables in the underlined content words. Check the answers as a class. Ask volunteers to say the sentences out loud, correcting the sentence stress if necessary.

Exercise 5 page 42

All four

Exercises 6–7 page 42

1 hot   **2** snow   **3** cold   **4** autumn   **5** red; orange
6 spring   **7** warm

Exercise 8 page 43

Answers will vary.

LANGUAGE DEVELOPMENT

Learning objectives

- Name seasons – *spring, summer, autumn*
- Use nouns and adjectives correctly to name types of weather – *I'm happy when it's sunny. We get a lot of storms in April. It's windy in autumn.*
- Name seven different colours – *white, black, orange*
- Use phrases to ask and answer questions about colour – *What colour is your family's car? It's red.*

- Use *there is/are* to talk about seasons, weather and places – *There are extreme temperatures in the winter. There's a lot of wind. There's a river.*

Exercise 1 page 44

a winter   **b** summer   **c** spring   **d** autumn
e the rainy season   **f** the dry season

Exercise 2 page 44

Answers will vary.

Exercise 3 page 45

From the top to the bottom row of the table, the picture numbers are: 3, 6, 2, 5, 1, 4

Exercise 4 page 45

1 sunny   **2** cloud   **3** rainy   **4** storms   **5** snow   **6** windy

Exercises 5–6 page 45

Answers will vary.

Optional activity

👤 👥 Prepare a worksheet with questions like: *Do you like to stay inside when it's sunny?*, *Do you like to go outside when it's windy?*, *Do you like to stay at home and read when it's rainy?*, *Are you afraid when it's stormy?*, etc. Students mingle with the rest of their classmates and ask the questions. After five minutes, ask students to share their findings with the class.

Exercise 7 page 46

orange 6   **red** 2   **green** 5   **white** 1   **yellow** 4   **blue** 3   **black** 7

Exercise 8 page 46

1 blue; green   **2** white   **3** green; red; orange
4 yellow; white   **5** white; black; grey   **6** *Answers will vary.*

Exercise 9 page 47

Countable nouns: river; rock; town; cloud; temperature
Uncountable nouns: water; wind; sand

Exercises 10–11 page 47

1 There's a   **2** There's   **3** There are   **4** There's
5 There's a   **6** There are   **7** There are   **8** There's

LISTENING 2

Learning objectives

- Understand key vocabulary for landscapes – *desert, forest, island*
- Listen and identify the main ideas and details in two presentations about landscapes and seasons

- Listen and note details in a table
- Synthesize information from a talk about a country's climate and two presentations about landscapes and seasons in a discussion

Lead-in

Point out the photos from Exercise 2. Ask students to guess where the photos could have been taken. Allow two to three minutes for discussion, then ask the pairs to share their ideas with the class. Tell students that they will find out from the Listening where two of the photographs were taken.

Exercise 1 page 48

1 **a** autumn **b** spring or summer **c** summer **d** spring or winter
2 It is sunny in all the photographs.
3 blue; green; orange; yellow; white; grey; red

Exercise 2 page 48

1 mountain 2 forest 3 island 4 sea 5 sky
6 desert 7 park

Exercise 3 page 49

1 b 2 a 3 c and d

Be flexible

👤 With a **more advanced class**, ask students to close their books and take notes while they listen. Students then use their notes to answer the questions.

Exercise 4 page 49

1 **a** spring **b** Turkey **c** forest **d** beautiful
2 **a** another **b** autumn **c** cold **d** park

Exercise 5 page 49

Daniela: *white* building; *blue* sea and sky
Altan: *red and orange* trees

Exercise 6 page 49

Answers will vary.

CRITICAL THINKING

Learning objectives

- Understand how visuals support content in a presentation
- Evaluate the best season to visit a place
- Evaluate and choose photographs for a talk
- Apply your ideas about a place to describe photos

UNLOCK TEACHER DEVELOPMENT

BE INFORMED

→ **Using visuals in a talk** is an important skill for students because: (1) Visuals make a talk more interesting; (2) They can be a quick and easy way of presenting a lot of information and data; (3) Using visuals makes the process of preparing a talk more interesting, so the outcome should also be better.

BE CONFIDENT

→ Develop this skill for yourself by doing the following activity:
Think of talks and presentations that you have been to, and ask yourself the following questions:
1 What kind of visuals had the biggest impact on you? Are there any you can still remember?
2 How did speakers use visuals effectively within their talk?
3 How did speakers use visuals poorly within their talk?

Lead-in

Go through the instructions with the class and focus on the Speaking task. Explain that the following sections of the unit will help them to prepare to describe photos of a place they want to visit. Point out that to give an interesting talk, you need time to ask and answer questions, take notes, plan and prepare. Emphasize that because the Speaking task for the unit focuses on a visual, it's very important to find an engaging and interesting photo.

UNLOCK TEACHER DEVELOPMENT

BE READY

Look at the Critical Thinking section in the Student's Book on pages 50–51.
→ Which elements of the lesson do you think your students will find easiest / most difficult / most useful? Why?
→ Are your answers true for all students in your class?
→ How can you adapt your teaching or the material to meet your students' needs?

BE FLEXIBLE

Depending on your class, Exercises 3 and 4 could be done digitally. Since many of your students may already be in an online group, they could post the photos and text there.

Exercise 1 page 50

1 snow next to flowers, trees, shrubs and grass **2** spring or summer **3** cold / cool / sunny **4** blue; white; green; orange; yellow; red **5** *Answers will vary.*
6 cold; snow; weather; spring; summer; sunny; temperature

Optional activity

Allow students to select a few photos before they choose the one for the Speaking task. Students then work in small groups and use the questions from Exercise 1 to evaluate the photos. Students discuss which photo is the most interesting; they can help each other select the best one for the task.

Exercises 2–5 page 51

Answers will vary.

UNLOCK TEACHER DEVELOPMENT

BE REFLECTIVE

Think about the following questions:

→ How confident are you about integrating the students' digital lives with their 'real' lives? (see *Be flexible* section.) Since the two are closely linked for many young people, this is an important consideration in your teaching. If you would like to do this, but do not feel confident, consider what training or additional support you might need.

→ What was your students' level of 'world knowledge'? Did different students have different levels of knowledge? Knowing this can help you plan better for future sessions.

BE COLLABORATIVE

Your development is more meaningful when it is shared. See page 14 for ideas on how to peer-collaborate. Why not share the ideas you generated in the *Be ready* section, and their outcome?

PREPARATION FOR SPEAKING

Learning objectives

- Use phrases for introducing photographs and starting presentations – *Good morning everybody. I'm going to talk about Samsun. OK, so here's a photo of the park.*
- Identify appropriate places for syllable stress and pauses in sentences
- Use adjectives with correct word order to describe seasons, weather and places – *There's a big mountain. There are white clouds in the sky. It's a sunny day.*

Exercise 1 page 51 and Exercises 2–3 page 52

a Good <u>morning</u>, everybody.
b I'm going to talk about <u>two photos</u> of a <u>place</u> in <u>spring</u>.
c OK, so <u>here's</u> my <u>first photo</u>.
d <u>Hello</u>, everybody! <u>I</u>'m Altan.
e I'm from <u>Samsun</u>. Samsun is in <u>Turkey</u>.
f Here's my <u>first</u> photo.
g Here's <u>another</u> photo of the <u>park</u>.

Exercise 4 page 52

OK, // so today I want to talk about a place with extreme temperatures. // Take a look at the photos. // What seasons do you see?

Exercise 5 page 52

Answers will vary. Suggested answer:

In photo 1, there is snow on a mountain (Mount Fuji in Japan). There are red leaves on the trees. It is autumn.

In photo 2, people are hiking on a mountain. They are very high up. There are white clouds in the blue sky.

Exercise 6 page 53

1 f **2** c **3** e **4** a **5** b **6** d

Exercise 7 page 53

Answers will vary.

Exercise 8 page 54

Possible answers:

1 There are white clouds in the sky.
2 It's a snowy day in winter.
3 There are some big mountains in Switzerland.
4 It's a sunny day in spring.
5 The trees are orange and red in the autumn.
6 It's a beautiful beach.

Optional activity

Students work in pairs and underline the stressed words in each sentence. Check their answers as a class. Allow students a couple of minutes to practise saying the sentences by stressing only the content words. Monitor and give feedback on sentence stress. The stressed words are:

1 white; clouds; sky **2** snowy; day; winter **3** mountains; Switzerland **4** sunny; day; spring **5** trees; orange; red; autumn **6** beautiful; beach

Exercise 9 page 54

1 It's sunny in the photo.
2 There are white clouds.
3 There's a big mountain.
4 The people are happy.
5 There's a green forest.
6 It's a rainy day.

SPEAKING TASK

Learning objectives

- Prepare for a talk by reviewing and adding to your notes
- Give feedback on another student's talk
- Respond to feedback on your talk
- Describe photos in a talk about a place you want to visit
- Listen and take notes on presentations about places
- Respond to feedback on your notes

Exercises 1–6 pages 55–56
Answers will vary.

RESEARCH PROJECT

Become a weather forecaster.

Divide the class into groups and ask them to research ways to monitor the weather in different places around the world. For example, one group could do an internet search for 'weather in London', another group could search for 'weather in Sydney' and another group 'weather in Mumbai'. Students could note information on how hot/cold the temperature is, how windy it is and whether it is raining/snowing, etc.

Each group could present the information they have found to the rest of the class as a weather forecast. They can see examples of weather forecasts on video-sharing websites, and could film and upload their own forecasts to the same or a similar website. Each group could also create a blog with the weather report for their chosen place and update this daily over the course of a week.

CLASSROOM APP

Exercise 1
Answers will vary.

Exercise 2
1 winter **2** stormy **3** black **4** rainy **5** dry **6** sunny
7 green **8** Spring

Exercise 3
1 is, rain **2** are, rivers **3** are, trees **4** is, town **5** is, sand

Exercise 4
1 temperature **2** island **3** mountain **4** autumn
5 spring **6** weather **7** water **8** desert

Exercise 5
Answers will vary.

Exercise 6A
1 white, sand, beach **2** men, black, snow **3** beautiful, trees, Japan **4** a, green, mountain **5** snowy, weather, very

Exercise 6B
Answers will vary.

UNIT OBJECTIVES

Watch and listen	Watch and understand a video about a kite festival in Australia.
Listening skills	Listen for main ideas.
Critical thinking	Understand surveys.
Grammar	Use the present simple.
Speaking skill	Use prepositions to talk about when things happen.
Speaking task	Interview students for a survey.
♻ **Teacher development**	Help your students become better at **understanding surveys**.

UNLOCK YOUR KNOWLEDGE

Background note

The photo shows two Egyptian men in traditional clothes, sitting on camels. The photo is taken in front of the pyramids in Giza, Egypt. The younger man is looking at his mobile phone. The photo shows how traditional and modern lifestyles can exist together.

Lead-in

Point out that the word *lifestyle* is a compound word, made from two words put together. Share short definitions of both words: *life = part of somebody's experience* and *style = a way of doing something*. Then show some photos of people, and with students, list short descriptions for their possible lifestyles. For example, a photo of a businesswoman = *busy, wakes up early*, etc.

page 59

1 Two men riding camels. One is also looking at a phone.
2–3 *Answers will vary.*

WATCH AND LISTEN

Learning objectives

* Listen and identify main ideas and details in a video about a festival
* Complete a set of inferences about the information in the video
* Practise talking about festivals

Exercise 1 page 60
Answers will vary.

Exercise 2 page 60
a 4   **b** 3   **c** 2   **d** 1

Exercise 3 page 60
1; 3; 4; 5

Exercise 4 page 61
1 a   **2** c   **3** b   **4** a   **5** b

Exercise 5 page 61
1 c   **2** a   **3** d   **4** b

Exercise 6 page 61
Answers will vary.

LISTENING 1

Learning objectives

* Understand key vocabulary for lifestyle – *play computer games, exercise, watch TV*
* Gain awareness of rising and falling intonation in open and closed questions and answers
* Listen and understand *where, who* and *why* in a discussion
* Listen and understand details
* Discuss healthy lifestyles

Lead-in

Point out that the Listening has multiple speakers and students will have to listen closely to track the different speakers. Tell them that Listening 1 is about the lifestyle of one group of people. Ask students to discuss in pairs what they think the lifestyles of the people on pages 62 and 63 are like. After five minutes, elicit ideas from the class.

Exercise 1 page 62

Answers will vary.

Exercise 2 page 62

1 c **2** f **3** a **4** g **5** b **6** d **7** e

Exercise 4 page 63

1 down **2** down **3** down **4** up **5** down **6** up

Exercise 5 page 64

1 b **2** c **3** c

Exercise 6 page 64

1 F; It is morning. **2** T **3** F; Abdul sleeps six or seven hours a night. **4** T **5** T **6** F; Sandra does not exercise.

Exercise 7 page 65

Answers will vary.

Be flexible

👥 👥👥 With a **more advanced** class, invite students to write tips for a healthy lifestyle. Give students ten minutes to brainstorm in pairs. Then ask students to write their tips on a shared document to display for the whole class. Ask students to rank the tips in order, from most important to least important, and discuss their opinions in small groups.

LANGUAGE DEVELOPMENT

Learning objectives

- Use the present simple to describe things people usually do – *They go to work at 8:30. She goes to work at 8:30. She doesn't work at weekends.*
- Use present simple questions to ask about things that people do – *Do you cook? Yes, I do. Does he cook? No, he doesn't. Where do they live?*
- Use common collocations to describe lifestyles. *I have a coffee. I don't make breakfast.*
- Ask and answer questions about lifestyle using collocations and present simple questions – *Do you eat out at restaurants? Yes, I do. Where do you do your homework? At the library.*

Exercise 1 page 66

1 have **2** gets up; goes **3** doesn't eat; has; starts **4** doesn't go **5** works **6** takes; walks **7** make **8** does; exercises **9** plays; goes **10** don't like

Exercise 2 page 67

1 Do you exercise? **2** Do you do homework? **3** Which computer games do you play? **4** Do you watch TV in the evening? **5** Who do you text at the weekend? **6** Where do you live? **7** What do you study at university?

Exercise 3 page 68

1 Do; don't **2** Does; does **3** Do; do **4** Does; doesn't

Exercise 4 page 68

1 Where do they live? **2** What does she study? **3** Where do you work? **4** When does he go to bed? / What time does he go to bed? **5** Who do you study with?

Exercise 5 page 68

1 Do you cook food for your family? **2** Do you do homework? **3** What do you do at home? **4** Where do you go with friends? **5** What smartphone do you like?

Exercise 6 page 68

Answers will vary.

Exercise 7 page 69

2 make **3** play **4** go **5** get **6** take **7** watch

Exercise 8 page 70

2 eat **3** have **4** watch **5** play **6** go **7** do

Exercises 9–10 page 70

Answers will vary.

Optional activity

👥 👥👥 Prepare paper slips with collocations from the table: *chat online, eat out at restaurants, eat at home, have coffee with friends, have dinner with friends, go out with friends, go to the cinema, do homework, go to the gym, play sports* and *play computer games*. Prepare enough slips for several pairs or groups. Cut the slips into halves and ask each pair or group to match the collocations. At the end, ask each pair or group to say one collocation and write it on the whiteboard. To make it more competitive, ask the groups to work quietly and raise a hand when they think they are finished. The group that correctly completes all the collocations first wins.

LISTENING 2

Learning objectives

- Understand key vocabulary for lifestyles – *busy, parents, study*
- Listen and understand *where, who* and *why* in a discussion
- Listen and note details in a questionnaire
- Synthesize information from two discussions about lifestyle

Lead-in

Ask students if they have been stopped on the street before to answer questions for a survey, or to hear about a group or organization's work. Discuss that this is a way for businesses, organizations and researchers to get information. You may want to point out that often most people have a name tag or other item that shows they are working for or belong to an organization. This helps people on the street know who they are.

Exercise 1 page 71

Answers will vary.

Exercise 2 page 71

1 study   **2** gym   **3** go out   **4** parents   **5** café   **6** busy

Exercise 3 page 72

1 Excuse me. / I'd like to   **2** Can I have / Sure. No problem.
3 Sorry / I'm afraid I don't.

Exercise 5 page 72

1 c   **2** a   **3** a

Exercise 6 page 73

A1 Y   **B1** study   **C1** Y   **C2a** goes to a gym   **C2b** Y
C2c Y   **C2d** N   **C3a** on Saturday afternoons   **C3b** a café

Exercise 7 page 73

Answers will vary.

CRITICAL THINKING

Learning objectives

- Use an ideas map to organize ideas from a survey
- Create an ideas map to plan a lifestyle questionnaire
- Write questions for a survey, using an ideas map

UNLOCK TEACHER DEVELOPMENT

BE INFORMED

→ **Understanding surveys** is an important skill for students because: (1) Surveys are frequently used for gathering academic research data; (2) Surveys are also a common business tool for getting information, such as customer feedback; (3) Students sometimes find it hard to know what questions to ask and the language that is required.

BE CONFIDENT

→ Develop this skill for yourself by doing the following activity:

Imagine you wanted to find out more about the teaching of critical thinking in your educational institution. Think about these questions:

1 Who would you ask?
2 What questions would you ask?
3 How long would your survey be?
4 How would you distribute it?

Lead-in

Go through the instructions with the class and focus on the Speaking task. Explain that the following sections of the unit will help them to prepare to interview students for a survey. Encourage students to look back at the questionnaire on page 73 as they write their questions for Exercises 4 and 5. Point out that students will want some simple *Yes/No* questions, so that the survey answers are easy to collect.

UNLOCK TEACHER DEVELOPMENT

BE READY

Look at the Critical Thinking section in the Student's Book on pages 74–75.

→ Which elements of the lesson do you think your students will find easiest / most difficult / most useful? Why?

→ Are your answers true for all students in your class?

→ How can you adapt your teaching or the material to meet your students' needs?

BE FLEXIBLE

When doing Exercise 4, students could write just two to three questions, and then share them with others to check that they are going in the right direction. Using feedback to improve a survey is a common technique, and it may be helpful to make students aware of this.

Exercises 1–2 page 74

Bottom left bubble:

Topic: Work / Study

Information: Work or study? What job? What do you study?

Right bubble:

Topic: Lifestyle

Information: Busy lifestyle? How do you relax? Exercise? Go to a gym? Go to the cinema? Go out with friends? When? Where?

Be flexible

👤 Challenge **advanced students** to think of other topic ideas on lifestyle, e.g. *sleep/eating habits*, etc. They could add them to the ideas map and generate details.

Exercises 3–5 page 75

Answers will vary.

UNL⊙CK TEACHER DEVELOPMENT

BE REFLECTIVE

Think about the following points:

→ If you have time, create a short survey based on what you thought about in *Be confident*. Try and get your colleagues to complete it.

→ Which aspect of the lesson did the students find more challenging: the conceptual (i.e. the content and subject matter) or the linguistic (i.e. forming the questions)? Understanding the strengths and weaknesses of your class will help you prepare better in the future.

BE COLLABORATIVE

Your development is more meaningful when it is shared. See page 14 for ideas on how to peer-collaborate. Why not share the ideas you generated in the *Be ready* section, and their outcome?

PREPARATION FOR SPEAKING

Learning objectives

- Use correct prepositions in time phrases – *at 1:00 pm, in the evening, on Wednesday*
- Pronounce third-person present simple verbs correctly

Exercise 1 page 76

2 at 6:00; in the morning   **3** in the evening
4 on Wednesdays   **5** at 3:00; in the afternoon
6 on Saturdays

Exercises 2–3 page 76

1 at   **2** at   **3** at   **4** on   **5** On   **6** at   **7** On   **8** at   **9** in
10 on   **11** On   **12** in   **13** On   **14** in

Be flexible

👤👥 Ask **lower-level students** to listen to the recording about Rabia one more time and follow the text as they listen. Students take turns saying the sentences in pairs. Allow a couple of minutes for practice. Monitor and give feedback on the pronunciation of the time expressions.

Exercise 5 page 77

texts 1; sleeps 1; needs 1; goes 1; studies 2; watches 2; chooses 2

Exercise 6 page 77

2 /z/   **3** /əz/   **4** /z/   **5** /əz/   **6** /s/   **7** /z/   **8** /s/

SPEAKING TASK

Learning objectives

- Prepare for an interview about lifestyle by reviewing and adding to survey questions
- Ask and answer questions using polite phrases
- Conduct an interview about lifestyle and take notes
- Present the results of your interview

Exercises 1–5 page 78

Answers will vary.

RESEARCH PROJECT

Create a lifestyle podcast.

Tell students that they are going to create a lifestyle podcast. Different groups in the class could think about a different topic, e.g. sport and exercise, technology use, holiday destinations or food. Students can use online tools to share the information that they find with the rest of their group.

Each group should create a short, two-minute podcast about their chosen topic. The podcast could include interviews with teachers or other students, a discussion, or advice. Students will need to plan the recording, record the podcast and then edit it. They can search online for free audio-editing software/apps. They could then share their podcast with the class to listen to and comment on.

CLASSROOM APP

Exercises 1–2

Answers will vary.

Exercise 3

1 does not start / doesn't start **2** gets up **3** do not have / don't have **4** do, exercise **5** does, work

Exercise 4

1 play **2** have **3** watches **4** eat **5** chats

Exercise 5

1 gym **2** busy **3** exercise **4** parents **5** homework
6 sleep **7** study **8** go online

Exercise 6A

1 at **2** in **3** on **4** at **5** on

Exercise 6B

Answers will vary.

UNIT OBJECTIVES	
Watch and listen	Watch and understand a video about Shanghai.
Listening skill	Listen for detail.
Critical thinking	Interpret maps and directions.
Grammar	Use prepositions of place; use the imperative.
Speaking skill	Give and ask for directions.
Speaking task	Ask for and give directions in a university town.
⟳ **Teacher development**	Help your students become better at **interpreting maps and directions**.

UNLOCK YOUR KNOWLEDGE

Background note

The photo shows the skyscrapers in the financial centre of London. There is a mix of old buildings and modern skyscrapers. The skyline is full of cranes, which suggests further construction and development in other parts of the city.

Lead-in

Ask students to think of a place they would like to visit. Allow them about five minutes to make notes about the place, e.g. its name, location, what can people do there, etc. Students work in small groups and tell each other about the place. Model the first sentence, *I would like to visit ...*. Ask volunteers to share ideas with the class.

page 81
1 The photo shows the London skyline. There are a lot of tall buildings in different shapes.
2–3 *Answers will vary.*

WATCH AND LISTEN

Learning objectives

- Listen and understand the main ideas in a video about cities
- Listen and understand detailed information
- Complete a set of inferences about the information in the video
- Practise talking about changes in cities

Exercise 1 page 82
Answers will vary.

Exercise 2 page 82
a 2   **b** 1   **c** 4   **d** 3

Exercise 3 page 83
1 T   **2** T   **3** F; He takes photos two times a year.
4 F; The city looks very different today.

Exercise 4 page 83
1 ten   **2** important   **3** changes   **4** different

Exercise 5 page 83
1 cities   **2** fast-growing   **3** like   **4** a lot

Exercise 6 page 83
Answers will vary.

LISTENING 1

Learning objectives

- Understand key vocabulary for places – *building, location, safe*
- Listen and identify stressed words in directions
- Listen and identify main ideas in a presentation about an app
- Listen and understand details

Lead-in

Prepare between three and five slides with photographs of objects, both singular and plural, and close and far away. Display each slide and describe the objects, using sentences starting with *this*, *that*, *here* and *there*. Then display the slides again and elicit the sentences from students.

Exercise 1 page 84
1 location   **2** library   **3** safe   **4** directions   **5** building
6 map

Exercise 2 page 85

1 this   **2** here; there   **3** there   **4** here

Exercise 3 page 85

Yes, the words are stressed.

Exercise 4 page 85

1 to locate people or places   **2** in a phone app
3 *Possible answers:* school; library; park; home;
neighbourhood; streets; people; school bus

Exercise 5 page 85

1 c   **2** c   **3** c

Exercise 6 page 86

1 T   **2** T   **3** T

4 F; The map shows the locations of three children.

5 F; One daughter is opposite the library, and one
daughter is by the school bus.

6 F; The teenagers do like the app.

Exercise 7 page 86

Answers will vary.

Be flexible

For a **more advanced class**, expand this
activity into a debate. Ask small groups to debate
the question: *Should people track their friends
and family?* Students then create a T-chart to list
the positives and negatives. Spur both sides of the
debate by adding questions, for example, *What age
is it OK for you to not be tracked? Do adults need
to be tracked? What are some situations where
it's good for people to know where you are? Why
do some people not want to be tracked? When
could it be dangerous to be tracked?* Then expand
the conversation to the whole group. Encourage
students to use examples to justify their thinking.

LANGUAGE DEVELOPMENT

Learning objectives

- Name common places in a city – *fountain,
  library, monument*
- Understand prepositions of place – *by, behind,
  between*
- Use prepositions of movement and place to
  describe a route through a city – *Go through the
  square. Go along the road. Go around the fountain.*
- Use the imperative form of the verb to give
  directions – *Turn left. Go down Main Road.*

Exercise 1 page 86

1 factory   **2** train station   **3** fountain   **4** bridge   **5** bank
6 museum   **7** park   **8** monument   **9** university   **10** library

Exercise 2 page 88

1 library   **2** bank   **3** monument   **4** factory   **5** museum
6 university   **7** train station   **8** fountain

Exercise 3 page 88

1 a   **2** b   **3** d   **4** g   **5** f   **6** h   **7** c   **8** e

---

Be flexible

For **lower-level students**, or those who need
additional speaking practice, provide an opportunity
to role play the dialogues and practise pronunciation.
Model pronunciation and intonation for them by
playing audio 4.3 again. Pause after each conversation.
Ask students to repeat the questions and answers
as they hear them on the recording. Then students
work in pairs and practise the short dialogues
from the audio. Monitor and give feedback on the
pronunciation of the vocabulary for places.

Exercise 4 page 88

a behind   **b** over   **c** in front of   **d** between   **e** in
f on the left; next to   **g** by   **h** opposite

Exercise 5 page 88

1 in front of   **2** next to / by   **3** behind   **4** between
5 on the left / right   **6** in   **7** over   **8** opposite

Exercise 6 page 89

1 out of   **2** go / turn left   **3** Go / Turn right   **4** up
5 around   **6** along   **7** over   **8** over   **9** through
10 by / next to / opposite   **11** go / turn right   **12** into

Exercise 7 page 90

1 Go / Turn   **2** Walk / Go   **3** Go / Turn   **4** Enter
5 Don't forget   **6** Go / Turn

Exercise 8 page 90

1 Turn the map the other way, please!

2 Look for the café on South Road.

3 Do not / Don't enter the building on Main Road.

4 Don't go along York Street to the gym.

5 Do not / Don't go east on West Park Street.

6 Don't turn left on Sun Street.

Exercise 9 page 90

Answers will vary.

LISTENING 2

Learning objectives

- Understand key vocabulary for cities – *shopping centre, playground, toilets*
- Understand a map
- Listen and understand *where, who* and *why* in a discussion about directions
- Listen and complete detailed directions
- Synthesize ideas from discussions about directions

Lead-in

Prepare students for Listening 2 by asking pairs to write directions from the campus to well-known nearby places (e.g. parks, museums, other campus buildings, etc.). Then ask students to compare their directions to those given by online navigation sites. Invite discussion and reflection. Ask: *Which directions are easier to follow, yours or the phone's? Why?*

Exercises 1–2 page 91
Answers will vary.

Exercise 3 page 92
A

Exercise 4 page 92
1 T   **2** T

3 F; The supermarket is between the bus station and the toy shop.
4 F; The playground is next to the shoe shop.
5 F; Entrance 3 is on East Street.   **6** T
7 F; The toilets are next to the stairs.   **8** T

Exercise 5 page 93
1 c   **2** b   **3** a

Exercise 6 page 93
1 cinema   **2** out of; left   **3** supermarket
4 east; right; next   **5** toilets   **6** opposite; next

Exercise 7 page 93
Answers will vary.

CRITICAL THINKING

Learning objectives

- Identify phrases used to give locations in directions
- Use a map to identify a route and directions
- Evaluate which routes on a map are the most direct

UNLOCK TEACHER DEVELOPMENT

BE INFORMED

→ **Interpreting maps and directions** is an important skill for students because: (1) It is a core life skill; (2) Students often lack confidence when doing this 'in public' so need more practice in terms of language; (3) Some students will have problems with spatial awareness, so need help in grasping the concepts.

BE CONFIDENT

→ Develop this skill for yourself by doing the following activity:
Think about a route which you walk or drive regularly. Which way do you normally go? Why? Are there alternative routes? What are the advantages/disadvantages of each?

Lead-in

Go through the instructions with the class and focus on the Speaking task. Explain that the following sections of the unit will help them to ask for and give directions in a university town. Then tell students they will prepare for this task by using Map 3 on page 92 to give directions.

UNLOCK TEACHER DEVELOPMENT

BE READY

Look at the Critical Thinking section in the Student's Book on pages 94–95.
→ Which elements of the lesson do you think your students will find easiest / most difficult / most useful? Why?
→ Are your answers true for all students in your class?
→ How can you adapt your teaching or the material to meet your students' needs?

BE FLEXIBLE

Show the relevance of what they are learning by getting the students to think about your educational institution. Ask them the best way to get from one place to another. In order to tell them whether or not they are correct, you may need to work this out for yourself. If time permits, ask students in pairs to ask and explain how to get from one part of the institution to another, e.g. *Can you tell me how to get from the library to the cafeteria?*

Exercise 1 page 94

2 in this   **3** there; on your right; next to   **4** here; behind
5 at   **6** opposite; next to

Exercises 2–3 page 94

Go in entrance 1. At path A, turn left. Go along path A. When you get to the food court turn right. It's there. It's behind the shoe shop.

Exercises 4–5 page 94

Answers will vary.

UNLOCK TEACHER DEVELOPMENT

BE REFLECTIVE

Think about the following points:

→ Discuss with colleagues (either face-to-face or electronically) the *Be confident* questions. Compare and contrast your responses.

→ Think about your own physical and spatial relationship with the educational institution you work in. Think about how you move between rooms and areas. Understanding the space in which you work can help you have a deeper understanding and connection with it.

BE COLLABORATIVE

Your development is more meaningful when it is shared. See page 14 for ideas on how to peer-collaborate. Why not share the activities you tried out in the *Be flexible* section opposite, and their outcome?

PREPARATION FOR SPEAKING

Learning objectives

* Listen and give directions with prepositions of movement and place
* Use correct word order in questions asking for directions
* Practise asking for directions
* Listen and understand questions used for asking directions
* Use correct sentence stress and intonation in questions and answers about directions

Exercise 1 page 95

2 Go; turn; follow   **3** Go; go

Optional activity

👤 To practise listening to and using the imperatives, play *Simon says* with the class. In the game, one player takes the role of 'Simon' and gives instructions using imperatives, e.g. *Pick up your pen.*, *Stand up.*, *Turn around.*, *Close your book.*, etc. The other players follow the commands only if they are preceded by the phrase *Simon says ....* Students are eliminated from the game if they do not follow the instructions immediately, misunderstand the instructions or follow instructions that are not preceded by the phrase *Simon says ....* The last student in the game wins. Model the game first, then allow volunteers to take over.

Exercise 2 page 95

1 opposite   **2** in   **3** through   **4** in front of; right   **5** at
6 along   **7** next to   **8** on; behind

Exercise 3 page 96

1 Where's the supermarket?
2 Is the Physics building near here?
3 How do I get to the Language Centre?
4 Can you tell me how to get to the History building?
5 I'm looking for the Maths building. Is it near here?

Exercise 5 page 96

1 Where   **2** to get   **3** near here   **4** How

Exercise 6 page 97

a Can you tell me how to get to the History building, please?
b Is the Physics building near here?
c How do I get to the Language Centre?

Exercise 7 page 97

1 Ex<u>cuse</u> me! <u>Where</u>'s the <u>stu</u>dent centre, please?
2 Ex<u>cuse</u> me! I <u>think</u> I'm <u>lost</u>. <u>How</u> do I <u>get</u> to the <u>Chem</u>istry building?
3 Ex<u>cuse</u> me! Can you <u>tell</u> me how to <u>get</u> to the <u>super</u>market?

Exercise 8 page 97

1 up   **2** up   **3** down

SPEAKING TASK

Learning objectives

- Ask for directions and identify locations on maps
- Give accurate directions to places on maps

Exercises 1–3 page 98
Answers will vary.

Exercise 4 page 99
University of Beta
1 B **2** E **3** D **4** A **5** C

Exercise 5 page 100
University of Alpha
1 D **2** C **3** E **4** B **5** A

RESEARCH PROJECT

Create a TV advertisement for a city.

Ask students to think about a city they know which is good to visit. They will need to find out about this city, e.g. things to do there, famous buildings, etc. They could do research online to find information.

Tell the class that they will be filming a TV advert to appeal to tourists visiting the city. They could do this as a whole class or in groups. Ask them to plan the advertisement by creating a script and/or storyboard. They will also have to think about who will direct and record the video, who will do the editing and who will present or narrate the advert. If different groups are creating advertisements, the class could vote on which city they would most like to visit.

CLASSROOM APP

Exercises 1–2
Answers will vary.

Exercise 3
1 museum **2** park **3** bridge **4** monument **5** bank
6 library **7** factory **8** fountain

Exercise 4
1 go, bridge **2** next to **3** Turn right **4** next to
5 opposite

Exercise 5
1 to watch films with my friends. , a playground for children. , a map.
2 so I go to a shopping centre. , when I use a really large car park. , I go to the food court.
3 but I can't find the building. , since it is a safe place.

Exercise 6A
1 Enter the car park on 12th Street.
2 Walk down Park Avenue to get to the bank.
3 Turn left at the corner and go over the bridge.
4 Go behind the library.
5 Go around the fountain and the toilets are on the left.
6 Turn right when you get to the museum.

Exercise 6B
Answers will vary.

UNIT OBJECTIVES	
Watch and listen	Watch and understand a video about a dangerous job.
Listening skills	Use your knowledge to predict content; listen for opinions.
Critical thinking	Identify criteria.
Grammar	Use *have to*; use *should*; use comparative adjectives.
Speaking skills	Compare people; ask for and give opinions and reasons; make a decision.
Speaking task	Choose a person for a job.
⊘ **Teacher development**	Help your students become better at **identifying criteria**.

UNLOCK YOUR KNOWLEDGE

Background note

The photo shows firefighters at a training facility. The firefighters are spraying water on an aircraft fire.

Lead-in

Create an ideas map to brainstorm information students think about before they apply for a job. Include *interest, pay, hours, skills needed, location and benefits*, *like a gym* or *travel expenses*. Then ask students to rank the items listed, based on how important each item is to them personally. You may want to spur the conversation by asking students to think about how important it is for them to work with people, be in a big city, be famous / have recognition and other factors.

page 103

1 firefighters / firefighting **2** *Answers will vary.*
Suggested answers: dangerous; difficult; interesting
3 *Answers will vary.*

WATCH AND LISTEN

Learning objectives

* Listen and identify the main idea in a video about working on a building
* Listen and understand details
* Organize inferences about the information in the video
* Practise talking about dangerous jobs

Exercise 1 page 104
1 b **2** d **3** a **4** c

Exercise 2 page 104
1 The building is very tall.
2 This building has a beautiful view.
3 The man has a very dangerous job.
4 These men work together.

Exercise 3 page 105
1 b **2** c **3** a

Exercise 4 page 105
1 F; It's 800 metres tall. **2** T
3 F; The men clean 24,000 windows. **4** T

Exercise 5 page 105
1 have a dangerous job **2** need special training
3 has many offices **4** is very famous

Exercise 6 page 105
Answers will vary.

LISTENING 1

Learning objectives

* Understand key vocabulary for careers advice – *advice, job, help*
* Gain awareness of weak forms of *have to*
* Listen and understand main ideas in a discussion about careers advice
* Listen and take detailed notes on opinions
* Give personal opinions on jobs
* Evaluate the skills needed for jobs

Lead-in

On the board, invite students to list people they talk to for advice on important decisions. Discuss the benefits of talking to somebody who knows them well versus talking to somebody they don't know. Then ask pairs or small groups to think of a time when they asked somebody for advice on an important decision, and reflect on the experience. Prompts could include, *What advice did you ask for? What did they say? Did it go well? Should you listen to others or make your decisions on your own? Discuss with a partner.*

Exercise 1 page 106

1 work **2** earns **3** job **4** helps **5** boring **6** hard
7 advice

Exercise 2 page 107

Answers will vary.

Exercise 3 page 107

1 f **2** b **3** a **4** d **5** c **6** e

Exercise 4 page 108

Answers will vary.

Exercise 5 page 108

1 weak **2** strong **3** weak **4** weak **5** strong **6** weak
7 weak

Exercise 6 page 109

1 b **2** a **3** c **4** a

Exercise 7 page 110

Mother: go to medical school; **Father:** be a doctor or engineer; **Adviser:** get a job

Optional activity

Students work in pairs and give each other advice on how to improve their English. Monitor and correct expressions giving opinions and advice. At the end, ask students to share their ideas with the class. Make sure students use the expressions from the Skills box on page 109. Write their ideas on the board, then discuss which ones are the most useful.

Exercise 8 page 110

Answers will vary.

LANGUAGE DEVELOPMENT

Learning objectives

- Understand the difference between *have* as a main verb and *have to* to describe what is necessary – *She has two jobs. She has to work.*
- Use the correct form of *have to* to describe what is necessary in different situations.
- Use *have to* to describe what is necessary in different jobs – *Teachers have to work very hard. Doctors have to work at night.*
- Use the correct form of *should* in sentences about careers advice – *They should go to medical school. I should not go to medical school.*
- Form comparative adjectives correctly – *bigger, better, more interesting*
- Use comparative adjectives to give your opinions on different subjects and jobs – *I think studying Medicine is more difficult than studying English.*

Exercise 1 page 111

1 has **2** has to **3** have **4** have **5** has **6** have to

Exercise 2 page 112

1 Students have to read a lot of books.
2 My teacher has to walk to school.
3 You don't have to study English.
4 Teachers don't have to work at night.
5 Do we have to learn this grammar?
6 What does a nurse have to do?

Exercises 3–4 page 112

Answers will vary.

Exercise 5 page 112

1 Paul should go to medical school.
2 Beatrice should not get a job next year.
3 Laura should ask for advice from her friend.
4 The students shouldn't miss their classes.

Be flexible

Create a stack of note cards with a variety of different jobs with one job per card. If possible, create multiple stacks so that students work in groups of three or four and each group has a stack of cards. One student turns over two cards, reads the jobs out loud and creates a comparison, e.g. *Being a racing car driver is more exciting than being a librarian.* The student must spell the comparative adjective correctly. Then it is the next student's turn. Students should use different adjectives. You may want to brainstorm adjectives with students and list them on the board.

In addition, provide **lower-level students** with a sentence frame for completing the task. For example: *Being a ... is ... than ....* You may want to point out the grammar of this construction: *being* is the *-ing* form of the verb *be* and both parts of the comparison need to include *being* before the job name. Also, the indefinite article *a* is used before the job name because the comparison is a generalization about the jobs.

Exercise 6 page 113

1 2   2 3   3 1   4 2   5 3   6 1   7 1   8 1   9 1   10 3

Exercise 7 page 113

1 more boring   2 more interesting   3 safer   4 easier
5 more difficult   6 nicer   7 bigger   8 smaller   9 better
10 more important

Exercise 8 page 114

1 bigger than   2 easier than   3 safer than   4 more
interesting than   5 more boring than   6 better than

Exercise 9 page 114

Answers will vary.

LISTENING 2

Learning objectives

- Understand key vocabulary for choosing a person for a job – *strong, kind, polite*
- Understand an advertisement for a job
- Understand information about two applicants for a job
- Listen and understand the main ideas in a conversation about choosing a person for a job
- Listen and identify details
- Synthesize information from two conversations about careers in a discussion

Lead-in

Students work in small groups and discuss any jobs they may have done in the past. Ask students to tell the group what job it was, how they got it and what they had to do. If students have never worked before, ask them to talk about what jobs people in their family have. At the end, ask group members to tell the class about their group members' jobs. Elicit new vocabulary, e.g. *apply for a job, have experience* and *look for a job.*

Exercise 1 page 115

Answers will vary.

Exercise 2 page 115

1 b   2 a   3 a   4 b   5 a   6 b

Exercise 3 page 115

1 University of Yukon / sports centre   2 fitness instructor
3 Can teach sport and exercise; is friendly and helpful; has experience; should be strong and fit; know three or more sports; speak English and French

Exercise 4 page 117

	Student A	Student B
1	man	woman
2	Alan Green	Lucy Lau
3	Portland, Oregon, US	Vancouver, Canada
4	English; French	English; French; Cantonese
5	football; basketball; karate; judo	Zumba; Pilates; yoga; tennis

Exercise 5 page 117

Answers will vary.

Exercise 6 page 117

They choose Lucy.

Exercise 7 page 118

1 a   2 b   3 c   4 b   5 a   6 b

Exercise 8 page 118

Answers will vary.

CRITICAL THINKING

Learning objectives

- Understand criteria
- Identify criteria in a job advertisement
- Evaluate candidates for a job
- Use a table to organize and compare information

UNLOCK TEACHER DEVELOPMENT

BE INFORMED

➔ **Identifying criteria** is an important skill for students because: (1) It is a key skill in academic life, e.g. deciding what to include in an essay; (2) It is a key skill when trying to get a job, e.g. writing a cover letter to match a job description; (3) For students who are not used to making choices, identifying criteria can be a difficult concept, so practice is needed.

BE CONFIDENT

➔ Develop this skill for yourself by doing the following activity:

Think about your job. If you had to write a job description for it, what would it look like? What criteria would be used to select the ideal candidate?

Lead-in

Go through the instructions with the class and focus on the Speaking task. Explain that the following sections of the unit will help them to prepare to choose a person for a job. Pay particular attention to the directions in Exercise 2: students work in a group to judge each person for the job, based on the criteria. Point out that each group member will only read about one person, take notes, and then tell the group about that person.

UNL⌾CK TEACHER DEVELOPMENT

BE READY

Look at the Critical Thinking section in the Student's Book on pages 119–121.

➜ Which elements of the lesson do you think your students will find easiest / most difficult / most useful? Why?

➜ Are your answers true for all students in your class?

➜ How can you adapt your teaching or the material to meet your students' needs?

BE FLEXIBLE

Ask your class the question in *Be confident* about your job description. It would be interesting to compare their answers with your own.

Find real-life examples of job descriptions in or around your educational establishment – on noticeboards or the institution's website for students or for teachers. Referencing these in your class will make the learning more relevant.

Exercise 1 page 119

1 nurse (at the Sports Centre)
2 a person who has experience in a hospital; speaks another language; knows about sport; is a hard worker
3 a person who is helpful; likes sport; is friendly
4 *Answers will vary.*

Exercise 2 page 120

The number of points and the evidence may vary.

Criteria	Inesh	Morena	Darren
has experience in a hospital	**Points:** 0 **Evidence:** still studying, so she isn't working in a hospital yet	**Points:** 1 **Evidence:** nurse in a small children's hospital	**Points:** 2 **Evidence:** nurse in a big hospital

Criteria	Inesh	Morena	Darren
speaks another language	**Points:** 2 **Evidence:** speaks Indonesian, Chinese, Spanish and English	**Points:** 1 **Evidence:** speaks Portuguese, Spanish and English	**Points:** 0 **Evidence:** speaks only English
knows about sport	**Points:** 0 **Evidence:** no evidence	**Points:** 2 **Evidence:** runs and does yoga; is strong and fit	**Points:** 2 **Evidence:** loves football and basketball and goes to a gym
is a hard worker	**Points:** 0 **Evidence:** no evidence	**Points:** 1 **Evidence:** she says that she is strong and fit, implies that she works hard	**Points:** 0 **Evidence:** no evidence
is helpful and friendly	**Points:** 1 **Evidence:** says she is polite and friendly	**Points:** 1 **Evidence:** says she is a friendly and helpful nurse	**Points:** 0 **Evidence:** no evidence

UNL⌾CK TEACHER DEVELOPMENT

BE REFLECTIVE

Think about the following points:

➜ Based on what you did in the *Be confident* section, think about areas of your job which you feel you could do better in. How can you improve these areas? Is there training which you could participate in?

➜ Look at the Better Learning blog for articles and resources around various topics that may help you to develop these areas: http://www.cambridge.org/elt/blog

BE COLLABORATIVE

Your development is more meaningful when it is shared. See page 14 for ideas on how to peer-collaborate. Why not share the ideas you generated in the *Be ready* section, and their outcome?

PREPARATION FOR SPEAKING

Learning objectives

- Pronounce comparatives adjectives with weak /ə/
- Pronounce consonant sounds correctly in *have to, have, has to* and *has*
- Use phrases to ask for and give opinions and reasons about job candidates – *What do you think about Lucy? I think that Lucy is perfect. Another reason is the fitness instructor has to teach popular sports.*
- Use phrases to make group decisions – *Let's review our ideas. So, do we all agree ...? Is everyone OK with this decision?*

Exercise 2 page 122

1 a **2** d **3** b **4** c

Exercise 3 page 122

1 more languages **2** more experience **3** better **4** bigger

Exercise 4 page 123

A: What do you think about Lucy?

B: I think that she should be the new fitness instructor.

A: Why do you think that?

B: Because she is a better teacher than Alan. Another reason is the fitness instructor has to teach popular sports.

Exercise 5 page 123

Answers will vary.

Exercise 6 page 123

we need to make a decision; So, let's review our ideas; Is everyone okay with this decision?

Exercise 7 page 124

Answers will vary.

SPEAKING TASK

Learning objectives

- Take part in a discussion evaluating job candidates
- Take part in making a group decision about job candidates

Exercises 1–4 page 124

Answers will vary.

RESEARCH PROJECT

Create a training video for an interview.

Ask students to think about different ways people should prepare for interviews. If possible, use a shared document for students to note their ideas. Encourage them to think about how to dress, how to prepare, how to greet the interviewer, what questions the interviewer might ask, how you might answer these questions and what question you might ask.

Tell students they are going to create a short video which teaches people how to prepare for an interview. Different groups in the class could present one aspect of this, e.g. how to dress. Ask them to plan the video by creating a script. They will also have to think about who will direct and record the video, who will do the editing and who will do the presenting. Each group shares their video with the class to discuss and comment on.

CLASSROOM APP

Exercises 1–2

Answers will vary.

Exercise 3

1 A chef has to be a good cook. **2** Do you have to go to university to get a good job? **3** Does a musician have to practise every day? **4** A scientist doesn't have to be strong. **5** A good teacher has to be interesting. **6** When you go for an interview, you have to be polite. **7** Does Joleen have to do an interview on Tuesday?

Exercise 4

1 kinder **2** more interesting **3** better **4** more important **5** worse

Exercise 5

1 It isn't interesting. **2** The person usually eats good food and exercises **3** They can usually lift heavy things **4** They get a lot of money. **5** It isn't easy to do. **6** They act in a good way. **7** It can help you. **8** It's like others in the same group.

Exercise 6

1 What do you think about **2** I think that Tom should be **3** Because he **4** I think that Daniel **5** Another reason is **6** Why do you think

Exercise 7

Answers will vary.

UNIT OBJECTIVES	
Watch and listen	Watch and understand a video about a famous house.
Listening skill	Listen for reasons.
Critical thinking	Evaluate ideas.
Grammar	Give an opinion with *should*.
Speaking skills	Give reasons; ask for and give an opinion; agree and disagree.
Speaking task	Discuss ideas for a new café.
↻ **Teacher development**	Help your students become better at **evaluating ideas**.

UNLOCK YOUR KNOWLEDGE

Background note

The photo shows Paro Taktsang, also known as the Taktsang Palphug Monastery, Taktsang Goemba or the Tiger's Nest Monastery, in the Paro valley in Bhutan. It is one of Bhutan's most sacred religious sites. It is situated high up on a steep cliff, overlooking a valley. To get to the Tiger's Nest requires a two-hour climb from the bottom of the valley. The trail to the monastery is extremely steep and has lots of twists and turns.

Lead-in

Ask students to think in pairs about one traditional building and one unusual building. What makes them traditional or unusual? Elicit ideas as a class.

page 127
Answers will vary.

WATCH AND LISTEN

Learning objectives

- Listen and understand main ideas and details in a video about a famous inventor's home
- Complete a set of inferences about the information in the video
- Practise talking about special homes

Exercise 1 page 128
Answers will vary.

Exercise 2 page 128
1 large **2** important **3** study **4** big

Exercise 3 page 129
1 T **2** F; Jefferson was important to American history.
3 T **4** F; The grounds around the house are large.

Exercise 4 page 129
1 40 **2** walls **3** convenient **4** study

Exercise 5 page 129
1 c **2** d **3** a **4** b

Exercise 6 page 129
Answers will vary.

LISTENING 1

Learning objectives

- Understand key vocabulary for buildings – *ceiling, floor, furniture*
- Gain awareness of linking in connected speech
- Listen and identify main ideas in an interview about restaurant design
- Listen for signals *why* and *because* to identify reasons
- Give opinions on colours
- Apply information to decide on the best colour for a restaurant

Lead-in

To review colours and places, display photos for students to describe the colours, e.g. *red, orange, blue, green*, etc. Correct any mistakes and list colours named on the board.

Exercise 1 page 130
Answers will vary.

Exercise 2 page 130

1 wall **2** floor **3** ceiling **4** wood **5** furniture **6** room

Exercise 3 page 131

c

Exercise 4 page 131

1 a **2** a **3** b **4** b

Exercises 5–6 page 132

1 b **2** d **3** c **4** a **5** e

Exercise 7 page 132

Answers will vary.

LANGUAGE DEVELOPMENT

Learning objectives

- Name items of furniture – *armchair*, *chair*, *lamp*
- Describe furniture, using a range of adjectives and nouns – *a comfortable chair*, *a leather sofa*

Exercise 2 page 134

Answers will vary. Suggested answers:

café: table; chairs; sofa; bookcase; armchair

home: table; chairs; sofa; lamp; bookcase; armchair

classroom: desk; table; chairs; bookcase

Exercise 5 page 135

1 plastic **2** metal **3** leather **4** uncomfortable
5 comfortable **6** glass **7** wooden

Exercises 6–7 page 135

Possible answers:

a glass table; a leather sofa; a plastic chair; a metal desk; a wooden bookcase; a metal lamp

Optional activity

👤 👥 Tell students that they are going to prepare an ideas map of their home. Draw an ideas map of your own home on the board as an example. Use *there is* and *there are* expressions as you explain one room. The model should have *My home* in the middle, and each branch should represent different rooms. Tell students that branching out from each room will be examples of typical furniture in the rooms. After explaining the furniture in one of your rooms, erase the example and tell students to make their own ideas maps. Students work on their ideas maps for 10–12 minutes. Then students explain their ideas maps in small groups.

LISTENING 2

Learning objectives

- Understand key vocabulary for buildings and location – *modern*, *quiet*, *far*
- Listen and identify main ideas, opinions and details in a conversation about a building
- Evaluate the design of buildings and rooms
- Synthesize information from an interview about restaurant design and a conversation about a building in a discussion

Lead-in

Tell students that, just like Listening 1, the speakers in Listening 2 are co-workers. Elicit important skills needed to work together professionally, such as asking for other opinions, being polite, staying on topic in a meeting, etc. Review questions and statements for *Asking for and giving opinions and reasons* (see page 123 of the Student's Book). Then make a list of ways that people politely agree and disagree with each other.

Exercise 1 page 136

1 expensive **2** noisy **3** quiet **4** modern **5** near
6 far **7** cheap

Exercise 2 page 136

Answers will vary.

Exercise 3 page 137

1 b **2** c **3** b

Exercise 4 page 138

1 big **2** yellow **3** wood **4** comfortable

Exercises 5–6 page 138

Answers will vary.

CRITICAL THINKING

Learning objectives

- Analyze images of cafés
- Evaluate the positive and negative aspects of the design, furniture and location of cafés
- Evaluate different locations for a new café

UNLOCK TEACHER DEVELOPMENT

BE INFORMED

→ **Evaluating ideas** is an important skill for students because: (1) Evaluation is one of the six specific critical thinking skills mentioned in Bloom's taxonomy; (2) Students sometimes look for evidence to support what they already think, rather than looking at both sides of an issue; (3) Students need practice in looking at issues from all sides.

BE CONFIDENT

→ Develop this skill for yourself by doing the following activity:

In a critical thinking survey by Cambridge University Press, teachers were asked to say whether they felt confident in their ability to develop their students' critical thinking skills. Look at the comments below and say whether they are positive or negative responses to this question.

'I personalize the critical thinking and make it relevant for them.'

'I didn't learn critical thinking myself so don't know what it feels like.'

'You have to do it because it is so important for their academic lives.'

'I'm sometimes not 100% clear what the book wants me to do.'

Lead-in

Go through the instructions with the class and focus on the Speaking task. Explain that the following sections of the unit will help them to prepare to discuss ideas for a new café.

UNLOCK TEACHER DEVELOPMENT

BE READY

Look at the Critical Thinking section in the Student's Book on pages 139–141.

→ Which elements of the lesson do you think your students will find easiest / most difficult / most useful? Why?

→ Are your answers true for all students in your class?

→ How can you adapt your teaching or the material to meet your students' needs?

BE FLEXIBLE

You could make Exercise 5 more interactive by dividing the class into four groups. Randomly give them one location (a, b, c or d) and tell them they have to make a case for the café to be there.

Exercise 1 page 139

1 Café B   **2** Café A   **3** Café C

Exercise 2 page 140

Answers will vary. Possible answers:

	positive things	**negative things**
Café A	It's easy to go there because it is in the centre of the city.	There are too many tourists.
Café B	It's modern. There's a lot of wood.	There aren't many tables. The chairs are not comfortable.
Café C	People can take beautiful photographs.	It's expensive to build. You can't go there when the weather is bad.

Exercise 4 page 141

Answers will vary. Possible answers:

a Positive: It's easy to go there. It's on the road to the capital city. **Negative:** It's far from the centre.

b Positive: It's good for travel. **Negative:** The buildings in the town are old. It's expensive.

c Positive: It's on the road to the airport. There are many hotels, so many people will come. **Negative:** It's noisy.

d Positive: It's quiet. There are a lot of tourists. **Negative:** It's very far from the roads. It's difficult to get to.

Optional activity

To provide additional practice with evaluating ideas, pairs of students can draw or create a similar three-column table to note the positive things and negative things of living in an apartment versus living in a house. Allow students up to ten minutes to complete the chart with their reasons. Students then work with another pair and present the reasons to each other. Each group has to decide whether they would prefer to live in an apartment or in a house. Monitor and make sure students give their reasons in complete sentences and support their ideas. Help with grammar and vocabulary for the task. At the end, each group presents their choice to the class and gives their reasons.

Exercise 5 page 141

Answers will vary.

UNL⊘CK TEACHER DEVELOPMENT

BE REFLECTIVE

Think about the following questions:

→ Evaluate your own lesson. What were the strengths and weaknesses? What went well and what did not go so well? If you taught the lesson again, what would you do differently?

→ Think again about the *Be confident* section. How would you have answered this question? What other positive or negative comments do you think were found in the survey?

BE COLLABORATIVE

Your development is more meaningful when it is shared. See page 14 for ideas on how to peer-collaborate. Why not share the ideas you generated in the *Be ready* section, and their outcome?

PREPARATION FOR SPEAKING

Learning objectives

- Use phrases to ask for and give opinions and reasons about going to different cafés – *I'd like to go to café A because it is in the city. Another reason is that it is outside.*
- Use phrases give opinions about a new school – *I think we should have computers. I don't think we should have a modern building.*
- Give and ask about opinions – *I think we should have big classrooms. What do you think?*
- Use phrases to agree and disagree – *Yes, I agree. I'm not sure. I don't agree.*

Exercise 1 page 142

People use the underlined phrases to give reasons, give opinions, ask for opinions or to indicate agreement.

Be flexible

👥 Ask **more advanced students** to write short dialogues in pairs to role play in front of the class. They should include eliciting an opinion on a building or design, sharing an opinion and agreeing or disagreeing. Ask students to pay attention to their tone of voice, and for the class to listen and note the phrases used to ask for and give opinions, as well as judge whether the person agreed or disagreed politely.

Exercise 2 page 142

Give a reason:

It's near some good roads.

Because the buildings in the centre are very old. They are cold in winter and hot in summer and they're very noisy. They're uncomfortable places.

It's quiet and it's not far from a big road.

It's pretty far from the town.

It's good for travel.

The buildings near the train station aren't cheap.

Give an opinion:

It's a good place.

I don't think we should go there.

The train station is good.

I think we should go to the park.

I think we should have a modern design with big windows.

Big windows are good.

Ask for an opinion:	**Agree or disagree:**
What about here?	I'm not sure.
What do you think?	Yes, I agree.
Why not?	
What about the design?	
What about you?	

Exercises 3–5 page 143
Answers will vary.

Exercise 6 page 144
1 you **2** blue **3** think **4** Mexican food

Exercise 7 page 144
1 D **2** A **3** D **4** A

Exercise 8 page 144
Answers will vary.

SPEAKING TASK

Learning objectives

- Review your notes to prepare for a discussion.
- Take part in a discussion of ideas for a new café
- Present ideas for a new café
- Evaluate other student's ideas for a new café

Exercises 1–5 pages 145–146
Answers will vary.

RESEARCH PROJECT

Plan and present your ideal home.

Ask each student to record ideas for their ideal home. Encourage them to think about rooms, size, garden, location and interior design (e.g. furniture, colours). Ask them to create a concept board and find images of some of the things they'd like in their ideal home.

Each student presents their concept board for their ideal home to the rest of the class. Ask presenters to give their opinion on items from the concept board and support their thinking with reasons. This can turn into a friendly competition where the class votes for the best house.

CLASSROOM APP

Exercises 1–2
Answers will vary.

Exercise 3
1 armchair   **2** table   **3** bookcase   **4** desk   **5** sofa
6 lamp **7** chair

Exercise 4
1 glass   **2** comfortable   **3** wooden   **4** metal   **5** leather

Exercise 5
1 wooden   **2** noisy   **3** ceiling   **4** expensive   **5** quiet
6 modern   **7** floor   **8** wall

Exercise 6A
1 give opinion   **2** agree/disagree   **3** ask opinion
4 give opinion   **5** give reason   **6** ask opinion

Exercise 6B
Answers will vary.

UNIT OBJECTIVES

Watch and listen	Watch and understand a video about special fruit in Japan.
Listening skill	Listen for numbers.
Critical thinking	Understand pie charts.
Grammar	Use the past simple.
Speaking skills	Introduce a report; talk about surveys.
Speaking task	Report the results of a survey.
⟳ **Teacher development**	Help your students become better at **understanding pie charts**.

UNL⦿CK YOUR KNOWLEDGE

Background note

The photo shows a display of Japanese cakes in Japan. Japanese-style cakes are very similar to Western-style cakes. Some of the cakes in the photo are chocolate cake, strawberry shortcake, fruit tart cake, roll cakes and choux pastries. Japanese cake is usually presented and sold in individual slices.

Lead-in

Bring in a variety of delivery menus representing different types of cuisines or alternatively, ask students to look at online menus. Invite pairs to discuss the foods they like and then identify what they would order for lunch. Use this as an opportunity to do an informal assessment on students' pronunciation of numbers and familiarity with food items. Invite students to tell you their order and the cost of their lunch. Make notes as necessary to document weak areas for added focus and instruction.

page 149
Possible answers:
1 pastries / cakes / desserts
2–3 *Answers will vary.*

WATCH AND LISTEN

Learning objectives

- Listen and identify main ideas and details in a video about luxury fruit in Japan
- Complete a set of inferences about the information in the video
- Practise talking about gifts

Exercise 1 page 150
Answers will vary.

Exercise 2 page 150
1 grapes   **2** fruit   **3** standing   **4** farmer

Exercise 3 page 150
1 F   **2** T   **3** T   **4** F   **5** T

Exercise 4 page 151
1 b   **2** b   **3** a   **4** c   **5** a

Exercise 5 page 151
1 expensive   **2** rich   **3** hard   **4** ordinary

Exercise 6 page 151
Answers will vary.

LISTENING 1

Learning objectives

- Understand key vocabulary for food – *meat, international, dish*
- Listen and discriminate between numbers with *-teen* and *-ty* endings
- Listen and identify the topic of a class discussion
- Listen and understand details and numbers
- Describe and give opinions on food

Lead-in

Ask the class where they typically buy their food. Is it made in their country? Is it from another country? How often do they eat food from other countries? Elicit ideas and discuss as a class.

Exercise 1 page 152

Answers will vary.

Exercise 2 page 152

1 b **2** c **3** f **4** g **5** a **6** e **7** d

Exercise 3 page 153

1 70; 17; Seventeen **2** 60; Sixteen; 60
3 Thirteen; Thirty; 13 **4** 15; Fifty; 15; 50

Exercise 4 page 153

b

Exercise 5 page 154

1 F; The average person in the UK eats meat once a day.

2 T **3** T **4** T

5 F; Only 20% of the students know how to cook traditional dishes.

Exercise 6 page 154

1 50/fifty **2** 14/fourteen **3** 20/twenty

Be flexible

👤👥 With a more **advanced class**, ask students to close their books and take notes while they listen. Explain that during lectures, we often write down important numbers and use key words to note down what these numbers refer to. Students listen and take notes. Allow students a couple of minutes to compare their notes with a partner. Monitor and check the quality of the notes. Students then use their notes to complete Exercise 6. If necessary, give advice on how students can improve their note-taking skills, e.g. listen to podcast, and take notes while they listen.

Exercises 7–8 page 154

Answers will vary.

LANGUAGE DEVELOPMENT

Learning objectives

- Use regular past simple verbs to complete positive and negative sentences.
- Ask and answer questions in the past simple – *Did both of your parents work? Yes, they did. Did your grandmother cook traditional dishes? Yes, she did.*
- Use irregular past simple verbs in positive and negative sentences – *I ate a big breakfast this morning. We went to a great new restaurant on Friday. She didn't do any cooking.*

- Name different types of food – *pizza, fries, tacos*
- Categorize different types of food – *Pizza is traditional food. Tacos are healthy food. Burgers are fast food.*
- Ask and answer questions about food – *Do you like traditional food? Do you like fast food? Yes, I do. I like fast food because it's easy.*

Exercise 1 page 155

1 lived **2** cooked **3** did not / didn't cook **4** worked
5 lived **6** watched **7** did not / didn't help
8 did not / didn't learn

Exercise 2 page 156

Answers will vary.

Exercise 3 page 156

2 Did you eat at a fast food restaurant this week?
3 Did you cook dinner last week?
4 Did you eat a big lunch yesterday?
5 Did you eat breakfast today?
6 Did you have a meal with friends last week?

Exercise 4 page 156

Answers will vary.

Exercise 5 page 157

1 did not / didn't make **2** ate **3** bought
4 was **5** did not / didn't do **6** came
7 did not / didn't have; went **8** read

Exercise 6 page 157

Answers will vary.

Exercise 7 page 157

1 I ate a big breakfast this morning.
2 Did you have fish for dinner last week?
3 They didn't cook dinner for their family last Sunday.
4 I learnt to cook from my father.
5 Did Kevin make dinner last night?
6 We went to a great new restaurant on Friday.
7 Emma didn't like her meal.
8 Did you have lunch with your parents yesterday?

Exercise 8 page 158

Possible answers:

meat: chicken; meatballs; sandwich meat
vegetables: lettuce; tomato; peppers; olives; salad; onions
other: noodles; pasta; tacos; cheese; chips; bread

Exercise 9 page 158

Possible answers:

1 H (also T – sandwiches are traditional) **2** T
3 T (also F – fast food) **4** H **5** T **6** F **7** F **8** T

Optional activity

👥 Prepare slips of paper with the names of the food pictured on page 158 (*sandwich, noodles, pizza, salad, tacos, chips, burger* and *pasta*). Then divide the class into teams. Students take turns to choose a slip of paper and describe the food for other teams to guess. Students may name the ingredients, say where the food is popular or how it's made, etc. The team that guesses the food vocabulary word correctly scores a point. Award bonus points for teams that can spell the word correctly. Play until all the words have been used.

Exercise 10 page 159

Answers will vary.

LISTENING 2

Learning objectives

- Understand key vocabulary for describing food and culture – *culture, home-cooked, enjoy*
- Understand pie charts
- Listen and identify main ideas in a student's report
- Listen and understand details
- Synthesize information from a discussion and a presentation about food

Lead-in

Explain that the student speaking in Listening 2 has already asked her survey questions, gathered the data and analyzed it. Point out that she put the results in pie charts on page 160. Explain that we often use visuals to show data because it helps us to understand the meaning of the data better.

Exercise 1 page 159

1 home-cooked   **2** meal   **3** healthy   **4** favourite
5 enjoy   **6** culture

Exercise 2 page 160

1 fast food restaurants   **2** Yes (because most people think food and family meals are important)
3 They enjoy it

Exercise 3 page 161

1 b   **2** c   **3** b

Exercise 4 page 161

1 T   **2** T   **3** T   **4** T
5 F; Traditions about eating have changed.

Exercise 5 page 161

Answers will vary.

Optional activity

👥 👥👥 Brainstorm additional questions about food habits and eating trends that students are interested in (e.g. *Do you buy a salad when you go to a fast food restaurant? Do you eat a healthy breakfast?*). Ask individuals to create a list of five *Yes/No* questions. Students switch questions with a partner to check their grammar and vocabulary, and then ask five other students their questions. Students practise answering with short answers, e.g. *Yes, I do.* or *No, I don't.* Interviewers should record results. With additional time, students can then get into small groups and discuss their results.

CRITICAL THINKING

Learning objectives

- Label sections of pie charts
- Understand information shown in pie charts about changes in food and culture
- Analyze which reasons have caused which changes in food cultures

UNL⌓CK TEACHER DEVELOPMENT

BE INFORMED

→ **Understanding pie charts** is an important skill for students because: (1) Pie charts are a common method for presenting data in many academic subjects, particularly Maths, Science and Engineering, because they are easy to understand; (2) Pie charts are also commonly used in the media and everyday life because of their simplicity.

BE CONFIDENT

→ Develop this skill by doing the following activity:
In the Cambridge University Press critical thinking survey, 1,000 teachers were asked to respond to the statement: 'I believe my students want to develop their Critical Thinking skills.' Their responses are presented in the pie chart below.

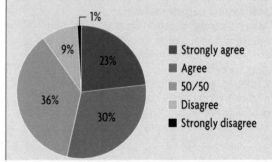

1 Quickly summarize the main findings presented in this pie chart.
2 What reasons do you think were given by the people who 'agreed' or 'strongly agreed' with the statement?
3 What reasons do you think were given by the people who 'disagreed' or 'strongly disagreed' with the statement?
4 How would you answer this question for your class(es)? Why?

Lead-in

Go through the instructions with the class and focus on the Speaking task. Explain that the following sections of the unit will help them to prepare to report the results of a survey. Make sure students understand that the words and phrases in the box on page 162 are for labelling the charts on page 160.

UNL⌀CK TEACHER DEVELOPMENT

BE READY

Look at the Critical Thinking section in the Student's Book on pages 162–164.
→ Which elements of the lesson do you think your students will find easiest / most difficult / most useful? Why?
→ Are your answers true for all students in your class?
→ How can you adapt your teaching or the material to meet your students' needs?

BE FLEXIBLE

If your students are already very familiar with pie charts, extend the skill practice by finding a more complex pie chart for students to analyze, perhaps one related to the academic subject(s) they are studying.

Exercise 1 page 162
Question 1
a: fast food sales   **b:** sales from other restaurants

Question 2
a: eating together is not important
b: eating together is important

Question 3
a: enjoy food   **b:** don't enjoy food

Exercise 3 page 163
1 Types of restaurants; Eating habits; Cooking habits
2 *Possible answers:* What type of restaurants do you go to? Do you eat with other people or alone? What type of meals do you eat?
3 **country A:** Yes; **country B:** Yes
4 **country A:** More; **country B:** Less
5 **country A:** No; **country B:** No
6 Country A: mostly home-cooked food; Country B: most responded with 'home-cooked food'

Exercise 4 page 164
Possible answers:
1 Fast food was not available.
2 Fast food is cheap and easy. International foods or international restaurants are more popular. People eat smaller lunches, such as fast food, which don't take as long. Families are not together because of work hours. People don't know how to cook. Traditional restaurants are more expensive.
3 People couldn't buy foods from other countries. Families ate big lunches together. Fast food was not available.
4 Families are not together because of work hours.
5 Fast food was not available.
6 Pre-made meals are available at supermarkets. People don't have time to cook.

Exercise 5 page 164
Answers will vary.

UNL⌀CK TEACHER DEVELOPMENT

BE REFLECTIVE

Think about the following questions:
→ How did your students respond to the lesson? Did you feel that they were interested in developing their critical thinking skills?
→ What aspects of the lesson enabled your students to link this critical thinking focus to their future academic studies?

BE COLLABORATIVE

Your development is more meaningful when it is shared. See page 14 for ideas on how to peer-collaborate. Why not share the pie chart you found in the *Be flexible* section opposite, and the impact it had in the class?

PREPARATION FOR SPEAKING

Learning objectives

- Understand and use phrases for introducing a report – *I think this is an interesting topic. There were three questions in my survey. My questions were on the topic of food and culture in France.*
- Pronounce the letter *u* correctly in different words in sentences about food surveys – *question, survey, result*
- Use phrases to present results of surveys using pie charts – *My last question was 'Is eating together with others important?'. So when you look here, 54% percent of all restaurant sales were from fast food places.*

Exercise 1 page 165
1 f   **2** d   **3** b   **4** a   **5** e   **6** c

Exercise 2 page 165
1 morning   **2** five   **3** traditional   **4** interesting
5 everybody   **6** fast   **7** three   **8** good

Exercises 3–4 page 166
Answers will vary.

Exercise 5 page 166
Answers will vary.

Exercise 6 page 166
1 my first question was
2 You can see here that
3 In one survey I read
4 My second question was
5 My last question was
6 So, when you look here

Exercise 7 page 167
Answers will vary.

SPEAKING TASK

Learning objectives

- Review your ideas to prepare for a survey
- Prepare an introduction for presenting the results of a survey
- Report the results of a survey using pie charts

Exercises 1–6 pages 167–168
Answers will vary.

RESEARCH PROJECT

Create an online cookery course.

Show the class some cookery videos on the internet. Divide the class into groups and tell them that each group needs to select a recipe it can make. Students could use a recipe known to them or choose a simple one from a cookbook or website. Each group could share its recipe with the rest of the class. Tell students that each group will make a video demonstrating how to make its recipe and then share these with the class to create a cookery course.

CLASSROOM APP

Exercise 1
Answers will vary.

Exercise 2
1 did, eat   **2** worked   **3** did, live   **4** made, was
5 Did, buy   **6** didn't cost / did not cost   **7** Did, help
8 cooked

Exercises 3–4
Answers will vary.

Exercise 5
1 healthy   **2** fish   **3** vegetables   **4** culture
5 home-cooked   **6** favourite   **7** meat **8** international

Exercise 6
1 My survey was about healthy food in your country.
2 There were three questions in my survey.
3 My first question was, 'Is traditional food healthy in your country?'
4 So, when you look here, you see 80% of the people said the food was healthy.
5 My second question was 'Do people in your country often eat fast food?'
6 This chart shows that most people in your country don't eat often eat fast food.

UNIT OBJECTIVES

Watch and listen	Watch and understand a video about travelling by road.
Listening skills	Listen for definitions; synthesize information.
Critical thinking	Synthesize information for a talk.
Grammar	Use the past simple; use *because* and *so*.
Speaking skills	Describe a topic; describe a problem; describe a solution; describe results.
Speaking task	Describe a transport problem, solution and results.
⊘ Teacher development	Help your students become better at **synthesizing information for a talk**.

UNLOCK YOUR KNOWLEDGE

Background note

The photo shows a canal in Amsterdam, the Netherlands, on a sunny morning. In the foreground, there are many bicycles, which have been locked to the canal bridge. Amsterdam is famous for its canals, and the photo shows boats and barges – a traditional type of boat used on canals. In the past, boats were the main form of transport in the city, but today, bicycles are the most popular. Many people also use public transport, including trams, metro, buses and ferries. There are also privately owned water taxis and water buses. Some people also drive.

Lead-in

Do a quick survey to see what transport students used to get to class (see page 178 of the Student's Book for examples). As a class, discuss the reasons for these results. Encourage students to state their opinion and give a reason (e.g. *I think most students walk because they live close to campus. I think most students take the bus because they get cheap tickets.*)

page 171

1 The photograph was taken in the Netherlands. Students may be able to guess this from the canal, the bicycles and the style of architecture.
2 **a** cars; vans **b** bikes; (canal) boats
3 *Answers will vary.*

WATCH AND LISTEN

Learning objectives

- Listen and understand facts and figures about roads in China
- Infer the reasons for building new roads in China
- Practise talking about road transport in your country and China

Exercise 1 page 172
Answers will vary.

Exercise 2 page 172
1 The city has many roads.
2 There is not much traffic in the country.
3 The road goes under the mountain.
4 There is a long bridge between the mountains.

Exercise 3 page 173
1 T 2 F; The largest builder of roads is China.
3 F; China has over 50,000 miles of highways.
4 T 5 F; The Sidu Bridge is the world's highest bridge.

Exercise 4 page 173
2; 5; 4; 1; 3

Exercise 5 page 173
1 b 2 c

Exercise 6 page 173
Answers will vary.

LISTENING 1

Learning objectives

- Understand key vocabulary for transport – *bus, metro, passenger*
- Listen and understand years – *1994 (nineteen ninety-four), 2017 (two thousand and seventeen / twenty seventeen)*
- Listen and take notes on the main ideas in a presentation about transport in London
- Listen and understand detailed information
- Describe which forms of transport you use and give reasons

Lead-in

Write the questions below on the board. Ask students to discuss the questions in pairs about the city or town they live in. Elicit responses from the class.

1 *What are the main ways to travel by public transport?*
2 *Do you need a ticket to ride?*
3 *How do passengers pay?*

Exercise 1 page 174

1 journey   2 bus   3 taxi   4 metro   5 train
6 passenger   7 ticket   8 travel

Exercise 2 page 175
Answers will vary.

Exercise 3 page 175

1 ticket   2 journey   3 passenger

Exercise 4 page 175

private: car; taxi
public: bus; metro; train

Exercise 5 page 175
Answers will vary.

Exercise 7 page 176

1 1,435   2 1,749   3 1,949   4 1,953   5 2,017

Exercise 8 page 176

The year 2017 can be pronounced twenty seventeen or two thousand and seventeen.

Exercise 9 page 176
Possible answers:

a a metro train / the Underground   b a man   c a lot of traffic and people   d somebody using an electronic ticket   e an electronic gate

Exercises 10–11 page 177
Possible answers:

1 Transport for London and Oyster cards (the electronic tickets)
2 takes care of private and public transport in London / takes care of people and passengers (who use transport)
3 eight million (three million private cars and taxis, five million public transport)
4 It opened in 1863, so it's more than 150 years old.
5 a kind of ticket / an electronic ticket

Exercise 12 page 177

1 cars, taxis, buses, trains   2 2003
3 (Paper) tickets were slow and/or London was bigger and more people lived and worked there.
4 By tapping a credit card; by paying online; by making a mobile payment with your phone

Exercise 13 page 177
Answers will vary.

LANGUAGE DEVELOPMENT

Learning objectives

- Use verb phrases to describe journeys on different forms of transport – *take the bus, go by car, go on foot*
- Use the correct form of irregular past tense verbs – *go → went, take → took, run → ran*
- Use *because* to give reasons and *so* to show results in sentences about transport – *He ran to the train station because he was late. I don't like to go by train, so I drive to work.*

Exercise 1 page 179

1 take   2 go   3 drive   4 go

Exercise 2 page 179
Answers will vary.

Be flexible

👥 👥 Provide additional practice for **lower-level students** with the transport collocations. Create a memory game for students to match verbs with nouns to make the collocations. Write the nine nouns: *bus, train, taxi, ferry, metro, car, bike, motorbike, foot* on cards. Then write nine verbs / verb phrases on more cards to match each noun.

Groups place the cards with the words facing down. Players take turns and uncover two pieces of paper at a time. If the halves match, they take the halves and score a point. If the halves do not match, the player puts the pieces of paper back in the same place. Students play until they match all the collocations.

Exercise 3 page 179

1 sat **2** took **3** went **4** drove **5** ran

Exercise 4 page 180

1 took **2** ran **3** sat **4** drove **5** went

Exercise 5 page 180

1 d **2** a **3** c **4** b **5** e

Exercise 6 page 180

Answers will vary.

LISTENING 2

Learning objectives

- Understand key vocabulary for transport problems and solutions – *accident, idea, pavement*
- Gain awareness of sound and spelling relationships in common consonant clusters – *wh /w/, ck /k/, ph /f/*
- Recognize words and phrases which signal definitions of new words while listening
- Listen and understand definitions of new words in a presentation about transport problems and solutions
- Listen and take detailed notes
- Synthesize information from two presentations in a discussion

Lead-in

As a way to anticipate the discussion in Listening 2, invite students to talk with a partner about a problem with transport in a city they are familiar with. After students talk, ask students to record the problem their partner discussed on one side of a T-chart. If possible, use a shared document so students' work can be displayed. Analyze the problems. Are they the same? What causes these problems? Then as a class, brainstorm solutions and add them to the other side of the T-chart.

Exercise 1 page 181

Answers will vary.

Exercise 2 page 181

1 idea **2** traffic **3** petrol **4** problem **5** accident **6** pavement

Exercises 3–4 page 182

Answers will vary.

Exercise 5 page 182

1 the cars can't move **2** air pollution **3** people can use bicycles for free **4** sharing a ride with other people

Exercise 6 page 183

1 traffic **2** cars **3** time **4** petrol **5** expensive **6** smog **7** bike-sharing programmes **8** car sharing **9** idea **10** self-driving **11** accidents

Be flexible

With a **more advanced class**, ask students to close their books and take notes in their notebooks rather than in the template in Exercise 6 on page 183. Ask students to compare their notes, and then use them to complete the task in Exercise 6. Monitor and give feedback on the quality of the notes. If necessary, point out any spelling mistakes and ask students to find the correct spelling in the Glossary. Point out places where abbreviations may be helpful for faster note-taking.

Exercise 7 page 183

1 too many cars **2** build a metro system **3** fewer cars on the road **4** people don't like walking on pavements **5** inside moving pavement **6** People get exercise, feel comfortable and don't drive.

Exercise 8 page 184

1 Because everyone uses a car. **2** They are slow and expensive and they cause pollution. **3** free bicycles and car sharing **4** Dubai **5** build a metro system / inside moving pavements

Exercise 9 page 184

Answers will vary.

CRITICAL THINKING

Learning objectives

- Remember and organize information from notes about transport problems and solutions in different cities
- Analyze transport problems, solutions and their results in a city
- Apply solutions to transport problems from other cities to the problems of a new city and predict their results
- Suggest new solutions to transport problems in a city and predict their results
- Evaluate solutions to transport problems in a city and choose the most effective solution

UNLOCK TEACHER DEVELOPMENT

BE INFORMED

➔ **Synthesizing information for a talk** is an important skill for students because: (1) A talk (or presentation) is a common form of assessment, so students need as much practice as possible; (2) Too often, students rely on one source of information, which makes the talk less interesting and too one-sided; (3) Students need encouragement to integrate as many sources as possible into their work.

BE CONFIDENT

➔ Develop this skill for yourself by doing the following activity:

Imagine you were going to give a talk about why critical thinking is important. What kind of sources would you include? Where would you find your background information? How could you make it as interesting as possible?

Would your answers to these questions change, depending on your audience? For example, if it were colleagues, parents or students?

Lead-in

Go through the instructions with the class and focus on the Speaking task. Explain that the following sections of the unit will help them to prepare to describe a transport problem, solutions and results.

UNLOCK TEACHER DEVELOPMENT

BE READY

Look at the Critical Thinking section in the Student's Book on pages 185–186.

➔ Which elements of the lesson do you think your students will find easiest / most difficult / most useful? Why?

➔ Are your answers true for all students in your class?

➔ How can you adapt your teaching or the material to meet your students' needs?

BE FLEXIBLE

Students could also research traffic-related problems in your own location. Personalizing the subject matter is a good way to engage lower-level students. This could be an extension or homework task. A further suggestion is to watch a video of a very effective talk which uses different source materials.

Exercise 1 page 185

Listening 1: problem: paper tickets very slow; **solution:** Oyster cards / credit cards / mobile payments / pay online; **result:** walk through gates faster

Listening 2: problem: traffic means it takes more time and petrol to travel around the city; too many cars in Dubai; people don't like to walk on the pavements outside; **solution:** free bicycles for people to use; car sharing; a self-driving car; build a metro; inside moving pavement or a moving walkway; **results:** there aren't as many cars; it can help stop accidents; fewer cars on the road; people get exercise, feel comfortable and don't drive

Exercise 2 page 185

Group A:

1 Traffic problems and solutions for the Santa Fe district of Mexico City

2 Too many cars on the road; pollution is bad; businesses have to pay a lot for car parks; people have to spend a lot of time driving to work (and so they feel tired at work) and spend a lot of money on petrol; no trains or high-speed buses or metro system

3 Sharing transport, such as car-sharing or bicycle-sharing

4 *Answers will vary.*

Group B:

1 Traffic problems in Melbourne

2 Public transport is not very good; people spend many hours in traffic – this is bad for their health.

3 self-driving cars　4 *Answers will vary.*

Exercises 3–4 page 186

Answers will vary.

UNLOCK TEACHER DEVELOPMENT

BE REFLECTIVE

Think about the following points:

➔ Did it work well in your class when you separated students into groups A and B? This can sometimes be challenging with lower-level students, or when students are not familiar with doing this. If it was difficult, think how you could do this more effectively next time.

➔ Prepare and deliver the talk which you planned in the *Be confident* section. Get feedback from your colleagues, not only about the content but about how you delivered it.

BE COLLABORATIVE

Your development is more meaningful when it is shared. See page 14 for ideas on how to peer-collaborate. Why not share the talk you showed students in the *Be flexible* section opposite, and its outcome?

PREPARATION FOR SPEAKING

Learning objectives

- Use words and phrases to describe a current topic or situation – *more and more, this means, with all of*
- Use past simple verb forms to describe a situation that used to be a problem – *Each passenger waited to buy a ticket, and then they went to the gate. This took a long time and more people started to live and work in London, so we needed a faster ticket system.*
- Pronounce *-ed* verb endings correctly when talking about the past
- Gain awareness of ways to describe solutions and results
- Use phrases to evaluate solutions and explain results – *I think it was a good solution. Why? Because ... That means ...*

Exercise 1 page 186

1 More and more   **2** This means   **3** because
4 With all of   **5** This is

Exercise 2 page 186

1 waited   **2** went   **3** put   **4** opened   **5** took   **6** took
7 started   **8** needed   **9** was

Exercise 3 page 187

went; put; took; was

Exercises 4–5 page 187

happened /d/	changed /d/	visited /ɪd/
guessed /t/	needed /ɪd/	waited /ɪd/
asked /t/	helped /t/	showed /d/
watched /t/	opened /d/	started /ɪd/

Exercises 6–7 pages 187–188

Answers will vary.

Exercise 8 page 188

1 They had to build a metro line.
2 People could cycle for free.
3 The cities started car sharing for workers.
4 There is a moving walkway.
5 The Oyster card is faster than paper tickets.
6 People can tap credit cards to pay.

Exercise 9 page 188

1 There was no public transport, so people had to drive everywhere. One solution was car sharing. That way, there were fewer cars and workers felt better.
2 There are a lot of bad drivers, so there are a lot of accidents. One solution is self-driving cars. So, these cars are safer because there are fewer accidents.
3 It took a long time because people waited to buy tickets and go through the gate. So Transport for London started Oyster cards. The result is that it is very fast and easy.

Exercise 10 page 189

Answers will vary.

SPEAKING TASK

Learning objectives

- Prepare to speak by organizing your notes
- Give a talk describing a transport problem in a city, the most effective solution and its result
- Listen and ask questions to understand another student's talk
- Evaluate solutions for transport problems in cities in a discussion

Exercises 1–6 pages 189–190

Answers will vary.

RESEARCH PROJECT

Research and share how transport may change in the future.

Divide the class into groups. Ask some groups to research different types of transport being used today. Ask the other groups to research future types of transport. Each group could think about what is good and bad about the different types of transport.

Determine the best way for the class to share the information which they have collected. Consider asking students to create and record video or audio presentations for the class to listen to and take notes on. Students could then vote on which form of future transport they would most like to use. Students could use an online voting system. Search for 'voting software' to view some of these.

Exercise 1

Answers will vary.

Exercise 2

1 go by   **2** take   **3** ride   **4** take   **5** drive

Exercise 3

1 because   **2** because   **3** so   **4** so   **5** Because

Exercise 4

1 train.   **2** the pavement.   **3** a solution.   **4** an accident.
5 petrol.   **6** an idea?   **7** a passenger.   **8** petrol.

Exercise 5

Answers will vary.

Exercise 6A

1 a problem   **2** a solution   **3** results   **4** a solution
5 a problem   **6** a solution

Exercise 6B

Answers will vary.

UNIT OBJECTIVES

Watch and listen	Watch and understand a video about the Grand Canal in Venice.
Listening skills	Predict content using visuals; distinguish fact from opinion.
Critical thinking	Decide if ideas are relevant.
Grammar	Use past simple statements and questions.
Speaking skills	Signpost an opinion; organize information for a presentation.
Speaking task	Give a presentation about an interesting place.
⊘ **Teacher development**	Help your students become better at **deciding if ideas are relevant**.

UNLOCK YOUR KNOWLEDGE

Background note

The photo shows traditional houses in Sulawesi, Indonesia. This type of house is called a *tongkonan* and is associated with the Toraja culture in Indonesia. The word *tongkonan* comes from a Toraja word for 'to sit' and it means 'a place where a family meets'. A *tongkonan* has a particularly large, unusually shaped roof. The inside of the house is small in comparison to the roof and is used mainly for sleeping, storage and for protection during bad weather. Toraja people spend most of their day outside the house.

Lead-in

Ask students for a show of hands as to who lives in a flat / an apartment and who in a house. Put them into groups of three or four. Ask students to think of the advantages and disadvantages of living in these different types of home. Allow two to three minutes for this, before inviting feedback from the class.

page 15
Answers will vary.

WATCH AND LISTEN

Learning objectives

- Look at photos of Venice and discuss how it differs from your own city
- Listen and understand main ideas in a video about Venice
- Listen and understand detailed information and figures
- Make inferences about opinions in the video
- Practise talking about canals and rivers
- Understand an advertisement for a gondola ride

Exercise 1 page 16
1 Italy   **2–3** *Answers will vary.*

Exercise 2 page 16
Answers will vary.

Exercise 3 page 16
1 T   **2** F; Most of the islands between the canals are little.
3 F; Today, Venice is important for tourists.   **4** T
5 F; The Grand Canal is the biggest canal in Venice.   **6** T
7 F; Another name for Venice is 'The city of bridges'.

Exercise 4 page 17
1 a lot of canals   **2** cars   **3** gondola   **4** stilts   **5** gold
6 stone

Exercise 5 page 17
1 117, 400   **2** two   **3** 300   **4** 30   **5** 15

Exercises 6–7 page 17
Answers will vary.

Exercise 8 page 17
1 no   **2** no   **3** at the Ca' d'Oro   **4** €20 per person
5 *Possible answer:* It is warmer during those months.
6 *Possible answer:* They want to keep people safe.

LISTENING 1

Learning objectives

- Understand key vocabulary for homes and places – *capital, ancient, apartment*
- Use visuals to understand a topic before you listen
- Gain awareness of typical spellings of vowel sounds
- Listen and identify speakers and topic in a podcast
- Listen and complete a set of detailed notes
- Evaluate how useful a set of notes is
- Give personal opinions on different places to live

Lead-in

Refer students back to the Lead-in at the beginning of the unit, when you asked about where they live, then ask them if they can think of other interesting places where people can live. Encourage students to be as creative as possible and put all reasonable ideas on the board. *Suggested ideas:* in an ice house (igloo), in caves, in trees, on a boat, underground, in tents, in skyscrapers

Exercise 1 page 18

a strange   **b** bridge   **c** rocks   **d** recognize   **e** cave
f ancient   **g** apartment   **h** capital

Exercise 2 page 19
Answers will vary.

Exercise 3 page 19
Photo a: cave, rock, strange, ancient
Photo b: strange, rock, ancient
Photo c: bridge   **Photo d:** bridge, strange

Exercises 4–5 page 20
/eɪ/: cave, strange, ancient, say
/ɒ/: rock, long
/ɪ/: bridge, built
/ʌ/: hundreds, under

Be flexible

👥👥 Copy the table onto the board and drill students through the IPA sounds and the words, starting by modelling the sound/word for them to repeat. Point out the first vowel sound is long and the other three are short. Demonstrate this by exaggerating the lengths. Then point to a sound/word and ask students to repeat. Encourage students to say the sound/word clearly and confidently. Gradually increase the speed at which you point, encouraging students to keep up by calling out the sounds/words as fast as you point to them. This gives students less time to think and helps with learning. Ask **more advanced students** to think of two more words with each of the sounds and add them to the chart.

Exercise 7 page 21
1 c   **2** b

Exercise 8 page 21
1 Tunisia   **2** 700   **3** 355   **4** Turkey   **5** 8,000
6 Florence, Italy   **7** 1345   **8** Azerbaijan   **9** 48   **10** 2,000

Exercise 9 page 21
Possible answer: The notes are useful because they help you remember the important information and key facts from the podcast.

Exercise 10 page 21
Answers will vary.

LANGUAGE DEVELOPMENT

Learning objectives

- Use past simple verbs in sentences about homes around the world – *They built the bridge in 1345. They were very strange buildings.*
- Differentiate between regular and irregular past simple verbs – *They made them out of rock. She lived there for 20 years.*
- Write past simple questions and statements about homes – *When did they build their house? Why did you move to your home? We moved here because my dad got a job here.*
- Use adjectives to ask questions about places – *Is it ancient? Is it a cheap place to live? Are the streets crowded?*

Exercise 1 page 22
1 changed   **2** went   **3** made   **4** was, destroyed
5 decided, needed, built   **6** put   **7** formed

Exercise 2 page 23
regular: destroyed, decided, needed, formed
irregular: made, was, built, put

Exercise 3 page 23
Answers will vary.

Exercise 4 page 23
1 did you live   **2** did you start   **3** Did you know
4 did you move   **5** Did you like

Exercises 5–6 page 23
Answers will vary.

Optional activity

👤 Students research another unusual home, possibly one suggested in the Lead-in for Listening 1 that didn't feature in the listening. *Suggested ideas:* on boats, in trees, underground, in tents

Exercise 7 page 24

a cheap **b** rural **c** ancient **d** expensive **e** crowded **f** modern **g** urban **h** popular

Exercise 8 page 24

1 urban **2** popular **3** rural **4** expensive

Exercise 9 page 24

Answers will vary.

LISTENING 2

Learning objectives

- Understand key vocabulary for places – *urban, lake, modern*
- Use a visual to predict and then identify the topic of a lecture
- Take detailed notes on advantages and disadvantages in a table
- Listen and use signal words and context to discriminate between facts and opinions
- Explain how you evaluate statements of fact and opinion
- Synthesize information from a podcast and a lecture about places to live in a discussion

Lead-in

Students work in pairs. They try to agree on the biggest advantage of living in the place they currently live and do the same with the biggest disadvantage. They then discuss whether that one advantage is enough to make them want to live there for a long time, or if the disadvantage is enough to make them want to move away.

Exercise 1 page 25

a field **b** area **c** modern **d** lake **e** traffic **f** urban **g** woods **h** is located

Exercise 2 page 25

Possible answers:

The photo shows an urban area. There are lakes and woods. It is a modern city. The woods are located next to a city.

Exercise 3 page 26

b

Exercise 4 page 26

Advantages: lots of trees help clean the city air; parks give people places to walk, so they are healthier; it's near mountains and the ocean so people can enjoy the outdoors easily during warm weather; you can enjoy ancient trees and walk near the ocean; you can have fun by Beaver Lake; the park helps make Vancouver one of the healthiest and cleanest cities in the world

Disadvantages: not much room for new buildings and homes; makes Vancouver expensive; crowded; very bad traffic; wild animals can be a problem

Exercise 5 page 26

2 In fact; F **3** As we know; F **4** I think; O
5 I personally feel; O **6** In my opinion; O

Exercise 6 page 26

You know that a sentence is fact because the signal word or phrase he uses tells us it is something that everybody knows or that it is officially recognized.

You know that a sentence is opinion because the signal word or phrase he uses tells us it is what he personally thinks.

Exercise 7 page 27

The tense often used to give facts is the present simple.

Exercise 8 page 27

Fact: In fact; As we know **Opinion:** I personally feel; In my opinion

Exercise 9 page 28

1 O **2** F **3** F **4** O

Be flexible

👤 👥 Students think of a place in their city or town that they know well. It can be a park, a restaurant, their school, etc. Tell them to write five to six statements about the place they chose. The statements should be a mixture of fact and opinion. When they have finished, they read their statements to a partner, adding in signal words when appropriate. Partners say whether each statement is a fact or opinion.

Exercise 10 page 28

Answers will vary.

CRITICAL THINKING

Learning objectives

- Evaluate the relevance of a set of ideas to a presentation
- Apply what you have learnt by choosing a new place and finding relevant ideas for a presentation
- Use a table to organize your notes into an outline for a presentation
- Evaluate another student's outline of a presentation

UNL⌀CK TEACHER DEVELOPMENT

BE INFORMED

➔ **Deciding if ideas are relevant** is an important skill for students because: (1) It is important to know that they don't have to use all their notes when giving a presentation; (2) Presentations in which students have not carefully selected the content are often difficult to follow; (3) Students often find it difficult to evaluate which ideas are more relevant than others.

BE CONFIDENT

➔ Develop this skill for yourself by doing the following activity:

1 *Imagine you are going to give a presentation to the other English teachers at your school about the importance of critical thinking for university-level study. Choose five facts from the list below which you would include.*

- How you think is as important as what you think.
- Critical thinking helps students create high-quality essays, by enabling them to synthesize ideas.
- Critical thinking can help students better organize their working practices (e.g. researching and collecting information).
- People who lack confidence in their beliefs or their actions are afraid of critical thinking.
- Employers highly value critical thinking skills, such as the ability to create surveys and interpret data.
- The ability for students to think for themselves can increase their self-reliance.
- Critical thinking develops confidence, and confidence is the most important academic skill.
- All academic subjects – sciences, social sciences, arts and humanities – require critical thinking skills.

2 *Now number the facts 1–5, where 1 is the most relevant to the topic and 5 is the least relevant*

Lead-in

Students begin to think about the Speaking task that they will do at the end of the unit. Give them a minute to look at the box and ask you any questions they might have.

UNL⌀CK TEACHER DEVELOPMENT

BE READY

Look at the Critical Thinking section in the Student's Book on pages 29–30.

➔ Which elements of the lesson do you think your students will find easiest / most difficult / most useful? Why?

➔ Are your answers true for all students in your class?

➔ How can you adapt your teaching or the material to meet your students' needs?

BE FLEXIBLE

Do Exercises 4 and 5 as a group project. Three students decide on the same place to find out information about. They should then share their research with each other. The individual student can then decide which facts to use in their presentation in Exercise 6, or they could do it as a group presentation; in which case, the same students can then work together on Exercise 7.

Exercises 1–7 pages 29–30
Answers will vary.

UNL⌀CK TEACHER DEVELOPMENT

BE REFLECTIVE

Think about the following questions:

➔ Share with a colleague (face-to-face or electronically) the five facts you chose in the *Be confident* section. See if they agree with your choices, or if they would have chosen different facts. Can you can reach a consensus?

➔ Do students in your class prefer to work by themselves or as a group? Knowing this will help you plan more effectively for future classes.

BE COLLABORATIVE

Your development is more meaningful when it's shared. See page 14 for ideas on how to peer-collaborate. Why not share what you learnt in the *Be ready* section?

PREPARATION FOR SPEAKING

Learning objectives

- Use phrases for signposting opinions – *I personally feel that most people would enjoy Vancouver. In my opinion, most people would enjoy Vancouver. It seems to me that most people would enjoy Vancouver.*
- Categorize the type of information in a talk
- Use phrases to signal the organization of information in a talk – *I'd like to give you some information about parks. Now let's talk about homes. The next topic is roads. Finally, let's look at tourism.*
- Use connected speech to say phrases which signal the organization of information in a talk

Exercise 1 page 31
Answers will vary.

Exercise 2 page 31
1 d   **2** a   **3** b   **4** c

Exercise 3 page 32
1 I'd like to talk about   **2** First of all,
3 I'd also like to talk about   **4** Finally,

Exercise 4 page 33
First‿of‿all, let's look‿at some‿of the positives.

Exercise 6 page 33
1 I'd like to give you some‿information‿about ...
2 Now let's talk‿about ...
3 The next topic‿is ...
4 Finally, let's look‿at ...

SPEAKING TASK

Learning objectives

- Prepare for a presentation by reviewing and adding to your notes
- Prepare an introduction and conclusion for your presentation
- Plan how to signal facts and opinions in your talk
- Give a presentation on an interesting place

Exercises 1–6 pages 33–34
Answers will vary.

RESEARCH PROJECT

Create a documentary about Alaska.

Divide the class into groups and ask each group to investigate a different aspect of Alaska, e.g. its geography, nature, history, industry or literature. Tell students that they need to find images, sounds, music and videos to create a class documentary entitled *Alaskan life: Past and present*. Students could create a wiki to share their research with the rest of the class.

The class will use the information from each group to create a short documentary film about Alaska. To plan the documentary, students will need to create a script or storyboard. They will also have to think about who in the class will direct the documentary, who will work the camera, who will edit the video, and who will present or narrate the documentary. They could then upload the film to a video-sharing website.

CLASSROOM APP

Exercises 1
Answers will vary.

Exercise 2
1 Did, live   **2** saw   **3** were   **4** didn't go; did not go
5 built   **6** made   **7** weren't; were not   **8** put

Exercise 3
1 ancient   **2** crowded   **3** cheap   **4** expensive
5 popular   **6** rural

Exercise 4
1 woods   **2** a lake   **3** bridges   **4** recognize   **5** traffic
6 strange   **7** located   **8** rock

Exercise 5
Answers will vary.

Exercise 6A
1 fact   **2** negative opinion   **3** fact   **4** fact   **5** positive opinion   **6** negative opinion

Exercise 6B
Answers will vary.

UNIT OBJECTIVES	
Watch and listen	Watch and understand a video about a festival of ice sculptures in China.
Listening skills	Take notes; listen for main ideas.
Critical thinking	Create a persuasive argument.
Grammar	Use present tense question forms; use the present continuous.
Speaking skills	Make suggestions; agree and disagree.
Speaking task	Choose an event from a festival and persuade your group to go to it.
⟳ **Teacher development**	Help your students become better at **creating a persuasive argument**.

UNL⟳CK YOUR KNOWLEDGE

Background note

The photo shows the Holi festival in India. Holi, also known as 'the festival of colours', is a spring festival that is celebrated in almost every part of India. It celebrates the end of winter and the start of spring, and the victory of good over evil. Holi lasts for a night and a day. It starts on the evening of Purnima – the Full Moon Day – when people meet with family and friends near bonfires. The next day is the festival of colours, when people meet in the streets and throw colourful powders and coloured water.

Lead-in

Write *festival* on the board and ask students if they know what it means or can give an example. Ask students why we have festivals. What purpose do they serve?

page 37

1 This festival is in India. It is also held in many other countries around the world.

2–3 *Answers will vary.*

WATCH AND LISTEN

Learning objectives

* Listen and identify main ideas in a video about a festival
* Listen and understand details and figures
* Listen and identify the meaning of unfamiliar words from their context in the video
* Practise talking about going to an ice festival

Exercises 1–2 page 38
Answers will vary.

Exercise 3 page 38
1 F   **2** F   **3** T   **4** T   **5** F

Exercise 4 page 39
1 Ice City   **2** 7,000   **3** clear   **4** competitions   **5** 16.8
6 a million / 1,000,000   **7** 5 January

Exercise 5 page 39
1 c   **2** b   **3** b   **4** a

Exercise 6 page 39
Answers will vary.

LISTENING 1

Learning objectives

* Understand key vocabulary for festivals – *activities, traditional, entertainment*
* Use visuals to identify topics before you listen
* Take effective notes by removing unnecessary words
* Listen and complete a brochure about three festivals with detailed notes
* Listen and understand detailed information
* Use emphatic stress to ask questions about festivals

Lead-in

Elicit the festivals students have already learnt about. Ask: *What type of festivals are these?* to elicit *cultural*. If students aren't able to answer, prompt them with some questions, for example, *Are they music festivals? Are they book festivals?* Once they have identified these festivals as cultural, ask students what other types of festivals they can think of. Accept all reasonable suggestions.

Exercise 1 page 40

1 b **2** a **3** a **4** a **5** a **6** a

Exercise 2 page 41

a culture, traditional, enjoy(ed), entertainment
b activity, traditional, culture, enjoy(ed), entertainment
c lecture, enjoy(ed)

Exercise 3 page 41

1 c **2** b **3** a

Exercise 4 page 41

Answers will vary.

Exercises 5–6 page 41

1 Date: ~~The festival is in~~ April and May
2 Activities: ~~You can see art and you can try~~ cooking

Exercise 7 page 42

1 UK **2** October **3** history **4** gravity **5** talk **6** April
7 stalls **8** lake **9** museums **10** January **11** February
12 sports **13** dance **14** fashion

Exercise 8 page 42

1 F; The Festival of Ideas is for anybody interested in arts and science.
2 T **3** T **4** F; They can have picnics under trees, go to food stalls, hire boats on the lake and go to museums.
5 T **6** T

Exercises 9–10 page 43

Answers will vary.

Exercise 11 page 43

interesting, event, come

Exercise 12 page 43

The important words are stressed: Well, it's an <u>interesting event</u> to <u>come</u> to.

Exercise 13 page 43

1 So, <u>what kinds</u> of <u>things</u> do <u>people learn</u>? (Note: The speaker also stresses 'So' as a way of getting the listeners' attention, but this is not one of the important words.)
2 Are there any <u>things</u> you <u>don't like</u> about it?
3 Do you <u>have many people here</u> from <u>other countries</u>?

Exercise 15 page 43

1 What <u>activities</u> do people <u>do</u> at <u>festivals</u> in their <u>free time</u>?
2 Which <u>festival</u> is <u>good</u> for <u>people</u> with <u>lots</u> of <u>hobbies</u>?
3 What did you <u>do</u> at the <u>Cherry Blossom Festival last weekend</u>?

Exercise 16 page 43

Answers will vary.

LANGUAGE DEVELOPMENT

Learning objectives

- Ask questions in the present simple – *Do you like festivals? Is the work interesting? What time does the festival start?*
- Use the present continuous to describe actions at festivals – *I'm eating traditional food. Are you visiting The Muscat Festival?*
- Use ideas maps to organize vocabulary records of collocations with *go to*, *take* and *have*
- Use collocations to ask and answer questions about festivals and celebrations.

Exercise 1 page 44

1 learn **2** concentrate **3** Are

Exercises 2–3 page 44

1 ~~Are~~ Do you like your job?
2 ~~Do~~ Are you a chef?
3 What time ~~is~~ does the festival start?
4 What kinds of food ~~are~~ do you have?
5 ~~Does~~ Is it all good?
6 Where ~~are~~ do people eat their lunch?
7 ~~Is~~ Do you like the food?
8 ~~Do~~ Is the work interesting?

Exercise 4 page 45

1 Do you like festivals? **2** When do you go home?
3 Are you a good cook? **4** When do you feel hungry?
5 What do you do for fun? **6** Do you like your school?

Exercise 5 page 45

Answers will vary.

Exercise 6 page 46

1 'm/am studying **2** 's/is enjoying **3** 're/are attending
4 's/is giving **5** 're/are having **6** 's/is; doing
7 are watching **8** Are; parking

Exercise 7 page 46

Answers will vary.

Optional activity

👥 Charades: Each student writes a one-word verb on a small piece of paper. The verb can be related to something one might see/do at a festival or celebration. Collect the papers. Divide the students into teams. One by one, students select one of the verbs and act it out. The first team to correctly guess the action wins a point. Teams must use correct present continuous forms (*She is dancing*). Extra points may be awarded if the team can use another form correctly (*They are dancing.*)

Exercise 8 page 47

go to: a celebration, university, an event, a lecture, a party

take: part, place, your time

have: a celebration, an event, fun, a lecture, a party, a problem

Exercise 9 page 47

1 take   **2** go to   **3** take   **4** Have   **5** have

Exercise 10 page 47

1 event   **2** your time   **3** concerts   **4** party/celebration

Exercise 11 page 47

Answers will vary.

LISTENING 2

Learning objectives

- Understand key vocabulary for holidays – *celebrate*, *costume*, *dish*
- Use visuals to identify topics in a conversation about holidays and celebrations
- Listen and complete the main ideas in a detailed set of notes
- Listen and understand detailed information
- Listen and identify phrases signalling examples
- Synthesize information from interviews about festivals and a conversation about holidays and celebrations, and evaluate advantages and disadvantages

Lead-in

Books closed. Ask students: *Do you eat any special food during celebrations in your country?* Encourage as many ideas as possible and ask follow-up questions, such as: *Do you eat this at home or in a restaurant? Do you invite family or friends to share it? Do you stay in your home or go to other people's homes?.* Also ask students: *Do you use special decorations for celebrations in your country? Do you usually give gifts? Do you do any special activities?.*

Exercise 1 page 48

a dish   **b** fireworks   **c** parade   **d** celebrate   **e** gift(s)   **f** costume   **g** decorate(d)

Exercise 2 page 48

a fireworks, celebrate   **b** parade, celebrate, costume   **c** decorate/decorated, dish, celebrate

Exercise 3 page 48

Answers will vary.

Exercise 4 page 49

1 Thanksgiving   **2** Family   **3** Traditional   **4** Food   **5** Canada   **6** US   **7** Pumpkin pie   **8** Stuffing   **9** Decorations   **10** Autumn colours   **11** Activities   **12** Canada   **13** US   **14** reasons

Exercise 5 page 50

1 F; He likes it because everyone can celebrate it.

2 F; Potatoes, corn and cranberries are from the Americas.

3 F; In the eastern US, sometimes oysters are used in the stuffing.

4 T   **5** T

Exercise 6 page 50

1 like   **2** such as   **3** For example   **4** for instance

Be flexible

👥 Students think of a festival or celebration they know about. In pairs, they give examples of the event's food, decorations and activities, using phrases they heard in Exercise 6 (*like, such as, for example, for instance*). For a **bigger challenge**, put the students in new pairs. Each has to report to the new partner on what the previous partner said, again, offering examples of the event's food, decorations and activities.

Exercise 7 page 50

1 like; such as   **2** for example; for instance

Exercise 8 page 50

Answers will vary.

CRITICAL THINKING

Learning objectives

- Understand a text about a festival
- Decide which events you would enjoy the most
- Select information from a text to best support your arguments
- Evaluate a poster and make suggestions for improvements

UNLOCK TEACHER DEVELOPMENT

BE INFORMED

→ **Creating a persuasive argument** is an important skill for students because: (1) Arguing is a difficult skill intellectually as well as linguistically, and so students need as much practice as possible; (2) It is important to be able to argue in different ways, depending on the audience; (3) It is important for students to understand the strategies for composing and developing a strong argument.

BE CONFIDENT

→ Develop this skill for yourself by doing the following activity:

1 *Complete the table with positives and negatives for the two statements below.*

	Positives	Negatives
Critical thinking is best taught within ELT, rather than as a separate subject.		
Parents should come to a critical thinking lecture at the start of every academic year, so they understand more about it.		

2 *Look at what you have written. Based on this information, are you more positive or negative about each of these statements? What would you try and persuade somebody to think about them?*

Lead-in

Students begin to think about the Speaking task that they will do at the end of the unit. Give them a minute to look at the box. As a class, you could spend a few minutes brainstorming some ideas for festival events for the Speaking task.

UNLOCK TEACHER DEVELOPMENT

BE READY

Look at the Critical Thinking section in the Student's Book on pages 51–53.

→ Which elements of the lesson do you think your students will find easiest / most difficult / most useful? Why?

→ Are your answers true for all students in your class?

→ How can you adapt your teaching or the material to meet your students' needs?

BE FLEXIBLE

As an optional project / homework extension to Exercise 6, students can create their own poster for National Day, or an event within it. They could print them and display them in class, or else share them electronically.

Exercises 1–6 pages 51–53
Answers will vary.

UNLOCK TEACHER DEVELOPMENT

BE REFLECTIVE

Think about the following questions:

→ How interested were your students in the main topic in the critical thinking section? If they were not that interested, is there a way you could have made it more interesting, e.g. with some background information about the UAE, or asking them to do some research before the lesson?

→ Is there anything that you do in your lessons which you think your colleagues might also like to try out? Could you persuade them to do this? How could you try and achieve this?

BE COLLABORATIVE

Your development is more meaningful when it's shared. See page 14 for ideas on how to peer-collaborate. Why not share what you learnt in the *Be ready* section?

PREPARATION FOR SPEAKING

Learning objectives

- Use phrases to make suggestions – *Visitors should try to go to the cake shop. Why not try this activity? How about driving to the festival?*
- Use phrases to respond to suggestions – *That's a great idea! I'm not sure that's a good idea.*

Exercise 1 page 54
1 You could look at this online.   **2** How about starting with cake?   **3** Why not try it yourself?

Exercise 2 page 54
2, 4, 5, 6

Exercise 3 page 54
2 Why not   **3** Shall we   **4** How about   **5** I'd suggest
6 Can we think about

Exercise 4 page 55

1 Shall 2 How about / Can we think about 3 could
4 how about / can we think about 5 could / shall

Optional activity

Role play: Tell students to imagine they are going to a festival or celebration. With a partner, they have to create a dialogue in which they are at the event and discussing which activities they want to see and do. They must use language that makes suggestions.

Exercise 6 page 55

No: (Oh,) I am not sure that's a good idea; (Hmm,) I might want to see some other things.

Yes: OK. Good idea; Yeah, that sounds good; Yeah, I'd love to! That's a great idea!; Sure! That sounds good.

SPEAKING TASK

Learning objectives

- Prepare to persuade others in a discussion about a festival by reviewing and adding to your notes
- Select one event on National Day to attend
- Take part in a discussion about which event to attend on National Day
- Present your decision and reasons for choosing an event to the class

Exercises 1–8 pages 55–57

Answers will vary.

RESEARCH PROJECT

Research and explain festivals and celebrations.

Divide the class into groups and work with them to produce some interview questions for people from different countries about festivals and celebrations. Students could interview people face-to-face or online in other countries. They will need to film / audio record the interview. Students should focus on the type of festival, customs, food, time and its function.

Each group will create a short video to explain the different festivals, using extracts from the interviews. Students will first need to create a script or storyboard. They will also have to think about who in the class will direct the video, who will work the camera, who will edit the video, and who will present or narrate the video.

CLASSROOM APP

Exercise 1

Answers will vary.

Exercise 2

Answers will vary.

Exercise 3

1 Do you like to cook a big meal for holidays like Thanksgiving?
2 This photo of traditional Japanese New Year's food looks delicious. How does it taste?
3 I am shopping for a birthday gift for my sister. Do you think she would like this scarf?
4 What music are we listening to now? I don't know this song.
5 Are you coming to the fireworks festival soon? I'm waiting for you by the park entrance.
6 Does your sister enjoy events like the Festival of Ideas?
7 What do people eat at the winter festival?
8 My parents aren't home right now. They are having a picnic at the Cherry Blossom Festival.

Exercise 4

1 a nice time 2 photos 3 a problem 4 part
5 university 6 events 7 place 8 care

Exercise 5

1 traditional 2 enjoyed 3 decorated 4 dish
5 costumes 6 gift 7 entertainment 8 activities

Exercise 6A

1 Shall we try going to the art fair?
2 You could try studying at the library.
3 How about taking a cooking class?
4 Can we think about going in the morning?
5 Why not eat out at that good restaurant near your house?

Exercise 6B

Answers will vary.

UNIT OBJECTIVES

Watch and listen	Watch and understand a video about fibre optic cables.
Listening skill	Listen for reasons.
Critical thinking	Evaluate advantages and disadvantages.
Grammar	Use *can / be able to*.
Speaking skills	Give a spoken report; give additional and contrasting information.
Speaking task	Present a report about a device or technology.
⌀ **Teacher development**	Help your students become better at **evaluating advantages and disadvantages**.

UNLOCK YOUR KNOWLEDGE

Background note

The photo shows a humanoid robot called InMoov. The robot was constructed in 2011 by the French sculptor Gaël Langevin, using 3-D printing technology. InMoov is unique, because it can be made by anybody with just a simple 3-D printer. The robot is controlled by a computer programme, and it can see, hear, talk and move. It is used in education to teach about 3-D printing, programming and robotics. It is also interesting for engineers and doctors, as it shows how 3-D printers could be used to make prosthetic limbs.

Lead-in

Write the word *technology* on the board. Ask students: *What do you think of when you see this word?* Brainstorm ideas onto the board and encourage students to be as creative and imaginative as possible.

page 59

1–3 *Answers will vary.*

4 *Possible answers:* It reduces face-to-face communication; We can become too reliant on it; It can harm eyesight and posture; People can become addicted to social media sites or online gaming; It can be abused to manipulate people and opinions.

WATCH AND LISTEN

Learning objectives

- Listen and identify main ideas and details in a video about fibre optic cables
- Listen and understand details
- Choose an inference about the implications of the information in the video
- Practise talking about the internet and technology

Exercises 1–2 page 60

Answers will vary.

Exercise 3 page 60

1 changes **2** Most **3** bottom **4** suddenly **5** Engineers **6** broken **7** weeks **8** ship

Exercise 4 page 61

a 2 **b** 5 **c** 3 **d** 1 **e** 4

Exercise 5 page 61

1 violent volcanic activity **2** ten years ago
3 Between Taiwan and the Philippines **4** heavy rocks
5 A special ship called the Wave Sentinel

Exercises 6–8 page 61

Answers will vary.

LISTENING 1

Learning objectives

- Understand key vocabulary – *accident*, *collect*, *disabled*
- Listen and identify consonant sounds – /s/ / ʃ/ and /tʃ/
- Use sound maps to organize vocabulary by sound
- Listen and complete a detailed set of notes on a radio programme about robots
- Listen for signal words and identify reasons
- Use signal words to link reasons and results
- Give opinions about robots

Lead-in

Write the word *robot* on the board and elicit from students what they think a robot is and what it does. (A robot is a machine that is programmed to do mechanical tasks in the way of a human.) Encourage students to be as creative and imaginative as possible in their ideas about what robots can do.

Exercise 1 page 62

1 a **2** b **3** b **4** a **5** a **6** b **7** b **8** b

Exercises 2–3 page 63

Answers will vary.

Exercise 4 page 63

a fish **b** disabled **c** suit **d** pollution **e** kitchen

Exercise 6 page 63

/s/: suit, disabled **/ʃ/:** fish, pollution **/tʃ/:** kitchen

Exercise 7 page 64

/s/: sort, robots, accident **/ʃ/:** station, short, wish, ocean **/tʃ/:** which, match, cheap

Exercise 8 page 64

1 sorts **2** cheap **3** wash **4** sea **5** shave

Exercise 9 page 64

Answers will vary.

Exercise 10 page 64

1 robots **2** cheaper **3** disabled **4** accidents **5** suit **6** in their own homes **7** luxury **8** information collection **9** pollution (in the water)

Exercise 11 page 65

Answers will vary.

Exercise 12 page 65

1 always really expensive **2** accident
3 new types of robots **4** robotic fish

Exercise 13 page 65

1 Thanks to **2** due to / because of **3** Since
4 Due to / Because of

Be flexible

Students work in pairs. Call out the beginning of sentences and tell them to finish each sentence with *since*, *because of*, *thanks to* and *due to*. They should think of as many ways to end the sentences as possible.

Sentences to give students and possible answers:

More businesses are starting to use robots (*since robots aren't as expensive as they used to be*).

Some disabled people can walk again (*thanks to robotic suits*).

Some people may need robots to help them do housework (*due to old age*).

Scientists use robotic fish (*because of pollution in the ocean*).

To provide a **bigger challenge**, students can then think of their own sentences about robots. Give a point for each correct sentence. The pair with the most points wins.

Exercise 14 page 65

Answers will vary.

LANGUAGE DEVELOPMENT

Learning objectives

- Use *can/can't* and *am/is/are* (not) *able to* describe ability in the present – *Robots are able to help people in their everyday lives. She can't do housework easily.*
- Use *was/were (not) able to* and *couldn't* to talk about ability in the past – *He wasn't even able to sit up on his own when a visitor came. He was able to stand up when he finally put on the robotic suit. He couldn't feel his legs when doctors touched them.*
- Describe actions and equipment related to technology – *I often use Wi-Fi. I forgot my password. I log in to my email every day.*
- Organize technology vocabulary by parts of speech

Exercise 1 page 66

1 am able   **2** was able to   **3** wasn't able to   **4** couldn't
5 wasn't able to   **6** Are you able to   **7** Were you able to

Exercises 2–3 page 67

Answers will vary.

Exercise 4 page 67

1 turn; on   **2** mouse / keyboard   **3** log in   **4** Wi-Fi;
go online / log in   **5** the cloud   **6** shut down / turn off

Exercise 5 page 68

Answers will vary.

Exercise 6 page 68

verbs: charge, surf, text
nouns: apps, battery, charger, keys, text

Exercise 7 page 68

1 keys   **2** apps   **3** surf   **4** text   **5** battery
6 charger; charge

Exercise 8 page 68

Answers will vary.

LISTENING 2

Learning objectives

- Understand key vocabulary for computers and memory – *stupid, memory, research*
- Listen for and practise saying /ə/ and /æ/ correctly in sentences with linking words
- Listen and complete a set of detailed notes on a report about computers and memory with main ideas and details
- Describe how you store information
- Synthesize information from a radio programme about robots and a report about computers and memory in a discussion

Lead-in

Ask students a few basic questions to check their memory (*Do you know your / your mother's mobile phone number? When did World War II begin and end? When did the Euro become official currency?*). Ask students how they find out answers they don't know. Ask them if they think computers affect their memory and if so, how?

Exercise 1 page 69

Answers will vary.

Exercise 2 page 70

a research   **b** stupid   **c** file   **d** location   **e** memory

Exercise 3 page 70

1 You will hear the main ideas <u>and</u> additional information.
2 You will hear the main ideas <u>as well as</u> additional information.

Exercise 5 page 71

1 d   **2** weak   **3** weak

Exercise 6 page 71

1 memory   **2** difficult   **3** websites   **4** information   **5** lazy

Exercise 7 page 71

6 information   **7** answer   **8** how   **9** put   **10** facts
11 location   **12** find

Exercises 8–10 page 72

Answers will vary.

Be flexible

Memory game: If the class is around 12 students, this can be done as a whole-group activity. If the class is large, divide students into several large groups. Tell them that they are going to invent a robot and they have to think of one sentence to describe what the robot can and can't do. Encourage them to use *can* and *can't* and vocabulary for technology. Each group should stand in a circle. The first student says his/her sentence (Possible sentence: *Our robot can cook dinner every night.*) The second student repeats the first student's sentence, and then adds his/her own (*Our robot can cook dinner every night and it can help us do our homework.*) This should continue around the circle, with each student adding the previous students' sentences. Follow-up discussion can be whether students think they have a good memory or not.

For a **bigger challenge**, ask students what they think the limit is on the number of (unrelated) things they can remember. (Estimates range between four and seven). Ask for suggestions on how to improve their memory of lists like this (examples could include writing things down rehearsing and mnemonics).

CRITICAL THINKING

Learning objectives

- Evaluate a set of opinions about using computers
- Analyze the advantages and disadvantages of a type of technology
- Evaluate another student's ideas
- Evaluate the importance of the advantages and disadvantages you listed

UNLOCK TEACHER DEVELOPMENT

BE INFORMED

→ **Evaluating advantages and disadvantages** is an important skill for students because: (1) When students think about the advantages and disadvantages of a particular topic, they may simply count the number of each and decide that the one with the most has the best argument; (2) Instead, students need to develop evaluation skills, so they can judge the quality of different arguments; (3) If students are unable to do this, then their arguments are likely to be weak and unbalanced.

BE CONFIDENT

→ Develop this skill for yourself by doing the following activity:

Look at the following opinions about critical thinking. Decide if they are advantages or disadvantages. Are the advantages or the disadvantages more important? Why?

- Students often don't like doing critical thinking.
- Being able to think critically can help students get into their university of choice.
- Students find doing critical thinking hard work.
- Critical thinking is an important skill for improving the quality of spoken and written content.
- Doing critical thinking in English classes means there is less time for developing grammar and vocabulary.
- Students may not think critical thinking is relevant to their everyday lives.
- Critical thinking can help young people succeed in a world which is changing quickly.

Lead-in

Students begin to think about the speaking task they will do at the end of the unit. Give them a minute to look at the box and ask you any questions they might have.

UNLOCK TEACHER DEVELOPMENT

BE READY

Look at the Critical Thinking section in the Student's Book on pages 73–74.

→ Which elements of the lesson do you think your students will find easiest / most difficult / most useful? Why?

→ Are your answers true for all students in your class?

→ How can you adapt your teaching or the material to meet your students' needs?

BE FLEXIBLE

When doing Exercises 4 and 5, you could also get students to compare different types of technology (e.g. internet TV and video conferencing) to see whether they have similar advantages (e.g. both have clear visuals) and disadvantages for each (e.g. may have streaming issues).

Exercise 1 page 73
Possible answers:
advantages: 2 and 3   **disadvantages:** 1, 4 and 5

Exercises 2–5 pages 73–74
Answers will vary.

UNLOCK TEACHER DEVELOPMENT

BE REFLECTIVE

Think about the following questions:

→ Think about the disadvantages to critical thinking which you identified in *Be confident*. How could you respond to or solve these challenges with your students?

→ Were your students particularly motivated or interested in this section because the focus was on computers, smartphones and tablets? If so, think about how you could build on this in future sessions.

BE COLLABORATIVE

Your development is more meaningful when it's shared. See page 14 for ideas on how to peer-collaborate. Why not share the evaluation activity you did in *Be confident*?

PREPARATION FOR SPEAKING

Learning objectives

- Use linking words and phrases to supply contrasting ideas – *but, however, on the other hand*
- Use linking words and phrases to supply additional information – *and, and also, as well as*
- Apply the criteria for a good introduction to choose the best introduction to a talk
- Apply the criteria for a good conclusion to choose the best conclusion to a talk

Exercises 1–2 page 75

1 However **2** but **3** On the other hand / However
4 but / however

Exercise 3 page 75

different information

Exercise 4 page 76

additional information

Exercise 5 page 76

1 a and **b** but
2 a but **b** and also
3 a as well as **b** However,

Exercise 6 page 76

1 b **2** b

Exercise 7 page 77

Answers will vary.

Exercise 8 page 77

finish

SPEAKING TASK

Learning objectives

- Prepare to present a report by completing an introduction and stating your arguments
- Prepare to use linking words to state your arguments
- Prepare a conclusion for your report
- Present a report on a technology
- Give feedback on another student's talk

Exercises 1–7 pages 77–78
Answers will vary.

RESEARCH PROJECT

Research and explain cutting-edge technology.

Divide the class into groups and assign each group a theme to do with technology, e.g. materials, computing, travel, space or food. Tell the class that they will be researching these different themes and then presenting them to the rest of the class. Each group will need to think about their theme as it is now, and how it may be developed in the future.

Each group will then prepare a ten-minute presentation, including time for questions. Students could develop presentation slides with their final research and refer to this during their presentation.

CLASSROOM APP

Exercises 1–2
Answers will vary.

Exercise 3

1 couldn't **2** can **3** couldn't **4** Were **5** could
6 couldn't **7** wasn't able to **8** Are you able to

Exercise 4

1 you need to go online. **2** I need to charge it.
3 log on to my work PC **4** turn off my smartphone
5 an app **6** keyboard **7** the cloud **8** charger

Exercise 5

1 disabled **2** luxury **3** collected **4** location
5 memory **6** research **7** stupid **8** developed

Exercise 6A

1 but **2** on the other hand **3** too **4** However
5 and **6** too **7** and **8** but

Exercise 6B
Answers will vary.

UNIT OBJECTIVES

Watch and listen	Watch and understand a video about the impact of oceans on climate.
Listening skill	Predict ideas from research.
Critical thinking	Evaluate effects.
Grammar	Use gerunds and infinitives; use future forms.
Speaking skill	Use linking words to explain cause and effect.
Speaking task	Give a presentation about climate change.
⟲ Teacher development	Help your students become better at **evaluating effects**.

UNLOCK YOUR KNOWLEDGE

Background note

The photo shows dark storm clouds and lightning over Monument Valley in Arizona, the USA. The valley is famous for its small, flat-topped hills with very steep sides. Monument Valley has a desert climate with hot summers and cold winters. In the summer, the temperature can reach around 38°C, but it usually drops significantly at night. Winters are cold and there is occasional snow, although it is unusual for the temperature to drop below freezing.

Lead-in

Ask students: *What's the weather like today?* Write the weather vocabulary they give on the board. Ask them: *What's the weather like in [month]?* Then ask them if they know of any other different types of weather from different places in the world.

page 81
Answers will vary.

WATCH AND LISTEN

Learning objectives

- Listen and understand details in a video about the impact of oceans on climate
- Understand the main ideas in the video
- Make an inference about the speaker in the video's implications
- Practise talking about climate and lifestyle

Exercise 1 page 82

1 There are five oceans: Arctic, Atlantic, Indian, Pacific, Southern   **2** Almost 70%   **3** *Answers will vary.*

Exercise 2 page 82

1 b, c, d   **2** a, e   **3** c   **4** *Answers will vary.*

Exercise 3 page 83

1 c   **2** a, b   **3** d, e   **4** mainly e

Exercise 4 page 83

1 False   **2** True   **3** False   **4** False   **5** False   **6** True
7 False

Exercise 5 page 83

1 b   **2** d   **3** c   **4** e   **5** a

Exercises 6–7 page 83
Answers will vary.

LISTENING 1

Learning objectives

- Listen and identify a speaker's mood from their intonation
- Practise using intonation to sound interested or bored
- Understand key vocabulary for weather and mood – *angry, cool, energy*
- Use your knowledge to predict the content of a presentation about weather and mood
- Listen and complete an ideas map with notes on main ideas
- Listen and identify reasons and detailed information
- Describe personal experience on the topic of weather and its impact on mood

Lead-in

Ask four students to tell you what they plan to do over the coming weekend. For the first two, respond with an interested *really* and the second two with a bored *really*. Then ask the class: *Do I think all those answers were interesting?* (no). Then ask the students: *How do you know?* (because of the way you said *really*). Ask students: *Do you think it's important to sound interested when you are listening to somebody?* (yes). *Why is it important?* (because it's polite and we want to encourage the speaker to continue speaking).

Exercise 1 page 84

1 N **2** I **3** N **4** I **5** N

Exercise 2 page 84

1 *Possible answer*: Intonation helps you understand others' moods and interest.

2 *Possible answer*: If you use the wrong intonation, people might misunderstand your mood or interest.

Be flexible

👥 Students work in pairs. Give them a simple dialogue. Assign some pairs to read the dialogue in an interested way and others to read it in a bored way. The class should choose the correct mood of each conversation. For example:

A: Hi.
B: Hello. How are you?
A: Good. It's my last day of school. I'm going on holiday tomorrow.
B: Are you?
A: Yes. What about you? Are you almost finished?
B: No, I still have to write a research report.
A: Really? What about?
B: The rainforest in Brazil.
A: Well that sounds interesting.
B: Yes, I suppose so.

Challenge **stronger students** to write their own dialogue in pairs and then act it out for the class. The class should then interpret the intonation that is used as interested or not interested.

Exercise 3 page 85

1 humid **2** dry **3** upset **4** cool **5** energy **6** angry
7 prefer

Exercise 4 page 85

Answers will vary.

Exercise 5 page 86

1 more upset / worse **2** tired **3** energy **4** to work
5 angry / angrier

Exercise 6 page 86

1 c **2** a **3** d **4** b

Exercise 7 page 86

1 Fourteen **2** Thirteen **3** light **4** more

Exercise 8 page 87

Answers will vary.

LANGUAGE DEVELOPMENT

Learning objectives

* Choose the correct verb form to use after particular verbs – *We want to learn more about global warming. I enjoy learning about science.*
* Use *will* and *going to* to talk about decisions and plans – *I think global warming is terrible, so I will do more to stop it. I'm going to present information about the forests next week.*
* Use *will* and *going to* to talk about predictions for the future – *I will / am going to get a great job.*

Exercise 1 page 87

1 c and e **2** b and d **3** a **4** c **5** b and d

Exercise 2 page 87

1 prevent **2** cut down **3** save **4** do **5** cause

Exercise 3 page 88

1 learning **2** to think **3** to visit / visiting **4** to watch
5 to go **6** listening **7** to study **8** to tell / telling

Exercises 4–5 pages 88–89

1 to learn / learning **2** to go **3** to read / reading;
to attend / attending **4** to study **5** talking **6** walking
7 to visit **8** to watch / watching **9** to invite / inviting

Optional activity

👤👥 Review present tense question forms from Unit 2. Give students a list of verbs and actions. They have to form questions using either gerunds or infinitives correctly, and then ask each other the questions. They have to decide which verbs can go with which actions. More than one answer may be correct.

Verbs: need, prefer, want, start, enjoy, like

Actions: study English, ride a bicycle, exercise, go to graduate school, cook dinner every day, watch scary films

Possible questions: 'Do you need to cook dinner every day?' 'Do you enjoy riding a bicycle?' 'Do you prefer to watch/watching scary films?'

Exercise 6 page 90
1 am leaving   2 am going to do   3 am going; will come
4 is talking / is going to talk   5 are going to drop
6 will be / are going to be

Exercises 7–8 page 90
Answers will vary.

LISTENING 2

Learning objectives

- Listen for and practise saying /ɒ/ and /əʊ/ correctly in sentences about the environment
- Use a visual to predict the content of a news report about an animal
- Understand key vocabulary for the environment – *unusual, become, discover*
- Read and summarize three main ideas in a text about climate change
- Read background information to predict the content of a news report about an animal
- Listen and complete a set of detailed notes with main ideas
- Listen and identify details
- Prepare and present ideas on a problem caused by climate change
- Synthesize ideas from a presentation about weather and mood and a news report about an animal in a discussion about global warming

Lead-in

Ask the class to think of different types of animals. List answers on the board. Then ask students if any of them are *endangered*. If yes, elicit reasons why these animals might be endangered.

Exercise 1 page 91
Group A: 1; **Group B:** 2

Exercise 2 page 91
1 don't   2 want   3 stop   4 known   5 cost

Exercises 3–4 page 91
Answers will vary.

Exercise 5 page 92
1 believe   2 look after   3 disappear   4 carefully
5 discover   6 become   7 unusual   8 save

Exercise 6 page 92
Possible answers:

1 climate or weather of forest   2 damage to the forest and its animals   3 research about the forest

Exercise 7 page 92
Answers will vary.

Exercise 8 page 93
2, 3, 5

Exercise 9 page 93
Answers will vary.

Exercise 10 page 93
1 problems   2 Cut   3 Damages   4 rain   5 45
6 disappear

Exercise 11 page 94
1 a   2 b   3 a   4 a   5 b

Optional activity

Tell students to divide a piece of paper in half. They write *clock* on one half and *phone* on the other. Play Listening 2 again. When students hear a word with the same vowel sound as *clock*, they hold up that paper. When they hear the same vowel sounds as *phone*, they hold up the other paper. Alternatively, do the same exercise with song lyrics that have those vowel sounds.

Exercise 12 page 94
North America: water shortages / drought
Brazil: damage to (rain) forests / forest fires
Pakistan: floods

Exercises 13–14 page 94
Possible answers:

1 Wildlife won't find water to drink and plants won't grow well, if at all, so there will be food shortages.
2 Damage to rainforests will cause wildlife to die or to move to new areas.
3 Wildlife will need to move to new areas to find dry land.

Exercise 15 page 94
Answers will vary.

CRITICAL THINKING

Learning objectives

- Compare your ideas about climate change in the Arctic with a fact file
- Understand cause and effect in climate change in the Arctic
- Evaluate events to decide if they have a cause-and-effect relationship
- Complete a cause-effect chain about climate change in the Arctic
- Create a cause-effect chain for climate change in another (type of) region

UNLOCK TEACHER DEVELOPMENT

BE INFORMED

➔ **Evaluating effects** by using a cause-effect chain is an important skill for students because: (1) Students commonly mix up 'time' relationships (i.e. where one thing happens *after* another thing) and 'causal' relationships (i.e. where one thing happens *because of* another thing); (2) When developing arguments, it is essential to not mix up these relationships; (3) Creating cause-effect chains is a very useful skill in all academic subjects.

BE CONFIDENT

➔ Develop this skill for yourself by doing the following activity:

Complete the cause-effect chain using the following phrases. Write them in the appropriate box.

A Students incorporate these skills into their academic practice.

B Students develop good critical thinking skills.

C Students can graduate with a good degree, or get promotion at work, especially if they continue to develop these skills.

D These skills can help students in either their working lives, or at college / university.

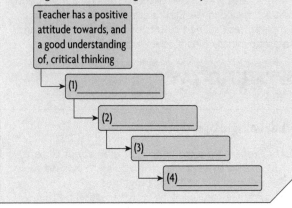

Teacher has a positive attitude towards, and a good understanding of, critical thinking

(1)

(2)

(3)

(4)

Lead-in

Students begin to think about the speaking task they will do at the end of the unit. Give them a minute to look at the box and ask you any questions they might have. It might be useful to give some of the preparation work for the final task as homework.

UNLOCK TEACHER DEVELOPMENT

BE READY

Look at the Critical Thinking section in the Student's Book on pages 95–97.

➔ Which elements of the lesson do you think your students will find easiest / most difficult / most useful? Why?

➔ Are your answers true for all students in your class?

➔ How can you adapt your teaching or the material to meet your students' needs?

BE FLEXIBLE

If you think your class may already have a decent understanding of environmental issues, get them to do Exercise 1 initially with the book closed. They can generate their own ideas before looking in the book.

Exercises 1–2 page 95

Answers will vary.

Exercise 3 page 96

2 sea levels rise

3 polar bears and other animals lose sea ice to hunt from

4 local people lose food sources

For the arrows: Melting polar ice could cause temperatures to rise; sea levels rising could cause polar ice to melt.

Exercise 4 page 96

Possible answers:

The cause-effect chain is a clear visual representation of how separate events are connected. It is easy to look at and refer to in a presentation.

Exercise 5 page 97

Answers will vary. Possible answers:

Africa: Temperatures rise. → By 2050, up to 600 million people won't be able to get drinking water. → Shortage of clean water will help diseases spread. → Drought will stop farmers from growing food. → Some land areas will be under the sea. → Some areas may lose up to 60% of animal species.

California: Temperatures rise. → Heat waves occur. → Less water is on the land. → Drought occurs. → Trees die. → Wildfires occur. → People lose homes and jobs.

Low-level lands: Temperatures rise. → Ice on land melts around the world. → Sea levels rise. → Low-level land around the world floods. → Land areas go under water. → Some people lose their home or country. → People have to find new homes or countries to live in.

Exercise 6 page 97

Answers will vary.

PREPARATION FOR SPEAKING

Learning objectives

- Use linking words to introduce causes – *because*, *because of*, *due to*
- Use linking words to describe effects – *so*, *therefore*, *consequently*
- Describe the relationship between burning fossil fuels and climate change, using linking words for causes and effects
- Describe the relationship between burning fossil fuels and climate change, using key vocabulary – *melt*, *smoke*, *trap*

Exercise 1 page 98

1 a cause **b** effect   **2 a** cause **b** effect   **3 a** effect **b** cause

Exercise 2 page 98

1 so   **2** Therefore   **3** As a result

Exercise 3 page 98

Possible answers:

2 As a result, more people had jobs.

3 So governments feel they need to take more action.

4 Therefore we need to find ways to protect them.

5 So I need to apply for a new one.

6 As a result, we keep in touch with our friends more often.

Exercises 4–5 page 98

Answers will vary. Possible answers:

1 The village flooded because of the heavy rainfall.

2 More people had jobs because of the new factory.

3 Governments may feel they need to take more action on global warming because more people are interested in it.

4 We need to find ways to protect rainforests because they are getting smaller.

5 I need to apply for a new passport because I've lost my old one.

6 We keep in touch with our friends more often due to easier communication.

Exercise 7 page 99

Possible answer:

Homes, factories, cars and planes all burn fossil fuels.

→ gases and smoke rise into the sky.

→ heat is trapped in the Earth's atmosphere.

→ temperatures rise.

→ ice caps in the Arctic and Antarctic melt.

→ global warming occurs / temperatures rise more.

Exercise 8 page 99

Possible answer:

Homes, factories, cars and planes all burn fossil fuels. As a result, gases and smoke rise into the sky. Consequently, heat is trapped in the Earth's atmosphere. Therefore, temperatures rise. As a result, ice caps in the Arctic and Antarctic melt and so global warming occurs.

SPEAKING TASK

Learning objectives

- Prepare for a group presentation about climate change by reviewing and adding to a cause-effect chain and allocating roles
- Prepare to use linking words to describe the causes and effects of climate change
- Give a group presentation on the effects of climate change on a (type of) region
- Listen and ask questions about other students' presentations about climate change
- Suggest solutions to the problem of climate change in a discussion

Exercises 1–6 page 100

Answers will vary.

RESEARCH PROJECT

Create a website to explain weather phenomena to children.

Divide the class into groups and assign each group a weather phenomenon such as rain, hail, wind, cloud, fog, snow and dust storms – or even tornadoes, hurricanes, cyclones or typhoons. Each group will need to find out how and why these phenomena occur and collect relevant video, audio and images. Students could use online tools to share ideas.

Students then use this information to create a website or eBook explaining the weather phenomena in a simple way to children. You can find guides and eBook software by searching online for 'create eBook'. The website/eBook could include the media collected by each group and quizzes for the children. The class can then find ways to publicize their creation to local schools as a resource.

CLASSROOM APP

Exercise 1
Answers will vary.

Exercise 2
1 cut down trees   2 do research   3 prevent global warming   4 cause forest fires   5 save wildlife
6 prevent forest fires

Exercise 3
1 'm taking   2 will probably   3 are going   4 'm going to
5 'll   6 'm going to   7 will probably   8 are going to

Exercise 4
1 look after   2 humid   3 upset   4 unusual   5 becoming
6 save   7 cool   8 energy

Exercise 5
Answers will vary.

Exercise 6A
1 consequently   2 so   3 As a result   4 Because
5 Because   6 therefore

Exercise 6B
[5] I had nowhere else to live, so I'm staying with my parents again.

[2] Without a car, I wasn't able to travel to work. Consequently, I lost my job.

[4] I didn't pay my rent; therefore, I lost my flat.

[1] I was late for work and driving too fast. As a result, I crashed my car.

[3] Because I didn't have a job, I had no money to pay the rent on my flat.

UNIT OBJECTIVES	
Watch and listen	Watch and understand a video about a chess master playing against a computer.
Listening skills	Listen for bias; listen for supporting opinions.
Critical thinking	Build a strong argument.
Grammar	Use the zero conditional and the first conditional; use adverbs of degree.
Speaking skills	Emphasize a point; ask for and give clarification.
Speaking task	Have a discussion about money in sport.
⟳ **Teacher development**	Help your students become better at **building a strong argument**.

UNL⟳CK YOUR KNOWLEDGE

Background note

The photo shows the Formula One Grand Prix at Yas Marina Circuit in Abu Dhabi, the UAE. Formula One, or 'F1', is one of the world's premier car racing competitions. A Formula One season consists of a series of races known as Grand Prix. The Yas Marina Circuit in Abu Dhabi is the only race that is held in the evening and is the last race in the F1 season. In the past, Formula One was limited to Europe but it has now become a global competition. It is one of the most popular sporting events worldwide – attracting over 400 million viewers in over 150 countries.

Lead-in

Ask students: *What do we call it when I ask you to do something in groups and the person/group that finishes first is the winner?* to elicit *race*. Write *race* on the board. Ask students if they can think of different sports races, to elicit ideas such as running, horse, camel, bicycle/bike/cycle, Formula One. Accept any reasonable suggestions. Point out that apart from *running*, these collocate with *race*.

page 103
1 The photo shows a Formula One / motorsport race.
2–3 *Answers will vary.*

WATCH AND LISTEN

Learning objectives

- Listen and understand the main ideas in a video about chess
- Listen and identify the sequence of events in a video about chess
- Listen and identify details
- Make inferences about the skills involved in chess
- Practise talking about computers, games and intelligence

Exercise 1 page 104
Answers will vary.

Exercise 2 page 104
1 and 2 are true

Exercise 3 page 104
1 F; Humans began playing chess nearly 1,500 years ago.
2 F; Garry Kasparov played a famous chess match against a computer.
3 T **4** T **5** F; A genius like Kasparov can think about three moves in a second.

Exercise 4 page 105
a first game **b** second game **c** second game
d first game **e** first game **f** second game

Exercise 5 page 105
1 a **2** b **3** b **4** b **5** b

Exercises 6–7 page 105
Answers will vary.

LISTENING 1

Learning objectives

- Gain awareness of emphasis and intonation when speakers correct themselves
- Practise using intonation and emphasis to stress correct information
- Understand key vocabulary for Sports Science – *champion, compete, intelligent*
- Listen, identify and correct main ideas in a presentation about a Sports Science project
- Listen and complete a set of detailed notes on unusual sports
- Identify phrases used for correcting mistakes

Lead-in

Say to students: *OK, we're going to have a test tomorrow ... Oh, sorry I mean on the day after tomorrow.* Make sure you clearly emphasize the correct day. Ask students: *What did I do there?* (gave the wrong information). Tell students that when people speak, they sometimes make mistakes and correct themselves. If they correct themselves, they often emphasize the correct version. They do this with intonation and stress to make sure the people listening hear the change clearly.

Exercise 1 page 106

1 Rosson   **2** golf   **3** 6.00   **4** Gymnastics   **5** Colombia

Exercise 2 page 106

1 The correct and incorrect words.   **2** down

Exercise 3 page 106

1, 2, 5 *Answers will vary.*
3 Formula One drivers don't race on motorbikes, they race in cars.
4 We don't use a football to play golf. We use a golf ball.

Exercises 4–5 page 107

1 strong   **2** intelligent   **3** compete   **4** champion
5 kick   **6** hit

Exercise 6 page 107

a 2   **b** 3   **c** 4   **d** 1

Exercise 7 page 108

1 intelligent   **2** hit   **3** chess   **4** boxing   **5** (soft) tennis
6 street   **7** money   **8** break   **9** six   **10** hardest   **11** feet
12 head   **13** Malaysia   **14** schools

Exercise 8 page 108

1 ~~boxing~~ chess   **2** ~~golf ball~~ tennis ball   **3** ~~a week~~ 6 days
4 ~~Indonesia~~ Malaysia

Exercise 9 page 109

1 sorry, I mean   **2** well, actually   **3** or rather   **4** no, not

Exercises 10–11 page 109

Answers will vary.

Optional activity

As an alternative to Exercises 10 and 11, put students into groups of four and give each group a familiar sport. Ask them to think of as many facts as they can about the sport. Allow about two minutes for this. Then put students into pairs, each pair from a different group, and ask them to tell their partner about the sport they have chosen. Remind them that if they make a mistake, they should correct it, using the phrases from Exercise 9 and the correct stress and intonation. Allow about four minutes for this, before inviting feedback from the class about the sports they chose.

Exercise 12 page 109

Answers will vary.

LANGUAGE DEVELOPMENT

Learning objectives

- Use the zero conditional to talk about facts – *If you play urban golf, you don't need to go anywhere special. If you hit the ball too hard, you might break something.*
- Use the first conditional to talk about real possibilities – *If you work hard, you will do well in the competition. If James wins the next race, he could compete in the Olympics this year.*
- Use adverbs of degree to modify adjectives – *The runner was not very fast. Tennis is too difficult. The tickets were really expensive.*

Exercises 1–2 pages 110–111

1 they get to keep the match ball
2 you have to leave the pitch
3 they often get injured
4 you win the game
5 you get three points
6 they will be the champions
7 you will need to buy golf clubs
8 you will have more strength
9 she might / will be successful
10 they might / will cancel it

Exercises 3–4 page 111

Answers will vary.

Exercises 5–6 page 112

2 pretty / really / very / extremely / too (S) **3** really / very / extremely (S) **4** pretty / really / very / extremely (S) **5** fairly / quite (W) **6** fairly / quite (W) **7** too (S)

Be flexible

👥 Students work in small groups. Write each of the adverbs of degree on small pieces of paper. Each student takes turns selecting a different adverb of degree. They have to use it to make a sentence that describes a sport of their choice. (*Possible answers: Playing football is really exciting. Watching tennis on television is fairly boring. The rules of cricket are extremely difficult to learn.*)

To **increase the challenge for more advanced students**, tell students to repeat the activity above, but to correct themselves using the expressions they have learnt (e.g., *It is fairly difficult, no, I mean, **really** difficult to play chess well.*) and change to a new adverb of degree.

Exercise 7 page 112

Answers will vary.

LISTENING 2

Learning objectives

- Understand key vocabulary for money and sport – *competition, fan, cost*
- Listen and understand bias in a discussion about paying athletes to train
- Listen and complete a set of detailed notes on opinions and supporting arguments
- Differentiate between supported and unsupported arguments
- Synthesize information from a presentation on unusual sports and a discussion about paying athletes to train

Lead-in

Divide students into small groups. Have them come up with a list of famous athletes (e.g. Serena Williams, Novak Djokovic, Lionel Messi, Naomi Osaka, etc.). Ask students to think about how much these people get paid to play their sport. Have groups rank the athletes from highest paid to lowest paid. Ask why they ranked them the way they did. Where does this money come from?

Exercise 1 page 113

a prize **b** charge **c** score **d** cost **e** salary **f** fan **g** support **h** competition

Exercise 2 page 114

1 Andre **2** Ian

Exercise 3 page 114

1 Ian is against corporate sponsors because he just enjoys watching sport.

2 Andre is for corporate sponsors because he used to be a sportsperson.

Exercise 4 page 114

1 sport **2** make money **3** Five **4** training
5 participate **6** companies **7** amounts **8** employees
9 sign **10** countries **11** adverts

Exercise 5 page 115

1 ○ **2** ○ **3** S **4** S

Exercise 6 page 115

Answers will vary.

CRITICAL THINKING

Learning objectives

- Remember information and arguments about athletes' pay
- Decide whether arguments about athletes' pay are adequately supported
- Create a persuasion map to plan a well-supported argument about athletes' pay

UNL⭘CK TEACHER DEVELOPMENT

BE READY

→ **Building a strong argument** is an important skill for students because: (1) Too often, students present arguments based on what they think or feel, rather than what they can show or demonstrate; (2) Arguing in this way is not sufficient at college/university, and students must learn how to use evidence; (3) Having a well-supported and strong argument increases students' confidence when presenting or writing.

BE CONFIDENT

→ Develop this skill for yourself by doing the following activity:

Read the arguments below. Do they have enough (E) or not enough (NE) support to persuade somebody to agree? (Note: it doesn't matter whether you agree with these statements; just consider whether they could be used to persuade others.)

- Some students are naturally good at critical thinking. ____
- The more students practise critical thinking skills, the more familiar they will become with them, and the better they can execute them. ____
- By sharing their own positive experience of critical thinking, teachers can encourage less confident students to try out new things, and to improve. ____
- Students who are good academically are always good at critical thinking. ____
- For students to develop their critical thinking skills, teachers must create an atmosphere in their classroom where students aren't afraid to make mistakes. ____

Lead-in

Students begin to think about the speaking task that they will do at the end of the unit. Give them a minute to look at the box and ask you any questions they might have. You could give some of the preparation for this as homework.

UNL🔒CK TEACHER DEVELOPMENT

BE READY

Look at the Critical Thinking section in the Student's Book on pages 116–118.

→ Which elements of the lesson do you think your students will find easiest / most difficult / most useful? Why?

→ Are your answers true for all students in your class?

→ How can you adapt your teaching or the material to meet your students' needs?

BE FLEXIBLE

An interesting additional task for Exercise 2 is to get students to add evidence to the arguments they marked as 'NE' so that they become persuasive.

Exercise 1 page 116
Answers will vary.

Exercise 2 page 117
1 E   **2** NE   **3** NE   **4** E   **5** E   **6** E

Exercises 3–6 page 117–118
Answers will vary.

UNL🔒CK TEACHER DEVELOPMENT

BE REFLECTIVE

Think about the following questions:

→ Follow the *Be flexible* advice for the exercise you did in *Be confident*. How could you strengthen the arguments which you thought did not contain enough evidence?

→ In Exercise 4, students had to work in groups of three or four. Did this work well? Did you set up and manage the exercise well, or could you have done this more effectively?

BE COLLABORATIVE

Your development is more meaningful when it's shared. See page 14 for ideas on how to peer-collaborate. Why not share what you learnt in the *Be ready* section?

PREPARATION FOR SPEAKING

Learning objectives

- Use signal words to emphasize points – *obviously, actually, definitely. Sports fans actually like to see adverts with athletes in them.*
- Use phrases to ask for clarification – *I'm afraid I didn't get that. What do you mean by ...? Can you give more detail?*
- Use phrases to clarify your meaning – *Sorry, let me explain ..., In other words ...,*

Exercise 1 page 119
1 definitely   **2** actually   **3** of course

Exercises 2–4 pages 119–120
Answers will vary.

Exercise 5 page 121
Part 1

1 I: Did you enjoy the game?

2 C: Yes, I thought we played well. We made a few silly mistakes, though.

3 I: Which mistakes did you make? Can you give some more detail?

4 C: Yes, sure. I thought that the ball went outside the court too much.
Also, our Tekong jumped off the ground once or twice.

5 I: What do you mean by Tekong?

6 C: That's the player who serves the ball during the match ...

Part 2

1 I: I hear that people are trying to get sepak takraw included in the Olympics.

Do you agree?

2 C: Definitely! I agree that it should be included. It's already in the Asian Games.

3 I: But even though it is in the Asian Games, can you explain more about why you support it?

4 C: Well, obviously, as a player I support it. But actually, even people who are not players want to see it in the Olympics.

5 I: Can you give some examples of why people want to see this sport in the Olympics?

6 C: Sure. One example is the excitement in the game from the players' amazing kicks ...

Be flexible

As an alternative to Exercise 5, photocopy the exercise and cut it into individual sentences. Put students into groups and give each group one set of sentences from Part 1. Ask them to find the first sentence (*Did you enjoy the game?*). Ask students to put the sentences in order to make a conversation. Next, give each group a set of sentences from Part 2. To make it more challenging, don't give them the first sentence. Ask them to put the sentences in order, to make a conversation. The first group to do this successfully for both parts is the winner. Circulate, monitor and give assistance where appropriate.

If students need **extra support**, identify the first turn in the sequence. Give students some hints:

- What do you expect as an answer to a *Yes/No question? Look for an answer among the sentences.*
- *Look for words and phrases that are repeated across the sentences.*

To **increase the challenge**, don't identify the speaker (in other words, don't include the identifiers I and C with the sentences).

Exercise 6 page 121

Possible answers:

What do you mean?: Sorry, I don't understand. Can you explain what you mean?

Can you give some more detail?: Can you give an example? / Can you explain what you mean?

Exercise 7 page 121

Asking a person to explain more: Can you give some examples? / Can you explain more?

Emphasizing: Definitely / obviously / actually

Exercise 9 page 121

1 DU   **2** EM   **3** DU   **4** DU   **5** EM

Exercises 10–11 pages 121–122

Answers will vary.

SPEAKING TASK

Learning objectives

- Prepare to take part in a panel discussion by reviewing and adding to a persuasion map
- Take part in a panel discussion about athletes' pay

Exercises 1–4 page 122

Answers will vary.

RESEARCH PROJECT

Become a sports commentator.

Find videos of sports commentators on the internet. When you have found one or two clips, show them to your students so that they can get an idea of the genre of sports commentary. Divide the class into groups and ask students to think about sports played in their own country. Assign each group one of these sports and then ask them to find an example of the sport. Students could search online, visit and film a sporting event, or arrange and film their own sporting event.

Each group will create a short video including sports commentary and clips of the event they attended, or an audio-recorded commentary to accompany an online sports video. Students could be spontaneous with their commentary, but they will probably feel more comfortable creating and reading from a script. For videos, each group will have to think about who will work the camera during filming, who will edit the video, and who will provide the commentary.

CLASSROOM APP

Exercises 1–2

Answers will vary.

Exercise 3

1 is   **2** might   **3** will have   **4** will love
5 won't be able to   **6** might   **7** might need   **8** will

Exercise 4

1 Marilyn is an extremely clever footballer.

2 Ian is quite strong.

3 Archie can play chess fairly well.

4 Sandra is quite good at tennis.

5 Karl is really good at karate.

6 Laura is fairly well-known as an athlete.

7 Rachel is not very good at sport.

8 Lydia is a pretty awful basketball player.

Exercise 5

Answers will vary.

Exercise 6A

1 I mean it's in the city, not in the countryside.

2 Obviously, it's good for your health.

3 It actually makes the game more fun!

4 Right, let me explain more clearly.

5 Sure. Look, there are three rules. The first one …

6 Can you give me an example of what I could do, please?

Exercise 6B

Answers will vary.

UNLOCK YOUR KNOWLEDGE

Background note

The photo shows an office worker at the offices of the online retailer Zappos. The woman is sitting in a cubicle in a messy office. There are books, novelty toys, plants and boxes everywhere. There are lots of cubicles and chairs, with people working close together. An office worker could do many different types of jobs, such as finance and accounting, administration, sales and marketing, or project management.

Lead-in

Ask students: *How do you go to work?* or *How do your parents go to work?* Write up all answers on the board. Then ask students: *How far do you / your parents have to travel?* Find out who lives nearest to their work and who lives furthest away. Then ask: *How long does it take you / your parents to get to work?* Find out who has the shortest and the longest journey times. Ask students: *Do you / your parents like making this journey every day? Why / Why not?*

page 125

1 She is working in an office, probably doing an administrative job.

2–4 *Answers will vary.*

WATCH AND LISTEN

Learning objectives

- Listen and identify details and main ideas in a video about chains of coffee shops
- Make an inference based on the information in the video
- Practise talking about coffee shop businesses

Exercises 1–2 page 126
Answers will vary.

Exercise 3 page 127
1 b   **2** b   **3** a   **4** b   **5** a

Exercise 4 page 127
1 Costa Coffee   **2** a British   **3** food   **4** lunch
5 headquarters   **6** quality

Exercise 5 page 127
b

Exercises 6–8 page 127
Answers will vary.

LISTENING 1

Exercise 1 page 128

1 earn **2** colleague **3** spends time **4** wastes time
5 profit **6** project **7** break

Lead-in

Write random numbers on the board and ask students to say what they are. The numbers can get larger, to check students know how to say them correctly. Begin to add in the example numbers in the box (½, ⅓, 0.27, 004 41789 830, 27%). Elicit the correct way to say them. Students read the information in the box to check their answers.

Exercise 2 page 129

1 forty-eight percent **2** a half / one half **3** a fifth / one fifth **4** thirty-one point five **5** a hundred and three / one hundred and three / one-oh-three **6** one thousand, five hundred and forty **7** six thousand and one **8** nought point nought one

Exercise 4 page 130

1 half **2** emails **3** 31.5 **4** 15 **5** jobs **6** earn
7 clothes **8** 19 **9** salaries

Exercise 5 page 130

1 F; Alika has not finished her research project. **2** T

3 F; She looked at how people spend and waste their time at work and why they don't work hard at their jobs. **4** T

5 F; She says productivity depends on how hard people work or how fast workers make things or provide services.

Exercise 6 page 131

Suggested answers:

1 5% of people wasted time at work texting friends and making plans for after work.

2 15% of people wasted time at work taking long coffee and lunch breaks.

3 31.5% of people wasted time at work talking to colleagues.

4 48% of people wasted time at work surfing the internet or writing personal emails.

5 33.5% wasted time because they didn't earn a good enough salary.

6 19% wasted time because they had to work too many hours.

Exercises 7–8 page 131

Answers will vary.

LANGUAGE DEVELOPMENT

Exercise 1 page 132

1 on the phone **2** in meetings / on the phone
3 working at a desk **4** taking breaks / working at a desk

Exercise 2 page 132

Possible answers:

2 The most amount of time is spent / People spent the most amount of time helping somebody else with their work.

3 More time is spent / People spent more time waiting for someone to finish their part of a project than going to meetings.

4 Less time is spent / People spent less time going to meetings than waiting for someone to finish their part of a project.

5 The least amount of time is spent / People spent the least amount of time filling in papers and forms.

Exercise 3 page 134

1 more important than **2** good as **3** worse than
4 more serious than **5** the funniest **6** the most interesting

Exercise 4 page 134

Answers will vary.

Be flexible

👤👥 Ask students to write four to six sentences using comparatives and superlatives. Start by eliciting some examples from the group work in Exercise 4. Write the examples on the board, e.g. *Lina thinks the most exciting job in the world is a doctor. Most people prefer to do a job inside.* Circulate, monitor and give assistance where appropriate.

You can **provide more structure** to this exercise by presenting the class with three things/people to compare. You can use visuals or just the words. It could be three sports figures, movie stars, cities, tourist destinations, etc. Start by brainstorming as a class the features that could be compared. Make sure students know that comparisons will be between two of the items, whereas superlatives focus on one out of the whole group.

Exercise 5 page 134

Possible answers:

1 Friendly colleagues is the least important thing to employees.
2 Great benefits are less important than interesting work to employees.
3 Interesting work is more important than friendly colleagues to employees.
4 Friendly colleagues are less important than great benefits to employees.
5 The company doing important work is less important than good pay to employees.

Exercises 6–7 pages 134–135

Answers will vary.

Exercise 8 page 135

1 wrote; down   2 ran out   3 wrote down   4 took over
5 found out   6 looked at   7 get by

Exercise 9 page 136

1 run out   2 found out   3 look at   4 get by
5 wrote; down   6 take over

Exercise 10 page 136

2 f   3 e   4 a   5 b   6 d

Exercise 11 page 136

Answers will vary.

LISTENING 2

Learning objectives

- Understand key vocabulary for business consultancy – *careless, customer, goal*
- Listen and complete a set of detailed notes on a conversation about business problems and solutions
- Listen and identify speakers' reactions to ideas
- Make inferences about the speakers' past discussion and their emotional responses
- Synthesize information from a conversation about a student project and a conversation about business problems in a discussion

Lead-in

Ask students: *How can employers increase the happiness of their workers?* (good benefits, good pay, interesting work). Ask students: *How can a business owner keep down the costs of running a business?* (use less paper, review expenses every month). Ask students: *How can business owners reach new customers?* (advertise on social media, offer discounts on products). Students then listen and see how their answers compare with the consultant's answers in the listening.

Exercise 1 page 137

1 goal   2 messy   3 weaknesses   4 skill   5 customer
6 strengths   7 careless   8 stress

Exercise 2 page 138

Answers will vary.

Exercise 3 page 138

1 happy   2 (organize) social events   3 paint the walls
4 find cheaper   5 profit   6 online sales
7 professional web designer   8 pop out (a bit more)
9 well organized   10 easy

Exercise 4 page 139

a 1   b 5   c 3   d 6   e 4   f 2

Exercise 5 page 139

a question   b question   c question   d statement
e question   f question; statement

Exercise 6 page 139

It sounds like a question because the intonation rises through the sentence.

Exercise 8 page 139

Possible answers:

1 They discussed Sam's business goals and his business's strengths and weaknesses.

2 Sam feels quite positive. The consultant makes a number of suggestions, and Sam says 'OK, great! I'll do that and bring it in next week'.

Be flexible

👥 Role-play: Students create a dialogue with Sam and the consultant at their next meeting. Sam tells the consultant whether his previous advice worked or not and asks for additional advice.

For **lower-level students** who may need extra support, before they write their dialogue, students should go back to the text (either listen again or review the script) and decide which topics of that conversation Sam and Joe are likely to return to. Choose three of them as the basis for the new dialogue.

Exercise 9 page 139

Answers will vary.

CRITICAL THINKING

Learning objectives

- Remember possible solutions to business problems
- Analyze the problems a business faces
- Suggest possible solutions for the business and predict its results

UNL⦶CK TEACHER DEVELOPMENT

BE INFORMED

→ **Identifying solutions to problems** is an important skill for students because: (1) The ability to identify solutions to problems is clearly a core life skill; (2) It is also an important academic skill, and a very common requirement in presentations (as well as in writing); (3) Students lack strategies, such as creating a problem-and-solution table, which can help them identify solutions.

BE CONFIDENT

→ Develop this skill for yourself by doing the following activity:

Below is a list of the some of the problems in teaching critical thinking identified by teachers in a critical thinking survey by Cambridge University Press. What possible solutions can you identify for each problem?

- 83% said they had had no specific training / coaching in teaching critical thinking skills.
- Only 21% agreed or strongly agreed that they had all the material to develop their students' critical thinking skills.
- Only half agreed or strongly agreed that they had the time to develop effective means to teach critical thinking skills.

Lead-in

Students begin to think about the speaking task that they will do at the end of the unit. Give them a minute to look at the box and ask you any questions they might have. It might be useful to give some of the preparation for this task as homework.

UNL⦶CK TEACHER DEVELOPMENT

BE READY

Look at the Critical Thinking section in the Student's Book on pages 140–142.

→ Which elements of the lesson do you think your students will find easiest / most difficult / most useful? Why?

→ Are your answers true for all students in your class?

→ How can you adapt your teaching or the material to meet your students' needs?

BE FLEXIBLE

If you have time after Exercise 5, students could present their 'possible results' and get feedback from others. Students could then redraft their problem and solution table, based on this feedback.

Exercise 1 page 140

2 a   **3** b   **4** d

Exercise 2 page 140

2 Save money and make more of a profit.

3 Get more online sales and new customers.

4 Website will be more attractive and easier to use and you'll get more online customers.

Exercises 3–5 pages 141–142

Answers will vary.

UNL⦶CK TEACHER DEVELOPMENT

BE REFLECTIVE

Think about the following questions:

→ How well could students complete the problem and solution table in Exercise 4? Some students find this very analytical, logical way of thinking difficult. If this is the case, is there anything you could change next time you work on something similar?

→ Think about the possible solutions for teaching critical thinking you identified in the *Be confident* section. If your solutions were implemented, what would the possible results be?

BE COLLABORATIVE

Your development is more meaningful when it's shared. See page 14 for ideas on how to peer-collaborate. Why not share what you learnt in the *Be ready* section?

PREPARATION FOR SPEAKING

Learning objectives

- Use phrases to suggest advice – *If you want to sell more, you should start by trying to improve your advertising. Why don't you start by trying to improve your advertising? Be careful not to offend your customers.*

Exercises 1–2 pages 142–143
Answers will vary.

Exercise 3 page 143

I think you should try to improve your shop.

If you want bring in more customers, you need to have a more interesting front window.

I think you should hire a window designer.

Inferred advice is to clean the shop and make it tidier.

Exercises 4–6 page 143
Answers will vary.

Optional activity

Tell students to imagine they are business owners who are having problems with their business. Give them several small pieces of paper and tell them to write one problem on each piece of paper. Encourage them to think of problems that haven't already been discussed in the unit. The problems can be serious or silly. Collect the problems and read them one by one to the class. At least three students should give advice, using different phrases, before moving on to the next one.

SPEAKING TASK

Learning objectives

- Review and add to your notes to prepare for a discussion
- Select language for introducing your advice
- Offer advice to the owner of a failing business
- Evaluate the advice you are given as the owner of a failing business

Exercises 1–4 page 144
Answers will vary.

RESEARCH PROJECT

Design the perfect workplace.

Ask students to search on the internet for information on different designs for workplaces, e.g. by searching 'creating an office for work and play' or 'creative office'.

Divide the class into groups and ask each group to design a workplace which will motivate and engage employees to produce high-quality work. Students could create an image collage, a floor plan (you can find free software by searching 'draw floor plan') or a 3-D model. Each group will present its design to the class and students can then vote on which work environment is the best.

CLASSROOM APP

Exercise 1
Answers will vary.

Exercise 2
1 more than   **2** the least interesting   **3** better
4 the most   **5** worse than   **6** less stressful than
7 friendlier than   **8** the most skilled

Exercise 3
1 I ran out of milk.
2 She wrote it down in her address book.
3 Lee took part in the game.
4 My supervisor looked at my report.
5 There are just enough supplies to get by.
6 We found out by using the internet.
7 I don't remember his address, so I'll have to look it up.
8 We didn't want to run out of coffee, so we made a lot.

Exercise 4
1 messy   **2** waste time   **3** break   **4** weakness   **5** earn
6 goal   **7** stress   **8** spend time

Exercise 5
Answers will vary.

Exercise 6A
1 I think you   **2** Be careful   **3** Why don't you
4 If I were   **5** If you want to   **6** Be careful
7 I wouldn't   **8** I think

Exercise 6B
Answers will vary.

UNIT OBJECTIVES

Watch and listen	Watch and understand a video about art made from rubbish in the sea.
Listening skill	Listen for attitude.
Critical thinking	Evaluate the importance of information.
Grammar	Use the past continuous and the past simple.
Speaking skills	Use correct time order; give examples and details.
Speaking task	Give a presentation about a remarkable person and his or her work.
⟳ Teacher development	Help your students become better at **evaluating the importance of information**.

UNLⓄCK YOUR KNOWLEDGE

Background note

The photo shows a free diver filming a humpback whale and her two calves, ten metres under the sea. The photograph was taken off the coast of Baja California, in Mexico. Free divers don't use scuba equipment but, instead, they rely on their ability to hold their breath underwater. Most free divers can stay underwater for three minutes or more, while champion free divers can hold their breath for up to ten minutes. Free divers have to be very physically fit, and carry out demanding training and preparation. The sport can be very dangerous, so free divers dive in pairs and are trained in rescue and emergency medical procedures.

Lead-in

Put students in small groups and ask them to make a list of three very unusual or very dangerous jobs and why they think they are unusual or dangerous. Give them three minutes to make the list, before inviting one person from each group to read out their list to the class and write the jobs on the board. Take a vote on which is the most unusual or dangerous job of all.

page 147
Answers will vary.

WATCH AND LISTEN

Learning objectives

- Listen and identify main ideas and details in a video about Kenyan beaches
- Identify an inference which can be made from the information in the video
- Practise talking about rubbish and recycled art

Exercise 1 page 148

1 Africa   2 Indian Ocean   3 *Answers will vary.*

Exercise 2 page 148

1 rubbish   2 picking up rubbish; making things from the rubbish   3 *Answers will vary.*

Exercise 3 page 149

1 are not   2 isolated from   3 daily   4 art   5 make
6 most   7 world

Exercise 4 page 149

1 e   2 a   3 h   4 d   5 f   6 g   7 c   8 b

Exercise 5 page 149

c

Exercises 6–7 page 149
Answers will vary.

LISTENING 1

Learning objectives

- Understand key vocabulary for creative people – *design*, *simple*, *achievement*
- Listen and identify the main ideas in a student presentation about creative people
- Listen and complete a set of detailed notes
- Give opinions on designers and inventors

Lead-in

Ask students if they know people who share the same qualities that are mentioned in the listening. Discuss as a whole class, and then students listen for which inventors are described in that way.

Do you know somebody who never gives up? What achievements have they made in their lives? (Sir James Dyson)

Do you know somebody who likes to play jokes on others? What is something funny he/she has done? (Arne Jacobsen)

Do you know somebody who is creative? In what ways do they show their creativity? (Sir Jonathan Ive)

Exercise 1 page 150

1 a **2** a **3** a **4** b **5** b **6** b **7** a **8** a

Exercise 2 page 151

Answers will vary.

Exercise 3 page 151

a hand dryer, Sir James Dyson **b** wheelbarrow, Sir James Dyson **c** iPhone, Sir Jonathan Ive **d** Egg chair, Arne Jacobsen

Exercise 4 page 152

1 painting **2** simple **3** modern **4** purpose **5** Art **6** students **7** problems **8** inventing **9** creative **10** simple **11** awards

Exercise 5 page 153

Answers will vary.

LANGUAGE DEVELOPMENT

Learning objectives

- Use -ed and -ing adjectives to describe feelings – *Stories about really simple inventions, like drinking straws, are pretty boring. I get bored when my internet connection isn't working.*
- Use past continuous verbs in positive and negative sentences – *He was studying Maths last spring. They weren't working at the time.*
- Use past continuous verbs with past simple verbs in sentences showing the time relationship between actions – *While he was working on his invention, he decided to go to university. When the fire alarm went off, we were presenting our project in class.*

Exercise 1 page 153

1 interesting **2** relaxing **3** frustrated **4** interested

Exercise 2 page 154

1 **a** The news **b** I
2 **a** I **b** She
3 **a** He **b** His idea
4 **a** My mum **b** story
5 **a** The walk **b** I
6 **a** idea **b** My friend

Exercise 3 page 154

1 fascinated **2** interested **3** excited **4** surprising **5** tired **6** boring

Be flexible

Put students into pairs. Ask them to write sentences, using each of the adjectives from Exercise 3. Allow about seven minutes for this. Put students with a different partner and ask them to compare their sentences. Did anybody have the same or similar sentences? Allow four minutes for this, before inviting feedback from the class.

For **more advanced students** who may need a more challenging activity, tell them to look at their answers to Exercise 3 and write sentences using the 'opposite' (-ing/-ed) adjective. In other words, if they used *fascinating* in the first gap, they should write a sentence with *fascinated*.

Exercise 5 page 155

1 was going **2** was working **3** were living **4** weren't studying; were cooking **5** were travelling **6** was preparing **7** was thinking **8** wasn't living

Exercise 6 page 155

Answers will vary.

Exercise 7 page 157

2 noticed **3** was watching **4** went **5** discovered **6** was working **7** was doing **8** happened **9** was waiting **10** realized **11** was **12** brought **13** was doing **14** blew **15** invented **16** made **17** was making **18** discovered **19** created

Exercise 8 page 157

1 When / While **2** was doing **3** saw **4** When / While **5** read (only if answer to number 4 is 'When') / was reading **6** realized **7** was working **8** when **9** dropped **10** was looking **11** when **12** found

LISTENING 2

Learning objectives

- Understand key vocabulary for describing interesting people – *remarkable, success, entrepreneur*
- Listen and take detailed notes on a student conversation about remarkable people
- Listen and understand attitudes
- Understand the use of intonation to show emotion or interest
- Practise showing enthusiasm and lack of enthusiasm through intonation
- Synthesize information from a student presentation about creative people and a student conversation about remarkable people in a discussion

Lead-in

Ask students: *Who is the most interesting person you know or know about?* Ask follow-up questions like: *Why do you think they are interesting? How do you know about them?*

Exercise 1 page 158

a retire **b** amazing **c** remarkable **d** situation
e entrepreneur **f** success

Exercise 2 page 158

Answers will vary.

Exercise 3 page 159

Person 1

Name: Sima Najjar

Job: Entrepreneur, former head of a modelling company. Worked with clothing designers

Why remarkable: Famous for website showing people how to do things in Arabic.

Person 2

Name: Yoshiro Nakamatsu

Job: Inventor

Why remarkable: Created more than 3,000 inventions like shoes for jumping, glasses the shape of eyes and fake hair for safety. Still inventing at the age of 90.

Exercise 4 page 159

1 They have to prepare a presentation on a remarkable person.

2 Yasmin

Exercise 5 page 159

1 not that **2** all of it **3** not very good **4** a lot about

Exercise 6 page 159

1 L **2** Y **3** Y **4** L **5** L

Exercise 7 page 160

Possible answers:

Sima Najjar

She is from Jordan.

She used to be the head of a modelling company.

She is an entrepreneur and former company leader.

She is a mother.

She is famous because she started a website with videos in Arabic showing people how to do things.

Her videos get one million views a month.

Yoshiro Nakamatsu

He was born in Japan.

He is now over 90 years old and he is still an inventor.

He has created than 3,000 inventions.

His inventions are unusual.

Some people don't think his inventions are real.

He didn't retire even after he reached the age of 90.

Exercise 8 page 160

a 2 and 4 ('s not great / doesn't sound ... extraordinary)
b 3 (a little more work)

Exercise 9 page 160

1 bad **2** hasn't prepared **3** bad **4** doesn't know anything

Exercise 10 page 161

Sentences 1, 2, and 3 sound enthusiastic.

Exercises 12–13 page 161

Answers will vary.

Optional activity

Put students into small groups. They make a set of cards with the names of the people and inventions that have been discussed in the chapter. Put one name or invention on each card. Next, one student at a time chooses a card and asks the student to their right what they think about the person or invention they chose. (For example, *What do you think about Dr Grace Murray Hopper?*). The student to the right answers with/without emotion and interest (*I think she was brilliant*), and the rest of the group decides whether he or she answers with appropriate emotion.

CRITICAL THINKING

Learning objectives

- Remember information about a remarkable person to complete an ideas map
- Evaluate information to decide what is important for a presentation
- Research information about a remarkable person who interests you
- Create an ideas map about a remarkable person
- Evaluate your ideas map and select information to use in a presentation

UNL⌀CK TEACHER DEVELOPMENT

BE INFORMED

➔ **Evaluating the importance of information** is an important skill for students because: (1) When preparing for a presentation, students often think in terms of quantity, not quality – but both should be considered; (2) A problem area for many students is including irrelevant information which does not answer the question in their work; (3) Whilst generating ideas is important, students also need to evaluate which ideas are the most important.

BE CONFIDENT

➔ Develop this skill for yourself by doing the following activity:

Look at the ideas map below for Bloom's revised taxonomy. Imagine you had to give a presentation at your educational institution about 'The importance of critical thinking in modern education'. Which information would you include or prioritize? What other information would you need to find out?

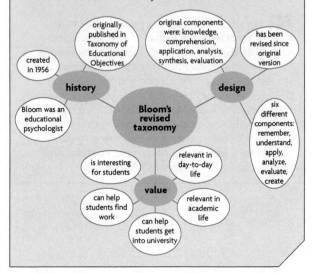

Lead-in

Students begin to think about the speaking task that they will do at the end of the unit. Give them a minute to read the box and ask any questions they might have.

UNL⌀CK TEACHER DEVELOPMENT

BE READY

Look at the Critical Thinking section in the Student's Book on pages 162–163.

➔ Which elements of the lesson do you think your students will find easiest / most difficult / most useful? Why?

➔ Are your answers true for all students in your class?

➔ How can you adapt your teaching or the material to meet your students' needs?

BE FLEXIBLE

An optional stage which you could add between Exercises 3 and 4 is that, before going online to conduct research, you could organize a whole-class 'mingle' activity where students ask each other whether they know anything about their chosen person. When they go online, they can check whether this information is correct.

Exercise 1 page 162

Company leader: a, Why is she famous: g, Videos: c, f, Personal life: e, Fashion: b, d

Exercises 2–5 page 163

Answers will vary.

UNL⌀CK TEACHER DEVELOPMENT

BE REFLECTIVE

Think about the following questions:

➔ Think about the ideas map in the *Be confident* section. How would you evaluate your own understanding of Bloom's taxonomy? Are you happy with it, or do you feel there is more you could learn?

➔ Did your students find it difficult to think of a 'remarkable person' (Exercise 3)? If so, for a similar future activity, how could you give them more direct suggestions?

BE COLLABORATIVE

Your development is more meaningful when it's shared. See page 14 for ideas on how to peer-collaborate. Why not share what you learnt in the *Be ready* section?

PREPARATION FOR SPEAKING

Learning objectives

- Use time phrases to sequence information – *Nowadays many people know about ...*, *In 1930, no one had tasted ...*, *After that, her chocolates ...*
- Use phrases to present supporting examples and details – *For example, ...*, *An important example ...*, *Equally important ...*
- Evaluate the information chosen for a student presentation

Exercise 1 page 164

1 Nowadays, **2** before **3** At that time **4** in **5** First **6** Then **7** When **8** After that **9** Finally

Exercise 2 page 165

1 such as **2** Another important example **3** Equally important

Exercise 3 page 165

1 for example / like **2** Another example **3** Another (important) example

Exercise 4 page 165

They included mostly information about his inventions.

They chose that information because it is the most relevant and interesting.

Be flexible

👥👥👥 Put students in small groups. Give each student in the group a different topic. Tell them to give as many examples as they can of the topic, without telling their group what the topic is. They should use phrases to introduce their examples. The rest of the group has to guess the topic. For example, if the topic is 'ways to improve your English', the student can say, *One example is to watch films in English. Another example is to read blogs and newspapers in English.* (Other possible topics: restaurants near our school, things to do on the weekend, how to stay fit.)

Increase the challenge for **more advanced students** by allowing them to pick their own topics. You should probably give one of the examples above to help guide their choices. Have the person who is 'it' write the topic down on a piece of paper first. You can add a 'getting warmer/colder' feature to help the process along.

SPEAKING TASK

Learning objectives

- Review your idea map and add additional ideas to prepare for your presentation on a remarkable person
- Select time phrases for ordering ideas in your presentation
- Give a presentation about a remarkable person

Exercises 1–5 page 166

Answers will vary.

RESEARCH PROJECT

Create a video about interesting people.

Tell students they are going to create a class video called, 'My remarkable classmates.' Each student should interview a classmate to find out something remarkable their classmate has done. (*Raised a family, moved abroad alone, is the first one in his/her family to go to university*). The interviewer should then prepare a short presentation on why their classmate is remarkable. One student should record each presentation to make a class video.

CLASSROOM APP

Exercises 1–2

Answers will vary.

Exercise 3

1 relaxing **2** surprising **3** interested **4** bored **5** frustrating **6** exciting **7** tired **8** fascinated

Exercise 4

1 was studying **2** invented **3** was working **4** weren't living; were not living **5** called **6** finished **7** were writing **8** was travelling

Exercise 5

1 remarkable **2** retire **3** situation **4** simple **5** complicated **6** purpose **7** use **8** achievement

Exercise 6A

1 Richie visited Hawaii when he was 11. When he was there, he got the idea for an invention to talk under water. After that, he improved his invention and began a company at age 13.

2 Felicia studied at university last year. At that time, she was single. After she graduated, she got married.

Exercise 6B

1 such as **2** Also **3** for example **4** One example **5** an important example **6** equally important **7** another example **8** such as

Exercise 6C

Answers will vary.

UNIT OBJECTIVES	
Watch and listen	Watch and understand a video about the Voyager space project.
Listening skill	Understand meaning from context.
Critical thinking	Find the best solution to a problem.
Grammar	Use the second conditional.
Speaking skills	Take turns in a discussion; show levels of agreement.
Speaking task	Discuss how to get children interested in space exploration.
⊘ **Teacher development**	Help your students become better at **finding the best solution to a problem**.

UNLOCK YOUR KNOWLEDGE

Background note

The photograph shows a radio telescope in Jeff Davis County, Texas, the USA. Radio telescopes are used to explore space. They have a radio receiver that can receive radio waves from objects in space. In the background of the photograph, we can see the stars of the Milky Way – the galaxy that contains our solar system. By observing the night sky, we can study the moon, stars, constellations, and other planets. Space sciences, known as astronomy and astrophysics, are important areas of study for many reasons. As well as learning more about space and how it works, astronomy and astrophysics play an essential role in developing technology and engineering that help us understand our own environment on Earth.

Lead-in

Write *space* on the board. If necessary, indicate, through the window, pointing towards the sky, that space is 'out there'. Ask students: *What do you know about space?* to elicit ideas such as *space travel, satellites that are used for TV, GPS systems*. Write all the ideas on the board, and encourage students to come up with as many different ideas as they can which derive from the main ideas above.

page 169

1 The photo shows a radio telescope, which is a form of radio receiver used in astronomy to detect radio waves emitted from objects in space (e.g. galaxies). This is how the telescope 'sees' these objects, rather than by detecting visible light like a normal telescope.

2–3 *Answers will vary.*

WATCH AND LISTEN

Learning objectives

- Listen and identify numbers and details in a video about the Voyager space project
- Explain the main ideas in a video about the Voyager space project
- Practise talking about space organizations
- Practise talking about sending messages

Exercise 1 page 170

1 Mercury, Venus, Mars, Earth, Jupiter, Saturn, Uranus and Neptune

2 *Possible answers:* stars, moons, suns, asteroids, comets

3 *Answers will vary.*

Exercise 2 page 170
Possible answers:
They are doing research.
They are analyzing data.
They are talking about a project.
They are explaining a project.

Exercise 3 page 170
1 1977   **2** years   **3** 11   **4** 17   **5** space   **6** 2012

Exercise 4 page 171
1 a   **2** b   **3** b   **4** a   **5** a

Exercise 6 page 171
1 to send back information to Earth   **2** no   **3** new things

Exercise 7 page 171
Answers will vary.

LISTENING 1

Learning objectives

- Listen and differentiate between easily confused words
- Understand key vocabulary for space travel – *beyond, explore, journey*
- Listen and complete a set of detailed notes on a radio programme about space travel
- Listen and understand detailed information
- Evaluate some issues related to space travel and explain your ideas

Lead-in

Write *sea* and *see* on the board and ask students to say them out loud. Ask students: *Do they sound the same or different?* to elicit *the same*. Then write *two* on the board and ask: *Can you think of any other words that sound the same as this?* to elicit *to* and *too*. Write these on the board to show the different spellings. Ask students if they can think of other examples, e.g. *there*, *their* and *they're*, *here* and *hear*, *right* and *write*. Tell students that there are many words in English that sound the same, but are spelt differently and have different meanings, but we know which one to use because of the context. If appropriate, you can tell the class that these are called *homophones*.

Exercise 1 page 172

1 sun/son   2 read/Red   3 whether/weather
4 ate/eight   5 There/their   6 Our/hour

Exercise 2 page 172

The words have the same pronunciation, but they have different spellings and meanings.

Exercise 3 page 172

1 The weather is really nice today.   2 I waited for an hour.
3 Are you going there later?   4 I read the book yesterday.
5 We ate our dinner.   6 I don't mind.

Optional activity

👥 Running dictation: Write several simple sentences using the words in Exercise 2 on page 172. Cut the sentences into strips and tape to the walls around the classroom. Students work in pairs. Their goal is to write all of sentences on the board correctly. To accomplish this, one student from each pair should walk around the room and read

the sentences. For each sentence, the student should read it and remember as much as he/she can and then dictate it to his/her partner. He/she may have to go back to the sentence more than once to remember it all. The second partner then writes the sentence on a piece of paper. The first partner moves on to the second sentence. The first pair to write all sentences correctly wins. Repeat the activity so students can switch roles.

Exercise 4 page 173

1 spacecraft   2 planet   3 explore   4 journey
5 surface   6 reach   7 path   8 beyond

Exercise 5 page 174

1 whether   2 sun   3 Red   4 sent   5 to

Exercise 7 page 174

1 2025   2 the sun   3 boulder (from its surface)
4 the moon   5 explore   6 (help) Test   7 A dead
8 heat   9 outside   10 4,000   11 hot

Exercise 8 page 175

1 T   2 F; Dwarf stars are not found in our solar system.
3 F; Lucy is smaller than Earth.   4 T
5 F; It's planned for the 2030s.

Exercise 9 page 175

Answers will vary. Possible answers:

1 Orion won't be able to land on Mars. Orion will help give NASA information to safely send people to Mars.
2 A white dwarf star is what is left when a star uses all its energy. Scientists call Lucy a cold star even though it burns at 2,700 degrees Celsius, because it's only half as hot as our sun.

Exercise 10 page 175

Answers will vary.

LANGUAGE DEVELOPMENT

Learning objectives

- Use vocabulary for describing problems and solutions to complete sentences – *issue, impact, alternative*
- Use the second conditional to describe imagined future situations – *If we had the right spacecraft, we would send people to Mars. If a very light spacesuit were invented, people could walk around on Mars easily.*
- Use the second conditional to make predictions – *If space travel were as easy as travelling on a plane, people would go to the moon on holiday. If the government stopped paying for space exploration, nobody would notice.*

Exercise 1 page 176

c solution   **d** impact   **e** problem   **f** issue   **g** alternative

Exercise 2 page 176

impact and effect; option and alternative; problem and issue (although *issue* focuses more on a topic and can be used to talk about problems as well)

Exercise 3 page 177

1 problem / issue   **2** issue / problem   **3** option
4 impact / effect / issue   **5** solution   **6** alternative
7 effect / impact

Exercise 4 page 178

2 met; wouldn't know   **3** could/would become; studied
4 were; would/could get   **5** weren't; would/could go
6 could/would think; understood   **7** would be; gave
8 happened; would be

Exercises 5–6 page 178

Answers will vary.

Be flexible

👥👥 Give each student a list of *if* clauses and ask them to complete each one with a main clause to make complete sentences. In small groups, students take turns reading their main clauses only. The rest of the group should decide which *if* clause the sentence goes with. In some cases, main clauses may fit with more than one *if* clause.

Example *if* clauses to hand out:

If we travelled to Mars together ...
If I worked for NASA ...
If I were an astronaut ...
If it were possible to live on the moon ...

Increase the challenge for **stronger students** by asking them to write their own *if* clauses about possibilities for the future. These should be sentences about the world, society, etc., not about their personal lives. Alternatively, students can work in pairs, with the first writing the *if* clause and the second student making the prediction.

LISTENING 2

Learning objectives

- Understand key vocabulary for funding – *option, private, evaluate*
- Use the introduction to a discussion to predict the content
- Listen to a discussion about paying for space exploration and complete a set of detailed notes
- Synthesize information from a radio programme about space travel and a discussion about paying for space exploration

Lead-in

Write the names of the three people mentioned in the listening and their job titles on the board (Dorota Loy, engineer for the space development project; Raj Padow, researcher in economics; Dr Jun Wu, professor of astrophysics). Ask students what each of these experts will probably say about space travel.

Exercise 1 page 179

1 a   **2** b   **3** a   **4** b   **5** a   **6** b

Exercise 2 page 180

Answers will vary.

Exercise 3 page 180

1 exploration   **2** benefits; options

Exercise 4 page 180

2

Exercise 5 page 180

Answers will vary.

Exercise 6 page 181

2, 4, 6

Exercise 7 page 181

1 governments   **2** important   **3** space works   **4** private companies   **5** money   **6** public/government and private   **7** the world   **8** individuals   **9** the internet

Optional activity

👥👥 Tell students that you are going to look at some more verb–noun collocations that they will hear in Listening 2. Write the following words on the board: *research, information, about biology, money, space programmes*. Students work in groups of three or four to write possible verbs to go with these nouns. If students need some assistance, write the verbs on the board and ask students to match the verbs to the nouns. (Verbs: *do, get, run, learn, spend*.) Allow about two minutes for this, before inviting feedback from the class. Answers are: *do research, get information, run space programmes, learn about biology, spend money*.

Exercises 9–10 page 182

Answers will vary.

CRITICAL THINKING

Learning objectives

- Remember and organize information from notes about paying for space exploration
- Evaluate possible solutions about space exploration
- Analyze the challenges involved in getting children interested in space exploration
- Complete an ideas map with challenges
- Suggest and organize alternative solutions to a problem in a table
- Evaluate your table and add support for your arguments to your table

UNLOCK TEACHER DEVELOPMENT

BE INFORMED

→ **Finding the best solution to a problem** is an important skill for students because: (1) Students are often quick to accept the first solution to a problem which they identify (since this is the easiest thing to do!); (2) Students need to be made aware that they should spend more time identifying multiple solutions to a problem, in order to find the best one; (3) When evaluating all the possible solutions, students should try and predict the possible result of each one as part of the process.

BE CONFIDENT

→ Develop this skill for yourself by doing the following activity:

One key problem identified in a critical thinking survey by Cambridge University Press of English teachers was that many teachers found it difficult to know how to improve the way they taught critical thinking.

Which of the following three strategies do you think would work best in your educational institution to solve this problem? Why?

1 Talking to colleagues about how you could work on this problem together, for example by holding training sessions on critical thinking on a regular basis.

2 Taking an online course, such as a MOOC in critical thinking, which could significantly increase your knowledge of what critical thinking is, and how to teach it.

3 Working with colleagues, senior management and students to raise awareness about the importance of critical thinking for academic study and the world of work.

Lead-in

Students begin to think about the speaking task that they will do at the end of the unit. Give them a minute to look at the box and ask you any questions they might have.

UNLOCK TEACHER DEVELOPMENT

BE READY

Look at the Critical Thinking section in the Student's Book on pages 183–185.

→ Which elements of the lesson do you think your students will find easiest / most difficult / most useful? Why?

→ Are your answers true for all students in your class?

→ How can you adapt your teaching or the material to meet your students' needs?

BE FLEXIBLE

This critical thinking section is quite long. If you feel there is too much material to get through in the time you have, consider getting the students to do Exercises 1 and 2 before the lesson.

Exercise 1 page 183

Funding space exploration can be very expensive, but should government or private money pay for it?

Exercise 2 page 183

Use money from the government and taxes to pay for it.

Find money from private companies to pay for it.

Use both private and public money to pay for space exploration.

Find money from private wealthy people.

Exercises 3–8 pages 183–185

Answers will vary.

UNLOCK TEACHER DEVELOPMENT

BE REFLECTIVE

Think about the following questions:

→ Compare your answer in the *Be confident* section with a colleague. Do you share the same opinion?

→ This is the last critical thinking section of the coursebook. How did you feel your students responded to the topic? How did you feel about it? Are there any changes you would make for the next time you teach this?

BE COLLABORATIVE

Your development is more meaningful when it's shared. See page 14 for ideas on how to peer-collaborate. Why not share what you learnt in the *Be ready* section?

PREPARATION FOR SPEAKING

Learning objectives

- Use fixed phrases to take turns in conversations – *I'd like to finish my point. Could I just say something? You haven't said much. What do you think?*
- Use fixed phrases for starting and ending discussions – *Would you like to start? Let me begin by asking ..., So, to conclude, ...*
- Use phrases to show different levels of agreement with other speakers – *I feel exactly the same. I see your point. I hear what you're saying, (but) ...*

Exercise 1 page 185

inviting somebody else to speak: a, f, g, i

interrupting: d, e, h

continuing to speak: b, c, j

Exercise 2 page 186

Suggested answers:

1 Why don't you start us off
2 Could I just say something
3 Let me just finish what I was saying
4 Would anybody like to say anything else about
5 you haven't said much. What do you think
6 What is your opinion

Exercise 4 page 186

1 S 2 F 3 S 4 S 5 F 6 F

Exercise 5 page 187

Possible answers:

1 I see your point   2 I hear what you're saying
3 I agree with you completely   4 You're absolutely right
5 I see your point   6 you have a point

SPEAKING TASK

Learning objectives

- Prepare to speak by reviewing and adding to your notes
- Take part in a discussion about getting children interested in space exploration
- Evaluate solutions for getting children interested in space exploration in a discussion

Exercises 1–7 page 188

Answers will vary.

RESEARCH PROJECT

Create a newsletter explaining space phenomena.

Divide the class into groups and ask them to research one of the following space phenomena: black holes, star types, supernovas, comets or meteors. There are various sources on the internet which explain these phenomena.

Tell students they are going to create a newsletter. The class will need to decide on a title for the newsletter. Each group should add the information they have collected on their space phenomenon to the newsletter. Each group should include a 300-word summary with a title for their space phenomenon.

CLASSROOM APP

Exercise 1

Answers will vary.

Exercise 2

1 options 2 alternative 3 effect 4 solutions
5 impact 6 issue 7 problems

Exercise 3

1 Would 2 were 3 could 4 became 5 would
6 recycled 7 send 8 lived

Exercise 4

1 evaluate 2 options 3 journey 4 planet 5 explored
6 public 7 surface 8 path

Exercise 5

Answers will vary.

Exercise 6A

1 **Showing strong agreement** I agree with you 100 percent; That's a good point

   Showing weak agreement You have a point; You could be right.

2 **Showing strong agreement** You're absolutely right; I feel exactly the same.

   Showing weak agreement I suppose so.; I hear what you're saying, (but) ...

Exercise 6B

Answers will vary.

LISTENING, SPEAKING & CRITICAL THINKING 3

UNIT OBJECTIVES

Watch and listen	Watch and understand a video about the mental skills of chimpanzees.
Listening skills	Take notes; listen for contrasting ideas; listen for signposting language.
Critical thinking	Create a talk for a specific audience; organize information for a presentation.
Grammar	Use modals for obligation, prohibition and advice.
Speaking skills	Use signposting language, introduce examples; express general beliefs.
Speaking task	Give a two-minute presentation about the human threats to an endangered species.
⟳ **Teacher development**	Help your students become better at **creating a talk for a specific audience**.

UNLOCK YOUR KNOWLEDGE

Background note

The photo shows a Tsaatan man using a reindeer to transport firewood out of a forest. The reindeer has the firewood and a chainsaw strapped to its back. The Tsaatan, or Dukha people, live in northern Mongolia, close to Russian Siberia. They are the largest group of nomadic reindeer herders in the world. They live in close harmony with their reindeer and move their villages depending on the seasons.

Animals such as horses, elephants and oxen have traditionally been used on farms to pull carts and move logs. Camels, donkeys, horses, dogs and reindeer have also been used for transport.

Lead-in

Make a table on the board to create a discussion about the advantages and disadvantages of animals for humans, and humans for animals. Ask a few volunteers to come to the board and fill in the table. When the table is complete, you can discuss whether the advantages outweigh the disadvantages.

advantages of animals for humans	advantages of humans for animals
disadvantages of animals for humans	disadvantages of humans for animals

page 15

1 The animals are reindeer. They are being used for transportation in a cold, northern region with few or no roads.

2 *Answers will vary.*

3 *Possible answers:* hunting, herding sheep, guiding the blind, carrying things, searching for people

WATCH AND LISTEN

Learning objectives

- Listen and identify main ideas in a video about the mental skills of chimpanzees
- Listen and understand details
- Practise talking about animal intelligence

Exercise 1 page 16

Answers will vary.

Exercise 2 page 16

Possible answers:

1 The goal is to find the exit.

2 I think the chimpanzee is thinking because she is watching very closely.

3 I think they are happy because they are laughing.

Exercise 3 pages 16–17

1 b **2** a **3** c **4** a **5** b

Exercise 4 page 17

1 DNS **2** T **3** F; Planning before acting is not just a human skill.

4 T **5** F; Chimpanzees can plan ahead for several days.

Exercise 5 page 17

Answers will vary.

LISTENING 1

Learning objectives

- Understand key vocabulary for working animals – *abuse, conditions, cruel*
- Listen and identify main ideas in a debate about using animals for work
- Use a T-chart to organize detailed notes
- Listen and complete a set of detailed notes
- Gain awareness of words that signal a contrast or difference – *yet, on the contrary, even though*
- Give personal opinions on working animals and prioritizing animals over humans

Lead-in

Spend a few minutes brainstorming different animals and write them on the board. Write three headings on the board: *Used for food; Used for work; Used for other purposes.* Ask students to come to the board (two or three students at a time) and put the animals into categories. This will probably create further discussion since some animals are used for more than one purpose. The use will also depend on which countries the students are from. Once the three categories are complete, discuss any disagreement about how the animals have been categorized.

Exercise 1 page 18

1 abuse **2** protect **3** cruel **4** suffer **5** conditions
6 issue **7** survive **8** welfare

Exercises 2–3 page 18

1 *Possible answers:* Poor people still need animals to survive. Not all animal use is abuse; domesticated animals wouldn't have been able to survive without humans. There are many animal lovers who help animals. Millions of children are treated worse than animals. People often care more about animals than poor people.

2 *Possible answers:* Animals' hard work and suffering aren't recognized. Animals have died in wars. They work long hours and live in difficult conditions and get very little reward. Technology can replace animals. Animals have no one to represent them and protect their rights. They may be abandoned when they get sick or too old. It's old-fashioned and cruel.

3 *Answers will vary.*

Exercise 4 page 19

dogs: protection, transport
horses: building, transport, war
elephants: building, transport, war
camels: transport, war

Exercise 5 page 19

cons (Ms Johnson's ideas): rights, cruel
pros (Dr Kuryan's ideas): skills, poor, survive

Exercise 6 page 20

1 Even though **2** On the contrary **3** Yet
4 Even though **5** Yet

Exercise 7 page 21

1 but/yet **2** However **3** Even though
4 On the contrary

Exercises 8–9 page 21

Answers will vary.

LANGUAGE DEVELOPMENT

Learning objectives

- Record word families by parts of speech in a table – *analysis, analyze, analytical, analytically*
- Use the correct word form to complete sentences about animals
- Differentiate between modal verbs showing obligation or lack of obligation, prohibition and advice – *Animals have to find food, water and a safe place to live in order to survive. You don't need to feed the chickens. Visitors to the zoo mustn't touch the animals. You should give some money to that animal rights organization.*

Exercise 1 page 22

noun	verb	adjective	adverb
abandonment	**abandon**	**abandoned**	
abuse	abuse	**abused/ abusive**	abusively
analysis	analyze	analytical	analytically
communication	**communicate**	**communicative**	communicative▶
connection	connect	**connected**	
damage	**damage**	damaged	
debate	debate	**debated/ debatable**	
environment		**environmental**	**environmental▶**
involvement	**involve**	involved	
protection	**protect**	**protected/ protective**	protectively
support/ supporter	support	**supportive**	supportively
survivor/survival	**survive**	**survivable/ surviving**	

Exercise 2 pages 22–23

1 analysis **2** survive **3** abandon **4** supporter
5 environmentally **6** communicate **7** involvement
8 protective **9** debate **10** abusive

Exercise 3 page 23

1 O 2 P 3 A 4 O 5 O 6 A 7 A 8 A

Exercise 4 page 24

1 a 2 a 3 b 4 a

Be flexible

👥👥👥 For **advanced students** who can benefit from more independent practice, provide open-ended speaking practice with modals. Put students into small groups. Give each group a stack of index cards and ask them to write one modal on each card and put the cards in a pile in the centre of their group, face down. Explain that they're going to use the modals to make sentences about how to treat animals humanely. The first student should take a modals card and make a statement using the modal they chose. The students should go around the group and continue until all the cards have been used.

Possible sentences: *Humans need to provide a warm place for domesticated animals to sleep. Farm animals such as horses mustn't be hit or treated cruelly.*

LISTENING 2

Learning objectives

- Understand key vocabulary for endangered species – *endangered, habitat, threat*
- Use visuals to predict the content of a presentation about the human threats to polar bears
- Use a T-chart to take notes on main ideas
- Listen and understand details
- Listen and note signposting language – *first, second, to summarize*
- Listen and understand the use of intonation to signal whether or not lists are complete
- Synthesize information from a debate about using animals for work and a presentation about the human threats to polar bears in a discussion

Lead-in

Brainstorm with the students some of the major threats that animals face. Explain that five major threats are: climate change; deforestation; overexploitation (overfishing, overhunting); invasive species (introduction of non-native species to an environment); and pollution. For each threat, discuss which animals are most likely to be impacted. The students can then move on to Exercise 3 on page 26 and discuss more specific threats to polar bears, and if any of the five major threats endanger them.

Exercises 1–2 page 25

1 a 2 b 3 a 4 a 5 b 6 a 7 a 8 a

Exercises 3–4 page 26

1 Photo 1 shows polar bear patrollers trying to keep polar bears away from where humans live. Photo 2 shows a polar bear on a small patch of ice because the ice is melting. Photo 3 shows a polar bear climbing aboard a ship.

2–3 *Possible answers:* The threats to polar bears are loss of sea ice habitat due to rising ocean temperatures, which makes it harder for polar bears to hunt; contact between humans and polar bears; and industrial development.

Exercise 5 page 26

human threats to polar bears	what people are doing to help polar bears
2 contact between humans and polar bears **3** industrial development	**4** reduce contact between humans and polar bears **5** governments have made laws which limit the amount of oil production **6** people are trying to stop climate change

Exercise 6 page 26

1 26,000 2 2050 3 negative 4 towns 5 safer 6 petrol

Exercise 7 page 27

1 First 2 Second 3 to summarize

Exercises 8–9 page 28

1 not complete **2** complete **3** complete
4 not complete

Be flexible

👥👥 Provide practice and support to **lower-level students** with intonation on lists. Make the task more meaningful by personalizing the content. Write the names of five types of food that you like on the board (e.g. *bananas, grapes, cheese, coffee, cakes* – any five will do). Call on one student to read the list out. Give feedback on the student's intonation. Next, ask each student to write their own list of five items personal to them. You could give examples, such as *favourite songs, countries I have visited, food I don't like*, etc. In pairs, the students read out their lists. Finish off by inviting some of the students to read their lists out to the class.

Exercise 10 page 28

1–2 *Answers will vary.*

CRITICAL THINKING

Learning objectives

- Analyze the target audience for presentations from their introductions
- Think about the objective of a speaker in a presentation about the human threats to polar bears
- Use a table to organize notes from the listening into an outline for a presentation
- Use a table to plan ideas for a presentation targeted at a specific audience
- Evaluate the suitability of your presentation for different audiences

UNL◯CK TEACHER DEVELOPMENT

BE INFORMED

→ **Creating a talk for a specific audience** is an important skill for students because: (1) In their academic and work lives, they are likely to give presentations to people with different backgrounds and knowledge; (2) Students can lose confidence if they 'misread' an audience, so it is important they have the tools to tailor their talks; (3) Students can find doing this very challenging, especially with regard to language level, and so need practice and experience.

BE CONFIDENT

→ Develop this skill for yourself by doing the following activity:

Imagine that you have been asked to give a talk on critical thinking to the following audiences. What differences in terms of (a) content and (b) language would there be?

- The head of your educational institution and senior managers / leaders
- A peer group of fellow teachers
- A group of parents
- A class of adolescent students

Lead-in

Students begin to think about the speaking task that they will do at the end of the unit. Give them a few minutes to look at the box and ask you any questions they might have.

UNL◯CK TEACHER DEVELOPMENT

BE READY

Look at the Critical Thinking section in the Student's Book on pages 29–31.

→ Which elements of the lesson do you think your students will find easiest / most difficult / most useful? Why?

→ Are your answers true for all students in your class?

→ How can you adapt your teaching or the material to meet your students' needs?

BE FLEXIBLE

In Exercise 4, some students may find it difficult to plan content for 'people at a professional conference' if they lack the required level of knowledge. If this is the case, ensure they choose one of the other groups. Afterwards, they can search online for experts talking about these topics to see how they talk about them. In Exercise 5, they can also be paired with a student who has experience of presenting to this group.

Exercise 1 page 29

1 B   **2** C   **3** A

Exercise 2 page 30

1 b   **2** a

Exercise 3 page 30

main idea	Polar bears are threatened by humans
supporting details	**Threats:** loss of sea ice habitat contact between humans and polar bears industrial development **What people are doing to help:** reduce contact between humans and polar bears governments have limited the amount of oil production people are trying to stop climate change
conclusion / summary	The main threat to polar bears is loss of habitat due to climate change. Related threats are human contact and industrial development. If people don't make changes quickly, polar bears may disappear.

Exercises 4–5 page 31

Answers will vary.

UNL⌀CK TEACHER DEVELOPMENT

BE REFLECTIVE

Think about the following points:

➔ The next time that you give any talk to a group, take particular care to think about your audience. After giving your talk, reflect on whether (a) the content and (b) the language were appropriate. If not, what changes would you make if you did it again?

➔ Think about the level of the language which you used in this class, and in your teaching in general. Is it appropriate for the level of your students?

BE COLLABORATIVE

Your development is more meaningful when it is shared. See page 14 for ideas on how to peer-collaborate. Why not share your ideas from the *Be reflective* section above, and their outcome?

PREPARATION FOR SPEAKING

Learning objectives

- Analyze the different parts of a presentation
- Use phrases for signposting the organization of ideas in a presentation – *First of all, ..., Furthermore, ..., In conclusion, ...*
- Use phrases for introducing examples – *For example, many species, such as the giant panda and the snow leopard, are endangered.*
- Use phrases to describe general beliefs – *It's often said that it's cruel to use animals for entertainment. It's believed that most polar bears will be gone by 2050 if nothing changes. It's widely known that climate change is a threat to polar bears.*
- Use correct stress in signposting phrases

Exercise 1 page 32

1 Keeping animals in zoos helps to protect them; it educates people about animals. We should support zoos.

2 Zoos protect animals; they educate our children; modern zoos are comfortable and in good condition.

---

3 Many endangered species (e.g. the giant panda, the snow leopard) are kept safe in zoos. The speaker learnt about exotic animals as a child after being taken to the zoo. Animals in zoos now have large areas which resemble their natural habitat.

4 Visit zoos; give financial support.

Exercise 2 page 32

1 c   **2** b   **3** a

Exercise 3 page 33

Possible answers:

1 I think that zoos are sometimes good for animals. For example, they breed endangered animals and release them into the wild.

2 You can see many exotic animals in zoos, such as lions, tigers and elephants.

3 Animals are sometimes unhappy in zoos. For instance, animals kept in cages that are too small show behaviour that isn't natural, like walking up and down in their cages repeatedly.

Exercise 4 page 33

Possible answers:

1 It's often said that animals should not be used in medical testing.

2 It's believed that dolphins are as smart as humans.

3 It's widely known that if insects continue to die out, it will affect the human food chain.

Optional activity

👤 Ask each student to write one sentence in their notebook about anything in the unit that is related to threats to animals. Give them a few minutes, monitoring and helping when necessary. Ask students to write their sentences on the board. As a whole class, decide which of the phrases in Exercise 4 is the best one to use with each sentence. Some of the sentences might not work with all of the phrases. For example, *Polar bears often get killed when they go near towns* is a fact, not a general belief, so using *It's believed that ...* isn't appropriate. The best phrase for this sentence is *It's widely known that ...*

Other possible sentences:

Loss of sea ice habitat is a great danger to polar bears. (Any of the three phrases would be OK here).

Climate change is a threat to many animals. (*It is widely known that ...* is the best choice here since the statement is a universal belief).

Exercise 5 page 33

2 example   **3** Another   **4** summarize   **5** short

SPEAKING TASK

Learning objectives

- Prepare for a presentation by reviewing and adding to your notes
- Make notes for an introduction and write a concluding statement
- Plan how to signpost supporting details
- Give and respond to feedback on a presentation
- Give a presentation about human threats to an endangered species

Exercises 1–7 page 34

Answers will vary.

RESEARCH PROJECT

Give a lecture on the most endangered species in the world.

Divide the class into groups and ask each group to investigate the most endangered species. Students can search for 'the top-ten endangered species in the world'. Give each group one of the animals listed and ask them to find out about their behaviour, diet, their natural environment and other interesting facts. Students could use online tools, such as a wiki, to share their initial research with the rest of the class.

Each group will then prepare a 15-minute presentation, including time for questions. Students could develop the wiki further with their final research and refer to this during their presentation, create slides using presentation software and produce a leaflet to email to the rest of the class.

CLASSROOM APP

Exercise 1

Answers will vary.

Exercise 2

1 connected **2** analytically **3** supportive **4** involved
5 protect **6** environment **7** abandon **8** communicative

Exercise 3

1 don't have to **2** should **3** need to **4** might
5 ought to **6** mustn't **7** have got to **8** could

Exercise 4

1 welfare **2** survive **3** issue **4** conditions
5 depend on **6** melt **7** source **8** threat

Exercise 5

Answers will vary.

Exercise 6

1 First / First of all **2** Another point is that / Furthermore
3 For example / For instance **4** In short / To summarize

Exercise 7

It's believed that; First; Furthermore; For example; Finally

UNIT OBJECTIVES	
Watch and listen	Watch and understand a video about offshore wind farms.
Listening skills	Listen for explanations; listen for counter-arguments.
Critical thinking	Make counter-arguments.
Grammar	Use modals to express future possibility.
Speaking skills	Link ideas with transition words and phrases; talk about advantages and disadvantages; give counter-arguments.
Speaking task	Take part in a debate about allowing a new wind farm near your town.
⟳ **Teacher development**	Help your students become better at **making counter-arguments**.

UNL⟳CK YOUR KNOWLEDGE

Background note

The photo shows a solar power station in Visonta, Hungary. There are hills, fields and a lake in the background. The photovoltaic solar panels convert energy from the sun into electricity. Using renewable energy, such as solar power, wind energy, hydropower, geothermal energy or biomass, can reduce the amount of carbon a country uses. These energy sources are cleaner and less polluting than traditional fossil fuels like oil, coal and gas. The main disadvantages of green energy are that it can be expensive to set up, and some people think it looks ugly in the natural landscape.

Lead-in

Start the lesson by asking students how their country produces its energy. For example, does it use mainly fossil fuels (such as oil, coal and gas)? Elicit ideas from the class and take notes on the board. On the left-hand side, write down any suggestions for traditional sources (but do not label the list) and on the right-hand side write down any alternative forms suggested (again, do not label the list). Once the students have given you all of their ideas, ask them to look at the list and to tell you what each side of the board represents (if you only have notes on one side of the board, add one or two ideas of your own on the other side). Elicit the answer using the information on the board. Then ask the class to discuss in pairs or small groups whether the question of sourcing energy is an issue in their country. Allow a minute for discussion, then elicit ideas from the class.

As a follow-up task, you could find images online using your search engine. Do a search on 'energy sources' and scroll through the different pictures, using a digital projector. As you do so, elicit the different types of energy sources displayed and ask the class whether they are considered traditional or alternative.

page 37

1 *Answers will vary.*

2 nuclear energy, oil, coal, natural gas, wind, geothermal, hydropower

3–4 *Answers will vary.*

WATCH AND LISTEN

Learning objectives

- Listen and understand main ideas in a video about offshore wind farms
- Listen and identify figures
- Practise talking about alternative energy and saving energy

Exercises 1–2 page 38

Answers will vary.

Exercise 3 page 39

1 T

2 F; The ship made it possible to build the turbines in the middle of the sea/water.

3 T

4 F; It was difficult to build the turbines in windy weather.

5 T

Exercise 4 page 39

1 12   **2** 175   **3** 120   **4** 3,000   **5** 500,000

Exercise 5 page 39

Answers will vary.

LISTENING 1

Learning objectives

- Understand key vocabulary for the environment – *alternative, environmental, resource*
- Use visuals to identify topic and details before you listen
- Gain awareness of linking sounds /j/ and /w/ in connected speech
- Identify main ideas and details in a lecture about hydroponic agriculture
- Take notes to complete a summary
- Listen and understand language signposting different types of explanations – *Hydroponics means growing plants in water*
- Give opinions and evaluate issues related to environmentally-friendly food production

Lead-in

Explain to students that when farming is done carelessly, it can threaten the environment. Elicit examples (land conversion and habitat loss, wasteful water consumption, pollution). Put students into small groups and assign each group an example threat. Each group should discuss how unsustainable farming causes their particular threat and come up with some possible solutions to prevent it. To prepare them for the listening, focus on wasteful water consumption and tell them they will hear about a company that has found a solution to this problem.

Exercise 1 page 40

1 b **2** a **3** b **4** c **5** b **6** c **7** a **8** b

Exercise 2 page 41

1 The topic of the lecture is growing fruits and vegetables using sunlight and seawater.

2 The first photo shows a man picking tomatoes in a greenhouse. The picture/diagram shows how seawater has its salt removed so it can be used to grow fruits and vegetables.

3 Solar power is used on this farm.

Exercise 3 page 41

1 w **2** j **3** j **4** w

Optional activity

👥 👥👥 Write the following on the board and ask the students to try and say them out loud in pairs or small groups, comparing the difference between the two:

/duː/ /aɪ/ /hæv/ /taɪm/ (= *do I have time*, with each word articulated individually)

/dəwaɪhævtaɪm/ (= *do I have time*, spoken naturally with the connecting /w/ sound and weak form in the word *do*)

Monitor the students as they practise saying the phrases out loud, giving feedback as appropriate. Note down the names of one or two students who are pronouncing the two examples well. Then call on one or more of these students to model the pronunciation of each example, and then ask the class which example sounds the most natural.

Exercise 4 page 42

1 water **2** in extreme climates **3** solar power
4 greenhouse **5** no pesticides **6** around the world
7 can help solve the global food problem **8** not known

Exercise 5 page 42

2 f **3** a **4** e **5** b **6** c

Exercise 6 page 43

1 100 **2** sun **3** (sea)water **4** 160 **5** 10,000
6 environment

Exercise 7 page 44

1 d **2** a **3** c **4** b

Exercise 8 page 44

1–2 *Answers will vary.*
3 *Possible answers:* It's expensive. It involves a lot of work. It requires a lot of technical knowledge.

LANGUAGE DEVELOPMENT

Learning objectives

- Record words with negative meanings by prefix in a table – *unnecessary, irresponsible, impossible*
- Add the correct negative prefixes to words in sentences about environmental issues
- Use modal verbs to express different degrees of certainty about the future of environmental issues – *Farming in the desert will/might/could solve the problem of the world food crisis.*

Exercise 1 page 45

in-: incorrect　　　　*dis-*: disadvantage

ir-: irresponsible　　　*im-*: impossible

Exercise 2 page 45

1 ir　**2** un　**3** dis　**4** in　**5** un　**6** im　**7** in　**8** dis
9 un　**10** dis

Optional activity

👥👥👥 Draw five circles on the board. Write a prefix in each circle. Start with *un-* and ask the students what negative words can be formed with it. They should start by looking at the words in Exercises 1 and 2 on page 45. For each word, draw a line outward from the circle and write the word at the end of the line, like an ideas map. After they've given the words from the exercises, they should think of any other words they know that can be made negative with *un-*. Follow the same procedure for the rest of the prefixes. Ask for volunteers to come to the board to complete the diagrams. If the students need extra help, give them the root words and they can match them to the correct prefixes.

Possible answers: *un-: limited, necessary, known, able, employed, familiar. in-: expensive, correct, complete, active, experienced. im-: possible, polite, patient. dis-: advantage, approve, agree, respect. ir-: responsible, replaceable.*

Exercise 3 page 46

1 may　**2** could　**3** might

Exercise 4 page 46

2 Not using fossil fuels might/could/may reduce climate change.

3 Taxing fossil fuels will reduce the use of cars.

4 Using solar energy won't lead to any environmental disasters.

Exercise 5 page 46

Answers will vary.

LISTENING 2

Learning objectives

- Understand key vocabulary for power sources – *benefit, pollute, affordable*
- Use your knowledge to predict the main ideas in a debate about nuclear power
- Take notes on speakers' opinions on the issue of nuclear power and their reasons
- Listen and identify details
- Listen and identify counter-arguments
- Synthesize information from a lecture about hydroponic agriculture and a debate about nuclear power in a discussion

Lead-in

Ask students to predict the answers to the following questions. They can listen to the debate to see if their answers are correct. (Answers: **1** a **2** b **3** b)

1 When can people return to live near Fukushima, Japan, following the 2011 nuclear disaster?

　a 20 years after　**b** 50 years after　**c** 10 years after

2 How many major nuclear accidents have occurred in the last 30 years?

　a 30　**b** 3　**c** 13

3 Turbines are dangerous for:

　a plants　**b** birds　**c** planes

Exercise 1 page 47

1 benefits　**2** risks　**3** long-term　**4** disasters
5 affordable　**6** opponent　**7** pollute

Exercises 2–3 page 48

Possible answers:

advantages: green, clean, cheap, unlimited

disadvantages: expensive, dangerous

Exercise 4 page 49

Emma

For or against?: against

Reasons: accident will have long-term effect on environment; building power plants pollutes the air; expensive

Jack

For or against?: for

Reasons: safe; doesn't pollute; always enough of it; cheap; can provide a huge amount of electricity; selling electricity helps the economy; makes a country less dependent on oil and gas; wind and solar energy can't solve climate change and are expensive

Exercise 5 page 49

1 a; c　**2** a; b; d　**3** a; d

Exercise 6 page 50

1 nuclear power is a big risk

2 nuclear power does not pollute the air

Exercise 7 page 50

1 *Possible answers:* **Similarities:** Both are green; both are unlimited; and both require advanced technology. **Differences:** Hydroponics is safe; nuclear energy is dangerous. Nuclear power is more expensive than hydroponics.

2–3 *Answers will vary.*

CRITICAL THINKING

Learning objectives

- Organize your notes on speakers' arguments and counter-arguments in a table
- Evaluate your position on an issue by listing advantages and disadvantages in a table
- Choose which arguments to use in a presentation
- Anticipate opposing points of view and prepare counter-arguments

UNLOCK TEACHER DEVELOPMENT

BE INFORMED

➔ **Making counter-arguments** is an important skill for students because: (1) A common challenge for students is that they present their argument 'in a vacuum', i.e. they do not consider the issue from all possible angles; (2) Having empathy and understanding other people's positions, needed to effectively counter-argue, is an important skill in the academic world, as well as in real life; (3) Acknowledging other people's arguments can actually strengthen the speaker's own argument, as it helps to show they have considered all points of view – sometimes students think this is a sign of weakness, when it is quite the opposite.

BE CONFIDENT

➔ Develop this skill for yourself by doing the following activity:

The leader of your educational institution has decided that the first lesson every day will be a compulsory one-hour session on critical thinking. Think of the advantages and disadvantages of doing this.

1 Decide what your position is: Overall, I am **for/ against** this decision.

2 The leader of your educational institution has asked you to email and say what you think. What three arguments would you make in support of your position?

3 What counter-arguments to an opposing position would you give to make your argument stronger?

Lead-in

Students begin to think about the speaking task that they will do at the end of the unit. Give them a few minutes to look at the box and ask you any questions they might have.

UNLOCK TEACHER DEVELOPMENT

BE READY

Look at the Critical Thinking section in the Student's Book on pages 51–52.

➔ Which elements of the lesson do you think your students will find easiest / most difficult / most useful? Why?

➔ Are your answers true for all students in your class?

➔ How can you adapt your teaching or the material to meet your students' needs?

BE FLEXIBLE

It can be useful sometimes to talk to your class about their actual critical thinking process. After doing Exercise 2, you could ask them to feed back about how/why they decided who they agreed with (Emma or Jack), and then how the conversation with their partner proceeded.

Exercise 1 page 51

	for / against nuclear power	arguments	counter-arguments
Emma	against	1 There are very few accidents caused by nuclear power plants. 2 Nuclear power doesn't pollute the air.	1 If there is an accident, it will be huge. 2 Machines that build the power plants pollute the air.
Jack	for	1 Nuclear power is a big risk. 2 It's expensive to build the plant. 3 Solar and wind energy are greener than nuclear energy.	1 There have only been three major nuclear accidents in the last 30 years. 2 Once the plant is there, it's inexpensive to produce energy. 3 Wind turbines aren't friendly for birds.

Exercise 2 page 51

Answers will vary.

Exercise 3 page 52

Possible answers:

advantages: safe, affordable, unlimited source of energy

disadvantages: ugly / takes up space, bad for wildlife/ birds, expensive

Exercises 4–5 page 52

Answers will vary.

UNLOCK TEACHER DEVELOPMENT

BE REFLECTIVE

Think about the following points:

→ When you make decisions in the classroom, how often do you consider the opposite points of view? Do you think you could/should do this more?

→ The ability to develop empathy and understanding of others' positions is a key item in the Cambridge Framework for Life Competencies (www.englishprofile.org/cflc), especially regarding the 'emotional development' competency. You might consider finding out more about this, if you think it would be useful in your practice.

BE COLLABORATIVE

Your development is more meaningful when it is shared. See page 14 for ideas on how to peer-collaborate. Why not share the ideas you generated in the *Be reflective* section, and their outcome?

PREPARATION FOR SPEAKING

Learning objectives

- Choose correct transition words and phrases for sequencing ideas, comparing and contrasting, adding ideas and summarizing – *first of all, on the other hand, in short, overall*
- Use words and phrases used to describe advantages and disadvantages in sentences about sources of energy – *The good thing about wind power is ..., The second drawback of solar energy is ..., There are many pros of solar energy...*
- Make counter-arguments using linking words and phrases – *yet, but, that's completely true*

Exercise 1 page 53

1 Also **2** On top of that **3** And yet **4** First of all
5 In addition

Exercise 2 page 54

2 And yet

3 First of all

4 Second

5 overall

6 comparison

7 addition

8 the other hand

Exercise 3 page 54

1 A **2** D **3** A **4** A **5** D **6** D

Exercise 4 page 55

Possible answers:

1 it is dangerous.

2 they don't pollute the environment.

3 it's unlimited.

4 it pollutes the environment.

Be flexible

👥 Provide **lower-level students** with an opportunity to use language for discussing advantages and disadvantages with a familiar topic. Using a familiar topic for the content allows students to focus on acquiring the academic language. Put students into small groups. They should brainstorm advantages and disadvantages of living in their town. When they are finished, ask the first group to tell you one advantage, using a sentence with one of the phrases from Exercise 3. The next group should give you another advantage, using a different phrase. Continue in this way until all of the phrases have been used. If students still have more advantages, they can now use repeat phrases. Follow the same process with disadvantages. Give each group that gives a correct sentence a point. The group with the most points wins.

Exercise 5 page 55

Possible answers (the rest will vary):

2 that's completely true **3** yet **4** but

Exercise 6 page 55

Answers will vary.

SPEAKING TASK

Learning objectives

- Prepare to persuade others in a discussion about wind power by reviewing and adding to your notes
- Choose language to present arguments and counter-arguments
- Evaluate your arguments and add additional support
- Take part in a group discussion about whether or not to build a wind farm near a town

Exercises 1–7 pages 55–56

Answers will vary.

RESEARCH PROJECT

Create an advert to sell 'green' energy sources.

Divide the class and ask them to think about alternative, 'green' sources of energy. Examples could be solar, tidal, geothermic, wind, hydroelectric and biomass. Give each group one of these to research in depth. Ask students to think about how that way of sourcing energy works, its advantages, and compare it to the process of getting energy from fossil fuels such as oil, gas and coal. Ask each group of students to produce a video to advertise their way of sourcing 'green' energy, using media of their choice, in order to 'sell' it to people. Videos can be uploaded to a video-sharing website.

CLASSROOM APP

Exercises 1–2
Answers will vary.

Exercise 3
1 incorrect   **2** responsible   **3** impossible   **4** unable
5 advantage   **6** unlimited

Exercise 4
1 will   **2** will   **3** could   **4** will   **5** will not   **6** will
7 could   **8** will

Exercise 5
1 solutions   **2** provides   **3** environmental   **4** crisis
5 long-term   **6** risks   **7** benefits   **8** Opponents

Exercise 6
1 to compare and contrast ideas
2 to add another idea
3 to explain a sequence of ideas
4 to summarize ideas
5 to compare and contrast ideas
6 to add another idea

Exercise 7
Answers will vary.

UNIT OBJECTIVES

Watch and listen	Watch and understand a video about the air travel revolution.
Listening skill	Listen for rhetorical questions.
Critical thinking	Evaluate problems and propose solutions.
Grammar	Use comparative and superlative adjectives.
Speaking skills	Give recommendations; expand on an idea.
Speaking task	Give a presentation on a transport problem and suggest solutions to solve the problem.
⊘ Teacher development	Help your students become better at **evaluating problems and proposing solutions**.

UNLOCK YOUR KNOWLEDGE

Background note

The photo shows a busy motorway junction in Shanghai, China, from above. Some of the problems with modern forms of transport are traffic jams and increased levels of air pollution, which can cause health problems. Pollution from cars, motorbikes and planes also has an impact on climate change. In the UK, more people use cars now than they did 50 years ago and, nowadays, fewer people travel by bus, bike or on foot. More people can also afford to take long plane journeys than they could in the past.

Lead-in

Explain the term 'car culture' (when the daily lifestyle of a particular place is built around using cars). Ask the students to discuss the following questions in small groups:

Are you from a 'car culture'? If yes, how does that affect the culture of your city? (*people have less contact with each other because they're isolated in cars, people might work in a city other than where they live, people are less active so more overweight, only people with enough money own a car*) If you're not from a car culture, what term would you use to define it? Ask them to think of a similar term to describe where they're from. (*metro culture, cycling culture*) How does it affect the culture of your city? (*people interact more because they're together on the metro, people get more exercise because they walk a lot, people are stressed because they have to wait for the train*)

page 59

Possible answers:

1 Modern transport causes pollution. More people are on the road causing congestion. People spend more time commuting. Public transport isn't good enough.
2 There are more cars on the road. Cars are more environmentally friendly. Safety and roads have improved. Air travel is cheaper and more popular.
3 Electric cars will become more common. There will be driverless vehicles / high-speed trains / space travel for tourists.

WATCH AND LISTEN

Learning objectives

* Listen and complete a summary of a video about the air travel revolution
* Listen and identify details
* Practise talking about transport

Exercises 1–2 page 60
Answers will vary.

Exercise 3 page 61
1 smaller 2 closer 3 business 4 commercial
5 busiest 6 larger

Exercise 4 page 61
1 in no time 2 Asia 3 sound 4 3,500 5 2016 6 over

Exercise 5 page 61
Answers will vary.

LISTENING 1

Learning objectives

- Listen and identify stressed syllables in nouns and verbs with the same form – *decrease, record, permit*
- Understand key vocabulary for fear of flying – *crash, cure, extreme*
- Listen and identify the main ideas in a radio programme about the fear of flying
- Listen and complete a detailed set of notes
- Evaluate the usefulness of tips for overcoming the fear of flying
- Listen and identify details
- Differentiate rhetorical questions from regular questions
- Practise talking about phobias

Lead-in

In order to get the students talking about the topic, ask them the following questions: *Would you like to be a flight attendant? What do you think flight attendant training consists of? What are the pros and cons of being a flight attendant?*

Exercise 1 page 62

a 2 **b** 1 **c** increase (noun); increase (verb)

Exercises 2–3 page 62

1 record **2** records **3** permit **4** permit **5** presents
6 present

Exercise 4 page 63

1 extreme **2** compare **3** crash **4** avoid **5** cure
6 consists of **7** scared **8** Safety

Exercise 5 page 64

Answers will vary.

Exercise 6 page 64

1 b **2** a **3** a **4** a

Exercise 7 page 64

1 reduce **2** engines **3** wings **4** normal **5** damaged
6 Avoid **7** flying **8** driving

Exercise 8 page 65

Answers will vary.

Exercise 9 page 65

1; 4; 6

Exercise 10 page 65

1 rhetorical **2** rhetorical **3** rhetorical **4** regular
5 regular **6** rhetorical **7** regular

Be flexible

Provide a creative writing opportunity for students to demonstrate rhetorical questions. Put students into pairs. (**For a mixed group, pair a higher-level student with a lower-level student.**) Give each pair a random object that you have nearby, such as a pen, paper clip, cup, glass, eraser, mobile phone or mouse. Give each pair five to ten minutes to write and rehearse a short radio advertisement for the object. Tell the students that the advert must include at least one rhetorical question. Monitor the class as they write and rehearse their advertisements, giving feedback as appropriate. Then ask each pair to perform their advertisement while the rest of the class tries to identify the rhetorical question(s).

Exercise 11 page 66

1 *Answers will vary.*

2 *Possible answers:* The most common phobias are about spiders, snakes, heights, open spaces and dogs.

3 *Possible answers:* Phobias can be cured by experiencing them in safe environments or by being exposed to the phobia for a long period of time.

LANGUAGE DEVELOPMENT

Learning objectives

- Understand key vocabulary for describing problems and solutions – *control, serious, figure out*
- Form comparative and superlative adjectives – *fast, faster than, the fastest*
- Identify stress in adverbial phrases used for modifying comparative and superlative adjectives
- Identify the form of phrases modifying comparative and superlative adjectives – *by far the most affordable, absolutely the healthiest, considerably more expensive*
- Complete sentences about transport, using comparative or superlative adjectives
- Use comparative and superlative adjectives and adverbials to describe transport in a city – *The underground is much faster than the bus. Driving is definitely the most expensive type of transport.*

Exercise 1 page 67

1 b **2** a **3** c **4** a **5** a **6** b **7** a

Exercise 2 page 68

Answers will vary.

Exercise 3 page 69

Adjective	Comparative form	Superlative form
safe	safer	the safest
comfortable	more comfortable	the most comfortable
healthy	healthier	the healthiest
dangerous	more dangerous	the most dangerous
thin	thinner	the thinnest
slow	slower	the slowest
relaxing	more relaxing	the most relaxing
noisy	noisier	the noisiest

Exercise 4 page 69

2 far   3 considerably   4 much   5 definitely   6 lot
7 considerably   8 absolutely

Exercise 5 page 69

1 1; 3; 4; 5; 6; 7

2 2; 8

3 1 a lot   2 by far   3 considerably   4 much
   5 definitely   6 a lot   7 considerably   8 absolutely

4 The words either mean 'very much' or 'a lot' or indicate
   certainty (definitely, absolutely).

Exercise 6 page 70

1 most direct   2 calmer   3 most serious
4 most comfortable   5 faster   6 more affordable
7 most appropriate   8 safer

Exercises 7–8 page 70

Answers will vary.

Be flexible

👥 Challenge **advanced students** with an
opportunity to think on their feet and generate
comparative and superlative forms. Write some
adjectives on small slips of paper (one adjective
per slip) and put them into a bowl or a hat. Divide
the students into teams. One student from the
first team should come to the front of the room
and select a slip of paper at random. They have
to think of one transport-related sentence using a
comparative form and one using a superlative form
of the adjective they have selected. You can use the
sentences in Exercise 7 as examples, but the students'
sentences must be different. Give a point for each
correct sentence. The team with the most points at
the end wins.

LISTENING 2

Learning objectives

- Understand key vocabulary for cycling – *injure,
  respect, convenient*
- Listen and understand main ideas in a
  presentation about cycling to work
- Listen and identify details
- Listen and take detailed notes on
  recommendations and results in a table
- Listen and identify phrases used to make
  recommendations
- Make recommendations about transport in a city
- Synthesize information from a radio programme
  about the fear of flying and a presentation about
  cycling to work in a discussion

Lead-in

Put the students into small groups. Tell them to
imagine they are City Council members. Because
of increasing traffic congestion, the city wants to
encourage residents to cycle to work. Ask students
to suggest three ways to encourage people to cycle
to work. If you want to take the discussion further,
elicit the suggestions from the groups, take the best
ones and assign one to each group. The group can
discuss any problems their suggestion may pose, and
possible solutions.

Exercise 1 page 71

a convenient   **b** pass   **c** injure   **d** respect   **e** solve
f fine   **g** prevent   **h** break the law

Exercise 2 page 71

Possible answers:

1 People cycle because it's cheap, good for your health,
   and in some places faster than driving.

2 Cycling is good for your health. It's cheaper than driving
   or using public transport. It's environmentally friendly.
   It's faster in busy places. It's easy to park a bike.

3 It's dangerous. Drivers can be rude or aggressive. It's not
   enjoyable in bad weather. Equipment can be expensive.
   It's difficult.

Exercise 3 page 72

1 to make the city more bicycle-friendly and/or to make it
easier for people to cycle to work

2 a safety   **b** storage   **c** convenience

Exercise 4 page 72

2; 4; 5; 6; 9; 10

Exercise 5 page 72

recommendations	possible results
1 give fines to drivers who drive in a cycle lane	prevent cars from hitting cyclists; save lives
2 wider cycle lanes	allows more bicycles to pass at the same time
3 add more cycle lanes	prevent cars from hitting bicycles; save lives
4 parking garages should have sections for bicycles	keep bicycles safe and dry while people are working
5 put cycle racks on buses	people wouldn't have to cycle at night or in bad weather people who live far from work could cycle part of the way to work and take public transport the rest of the way

Exercise 6 page 73

1; 3; 5; 7; 8

Exercise 7 page 73

Answers will vary.

Optional activity

👥👥 Each pair from Exercise 7 should decide on their best idea and present it to the class. The class can then vote on the best three proposals. You could divide the class into three groups and tell them to further develop one of the proposals. *What exactly would be involved? What other considerations might there be? Which interested parties should be consulted? How much might the proposal cost if carried out? What research must be carried out in order to present a more detailed proposal?* Tell each group that they must research the proposal in more detail for the next lesson using English language websites (as far as possible). They must then present the more detailed outline of the proposal during the next lesson. Give the groups five to ten minutes to finalize their proposal at the start of the next lesson, then invite each group to present their ideas in under five minutes. Once each proposal has been presented, the class should vote on which was the best. Give each student two votes (to avoid the problem of them voting for their own proposal).

Exercise 8 page 73

1 *Possible answers:* An accident while flying is likely to be more serious than while cycling. People understand how bicycles work, but not how planes work. People feel in control on a bicycle. The thought of dying in a plane crash is more terrifying. There are no disaster movies about cycling.

2 *Answers will vary.*

CRITICAL THINKING

Learning objectives

- Use a table to organize your notes on transport problems, solutions and predicted results
- List problems and propose solutions to transport problems in your city
- Predict the results of solutions to transport problems in your city
- Decide which solutions are the best

UNL⌀CK TEACHER DEVELOPMENT

BE INFORMED

→ **Evaluating problems and proposing solutions** is an important skill for students because: (1) Students may sometimes think that there is only one possible solution to a problem, when in fact there may be multiple solutions; (2) It can take time to develop this awareness for a whole range of different reasons (e.g. social / cultural); (3) Even when students have the critical awareness that more than one solution may be possible, they may find it difficult to evaluate which solution is best.

BE CONFIDENT

→ Develop this skill for yourself by doing the following activity. (Note: this is the same activity as students are asked to do in Exercises 3–5.)

Think about the transport problems in your city or country. Write a list of the problems.

1 Choose a transport problem. Write it in the *problems* column of the presentation planning table below.

2 What are some possible solutions to the problem? Write them in the *proposed solutions* column.

problems	proposed solutions	predicted results

3 What do you predict the results would be of each solution? Write your ideas in the *predicted results* column above.

4 Which solution do you think is best? Circle it.

Lead-in

Students begin to think about the speaking task that they will do at the end of the unit. Give them a few minutes to look at the box and ask you any questions they might have.

UNL⌀CK TEACHER DEVELOPMENT

BE READY

Look at the Critical Thinking section in the Student's Book on pages 74–75.

→ Which elements of the lesson do you think your students will find easiest / most difficult / most useful? Why?

→ Are your answers true for all students in your class?

→ How can you adapt your teaching or the material to meet your students' needs?

BE FLEXIBLE

It may be interesting – and instructive – for students to compare their work in Exercises 3–5 with what you did. This act of sharing can be motivating for weaker / more reluctant students and shows that you are fully engaged in the critical thinking aspect of this course.

Exercise 1 page 74

Possible answers:

problems	proposed solutions	predicted results
cycling is dangerous	give fines to drivers who drive in a cycle lane wider cycle lanes add more cycle lanes	prevents cars from hitting bicycles; saves lives
people don't have anywhere to store their bicycles when they're at work	parking garages should have sections for bicycles	keeps bicycles safe and dry while people are working
riding a bicycle to work is inconvenient	put cycle racks on buses	people wouldn't have to cycle at night or in bad weather

Exercises 2–5 pages 74–75

Answers will vary.

Optional activity

👥 Give students a list of solutions that some cities have tried in order to solve their transport problems. Put students into groups and assign each group one or two solutions. Each group should discuss the possible results of their solution(s). They can then discuss whether their city has implemented this solution. If yes, does it work well? If no, could it work?

Possible transport solutions: *bike sharing scheme, ferry system, company shuttles to take employees to work, charging a congestion tax for cars who drive in the busiest parts of a city, taxi-sharing scheme.*

UNL⌀CK TEACHER DEVELOPMENT

BE REFLECTIVE

Think about the following questions:

→ Did you come up with similar or different points to your students for the task in the *Be confident* section? How do you explain any differences?

→ How did it feel doing a student book activity? Did it allow you to develop empathy with your students at all – to see things from their point of view? Going forward, if you have time, it may be useful and interesting to actually do more student book activities yourself before teaching them in the class.

BE COLLABORATIVE

Your development is more meaningful when it is shared. See page 14 for ideas on how to peer-collaborate. Why not share the ideas you generated in the *Be reflective* section, and their outcome?

PREPARATION FOR SPEAKING

Learning objectives

- Use phrases for giving recommendations about what should be done about problems caused by eating while driving – *I think it would be better if they closed drive-through restaurants.*
- Use phrases for expanding on ideas to support your opinions on the problems caused by eating while driving – *This is because they only encourage drivers to buy food and eat it while they drive.*

Exercise 1 page 76

Answers will vary.

Exercise 2 page 76

2 I think it would be better if **3** I think it would be much better if **4** The best thing would be **5** I'd suggest that

Exercise 3 page 77

b 1 **c** 4 **d** 2

Exercise 4 page 77

Answers will vary.

SPEAKING TASK

Learning objectives

- Prepare to give a presentation on a transport problem in a city and suggested solutions
- Prepare to use phrases to make suggestions
- Make notes about how you will expand on your ideas with reasons and examples
- Respond to feedback from other students on your presentation
- Give a presentation on a transport problem in a city and suggested solutions

Exercises 1–5 page 78

Answers will vary.

RESEARCH PROJECT

Create a presentation about a city's transport system.

Divide the class into groups and give them a list of the top ten cities in the world for transport. Ask groups to research their assigned city's transport system and prepare a presentation on why it is listed in the top ten. Ask them to consider the various modes of transport the city offers, their environmental impact and their convenience and reliability. Students can use online tools such as a wiki to share information on this topic. Once students have researched the different stages, ask them to use presentation software to create a presentation including pictures, narration, sound effects and music. The class can then vote for the best presentation, based on how clear it is, how interesting it is and the quality of information presented. There are free online voting systems to enable this. Search for 'voting software' to view some of these.

Top ten cities for transport (according to Lonely Planet in 2017): 1. Hong Kong 2. Zurich 3. Paris 4. Seoul 5. Prague 6. Vienna 7. London 8. Singapore 9. Stockholm 10. Frankfurt

CLASSROOM APP

Exercise 1

Answers will vary.

Exercise 2

1 trouble **2** impact **3** method **4** solve **5** figure out **6** control **7** serious **8** influence

Exercise 3

1 bigger **2** most interesting **3** more relaxing **4** a lot slower **5** the noisiest **6** by far **7** scarier **8** faster

Exercise 4

1 prevent **2** convenient **3** avoid **4** fine **5** scared **6** injured **7** safety **8** compared

Exercise 5

Answers will vary.

Exercise 6

1 From my own experience, **2** This is because **3** Last week, **4** Personally,

Exercise 7

1 In my opinion, public transport should be free. This is because it would encourage people not to drive, so there would be less traffic and pollution. Personally, I prefer to drive to places when I'm with friends because it's cheaper than taking the subway.

2 I'd like to see the minimum driving age increased to 21. The reason for this is that it is too dangerous for teenagers to drive. From my own experience, I can tell you that they drive too fast and often don't focus on the road.

3 I'd suggest we pass a law that people have to wear bike helmets. This is because the law will save lives. Personally, I sometimes don't bother with things like helmets unless I'm told that it's the law!

UNIT OBJECTIVES	
Watch and listen	Watch and understand a video about the Chinese tradition of moon cakes.
Listening skills	Identify cause and effect; listen for opinions.
Critical thinking	Create a convincing argument.
Grammar	Use dependent prepositions.
Speaking skills	Be polite in a discussion; use adverbs for emphasis; use phrases with *that*.
Speaking task	Take part in a discussion about whether special occasions have become too commercial.
⟳ **Teacher development**	Help your students become better at **creating a convincing argument**.

UNL⟳CK YOUR KNOWLEDGE

Background note

The photo shows the Yi Peng Festival in Chiang Mai, Thailand. The festival is celebrated at the end of the rainy season, on the night of the full moon in November. As part of the celebrations, it is a tradition to release lanterns into the night sky. The flames in the lanterns represent knowledge. During this time, in other parts of Thailand, people celebrate the Loy Krathong Festival, where people float boats shaped like lotus leaves in rivers and ponds. This custom is meant to bring people good luck and fortune.

Lead-in

Ask students to think about customs they share with their families. These can range from special holidays such as New Year's Eve or Ramadan to gathering together for weekly dinners with their extended family. The students should also think about whether these customs have changed over the past 50 years or so. They should consider the following aspects of the customs: food, clothing, gifts given and received, music, dancing, games.

Once the students have thought individually, put them into small groups. The groups should briefly describe the customs on their list and whether or not they've changed over the past 50 years.

page 81

1 The photo is of Chiang Mai, Thailand. This is the tradition of launching sky lanterns to celebrate the full moon in the 12th month of the Thai calendar, as part of the Yi Peng festival.

2–3 *Answers will vary.*

WATCH AND LISTEN

Learning objectives

- Listen and understand main ideas in a video about Chinese traditional moon cakes
- Listen and identify the order of stages in a process
- Listen and understand details
- Practise talking about food and special occasions

Exercise 1 page 82

1 A harvest is the time of year when crops are cut and collected.

2–3 *Answers will vary.*

Exercise 2 page 82

1 Hong Kong; celebrated by Chinese people across the world   **2** butter and sugar   **3** wrap the filling in a thin layer of pastry   **4** pastry; filling; decoration

Exercise 3 page 83

1 People get together with family and friends to watch the moon, admire the lights and eat the traditional sweet of this festival.

2 Moon cakes. They are so named because the festival takes place during the full moon.

3 No, the recipe is quite complicated.

Exercise 4 page 83

2 a   **3** g   **4** c   **5** f   **6** h   **7** d   **8** b

Exercise 5 page 83

1 The Mid-Autumn Festival is celebrated by Chinese people across the world.

2 Chinese people don't make moon cakes at home – the recipe is too complicated.

3 Moon cakes have sweet or savoury fillings.

4 The decorations on top of moon cakes can be Chinese letters or patterns, like flowers.

5 After the moon cakes are made, they are left for the pastry to soften.

Exercise 6 page 83

Answers will vary.

LISTENING 1

Learning objectives

- Understand key vocabulary for customs in the modern world – *multicultural, die out, generation*
- Listen and understand main ideas in a podcast
- Listen and complete a set of detailed notes
- Listen and identify phrases used to signal cause and effect – *Due to ..., The reason for this is ..., That's why ...*
- Identify causes and effects in sentences about cultural traditions
- Gain awareness of the pronunciation of /d/ and /t/ at the end of words in connected speech
- Talk about traditions and customs in your country and abroad

Lead-in

Show students the table below and ask them to copy it onto paper. Students will conduct a survey with their classmates. Note that when asking questions, students will need to turn the 'Find somebody who ...' statements into questions (*Do you give cards for birthdays?*). If necessary, elicit all questions before students begin asking each other. For each question, students should find somebody who answers *yes*. The students should do their best to ask one question per classmate. If they get an answer of *yes*, encourage them to ask questions to find out more information (*Which restaurant? What do you order?*).

find somebody who ...	name	more information
eats in restaurants at least twice a week		
eats dinner at a dining-room table most evenings		
gives cards for birthdays, anniversaries, etc.		
eats a home-cooked meal on special holidays		
plays games with family members		

Exercise 1 page 84

1 b **2** a **3** b **4** b **5** b **6** a **7** b **8** a

Exercise 2 page 85

1 A tradition is a custom or way of behaving that has continued for a long time in a group of people or a society.
2 *Answers will vary.*

Exercise 3 page 85

1 an anthropologist and author **2** whether traditions are adapting to the modern world or dying out

Exercise 4 page 85

a (shaking hands)

Exercise 5 page 86

Effects of modern technology on traditions

	old tradition	new tradition
preparing holiday food	people spent a lot of time and effort preparing special meals for celebrations	we prepare food more quickly because of modern kitchens and supermarket food
recipes	people used cookery books	people find recipes on the internet
where people eat holiday meals	at home	sometimes at restaurants

Exercise 6 page 87

1 That's why **2** because **3** due to **4** This is because
5 because

Exercise 7 page 87

1 Anthropology, in a general sense, is the study of humanity. I know that's not very exact. That's why we have many types of Anthropology, like Linguistic anthropology and Social anthropology.
2 Some traditions die out because our way of life changes.
3 Now, due to developments in technology, people spend more time interacting with other people over the internet
4 But now we don't have to work so hard. This is because we have modern kitchens and supermarket food.
5 In the United States, on Thanksgiving, which is one of the biggest celebrations, many families go to restaurants because they don't want to spend their holiday working in the kitchen.

Exercise 8 page 87

1 Because 2 That's why 3 This means that 4 because
5 Because of

Exercise 9 page 88

1 effec(t) 2 spen(t) lo(t) an(d) 3–4 bu(t) no(t) 5 sen(t)
importan(t) 6 don'(t) an(d)

Exercise 10 page 88

Answers will vary.

Be flexible

👥 For more **advanced students** who can independently apply the skill of connecting /t/ and /d/ sounds at the end of words, ask them to write down their own answers to the questions in Exercise 10. They should mark the letters that shouldn't be pronounced clearly due to connected speech and then practise saying their sentences to a partner.

Adapt this activity for **lower-level students** by asking them to write their answers and then find three examples of where the sounds are not pronounced clearly. Encourage them to use online dictionaries to check the spelling of words and verify the sounds before they share aloud. Providing specific numbers and limiting the number of items or choices can make many tasks more approachable for struggling students.

LANGUAGE DEVELOPMENT

Learning objectives

- Organize words with common suffixes by part of speech
- Use the correct word forms to complete sentences
- Choose the correct dependent preposition to use after particular verbs – *adapt to, talk about, benefit from*
- Use verbs with dependent prepositions to ask and answer questions
- Use the correct dependent prepositions after adjectives

Exercise 1 page 89

adjective: digital, hopeful, political, professional, successful, unbelievable, unforgettable, useless

verb: digitize, frighten, organize, recognize, specialize, weaken

noun: agreement, celebration, communication, connection, excitement

Exercise 2 page 89

Answers will vary.

Exercise 3 page 90

1 celebration 2 acceptable 3 agreement 4 political
5 frightens 6 specialize

Exercise 4 page 90

1 harmless 2 useful; reliable; careful 3 enjoyable
4 thoughtful

Exercise 5 page 90

Answers will vary.

Exercise 6 page 91

1 to 2 to 3 about 4 with 5 about 6 to
7 about 8 at

Exercise 7 page 91

Answers will vary.

Exercise 8 page 91

1 in 2 to 3 about 4 for 5 by 6 for

Be flexible

👥👥 Provide **lower-level students** with an activity to practise using dependent prepositions and speaking more spontaneously. Write some verbs and adjectives that are followed by dependent prepositions on slips of paper and put them in a bowl or a hat. Ask a student to select one and ask another student in the class a question, using the word they selected and the correct preposition. Invite the students to evaluate if the expression is correct after the student poses the question. Then a different student answers the question and he or she is the next one to select a slip of paper and ask a question. You can do this as a whole-class activity or divide the students into groups if the class is large.

LISTENING 2

Learning objectives

- Understand key vocabulary for gift-giving customs – *behaviour, commercial, obligation*
- Listen and identify the main ideas in a discussion about gift-giving customs
- Listen and take detailed notes on arguments about the commercialization of special occasions
- Listen and identify phrases for signposting opinions, agreeing and disagreeing – *Personally, I …; I couldn't agree more.; I'm not convinced.*
- Synthesize ideas from a podcast about customs in the modern world and a discussion about gift-giving customs

Lead-in

Tell the students to imagine they have been invited to a graduation party. The graduate has requested that people not buy gifts or give money, but instead create something the graduate can remember each guest by. The 'gift' can be anything that doesn't cost money. Give students a few minutes to think of something. Then they can pretend they are at the party, mingling and asking each other what gift they gave the graduate. If your class needs some extra help, you can brainstorm ideas with them first.

Possible ideas: *sing a song, recite a poem, draw a picture, give a photograph of you with the graduate*

Exercise 1 page 92

1 obligation **2** graduate **3** personal **4** behaviour
5 thoughtful **6** occasions **7** event **8** commercial

Exercise 2 page 92

1 *Possible answers:* anniversary; graduation; wedding; engagement; new baby; passing a test

2 *Answers will vary.*

Exercise 3 page 93

b

Exercise 4 page 93

Answers will vary.

Exercise 5 page 93

yes	no
1 giving gifts is an obligation	**1** giving a gift shows you were thinking of somebody
2 have to spend money – could spend on more important things	**2** graduation gifts are practical – young people need gifts and money
3 better to spend time with a person than to spend time shopping	**3** gifts remind people of the person who gave the gift
4 too much focus on opening gifts	

Exercise 6 page 93

Answers will vary.

Exercise 7 page 94

2 seems **3** agree **4** disagree **5** not convinced
6 why not **7** don't agree

Exercise 8 page 94

Answers will vary.

CRITICAL THINKING

Learning objectives

- Organize and analyze arguments about the commercialization of special occasions in a table
- Organize ideas about the commercialization of special occasions in your own country in a table
- Evaluate arguments about the commercialization of special occasions in your country and list supporting ideas

UNLOCK TEACHER DEVELOPMENT

BE INFORMED

→ **Creating a convincing argument** is an important skill for students because: (1) There is a common misunderstanding about what constitutes a 'convincing' argument, and it is important that students have the correct tools to be able to do this; (2) One misapprehension is to think that if somebody uses complicated words, or says something very forcefully, their argument must be correct; (3) Students need to develop the skill to examine an argument's underlying evidence and reasons, in order to evaluate its strength.

BE CONFIDENT

→ Develop this skill for yourself by doing the following activity:

Look at the following arguments about whether seven-year-olds should be taught critical thinking. Do you agree or disagree with them?

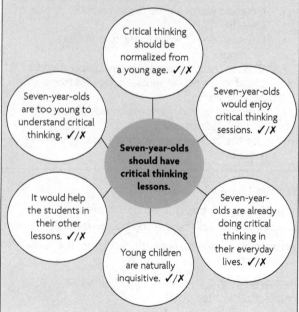

For the arguments which you have ticked, and agree with, how could you make them more convincing? Can you think of any other points to support your position?

Lead-in

Students begin to think about the speaking task that they will do at the end of the unit. Give them a few minutes to look at the box and ask you any questions they might have.

UNL*C*CK TEACHER DEVELOPMENT

BE READY

Look at the Critical Thinking section in the Student's Book on pages 95–96.

→ Which elements of the lesson do you think your students will find easiest / most difficult / most useful? Why?

→ Are your answers true for all students in your class?

→ How can you adapt your teaching or the material to meet your students' needs?

BE FLEXIBLE

After doing Exercise 4, an optional extension would be to get students to revise/recycle what they learnt about counter-arguments in Unit 2. Can they think of any counter-arguments to the three reasons given?

Exercise 1 page 95

Answers will vary for ✓ or ✗.

	argument
Special occasions have become too commercial.	giving gifts is an obligation
	have to spend money – could spend on more important things
	better to spend time with a person than to spend time shopping
Special occasions have not become too commercial.	giving a gift shows you were thinking of somebody
	graduation gifts are practical – young people need gifts and money
	gifts remind people of the person who gave the gift

Exercises 2–4 pages 95–96

Answers will vary.

UNL*C*CK TEACHER DEVELOPMENT

BE REFLECTIVE

Think about the following questions:

→ Compare your responses in the *Be confident* section with a colleague. Do you agree or disagree with each other on the points?

→ Based on the responses to the questions in the *Be confident* section, are there any changes which you would advocate at the place where you teach?

BE COLLABORATIVE

Your development is more meaningful when it is shared. See page 14 for ideas on how to peer-collaborate. Why not share the ideas you generated in the *Be flexible* section, and their outcome?

PREPARATION FOR SPEAKING

Learning objectives

- Use phrases for being polite in a discussion – *You may be right, but ..., What do you think? Excuse me, can I say something?*
- Use adverbs to emphasize your opinions – *I strongly believe that people spend too much money on gifts. Yes, that's completely true. It's absolutely not true.*
- Use emphatic stress on adverbs to emphasize your opinions – *I completely agree that holidays have become too commercial. I absolutely disagree that we should stop giving gifts on Mother's Day. I really think that we should give fewer gifts.*
- Use phrases followed by *that* to express the opinions of yourself and others – *I think that ..., many people believe that ..., I doubt that ...*

Exercise 1 page 97

1 I see your point   **2** You may be right, but
3 I understand, but   **4** I'm sorry to interrupt, but
5 I disagree

Exercise 2 page 97

Answers will vary.

Exercises 3–4 page 98

Answers will vary.

Exercise 5 page 98

1 strongly   **2** absolutely   **3** really   **4** completely

Exercise 6 page 99

1 P **2** O **3** P **4** O **5** P **6** O **7** P **8** O

Exercises 7–8 page 99

Answers will vary.

SPEAKING TASK

Learning objectives

- Prepare for a group discussion about the commercialization of special occasions by reviewing your notes and adding new information
- Plan the language you will use to make arguments and acknowledge other arguments
- Respond to feedback on your performance in a discussion
- Give feedback on others' performances in a discussion
- Take part in a discussion about the commercialization of special occasions

Exercises 1–6 pages 99–100

Answers will vary.

RESEARCH PROJECT

Discuss customs and traditions with students in another country.

Ask the class to think about their own customs and traditions. You could ask them to think about special foods, culture, time of year and why they are important. Students can use online tools to share their ideas with each other. Tell the class they will be contacting students in other countries to find out about customs and traditions in those countries. You can search for 'international school collaboration' in advance to explore the options for doing this. Students can send audio/video messages to other students or set up online live video sessions to discuss customs and traditions.

CLASSROOM APP

Exercise 1

Answers will vary.

Exercise 2

1 less **2** en **3** ment **4** able **5** ize **6** al **7** ion **8** ful

Exercise 3

1 about **2** to **3** by **4** about **5** for **6** at **7** with **8** for

Exercise 4

1 thoughtful **2** generation **3** anniversary **4** obligation **5** interact **6** behaviour **7** graduate **8** occasions

Exercise 5

Answers will vary.

Exercise 6

1 your point **2** interrupting **3** interrupt **4** opinion **5** Excuse me **6** right

Exercise 7

1 I disagree **2** I see your point **3** I'm sorry to interrupt **4** What's your opinion? **5** You may be right

UNIT OBJECTIVES	
Watch and listen	Watch and understand a video about tackling the problem of obesity in children.
Listening skills	Listen for attitude; identify references to common knowledge.
Critical thinking	Brainstorm and evaluate ideas using an ideas map.
Grammar	Understand and use phrasal verbs.
Speaking skills	Use problem–solution organization; present persuasively.
Speaking task	Give a presentation to a group of students about an idea for a health product or programme.
♻ **Teacher development**	Help your students become better at **brainstorming and evaluating ideas using an ideas map**.

UNLOCK YOUR KNOWLEDGE

Background note

The photo shows people practising t'ai chi on a rooftop in Shanghai, China. T'ai chi is a form of exercise that involves slow movements and deep breathing. T'ai chi is a low-impact exercise and is suitable for people of any age and fitness. It is said to reduce stress and anxiety and increase flexibility and energy levels. In addition to regular exercise, people who want to stay fit and healthy should follow a healthy diet and not smoke.

Lead-in

Write the word *diet* on the board and elicit its meaning(s) from the class. The word has three distinct meanings, the first two of which are related to food. Students do not need to know the third meaning for the purposes of this unit.

1 the food and drink usually eaten or drunk by a person or group: *Diet varies between different countries in the world.*

2 an eating plan in which somebody eats less food, or only particular types of food, because they want to become thinner or for medical reasons: *The doctor put me on a low-salt diet to reduce my blood pressure.*

3 a particular type of thing that you experience or do regularly, or a limited range of activities: *The TV only offers a diet of comedies and old films every evening.*

Elicit from the class whether people in their country have, generally speaking, a healthy diet. Encourage discussion where there is disagreement. At this stage, keep the discussion fairly general. Students will have the opportunity to discuss their own attitude towards diet and fitness later. You could also ask them what can happen when people have a poor diet.

page 103

1 *Possible answers:* The people are doing t'ai chi. T'ai chi is a form of Chinese exercise that involves a series of slow movements. It makes your muscles stronger, makes you more flexible, improves balance and can reduce stress.

2–3 *Answers will vary.*

WATCH AND LISTEN

Learning objectives

- Listen and identify the main ideas in a video about the health problem of obesity in children
- Listen and complete a set of notes with figures
- Listen and understand details
- Practise talking about childhood health

Exercises 1–3 page 104

Answers will vary.

Exercise 4 page 105

1; 2; 4; 5

Exercise 5 page 105

1 1975 **2** 19% **3** 1 in 10 **4** 1.6% **5** 1 in 5 **6** 60%

Exercise 6 page 105

Some answers are paraphrased.

1 being overweight or obese than being underweight

2 be more active

3 a sandwich with a protein filling and salad.

4 crisps

5 help children control their weight / control what they eat at lunch

Exercise 7 page 105

Answers will vary.

LISTENING 1

Learning objectives

- Understand key vocabulary for health – *illness, overweight, habit*
- Listen and understand main ideas in a podcast about why some people live a long life
- Listen and complete detailed notes on opinions
- Listen and use speakers' intonation to understand their attitudes
- Listen for adjectives and rhetorical questions which communicate a speaker's attitude
- Understand fixed phrases referring to common knowledge – *There is no doubt that ..., Everyone knows that ..., Most people think that ...*
- Evaluate and discuss healthy and unhealthy lifestyles

Lead-in

Tell students they're going to interview classmates about their daily lifestyles. In small groups, ask students to brainstorm interview questions. (Possible questions: *What do you eat on a typical day? What foods do you avoid eating? What do you do for physical activity every day? Do you spend a lot of time watching television or playing video games?*) They can also ask each other about their family genes (*Do people in your family tend to live long? If yes, do you think it's because they have healthy lifestyles or healthy genes?*) Once the groups have thought of questions, students should walk around the classroom and interview each other. When everyone has finished, ask for volunteers to share interesting information they have learnt. Take a class vote on whether students think a healthy lifestyle or good genes are more important for a long life.

Exercise 1 page 106

a unhealthy   b work out   c prove   d illness
e overweight   f habit

Exercise 2 page 106

Possible answers:

1 Photos **a** and **c** show people eating an unhealthy and healthy diet. Photos **b** and **d** show people being active and inactive.

2 A lifestyle of not being active and eating unhealthy food can lead to obesity and health problems. Leading a healthy lifestyle is much better for us.

3 Your genes affect how likely or unlikely you are to get certain diseases, like diabetes. Having an unhealthy lifestyle increases the chance of getting these diseases.

Exercise 3 page 107

1 No, they don't. Some older people may have eaten an unhealthy diet or not exercised regularly.

2 Genes are more important than lifestyle for having a long life.

Exercise 4 page 107

1 it's great news!

2 the key to a healthy life is to enjoy yourself.

3 get too worried about healthy eating and exercise!

4 genes are more important than our lifestyle.

5 exercise and eat well.

6 it's always better to have a healthy lifestyle.

7 bad health habits increase the chances of getting a serious illness.

8 be careful and look after myself because I don't know if I have good genes!

Exercise 5 page 108

1 excited: the speaker's voice goes up and down a lot

2 certain: emphasis on *no question* and *happy people live longer*

3 critical of people for getting worried: emphasis on *ridiculous*

4 certain/sarcastic: emphasis on *certainly*

5 serious/neutral: voice doesn't go up and down much

Optional activity

Ask students to read the Skills box and to discuss in pairs what kinds of clues can help us decide what a speaker is thinking or feeling. Allow a few minutes for discussion, then elicit ideas from the class.

(Possible answers include: *the language people use, intonation, body language and whether or not the speaker maintains eye contact*. Note that to a certain extent, all of these suggestions may be culturally specific. You could ask your students to discuss ways that people in their culture show agreement and disagreement, then ask them to contrast this with another culture that they know about.)

Exercise 6 page 109

Extract 1: Positive; speaker's voice goes up at the end.

Extract 2: Negative; speaker's voice goes down at the end, using a positive adjective with sarcastic intonation.

Extract 3: Negative; using a rhetorical question.

Extract 4: Negative; using a rhetorical question; voice doesn't go up and down a lot; question ends on a falling tone, which suggests that the speaker doesn't expect an answer.

Extract 5: Positive; intonation goes up and down.

Extract 6: Negative; voice doesn't go up and down much; doesn't stress *great*, but stresses *some* and *I* (after *but*).

Exercises 7–9 page 110

Answers will vary.

LANGUAGE DEVELOPMENT

Learning objectives

- Identify and work out the meaning of phrasal verbs in context – *come down with, take up, try out for*
- Use phrasal verbs in a discussion about healthy lifestyles
- Use adjectives to describe well-being – *cultural, physical, emotional*

Exercise 1 page 111

2 came down with   **3** take up   **4** try out for   **5** give up
6 sign up (for)   **7** join in   **8** get over

Exercise 2 page 111

Answers will vary.

Exercise 3 page 112

1 come down with   **2** give up   **3** sign up (for)   **4** join in
5 try out (for)   **6** get over   **7** take up   **8** cut down on

Exercise 4 page 112

1 given up   **2** get over   **3** signed up   **4** taken up
5 tried out   **6** cut down on

Exercises 5–6 page 112

Answers will vary.

Be flexible

👥 Support **lower-level students** with the meaning of phrasal verbs by acting out the meanings in a game of Charades. Divide the class into teams. Write some phrasal verbs on separate slips of paper, fold them and put them in a hat or bowl. Students can come to the front of the room, select one, and act out the phrasal verbs. (You may want to first display the list of phrasal verbs and give students or pairs up to five minutes to discuss ways to act out them out. This will also help them more readily identify the answers.) The first team to call out the correct answer wins a point. For a bonus point, give the team about one minute to think of a sentence using the phrasal verb.

Exercise 7 page 113

1 emotional   **2** social   **3** intellectual   **4** personal
5 Physical   **6** cultural   **7** educational

LISTENING 2

Learning objectives

- Understand key vocabulary for health and well-being – *relax, stress, treatment*
- Listen and identify the topics of four presentations about programmes to improve your health
- Listen and take detailed notes on the benefits of four health programmes
- Synthesize information from a podcast about why some people live a long life and four presentations about health programmes in a discussion

Lead-in

Hold a class discussion. Ask students what the benefits of physical activity are in addition to improving physical health (can lead to improved self-confidence, better concentration, ability to work on a team and get along with others, can reduce pain and build bone strength).

Exercise 1 page 114

1 c   **2** a   **3** b   **4** b   **5** a   **6** b   **7** c   **8** a

Exercise 2 page 115

Answers will vary.

Exercise 3 page 116

1 taekwondo   **2** a football club   **3** a cycling tour
4 acupuncture

Optional activity

👤👥 For homework, ask students to research holidays that focus on health and fitness. These can include cycling tours, yoga retreats, extended walking tours, multi-day rafting or kayaking trips, or anything else that interests them. They can research what the holiday consists of, what countries it takes place in, a sample daily itinerary and what the benefits of this type of holiday are. The students can present their findings in small groups. The groups can discuss whether they would ever want to take a holiday like this, and why they think these types of holiday are growing in popularity.

Exercise 4 page 116

Programme 1: improves health and well-being; improves concentration; makes you feel good about yourself; improves confidence; reduces stress

Programme 2: improves social life; improves intellectual performance; improves physical fitness; improves team-building skills

Programme 3: exercise; fascinating cultural experience; improves memory and thinking skills

Programme 4: reduces pain; helps people lose weight

Exercise 5 page 116

Answers will vary.

CRITICAL THINKING

Learning objectives

- Organize your notes about the benefits of a health programme into an ideas map
- Discuss and evaluate different ideas for health programmes
- Add the benefits of the health programme you discussed to an ideas map

UNLOCK TEACHER DEVELOPMENT

BE INFORMED

→ **Brainstorming and evaluating ideas using an ideas map** is an important skill for students because: (1) Ideas maps can help students to identify what they already know about a subject, and to realize they know more than they think they do; (2) They are a useful way of organizing information when students are listening and have to be selective in what they write down; (3) Ideas maps can be particularly useful in showing the connections between the topic, main ideas and details.

BE CONFIDENT

→ Develop this skill for yourself by doing the following activity:

Watch the video, '21st Century Skills', by Ceri Jones at the Cambridge Better Learning Conference. Looking at just the section from 04:05 to 08:35, take notes using an ideas map on the presenter's ideas about 21st Century Skills: **www.youtube.com/watch?v=1v92oyTFAAk**. *Review your ideas map and add any ideas from your own teaching. Do you agree with everything you have written in your ideas map? Why / Why not?*

Lead-in

Students begin to think about the speaking task that they will do at the end of the unit. Give them a few minutes to look at the box and ask you any questions they might have.

UNLOCK TEACHER DEVELOPMENT

BE READY

Look at the Critical Thinking section in the Student's Book on pages 117–118.

→ Which elements of the lesson do you think your students will find easiest / most difficult / most useful? Why?

→ Are your answers true for all students in your class?

→ How can you adapt your teaching or the material to meet your students' needs?

BE FLEXIBLE

When doing Exercise 2, encourage the students to be as open-minded and inventive as possible. One of the main advantages of using an ideas map is that it can encourage new, interesting and innovative ideas. They should not 'edit' themselves too much at this stage.

Exercises 1–4 pages 117–118

Answers will vary.

Optional activity

Tell students they will contribute to several ideas maps about the benefits of health-related activities. If space allows, students should spread out around the room. Give each student a large piece of paper to tape to the wall, a marker to write with, and a health-related activity to write in the main circle of their ideas map (examples of health-related activities: *spending time with friends, vegetarian diet, team sports*). Each student should begin their ideas map with their assigned activity in the middle circle. They should add one benefit to an outside circle. Students should then move to the ideas map on their right, look at the new activity, and add one benefit to an outer circle. After filling in one outer circle on each map, students should move to the next map. The ideas maps are complete when they each have five or six outside circles. When they are finished, tell students to go to their original ideas maps. They can discuss with a partner what ideas they like the best and why.

UNLOCK TEACHER DEVELOPMENT

BE REFLECTIVE

Think about the following questions:

→ Look back at the ideas map which you created. Is it still clear to you? Do the notes help you remember the key points? If the answer is 'no', then you may need to rethink the way in which you take notes using an ideas map.

→ Did your students find it easy or difficult to come up with new and original ideas by themselves? Some students find it easy to do this, whilst others find it very challenging. How can having an awareness of this help you plan future sessions more effectively?

BE COLLABORATIVE

Your development is more meaningful when it is shared. See page 14 for ideas on how to peer-collaborate. Why not share the video and ideas you generated in the *Be confident* section opposite, and their outcome?

PREPARATION FOR SPEAKING

Learning objectives

- Identify the key content features of a problem–solution presentation about a health programme
- Understand the organization of a problem–solution presentation about a health programme
- Use imperative verb forms to write persuasively – *Buy our new product! Be kind to your body. Join us.*
- Use positive adjectives which make a message more persuasive – *exciting, terrific, fascinating*

Exercise 1 page 119

1 to engage the audience and make them think about the topic

2 to make listeners think about their own problems; as it is likely that many people would answer 'yes' to some of them, this sets up the presentation as a solution to the audience's problems

3 focusing on work, feeling stressed, wanting to get more exercise

4 taekwondo

5 to try to make the reader believe it is common knowledge that taekwondo is helpful

6 it has been shown to improve your concentration and make you feel good about yourself

7 the date of the first free introductory class

Exercise 2 page 119

specific information about the place, time, etc. 4
background information about the programme 3
introduction of the solution 2

Exercise 3 page 120

2 check out   3 join   4 learn; visit

Exercise 4 page 120

1 Imperatives often make the listener want to take action.

2 Imperatives are used in the presentations because the presenters want to persuade the listeners to do something – sign up for a course, group, etc.

Exercise 5 page 120

2 Buy one and get one free.

3 Hurry and purchase a ticket now.

4 Don't forget that our shops are open on Sundays.

5 Register for our course before it's too late!

Be flexible

👤 Provide **advanced students** with the opportunity to analyze authentic persuasive language and deepen their understanding of imperatives and adjectives. The task is for students to find examples of the use of imperatives and adjectives in advertisements, and to consider how effective they are. Students can then rewrite a version of the advertisement without using any imperatives or adjectives and compare the effectiveness of this against the original. Invite students to discuss the following questions: *Which version is more honest? Which version is more persuasive? What effect do imperatives have? What is the effect of adjectives?*

This can be done as a homework assignment. If internet access is available in class, you could also do this during lesson time. This would give you the opportunity to discuss the language used in advertisements in more detail with your students and give guidance to make this task appropriate for **lower-level students**. The task may also provide insight into students' interests as illustrated by the advertisements they decide to look at. This can then help inform your choice of tasks and extra materials in future lessons.

Exercise 6 page 121

1 new; exciting   **2** social; intellectual; physical, team-building   **3** terrific; fascinating; cultural; best   **4** interested; alternative   **5** traditional (Chinese)   **6** great; easy

Exercise 7 page 121

Answers will vary.

SPEAKING TASK

Learning objectives

- Prepare to give a presentation on a health programme by reviewing your notes and adding new information
- Organize the content of a presentation on a health programme
- Prepare persuasive language to use in a presentation
- Respond to feedback on your presentation by making it more persuasive
- Give a presentation on a health programme

Exercises 1–7 pages 121–122

Answers will vary.

RESEARCH PROJECT

Create an interactive menu.

Ask students to brainstorm healthy foods. In groups, students can then think about creating a menu which includes these healthy foods. Each group could use online tools to write a blog entry to share their menu with the rest of the class.

The menus can be used to create a class website (search for 'create free website'). Students can upload pictures, video and audio clips to add information about each menu item, e.g. calories, fat and alternative choices. This website can be promoted around the learning environment.

CLASSROOM APP

Exercise 1

Answers will vary.

Exercise 2

1 out   **2** on   **3** for   **4** into   **5** over   **6** up   **7** up   **8** with

Exercise 3

1 physical   **2** emotional   **3** cultural   **4** personal   **5** social   **6** educational   **7** intellectual

Exercise 4

1 work out   **2** habit   **3** unhealthy   **4** Participating   **5** performance   **6** treatment   **7** reduce   **8** mental

Exercise 5

Answers will vary.

Exercise 6

1 to attract the listeners' attention

2 to introduce a solution

3 to give background information

4 to give specific information about the programme

Exercise 7

Introduce the problem(s) with rhetorical questions. Introduce the solution. Give background information about the solution. Give specific information about the solution.

UNIT OBJECTIVES	
Watch and listen	Watch and understand a video about a boy with a prosthetic hand.
Listening skills	Understand references to earlier ideas; understand lecture organization.
Critical thinking	Summarize information using *Wh-* questions.
Grammar	Use passive verb forms.
Speaking skills	Preview a topic; organize ideas; explain how something is used.
Speaking task	Give a presentation about an invention or discovery which has changed our lives.
⊘ **Teacher development**	Help your students become better at **summarizing information using *Wh-* questions**.

UNLOCK YOUR KNOWLEDGE

Background note

The photo shows a replica of a very early computer called 'Difference Engine No 2'. It was designed by the British computing pioneer Charles Babbage (1791–1871) between 1847 and 1849. It would have weighed around 15 tonnes and been 2 metres tall. It was able to perform a complex series of calculations automatically and print the results. The replica was built by the Science Museum in London, the UK; construction began in 1985, this main section was completed in 1991, and the entire model in 2000. Difference Engine No 2 was never constructed in Babbage's lifetime, because it was too expensive and difficult to make at that time.

Some of the most important inventions and discoveries in the last 20 years have been digital television, Wi-Fi, Bluetooth, GPS systems, LED lightbulbs, MP3 players, hybrid cars, social media networks, e-readers, instant messaging, digital cameras and smartphones.

Lead-in

Tell students the wheel was invented around 3,500 BCE and the internet was invented thousands of years later. In small groups, ask students to brainstorm everything they can think of that was invented in between those years. The students can rank the top ten in order of importance and write their lists on the board.

page 125

Answers will vary.

WATCH AND LISTEN

Learning objectives

- Listen and complete a summary of a video about a boy with a prosthetic hand
- Listen and understand details
- Practise talking about the ideas emerging from the video

Exercises 1–2 page 126

Answers will vary.

Exercise 3 page 127

1 prosthetic / new   **2** expensive   **3** college   **4** 3D
5 normal   **6** successful   **7** new / prosthetic

Exercise 4 page 127

1 Holden Mora is <u>seven</u> ~~17~~ years old.
2 Jeff Powell built the hand using instructions from <u>the internet</u> ~~his professor~~.
3 The printer builds the parts in under <u>24</u> ~~44~~ hours.
4 Holden <u>can</u> ~~cannot~~ hold things with his artificial hand.
5 <u>Jeff Powell</u> ~~Holden~~ is now raising money to build hands for other kids.
6 Holden hopes other <u>children</u> ~~teachers~~ can have the best kind of hands, too.

Exercise 5 page 127

Answers will vary.

LISTENING 1

Learning objectives

- Understand key vocabulary for inventions – *design, develop, device*
- Listen and identify the order of main ideas in a museum tour about inventions
- Listen and complete a set of detailed notes about inventions
- Understand referencing to ideas which were mentioned earlier
- Understand the use of weak and strong forms of small words in sentences
- Evaluate and explain the importance of different inventions

Exercise 1 page 128

1 designed **2** Scientific **3** discover **4** invented
5 device **6** develop **7** diagram **8** technology

Exercise 2 page 129

1 d (invented 953) **2** c (invented in the thirteenth century, 1268) **3** a (invented in the ninth century) **4** b (invented 1206)

Lead-in

Ask students to speculate what people did before the items in Exercise 2 were invented. For example, how did people with poor vision see clearly before glasses were invented? They'll only hear the answer to one invention (the fountain pen) in Listening 1. For the others, the discussion can come from speculation.

Exercise 3 page 129

1 d **2** c **3** a **4** b

Exercise 4 page 130

1 pen **2** 953 **3** Africa **4** ink **5** glasses **6** thirteenth
7 Italy **8** read **9** twelfth **10** Turkey **11** engineer
12 gardens **13** farms **14** car **15** ninth **16** China
17 scientists **18** live

Exercise 5 page 130

1 953 **2** the Middle/Dark Ages **3** glasses
4 (the invention of) gunpowder

Exercise 6 page 131

1 and; and the; to **2** The; of; the **3** The; a; to; in a
4 of the; of

Exercise 7 page 131

1 b **2** c **3** a

Exercise 8 page 132

Answers will vary.

Be flexible

👥 Ask students to write down their answers to the questions in Exercise 8. They should then note in their answers the small words that are not usually stressed (*a, an, the, do, does, to, from, at, of*). They can read their answers to a partner, sometimes stressing the small words and sometimes not. They can discuss with their partner how the different stress changes the meaning of the word and the sentence.

Provide more guidance with this task for **lower-level students**. If possible, ask students to write their answers onto a shared document to display to the class. Then students can take turns reading their sentences to the group, choosing either to stress the small words or not. Ask the class to first identify any stressed words they hear and then discuss how the meaning changes when the word is stressed (or not).

Exercise 9 page 132

Answers will vary.

LANGUAGE DEVELOPMENT

Learning objectives

- Understand three different meanings of *make* – *force, cause* and *produce*
- Identify the meaning of *make* in collocations – *make a comparison, make a decision, make a difference*
- Recognize passive verbs – *The digital computer was invented in 1936. The first glasses were held in front of the eyes. It was first used for watering gardens.*
- Describe inventions and discoveries, using passive verb forms

Exercise 1 page 133

2 F **3** C **4** P **5** C **6** F

Exercise 2 page 133

1 b **2** a **3** b **4** b **5** a **6** b **7** a **8** a

Exercise 3 page 134

1 were brought **2** was made **3** were invented; were held / balanced; were developed **4** was (first) used
5 was invented; were written

Exercise 4 page 134

2 The law of gravity was discovered by Isaac Newton in the seventeenth century.

3 The first computer chip was invented in the 1950s.

4 The first smartphone was created after 1997.

5 Penicillin was first discovered in 1928 by Alexander Fleming.

Exercise 5 page 135

1 was discovered   **2** was invented   **3** designed   **4** were developed   **5** was written   **6** was created   **7** download
8 were sent   **9** was taken   **10** developed

Exercise 6 page 135

1 ~~were created~~ was created   **2** ~~is discovered~~ was discovered   **3** ~~was print~~ was printed   **4** ~~was wrote~~ was written   **5** no error   **6** ~~was invented~~ invented

Exercise 7 page 135

Answers will vary.

Be flexible

👥👥 Provide **advanced students** with an opportunity to identify passive verb forms in authentic texts. For homework, ask students to search online for an article about important inventions. They should find a short article that looks interesting to them. They should read the article and underline all instances of the passive voice and all instances of the active voice. In class, they can share their articles in small groups and explain why the passive voice was used in some sentences. You may want to provide additional challenge by asking students to use the passive verb forms they found in their own sentences to discuss the inventions from the unit.

For **lower-level students**, provide more controlled practice. Use the transcript from Listening 1 instead of an article and ask students to identify four passive verb forms (e.g., *is called, were brought, was made, were invented*). Ask students to share aloud examples and challenge them to find more passive verb forms as you verify they are on track. Then contrast the passive voice sentences with active voice sentences from Listening 1 and invite students to share their thoughts on why the passive voice was used.

LISTENING 2

Learning objectives

- Understand key vocabulary for technology – *install, industry, app*
- Listen and understand the organization and main ideas in a lecture about the history of smartphone apps
- Listen and complete a set of detailed notes
- Identify phrases which signpost the organization of ideas in a lecture – *We'll start by discussing ..., We will then discuss ..., I'd like to start by talking about ...*
- Synthesize information from a museum tour about inventions and a lecture about the history of smartphone apps in a discussion

---

Lead-in

Tell students to imagine they're planning a weekend trip to a city they've never been to before. In small groups, ask them to brainstorm the various things they'll need to know in order to plan their weekend (how to get there, the weather, good restaurants, things to do, opening and closing times of places). Now tell them to imagine their trip is taking place before the invention of computers and smartphones. They should discuss how they will find out the information they need to know. When they are finished, tell them they can now plan the trip using their smartphones. They should discuss which apps they would use for each aspect of the planning.

Exercise 1 page 136

1 access   **2** app; install   **3** create   **4** users   **5** product
6 industry   **7** allow

Exercise 2 page 136

1 and 3 *Answers will vary.*

2 At the time this book was published, 25 billion apps were downloaded every year.

Exercise 3 page 137

a 2   **b** 3   **c** 1

Exercises 4–5 page 137

Answers will vary.

Exercise 6 page 137

Possible answers:

1 internet   **2** checking emails   **3** sending texts   **4** first app store   **5** internet browsers   **6** 180 billion

7 go to bookshop or library – guidebooks; get audio books; get maps; look up directions on computer, print them; pack CDs, camera, torch, list of phone numbers and addresses; passenger reads directions; ask for directions if you get lost

8 read reviews; book hotel with travel app; use GPS; use music app; listen to podcasts

9 software engineers   **10** helpless   **11** patient

Exercise 7 page 138

2 We will then discuss   **3** I'd like to start by talking a little bit about   **4** I'm going to briefly talk about   **5** Now I'd like to mention   **6** In the next part of the lecture, I'll discuss

Exercise 8 page 138

Answers will vary.

Optional activity

👤 If some of your students have smartphones, you could ask them to research ways that their phones could be used to help them learn English, both inside the classroom and outside. Tell them that they should focus on three aspects of smartphone use:

1 useful apps designed specifically for students of English

2 apps that provide useful practice, but which were not designed primarily for students of English (e.g. English language news apps, podcast apps, etc.)

3 ways that they can use their smartphones as the basis of discussion tasks (e.g. taking photographs of things they see during the week to discuss in class, taking photographs of their family to describe in class)

Students should be ready to talk about their ideas during the next lesson, and to recommend particular apps and tasks to the other students in the class.

CRITICAL THINKING

Learning objectives

- Use *Wh-* questions to complete an ideas map about an invention from the Listening sections
- Use *Wh-* questions to create an ideas map about one of four inventions
- Suggest ideas for another person's ideas map

UNLOCK TEACHER DEVELOPMENT

BE INFORMED

➜ **Summarizing information using *Wh-* questions** is an important skill for students because: (1) Taking a question-based approach to research can help students identify rich, interesting and relevant background information; (2) Adopting this approach should also result in your students' writing being more argumentative and less descriptive; (3) This process is also very structured and focused, and leads on directly from their ideas maps (see Unit 5).

BE CONFIDENT

➜ Develop this skill for yourself by doing the following activity:

What is your response to these questions about critical thinking?

1 Why is critical thinking important for both 'academic' and 'real' life?

2 What are the best strategies for developing your students' critical thinking skills?

3 Where is the best place for critical thinking skills to develop?

4 When should students first start to learn about critical thinking?

5 Who should be responsible for developing critical thinking skills?

6 How should students apply what they learn about critical thinking in the classroom to real life?

Lead-in

Students begin to think about the speaking task that they will do at the end of the unit. Give them a few minutes to look at the box and ask you any questions they might have.

UNLOCK TEACHER DEVELOPMENT

BE READY

Look at the Critical Thinking section in the Student's Book on pages 139–140.

➜ Which elements of the lesson do you think your students will find easiest / most difficult / most useful? Why?

➜ Are your answers true for all students in your class?

➜ How can you adapt your teaching or the material to meet your students' needs?

BE FLEXIBLE

Exercise 5 could be done as a 'doughnut' activity. Half the class form the 'inner ring' of the doughnut, and hold up their books showing their ideas map. The other half form the 'outer ring' of the doughnut, and give feedback. After 60 seconds, the outer ring moves one place to the left, and gives feedback to the next student. After four or five turns, the inner ring and outer ring swap places. Then repeat.

Exercises 1–5 page 139–140

Answers will vary.

UNLOCK TEACHER DEVELOPMENT

BE REFLECTIVE

Think about the following points:

→ Share your answers to the questions in the *Be confident* section with your colleagues, perhaps via a discussion app. Could the questions be used as part of staff training on critical thinking?

→ Did most students talk about one of the inventions suggested in Exercise 3, or did they come up with their own one? Reflecting on this can tell you something about how confident students are in coming up with their own ideas.

BE COLLABORATIVE

Your development is more meaningful when it is shared. See page 14 for ideas on how to peer-collaborate. Why not share how the *Be flexible* exercise went, and its outcome?

PREPARATION FOR SPEAKING

Learning objectives

- Use phrases in the introduction to a presentation to signpost organization of ideas – *I'd like to begin my talk by looking at ..., After that, I'm going to explain ..., Then, I'll discuss ...*
- Understand the organization of information in a presentation
- Use phrases to explain how a device is used – *GPS allows us to find our way. The mobile phone helps people stay in touch.*

Exercise 1 page 141

2; 3; 5

Exercise 2 page 141

Answers will vary.

Exercise 3 page 142

a 6   **b** 2   **c** 5   **d** 3   **f** 7   **g** 4

Exercise 4 page 143

1 allows us   **2** helps people to   **3** are useful for
4 makes it   **5** Without

Exercises 5–6 page 143

Answers will vary.

Be flexible

👥 Provide **lower-level students** with support and practice in using phrases to explain how something is used. Write the phrases from the box in Exercise 4 on the board. Write one invention on the board (for variety, use different inventions than the ones in Exercises 4 and 5). Ask a volunteer to give an example sentence using one of the phrases *(The aeroplane is useful for travelling a long distance in a short time.)*. Put a tick next to that phrase so it's not used again. Ask the next volunteer to use the same invention with a different phrase *(Without the aeroplane, people would still have to travel by ship to cross the ocean.)*. Continue with the same invention until all the phrases have been used, and then repeat the process with a new invention. In this way, you provide targeted support for **lower-level students** in generating academic language while thinking on their feet.

SPEAKING TASK

Learning objectives

- Review and organize your notes in sequence to prepare for a presentation about an invention
- Prepare an introduction which previews your presentation
- Select language to explain how your invention is used
- Give a presentation on an invention
- Take part in a discussion to evaluate the importance of an invention

Exercise 1–5 page 144

Answers will vary.

RESEARCH PROJECT

Invent and present a new mobile app.

Ask students to brainstorm all the different things mobile apps can do. Examples may include: giving driving and walking directions, paying bills, paying people you owe money to, producing and editing films, creating music or editing photos. In groups, ask students to think about what else they wish there was a mobile app for.

Each group should design a new mobile app which allows them to do these new things. The assignment should include a description of the app's main purpose, how it works, who will find it most useful, and what image it will show on a smartphone screen. Each group can present their invention and vote for the best one.

CLASSROOM APP

Exercises 1–2

Answers will vary.

Exercise 3

1 contribution   **2** attempt   **3** decision   **4** improvements
5 public   **6** progress   **7** comparison   **8** difference

Exercise 4

1 was invented   **2** were taken   **3** wrote   **4** was discovered
5 were sent   **6** built

Exercise 5

1 User   **2** diagram   **3** scientific   **4** industry   **5** install
6 technology   **7** device   **8** access

Exercise 6

1 making   **2** Without   **3** make it   **4** to stay cool
5 help people to

Exercise 7

Answers will vary.

UNIT OBJECTIVES	
Watch and listen	Watch and understand a video about College of Art graduate, Christopher Raeburn.
Listening skills	Take notes on main ideas and detail; identify auxiliary verbs for emphasis.
Critical thinking	Create a purpose statement; evaluate interview questions.
Grammar	Make predictions and talk about expectations for the future.
Speaking skills	Ask for opinions and check information; ask follow-up questions.
Speaking task	Take part in an interview to find attitudes about uniforms and dress codes.
♻ **Teacher development**	Help your students become better at **creating a purpose statement** and **evaluating interview questions**.

UNL♻CK YOUR KNOWLEDGE

Background note

The photo shows fashion models walking down a catwalk, with British model Cara Delevingne at the front, while people in the audience watch and take photos on their phones. The photo was taken during London Fashion Week, which showcases fashion designers from around the world.

Fashion changes with time and usually reflects popular culture. For example, fashion can be influenced by celebrities, advertising, television shows, athletes, musicians, books, music and even politics. Young people often want to wear different clothes from their parents to show that they are young, new and modern.

Lead-in

Ask the class to write down the names of any designer-branded clothes that they are wearing (e.g. Levi's, Calvin Klein, Anita Dongre). For any shop-branded clothes (e.g. Esprit, H&M, Gap), they should write down the name of the store where the item was bought. Give the students a strict time limit of one minute to do this and tell them not to look at any of their labels – they must do the task from memory. Then ask the students to work in pairs and compare their lists. Invite comments from the class of which brands of clothing are the most popular.

page 147

1 *Possible answers:* The people in the photo are modelling clothes on a catwalk as part of a fashion show.

2–5 *Answers will vary.*

WATCH AND LISTEN

Learning objectives

- Listen and understand the main idea in a video about a fashion designer
- Listen and understand details
- Listen and identify the meaning of unfamiliar words and phrases from their context in the video

Exercise 1 page 148

Answers will vary.

Exercise 2 page 148

1 England   **2** England   **3** recycled

Exercise 3 page 149

he uses recycled materials

Exercise 4 page 149

1 T   **2** F; Christopher uses other spare military materials, like parachute material.   **3** F; Christopher employs local people in England to make his clothes.   **4** T   **5** T   **6** T   **7** F; Christopher gets the ideas for his designs firstly from the original fabric or piece of clothing. Then he adds ideas he gets from other places.

Exercise 5 page 149

1 b   **2** a   **3** a   **4** b   **5** b   **6** a

Exercise 6 page 149

Answers will vary.

LISTENING 1

Learning objectives

- Understand key vocabulary for fashion – *design, fabric, practical*
- Use visuals to predict the topic of a discussion about fashion
- Listen and complete the outline of a discussion about fashion
- Listen and note speakers' opinions in a table
- Understand and use full forms of auxiliary verbs for emphasis
- Gain awareness of unstressed vowel omission – *every* /ˈev·ri/, *family* /ˈfæm·li/, *several* /sev·rəl/
- Express personal opinions on fashion

Lead-in

Put students in pairs. Tell them they will hear the term 'smart fabrics' in the discussion about clothes of the future. Give them a few minutes to think about what that term might mean. With their partner, they should think of a definition for 'smart fabric' and at least one example of a piece of clothing that could be designed using smart fabric.

Exercise 1 page 150

1 fabric   **2** local   **3** useless   **4** convert   **5** Smart
6 practical   **7** focus on   **8** design

Be flexible

👥 Provide **advanced students** with the opportunity to be creative, think on their feet, and showcase their skills in front of the class. Ask the students to get into pairs (A and B) and tell them that they are going to perform a series of 60-second role plays. You will call out the number of one of the statements from Exercise 1. Student A must read out the statement, Student B must respond and then the two students together must improvise a dialogue for 60 seconds. They must continue talking until you call out the next number for Student B to read out. Continue like this until you have called out all of the numbers, then quickly elicit summaries of some of the role plays from the class. You may want to model this task with a student as an example.

The most successful statements for this activity are: 3, 6 and 8. The other statements can also be used, although they may demand a little more thought when setting a context for the dialogue.

Exercise 2 page 150

Answers will vary.

Exercise 3 page 151

1 future   **2** community   **3** environmentally
4 conditions   **5** energy   **6** electricity   **7** Smart   **8** kill
9 temperature   **10** sports   **11** ill   **12** lights   **13** dress
14 colour

Exercise 4 page 152

type of clothing	adjective(s)	speaker's opinion (*P* or *N*)
eco-clothes	interesting	P
fabrics *which* regulate body temperature	amazing	P
fabrics *which* prevent people from getting ill	cool	P
dress made of lights	*(not very)* practical useless	N

Exercise 5 page 152

1 a I've been <u>reading</u> about fashion of the future.
  b I <u>have</u> been reading about fashion of the future.

2 a <u>That's</u> amazing.   **b** That <u>is</u> amazing.

3 a I agree that it's <u>not</u> very practical.
  b I <u>do</u> agree that it's not very practical.

4 a I think it'll be <u>interesting</u>.
  b I <u>do</u> think it'll be interesting.

Exercise 6 page 153

1 I <u>do</u> believe they can be used to make sports clothing.

2 It <u>does seem</u> we have a lot of ideas for the future of fashion.

3 I <u>do</u> agree.

4 I <u>do</u> like the idea of clothes which help people with health problems.

5 She <u>does buy</u> a lot of clothes.

Exercise 7 page 153

1 interesting   **2** typically   **3** temperature   **4** finally
5 different

Exercises 8–9 pages 153–154

Answers will vary.

LANGUAGE DEVELOPMENT

Learning objectives

- Understand the meaning of common idioms – *over the top, give me a hand, keep an eye on*
- Use *will* and *going to* to talk about predictions and expectation for the future – *In the future, we'll probably wear clothes which can regulate body temperature. It's about future fabrics and how we're going to use them.*
- Use the future continuous to talk about predictions and expectation for the future – *A few years from now, we'll probably be using this fabric to charge our phones. In the future, we're going to be wearing clothes which regulate our temperature.*

Exercise 1 page 154

1 give me a hand   **2** not really into   **3** are up for
4 I'm not a fan of   **5** over the top   **6** keep my eye on
7 go for it

Exercise 2 page 154

b 7   **c** 2   **d** 3   **e** 1   **f** 4   **g** 5

Be flexible

👥 Once the class is clear as to the meaning of the idioms in Exercises 1 and 2, ask the students to look at them again and underline those they would feel most comfortable using. They should then practise using these during a discussion with a partner (either one of the discussion tasks from the book, or a topic of their own choice). The aim of the discussion is to try and sound as natural as possible when using the idioms.

Support **lower-level students** in acquiring these forms by providing the first line of a dialogue for partners to create the response to and then role play. Instruct students to use one of the idioms in their response. In this way, you give guidance with additional contexts to use the idioms in and traction with producing them (e.g. *Are you a fan of homework? / I'm not a fan.; I'm thinking about going to graduate school. / Go for it!; Can you watch my laptop for a second while I get a coffee? / Sure. I'll keep my eye on it.*)

Exercise 3 page 155

1 will be printing / are going to be printing

2 will be wearing / are going to be wearing

3 won't be using / aren't going to be using; will be doing / are going to be doing

4 will be making / is going to be making; will be living / is going to be living

Exercises 4–5 page 156

Answers will vary.

LISTENING 2

Learning objectives

- Understand key vocabulary for fashion – *collection, style, individual*
- Listen and understand the main ideas in an interview with a fashion designer
- Listen and take detailed notes to complete an outline form of an interview
- Listen and understand details
- Make inferences about the ideas in the interview
- Synthesize information from a discussion and an interview about fashion

Lead-in

Put students into small groups. Write the following questions on the board for discussion: *Have you ever travelled somewhere where you stood out because of how you were dressed? If yes, explain. If no, where is a place you might travel to where your style of dress would probably be very different from the local people?* Give groups about five minutes to discuss the questions and then ask students to tell you anything interesting that came up in their conversation. Finally, tell them they will hear an interview with Aysha Al-Husaini, a Muslim fashion designer who grew up in New York. Ask students if they think she stood out because of how she dressed.

Exercise 1 page 156

a admire   **b** modest   **c** unique   **d** collection
e individual   **f** combine   **g** confidence   **h** style

Exercise 2 page 157

Answers will vary.

Exercise 3 page 157

1 She's a talented fashion designer.   **2** Qatar
3 unique designs that combine traditional Muslim fashion with French chic

Exercise 4 page 158

Possible answers:

1 growing up in New York   **2** problems dressing in modest way   **3** tried to combine culture with fashion **4** Muslim clothes   **5** people think of *burkas*   **6** teachers – how to create fashion without miniskirts and sleeveless shirts?
7 fashion = more than showing body   **8** style = traditional chic   **9** young designers reusing traditional styles
10 popular outside the US – Doha, Dubai, etc.

Exercise 5 page 158

1 F; Aysha grew up in New York.

2 DNS **3** T **4** DNS **5** T **6** T **7** T

8 F; In China and India, you can see that many traditional styles are being reused by young designers.

9 F; Aysha receives requests for her clothes from women in Malaysia and Singapore and she might open stores there some day.

Exercise 6 page 159

1 Yes – the host says that Aysha's collection made a great impression on the audience at Fashion Week in Doha.

2 Yes – Aysha says that she had problems with dressing modestly and that her friends thought her clothes were strange.

3 No – Aysha says she thinks that there's a misunderstanding of Muslim clothes and that most people only think of a *burka*.

4 No – when she started at design school, her teachers asked her how she was going to stay in the fashion business if she wouldn't design miniskirts or sleeveless shirts.

5 Yes – the host says that her collection made a great impression at Doha's Fashion Week, she sells her collection in big cities, and she gets requests from other countries where she may also open stores.

Exercise 7 page 159

Answers will vary.

Optional activity

Tell students they will research a fashion designer for homework. Tell them about Fashion Forward Dubai, which is the biggest fashion event in the Middle East. They should go to the Fashion Forward Dubai website and find a designer that interests them. Then they should do further biographical research on the designer. They should find out where the designer is from, what type of clothes he/she designs and what his/her design influences are. Students can then be put into small groups to share their information. You can also ask them to compare their designer with Aysha Al-Husaini.

CRITICAL THINKING

Learning objectives

- Analyze purpose statements for interviews and identify the most useful one
- Discuss the topic of dress codes
- Write a purpose statement for an interview about attitudes to uniforms and dress codes
- Evaluate the effectiveness of interview questions against a set of criteria
- Create a list of questions for an interview
- Evaluate and improve your questions for an interview

UNLOCK TEACHER DEVELOPMENT

BE INFORMED

➔ **Creating a purpose statement** and **evaluating interview questions** are important skills for students because: (1) Students may have very little experience of conducting interviews, and so need to understand the basics; (2) Along with good interview questions, creating a purpose statement can help ensure the quality of the interview and therefore the greater likelihood that it will produce the data desired; (3) Creating a clear purpose statement and developing good, clear questions can help increase students' confidence in conducting interviews, which is crucial, as they may be nervous or anxious about doing them.

BE CONFIDENT

➔ Develop these skills for yourself by doing the following activity:

Imagine that you are going to interview a world expert on critical thinking.

1 Write a short (30–40 words) statement beginning, 'The purpose of this interview is...', to show what the goal of your interview would be.

2 Write a list of specific questions (around three to five) you would ask him or her about critical thinking.

Lead-in

Students begin to think about the speaking task that they will do at the end of the unit. Give them a few minutes to look at the box and ask you any questions they might have.

UNL🔒CK TEACHER DEVELOPMENT

BE READY

Look at the Critical Thinking section in the Student's Book on pages 160–162.

→ Which elements of the lesson do you think your students will find easiest / most difficult / most useful? Why?

→ Are your answers true for all students in your class?

→ How can you adapt your teaching or the material to meet your students' needs?

BE FLEXIBLE

As an optional 'at home' or 'project' task, get students to actually ask relevant people (e.g. teachers, parents, the principal) the questions they create in Exercise 6. This would make the task more realistic, and take critical thinking outside of the classroom. Take feedback at the beginning of the next lesson after they have done this work.

UNL🔒CK TEACHER DEVELOPMENT

BE REFLECTIVE

Think about the following questions:

→ Look again at the list of questions which you wrote in the *Be confident* section. What would your answers to these questions be? Ask a colleague (either in person or electronically) their responses.

→ If your students did the *Be flexible* task suggested, what happened? What did they discover? Is there any practical impact which this research could have on your educational institution?

BE COLLABORATIVE

Your development is more meaningful when it is shared. See page 14 for ideas on how to peer-collaborate. Why not share the ideas you generated in the *Be confident* section, and their outcome?

PREPARATION FOR SPEAKING

Learning objectives

- Use indirect questions to ask about opinions – *Do you think that most people know much about Muslim clothes? Can you tell me how you feel about Muslim fashion?*
- Use indirect questions to check your understanding – *Do you mean that Muslim women sometimes have a hard time finding fashionable clothes? Are you saying that there is a need for fashionable clothes for Muslim women?*
- Use phrases and follow-up questions to ask for more information – *Can you explain why you decided to design fashions for Muslim women? Could you expand on that point? You mentioned that when you were a teenager, your friends thought you dressed strangely in the summer. How did you feel about that?*
- Express opinions on fashion and ask follow-up questions

Exercise 1 page 160

Statement 1 states an incorrect goal. The goal of the interview isn't to explore fashions from around the world.

Statement 2 has more than one sentence.

Statement 3 is best because it is one sentence, it clearly states the goal, and it uses the qualitative phrase *learn about*.

Exercise 2 page 160

Possible answers:

1 A dress code is a set of rules about what types of clothes students or employees must wear and/or aren't allowed to wear.

2 Reasons for dress codes include: it makes sure that people look professional; in schools, dressing appropriately shows respect; it makes sure that people dress modestly

Exercise 3 page 160

Answers will vary.

Exercise 4 page 162

1 c   2 a   3 e   4 d   5 b

Exercises 5–6 page 162

Answers will vary.

Exercise 1 page 163

1 Are you saying that   2 How do you feel about
3 Would you say that   4 Can you tell me

Exercise 2 page 163

Possible answers:

1 What do you think is the best way to dress for a job interview

2 Would you say that I should wear a suit even if I don't usually wear one

3 Are you saying that my skills are less important than what I look like

4 Do you mean that you're really going to wear jeans and a T-shirt to your job interview

Exercise 3 page 164

Possible answers:

1 Can you explain why you're planning to do that?

2 Could you expand on that point?

3 What do you mean by 'too young'?

4 Can you tell me more about that?

5 Why do you think that students do better when they wear a uniform?

Exercises 4–6 page 165

Answers will vary.

SPEAKING TASK

Learning objectives

- Review your questions and make them polite to prepare for your interview on attitudes to uniforms and dress codes
- Respond to feedback from another student on your questions
- Conduct an interview on attitudes to uniforms and dress codes
- Take part in an interview on attitudes to uniforms and dress codes as an interviewee

Exercises 1–8 page 166

Answers will vary.

RESEARCH PROJECT

Design and present clothes for the future.

Ask students to think about different environments that people live in, e.g. indoor, rainy or hot. Now ask them to think about different types of clothing and accessories for different parts of the body like hats, jackets, watches, trousers and bags. Then ask them to imagine how these clothes could be designed to help people in their environment, e.g. a hat may have a cooling system to help people keep cool, or a watch could be a communication device.

Students could use online tools to share ideas. In groups, ask students to design and present an item of 'smart' clothing or an accessory like the ones they have been thinking about. As an additional activity, one group could interview another group about their design and upload this using online tools to share audio recordings.

CLASSROOM APP

Exercises 1–2

Answers will vary.

Exercise 3

1 a hand   **2** over   **3** into   **4** up   **5** for   **6** on   **7** of

Exercise 4

1 plan   **2** prediction   **3** prediction   **4** prediction   **5** plan   **6** prediction

Exercise 5

1 practical   **2** collection   **3** fabric   **4** modest   **5** convert   **6** unique   **7** local   **8** admire

Exercise 6

1 Can you explain why you feel that way?

2 Why do you think that fashion is so popular?

3 What you mean by 'fashionista'? What do you mean by fashionista?

4 How did you feel about that?

5 Can you tell me more about your style?

Exercise 7

1 Can you explain why you feel that way?

2 Could you expand on that point?

3 What do you mean by 'hipster'?

4 So, why do you think that so many people are interested in fashion?

5 Can you tell me about how you first got interested in fashion?

UNIT OBJECTIVES	
Watch and listen	Watch and understand a video about workshops for entrepreneurs.
Listening skill	Understand paraphrases.
Critical thinking	Evaluate arguments.
Grammar	Use conditional sentences.
Speaking skills	Use gerunds as subjects to talk about actions; present reasons and evidence to support an argument; use paraphrases.
Speaking task	Take part in a discussion about whether young people should be allowed to have credit cards.
↻ **Teacher development**	Help your students become better at **evaluating arguments**.

UNL⊘CK YOUR KNOWLEDGE

Background note

The photo shows a luxury car driving through a modern city. Like jewellery and designer clothes, people often buy luxury cars to show that they are wealthy. Some people also think it is worth spending money on designer clothes and cars because they are better quality or because they like them, whereas other people prefer to spend their money on other things.

Lead-in

Write some common sayings about money on the board. Discuss their meanings. Ask students to discuss in small groups whether they agree or disagree with the sayings and if they know of any additional ones they can share with the class.

Examples of common sayings: *Money can't buy happiness. Money makes the world go round. The best things in life are free. Money doesn't grow on trees. A fool and his money are soon parted. You have to spend money to make money.*

page 169

Answers will vary.

WATCH AND LISTEN

Learning objectives

- Listen and understand main ideas in a video about workshops for entrepreneurs
- Listen and understand detail
- Practise talking about different kinds of businesses

Exercises 1–2 page 170

Answers will vary.

Exercise 3 page 171

1 equipment / machinery   **2** products / things   **3** children
4 iPad   **5** computer servers   **6** locations / places

Exercise 4 page 171

1 F; TechShop attracts people who like to work for themselves.

2 DNS

3 F; Most people at TechShop like to build / make things.

4 F; Some of the inventors are now selling their products online / in stores.

5 T

6 F; The success of TechShop shows that many people without a lot of money have great ideas.

Exercise 5 page 171

Answers will vary.

LISTENING 1

Learning objectives

- Understand key vocabulary for money – *save money, afford, debt*
- Listen to the introduction to a podcast about millionaire lifestyles and predict the content of the podcast
- Listen and identify main ideas
- Listen and complete a set of detailed notes with numbers and percentages
- Identify phrases that signal paraphrases – *that is, to put it another way, in other words*
- Identify paraphrases in sentences
- Gain awareness of silent letters in English sound and spelling relationships – *debt, answer, yacht*
- Explain and justify your opinions on advice from a podcast
- Take part in a discussion to evaluate advice from a podcast

Lead-in

Write the phrase *financially savvy* on the board. Explain that it means being smart about how to save and spend money. Tell students they are going to work together to write a list called 'Ten tips for being financially savvy'. Begin brainstorming ideas as a group (don't borrow money if you don't have to, only buy new clothes when you need them, limit your holidays). Then put them into small groups and ask the groups to agree on five tips for being financially savvy. Once the groups have done this, ask for volunteers from each group to come to the board and write their five tips. As a whole class, vote on the best ten tips.

Exercise 1 page 172

1 b   **2** b   **3** a   **4** b   **5** a   **6** b   **7** a

Exercise 2 page 172

Answers will vary.

Exercise 3 page 173

Possible answers:

1 Richer people live very ordinary lives and not lavish ones.   **2** *Wealthy* means 'rich'.   **3** the behaviour of wealthy people

Exercise 4 page 173

Answers will vary.

Optional activity

You could also set up Exercise 4 as a pair work ranking activity. Ask the students to work on their own and number the statements 1–8: 1 = the truest, 8 = the least true. When they have finished ranking the statements, ask them to discuss their ranking in pairs and to agree on a common ranking.

Exercise 5 page 173

The following are true, according to the podcast: 2; 3; 4; 5; 7

Exercise 6 page 173

1 75   **2** 50   **3** 20   **4** 65   **5** average   **6** 86

Exercise 7 page 174

1 live within your means / don't spend more money than you have
2 show off / showing other people that they might be wealthy
3 frugal / careful about how she spends her money
4 was economically disadvantaged / didn't have much money

Exercise 8–9 page 175

1 yacht   **2** sign   **3** designer   **4** debt   **5** doubt
6 answer

Exercises 10–11 page 176

Answers will vary.

LANGUAGE DEVELOPMENT

Learning objectives

- Use collocations with *pay* and *money* to complete sentences – *borrow money, pay in cash, spend money*
- Use the zero conditional to talk about general facts, truths and habits – *If people have a lot of money, they are happier*
- Use the first conditional to talk about real possibilities – *If we save a little money each month, we'll be able to afford a holiday in the summer*
- Use conditional sentences to give advice – *If you want to be rich, save a lot of money!*

Exercise 1 page 177

1 make money   **2** pay in cash   **3** pay off   **4** pay a fine
5 lose money   **6** borrow money   **7** save money
8 owe money   **9** raise money   **10** spend money

Exercise 2 page 178

1 A 2 T 3 T 4 A

Exercise 3 page 178

1 If you want to save money, ~~you~~ don't buy lots of expensive things.

2 If you have time, ~~listened~~ listen to this podcast.

3 If I have money, I always ~~bought~~ buy new clothes.

4 If you ~~will~~ pay off all your debts, you will be happier.

5 If I lose my job, I *will* look for a new one.

Be flexible

👥👥 Turn this error-correction activity into a game by adopting the easy-first procedure, a technique that works especially well when you have two or more short exercises together. Write the question numbers on the board and ask the students to complete the exercise in teams. When the teams have finished answering the questions, ask the first team to choose the number of a question that they are sure they can answer correctly. If the team answers the question correctly, circle the question number with the team's colour and move on to the next team. Continue like this until all of the questions have been answered. The team with the most numbers at the end is the winner. The group work in this activity supports **lower-level students** and engages them in reflecting on and evaluating their work.

Exercise 4 page 179

1 g 2 d 3 a 4 e 5 f 6 c 7 b 8 h

Exercise 5–6 page 179

Answers will vary.

LISTENING 2

Learning objectives

- Understand key vocabulary for financial support for students – *encourage, minimum wage, responsible*
- Use the introduction to a discussion about whether university students should be paid for good grades to predict the arguments
- Listen and note the main arguments for and against students being paid
- Listen and take detailed notes on figures
- Identify the opinion of speakers in a discussion
- Synthesize information from a podcast about millionaire lifestyles and a discussion about whether college students should be paid for good grades

---

Lead-in

Ask *Do you think paying students for getting good grades will help them stay at university?* Allow a few minutes for students to share their ideas with the class. Ask *What are some ways to keep students at university until they graduate?* Give students a few minutes to discuss with a partner and then ask them to share their ideas with the class.

Exercise 1 page 180

1 encouraged 2 minimum wage 3 responsible
4 manage 5 decision 6 sense 7 services

Exercise 2 page 181

Answers will vary.

Exercise 3 page 181

Possible answers:

for: 1 encourages students to finish education and get a good job

2 shows students that they're treated like adults

3 gives students a sense of responsibility

4 students choose to study rather than going to work

5 gives students an option: stay at university and be paid or minimum-wage job

6 not all parents interested in education; need to show students a reason for studying

against: 1 won't solve problems / reduce drop-out rates; will just cover them up

2 money better spent on student services and advisers to help students manage their time better

3 sends the wrong message

4 students will take easy courses for good grades

Exercise 4 page 181

1 760; Students in Denmark are paid €760 a month to attend university.

2 6; Students receive the payments for a maximum of six years.

3 18; Students receive the payments starting at the age of 18.

4 25; The dropout rate at Dr Hassan's university is over 25%.

Exercise 5 page 182

1 b 2 a 3 b

Exercise 6 page 182

1 <u>I understand that</u> many students drop out of university because of financial problems. ...(However,) will paying students really encourage them to continue?

2 <u>I can see your point,</u> (but) we have already spent a lot on student services.

3 <u>I realize that</u> students need encouragement to stay at university, (but) are we going in the right direction?

Exercise 7 page 182

Answers will vary.

Be flexible

👥 Provide challenge for more **advanced students**. Ask them to create a role play using vocabulary and ideas from the unit. Put students into pairs. Student A is a university student who is thinking about dropping out. Student B is an adviser who is trying to convince the student to stay at university. The student should give several reasons why he/she can't stay at university and the adviser should try to give solutions to each problem. Encourage students to use new vocabulary from the unit in their role play. Ask students to write their role play down (about eight to ten lines of dialogue is enough), rehearse it, and then perform it for the class or for another pair.

Adapt the activity for **lower-level students** by first brainstorming ideas for them to base their dialogue on. Use a two-column chart and with students, list problems on one side and possible solutions on the other.

CRITICAL THINKING

Learning objectives

- Organize information from notes about paying students for good grades into arguments and supporting details
- Read and understand the financial difficulties young people face
- Evaluate the advantages and disadvantages of allowing young people to have credit cards
- Organize your ideas about credit cards for young people into arguments and supporting details

UNLOCK TEACHER DEVELOPMENT

BE INFORMED

➜ **Evaluating arguments** is an important skill for students because: (1) When researching any topic, students will come across arguments in favour and arguments against, and they need to know how to deal with this situation; (2) Having a logical and structured approach to this can help students more easily identify what their own opinion is; (3) This approach can help students identify, and therefore address, counter-arguments. This will strengthen their own argument.

BE CONFIDENT

➜ Develop this skill for yourself by doing the following activity:

1 *Look at the following arguments about whether universities should set critical thinking entry exams for students. Are they for or against this position?*

  1 'It is important to formally assess a student's ability to think critically.'

  2 'An exam is not the appropriate mechanism to evaluate a student's ability to think critically.'

  3 'Critical thinking is important for university study, and so should be assessed like other subjects – through an exam.'

  4 'Critical thinking should be assessed by looking at the student's written work and by interviewing them.'

2 *Can you think of any other arguments in favour of or against this position? What is your own personal view?*

Lead-in

Students begin to think about the speaking task that they will do at the end of the unit. Give them a few minutes to look at the box and ask you any questions they might have.

Exercise 1 page 183

arguments which support the position	arguments which oppose the position
Argument 1: pay students to encourage them to finish their education	**Argument 1:** money would be better spent on student services
Supporting detail: in Denmark, university students are paid to go to university.	**Supporting details:** students drop out due to stress and poor time management advisers can help students learn to manage their time better, and they'll be more likely to graduate
Argument 2: gives students a sense of responsibility	**Argument 2:** sends the wrong message
Supporting details: young people often choose to work and make money instead of staying at university gives students the choice to work for minimum wage or stay at university not all parents are interested in education; need to show students a reason for studying	**Supporting details:** some students will take easy courses to get high grades should reward excellent schools and teachers, not students

Exercise 2–5 pages 183–184

Answers will vary.

PREPARATION FOR SPEAKING

Learning objectives

- Use gerunds as subjects to focus on an action – *Doing small jobs for money teaches children how to be responsible.*
- Describe money-related issues in sentences with gerunds as subjects
- Use phrases to present reasons and evidence to support an argument – *One effect of being a couple is that it's easier to save money. Because of that, students will do better at university and will be more likely to graduate. Due to the high cost of living, we had to move out of the city.*
- Use paraphrases to clarify your ideas – *Millionaires often have simple lifestyles. That is, they don't buy a lot of expensive things. I can't afford to buy a new car right now. In other words, I don't have enough money for a car.*

Exercise 1 page 185

1 <u>Learning</u> should be about studying new things and improving yourself.

2 <u>Saving money</u> is not easy if you have bills to pay.

3 <u>Reading books about millionaires</u> is not a good way to get rich.

4 <u>Teaching children about money</u> should start at an early age.

Exercise 2 page 185

2 Teaching children to save money is very important.

3 Paying children to study can encourage them.

4 Giving children money at an early age can spoil them.

5 Learning about money is difficult when you're a child.

6 Not having much money makes it difficult to start a family.

Exercise 3 page 186

Answers will vary.

Exercise 4 page 186

1 As a result   2 One effect of   3 Due to   4 In my experience   5 As a consequence of   6 Because of that

Exercise 5 page 187

Answers will vary.

SPEAKING TASK

Learning objectives

- Prepare to speak by reviewing and adding to your notes
- Evaluate the strength of your arguments and improve them by adding support where possible
- Take part in a discussion about whether young people should be allowed to have credit cards

Exercises 1–5 page 188

Answers will vary.

RESEARCH PROJECT

Create an eBook to help people budget their finances.

Divide the class into groups. Ask each group to search online for 'budget your finances'. Give each group a different area to focus on, e.g. how to save money, how to create a budget, why it is important to budget. Students should make notes of their findings.

Tell the class they will be creating a class eBook using the information they have gathered (you can find guides and eBook software by searching for 'create eBook'). Each group will write a different section based on their research area, including information, advice and explanations of any specialist financial vocabulary. They will then combine their sections in an eBook which can be shared with the class.

CLASSROOM APP

Exercise 1

Answers will vary.

Exercise 2

1 raising   2 saving   3 make   4 in cash   5 fine   6 owe   7 spent   8 off

Exercise 3

1 will move   2 like   3 become   4 feel   5 snows   6 gets

Exercise 4

1 millionaire   2 debt   3 afford   4 payment   5 decision   6 manage   7 encouraged   8 minimum wage

Exercise 5

Answers will vary.

Exercise 6

1 As   2 to   3 of   4 As   5 experience

Exercise 7

Answers will vary.

LISTENING, SPEAKING & CRITICAL THINKING 4

GLOBALIZATION UNIT 1

UNIT OBJECTIVES	
Watch and listen	Watch and understand a video about US basketball stars bringing the American league to China.
Listening skills	Activate prior knowledge.
Critical thinking	Analyze and use data in pie charts; use data to support an argument.
Grammar	Use modals of present and past probability.
Speaking skills	Present data; describe a pie chart; draw conclusions from data.
Speaking task	Give a presentation using data from a pie chart.
⟳ **Teacher development**	Help your students become better at **using data to support an argument**.

UNL⟳CK YOUR KNOWLEDGE

Background note

The photo shows the ancient ruins of the Colosseum in Rome, Italy. Between the arches, we can see a large billboard displaying an advertisement for a globally recognized Japanese car manufacturer. In front of the arches, there are several tourists, from different countries and cultures. The photograph shows some of the effects of globalization. Globalization has had both positive and negative effects on cultures. On the one hand, global media and technology allow ideas, books, works of art and cinema to be spread across the world. On the other hand, the spread of global chains – like food, clothing and car manufacturers – has reduced cultural diversity around the world.

Lead-in

Students work in small groups to think of a country starting with each letter of the alphabet, plus the nationality adjective for each country. The first team to find at least 20 countries and nationality adjectives beginning with different letters is the winner. Note that there are no countries beginning with the letter *X* or *W*, and only one beginning with *O* (Oman), *Q* (Qatar) and *Y* (Yemen).

As a follow-up, when you are checking the lists of countries, elicit which part of the world they are in (e.g. the Middle East, Central America, North Africa, etc.).

page 15

Answers will vary.

WATCH AND LISTEN

Learning objectives

- Listen and understand main ideas in a video about the National Basketball Association (NBA)
- Listen and note supporting details for main ideas
- Make inferences about the NBA, its fans and its players
- Practise talking about international sport

Exercises 1–2 page 16

Answers will vary.

Exercise 3 page 17

1 T   **2** F; The game is already very popular.
3 F; The teams played two pre-season matches.
4 F; Jeremy Lin is Chinese American.   **5** T

Exercise 4 page 17

1 These US basketball stars are opening NBA-sponsored facilities ... one way for the American league to promote itself ... it gives people a chance to experience the NBA ... close up.

2 The Chinese market is worth nearly $150,000,000 in merchandising and broadcast deals, 5% of the NBA's income.

3 An honour to play in the first game ... ever in Shenzhen ... we've had an incredible few days here ... We had a terrific time here in Shenzhen ... a fabulous city ... It's a great city.

Exercises 5–6 page 17

Answers will vary.

LISTENING 1

Learning objectives

- Understand key vocabulary for the food industry – *consumers, produce, imports*
- Use background knowledge to predict the topics in a radio programme about the global food industry
- Listen and complete a set of detailed notes
- Listen and understand details
- Listen and identify the reporter's opinions
- Listen and note words with consonant clusters accurately
- Give personal opinions on the food industry

Lead-in

Ask students to write down what they ate for dinner last night / lunch today. Write some of the items on the board. Then ask them where they think each of the foods came from. Chances are that at least some of the items are imported. Ask them to think about how this might be different from a dinner / lunch in their country 50 years ago. This can be done in small groups or led by you.

Exercise 1 page 18

1 a   **2** c   **3** f   **4** d   **5** g   **6** b   **7** e

Exercise 2 page 19

Answers will vary.

Exercise 3 page 19

Topics 1, 2 and 7

Exercise 4 page 20

1 how globalization allows us to taste food from different cultures around the world   **2** David Green   **3** fruit
4 vegetables   **5** healthily   **6** Bananas   **7** Kiwis
8 South Africa   **9** 8,500   **10** 9,600   **11** 11,100   **12** local
13 transported it across the country
14 increases production costs   **15** 48,000 kilometres
16 supply chain   **17** footprint

Exercise 5 page 20

1 T   **2** F; David doesn't really think about where his food comes from.

3 F; The global food industry allows people all over the world to eat a huge variety of fresh fruit and vegetables.

4 F; You can only really be sure how far something has travelled if you purchase it directly from a farm or if you grow it yourself.

5 F; Even something that looks like it's local can have a big impact on the environment.

Exercise 6 pages 20–21

1 a   **2** b   **3** a

Exercise 7 page 21

1 abroad   **2** grow   **3** find   **4** produced   **5** timed
6 Flying   **7** pass   **8** cost

Optional activity

👤 Ask students to read along with the script as they listen to the first section again. Tell them to underline the words with consonant clusters. Ask whether it is more difficult for them to hear the clusters that come at the beginning / middle / end of words. (Most find the end most difficult.) Point out (1) that you cannot always tell how a cluster sounds from the written word, and (2) that word-final clusters often carry important information, like tense or number (e.g. *talked*).

Answer:

Today on *The world close up* – The 48,000-kilometre fruit salad. With globalization, the world has become a smaller place. On last week's programme, we talked about how people around the world are watching foreign TV programmes, wearing clothes from other countries and working at companies with several international offices. On this week's programme, let's look at how globalization allows us to taste food from different cultures around the world, without leaving the country.

Exercise 8 page 21

1 support   **2** three   **3** Firstly   **4** sixth   **5** climate
6 state   **7** trap   **8** growing   **9** would   **10** rain

Exercise 9 page 22

Answers will vary.

LANGUAGE DEVELOPMENT

Learning objectives

- Understand the level of certainty communicated by different modal verbs of present and past probability – *must, can't, could, might, may*
- Use modals of present and past probability to describe your ideas about where things and people are from – *These avocados must have come from Mexico. The supermarket might have imported the bananas from Colombia. Abdul can't be from Oman.*
- Use correct vocabulary to complete a text about globalization – *goods, import, multinational*

Exercise 1 page 23

1 may have bought **2** must be **3** must have lost
4 might send **5** can't be **6** must have lived

Exercise 2 page 23

1 very unlikely **2** a possibility **3** a possibility
4 only logical conclusion **5** only logical conclusion
6 a possibility

Exercise 3 page 23

1 must be

2 must have been

3 might / may / could contain

4 might / may / could have been

5 couldn't / can't have been

Exercise 4 page 23

Answers will vary.

Be flexible

Ask students to review the script for Listening 1, looking for modals of past probability, and answer the question below:

How certain is the reporter about the journeys of the following items: bananas, grapes, blueberries, kiwis, lettuce? How can you tell?

Answer:

He is quite certain about the first four but less certain about the lettuce:

The bananas from Colombia <u>must have travelled</u> more than 8,500 kilometres ..., the grapes from South Africa <u>must have come</u> more than 9,600 kilometres, and the Argentinian blueberries nearly 11,100 kilometres. The kiwi from New Zealand? That <u>must have flown</u> about 18,800 kilometres.

This lettuce <u>may be</u> local, but the farm it came from <u>could have transported</u> it across the country and then put it into this plastic packaging ... this local lettuce <u>might have travelled</u> ... up to 500 kilometres.

To challenge **stronger students**, bring in some photos of people from magazines and ask students to make guesses about them (e.g. *He might be a film star. This photo couldn't have come from recent magazine. Her hat must be very expensive.*).

Exercise 5 page 24

1 transport **2** goods **3** imported **4** supply chain
5 produce **6** purchase **7** multinational **8** prosperity
9 outsourcing

LISTENING 2

Learning objectives

- Understand key vocabulary for the film industry – *multinational, goods, production costs*
- Use a T-chart to take notes on main ideas on a presentation on the global film industry
- Listen and identify main ideas and details
- Identify language linking cause and effect – *therefore, since, in order to*
- Understand and describe ideas about cause and effect in the international film industry
- Describe a film and make deductions about its production
- Describe and give opinions on the globalization of the film industry
- Synthesize ideas from a radio programme about the global food supply chain and a presentation about the international film industry

Lead-in

Ask students to name recent films or a TV series they have seen and where they were made. Before the lesson, look up a few popular films you think your students may have seen and find out about their locations. Alternatively, you could ask about classic films like *Lord of the Rings* (New Zealand), *Indiana Jones* (San Francisco), *Casablanca* (Arizona), *Amadeus* (Prague), etc.

Exercise 1 page 25

1 b **2** a **3** a **4** b **5** b **6** a **7** a

Exercise 2 page 25

Answers will vary.

Exercise 3 page 26

	countries	reasons
1	Canada	– big discount on labour – tax credits – digital effects discount
2	Mexico	– free from taxes – brings jobs to Mexico
3	United Arab Emirates	– tax incentives – great locations – rebate on production costs – organizes permits, visas, customs clearance, script approval
4	Jordan	– tax incentives (avoiding VAT) – great locations

Exercise 4 page 26

a 1 **b** 3 **c** 2 **d** 4

Exercise 5 page 26

Overseas: 25%; Overseas and domestic: 50%; Domestic: 25%

Exercise 6 page 27

1 In order to get this tax credit

2 Since films made in Mexico are considered exports

3 Jordan helps producers avoid taxes

Exercise 7 page 27

1 In order to **2** Since **3** Therefore

Exercises 8–10 page 27

Answers will vary.

CRITICAL THINKING

Learning objectives

- Understand data about the global food industry in a pie chart
- Analyze which statements are supported by data in a pie chart
- Evaluate statements of opinion on the global food industry and give your opinion
- Analyze and support your arguments with data from a pie chart

UNL🔒CK TEACHER DEVELOPMENT

BE INFORMED

➔ **Using data to support an argument** is an important skill for students because: (1) To make strong, convincing arguments, you need strong, reliable data; (2) Should students fail to do this, their essays will not be based on facts; they will sound more like opinions; (3) Pie charts are a common way of presenting data and are used in many subjects, so students will need to be aware of how they are used.

BE CONFIDENT

➔ Develop this skill for yourself by doing the following activity:

The pie chart contains data from a survey on critical thinking conducted by Cambridge University Press.

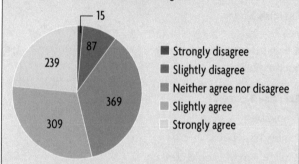

Responses of 1019 teachers to the statement 'I believe my students want to develop their critical thinking skills.'

- 15
- 87
- 239
- 369
- 309

■ Strongly disagree
■ Slightly disagree
■ Neither agree nor disagree
■ Slightly agree
■ Strongly agree

Does the data in the pie chart support or oppose the following statements?

1 The mode response was that people neither agreed nor disagreed.

2 A sizeable minority of respondents disagreed with the statement.

3 Most people were in general agreement with the statement.

4 About a quarter of respondents had a strong view.

Lead-in

Give students a minute to read the speaking task they will do at the end of the unit and keep it in mind as they do the next exercises. Ask them to brainstorm in groups about some possible ideas. Suggest they think about what can be done in both developing and developed countries. Tell them to keep their brainstorming notes for later, when they begin to develop their presentations.

UNL🔒CK TEACHER DEVELOPMENT

BE READY

Look at the Critical Thinking section in the Student's Book on pages 28–30.

➔ Which elements of the lesson do you think your students will find easiest / most difficult / most useful? Why?

➔ Are your answers true for all students in your class?

➔ How can you adapt your teaching or the material to meet your students' needs?

BE FLEXIBLE

When students do Exercise 5, question 4, it may be useful to encourage them to share any general sources of information. Otherwise, they may spend a lot of time searching for websites. Their time can then be maximized by looking for supporting information.

Exercise 1 pages 28–29

1 the percentage of profit for each step in the process; there are nine activities or steps in the process
2 *Answers will vary.*
3 They would increase; the other percentages would decrease.

Exercise 2 page 29

1 O   **2** S   **3** O   **4** O

Exercise 3 page 29

Possible answers:

1 the cost of storing, advertising and paying workers
2 The workers are paid little
3 Plantation owners have to pay for the land and growing supplies and workers do not.
4 It would increase. Other costs would also increase.

Exercises 4–5 page 30

Answers will vary.

UNL⊙CK TEACHER DEVELOPMENT

BE REFLECTIVE

Think about the following questions:

→ What would the pie chart in the *Be confident* section look like if you were to ask the opinions of teachers at your educational institution?

→ How confident were your students in using charts and data? Understanding their current level of knowledge in this area will help you during the course.

BE COLLABORATIVE

Your development is more meaningful when it is shared. See page 14 for ideas on how to peer-collaborate. Why not share the ideas you generated in the *Be ready* section, and their outcome?

PREPARATION FOR SPEAKING

Learning objectives

- Use phrases to complete the introduction to a presentation about specific data
- Use phrases to describe the data in a pie chart – *The largest part of the cost is administration. Labour accounts for 18% of the cost. Together, they make up 12% of the price you pay.*
- Use phrases for drawing conclusions from the data in a pie chart – *This data shows that the raw ingredients only account for 12% of the price you pay. In summary, the data shows that the two biggest parts of the cost of a cup of coffee are administration and labour.*

Exercises 1 and 2 page 31

1 I'd like to talk about   **2** a lot of discussion   **3** Many people believe   **4** others have pointed out   **5** They say
6 would like to show   **7** look at   **8** consider

Exercise 3 page 32

1 The largest part; more than a quarter of   **2** accounts for
3 each make up; a total of   **4** Three parts are related to; they make up

Exercise 4 page 33

a 3   **b** 1   **c** 5   **d** 7   **e** 6   **f** 2   **g** 4

Exercise 5 page 33

1 e   **2** a   **3** d   **4** c   **5** b

Be flexible

👥 Students work in pairs to re-tell this extract of the presentation, using the phrases from Exercises 4 and 5. When they have finished, you could play the extract again for them to compare it with their versions. Afterwards, ask some volunteers to re-tell the extract for the class.

Give **weaker students** more support. Students can practise presentation skills with familiar content by presenting the banana data in the pie chart on page 28.

Exercise 6 page 33

Possible answers:

fixed costs: tax, rent, labour; variable costs: cup / sugar / lid, coffee, milk, administration

SPEAKING TASK

Learning objectives

- Prepare for a presentation on how we can ensure that workers in developing countries are paid fairly for the goods and services we import, by organizing your notes
- Add support to your notes
- Write a conclusion for your presentation
- Give a presentation on how we can ensure that workers in developing countries are paid fairly for the goods and services we import
- Listen to and give feedback on other students' presentations

Exercises 1–5 page 34

Answers will vary.

RESEARCH PROJECT

Make a presentation about food journeys.

Divide the class into groups and ask each group to compile a list of their favourite foods. The groups research one of these foods, including where it comes from, its effect on health, how it is produced and how many miles it travels to get to their country. Students could use online tools to record and share their research.

The information could be used for group presentations. Alternatively, the class could collate their information, producing a world map showing 'food routes' for each of the foods they have researched, or a graph to show the distances the food has travelled. The data could form a starting point for thinking about the environmental or health impact of different foods.

CLASSROOM APP

Exercises 1–2

Answers will vary.

Exercise 3

1 These watches could come from Switzerland, but I'm not sure.
2 My new computer can't be from Mexico because there isn't a computer company there.
3 Both
4 Juan must have lived in Dubai because he speaks fluent Arabic and he told me his dad worked in the UAE.
5 The sweater must have been made overseas because I saw the label that says 'Made in the USA.'
6 Both

Exercise 4

1 goods 2 prosperity 3 imported 4 multinational
5 purchase 6 outsourcing 7 supply chain 8 transport

Exercise 5

1 consumers, discount 2 production costs, overseas, labour
3 profit, investigate

Exercise 6

1 I'd like to talk about 2 others have pointed out
3 They say 4 consider 5 would like to show
6 a lot of discussion

Exercise 7

Answers will vary.

UNIT OBJECTIVES

Watch and listen	Watch and understand a video about a school where students work on real science.
Listening skills	Listen for advice and suggestions; make inferences.
Critical thinking	Prioritize criteria; use priorities to evaluate options.
Grammar	Use the future continuous; state preferences with *would*.
Speaking skills	Give an opinion and make suggestions; agree and disagree respectfully; compromise and finalize a decision.
Speaking task	Decide as a group which candidate should receive a scholarship.
○ Teacher development	Help your students become better at **prioritizing criteria** and **using priorities to evaluate options**.

UNLOCK YOUR KNOWLEDGE

Background note

The photo shows scientists working in a laboratory. Careers in dentistry, medicine, law, architecture, science and research usually require several years of undergraduate and postgraduate study and a long period of on-the-job training. There are many well-paid careers that don't require a great deal of academic education. For example, commercial pilots, air traffic controllers, power plant operators, nurses, transport inspectors, electricians and line supervisors usually need to have finished secondary school and have completed further education, training or work until the age of 18 and/or have a specialized bachelor's degree. However, many of these careers require a great amount of on-the-job training.

Lead-in

Write the following quotes about education on the board. Students work in pairs to decide what each quote means and if they agree with the opinion in them. You may need to support them to make sure they understand some of the more difficult words and structures in the quotes. When they are ready, open up a class discussion on the quotes. You could have a class vote to decide on the best quote.

1 'Live as if you were to die tomorrow. Learn as if you were to live forever.' (Mahatma Gandhi, Indian independence leader)

2 'I have never let my schooling interfere with my education.' (Mark Twain, American author)

3 'Education is the most powerful weapon which you can use to change the world.' (Nelson Mandela, former President of South Africa)

4 'When you know better you do better.' (Maya Angelou, American author and poet)

5 'Kids don't remember what you try to teach them. They remember what you are.' (Jim Henson, American film and TV director and producer, creator of 'Sesame Street' and 'The Muppets')

page 37
Answers will vary.

WATCH AND LISTEN

Learning objectives

- Listen and understand main ideas in a video about the Langton School science programme
- Identify the opinions of speakers in the video
- Make inferences about science programmes
- Practise talking about science curriculums

Exercises 1–2 page 38

Answers will vary.

Exercise 3 page 39

1 T   **2** F; The school ignores the official government science curriculum.
3 F; Instead of just learning to pass the exam, the students contribute to science, do science and live science.
4 T   **5** T

Exercise 4 page 39

1 c   **2** a   **3** d   **4** b

Exercises 5–6 page 39

Answers will vary.

LISTENING 1

Learning objectives

- Understand key vocabulary for careers – *academic, acquire, adviser*
- Listen and identify main ideas and details in a meeting between a student and a careers adviser
- Listen for words signalling advice – *You should (consider) ..., I recommend ..., Wouldn't you rather ...?*
- Listen and complete details in a list of advice
- Listen and understand how certain a speaker is from their intonation
- Use language for certainty and uncertainty to describe ideas about careers – *I wonder if I should try something more vocational. Maybe you should consider Mechanical Engineering, then. Okay, but I'm not sure if that would be for me.*
- Evaluate careers advice

Lead-in

Put students in pairs or small groups. If they are students who have not decided on their career, ask them to discuss their possible career paths and why they think they might like a particular field. If they have already chosen their fields, they can discuss what motivated their choices.

Exercise 1 page 40

Answers will vary.

Exercise 2 pages 40–41

1 internship   **2** academic   **3** mechanical   **4** acquire
5 understanding   **6** adviser   **7** vocational   **8** specialist

Exercise 3 page 41

Answers will vary.

Exercise 4 page 41

1 what to do a degree in   **2** Engineering   **3** talk to some engineers, visit a careers fair and contact a Computer Engineering firm

Exercise 5 page 41

1 Engineering   **2** Mechanical   **3** academic
4 manual work   **5** talk to somebody
6 designing and making things

Exercise 6 page 42

1 Maths; Physics   **2** Mechanical   **3** Engineering
4 degrees   **5** universities; courses   **6** careers
7 graduates; jobs   **8** Computer; visit

Exercise 7 page 43

2 C   **3** C   **4** C   **5** U   **6** U   **7** C   **8** U

Exercise 8 page 43

Answers will vary.

Exercise 9 page 43

certain: definitely, for sure
uncertain: wonder, consider, not sure

Be flexible

Show students the sentences below. Ask them to underline the expressions in each sentence that they could use in other situations to express their opinions or question those of others. Ask them to write 'C' (certain) or 'U' (uncertain) next to each sentence. Check answers with the class.

1 Looking at your file, <u>I couldn't agree more!</u> (C)
2 Engineering jobs are <u>definitely</u> popular. (C)
3 <u>I think I could</u> do that. (U)
4 You <u>should definitely</u> attend that. (C)
5 <u>I'm sure we could</u> arrange for you to talk with them. (C)
6 <u>You might want to</u> try contacting a Computer Engineering firm here in the city, then. (U)
7 In fact, <u>I could</u> help you with that. <u>We could probably</u> arrange a visit for you. (U)

You can challenge **stronger students** by asking them to read the statements above with appropriate intonation to mark certainty/uncertainty.

Exercise 10 page 43

2 I wonder if I should study something technical.
3 I am certain I should try something more vocational.
4 You should definitely consider Mechanical Engineering, then.
5 Okay. I am sure that is for me.

Exercise 11 page 43

Answers will vary.

LANGUAGE DEVELOPMENT

Learning objectives

- Use the future continuous to talk about careers and holidays: plans and predictions – *Are you going to be working at Head Office next week? We will be taking a holiday after the exams.*
- Use the future continuous with adverbs of certainty – *I definitely won't be studying Nursing. I probably won't be having much fun until after final exams are finished. Ada is certainly going to be attending the careers fair.*
- Describe and ask about careers preferences with *would* – *Ada would prefer an internship at an Engineering company. I'd rather take a vocational course. Would you rather start work straight after graduation?*

Exercise 1 pages 44–45

1 will be studying   **2** is going to be using   **3** Will; be visiting   **4** will be taking   **5** will be attending   **6** will be calling   **7** Is; going to be choosing   **8** is going to be working

Exercise 2 page 45

Possible answers:

1 I certainly won't be studying on Friday night.

2 I will definitely be studying next week because I have an exam.

3 I probably won't be attending the match on Thursday afternoon …

4 I will likely be asking for help before Tuesday.

Exercise 3 page 45

Answers will vary.

Be flexible

👥 Ask students to work in pairs. Tell them to make predictions about what famous people will be doing in ten years. Encourage them to offer amusing or unlikely activities. If the names below are either inappropriate or unknown, ask students for the names of famous living people and create a list of six to eight people for the whole class before they begin the pair work. Remind them to explain what the person *will be doing*.

Melinda Gates, Jackie Chan, Donald Trump, Cristiano Ronaldo, Angela Merkel, Serena Williams

Reduce the challenge for **lower-level students** by asking one member of the pair to start the sentence (*In ten years, Serena Williams will be …*) and the second person to finish it (*… training a new player*).

Exercise 4 page 46

1 take   **2** to work   **3** participating   **4** to stay   **5** working   **6** see

Exercise 5 page 46

Answers will vary. Possible answers:

1 Would you prefer to work for a lot of money or for career satisfaction?

2 I'd rather study a diploma course.

3 Would they like to apply to a university in Riyadh?

4 He'd rather study Medicine.

5 Would she like to take a theoretical course?

6 I'd rather not start working right away.

LISTENING 2

Learning objectives

- Understand key vocabulary for describing professions – *manual, medical, technical*
- Take notes on the pros and cons of different career paths in a conversation between students about the medical profession
- Summarize a speaker's position on job preference
- Identify and evaluate opinions expressed by different speakers
- Make inferences about speakers' true opinions using tone and pitch
- Synthesize information from a meeting between a student and a careers adviser and a conversation between students about the medical profession in a discussion

Lead-in

Ask students to brainstorm about medical careers. Everyone knows about doctors, but what other careers are there in the medical field (e.g. midwife, radiologist, nurse, nutritionist)? What kind of training/education do these different careers require?

Exercise 1 pages 46–47

1 medical   **2** technical   **3** physical   **4** manual   **5** professional   **6** complex   **7** secure   **8** practical

Exercise 2 page 47

Answers will vary.

Exercise 3 page 48

Answers will vary. Possible answers:

emergency medical technician (EMT)	A&E (Accident and Emergency) nurse
Pros: exciting, takes less time, can become a specialist **Cons:** tough, physical job	**Pros:** pay is better **Cons:** takes more time

Exercise 4 page 48

EMT

Possible answers:

Adam wants to help people and have a practical and secure job. He wants to start work quickly. He doesn't want to do a lot more complex studying.

Exercise 5 page 48

1 medical student   **2** Adam   **3** Adam   **4** Adam
5 Adam   **6** medical student   **7** medical student   **8** Adam

Exercise 6 page 49

Possible answers:

Evidence: Adam talks about what an EMT does and what an A&E nurse does. Also, the course content, qualifications, who you work with after qualifying. They could also give figures for pay, specific course length, etc.

Exercise 7 page 49

Possible answers:

1 The medical student probably thinks Adam should do the EMT course, because he is so enthusiastic about it.

2 Helping people, being independent and making decisions on his own. He speaks more and his tone is more positive when he talks about these factors of the EMT job.

Optional activity

Ask students to review Listening 1 (either read the script or listen again). What can they infer? What does the adviser think Laura should do? What is the evidence for this conclusion? Does Laura change her mind about her plans during the interview? What is the evidence for this conclusion?

Suggested answers:

The adviser thinks she should study Mechanical Engineering: *Maybe you should consider Mechanical Engineering, then – as a start anyway. That's a good, basic Engineering degree – it covers the basic subjects. Mechanical Engineers often go on to become specialists in lots of different areas.* Then later, the adviser returns to this: *I suggest you find out more about engineering courses.*

Laura consents to investigating the possibility of an engineering career after the adviser offers to put her in touch with practising engineers.

Exercise 8 page 49

Answers will vary.

CRITICAL THINKING

Learning objectives

- Evaluate and rank criteria relating to choice of profession
- Evaluate and rank criteria relating to a scholarship
- Justify how you ranked criteria
- Evaluate and rank the value to society of different courses of study

UNLOCK TEACHER DEVELOPMENT

BE INFORMED

→ **Prioritizing criteria** and **using priorities to evaluate options** are important skills for students because: (1) Students may have very little experience of using criteria to make decisions, and the concept may be very new; (2) They may be unfamiliar with the concept of 'weighting', whereby different criteria are given different levels of importance; (3) Critical thinking topics are relevant not only to their academic work but also to practical work – for example, when applying for scholarships, university places or jobs.

BE CONFIDENT

→ Develop these skills for yourself by doing the following activity:

Imagine that your educational institution is going to award a prize for critical thinking. Five criteria have been agreed upon. How would you prioritize these criteria? (1 = most important, 5 = least important)

1 Can learners distinguish between reasoned and logical arguments? ___

2 Can learners understand the connections between ideas? ___

3 Can learners organize their thoughts and approach problems in systematic ways? ___

4 Can learners identify and understand arguments in texts? ___

5 Can learners reflect on their own assumptions, beliefs, values and judgements? ___

Lead-in

Give students a minute to read the speaking task they will do at the end of the unit and keep it in mind as they do the next exercises. Ask them to brainstorm in groups for a few minutes. What kind of student makes a good candidate for a scholarship? Tell them to keep their brainstorming notes for later, when they begin preparing for their discussions.

UNLOCK TEACHER DEVELOPMENT

BE READY

Look at the Critical Thinking section in the Student's Book on pages 50–52.

→ Which elements of the lesson do you think your students will find easiest / most difficult / most useful? Why?

→ Are your answers true for all students in your class?

→ How can you adapt your teaching or the material to meet your students' needs?

BE FLEXIBLE

An alternative way of starting Exercise 2, in particular for classes who know each other well, is to begin by getting students to predict their partner's responses.

Exercises 1–5 pages 50–52

Answers will vary.

UNLOCK TEACHER DEVELOPMENT

BE REFLECTIVE

Think about the following questions:

→ The questions in the *Be confident* section were asked in a critical thinking survey of teachers by Cambridge University Press. In the survey, the criteria were prioritized as follows: *5, 3, 2, 1, 4*. Were your answers the same? Why / Why not?

→ Did students have any practical or real-life experience of the critical thinking focus (e.g. when applying for a job or university place)? Getting students to link the theory of critical thinking with the reality is a very effective tool.

BE COLLABORATIVE

Your development is more meaningful when it is shared. See page 14 for ideas on how to peer-collaborate. Why not share the ideas you generated in the *Be ready* section, and their outcome?

PREPARATION FOR SPEAKING

Learning objectives

- Discriminate between phrases for giving an opinion and making suggestions – *I think the most important factor is probably financial need. Why don't we rank the proposed courses of study according to their contribution to society? I feel it's important to really focus on the applicants' potential contribution to society.*
- Discriminate between formal and informal language for agreeing and disagreeing – *Sorry, but I have to disagree. Yes, I can see that. Yes, but it seems like a great way to really help people.*
- Use formal language to agree and disagree respectfully with opinions about careers
- Complete phrases for compromising and finalizing a decision – *I see. That's understandable. OK, I see your point. I think we've come to an agreement.*
- Communicate certainty and uncertainty using intonation

Exercises 1 and 2 page 53

1 e **2** d **3** a **4** f **5** c **6** b

1, 2 and 6 give an opinion; 3, 4 and 5 are suggestions.

Exercise 3 page 54

1 D **2** A **3** A **4** D **5** D **6** D **7** A

1, 2, 4, 6 and 7 are formal responses; 3 and 5 are informal.

Exercise 4 page 54

Answers will vary.

Optional activity

You could turn the statements from Exercise 4 into a full class discussion, where everyone has a chance to express their real opinion on all six statements. Encourage students to use the language from Exercise 3 to do this.

Exercises 5–6 page 55

1 understandable **2** point **3** right **4** that **5** decision **6** agreement

Exercise 7 page 55

1 C **2** C **3** U **4** U **5** C **6** U

Exercise 8 page 55

Answers will vary.

SPEAKING TASK

Learning objectives

- Take part in a group discussion and rank candidates for a scholarship
- Decide which candidate should receive a scholarship
- Present and justify ideas about who should receive a scholarship (one student per group only)

Exercises 1–5 page 56

Answers will vary.

RESEARCH PROJECT

Create a video about a course at university.

In groups, ask the class to make a list of some of the courses on offer at universities in their country. Each group should then choose one to research, finding out how long the course is, the topic areas it covers, student opinions for studying it, and what types of career the course can lead to. Students could find this information online or by contacting the university and/or students directly.

Each group then produces a five-minute video about the course for people considering studying that subject at university. Students will need to create a script, think about who in the group will film the video, who will edit it, and who will present the information. The videos could then be uploaded to a video-sharing website.

CLASSROOM APP

Exercises 1–2

Answers will vary.

Exercise 3

1 We will be studying for the entrance exams this spring.
2 We are going to be taking business classes next year.
3 Will you be studying engineering at university?
4 Are you going to visit your sister in the holidays?
5 I won't be taking time off from work.
6 I will probably be studying nursing like my mum.
7 Juan is definitely going to be auditioning for the school play.
8 Ali certainly won't be practising football until after his final exams are over.

Exercise 4

1 learn   2 working   3 to eat   4 to be   5 get   6 to bake   7 start   8   to go

Exercise 5

1 manual   2 physical   3 professional   4 technical   5 complex   6 medical   7 practical   8 secure

Exercise 6A

1 to concentrate on learning English   2 getting
3 consider both academic and vocational career options
4 studying the humanities is just as important as studying the sciences   5 applying at colleges in Europe
6 to consider colleges that are international

Exercise 6B

Answers will vary

UNIT OBJECTIVES	
Watch and listen	Watch and understand a video about a device which provides instant results to 33 tests.
Listening skills	Identify contrasting opinions; strengthen points in an argument.
Critical thinking	Analyze background and motivation.
Grammar	Use the third conditional; use the second conditional for unreal situations.
Speaking skill	Create persuasive arguments.
Speaking task	Role play a debate.
⟳ **Teacher development**	Help your students become better at **evaluating arguments**.

UNL⟳CK YOUR KNOWLEDGE

Background note

The photo shows a woman comforting her son after his first flu vaccination. Currently, in the UK, most children are vaccinated against diphtheria, tetanus, whooping cough, polio, Haemophilus influenzae type B and hepatitis B, among other diseases. Other diseases that are preventable with vaccination are chickenpox, flu, measles, mumps, rubella, meningitis, tuberculosis and yellow fever. There are still many diseases without a high-efficacy vaccine, such as malaria, dengue fever and many others. Diseases spread differently – some are spread through coughing, sneezing or by touch, and some are spread through water or by insects. Vaccines help stop the spread of disease and save lives. However, some people believe that vaccines are not safe, and could cause other illnesses and health conditions.

Lead-in

Students work in teams to brainstorm medical vocabulary for the following categories. (You could add your own categories to make the exercise more challenging.)

* illnesses
* people involved in medicine
* places involved in medicine
* medical equipment
* medical verbs
* medical procedures (ways of helping sick people)

The first team to think of at least four words in each category, or alternatively 24 words in total, is the winner.

page 59

Answers will vary.

WATCH AND LISTEN

Learning objectives

* Listen and understand main ideas in a video about a medical innovation
* Listen and understand details
* Make inferences about the ideas in the video and their wider implications
* Practise talking about healthcare technology

Exercises 1–2 page 60

Answers will vary.

Exercise 3 pages 60–61

1 T

2 T

3 F; The patients are mainly the underprivileged.

4 F; The government plans to open 1,000 such community clinics.

5 T

6 F; India spends less than 1.5% of its GDP on public health.

Exercise 4 page 61

1 making all the difference; instant results of; storing medical records

2 made for the top one percent of the world; work in conditions and environments that are not necessarily very friendly

3 1.5% of its GDP on public health; medical cost

Exercises 5–6 page 61

Answers will vary.

Learning objectives

- Understand key vocabulary for disease – *contract*, *factor*, *infected*
- Use a text and a map to predict the main ideas in a seminar about pandemics
- Listen and take notes on the main causes of pandemics
- Listen and complete a detailed set of notes with opinions
- Listen and understand speakers' attitudes from intonation in question tags
- Evaluate risks and make suggestions and predictions about pandemics

Lead-in

Ask students to brainstorm about major outbreaks of infectious diseases in recent history (e.g. SARS, MERS, avian flu, Ebola). What steps did governments take to stop the spread of these diseases? Make a list on the board.

Exercise 1 page 62

a occur   b recover   c contract   d infected
e prevention   f outbreak   g treatment   h factor

Exercise 2 page 63

1 people's general health, how close they live together
2 large populations, people living close together, many international travellers, wealthier countries
3 high-risk countries are in dark blue; low-risk countries are in light blue

Exercise 3 page 63

See answers for Exercise 2.

Exercise 4 page 63

1 Possible causes of pandemics: poor general health, lack of vaccines

2 Possible factors making a country high risk: large populations living close together, many international travellers

Exercise 6 page 64

1 may not be effective this year
2 might not work
3 before they even know they have them
4 set up a system for checking if people have a disease
5 have a terrible effect on the economy
6 stop a lot of people going to work and it could separate families

Exercise 7 page 65

3 U   4 A   5 A   6 A   7 A   8 A

Exercise 8 page 65

1 b   2 a   3 a

Optional activity

👥 Take a section of the script and break it into sentences. Ask students to work in pairs to create tag questions for each, trying both types of intonation. One creates the tag question and the other has to guess the meaning – seeking agreement or expressing uncertainty. These are more challenging than the examples on page 65 because there are two clauses, so remind students that the tag should be based on the *main* verb in the *final* clause (bolded in the examples below):

1 They should give a vaccine to people as soon as an outbreak occurs, because prevention **is** generally much easier than treatment, (isn't it?)

2 When governments focus on the prevention of disease, pandemics **become** very rare, (don't they?)

Exercise 9 page 65

Answers will vary.

LANGUAGE DEVELOPMENT

Learning objectives

- Identify the meaning of health science vocabulary from context – *aid*, *antibiotic*, *prevention*
- Use the third conditional to describe the consequences of hypothetical past actions to complete a conversation about a pandemic – *If she had gone to school that day, she would have caught the flu. If you had gone on your trip, you might have caught the virus.*
- Use the correct form of verbs in second conditional sentences about illnesses – *If people stopped having vaccines, there would be pandemics. If people got vaccinated, they could avoid many illnesses.*

Exercise 1 page 66

1 a   2 a   3 a   4 a   5 b   6 b   7 b   8 a

Exercise 2 pages 67–68

1 had developed   2 might not have happened
3 might have survived   4 had found   5 hadn't focused
6 could have discovered   7 had questioned
8 would have realized   9 had allowed
10 wouldn't have called

Be flexible

👥 Ask students to think about regrets they have about something they did or didn't do. Why do they regret it? What should they have done instead? Tell them to make a list. Then in pairs, they exchange lists and ask each other questions. The phrase in bold in the example below can be used for each question.

Example of a regret + reason from Student 1's list: *I chose an arts degree. It's been really hard to find a job.*

Student 2 asks: *If you had realized the difficulty of finding a job with an arts degree, **what would you have done differently**?*

Student 1 responds: *If I had realized that, I would have done a degree in medicine.*

Then students change roles and repeat the process.

If this activity is too easy for **more advanced students**, increase the level of difficulty by asking them to talk about the result of a negative condition.

*If the government **hadn't provided** financial assistance, I couldn't have done a university degree.*

*If I **hadn't stayed** home from school last week, I would have caught the flu.*

Exercise 3 page 68

Answers will vary. Possible answers:

2 If it were available **3** If there weren't an outbreak
4 we might need the vaccine **5** she wouldn't be worried

LISTENING 2

Learning objectives

- Understand key vocabulary for medicine – *clinical, controlled, precaution*
- Predict, listen and understand main ideas in a debate about flu vaccinations
- Create a T-chart to organize notes on main ideas
- Listen and take notes on main ideas
- Listen and understand details
- Identify different techniques for supporting arguments
- Synthesize ideas from a seminar about pandemics and a debate about flu vaccinations in a discussion

Lead-in

Ask students if they were vaccinated as children. For what diseases? What do they know about these diseases (e.g. the morbidity rate of smallpox)? Have they continued to get vaccinations? Against what diseases?

Exercise 1 page 69

1 prove **2** clinical **3** researchers **4** precautions
5 in favour of **6** controlled **7** data **8** trials

Exercise 2 page 69

1 don't agree **2** believe **3** haven't **4** Some

Exercise 3 page 70

See answers for Exercise 2.

Exercise 4 page 70

Possible answers:

Dr Sandra Smith: Overall, flu vaccination is a good idea. New flu vaccines need to be made each year as the virus changes. No evidence that flu vaccine is harmful. Certain people should definitely have the flu vaccine, such as children, people over 65, pregnant women and anybody who already has a serious illness.

Mark Li: The flu vaccine isn't a good idea. It isn't scientifically tested. The flu vaccine can make you ill. Nobody should have the flu vaccine.

Exercise 6 page 70

1 F; Hundreds of thousands of people get ill from the flu every year. **2** F; The majority of the population does not receive the flu vaccine. **3** T **4** F; He is not against all vaccines, just some. **5** F; There is no scientific evidence that the vaccine doesn't work. **6** F; There is no scientific evidence that the flu vaccine makes people ill.

Exercise 7 page 71

1 d **2** c **3** a **4** e **5** b

Optional activity

👤 Students underline the parts of the examples in Exercise 7 that they could use in the debates in the final speaking task.

Exercise 8 page 71

Answers will vary.

CRITICAL THINKING

Learning objectives

- Use background information to analyze the motivation behind speakers' arguments about vaccinations
- Hypothesize about the opinions of medical professionals on a range of healthcare issues
- Analyze and note your group's background and motivation in preparation for a role play debate

UNLOCK TEACHER DEVELOPMENT

BE INFORMED

→ **Evaluating arguments** is an important skill for students because: (1) Different people / organizations can interpret the same thing in very different ways; (2) Sometimes people can sound very convincing (e.g. by using complicated language), when the actual content of their argument is weak; (3) When writing essays, you are not assessed on the number of arguments you make, but on the quality of your arguments.

BE CONFIDENT

→ Develop these skills for yourself by doing the following activity:

Imagine that a group of teachers were asked the following question: 'Are your students good at critical thinking?'. These are some of the responses.

'My students are poor critical thinkers because they do not enjoy it.'

'My students are really good at critical thinking, so I must be a good teacher.'

'My students do not have any opportunity to practise critical thinking, so they do not improve.'

'My students work hard to improve their critical thinking skills, because they see its relevance to their studies and lives.'

1 Which of these arguments are the strongest? Which are the weakest?

2 What is the problem with the arguments which are poorly supported? How could they be improved?

Lead-in

Give students a minute to read the speaking task they will do at the end of the unit and keep it in mind as they do the next exercises. Have them brainstorm in groups for a few minutes, by asking, *What do you think? Of course, it would be nice if healthcare were free, but it's never really free. Somebody has to pay. Who pays in a 'free' system?* Tell them to keep their brainstorming notes for later, when they begin to prepare for their debates.

UNLOCK TEACHER DEVELOPMENT

BE READY

Look at the Critical Thinking section in the Student's Book on pages 180–182.

→ Which elements of the lesson do you think your students will find easiest / most difficult / most useful? Why?

→ Are your answers true for all students in your class?

→ How can you adapt your teaching or the material to meet your students' needs?

BE FLEXIBLE

Think of a recent event (e.g. in the news, or in your school/college) where different people have different opinions about the same thing. This would make an interesting introduction to the topic, and offer a good opportunity to apply this knowledge.

Exercises 1–2 pages 72–73
Answers will vary.

Exercises 3–4 page 73

1 M **2** S **3** S **4** M **5** M **6** S

Exercise 5 page 73
Possible answers:

1 **ML:** it's natural, it's better than modern medicine; **SS:** it isn't proven to work, it doesn't help you

2 **ML:** this is what people have always done and it works; **SS:** medicine is much more effective than food

3 **ML:** they're just trying to make you think you're ill and sell you a cure; **SS:** it's a valuable way for people to learn about how to treat illnesses

4 **Both:** exercise has been proved to have positive health benefits

5 **ML:** the fever is a natural part of the illness, you don't need to give the child medicine; **SS:** paracetamol or ibuprofen will help the child feel better

6 **ML:** this may be a good idea, but clinical treatment may still not work for everyone; **SS:** this is the best thing we can do to prevent illness and disease

Exercises 6–7 page 74
Answers will vary.

UNLOCK TEACHER DEVELOPMENT

BE REFLECTIVE

Think about the following questions:

→ Evaluate how successful your teaching of critical thinking was. Which part was most successful? Which part was least successful? Why?

→ If you heard a teaching colleague make one of the weak arguments (or similar) in the *Be confident* section opposite, what might you say to them?

BE COLLABORATIVE

Your development is more meaningful when it is shared. See page 14 for ideas on how to peer-collaborate. Why not share the ideas you generated in the *Be flexible* section, and their outcome?

PREPARATION FOR SPEAKING

Learning objectives

- Identify different strategies used in persuasive arguments – personal examples, challenging questions, persuasive language, addressing opposing arguments, presenting factual support for a position
- Create persuasive arguments using a variety of techniques

Exercise 1 page 76

1 d **2** a **3** e **4** b **5** c

Exercises 2–3 page 77

Answers will vary.

Be flexible

👥 Ask students to work in pairs to create persuasive statements that include the elements listed in Exercise 1 (personal example, challenging questions, etc.) for or against raising the price of cigarettes as a way to make people give up smoking (or choose another health-related issue). They should use just one element per statement. Then they compare their work to another pair's work.

Provide more support for **weaker students** in the class. Tell them to think about the background and point of view of the person who might make each of the statements in the optional activity above (i.e. their background, personal and professional motivations, and role in society – see the Skills box on page. 72). What kind of person would say this? Why might he or she have this opinion?

SPEAKING TASK

Learning objectives

- Prepare to role play a debate between representatives of an aid organization and a drug company by allocating roles, and reviewing and adding to notes
- Prepare an opening statement of your position for a debate
- Anticipate opposing positions and prepare counter–arguments
- Take part in a debate between representatives of an aid organization and a drug company

Exercises 1–7 pages 77–78

Answers will vary.

RESEARCH PROJECT

Create a podcast about deadly diseases.

Ask students to think about diseases which used to be very common or deadly, but which are now under control or treatable (smallpox, polio, etc.). Divide the class into groups and ask each group to research one of these diseases, including how it is/was spread, treatment and prevention, and the long-term effects of the illness.

Each group then creates a three-minute podcast of this information to share with other groups. This could be shared in class or using online tools. The podcasts could also be used as the basis for short listening tests, whereby each group prepares one or two tasks for the rest of the class, based on their recording.

CLASSROOM APP

Exercise 1

Answers will vary.

Exercise 2

1 recover   **2** trials   **3** prevention   **4** aid   **5** urgent
6 antibiotic   **7** treat   **8** virus

Exercise 3

1 she had taken vitamins, she would not have got sick.
2 If you had gone to the doctor, you might have got some antibiotics.
3 The school could have avoided closing if it had had a school nurse to treat students when the flu started spreading.

4 If I had got the flu vaccine, I wouldn't have got sick when the flu spread.

5 I wouldn't have needed an antibiotic if I had listened to my doctor and rested more.

6 The government could have prevented a flu outbreak if it had offered vaccines to the citizens.

Exercise 4

1 stopped   **2** recommended   **3** were   **4** be
5 close   **6** were

Exercise 5

1 trials   **2** prove   **3** researcher   **4** clinical   **5** controlled
6 precautions   **7** in favour of   **8** data

Exercise 6

Answers will vary.

Exercise 7

1 giving personal examples   **2** addressing the opposing argument   **3** asking challenging questions   **4** presenting support for a position   **5** giving personal examples
6 presenting support for a position

UNIT OBJECTIVES

Watch and listen	Watch and understand a video about cloning endangered species.
Listening skills	Distinguish main ideas from details; take notes on main ideas and details.
Critical thinking	Organize information in a presentation.
Grammar	Use multi-word prepositions; use the past perfect.
Speaking skills	Give background information and explain a problem; use signposting language in a presentation.
Speaking task	Give a problem and solution presentation.
⊘ Teacher development	Help your students become better at **organizing information in a presentation**.

UNLOCK YOUR KNOWLEDGE

Background note

The photo shows industrial vehicles sorting out logs at a sawmill on Vancouver Island, British Columbia, Canada. Deforestation means removing trees from an area to make space for agriculture, urbanization or transport. British Columbia has experienced heavy deforestation. Some negative effects of deforestation include destroying the natural environment of animals, causing an increase in carbon dioxide and greenhouse gas emissions, and soil erosion.

Other ways that humans have an impact on the environment include farming, fishing, energy production, mining, transport and manufacturing. Certain man-made materials, such as plastics, paint and chemicals, can have a negative effect on the environment. Some ways we can use natural resources responsibly are by reducing what we use, recycling and re-using things we already have.

Lead-in

Write the following questions on the board for students to discuss in small groups.

1 What does the word *environment* mean to you?
2 What are some examples of threats to the environment (a) in your country, (b) in other countries?
3 Do you think it is important for us to protect the environment? Why / Why not?
4 Do you do anything to help the environment?

page 81

Answers will vary.

WATCH AND LISTEN

Learning objectives

- Listen and identify main ideas in a video about cloning endangered species
- Listen and understand details
- Make inferences about the successes and dangers of cloning based on the information in the video
- Practise talking about endangered species

Exercises 1–2 page 82

Answers will vary.

Exercise 3 page 83

b

Exercise 4 page 83

1 because the cloning of the banteng is the most successful cloning yet

2 by injecting the banteng's genetic material into the egg of a living cow

3 because it is pointless being able to produce more endangered animals unless we protect the habitat and deal with the root causes of endangerment

Exercises 5–6 page 83

Answers will vary.

LISTENING 1

Learning objectives

- Understand key vocabulary for the environment – *adapt*, *coastal*, *conservation*
- Predict and listen and understand how details relate to main ideas in a lecture about habitat destruction
- Listen and complete a set of detailed notes
- Use detailed notes to complete a summary
- Identify the speaker's opinion on human activities and habitat destruction
- Gain awareness of the use of pauses in prepared speech
- Describe habitats and wildlife in areas you know well

Lead-in

Ask students to think about the impact of human activity on the environment and, specifically, on other organisms. In pairs or small groups, they make two lists: (1) animals that have suffered as a result of human activity; and (2) animals that have thrived as the result of human activity or living near humans. If they have trouble with the second, prompt them by asking them to think about pests (e.g. rats, insects, monkeys). Pairs exchange and compare their lists.

Exercise 1 page 84

1 conservation **2** habitats **3** waste **4** coastal **5** adapt **6** exploit **7** impact **8** modify

Exercise 2 page 85

Planet Earth is dynamic and always changing.

i, g, b, e, c, j

Habitat destruction hasn't been bad news for all animals.

f, h, a, d

Exercise 3 page 85

See answers for Exercise 2.

Exercise 4 page 86

Suggested answers:

1 10% **2** natural (causes) **3** 800 square kilometres **4** rivers were blocked **5** 16 million **6** 9 million **7** fragmentation **8** fish and other sea life **9** Africa and Asia **10** Australia, Europe, Japan, North America **11** Mumbai **12** diets **13** fruit, plants, nuts and rodents **14** rubbish **15** pollution **16** resources **17** waste

Exercise 5 page 87

1 10,000 **2** rainforest **3** 9 **4** 160,000 **5** rubbish **6** pollution

Exercise 6 page 87

1 a **2** b **3** a

Exercise 7 page 88

Answers are in the Student's Book.

Exercise 8 page 88

One other animal that is as at home in the city as in the countryside [/ /] is the raccoon. [/ /] In fact, [/ /] raccoons are so at home in the city that the number of city raccoons has increased. [/ /] Raccoons have different diets depending on their environment. [/ /] Common foods include fruit, [/ /], plants [/ /], nuts [/ /] and rodents. [/ /] Much like the foxes of London, [/ /] raccoons living in the city are known to eat rubbish out of bins, [/ /] steal food from people's homes [/ /] and occasionally bite people.

Exercise 9 page 88

Answers will vary.

Be flexible

👥 Tell students to look at the script for Listening 1 on page 208. In pairs, students choose one paragraph (or part of a paragraph) from the lecture and insert pause symbols (/ /) where appropriate. They practise saying their paragraphs, paying particular attention to the pauses. When they are ready, ask volunteers to present their ideas to the class. Play the recording again to compare students' ideas with the original.

You could provide **weaker students** with more support by choosing one paragraph for the whole class to work with. Students should still work in pairs. Note that even if students' versions are different, this does not necessarily mean that they are wrong. If students are still having difficulty, play the recording again so that students can compare their ideas with the original.

Exercise 10 page 88

Answers will vary.

LANGUAGE DEVELOPMENT

Exercise 1 page 89

1 b   2 e   3 a   4 d   5 c

Exercise 2 page 89

1 Based on   2 due to   3 According to   4 instead of
5 as well as   6 except for

Exercise 3 page 90

Answers will vary.

Exercise 4 page 91

1 wrote   2 had spent   3 did   4 had; published
5 began   6 used   7 sprayed   8 had heard   9 decided
10 had released   11 attacked   12 responded

Exercise 5 page 91

1 settled; had been   2 began; had used   3 had not /
hadn't noticed; saw   4 erupted; had evacuated

Optional activity

👥 Give out slips of paper, each with a time in the past (or implied time in the past), for example, *by 2010, by last October, by my 15th birthday, when I got my first job*. Students work in pairs. They say something they had already completed by that time (using the past perfect). Offer an example:
*When I moved to Istanbul, I **had** already **finished** my degree.*

Exercise 6 page 92

1 adapted   2 survived   3 declined   4 extracted
5 impacted   6 affect   7 occurred   8 exploited

LISTENING 2

Lead-in

Ask students if they have ever been to a desert, and if so, to describe what it was like. Would they want to live there? Why / Why not? (If nobody has been to a desert, have a picture of the desert ready to help them imagine it.)

If the students live in a desert country, ask them to describe how living in a desert country/community is different from life in more temperate and wetter habitats. How is their daily life affected by the habitat?

Exercise 1 page 93

Answers will vary.

Exercise 2 page 93

a mining   b natural gas   c minerals   d diamond
e harsh   f wilderness   g copper

Exercise 3 page 94

Suggested answers:

1 Decline and destruction of deserts   2 exploit
3 ecosystem   4 dust and dirt   5 die   6 soil   7 manage
8 technological

Exercise 4 page 94

a 6   b 7   c 1   d 8   e 2   f 3   g 5   h 4

Exercise 5 page 94

1 25%   2 North Africa   3 copper, gold and other metals
4 hot and dry, with stable soil   5 Arabian oryx   6 solar

Exercise 6 page 95

1 b   2 a   3 c

Exercise 7 page 95

a background information   **b** offer a solution
c explain a problem

Optional activity

👥 Write the following words and phrases from Listening 2 in two columns on the board. Students work in pairs to make collocations. They could check their answers in the script on pages 209–210, or listen to the recording again. In class feedback, make sure everyone understands all the collocations.

1 threats	a variety of
2 background	b available
3 freely	c dwellers
4 power	d habitat
5 city	e information
6 a wide	f life
7 animal	g generation
8 way of	h to this environment

Exercise 8 page 95

Answers will vary.

CRITICAL THINKING

Learning objectives

- Complete an outline of a presentation with main ideas and details
- Understand the key features of an outline of a presentation
- Research and create an outline of a presentation on an environmental topic
- Give and respond to feedback on the outline of your presentation

UNL⟳CK TEACHER DEVELOPMENT

BE INFORMED

→ **Organizing information in a presentation** is an important skill for students because: (1) Students often find giving presentations difficult, and having some kind of clear structure to follow would help them become better at this; (2) Developing an outline as part of their planning can help to clarify the connections between main points, specific examples and details; (3) It can help them follow lectures and speeches more easily.

BE CONFIDENT

→ Develop this skill for yourself by doing the following activity:

Look at the example of an outline on page 96 of the Student's Book. Create a similar outline for a short presentation on the topic below.

Topic: Why critical thinking is important for young people

Introduction (background information):

_____

I. Main idea: _____
  A. Detail: _____
    a. Example: _____
    b. Example: _____
  B. Detail: _____

II. Main idea: _____
  A. Detail: _____
    a. Example: _____
  B. Detail: _____
    a. Example: _____

Solutions: _____
_____
_____
_____
_____
_____
_____
_____
_____

What did you learn by doing this task?

Lead-in

Give students a minute to read the speaking task they will do at the end of the unit and keep it in mind as they do the next exercises. Ask them to brainstorm in groups for a few minutes about where they can find information about both the problem and the solution. Tell them to keep their brainstorming notes for later, when they begin to develop their presentation.

BE READY

Look at the Critical Thinking section in the Student's Book on pages 96–97.

→ Which elements of the lesson do you think your students will find easiest / most difficult / most useful? Why?

→ Are your answers true for all students in your class?

→ How can you adapt your teaching or the material to meet your students' needs?

BE FLEXIBLE

Students do not necessarily need to be restricted to the topics given in Exercise 3. Let them research a different topic (as long as it is relevant) if they have a particular interest in it. It may be that particular topics may be more relevant depending on where they live (e.g. global warming if living in country affected by it).

Exercise 1 page 96

Topic: Decline and destruction of deserts

Introduction (background information): <u>Desert environment and wildlife</u>

I. Main idea: <u>Human survival</u>

A. Detail: <u>People in deserts</u>

  a. Example: Topnaar

  b. Example: Bedouins

B. Detail: <u>People in cities</u>

II. Main idea: <u>Plant and animal survival</u>

A. Detail: <u>Desert plants</u>

  a. Example: Acacia tree

B. Detail: <u>Desert animals</u>

  a. Example: Arabian oryx

Solutions: Manage desert resources carefully instead of abusing them; apply technological solutions; <u>use wind and solar energy</u> to provide clean energy in existing desert cities

Exercise 2 page 97

1 T 2 T

3 F; The outline doesn't tell the speaker exactly what to say in the presentation.

4 F; The outline includes only relevant details about the talk.

Exercises 3–5 page 97

Answers will vary.

UNLOCK TEACHER DEVELOPMENT

BE REFLECTIVE

Think about the following questions:

→ Is there an opportunity for you to give the presentation you planned in the *Be confident* section? If not in person, perhaps you could record it and share with colleagues, and they could do the same.

→ Some students can feel scared or anxious when giving a presentation. Did creating an outline and organizing the information give your students more confidence when thinking about doing their presentation for the speaking task?

BE COLLABORATIVE

Your development is more meaningful when it is shared. See page 14 for ideas on how to peer-collaborate. Why not share the ideas you generated in the *Be ready* section, and their outcome?

PREPARATION FOR SPEAKING

Learning objectives

- Understand the function of sentences giving background information and explaining a problem
- Use signposting language to give examples, to signal transition and to give conclusions – *Let's begin by looking at background information. A good example of this is Egyptian cotton. But what does this mean for the rest of the world?*

Exercise 1 page 98

1 a **2** b **3** e **4** d **5** f **6** c

Optional activity

👤 Ask students to review the following extract from the audioscript of Listening 2 (Track 4.5 on page 209–210), which gives background information at the beginning of the lecture:

'Let's begin by looking at some background information from the United Nations Environment Programme. The United Nations reports in *Global Deserts Outlook* that the Earth's deserts cover about 33.7 million square kilometres, or about 25% of the Earth's surface. Deserts are home to 500 million people, or about 8% of the world's population.'

How did the background information help them to understand the rest of the lecture? If they hadn't read this background information, what would have been difficult to understand in the lecture? (This question also gives practice in the third conditional.)

Exercise 2 page 99

1 e **2** g **3** d **4** f **5** c **6** a **7** h **8** b

Exercise 3 page 99

1 c **2** f **3** d **4** h **5** a **6** e **7** g **8** b

SPEAKING TASK

Learning objectives

- Prepare for a presentation about a change in the environment by reviewing your notes and adding new information
- Prepare an introduction for your presentation
- Review your solutions and select signposting language to signal your conclusions
- Give a presentation about a change in the environment and discuss possible solutions

Exercises 1–6 page 100

Answers will vary.

RESEARCH PROJECT

Create a website about an environmental threat.

Ask students to make a list of different environmental problems and then decide on one which they consider may be a real threat to them (desertification, flooding, droughts, destruction of trees, loss of biodiversity, etc.). Students could use online tools to share and discuss their ideas.

Students create a class website outlining the causes and dangers of their chosen environmental threat, as well as what can be done about it. If they are not sure how to start, suggest that they search 'create free website'. They could include audio clips, videos and images on the website.

CLASSROOM APP

Exercises 1–2

Answers will vary.

Exercise 3

1 to **2** on **3** to **4** to **5** from **6** with **7** of **8** as

Exercise 4

1 moved; had caused **2** had begun; covered
3 had lectured; hadn't lectured
4 were discovered; hadn't paid attention

Exercise 5

1 adapt **2** diamond **3** coastal **4** harsh **5** modify
6 waste **7** conservation **8** exploit

Exercise 6

1 give an example **2** start a new topic **3** make a conclusion **4** give an example **5** start a new topic

UNIT OBJECTIVES	
Watch and listen	Watch and understand a video about skyscrapers.
Listening skills	Understand figurative language; understand strong and tentative suggestions.
Critical thinking	Compare and evaluate solutions.
Grammar	Use *will* and *be going to* for predictions and expectations.
Speaking skills	Present a problem; make polite suggestions; respond to suggested solutions.
Speaking task	Discuss a housing problem and possible solutions.
↻ **Teacher development**	Help your students become better at **comparing and evaluating solutions**.

UNLOCK YOUR KNOWLEDGE

Background note

The photo shows the Hotel Marqués de Riscal in Elciego, Spain. The hotel was designed by the award-winning Canadian architect, Frank Gehry, and was opened in 2006. Gehry's design has angled walls, zigzag windows and curved lines, and uses unusual materials. It is a small luxury hotel located in an agricultural region in northwest Spain, among famous Spanish vineyards. The hotel attracts a lot of visitors to the area. Other famous buildings by Gehry include the Guggenheim Museum in Bilbao, Spain, and the Walt Disney Concert Hall in Los Angeles, California, the USA.

Lead-in

On the board, write *Architectural Wonders of the World*. Elicit briefly from the class what the phrase means. Students work in small groups to brainstorm a list of ten examples of architectural wonders. When they are ready, ask volunteers from each group to present their ideas to the class. Discuss with the class similarities and differences between their lists. If some students have never heard of some of the wonders, ask the student who suggested it to explain what it is and why it is so special.

page 103

1 This is the Hotel Marqués de Riscal in Elciego, Spain. It was designed by Frank Gehry.

2–3 *Answers will vary.*

WATCH AND LISTEN

Learning objectives

- Listen and understand main ideas in a video about skyscrapers
- Listen and complete a set of notes with details
- Make inferences about architecture
- Practise talking about buildings

Exercises 1–2 page 104

Answers will vary.

Exercise 3 page 105

1 F; Skyscrapers originated in Chicago.   **2** T
3 F; The first skyscraper was completed in 1889.   **4** T   **5** T

Exercise 4 page 105

1 a fire in 1871   **2** Chicago   **3** Michigan Avenue, Chicago
4 300,000 corporations in the United States   **5** American corporate success

Exercises 5–6 page 105

Answers will vary.

LISTENING 1

Learning objectives

- Understand key vocabulary for property development – *investment, contemporary, potential*
- Listen and understand main problems discussed by two property developers
- Listen and complete detailed notes on solutions
- Understand the meaning and function of figurative language – *biting off more than we can chew, a new lease of life, a potential goldmine*
- Create personalized examples using figurative language
- Understand the use of contrastive stress to emphasize alternatives in discussions
- Give opinions on the renovation and uses of old or historical buildings

Lead-in

Students work in small groups. Ask them to think about an area in their city that has become more popular in recent years, where there has been a lot of building. What was the area like before the building started? Were old buildings demolished? Were they repaired? If so, how do they look now? Ask if they prefer new buildings, modern buildings, or old buildings that have been repaired so that they are functional in today's world. Why?

Exercise 1 page 106

a transform   **b** collapse   **c** contemporary   **d** feature
e anticipate   **f** potential   **g** obtain

Exercise 2 page 106

Answers will vary.

Exercise 3 page 107

1 the Westside area itself   **2** the poor condition of the warehouse

Exercise 4 page 107

Suggested answers:

1 development; transform

3 Renovate; potential

4 the area; new, modern

5 old architectural

6 contemporary; steel; glass

7 wooden beams; brick; building; building

8 shops; apartments; offices

Exercise 5 page 107

Suggested answers:

1 At the beginning of the conversation, only one developer thinks a building development in Westside is a good idea.

2 There is some development going on in Westside.

3 There has not been much investment in the area in the past 20 years.

4 Only one developer thinks the best idea is to knock down the warehouse.

5 The developers do not need to choose between a contemporary building style and a traditional one.

6 The building can offer floor space for some shops.

7 Shops would not have to be on the second floor. They could be on the ground floor.

8 Renovation would not mean removing all the original features of the building.

Exercise 6 page 108

1 b   **2** d   **3** c   **4** a

Exercise 7 page 108

Supports knocking the building down: 1, 3; because they have negative connotations
Supports converting and modernizing it: 2, 4; because they have positive connotations

Exercises 8–9 page 108

Answers will vary.

Optional activity

Write the following statements on the board (without the words underlined). Ask students to identify any figurative language.

1 I love being an architect. When I am designing buildings, my mind is on fire with hundreds of ideas.

2 The lines of the building seem to dance in the sunlight.

3 I've seen this building a million times, but I never really understood it before.

4 I like this building because it has lots of curves instead of straight lines. (X)

5 Your home is your castle.

6 The building is just tall enough to peek over the bank in front of it.

Students can then think of statements using figurative language to describe the buildings where they live, work or go to school, and share their statements with their classmates.

Exercise 10 page 109

1 It <u>looks</u> as though it's about to <u>collapse</u>!

2 Really? I think the project is going to be a <u>great</u> success.

3 Couldn't we do <u>both</u>? We'll maintain more of a connection to the past if we include the <u>old</u> building as part of the <u>new</u> one.

Exercises 11–12 page 109

Answers will vary.

LANGUAGE DEVELOPMENT

Learning objectives

- Use *will* and *be going to* to describe your predictions and expectations about buildings in the future – *Perhaps I'll study Architecture, so I can work to restore old buildings to their former glory. I'll definitely consider buying a house. A lot of people are going to move into the luxury apartments that are being built in the city centre.*
- Use academic vocabulary for architecture and transformation to complete sentences – *Architecture can transform the way people interact with the world. The people working inside maintain a connection with nature. Suitable sites can be difficult to identify as cities expand.*

Exercise 1 page 110

1 The building I want to move into was bought by a developer. It's definitely going to be renovated before I move there.

2 The construction team probably isn't going to begin work until next month.

3 The supporting walls are already up. The developers will probably complete the building soon.

4 The developer is drawing up his plans now. Maybe he will send me the plans for the apartments on Friday.

5 I will certainly help you with your Architecture assignment now.

6 Farah is off work on Friday. Perhaps she will help you study for the Architecture test.

Exercise 2 page 111

Answers will vary.

Exercise 3 page 111

1 contribute   **2** transform   **3** maintain   **4** expand
5 anticipate   **6** abandon   **7** convert   **8** acquire

Exercise 4 page 112

1 expand   **2** transform   **3** contributed   **4** anticipate
5 convert   **6** acquire   **7** abandon   **8** maintain

Optional activity

Ask students to make predictions about how their city will look in 25 or 50 years. What buildings will still be there? Will there be big changes or will things still look much the same? They should use the vocabulary of architecture and transformation, as well as adverbs of certainty. (If you plan for some students to do the optional *Be flexible* activity for Listening 2, tell them to save their work for later.)

LISTENING 2

Learning objectives

- Understand key vocabulary for housing development – *adequate, existing, appropriate*
- Take notes on proposed solutions to housing problems in a housing development meeting
- Listen and identify main ideas and details
- Identify language which shows whether suggestions are strong or tentative – *What about more, smaller, lower buildings? In my view, the only viable option is to use brick. I strongly recommend that you reconsider this.*
- Synthesize information from a discussion between two property developers and a housing development meeting in a discussion

Lead-in

Have small-group discussions about what happens when communities and neighbourhoods change. Sometimes the people who have lived in these places for a long time don't like the changes. What kinds of objections do they often have? Ask students to make a list, then compare their lists with other groups.

Exercise 1 page 112

a existing   **b** controversial   **c** adequate   **d** sympathetic
e ambitious   **f** appropriate   **g** concerned

Exercises 2–4 page 113

Answers will vary.

Exercise 5 page 113

Possible answers:

1 use reflective glass; make the building lower
2 reflect the size and materials of the other buildings in the area
3 position the new building near the edge of the site

Exercise 6 page 114

1 C   2 D   3 A   4 B

Exercise 7 page 114

1 D   2 D   3 C   4 C   5 C   6 C   7 D   8 D

Exercise 8 page 115

1 T   2 S   3 T   4 S   5 T   6 S

Be flexible

👥 In pairs, ask students to review Listening 1 and identify strong and tentative suggestions in the script. Some examples include:

strong: *I strongly suggest that you reconsider this.*

tentative: *We could consider using reflective glass instead, then.*

Provide more challenge for **stronger students** by asking them to return to the predictions they wrote for the optional activity in Listening 1. Tell them to write a strong or tentative suggestion about each of the buildings or areas in their statements.

Exercise 9 page 115

Answers will vary.

CRITICAL THINKING

Learning objectives

- Identify the problems with an apartment building and the requirements of a replacement building
- Evaluate three buildings against the project requirements

UNL○CK TEACHER DEVELOPMENT

BE INFORMED

➔ **Comparing and evaluating solutions** is an important skill for students because: (1) There is often more than one solution to a problem; (2) Students need the tools to be able to decide which of several solutions is the best in specific circumstances; (3) This is a useful skill not only in academic life, but also in day-to-day life and the world of work.

BE CONFIDENT

➔ Develop this skill for yourself by doing the following activity:

The leader of your educational institution wants to improve the way critical thinking is taught. Which of the three solutions (A, B or C) do you think is best? Why?

solution A	solution B	solution C
-Students do compulsory critical thinking classes in the afternoon instead of sport. -Critical thinking assessed through internal and external exams. -Students encouraged to find critical thinking resources by themselves.	-Students do optional extra critical thinking classes instead of sport. -Critical thinking assessed through written exams. -More critical thinking books should be provided in the library.	-All critical thinking teaching takes place in English language lessons. -Critical thinking assessed through spoken assessments. -More online critical thinking resources should be provided.

If you do not think any of these solutions worked well, how did you decide what was more or less important in order to reach a decision?

Lead-in

Give students a minute to read the speaking task they will do at the end of the unit and keep it in mind as they do the next exercises. Ask them to brainstorm in groups for a few minutes. The oil company (mentioned in the speaking task) faces a number of challenges. Which do they think will be the easiest to solve? Which will be the hardest? Tell them to keep their brainstorming notes for later, when they begin to prepare for their discussion.

UNL○CK TEACHER DEVELOPMENT

BE READY

Look at the Critical Thinking section in the Student's Book on pages 116–118.

➔ Which elements of the lesson do you think your students will find easiest / most difficult / most useful? Why?

➔ Are your answers true for all students in your class?

➔ How can you adapt your teaching or the material to meet your students' needs?

BE FLEXIBLE

An interesting extension to Exercise 3 would be to ask whether any groups were unable to reach a group decision. It would be very valuable to understand why it was not possible to reach a consensus. You could also ask those groups who reached a decision what they did; for example, how they prioritized different criteria.

Possible answers:

problems	project requirements	A	B	C
crowded apartments	must have more space	✗	✓	✓
200 workers and 50 families need homes	must accommodate all people	✗	✗	✓
too far from school and offices	must be closer	✓	✓	✗
workers have to move out in one year	must be complete in one year	✓	✓	✓
only £3.8 million to spend	must cost less than £3.8 million	✓	✗	✗

Exercise 3 page 118

Answers will vary.

UNL⌬CK TEACHER DEVELOPMENT

BE REFLECTIVE

Think about the following questions:

→ Would any of the solutions in the *Be confident* section (or a combination of the solutions) further develop the teaching of critical thinking in your educational institution?

→ If you answered 'yes' to the question above, is there any way you can make changes within your place of work? Would it be worth speaking to colleagues to share ideas?

BE COLLABORATIVE

Your development is more meaningful when it is shared. See page 14 for ideas on how to peer-collaborate. Why not share the ideas you generated in the *Be ready* section, and their outcome?

PREPARATION FOR SPEAKING

Learning objectives

- Use contrastive stress to identify problems and suggest solutions
- Recognize fixed phrases for presenting a problem – *The problem is ...*, *The main issue is ...*, *We need to find a way around ...*
- Use phrases to make polite suggestions – *Should we consider ...? How about ...? Have you thought about ...? Why don't we ...?*

- Respond to suggested solutions
- Emphasize a word or idea to signal a problem
- Use phrases to accept or reject solutions – *That's a great idea, but I'm not sure it addresses the problem. We thought that might be an option at first, but now we realize it won't work. I like your thinking. I agree completely.*

Exercise 1 page 118

2 The main <u>issue</u> is that most retailers don't want to do business here.

3 The main issue is that most <u>retailers</u> don't want to do business here.

4 The main issue is that most retailers don't want to do business <u>here</u>.

Exercise 2 page 118

a 3   **b** 1   **c** 4   **d** 2

Optional activity

👥 Students work in pairs to take turns to read the sentences from Exercise 1 in a mixed-up order to their partner, who has to listen and provide the correct explanation for the emphasized word.

Exercise 3 page 119

1 We need to find a way around the problem of high prices.

2 The problem is that we don't have enough time.

3 The main issue is that people don't like our design.

4 We need to find a way around the problem of attracting business.

5 The main issue is that the building is collapsing.

6 The problem is that nobody wants to live in the area.

Exercise 4 page 120

Answers will vary. Possible answers:

1 Could we increase the budget?

2 Can I suggest we increase the budget?

3 Why don't we increase the budget?

4 Should we consider increasing the budget?

5 How about increasing the budget?

6 Have you thought about increasing the budget?

Exercise 5 page 120

Answers will vary. Possible answers:

2 Can I suggest we reduce the height?

3 Why don't we turn the waste ground into a park?

4 Should we consider building a rooftop garden?

5 How about having more, larger units?

6 Have you thought about offering lower rents?

Exercise 6 page 120

Answers will vary.

Exercise 7 page 121

1 reject **2** accept **3** accept **4** reject **5** reject
6 accept

Exercise 8 page 121

Answers will vary.

SPEAKING TASK

Learning objectives

- Allocate roles for a role play discussion of problems and possible solutions
- Discuss problems with proposed solutions

Exercises 1–6 pages 121–122

Answers will vary.

RESEARCH PROJECT

Create a gallery of architecture for an exhibition.

Ask groups of students to research different types of 'green' or 'eco' architecture by searching 'green buildings' or 'green architecture', noting down as many features of these buildings as they can. Students could use online tools to share their research.

Each group should then choose a particular building they discovered during their research. Ask them to find out why the building was built and what makes it special. Tell them that the class will be setting up an exhibition to present their building to the public. Students will need to decide how to present the information, who to invite, and how they can make the exhibition interactive for visitors (enable visitors to vote for their favourite building, provide a downloadable audio tour, etc.). They then present their gallery of ideas to the class.

CLASSROOM APP

Exercises 1–2

Answers will vary.

Exercise 3

1 This building will definitely help the city because it has both retail and residential space.
2 Many people are certainly going to need low-income housing in this part of the city.
3 Angelino will definitely consider architecture as his major.
4 I will probably visit the Guggenheim when I am in New York just to see the building design.
5 I'm not going to propose a plan for the school's design competition.
6 Maybe I'll focus on modern design because that is more creative.

Exercise 4

1 obtained **2** transform **3** collapsed **4** sympathetic
5 concerned **6** existing **7** potential **8** anticipate

Exercise 5

Answers will vary.

Exercise 6

1 Could we import the products for a cheaper price?
2 Why don't we ask other architects to submit designs?
3 Can I suggest we build a taller building, rather than a wider building, so that we don't use so much space?
4 Have you thought about having a town hall meeting to explain everything?
5 How about having a fundraiser to make more money for a second building?
6 Should we consider different types of parking lots?

UNIT OBJECTIVES

Watch and listen	Watch and understand a video about a South Korean island aiming for zero emissions.
Listening skills	Understand digressions; understand persuasive techniques.
Critical thinking	Analyze and evaluate problems and solutions.
Grammar	Connect ideas; use the passive voice.
Speaking skills	Ask for input in a discussion; summarize and keep a discussion moving; deal with interruptions and digressions.
Speaking task	Participate in a discussion about an energy problem and possible solutions.
⌀ Teacher development	Help your students become better at **analyzing and evaluating problems and solutions**.

UNLOCK YOUR KNOWLEDGE

Background note

The photo shows steam rising from chimneys at a coal-fired power station in West Virginia, the USA. In front of the power station, there are residential houses and cars. Apart from coal, other fuels that are used to produce electricity for our homes include natural gas, nuclear power and natural sources, such as solar, wind and hydropower. Before electricity was discovered, people used candles and oil lamps for lighting. For heating, they burnt wood on fires.

Petroleum is the main source of energy for transportation. Before cars were invented, people used horse-drawn coaches or steam-powered railway trains.

Lead-in

Tell students to imagine that we live in a world without electricity, where all our electrical appliances have stopped working suddenly and permanently. Students work in small groups to discuss the possible impacts of this change on our lives. You could use these questions to focus their attention:

1 What would happen in the first week after this change?

2 What would happen in the first year after this change?

3 What would happen 20, 50 or 100 years after this change?

When they are ready, ask volunteers from each group to present their ideas to the class.

page 125

Answers will vary.

WATCH AND LISTEN

Learning objectives

- Listen and understand main ideas in a video about carbon emissions
- Listen and complete a detailed summary of the ideas in the video
- Make inferences about South Korea and the global environment
- Practise talking about carbon emissions and renewable energy

Exercises 1–2 page 126

Answers will vary.

Exercise 3 page 126

1 F; A country that achieves carbon neutrality will balance its carbon emissions with other actions.   **2** T   **3** T   **4** DNS
5 F; Jeju Island plans to have only electric vehicles by 2030.   **6** T

Exercise 4 page 127

1 emissions   **2** neutrality   **3** balance   **4** trees   **5** zero
6 2030   **7** wind   **8** solar   **9** electric   **10** charge

Exercise 5 page 127

2, 3 and 4 are true.

Exercise 6 page 127

Answers will vary.

LISTENING 1

Learning objectives

- Understand key vocabulary for energy – *capacity*, *cycle*, *reservoir*
- Listen and identify main ideas in a radio programme about the island of El Hierro, Spain
- Listen and complete two sets of detailed notes about El Hierro
- Recognize digressions from the main topic
- Listen and understand the use of intonation to communicate attitudes and emotions
- Describe your knowledge of alternative energy sources

Lead-in

Ask students to imagine living on an island far away from major population areas. What might be some of the challenges of living there? What might be some of the attractions?

Exercise 1 page 128

1 element **2** consistent **3** reservoir **4** mainland
5 cycle **6** network **7** generate **8** capacity

Exercise 2 page 129

1 Government **2** Population **3** Area **4** mainland

Exercise 3 page 129

Answers will vary.

Exercise 4 page 129

1 c **2** a **3** c

Exercise 5 page 130

1 seafood restaurant **2** five years **3** Madrid
4 tough **5** relaxing **6** the sea **7** quiet **8** traffic
9 banking **10** independent **11** oil **12** 40,000
13 mainland **14** over 1.7 million euros

Exercise 6 pages 130–131

1 3,000 **2** 35 **3** turbines **4** 11 **5** 3,500 **6** water
7 dam **8** volcano **9** 500,000 **10** sea level **11** cycle
12 hill **13** drinking **14** agriculture **15** seawater
16 mainland

Exercise 7 page 131

1 R **2** D **3** D **4** D **5** D **6** R

Optional activity

Ask the class: *How does the reporter help end Pedro's digression and redirect the conversation?* Discuss the answer as a whole group.

Answer:

He summarizes what he believes is Pedro's answer to the original question about what is great about El Hierro, and then asks for further information in answer to the same original question.

Exercise 8 page 131

1 b **2** c **3** a

Exercise 9 page 132

a 2 **b** 3 **c** 1

Exercise 11 page 132

1 sarcastic **2** surprised **3** encouraging **4** bored
5 encouraging

Exercise 13 page 132

Answers will vary.

LANGUAGE DEVELOPMENT

Learning objectives

- Connect ideas using transition words and phrases – *It's a real challenge living here. On the other hand, we all love it. The houses use solar energy. What's more, they have water-recycling systems. Dams can damage habitats, so they have to be planned carefully.*
- Use the passive voice to describe processes – *Energy is generated by wind turbines. The water is pumped up the hill. Different machines are used to convert the energy.*
- Identify the meaning of academic vocabulary for networks and systems – *decline*, *potential*, *challenge*

Exercise 1 page 133

giving extra information: *in addition, moreover, furthermore*

comparing and contrasting: *even so, nevertheless*

explaining a result: *therefore, and as a result*

Exercise 2 page 134

Answers will vary. Possible answers:

1 City life is stressful. On the other hand, island life is relaxing.

2 The houses use solar electricity. Furthermore, they have water-recycling systems.

3 Dams can damage habitats. As a result, they have to be planned carefully.

4 The wind blows for 35% of the year. Nevertheless, that isn't enough to provide all of the island's electricity.

5 This electric car can go just over 99 kilometres per hour. Moreover, the battery can be charged using solar power.

6 The system requires that water moves from a high place to a lower place, so we've placed a water tank on a hill.

Be flexible

👥 Elicit other transition words and phrases from students and ask them to state their function. Make a table on the board.

word/phrase	function
besides	addition
whereas	contrast
instead	contrast

👥 Provide an extra challenge for **more advanced students**. Students work in pairs. Give them a list of possible topics (e.g. *their city, university, a political leader*). The first student makes a statement about it; the second student adds similar or contrasting information, using transition words or phrases. Students should take turns going first or second.

Exercise 3 page 135

1 P   2 P   3 A   4 P   5 A   6 A

Exercise 4 page 135

1 is used   2 is created   3 are found   4 be extracted
5 are caused   6 are drilled   7 is supplied   8 can be used

Exercise 5 page 135

2 Water is pumped up the hill.   3 Salt is taken out of the seawater.   4 Supplies are transported from the mainland.
5 In the past, all the power was produced by oil.
6 Wind turbines are blown by the wind.

Exercise 6 page 136

1 generation   2 element   3 capacity   4 source
5 challenge   6 network   7 potential   8 decline

LISTENING 2

Learning objectives

- Understand key vocabulary for saving energy – *consumption, volume, maintenance*
- Listen and complete a set of notes on main ideas in a chaired meeting about saving energy in an office

- Listen and understand details
- Identify different types of persuasive technique – challenging a point: *I see your point. Even so, ...*; asking a question: *Don't you think that solar panels are a good idea?*; reassuring: *Trust me when I say ...*
- Synthesize information from a radio programme about the island of El Hierro, Spain, and a chaired meeting about saving energy, in a discussion

---

Lead-in

Divide students into two teams and ask them what they do to save energy at home. Teams then share their ideas, and the team with the most unusual ideas wins. Students should keep their lists for the follow-up optional activity.

Exercise 1 page 136

Answers will vary. Possible answers:

1 computers, lights, photocopiers, printers, coffee machines, heating, air conditioning, etc.

2 turn off screens on computers when not using them, turn off lights when nobody is in a room / at night, turn off heating / air conditioning at weekends, etc.

3 save money, help the environment

Exercise 2 page 137

1 consumption   2 maintenance   3 experimental
4 efficient   5 limitations   6 function   7 volume
8 drawback

Exercise 3 page 137

1 solar panels (large scale)   2 low-energy   3 natural light
4 computer screens   5 air conditioning   6 photocopier
7 water (large-scale)

Exercise 4 page 138

1 solar panels   2 quickly   3 Cleaning   4 two
5 air conditioning   6 Maintenance   7 green   8 simple

Exercise 5 page 138

1 aren't   2 expensive   3 good   4 one   5 low   6 cost

Exercise 6 page 139

1 b   2 d   3 a   4 e   5 c

Exercise 7 page 140

1 d   2 c   3 e   4 b   5 a

Optional activity

👥 Ask students to take out the lists they wrote of suggestions for saving energy at home (or they can create them here). Students work in pairs to make suggestions and respond to suggestions, using the persuasive techniques from the lesson. For example:

Student 1: *I put a sign above the light switches to remind everyone in my family to turn off the light when they leave a room.*

Student 2: *That's a nice idea, but does anybody pay attention? (asking a question)*

Exercise 8 page 140

Answers will vary.

CRITICAL THINKING

Learning objectives

- Remember solutions to energy-saving problems
- Identify sources of energy wastage at a university or workplace
- Evaluate and rank problems with energy use at a university or workplace
- Propose solutions for each problem you prioritized

UNL⌀CK TEACHER DEVELOPMENT

BE INFORMED

→ **Analyzing and evaluating problems and solutions** is an important skill for students because: (1) Problem-solution essays/presentations, whereby students are expected to outline a problem and then evaluate possible solutions, are commonly used in many academic subjects; (2) To do this effectively, students need to fully understand the reasons and causes behind a problem; (3) Having done this, students can effectively evaluate the potential solutions, some of which may be large in scale, while others are smaller in scale.

BE CONFIDENT

→ Develop this skill for yourself by doing the following activity:

Look at the following common educational problems.

1 a student consistently fails to do their homework

2 the class seems bored whenever you teach critical thinking

3 the exam results for your educational institution are very poor

Think about (1) what might be the cause of these problems, and (2) what the possible solutions are. Create a table like the one below and fill in the causes and solutions.

problems	1	2	3
causes			
possible solutions			

For each case, identify what you think is the best possible solution.

Lead-in

Give students a minute to read the speaking task they will do at the end of the unit and keep it in mind as they do the next exercises. Ask them to consider in groups whether their ideas for saving energy at home work equally well for this project. Ask them to keep a list of the ideas they think would be useful in the workplace or at a university.

UNL⌀CK TEACHER DEVELOPMENT

BE READY

Look at the Critical Thinking section in the Student's Book on pages 141–142.

→ Which elements of the lesson do you think your students will find easiest / most difficult / most useful? Why?

→ Are your answers true for all students in your class?

→ How can you adapt your teaching or the material to meet your students' needs?

BE FLEXIBLE

In Exercise 4, consider trying to link the learning to the students' lives, particularly in terms of small-scale solutions to energy use problems. Get them to reflect on whether there are things they could do in their own lives which would have an impact.

Exercise 1 page 141

solar panels, low-energy light bulbs, clean dirty windows, turn off computer screens, turn off air conditioning; get rid of one photocopier, solar water-heating system

large-scale solutions: solar panels and solar water-heating system

Exercises 2–4 pages 141–142

Answers will vary.

UNLOCK TEACHER DEVELOPMENT

BE REFLECTIVE

Think about the following questions:

→ Can you share your answers from the *Be confident* section with a colleague, either in person or electronically? Were they similar or different? Is there anything practical you could do with the solutions you generated?

→ Were students successfully able to distinguish between large- and small-scale solutions? Did you get the feeling that they believed they could make a difference to energy use through personal action? Hopefully one of the key things students learn through developing their critical thinking skills is that how they think and what they do matters.

BE COLLABORATIVE

Your development is more meaningful when it is shared. See page 14 for ideas on how to peer-collaborate. Why not share the ideas you generated in the *Be ready* section, and their outcome?

PREPARATION FOR SPEAKING

Learning objectives

- Use phrases for keeping a discussion moving to complete a dialogue – *What do you think? We'd better move on to the next point. Does anybody have anything to add?*
- Rephrase ways to deal with interruptions and digressions more politely – *Excuse me, but I'd just like to finish this point. Could you possibly give me one more minute? Would you mind if I finish this last point?*
- Use a neutral tone of voice to avoid sounding challenging or argumentative

Exercise 1 page 142

1 b   2 a   3 c

Exercises 2–3 page 142

1 c   2 a   3 b

Optional activity

👥 Ask students to look back at the script from Listening 2 in Unit 5, on pages 211–212. Put students in groups and take the roles of John, Maria, Tom and Jamal. However, they should not just read the script. They should add expressions from the Skills box on page 142. Since Tom and Jamal called the meeting, one or both of them should chair the meeting and be responsible for keeping the meeting moving. The others can ask for input and summarize.

Exercise 4 page 143

Answers will vary. Possible answers:

1 Could you please wait until I've finished speaking?

2 Would you mind explaining what you mean?

3 Sorry, that isn't really what we're talking about.

4 Sorry, but would you mind waiting until Tom finishes speaking?

Exercise 5 page 143

3 A   4 N   5 N   6 A

Exercise 6 page 143

Answers will vary.

SPEAKING TASK

Learning objectives

- Understand an agenda to have a meeting about how energy can be saved in a place of work or study
- Prepare for a meeting by reviewing your table of problems and solutions and adding new ideas
- Allocate roles for your meeting by dividing up the agenda points
- Role play a meeting about how energy can be saved in a place of work or study
- Evaluate your solutions and any conclusions you reached

Exercises 1–6 page 144

Answers will vary.

RESEARCH PROJECT

Write a blog about saving energy.

Ask students to research different ways energy is wasted (e.g. by not turning off lights). Then ask them to answer the following questions: *How is my learning environment wasting energy? What can I do to help reduce this*? Use online tools to list the problems and to come up with solutions.

Students each create a week-long blog in which they record what they have done to save energy every day. Students could follow each other's blogs and vote for the best energy-saving student at the end of the week.

CLASSROOM APP

Exercise 1

Answers will vary.

Exercise 2

1 Nevertheless   **2** What's more   **3** Therefore   **4** Moreover
5 Even so   **6** so

Exercise 3

1 is generated   **2** suggested   **3** was sent   **4** are caused
5 can save   **6** were considered

Exercise 4

1 drawback   **2** network   **3** generate   **4** efficient
5 volume   **6** element   **7** capacity   **8** functions

Exercise 5

Answers will vary.

Exercise 6

1 Asking for input   **2** Summarizing   **3** Keeping a discussion moving   **4** Dealing with interruptions or digressions   **5** Dealing with interruptions or digressions   **6** Keeping a discussion moving
7 Summarizing   **8** Asking for input

ART AND DESIGN

UNIT 7

UNIT OBJECTIVES

Watch and listen	Watch and understand a video about the African contemporary art market.
Listening skills	Infer opinions; distinguish fact from opinion.
Critical thinking	Use debate statements and responses; prepare for a debate.
Grammar	Use relative clauses.
Speaking skills	Express contrasting opinions; restate somebody's point; use language for hedging.
Speaking task	Participate in an informal debate.
⌀ Teacher development	Help your students become better at **using debate statements and responses** and **preparing for a debate**.

UNLOCK YOUR KNOWLEDGE

Background note

The photo shows a temporary art installation called *Runway*. The installation was initially displayed in March 2017 on California's waterfront in Santa Barbara, the USA. The design won a competition run by the Museum of Contemporary Art Santa Barbara. It was created by Molly Hunker and Greg Corso, artists who are part of a New York group called SPORTS. The sculpture is constructed of three structures made of very thin steel rods and is painted blue, yellow and pink.

Lead-in

Before the lesson, search the internet for images of works of art. Use search terms such as *painting*, *modern art* or *sculpture*. Print out a range of images and stick them up around the classroom. Keep a record of where you found each picture, so that you can tell students who the artist is, if they want to know.

Tell students to walk around the classroom and look at the pictures as if they were in a gallery. When everybody has had a chance to look at the pictures, ask volunteers to say which images they liked best, and explain why they liked them. As a follow-up, you could hold a class vote to decide on their favourite picture.

page 147
Answers will vary.

WATCH AND LISTEN

Learning objectives

- Listen and understand main ideas in a video about African art

- Complete a detailed summary of the ideas in the video
- Make inferences about the art and artists in the video
- Practise talking about art

Exercises 1–2 page 148
Answers will vary.

Exercise 3 pages 148–149
1 a   2 c   3 a

Exercise 4 page 149
1 contemporary   2 collectors   3 demand   4 an auction
5 media   6 discarded

Exercises 5–6 page 149
Answers will vary.

LISTENING 1

Learning objectives

- Understand key vocabulary for street art – *vandalism*, *self-expression*, *composition*
- Listen and identify main ideas and opinions in a radio report about graffiti
- Listen and take detailed notes on opinions
- Make inferences about who made particular statements of opinion
- Understand the connotations of words used to describe street art
- Make inferences about opinions based on the connotations of their language
- Use correct stress when it varies on different members of word families – *de-co-rate* > *de-co-ra-tion*; *ar-tist* > *ar-tis-tic*
- Express personal opinions on street art

Lead-in

Either print out images or display digital images by famous street artists. (Possible candidates include: Roa, Vhils, c215, Eduardo Kobra, Shepard Fairey, Iheart, Collin van der Sluijs.) Be sure that the images are not too controversial or inappropriate for your students. Ask: *Are these images art? How do they compare to the images in museums?* (Or if you have used the unit Lead-in activity, use those for comparison.)

Exercise 1 page 150

a identity **b** right **c** vandalism **d** self-expression
e comment **f** composition **g** creativity **h** criticism

Be flexible

👥 Students work in pairs to write a paragraph using all eight words in bold from Exercise 1, using dictionaries if necessary. When they are ready, ask volunteers to read their paragraphs to the class.

Fitting all eight words into one paragraph may be too challenging for **lower-level students**. To reduce the level of challenge, ask them to choose just five words or to write individual sentences for each of the eight words.

Exercise 2 page 151

Answers will vary.

Exercise 3 page 151

1 c **2** a **3 a** yes **b** no **c** yes **d** yes **e** yes

Exercise 4 page 151

Answers will vary. Possible answers:

Alex: interesting to look at; distinctive style; decorates the area

office worker: no right to spray paint their message; art is in a gallery

police officer: creative; expressive; should get permission

Simone: expressive; colour and composition work well; could make a lot of money

Joseph: wishes he'd done it; good way of expressing ideas; communicates a message

Exercise 5 page 152

a 3 **b** 2 **c** 1 **d** 2 **e** 4 **f** 1 **g** 5 **h** 5 **i** 4 **j** 3

Exercise 6 page 152

Answers will vary.

Exercise 7 page 152

1 this artist; very creative; a piece of art; artistic, expressive; artwork

2 vandalism; the area's mystery graffiti artist; our illegal painter; this piece of vandalism

3 *Answers will vary. Possible answer*: The police officer seems to like the painting more. The police officer's personal and professional opinions are different. The reporter should be neutral but seems to dislike the graffiti.

Exercise 8 page 153

3 com-<u>mu</u>-ni-cate, com-mu-ni-<u>ca</u>-tion
4 cre-<u>ate</u>, cre-<u>a</u>-tion
5 ex-<u>hib</u>-it, ex-hi-<u>bi</u>-tion
6 re-com-<u>mend</u>, re-com-men-<u>da</u>-tion
7 ac-<u>tiv</u>-i-ty, <u>ac</u>-tive
8 <u>ar</u>-tist, ar-<u>tis</u>-tic

Exercises 9–10 page 153

Answers will vary.

LANGUAGE DEVELOPMENT

Learning objectives

- Use the correct relative pronouns in relative clauses to provide information about a noun – *Art that is painted illegally on city buildings is called graffiti. Graffiti, which is often painted on city buildings without permission, is a big topic of debate right now. The person who painted the graffiti is very creative.*
- Differentiate between defining and non-defining relative clauses
- Use defining and non-defining relative clauses to write sentences about art

Exercise 1 page 154

1 who; <u>Ray Noland</u> **2** whose; <u>The people</u>
3 where; <u>The museum</u> **4** when; <u>Mondays</u>

Exercise 2 page 155

2 ND: The painting includes the figure of Marianne, <u>who represents the victory of the French Republic over the monarchy</u>.

3 D: The painting <u>that Botticelli painted on the walls of the Tuscan Villa Lemmi</u> is located in the same room as Luini's *Adoration of the Magi*.

4 ND: Marianne, <u>whose image appears on small stamps and euro coins</u>, is also depicted as a statue at the Place de la République in Paris.

5 D: People <u>who visit the Louvre</u> can use cameras and video recorders, but not flash photography.

6 D: The Louvre is the museum <u>where *The Da Vinci Code* was filmed</u>.

Exercise 3 page 155

Answers will vary. Suggested answers:

2 The Prado museum, which is located in Madrid, displays a collection of paintings by El Greco.   **3** I like art which/that is bright and colourful.   **4** *The Mona Lisa*, which Da Vinci painted around 1503, hangs in the Louvre.   **5** Pieces of art which/that are famous are expensive to buy.

Be flexible

👥 This activity is a bit of a trap, but will help students remember the difference between the two types of clauses. Ask them to work in pairs to write defining and non-defining relative clauses about each of the following nouns and noun phrases. Some students should discover that the proper nouns will not permit defining relative clauses.

- street art
- modern art
- Pablo Picasso
- the Louvre Museum
- artists

Have **stronger students** read their sentences aloud, using the correct intonation for each clause type.

Exercise 4 page 156

Answers will vary.

LISTENING 2

Learning objectives

- Understand key vocabulary for art – *analyze, appreciate, display*
- Listen and take detailed notes on opinions in an informal debate about public art
- Identify main ideas using your notes
- Listen and complete a set of detailed notes
- Distinguish facts presented in the debate from opinions
- Synthesize information from a radio report about graffiti and an informal debate about public art in a discussion

Lead-in

Ask students to discuss the function of public art. Start by saying that we all know about art in museums, but what about art in public spaces, such as plazas, in front of government buildings, on university campuses, or even in hotels or shopping centres? What is the purpose of this kind of art? Does it in some way help the people who see it? Does it have an economic purpose? Tell students to take notes and keep them, as they may be useful for the final project.

Exercise 1 page 156

1 appreciate   **2** analyze   **3** focus on   **4** display
5 interpret   **6** reject   **7** restore   **8** reveal

Exercise 2 page 156

Answers will vary.

Exercise 3 page 157

Answers will vary. Possible answers:

Robert: they need to find out how much new art would cost; thinks Sandra is right; they need to do more research

Bilal: not really sure that paying for art is an appropriate way to spend public money; the art doesn't really benefit the city's population; more people would use and benefit from a leisure centre; public art is a waste of money

Ahmad: art is an important part of any culture; art can help make us proud of our city; people enjoy looking at it; the location of the artwork rather than the artwork itself is the problem; moving it might solve the vandalism problem; children need to see art in public places; balance investment in leisure activities and public art

Azra: art can have a very positive effect on people

Sandra: not sure a leisure centre would be popular enough; consider moving the sculpture; could be a tourist attraction

Claudia: public safety issue; artwork really is causing more problems than it's worth

Exercise 4 page 157

Tick: 1, 3, 5, 6, 8

Exercise 5 page 158

Suggested answers:

1 how much new art will cost
2 analyze the pieces we have
3 gather data and opinions
4 a survey
5 climb on it and write graffiti on it
6 the location
7 a different location
8 choose / determine a new project
9 see art in public places
10 explore options

Exercise 6 page 159

1 F   **2** O   **3** F   **4** F   **5** O   **6** O   **7** F   **8** O

Optional activity

🧍 Students return to Listening 1 and identify expressions of fact and of opinion in the script.

Exercises 7–8 page 159

Answers will vary.

CRITICAL THINKING

Learning objectives

- Understand the function of different statements in debates
- Create two lists of reasons to support different sides of an argument about how to spend public money
- Evaluate arguments in order to choose a position
- Develop support for your arguments
- Research facts and examples to counter opposing points of view

UNLOCK TEACHER DEVELOPMENT

BE INFORMED

➔ **Using debate statements and responses** and **preparing for a debate** are important skills for students because: (1) Although students may not participate in debates on a frequent basis either academically or in real life, the core skills needed to do well in them are extremely useful for effective speaking and argument; (2) An example of one such skill is to research reasons and evidence, which not only support your own position, but also the opposing positions; (3) It helps to develop the skill of preparing quality notes before speaking in public, which is also ideal preparation for giving presentations.

BE CONFIDENT

➔ Develop these skills for yourself by doing the following activity:

Think of reasons to support each of the statements below. Write a maximum of four reasons for each statement in the T-chart.

critical thinking should be taught as a standalone subject	critical thinking should be taught as an integrated component of ELT

Look at what you wrote in the T-chart. Decide which statement and reasons you agree with most.

Lead-in

Give students a minute to read the speaking task they will do at the end of the unit and keep it in mind as they do the next exercises. Ask them to review their notes from the Lead-in activity for Listening 2 (or, if they have not done it, have them complete it now) and to brainstorm the *value* of the functions they listed. Tell them to keep their brainstorming notes for later, when they begin to prepare for their debates.

UNLOCK TEACHER DEVELOPMENT

BE READY

Look at the Critical Thinking section in the Student's Book on pages 160–161.

➔ Which elements of the lesson do you think your students will find easiest / most difficult / most useful? Why?

➔ Are your answers true for all students in your class?

➔ How can you adapt your teaching or the material to meet your students' needs?

BE FLEXIBLE

If you have time, an interesting additional activity you could do after Exercise 5 would be for students to repeat Exercises 3–5, but this time they should focus on the statement they do not agree with. Doing this will help them see the argument from the other side.

Exercise 1 page 160
1 a **2** b **3** d **4** c

Exercises 2–5 page 161
Answers will vary.

UNLOCK TEACHER DEVELOPMENT

BE REFLECTIVE

Think about the following questions:

➔ Look back at the reasons you wrote in the *Be confident* section. Which of the statements and reasons do you agree with the most? Why? Do your colleagues have the same opinion?

➔ How much experience had your students had of debating beforehand? Was this a new skill for them, or had they done it before? What influence did this have on how well they could perform?

BE COLLABORATIVE

Your development is more meaningful when it is shared. See page 14 for ideas on how to peer-collaborate. Why not share the ideas you generated in the *Be ready* section, and their outcome?

PREPARATION FOR SPEAKING

Learning objectives

- Use phrases to express contrasting opinions –
  *We take it for granted that ..., However, ...
  People tend to believe (that) ..., Nevertheless, ...
  It seems like ..., In reality, ...*
- Argue against points by restating them
- Clarify points by restating them
- Make points politely using hedging language –
  *I'm not an expert, but ... For me, ... Personally,
  I'm not really sure ...*
- Respond to points politely using hedging
  language – *I see what you're saying, but
  maybe ... You may be right, but I wonder if ...
  You could say that. However, ...*
- Use correct stress in hedging language to
  acknowledge other opinions

Exercise 1 page 162

1 The speaker thinks it's an artistic piece of work.
2 This looks like   **3** but, in fact

Exercise 3 page 163

1 Many people think that public art has no long-term
cost. However, cleaning and maintenance need to be
considered.

2 It seems like the new sculpture is very popular, but
actually a thousand people have signed a petition to have
it removed.

3 It looks like the government wasted a lot of money on
the sculpture. The fact of the matter is it was donated to
the city.

Exercise 4 page 163

1 Y   **2** N   **3** N   **4** Y

Exercises 5–6 page 164

Answers will vary.

Exercise 7 page 165

Answers will vary. Suggested answers:

2 I'm not an expert, but ...   **3** All I know is, ...   **4** For me, ...
5 You could say that; however, actually ...   **6** That's true in
part, but I think ...   **7** You may be right, but I wonder if ...
8 I see what you're saying, but maybe ...

Exercise 8 page 165

Answers will vary.

SPEAKING TASK

Learning objectives

- Prepare to take part in an informal debate by
  evaluating your arguments and choosing those
  you will use
- Prepare to take part in an informal debate
  by considering how to address alternative
  arguments
- Take part in an informal debate about whether
  public money should be spent on public art

Exercises 1–5 pages 165–166

Answers will vary.

RESEARCH PROJECT

Create a TV programme discussing art and opinion.

Divide the class into groups. Ask each group to
search for works by a famous artist and to decide on
one they all like. Tell them to write some background
notes on the artist and then develop a brief critique
of the work. Critiques usually have four steps: (1)
Describe it. Tell somebody who cannot see it what
it looks like. (2) Analyze it. How does the artist use
colour, lines and shapes, composition and texture?
(3) Interpret it. What do you think the artist wanted
to say with this piece? What is your response to it?
How does it make you feel? What does it remind
you of? (4) Evaluate it. This does *not* mean saying the
piece is good or bad. Instead, say why you think it is
or is not successful. Does it express the message that
the artist intended?

Each group's critique will then contribute to a script
for an 'Art Critic' TV programme, which students will
produce as a class. The resulting video can then be
uploaded to a video-sharing website.

Exercises 1–2

Answers will vary.

Exercise 3

1 who **2** which **3** when **4** where **5** whose
6 which **7** which **8** who

Exercise 4

1 criticism **2** display **3** restore **4** self-expression
5 appreciate **6** focus on **7** reject **8** reveal

Exercise 5A

1 Restating an opposing opinion **2** Disagreeing
3 Hedging **4** Hedging **5** Introducing an opposing opinion
6 Disagreeing

Exercise 5B

1 In other words, galleries should be free?

2 They might want to focus on other subjects, like
science.

3 At first, it looks as if

4 I see what you're saying, but maybe

5 So what you're saying is that

UNIT OBJECTIVES

Watch and listen	Watch and understand a video about a Japanese woman who designed a mobile app at the age of 82.
Listening skill	Understand specific observations and generalizations.
Critical thinking	Analyze and use data from a line graph.
Grammar	Use verbs with infinitives or gerunds.
Speaking skills	Reference data in a presentation; explain details and trends in a graph; explain causes and effects.
Speaking task	Give a presentation using graphical data.
⟳ **Teacher development**	Help your students become better at **analyzing and using data from a line graph**.

UNL⌀CK YOUR KNOWLEDGE

Background note

The photo shows women in their 70s practising taekwondo at a local gym in Incheon, South Korea. Taekwondo is a Korean martial art that uses a lot of jump kicks and punches. Because it involves physical contact, it may not always be recommended for older people. Some other things that many people are not able to do as they get older are driving a car, climbing stairs, physical work and extreme sport. Some of the things that people might be able to do when they are older are travelling, spending more time on hobbies and interests, going to the theatre and restaurants, and spending more time with friends and family.

Lead-in

Write the following discussion topic and questions on the board:

Some experts believe that the first person who will live to 200 years old is already alive now. How could this be possible? Would you like to be that person? Why / Why not?

Students discuss the questions in small groups. After a few minutes, open up the discussion to include the whole class.

page 169
Answers will vary.

WATCH AND LISTEN

Learning objectives

- Listen and understand main ideas in a video about an elderly coder
- Complete a detailed summary of the ideas in the video
- Identify inferences which can be made from the information in the video
- Practise talking about ageing

Exercises 1–2 page 170
Answers will vary.

Exercise 3 page 171

1 F; Wakamiya worked in banking before she retired.
2 F; She had never used a computer before she retired.
3 T **4** T **5** F; Wakamiya's app uses figures from traditional Japanese culture.

Exercise 4 page 171

1 sixty **2** her elderly mother **3** bought a computer
4 designed for young people **5** weren't interested
6 design her own app **7** the Japanese festival
Hinamatsuri **8** an app developers' conference

Exercise 5 page 171

1 She was a banker before it was common for women in Japan to have such jobs. / Over the next 20 years, she taught herself about computers and the internet. / So, she did what she had always done: she did it herself.
2 She contacted app designers and asked them to develop games for older users, but nobody was interested. **4** Tim Cook, the head of Apple, heard about Wakamiya and her app. Calling her work 'inspiring', he invited her to an app developers' conference.
3 and **5** cannot be inferred.

Exercise 6 page 171
Answers will vary.

LISTENING 1

Learning objectives

- Understand key vocabulary for retirement finances – *asset, dependent, ensure*
- Listen and identify main ideas in a finance podcast
- Listen and complete a set of detailed notes with numbers and percentages
- Differentiate between specific and general observations
- Identify various types of elision and intrusion in native speaker connected speech
- Express personal opinions on generational finances

Background note

There are two main types of property: *personal property* (physical things such as cars, furniture and electrical appliances) and *real property* (buildings and land). In business contexts, the term *property* is often used with this second meaning (e.g. a property developer buys and sells real property, not personal property).

A person or company's *assets* include his/her/its personal and real property, as well as money and other non-physical assets, such as share certificates and intellectual property. The opposite of *assets* is *liabilities*, which is everything that a person or company owes to others.

Lead-in

Students think of an older person (65+) they know. Each student briefly describes the person to the class. Is she/he active? Still working? If so, why? If not, how does she/he spend her/his time? If you have a homogeneous group of students (all from the same country), as a class, develop a profile of older people. (This can help with the instruction on generalizations later.) If you have students from many different countries, they can compare and contrast these specific examples. (This can help with the instruction on specific observations later.)

Exercise 1 page 172
Answers will vary.

Exercise 2 page 172
1 retirement **2** generations **3** permit **4** dependents
5 ensure **6** pension **7** property **8** assets

Exercise 3 page 173
Tick: 1, 3, 5, 6, 7

Exercise 4 page 173
1 500 billion **2** 60 **3** 26 **4** 65 **5** 500,000
6 $^2/_3$ / two-thirds **7** 18

Optional activity

Write the following phrases from the listening on the board. Students work in pairs to discuss what the underlined words and phrases mean. When they are ready, discuss the answers with the class.

1 They're spending it on <u>meals out</u>.

2 I think <u>we've earned it</u>.

3 We <u>babysit</u> our grandchildren regularly.

4 We <u>might as well</u> enjoy life.

5 We've <u>done our part</u> as parents.

Exercise 5 page 174
3 S **4** S **5** G **6** S **7** G **8** G

Exercise 6 page 175
1 dropped /d/ **2** vowels joined with /w/ **3** dropped /d/
4 vowels joined with /w/ **5** vowels joined with /j/
6 dropped /t/ **7** dropped /d/

Exercise 8 page 175
Answers will vary.

LANGUAGE DEVELOPMENT

Learning objectives

- Choose the correct verb form to use after particular verbs including those with indirect objects – *We'll consider travelling after retirement. Our savings allow us to do what we want to do. We want him to agree with our plans.*
- Use academic verbs for support and assistance to complete sentences about the ageing population – *permit, devote (oneself) to, cooperate*

Exercise 1 pages 177
1 to visit **2** going **3** to meet **4** to babysit **5** working
6 gardening **7** to save **8** playing

Exercise 2 page 177
1 We always advise our daughters to enjoy life.

2 We want to encourage other people to retire early.

3 We managed to save enough money when we were working.

4 Our friends recommend spending our savings on a holiday.

5 We refuse to spend our retirement at home.

6 I won't force my children to look after me.

7 We do not need to delay retiring, because we saved a lot of money when we were working.

8 The financial adviser wants you to work until you are 65 years old.

Exercise 3 page 178

Answers will vary. Suggested answers:

2 Trina considered moving to a new city. **3** Her financial consultant advised her to change her pension plan.
4 We would never threaten to leave our children without any inheritance.

Exercise 4 page 178

1 c **2** a **3** f **4** b **5** e **6** d **7** g **8** h

Exercise 5 page 178

1 cooperate **2** permit **3** ensure **4** contribute **5** assist **6** indicate **7** devote **8** participate

---

Be flexible

👤👥👥 Students work alone to write the nouns derived from the academic verbs in Exercise 5. They check in pairs and feed back. Note that there is no noun derived from the verb *ensure*.

Ask **stronger students** to write sentences with the noun forms they have written, then compare sentences.

LISTENING 2

Learning objectives

- Understand key vocabulary for discussing the elderly – *ancestors, contribute, institution*
- Create a T-chart to organize notes on main ideas in two student presentations on ageing in different countries
- Listen and take notes on main ideas and details in T-charts
- Evaluate whether ideas presented by speakers are causes or effects
- Synthesize information from a finance podcast and two student presentations on ageing in different countries in a discussion

---

Lead-in

Students work in pairs to describe their grandparents' living situation. Do/Did they live on their own? With their children or other family? In a care home? If you have a homogeneous class (all from the same country), ask them to make generalizations about the living situations of the elderly. If you have students from many different countries, ask students if it is possible to make generalizations about their country from their specific examples.

Exercise 1 page 179

1 b **2** a **3** b **4** c **5** c **6** b **7** a **8** c

Exercises 2–3 page 180

Answers will vary.

Exercise 4 page 180

Answers will vary. Possible answers:

Mika, Japan

Importance of family: – extended family not so important

Figures explaining how population is changing:

- highest life expectancy in the world
- low fertility rate
- people wait longer to get married
- fewer young people to care for elderly
- more care centres

Solution: – government has citizens pay income tax to help elderly

Ahmet, Turkey

Most households have elderly people living in them.

Drawbacks: – caregivers and old people aren't free to do what they like

- older people don't like how things are done
- living closely together causes tensions

Benefits: – older people help with domestic jobs and childcare

- older people have a sense of responsibility

Challenge: – elderly population is growing

Solution: – continue caring for elderly at home

Exercise 5 page 180

1 Mika: Japan; Ahmet: Turkey **2** Mika **3** Ahmet
4 Mika: importance of family in her country, how population is changing with fewer young people and how government is helping by making citizens pay a tax;
Ahmet: drawbacks and benefits of older people living in households with younger people, challenges of the situation and possible solutions

Exercise 6 page 181

	Mika	**Ahmet**
country	Japan	Turkey
population today	127 million	81 million
% 65 or older today	26%	6%
% of households with older people	no information	80%
expected population in 2050	99 million	92 million
expected % 65 or older in 2050	35%	20%

Optional activity

👥 In small groups, students try to reproduce how the graph that Ahmet refers to might look. (A line graph that supports Mika's presentation appears on page 182. Don't point it out to the class but if they see it, it's not a problem; Ahmet's data is slightly different anyway.) It could be a line graph or a bar graph, or even two pie charts. Ask students why they chose a specific graph type and if others might work equally well. Ask them to show a rough sketch of their graph(s).

Exercise 7 page 181

1 E **2** C **3** E **4** C **5** E **6** E

Exercise 8 page 181

Answers will vary.

CRITICAL THINKING

Learning objectives

- Analyze data in line graphs about ageing populations
- Use data in line graphs to make predictions
- Evaluate the implications of your predictions
- Relate additional information to the features of line graphs

UNL⌂CK TEACHER DEVELOPMENT

BE INFORMED

→ **Analyzing and using data from a line graph** is an important skill for students because: (1) When giving a presentation, students can use graphs to present a substantial amount of information in a clear and concise way; (2) It makes students think about graphs more clearly, rather than simply inserting them into their presentations without thinking about their use or how to fully exploit them; (3) Students need to know how to analyze and explain graphs effectively in order to support their arguments.

BE CONFIDENT

→ Develop this skill for yourself by doing the following activity:

Look at the line graph below. What three key features of this line graph would you talk about in a presentation?

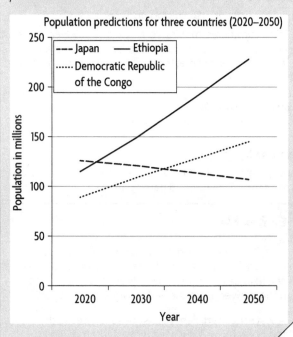

Population predictions for three countries (2020–2050)

Lead-in

Give students a minute to read the speaking task they will do at the end of the unit and keep it in mind as they do the next exercises. Ask them to brainstorm their own country in groups for a few minutes. Do they think the population is ageing? As quickly as in Japan*? Tell them to keep their brainstorming notes for later, when they begin to develop their presentation.

*If your class is in Japan, as an alternative, ask students to brainstorm how this trend might affect them personally. If your class is in Turkey, ask them if they think the current trend is likely to continue and why.

BE READY

Look at the Critical Thinking section in the Student's Book on pages 182–184.

→ Which elements of the lesson do you think your students will find easiest / most difficult / most useful? Why?

→ Are your answers true for all students in your class?

→ How can you adapt your teaching or the material to meet your students' needs?

BE FLEXIBLE

After doing Exercise 2 by themselves, you could introduce an optional stage where the students compare their predictions. You could even put students into groups of two to three, and tell them that they have to agree on a set of three predictions.

Exercise 1 page 182

1 approximately 29 million   **2** approximately 17 million
3 approximately 24 million   **4** ages 15 to 64
5 people 14 and under

Exercise 2 page 183

Answers will vary. Possible answers:

1 The 0–14 population will continue to decline.
2 The 15–64 population will also decline more.
3 The over-65 population will decrease, but more slowly.

Exercise 3 page 183

Answers will vary. Possible answers:

There will be fewer working people to pay taxes and to look after older people, and more older people who need healthcare and pensions. The government will need to increase spending on these areas but will have less tax money to fund it.

Exercise 4 page 183

1 *Answers will vary. Possible answers:*

Country A: Increasing total population then falling slightly; Increasing over-65 population

Country B: Decreasing total population; Rising and then falling over-65 population

Country C: Increasing total population; Fairly steady over-65 population

2 *Answers will vary.*

Exercises 5–6 page 184

Answers will vary.

BE REFLECTIVE

Think about the following questions:

→ How did you feel about doing the activity in the *Be confident* section? Were you easily able to identify the main points you would talk about, or did you find it challenging?

→ Overall, how did you feel about how you taught critical thinking for this level? If/When you teach it again, would you do anything differently?

BE COLLABORATIVE

Your development is more meaningful when it is shared. See page 14 for ideas on how to peer-collaborate. Why not share the ideas you generated in the *Be ready* section, and their outcome?

PREPARATION FOR SPEAKING

Learning objectives

- Use specific language to explain details and trends in graphs – *The population of over-65s will skyrocket from 4,000 to 24,000 people. You can see that the growth in the population remains steady. The population is predicted to fall slowly.*
- Use fixed phrases to explain cause and effect in sentences about populations – *was brought about by, can be traced back to, was due to*
- Use contrastive stress for emphasizing significant figures when describing trends and statistics

Exercise 1 page 185
1 Z   **2** Y   **3** Y   **4** Z   **5** Y   **6** Z

Exercise 2 page 186
Answers will vary.

Exercise 3 page 186
1 c or e   **2** c or e   **3** a   **4** b   **5** d

Exercise 4 page 187
Answers will vary. Possible answers:

2 A population decrease was brought about by people moving out of the country.   **3** A population increase can be traced back to an increase in people over 65.
4 The steady population was due to the high number of people over 65.

Exercise 5 page 187

2 The population of Country E will be <u>77 million</u> in <u>2050</u>. This number is <u>much larger</u> than the figure of <u>1.4</u> million for Country <u>D</u> in <u>2050</u>.

3 By <u>2050</u>, Country <u>D's</u> population will rise to <u>1.78 million</u> people. The population for Country <u>E</u> <u>also</u> peaks in 2050 with <u>9.2 million</u> people.

SPEAKING TASK

Learning objectives

- Prepare to give a presentation on how ageing has changed a country's population by reviewing and adding to your notes
- Plan the language you will use in your presentation to describe supporting data and predictions
- Give a presentation on how ageing has changed a country's population over time and the impact this is likely to have on its society in the future

Exercises 1–5 page 188

Answers will vary.

RESEARCH PROJECT

Create an 'infographic' showing the effects of an ageing population.

Divide the class into groups and explain that each group will be responsible for researching one of the effects an ageing population can have on a country. These could include issues related to work, retirement, healthcare, taxation, education and the economy. Each group researches one of these areas, using online tools to share ideas and research.

Using a slideshow app or infographics software (search 'infographics'), each group designs infographics to show and share the information they have found with the rest of the class.

CLASSROOM APP

Exercises 1–2

Answers will vary.

Exercise 3A

1 can be followed by an infinitive
2 can be followed by either an infinitive or a gerund
3 can be followed by a gerund
4 can be followed by a gerund
5 can be followed by an infinitive
6 can be followed by a gerund
7 can be followed by either an infinitive or a gerund
8 can be followed by an infinitive
9 can be followed by either an infinitive or a gerund

Exercise 3B

1 to interview   **2** driving   **3** working   **4** retiring
5 to stop   **6** moving   **7** to travel   **8** to save

Exercise 4

1 permit   **2** participate   **3** devote   **4** indicate   **5** assets
6 pension   **7** ensure   **8** responsibility

Exercise 5A

1 cause; effect   **2** effect; cause   **3** cause; effect
4 effect; cause

Exercise 5B

Answers will vary.

CONSERVATION UNIT 1

UNIT OBJECTIVES	
Watch and listen	Watch and understand a video about endangered birds in Indonesia.
Listening skills	Listen to introductions; identify rhetorical questions as signposts.
Critical thinking	Analyze issues.
Grammar	Use parallel structures in comparisons.
Speaking skill	Challenge other points of view.
Speaking task	Have an informal debate.
⊘ **Teacher development**	Help your students become better at **analyzing issues**.

UNL⊘CK YOUR KNOWLEDGE

Background note

The photo shows a large area of rice fields, and a farm, in Asia. Rice farming is one of the largest sources of methane – a greenhouse gas which contributes to global warming. Certain farming practices, such as large-scale intensive farming, can also affect the environment by causing loss of animal habitats, destruction of ecosystems, wasteful water consumption, soil erosion and degradation, and pollution.

Lead-in

Ask students to consider the simple act of boiling water. What is the impact on the environment? Ask them to offer ideas (e.g., energy to boil water, the water itself). They may be surprised to learn about the large amount of wasted energy in this process, specifically when we fill the kettle with more water than is needed. One estimate is that the amount of energy required to boil all that excess water for one day, for all the kettles in the UK, would power all of the streetlights in the UK for one night.

page 15
Answers will vary.

WATCH AND LISTEN

Learning objectives

- Listen and understand main ideas in a video about an endangered species
- Listen and complete a set of notes with detailed information
- Practise talking about endangered species

Exercises 1–2 page 16
Answers will vary.

Exercise 3 page 16
a

Exercise 4 page 17

1 F; The *cendrawasih* bird of paradise is becoming increasingly difficult to see / spot in the Indonesian jungle.
2 T 3 F; There are 41 species of bird of paradise found in Indonesia.
4 T 5 F; The forest where the *cendrawasih* live is protected by law.
6 F; Tourism by birdwatchers is the only chance for survival for the *cendrawasih*.

Exercise 5 page 17

1 Habitat 2 Destructive 3 logging 4 agricultural
5 banned 6 smuggled 7 remaining 8 economy
9 homestays

Exercise 6 page 17
Answers will vary.

LISTENING 1

Learning objectives

- Understand key vocabulary for agriculture — *fertile, yields, starvation*
- Listen to the introduction to a lecture and use it to preview the lecture's topic and structure
- Listen and understand the main ideas signalled by rhetorical questions in a lecture about sustainable agriculture
- Listen and complete a set of notes with detailed information
- Understand a speaker's opinions on a range of issues related to sustainable agriculture
- Listen and understand the use of intonation to indicate whether an idea is complete or not
- Express personal views and explain current issues relating to sustainable agriculture

Lead-in

Ask students to think about what they ate in the last 24 hours. Where do most of the fruit, vegetables, and grain come from in their country? Do they come from small family-owned farms, or large, industrial farms? Are they imported from abroad? How much do students know about the origin of their food?

Exercise 1 page 18

a loosen   **b** abundant   **c** conversion   **d** starvation
e yields   **f** viable   **g** fertile   **h** nutrients

Exercise 2 pages 18–19

Possible answers:

1 **sustainable agriculture:** a way of farming that can be continued because it provides food while protecting the environment and people's health
2 **erosion:** the fact of soil, stone, etc. being gradually damaged and removed by the waves, rain or wind; **retention:** the ability to keep or continue having something; **diversify:** to begin to make something varied or different

Exercise 3 page 19

1 a, d, e, f   **2** a, c   **3** b, c

Exercise 4 page 20

1 growing huge amounts of the same crop in the same fields, year after year; it produces huge amounts of food; it is not sustainable
2 soil and water
3 They can reduce vulnerability to pests and soil erosion.
4 higher labour costs and the belief that sustainable agriculture has lower yields

Exercise 5 page 20

1 of intensive farming techniques   **2** chemical fertilizers
3 using animal waste, crop rotation, planting cover crops
4 erosion   **5** wind, water   **6** 70; of the water used in the world today   **7** rain, underground reserves   **8** planting cover crops; redesigning fields to trap rainwater

Exercise 6 pages 20–21

1 b   **2** b   **3** a   **4** a

Exercise 7 page 21

1 I   **2** C   **3** I   **4** C   **5** I   **6** I   **7** I   **8** C

Exercise 8 page 21

Answers will vary.

LANGUAGE DEVELOPMENT

Learning objectives

- Use parallel structure in sentences containing comparisons to write about agriculture — *Wind causes more coastal flooding than rain does. Today, farmers grow more wheat than they grew in the past. Wheat farms in China produce more than those in India do.*
- Understand and recognize common expressions used to attribute responsibility and blame — *shirk the blame, hold somebody accountable, have somebody to thank for something*

Exercise 1 page 22

Possible answers:

1 Wind causes more coastal flooding than rain does/ causes.
2 Some people say farmers should not grow almonds because they need more water than wheat and other grains do/need.
3 The cost of labour in organic farming is higher than (it is) in traditional farming.
4 Farms take up a higher proportion of the land in Turkey than they do in Saudi Arabia/farms in Saudi Arabia do/ take up.

Exercise 2 page 23

Possible answers:

1 Farms in India produced more wheat in 2012 than they did/produced in 2013.
2 The production of wheat is greater in China than in the United States.
3 European Union farms produce more wheat than those/farms in China (do/produce).

Optional activity

👤 Ask students to compare two things using parallel structure. This could be two universities in their country, two sports teams, etc. Make sure they understand they must compare something about the two things (e.g. size of student body). For example:

The environmental footprint of Vietnam is smaller than that of Japan.

People in the United Arab Emirates have a greater impact on the environment than the people in Saudi Arabia do.

Exercise 3 page 23

Answers will vary.

Exercise 4 pages 24–25

1 point the finger at; to blame   **2** falls on the shoulders
3 credited with   **4** shirk the blame / their responsibilities; held to account   **5** step up and accept responsibility
6 took credit

LISTENING 2

Learning objectives

- Understand the information and implications communicated by a line graph showing greenhouse gas emissions in different parts of the world
- Understand key vocabulary for global responsibility for climate change – *shameful, accelerate, sanctions*
- Listen to an announcement for a radio show and use it to preview the show's content
- Listen, understand and summarize the position of each participant in a panel discussion of global responsibility for climate change
- Synthesize information from a lecture and a radio programme about environmental issues in a discussion

Lead-in

If students completed the optional activity for Language development, they will have seen the term *environmental footprint*. Otherwise, you can introduce the term now. Ask students how they think this figure is calculated. Possible answers include use of land and sea resources, fuel use, carbon release, landfill use. List their ideas on the board.

Exercise 1 page 25

Possible answers:

1 They are rising.

2 Non-OECD countries passed OECD in carbon emissions around 2006.

3 Non-OECD countries will continue to increase their carbon emissions at a faster and higher rate than OECD countries. OECD emissions may be stabilizing or falling.

4 *Answers will vary.*

Exercise 2 page 26

1 b   **2** c   **3** a   **4** a   **5** b   **6** c   **7** b   **8** a

Exercise 3 page 27

1 *Answers will vary.*   **2** a   **3** c

4 **boycott:** the refusal to buy a product or take part in an activity as a way of showing strong disapproval; **economic sanction:** an official action against a government that affects its economy by forcing it to behave differently, or as punishment for its behaviour.

5 *Answers will vary.*

Be flexible

👤 Ask students to listen to the introduction (the moderator's section) and check their answers to Exercise 3, questions 1 and 2.

Provide **lower-level students** with more support by letting them read the script as you play the audio a second time. If time allows, students can practice reading the script aloud.

Exercise 4 page 27

Grace Chin b; Russell Sanchez c; Dara Staples d; Vijay Gupta a

Exercise 5 page 28

Answers will vary.

Exercise 6 page 29

Possible answers:

1 Developed countries, such as the USA, have very high per capita emissions; the developing world can't afford to change their practices.

2 Developing countries have very high overall CO_2 emission rates, and practices such as cutting down forests are making the problem much worse. They know the environmental consequences, so they should stop doing it.

3 He wants developed countries to stop buying the right to cause environmental damage (with carbon credits and e-waste dumping), and start supporting developing countries in more meaningful ways.

4 The planet is warming up too quickly for us to continue talking about the issues, or to allow any countries to increase their emissions. The planet will not survive without immediate action.

Exercise 7 page 29

Possible answers:

1 The USA and other developed countries should make changes, even if they're expensive.

2 It's a good idea to boycott products whose manufacture causes significant negative environmental effects.

3 Economic development and resource extraction will not be useful to the people of Bangladesh if their land is under water.

4 Pointing fingers and blaming one another doesn't help.

Exercise 8 page 29

Answers will vary.

CRITICAL THINKING

Learning objectives

- Remember personal experiences and real-world knowledge of national parks
- Analyze information about the challenges facing national parks to understand implications for the future if the problems are not addressed
- Evaluate the seriousness of different challenges facing national parks
- Understand and evaluate two possible missions of national parks
- Evaluate and explain your own position on the mission of national parks

UNLOCK TEACHER DEVELOPMENT

BE INFORMED

→ **Analyzing issues** is an important skill for students because: (1) Before deciding what they think about a particular issue, they need a good understanding of its background and the core related information; (2) In an era of 'fake news', and questions being raised about the very nature of 'truth', the ability to critically evaluate this background information is crucial; (3) Having determined whether such information is true, students need to identify the relevance of this information and whether/how it supports their position.

BE CONFIDENT

→ Develop this skill for yourself by doing the following activity:

Imagine that you are giving a presentation about businesses in your local area. Which of the following sources would you consider using? Think about (a) whether they are likely to be true, and (b) if they are relevant.

'Local businesses are doing really well, and we should all be very pleased.' – **Current town mayor**

'Local business has shown steady growth of 3% per year over the last decade.' – **University research**

'It's hard to be a business here. We need more tax breaks.' – **Local café owner**

'There has been a significant increase in the population over the last year.' – **Statistics agency**

'Business is going downhill fast. We need change.' – **Previous town mayor**

'The number of people 'buying local' is increasing.' – **Local trade association**

'Buying online is more attractive for people.' – **Online shopping company**

Lead-in

Give students a minute to read the speaking task they will do at the end of the unit. Then ask them to brainstorm the issue, and to keep their brainstorming notes for later, when they develop their ideas for the debate.

UNLOCK TEACHER DEVELOPMENT

BE READY

Look at the Critical Thinking section in the Student's Book on pages 30–32.

→ Which elements of the lesson do you think your students will find easiest / most difficult / most useful? Why?

→ Are your answers true for all students in your class?

→ How can you adapt your teaching or the material to meet your students' needs?

BE FLEXIBLE

Get students to compare possible consequences for two or three of the issues in Exercise 2. Reflecting on the similarities and differences may help them focus on relevance, and stronger students may support students who find the exercise challenging.

Exercise 1 page 30

Answers will vary.

Exercise 2 pages 30–31

Possible answers:

Neighbours: The parks can be polluted or littered by neighbouring businesses or homes, damaging the habitat and the animals that live there. Wild animals from the park could catch diseases from domestic animals when they go out of the park; they could bring these diseases back into the park and damage the population. Hunting and poaching can cause species to go extinct.

Non-human visitors: Invasive species could replace native species, damage the habitat and disrupt the park's ecosystem. Any loss of species disrupts the ecosystem and could cause the park to lose its value as an attraction and as a preserve for wildlife.

Climate change: The landscape of parks could change drastically. Animals will die or leave the park. Migrating species will go to new places.

Popularity: Building roads and services for visitors could damage the habitat, but if these are not built, visitors might not come. If people do not visit the park, the park may not have enough funding to protect wildlife from hunters or be able to justify its status as a park.

Natural resources: The extraction of natural resources could lead to environmental pollution, such as oil spills or polluted river water, which are disastrous for animal species. Deforestation of parkland reduces the size of the habitat and may result in species being lost.

Exercise 3 page 32

Answers will vary.

Exercise 4 page 32

1 neighbours; non-human visitors; popularity; natural resources

2 **Mission A:** They are trying to get $6.2 billion to help protect the park from threats. **Mission B:** They had 5.5 million visitors last year and they spent all their budget on maintaining services for them.

Exercises 5–6 page 32

Answers will vary.

UNL⌀CK TEACHER DEVELOPMENT

BE REFLECTIVE

Think about the following questions:

→ If you reflected on the subject matter before the lesson, did it help you teach the critical thinking skill more effectively?

→ How did your students respond to the lesson? Did you feel that they were interested in developing their critical thinking skills?

BE COLLABORATIVE

Your development is more meaningful when it is shared. See page 14 for ideas on how to peer-collaborate. Why not share the ideas you generated in the *Be ready* section, and their outcome?

PREPARATION FOR SPEAKING

- Use appropriate phrases to challenge other points of view on environmental issues – *That doesn't follow. That may be true, but ..., On the contrary, ...*
- Use rising or falling intonation to indicate whether an idea is complete or not

Exercise 1 page 33

1 a   2 c   3 d   4 b

Exercises 2–3 page 33

Answers will vary.

Be flexible

Ask students to work in small groups. Each group thinks up a clearly false scientific idea, but with a grain of truth in it (as in the Mars example) and presents it to another group. Members of the other group use polite, academic language to refute to proposal. Possible examples include:

- *Smiling can make you happy.*
- *Groups are more creative than individuals.*
- *Eating wheat is bad for your health.*
- *You are either right- or left-brain dominant.*
- *Cows can sleep standing up.*

If you provide students with the set of examples above, they may simply use those. **For a greater challenge,** (1) make sure students elaborate the example beyond a single sentence so that other students have something to agree or disagree with; and (2) ask students to think of their own examples.

Exercise 4 page 33

Answers will vary.

SPEAKING TASK

Learning objectives

- Prepare for a debate by writing a statement expressing your position
- Anticipate opposing points of view and prepare counter-arguments for a discussion
- Take part in an informal debate by stating your position and countering an opposing point of view

Exercises 1–6 page 34

Answers will vary.

RESEARCH PROJECT

Give a group presentation on how a national park is balancing its missions.

Ask students to do some research on how a national park (either in their own country or in another country, but not the Grand Canyon) is balancing their two missions. What attractions does the park offer? Who are its visitors? Is it an important source of income for the country? What have been the greatest challenges? Has the park had to limit the number of visitors or cars?

The information could be used for group presentations. Alternatively, the class could collate their information, compiling a series of international park profiles, or a series of environmental problems relating to national parks and how we can solve them.

CLASSROOM APP

Exercises 1–2

Answers will vary

Exercise 3

1 The winters in the 20th century have been warmer than those in earlier centuries.
2 The fields on the north side of the farm are more fertile than the land on the south side.
3 Some agricultural practices in the developing world don't harm the land as much as those used in developed countries.; Some agricultural practices in the developing world don't harm the land as much as those used in developed countries do.
4 Cities in the interior are in less danger than the cities on the coast
5 Damage to the forests has been even more dramatic than the damage to oceans.
6 Children in cities experience more environmental threats than the children in rural areas do.; Children in cities experience more environmental threats than those who live in rural areas.

Exercise 4

1 responsible for   2 thank for   3 be held to account for   4 took credit for   5 point the finger at

Exercise 5

1 viable   2 abundant   3 nutrients   4 dispose of   5 unprecedented   6 accelerate   7 burden   8 combat

Exercise 6

Answers will vary

Exercise 7A

1 Not necessarily
2 That's not necessarily the case
3 That may be true but
4 On the contrary
5 That doesn't follow

Exercise 7B

Answers will vary

UNIT OBJECTIVES

Watch and listen	Watch and understand a video about designer bikes in France and Japan.
Listening skills	Use a table to take notes on main ideas and detail; review and organize notes.
Critical thinking	Evaluate pros and cons.
Grammar	Use degree expressions.
Speaking skill	Acknowledge other arguments.
Speaking task	Give a group presentation.
⊘ **Teacher development**	Help your students become better at **evaluating pros and cons**.

UNL⊘CK YOUR KNOWLEDGE

Background note

The photo shows a 3D printer printing a hand. With 3D printing, a designer can print any design using just the materials and a detailed drawing. This allows designers to test new designs and improve their products at a very low cost. Some predict that, in the future, 3D printing will be available to anybody. This technology would allow us to manufacture our own consumer goods, such as domestic appliances, gadgets, shoes and other items of clothing. It also has applications in healthcare, being used to print replacement body parts and organs.

Lead-in

Students work in groups. Tell them to walk around the room, into the hallways, and to other areas they are allowed access to in the building, in order to look at the design of everyday objects (door handles, taps, chairs, etc.). They choose one and report back to the class. Is the design of the object good or bad? Why? For example, they might say that the design makes the purpose of the object clear. The goal is for them to consider why design matters, even for everyday objects.

page 37
Answers will vary.

WATCH AND LISTEN

Learning objectives

- Listen and identify main ideas in a video about bicycle design
- Listen and understand detailed information
- Practise talking about luxury products and status symbols

Exercises 1–2 page 38
Answers will vary.

Exercise 3 page 39
3, 1, 2, 5, 4

Exercise 4 page 39
Answers will vary. Possible answers:
1 gap in the market   **2** has recognized Japanese talent in this area (bicycle design)   **3** personalizing (posh cycling) accessories   **4** wealth and social status

Exercise 5 page 39
1 a carbon-fibre frame; a silent chain   **2** €8,000
3 €15,000   **4** mahogany   **5** *Possible answers:* leather saddle bags; hand-painted bells; keyrings in leather

Exercise 6 page 39
Answers will vary.

LISTENING 1

Learning objectives

- Understand key vocabulary for a discussion of the implications of 3D printing – *customize, downside, mass production*
- Use visuals to explain traditional supply chains
- Listen and identify the main ideas in a presentation about the implications of 3D printing
- Listen and use a table to organize main ideas and details
- Listen and take detailed notes
- Review and organize detailed notes in outline format
- Gain awareness of, and identify word stress in, multi-syllable words
- Explain and imagine potential implications of 3D printing in a discussion

Lead-in

Ask if students have ever used a 3D printer or used an object printed by one. Ask volunteers to describe their experiences with 3D printing. If nobody volunteers, have a photo of a 3D printed object ready to show them. Ask them to speculate on how a 3D printer works. What is the 'ink' in a 3D printer?

Exercise 1 page 40

Answers will vary.

Exercise 2 pages 40–41

1 junk **2** customize **3** fabric **4** downside
5 foundation **6** rejection **7** drastically
8 mass production

Exercise 3 page 41

Possible answer: Raw materials are sent to a supplier. The supplier sends materials to the assembly plant where the parts are put together into a product. The products are sent out for distribution. They are taken to retail businesses where they are sold to consumers.

Exercise 4 page 41

1 b **2** a **3** b **4** a **5** b

Exercise 5 page 42

Possible answers:

1 assembly **2** supply chain **3** on the spot (where it was needed) **4** lighter **5** to maintain stock levels **6** ship goods **7** waste / environmental footprint

Exercise 6 pages 42–43

1 F; 3D printing has been around since the 1980s.
2 T **3** F; Clothing is printed using a type of plastic.
4 F; 3D printing could shift the production of clothing away from large facilities in the developing world.
5 DNS **6** F; One man printed part of an aeroplane as a single piece.
7 T **8** DNS

Exercises 7–9 page 43

Answers will vary.

Be flexible

Tell students to go back to the diagram in Exercise 3. Say that they should describe the manufacturing process again, this time considering the information from the lecture. Where has the process been disrupted? (Basically the supplier, assembly plant and distribution network have been eliminated.)

Support **lower-level students** by asking them to go through each of the steps one by one. Ask them as a group to describe how 3D printing has changed any of the steps in the process.

Exercise 10 page 44

1 a tech-<u>no</u>-lo-gy **b** <u>pro</u>-cess **c** <u>ob</u>-ject
2 a com-<u>pu</u>-ter **b** <u>soft</u>-ware **c** sce-<u>nar</u>-i-os
3 a dra-<u>ma</u>-tic **b** bi-o-<u>med</u>-i-cal **c** re-<u>search</u>
4 a at-<u>tracts</u> **b** pos-si-<u>bil</u>-i-ty **c** <u>cus</u>-tom-iz-ing
5 a pro-<u>duc</u>-tion **b** fa-<u>cil</u>-i-ties **c** <u>in</u>-dus-try
6 a <u>el</u>-e-ments **b** foun-<u>da</u>-tion **c** man-u-<u>fac</u>-tur-ing
7 a en-tre-pre-<u>neur</u> **b** <u>fac</u>-to-ries **c** as-<u>sem</u>-bled

Exercises 11–12 page 44

Answers will vary.

LANGUAGE DEVELOPMENT

Learning objectives

- Use phrases with *by* to describe causes – *By printing it as one piece, he created a part that was five times stronger.*
- Use phrases to describe effects – *The blouses appear on shelves the following week, encouraging the trend.*
- Use degree expressions with infinitives to compare something with a standard – *too high to be practical; cheap enough to replace annually*

Be flexible

👤 Write these sentences on the board and have students identify whether the phrases express a cause or effect. (The phrases are underlined.)

1 <u>By changing the shape of the door handle</u>, the designer has made its function (to push or pull) more obvious. (cause)

2 The new design takes into account all of the feedback we have received, <u>thus improving the user experience</u>. (effect)

3 We believe we have become a more responsible company <u>by paying attention to the long-term social and economic impact of our products</u>. (cause)

Give **stronger students** a bigger challenge. You can return to these sentences after students have done some of the exercises and ask them to transform them into the opposite type. For example, the first one would be: *The designer has changed the shape of the door handle, making its function (to push or pull) more obvious.*

Exercise 1 page 45

Possible answers: **1** By designing new products
2 By advertising regularly   **3** By working overnight
4 By collaborating as a team   **5** By using a 3-D printer

Exercise 2 page 45

1 making it psychologically easier to throw things away
2 leaving assembly plants in developing countries out of the process
3 giving hope to those on transplant waiting lists

Exercises 3–5 page 46

Answers will vary.

LISTENING 2

Learning objectives

- Understand key vocabulary for planned obsolescence – *backlash, innovation, resent*
- Listen and identify the main topics in a group presentation about planned obsolescence
- Listen and take notes in outline form on main ideas and details
- Use your notes to summarize the most important ideas from a presentation on planned obsolescence
- Understand and identify the attitude of the presenters to planned obsolescence

- Understand and respond to an infographic on value clothing, explaining the facts and their implications
- Synthesize information from two presentations about design in a discussion

Lead-in

Show students the graph below. Ask if the figures surprise them. Ask them the possible causes and effects of this rapid replacement rate (e.g. how frequently consumers buy a new phone).

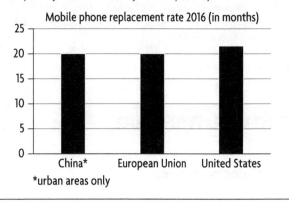

Mobile phone replacement rate 2016 (in months)

*urban areas only

Optional activity

👥 Write the words below on the board, without stress markers. Ask students to underline the stressed syllable in these words and then check their answers by listening to the audio. (Stress indicated below.)

obso'lescence	phe'nomenon	de'liberate
inno'vation	'durable	elec'tronics
'attitude	e'normous	'penalties

Exercise 1 page 47

a resent   **b** issued   **c** innovation   **d** circumvent
e devised   **f** backlash   **g** finite   **h** obstacle

Exercise 2 page 47

1 old electronics   **2–3** *Answers will vary.*

Exercise 3 page 48

Answers will vary.

Exercise 4 page 48

b, c, d, e, f

Exercises 5–7 page 49

Answers will vary.

Exercise 8 page 49

d

Exercise 9 page 50

Possible answers:

1 Value clothing is low-cost clothing which allows people to keep up-to-date with the latest fashions on a budget.

2 Educated people with higher incomes have started to shop at value retailers. This has resulted in 24.9% market growth for this sector of the clothing industry.

3–4 *Answers will vary.*

5 more clothes being made overseas; fewer jobs in manufacturing in the UK; more jobs in manufacturing in the developing world; transportation of goods from the developing world to the UK, which has a negative environmental impact; more waste going into the environment; more retail jobs in the UK, but less business for high-end retailers; more pressure on high-end retailers to reduce prices

Exercise 10 page 50

Answers will vary.

CRITICAL THINKING

Learning objectives

- Analyze the principles of planned obsolescence for various consumer products
- Analyze the pros and cons of planned obsolescence for various consumer products
- Evaluate and suggest reasons why consumers purchase goods and services, using your own experience
- Evaluate which planned obsolescence scenarios are used for different consumer products

UNLOCK TEACHER DEVELOPMENT

BE INFORMED

→ **Evaluating pros and cons** is an important skill for students because: (1) Most situations, both in the academic world and real life, are not clear cut – they are not black and white, but rather different shades of grey; (2) Different people evaluate the same information in different ways, or they might give more weight to a particular pro or con; (3) Students commonly make the mistake of thinking that the 'correct' answer is the average of two extreme positions.

BE CONFIDENT

→ Develop this skill for yourself by doing the following activity:

Look at the following three areas of critical thinking. Think of arguments for and against each. When you have identified at least one argument for each, consider what your own view is.

Use of class time

Critical thinking is a good use of class time because …

Critical thinking is not a good use of class time because …

Relevance to academic study

Critical thinking is relevant to academic study because …

Critical thinking is not relevant to academic study because …

Stand-alone subject

Critical thinking should be taught as a stand-alone subject because …

Critical thinking should not be taught as a stand-alone subject because …

Lead-in

Give students a minute to read the speaking task they will do at the end of the unit. Give them a few minutes to brainstorm possible products. Tell them to keep their brainstorming notes for later, when they begin to develop their presentations.

UNLOCK TEACHER DEVELOPMENT

BE READY

Look at the Critical Thinking section in the Student's Book on pages 51–53.

→ Which elements of the lesson do you think your students will find easiest / most difficult / most useful? Why?

→ Are your answers true for all students in your class?

→ How can you adapt your teaching or the material to meet your students' needs?

BE FLEXIBLE

In Exercise 2, get students to reflect about their own personal experience, i.e. matching their own purchasing behaviour to these theoretical reasons.

Exercises 1–5 pages 51–53

Answers will vary.

UNL⌀CK TEACHER DEVELOPMENT

BE REFLECTIVE

Think about the following points:

→ Did your students have similar or different opinions on the subject matter in this unit? Knowing whether or not your class holds diverse opinions can help you plan future lessons more effectively.

→ If you did any activities that were not in the book which worked well, share these with your colleagues and tell them why it was successful.

BE COLLABORATIVE

Your development is more meaningful when it is shared. See page 14 for ideas on how to peer-collaborate. Why not share the strategies you explored in the *Be ready* and *Be flexible* sections, and their impact on the lesson?

PREPARATION FOR SPEAKING

Learning objectives

- Use correct stress in compound nouns and noun phrases when speaking
- Use appropriate structures with concession expressions to acknowledge other points of view when talking about planned obsolescence – *Planned obsolescence clearly benefits manufacturers; that said, it can also be seen as providing some consumer benefits.*

Exercise 1 page 53

1 clothing industry 2 complex devices 3 backlash
4 design policy 5 digital locks 6 fast fashion
7 finite lifespan 8 runway 9 tech sector

Exercises 2–3 page 53

Answers will vary.

Exercise 4 page 54

1 c 2 b; d 3 a 4 e

Exercises 5–6 page 55

Answers will vary.

Be flexible

👥 Bring in advertisements for two comparable (similarly desirable) products. Ask students which product they prefer, naming pros and cons of each and using the expressions they have learnt.

Challenge **more advanced students** to bring in their own product advertisements and ask classmates to express their preferences.

SPEAKING TASK

Learning objectives

- Prepare for a group presentation on planned obsolescence by assigning roles
- Prepare for your part of the group presentation by developing talking points
- Give and respond to feedback in order to develop your part of the presentation
- Give a group presentation on planned obsolescence

Exercises 1–4 pages 55–56

Answers will vary.

RESEARCH PROJECT

Develop a group presentation on e-waste.

Do some research on e-waste, including causes and consequences. Divide the class into small groups to investigate separate aspects of the issue. Possibilities include:

- role of product obsolescence in e-waste
- amount and origin of e-waste
- environmental impact
- possible security risks
- health hazards
- alternatives (e.g. recycling)
- laws in different countries
- developed v developing world's roles

If your students are creative or perhaps in an arts curriculum, they may wish to create a graphic (infographic, map, etc.) to support their presentation. Students then give their presentations to the class. Afterwards, they can discuss whether any findings surprised them, and any actions they could take.

CLASSROOM APP

Exercises 1–2

Answers will vary.

Exercise 3

1 effect **2** cause **3** cause **4** effect **5** effect **6** cause **7** cause

Exercise 4

1 too big to fit in your pocket.

2 enough money to start the business

3 safe enough to give to children

4 too small to see without my glasses.

5 enough in this course to move

6 too many ideas to fit into one paper.

7 enough room to let everyone enter

Exercise 5

1 rejection **2** fabric **3** obstacles **4** foundation
5 backlash **6** downside **7** junk **8** innovation

Exercise 6

1 Granted; On the one hand; Many people think; Many people think that
   but; on the other hand; some others say that

2 Granted; On the one hand
   But; on the other hand

3 said; Having said that

4 There are two ways

5 Many; Some
   others; some

Exercise 7

Answers will vary.

UNIT OBJECTIVES

Watch and listen	Watch and understand a video about internet security.
Listening skills	Listen for facts and supporting information; listen for opinion.
Critical thinking	Elicit information in surveys; analyze data.
Grammar	Use subject-verb agreement with quantifiers.
Speaking skills	Present survey data; present conclusions from research.
Speaking task	Present survey data and conclusions.
⟳ **Teacher development**	Help your students become better at **eliciting information via surveys and analyzing data**.

UNLOCK YOUR KNOWLEDGE

Background note

The photo shows a person paying for a ticket on the London Underground, the UK, using a smartwatch and a contactless payment device. Almost half of all Underground and rail journeys in London are paid for with contactless payment methods, including bank cards and mobile phones. Contactless payments don't require a signature or PIN, and are limited to small amounts. However, the system could be used to steal credit card information. When used for transport, this type of system could also contain information about where somebody is, how they travel and their daily routine, which could also be used to build a personal profile, target advertising or be used by thieves.

Lead-in

Ask students to brainstorm what could happen if their passport were stolen. What could a criminal do with their personal information? Make a list on the board.

page 59
Answers will vary.

WATCH AND LISTEN

Learning objectives

- Listen and identify the main idea in a video about a ransomware attack
- Listen and understand detailed information
- Listen and identify the meaning of unfamiliar words and phrases from their context in the video
- Practise talking about ransomware and network security

Exercises 1–2 page 60
Answers will vary.

Exercise 3 page 61
b

Exercise 4 page 61

1 a cyber-security firm   **2** X-Peter   **3** one hundred thousand   **4** the same or more serious   **5** one
6 on bank machines and bureaucrats' desks (across the nation / Ukraine)

Exercise 5 page 61
1 b   **2** c   **3** a   **4** c

Exercise 6 page 61
Answers will vary.

LISTENING 1

Learning objectives

- Understand key vocabulary for privacy and the law– *encryption, compel, legitimate*
- Listen to an introduction and use it to preview the format of a discussion about privacy
- Listen and identify speakers' points of view and understand whether or not they support their views with facts, and if so, how
- Understand the use of idioms in the context of a discussion about privacy
- Gain awareness of and identify sentence stress
- Explain your views on privacy and the law, and the implications of technology in crime and law enforcement

Lead-in

Ask students to focus on the target word *trade-off*. Ask them to think of some situations that exemplify the term. Here are some to get them started:

price v quality in consumer products

spending now v saving for the future

taking a job for a lower salary now v going back to university for a higher degree

Exercise 1 page 62
Answers will vary.

Exercise 2 pages 62–63
1 b **2** a **3** a **4** c **5** b **6** c **7** a **8** c

Exercise 3 page 63
1 b **2** c **3** private individuals; break into
4 *Answers will vary.*

Exercises 4–5 pages 64–65

speaker	answer	notes	type of support
Joel	Q1 Y Q2 ?	*Answers will vary.*	opinions
Lauren	Q1 N Q2 N	*Answers will vary.*	facts – published report
Dave	Q1 Y Q2 Y	*Answers will vary.*	facts – law, personal experience / own expertise
Karina	Q1 Y Q2 N	*Answers will vary.*	facts – law, own expertise
Tony	Q1 Y Q2 Y	*Answers will vary.*	opinions
Miku	Q1 Y Q2 N	*Answers will vary.*	opinions, own expertise

Exercise 6 page 65
1 c **2** b **3** b

Exercise 7 page 66

1 We'll take <u>questions</u> and <u>comments</u> from <u>list</u>eners at the <u>end</u> of the <u>programme</u>.
2 Joel, <u>should</u> companies have to <u>hand</u> over infor<u>mation</u> about their <u>customers</u>?
3 <u>Law</u> en<u>forc</u>ement is made <u>more</u> <u>diffi</u>cult with<u>out</u> <u>access</u> to <u>this</u> kind of infor<u>mation</u>.
4 I think the ma<u>jor</u>ity of these <u>agencies</u> have their <u>own</u> experts.
5 With<u>out</u> <u>evi</u>dence from sur<u>veill</u>ance that's ad<u>miss</u>ible in <u>court</u>, <u>we</u> <u>don't</u> have a <u>hope</u> of <u>putt</u>ing them a<u>way</u>.
6 The infor<u>mation</u> on <u>that</u> phone <u>does</u>n't belong to the <u>tech</u> company; it be<u>longs</u> to a <u>private</u> indi<u>vid</u>ual.
7 That <u>might</u> be <u>true</u> if we were talking about the <u>physical</u> <u>world</u> – <u>like</u> un<u>lock</u>ing the <u>door</u> to your a<u>part</u>ment.

Be flexible

Ask students to take roles from the script and read it aloud together, using correct sentence stress.

Before they do this, allow **lower-level students** to listen again and mark the script for stress.

Exercise 8 page 66
Answers will vary.

LANGUAGE DEVELOPMENT

Learning objectives

- Use noun phrases with *of* to talk about proportions – *the majority of people, fifty percent of the data, some of the cookies*
- Use quantifiers as subjects – *75% believe they are safe. Some were lost, but most have been saved.*
- Make verbs agree with the correct noun in noun phrases with *of* to talk about proportions and when using quantifiers as subjects – *75% of people believe they are safe. Some of the data was lost, but most has been saved.*
- Use collocations to describe online activity and the law – *clear your cookies, identity theft, secure network*

Exercise 1 page 67
1 offer **2** are **3** contains **4** is

Exercise 2 page 67
1 say **2** prefer **3** have **4** was **5** choose

Be flexible

👥 Ask students to work in pairs. One person starts a sentence with a quantifier + noun. The other person completes it. They should come up with at least five examples.

Ask **stronger students** to create sentences with pronouns that express quantity as the subject. They work in pairs. One student creates the sentence and the second student infers what the pronoun refers to. (Note: many answers could be correct.) For example, *Most don't read the policy statement before ticking 'agree'.* Possible answers include *people, readers, users*, etc. The point is that the answer for this example must be plural and countable.

Exercise 3 page 68

1 surfing the internet / web / net **2** secure network
3 search engine **4** clear (your) cookies

Exercise 4 page 68

1 law-abiding **2** law enforcement **3** combatting crime
4 public safety

LISTENING 2

Learning objectives

- Understand key vocabulary for internet security – *trace, offline, target*
- Listen and take notes in table form on main ideas and details, in a group presentation about internet security
- Listen, identify and understand definitions of key terms
- Organize detailed notes and use them to review the most important ideas in a presentation
- Gain awareness of words and phrases which signal whether a speaker is presenting facts or opinions
- Differentiate between and facts and opinions in statements about internet security
- Synthesize information from a discussion about privacy and a presentation about internet security, and use in a discussion

Lead-in

Ask students to consider all of the online activities listed in Exercise 1 on page 69. What are the advantages of doing them online instead of in person, in print, etc.? Responses should include *speed, convenience, wider audience* and *community*.

Exercises 1–2 page 69

Answers will vary.

Exercise 3 page 70

a taking steps **b** move on **c** disable **d** targeted
e retailers **f** personalize **g** offline **h** traced

Exercise 4 page 70

Answers will vary.

Exercise 5 page 71

Possible answers:

1 a way for companies to track your browsing activity and use it to send you advertisements that specifically target you
2 a small text file which is downloaded onto your browser when you visit a site and which saves information about what you do while you're on the site
3 a cookie which is sent to your browser by the advertiser when you click on an advert, and which identifies you across all websites that advertisers use
4 cookies which are transmitted over a secure network, sent in a type of code
5 a browser option that allows you to surf without information being collected on your activity
6 cookies that save information about you, but are stored *outside* of your browser
7 a tiny invisible graphic on web pages that can tell the server you're on a specific page

Exercise 6 page 71

1 N **2** F **3** F **4** O **5** F **6** O / F (first half opinion, second half fact) **7** N **8** F **9** O / F (first half opinion, second half fact) **10** O

Exercise 7 page 72

Answers will vary.

Exercise 8 page 72

1 a **2** b **3** b **4** a and b **5** a

Be flexible

👥 Tell students to review the script for Listening 1 to find expressions of opinion. Perhaps have them find five examples and then identify the signal(s) for each. Some possibilities:

- *The police should have as much information as possible in order to keep us safe.* (Signal: should)
- *I think if the information is limited to metadata – you know – phone numbers, dates, times – that kind of thing, it's fine.* (Signals: I think, it's fine)

You may also want to extend this activity to have **stronger students** identify expressions of opinion that are more implicit, i.e. those that do not have signals. Ask students to restate the ideas using concise language and signals. For example:

Well, if I have a contract with a private company for phone service or web access or whatever, that's between me and the company. (= I don't think private companies should give access to the government.)

Exercise 9 page 72

Answers will vary.

CRITICAL THINKING

Learning objectives

- Remember information from a discussion about privacy and a presentation about internet security
- Apply classification information as behaviour or opinion
- Evaluate the strengths and weaknesses of different questions for use in a survey
- Create an effective survey for your target respondents on the topic of online security or privacy

UNLOCK TEACHER DEVELOPMENT

BE INFORMED

➔ **Eliciting information via surveys and analyzing data** are important skills for students because: (1) They are required in many academic subjects, across different disciplines; (2) Many jobs use surveys to gather information, which then needs to be analyzed; (3) Students find it particularly challenging to disaggregate data (i.e. separate it to identify trends and differences between different demographics).

BE CONFIDENT

➔ Develop this skill for yourself by doing the following activity:

1 *What makes a good survey? Think whether you agree or disagree with these statements.*

  a The questions asked should be straightforward.

  b The language used should be very simple.

  c Respondents should have to answer every question.

  d You should use the same number of ranking options in each question.

  e You should combine several questions together into one.

2 *Imagine you are creating a survey for teachers about their experience of critical thinking in the classroom. What questions would you ask? What do you think their responses would be?*

Lead-in

Give students a minute to read the speaking task they will do at the end of the unit. Then give them a few minutes to brainstorm the use of surveys. Tell them to keep their brainstorming notes for later, when they begin to develop their presentations.

UNLOCK TEACHER DEVELOPMENT

BE READY

Look at the Critical Thinking section in the Student's Book on pages 73–74.

➔ Which elements of the lesson do you think your students will find easiest / most difficult / most useful? Why?

➔ Are your answers true for all students in your class?

➔ How can you adapt your teaching or the material to meet your students' needs?

BE FLEXIBLE

Before looking at the critical thinking section in the book, you could ask your class (1) to briefly share their experiences of completing surveys, and (2) if/when surveys are used in their academic subjects (and what they are used for).

Exercises 1–6 pages 73–74

Answers will vary.

UNLOCK TEACHER DEVELOPMENT

BE REFLECTIVE

Consider the following questions:

➔ Think about any survey or questionnaire you have created in the past. Based on what you have learnt in this unit, what changes would you make? If you were to create another in the future, what would you do?

➔ What aspects of the lesson enabled your students to link this critical thinking focus to their future academic studies?

BE COLLABORATIVE

Your development is more meaningful when it is shared. See page 14 for ideas on how to peer-collaborate. Why not share the ideas you generated in the *Be ready* section, and their outcome?

PREPARATION FOR SPEAKING

Learning objectives

- Conduct a survey using correct rising or falling intonation in open and closed questions
- Use appropriate phrases to present survey data displayed in visuals: *This pie chart compares ..., The majority of respondents said ...*
- Present the conclusions of your research using appropriate words and phrases: *Survey results indicate that ..., Taking all the results into account, ..., This stands in contrast to ...*

Exercise 1 page 75

1 b   2 a   3 a   4 a   5 b

Exercises 2–3 page 75

Answers will vary.

Exercises 4–5 pages 76–77

Answers will vary.

Optional activity

Tell students to review their data analysis from Critical Thinking, Exercise 3. In their groups, they should determine what conclusions, if any, they can draw based on their analysis. Then they practise stating these conclusions, using the expressions in the Skills box on page 76.

SPEAKING TASK

Learning objectives

- Prepare for a group presentation on online security or privacy by evaluating the effectiveness of your survey data and questions
- Develop graphic support for your presentation to communicate the results of your survey
- Prepare for a group presentation on online security or privacy by assigning roles
- Prepare for (your part of) a presentation on online security or privacy by developing structured talking points
- Present and respond to feedback on the conclusions you have made from the survey data
- Give feedback on the conclusions others present to you from their survey data
- Give an individual or group presentation on online security or privacy

Exercises 1–8 pages 77–78

Answers will vary.

RESEARCH PROJECT

Develop a podcast on identity theft, with the goals of informing consumers about the problem and giving information about how to deal with it.

Students work in groups and research different aspect of the topic, including:

- What is identity theft and what are the different types?
- How does it happen?
- How can you prevent it?
- What should you do if you have been a victim?

If possible, they could record an interview with somebody who has experienced this problem. If this is not possible, they can include a profile(s) of a victim(s) they have read about online or in the news.

Each group then creates a three-minute podcast of this information to share with other groups. This could be shared in the lesson or using online tools.

CLASSROOM APP

Exercise 1

Answers will vary.

Exercise 2

1 have   2 say   3 understand   4 have   5 are; cost
6 pay

Exercise 3

1 network   2 cookies   3 search   4 enable   5 surfing
6 engines

Exercise 4

1 personalize   2 target   3 insight   4 compel
5 trade-off   6 trace   7 livelihood   8 move on

Exercise 5

Answers will vary.

Exercise 6

1 into account   2 indicates; suggests   3 it is clear; it follows; we can conclude; it can be concluded
4 it can be concluded; we can conclude
5 clearly demonstrates; demonstrates

Exercise 7

Answers will vary.

UNIT OBJECTIVES	
Watch and listen	Watch and understand a video about the tech hub in East Africa.
Listening skills	Listen for definitions; understand figurative language; identify figurative language.
Critical thinking	Persuade your audience in a business presentation.
Grammar	Emphasize and contrast.
Speaking skills	Craft a mission statement; craft a pitch.
Speaking task	Make a pitch to get funding for a new venture.
⟳ **Teacher development**	Help your students become better at **persuading your audience in a business presentation**.

UNLOCK YOUR KNOWLEDGE

Background note

The photo shows people in China queueing outside the American coffee chain, Starbucks. In the last 20 years, e-commerce and globalization have changed the way people buy and consume goods. Many online businesses, like Amazon, have become extremely successful, and other long-established high street brands have disappeared. Consumer demands have also changed. Nowadays, customers expect a high level of service, speed, choice, easy-to-recognize branding and good value for money. Consumers can also share their experiences online, which makes business more consumer-driven.

Lead-in

Ask students what influences the decisions they make about how and where they spend their money. Where do they get information to help them make those decisions? What factors are most important to them? They should provide examples (e.g., *I ask my friends about the best places to eat. Good value is most important to me.*) Make a chart on the board like the one below to list their ideas. (Note: be aware that money can be a sensitive issue and that students may not wish to speak too personally about how they spend their money.)

What	Information source	Important factor
restaurants	friends	value

page 81
Answers will vary.

WATCH AND LISTEN

Learning objectives

- Listen and understand the main ideas in a video about business opportunities in mobile app development
- Listen and understand detailed information
- Listen and identify the meaning of unfamiliar words and phrases from their context in the video
- Practise talking about app development and business opportunities

Exercises 1–2 page 82
Answers will vary.

Exercise 3 page 83

1 T   **2** F; Ugandan tech companies are developing apps for local markets.   **3** DNS   **4** T   **5** F; Increasingly, people want to invest in African tech companies.

Exercise 4 page 83

1 *Possible answers:* gaming app / smartphone app / app   **2** access the web   **3** developer challenge   **4** publicity and mentoring   **5** mobile money   **6** young people   **7** markets   **8** creators

Exercise 5 page 83

Answers will vary. Possible answers:

1 achieved; accomplished

2 increasing numbers of people

3 young people who are very clever and successful

4 cause something to make progress

5 situation where something is getting a lot of attention

6 time when an industry suddenly increases in size and makes a lot of money

7 encouraged   **8** workplaces where people share their ideas

9 begin to make money in   **10** producing a lot of money

Exercise 6 page 83

Answers will vary.

LISTENING 1

Learning objectives

- Understand key vocabulary for business innovation – *venture, disruptive, buzzwords*
- Listen to an introduction and use it to predict the content of a lecture about disruptive innovation
- Listen and use questions about main ideas to structure detailed notes on a lecture
- Listen and identify definitions of key terms
- Understand the use of figurative language in the context of a lecture about disruptive innovation
- Gain awareness of the way that speakers use pauses to indicate thought groups
- Identify pauses which indicate thought groups in a speaker's words
- Explain your experience of online innovations

Lead-in

Ask students for an example of a definition. If they need prompting, suggest some possibilities, such as *user interface, entrepreneur, inventory, marketing*. It is likely that they will use the standard format with the verb *to be* as in *User interface is …* or possibly, *the definition of user interface is …*.

Tell them that this is indeed a common form of giving definitions in presentations, but there are many others, which they will learn about in this unit.

Exercise 1 page 84

1 c 2 a 3 a 4 a 5 c 6 a 7 c 8 b

Exercises 2–4 page 85

Answers will vary.

Exercise 5 page 85

b, c and d are all discussed; *Answers will vary.*

Exercise 6 page 86

1 d 2 a 3 b 4 f 5 c 6 e 7 g

Be flexible

👤 Ask students to find the signals that the speaker uses to explain the definitions of each of the terms in Exercise 6. You may wish to do this activity and Exercise 6 simultaneously, so students do not have to go through the process twice. Allow **weaker students** to read the script as they listen.

Exercise 7 page 87

Possible answers:

engine: literal: the thing that powers a machine

friction: figurative: something that slows a process, or makes it more difficult

harnessing: literal: using apparatus to control a powerful animal, usually in order to use its power for work; figurative: using the power of something to create something useful

casualty: literal: somebody who dies or is very seriously hurt because of an action that person was not responsible for, often used for non-military people injured or killed in war; figurative: something that becomes obsolete

Exercise 8 page 88

Possible answers:

1 With IBM's new, smaller model however / computers became accessible / to an entirely new group of customers.

2 The internet has become the engine / of disruptive innovation / in dozens of markets / from travel / to publishing / to insurance.

3 Firstly / suddenly / anybody with a computer / and a network connection / could access all kinds of information / information that had previously only been available / to professionals.

4 Travel sites / such as Expedia / and Kayak / aggregate information / on dozens of airlines and car rentals / and thousands of hotels / allowing customers to compare / and make their choices / from a single site.

5 With online transactions / there is no need for people / no need for interaction / which could slow things down.

Exercises 9–10 page 88

Answers will vary.

LANGUAGE DEVELOPMENT

Learning objectives

- Use phrases to emphasize contrast and extremes in sentences about businesses – *Customers no longer have to visit different websites, let alone different shops. Too much choice may lead to indecision, even decision-making paralysis. The company's owner is talented and intelligent, not to mention rich.*
- Understand the connotations of academic alternatives to common words and phrases and use them in sentences: *stop using = abandon – A lot of people have abandoned physical shops completely and make all purchases online.*

Exercise 1 page 89

1 let alone   **2** even   **3** even   **4** not to mention
5 let alone   **6** not to mention / let alone

Exercise 2 page 90

Answers will vary.

Be flexible

👤 Ask students to create their own sentences with *even* and *let alone*. This will be challenging, so give them a frame to start them off:

- situation/characteristic X, sometimes even situation/characteristic Y
  e.g. *The temperatures in Iraq can reach the 30s (°C), sometimes <u>even</u> the 40s.*
  She can be unpleasant, sometimes <u>even</u> hostile.
- I can't X, let alone Y.
  e.g. *I can't read Mandarin, <u>let alone</u> write it.*

Ask **stronger students** to create their own sentences using *not to mention.*

Exercise 3 page 90

Answers will vary.

Exercise 4 page 90

1 analyze   **2** abandoned   **3** traces   **4** emerged
5 venture   **6** primary   **7** options   **8** large

Exercise 5 page 91

Answers will vary.

LISTENING 2

Learning objectives

- Understand key vocabulary for non-profit organizations – *donor, worthy, enterprise*
- Listen and understand the main ideas in a presentation about non-profit organizations
- Listen, identify and take detailed notes on the definitions of key terms in a presentation about non-profit organizations
- Understand the use of figurative language in the context of a lecture about non-profit organizations
- Use figurative imagery to describe non-profit organizations
- Gain an awareness of words and phrases which signal whether a speaker is presenting facts or opinions
- Synthesize information from a lecture about disruptive innovation and a presentation about non-profit organizations in a discussion

---

Lead-in

Bring in an image or poster for an international aid agency. Ask students what they think motivates people to donate (or not) to organizations like these, for example, is it only when there is a crisis?

Exercise 1 page 91

1 overview   **2** worthy   **3** status   **4** scope   **5** donors
6 oversight   **7** concisely   **8** enterprise

Exercise 2 page 92

1 Myanmar   **2** *Answers will vary.*

Exercise 3 page 92

Answers will vary.

Exercise 4 page 92

1 T   **2** F; The main difference between non-profits and for-profits is that non-profits are established to achieve some sort of social good. Non-profits make revenue but all of it must be returned to the organization.

3 F; All of the revenue (which includes donations) must be returned to the organization. Most of this money should be used for the organization's programmes, but some of it must be used for the administration of the organization.

4 T   **5** DNS

6 F; Non-profits are learning from the for-profit sector about how to harness market forces, but so that they can use the revenue for good.

Exercise 5 page 93

1 an organization that achieves social good
2 the purpose of the organization
3 donations, grants, money from fundraising
4 activities that provide direct benefits to people who need help
5 the value of a for-profit company which can be distributed among shareholders
6 the five or more people who have oversight over an organization
7 raising money from donors, grants, etc. to fund the non-profit's activities

Exercise 6 page 93

1 Non-profit organizations   **2** equity   **3** revenue
4 fundraising   **5** programmes   **6** mission   **7** board of directors

Exercise 7 page 94

1 lifeblood of a non-profit; *Answers will vary.*
2 a child that is always hungry; *Answers will vary.*
3 starvation budget; *Answers will vary.*
4 harness market forces; *Answers will vary.*
5 make your mark; *Answers will vary.*

Exercise 8 page 94

nuts and bolts: 1 mechanical pieces of machinery
2 the small but important details of how it works

wheels of commerce turn: 1 mechanical, interconnected machinery
2 getting things to run smoothly or as they should

Exercises 9–10 page 94
Answers will vary.

Be flexible

Tell students to think about figurative language in technology. Display the following terms and elicit their meanings. In what sense are they figurative? What is the literal meaning on which each is based?

- digital footprints
- digital fingerprints
- search engine
- surfing the web
- the cloud
- data mining

Why is figurative language frequently found in emerging technology? (It is frequently used because it makes the unfamiliar seem more familiar.)

Challenge **stronger students** to analyze the figurative language in the Skills box on page 93. Which expressions involve personification? Which involve idioms or comparisons with other experiences?

Exercise 11 page 94
Answers will vary.

CRITICAL THINKING

Learning objectives

- Understand the potential of P2P and non-profit venture propositions
- Analyze and evaluate P2P and non-profit venture propositions from the perspective of investors/donors
- Create a P2P or non-profit venture proposition

UNLOCK TEACHER DEVELOPMENT

BE INFORMED

→ **Persuading your audience in a business presentation** is an important skill for students because: (1) If they are going to succeed in today's extremely competitive business world, students need to be able to persuade others; (2) Students can underestimate the challenges of giving business presentations. It is important they understand how to deliver them most effectively; (3) The more practice students have, the better they will be able to develop the difficult skill of persuasion. Feedback from you and fellow students will help with this.

BE CONFIDENT

→ Develop this skill for yourself by doing the following activity:

Imagine that you are teaching a new class at the beginning of the academic year. The students say that they are not interested in learning about critical thinking. How would you convince them that (1) critical thinking is important, and (2) critical thinking is fun?

Lead-in

Give students a minute to read the speaking task they will do at the end of the unit. Give them a few minutes to brainstorm what they know about making a pitch. Tell them to keep their brainstorming notes for later, when they begin to develop their pitches.

UNLOCK TEACHER DEVELOPMENT

BE READY

Look at the Critical Thinking section in the Student's Book on pages 95–97.

→ Which elements of the lesson do you think your students will find easiest / most difficult / most useful? Why?

→ Are your answers true for all students in your class?

→ How can you adapt your teaching or the material to meet your students' needs?

BE FLEXIBLE

Get together a collection of unusual items. Divide the class into groups. Randomly give each group one of these items. Together, they must create a business 'pitch', which they then present to the rest of the class. At the end, the class votes on which item they would invest their money in.

Exercises 1–5 pages 95–97
Answers will vary.

UNLOCK TEACHER DEVELOPMENT

BE REFLECTIVE

Think about the following points:

→ You could ask a colleague to role play the task the class described in the *Be confident* section, by pretending to not be interested in critical thinking. Try your arguments on them and see if you are successful in changing their mind!

→ Did anything about the students' responses surprise you in this lesson? If so, why? How could you use that information in future lessons?

BE COLLABORATIVE

Your development is more meaningful when it is shared. See page 14 for ideas on how to peer-collaborate. Why not share the persuasive techniques you experimented with in the *Be confident* section, and the response they received?

PREPARATION FOR SPEAKING

Learning objectives

- Develop an effective mission statement for a P2P or a non-profit venture proposition
- Craft a pitch to investors/donors by considering how to get their attention, appeal to their emotions and leave a lasting impression

Exercise 1 page 98

Possible answer: Our mission is to offer educational assistance to low-income teens within their own communities.

Optional activity

👤 Ask students to find mission statements of well-known companies or non-profit organizations online. Many companies publish their mission statement on their home page, but they can be found easily by simply searching for the company or organization name and 'mission statement'. Ask students to analyze the statements, using the three bullet points in the Skills box on page 97.

Exercises 2–5 pages 98–99

Answers will vary.

SPEAKING TASK

Exercises 1–5 page 100

Answers will vary.

RESEARCH PROJECT

Give a presentation on for-profit and non-profit business collaborations.

This project could be a series of group presentations. Alternatively, the class could collate their information, compiling a series of business/organization profiles.

Ask students to do some research on for-profit and non-profit collaborations. How can businesses work with non-profit organizations for the benefit of both? Students should work in small groups. The groups can be organized in two ways. The simplest is for each group to look at a separate collaboration (e.g., Oxfam with Swiss Re). Alternatively, they could research and then present different types of collaboration (e.g. a business that donates a portion of its profits to a non-profit; employees of a for-profit business that give time to a non-profit; direct grants or donations, etc.).

CLASSROOM APP

Exercises 1–2

Answers will vary.

Exercise 3

1 let alone   **2** not to mention   **3** even   **4** let alone
5 even   **6** let alone   **7** not to mention

Exercise 4

1 emerged   **2** options   **3** considerable   **4** primary
5 abandoned   **6** traces   **7** venture   **8** analyzed; analyzes

Exercise 5

1 buzzword   **2** transaction   **3** wary   **4** enterprise
5 oversight   **6** worthy   **7** status   **8** scope

Exercise 6

1 use imagery or figurative language   **2** make them feel special   **3** tell a story   **4** make them nervous   **5** appeal to emotions

UNIT OBJECTIVES

Watch and listen	Watch and understand a video about scientific research into dementia.
Listening skills	Listen for generalizations and summaries; listen for dependency relationships.
Critical thinking	Synthesize information from multiple sources.
Grammar	Use noun clauses with *wh-* words and *if / whether*.
Speaking skills	Talk about research; incorporate visual support.
Speaking task	Give a group presentation synthesizing research.
☉ Teacher development	Help your students become better at **synthesizing information from multiple sources**.

UNLOCK YOUR KNOWLEDGE

Background note

The photo shows a crowd of people; the focus is on their faces. Some people have an excellent memory for faces, whereas other people find it hard to remember what people look like. Skills and abilities like these are influenced by characteristics we are born with and inherit from our parents, but also by other things that we learn through our environment and experiences. This is the focus of one of the great psychological debates: are we influenced more by our nature (what we are born with) or our nurture (how we are brought up)?

Lead-in

Write these statements about the brain on the board, and ask students to read and respond to them. Check to make sure students understand any difficult words and structures. When they are ready, begin a class discussion of the statements. You could have a class vote to decide on the most fascinating statement.

- Tears come from the heart and not from the brain.
- One of the most complicated objects in the known universe is sitting on your shoulders.
- The function of the body is to carry the brain around.
- For some reason, chewing gum gets my brain going.

page 103
Answers will vary.

WATCH AND LISTEN

Learning objectives

- Listen and identify the main idea in a video about dementia research
- Listen and complete a set of detailed notes
- Make inferences about the implications of the ideas in a video about dementia research
- Practise talking about technology and its role in psychology research

Exercises 1–2 page 104
Answers will vary.

Exercise 3 page 104
b

Exercise 4 page 105
1 virtual reality game   2 through simple mazes   3 spatial awareness   4 struggling and dying   5 Functional
6 triple   7 known cure   8 mobile devices
9 normal healthy   10 measurable differences

Exercise 5 page 105
Answers will vary. Possible answers:

1 because of the huge increase in dementia sufferers that is currently predicted; to prevent the number of dementia sufferers from tripling by 2050

2 by installing the game on their devices; by promoting the game to their customers; by funding part of the research; by providing technical support to game players; by providing technological expertise

3 a more detailed understanding of how people navigate; a more detailed understanding of the parts of the brain involved in navigation; a more detailed understanding of the early brain changes in dementia sufferers; a way to diagnose early brain changes that indicate dementia, using *Sea Hero Quest*

Exercise 6 page 105

Answers will vary.

LISTENING 1

Learning objectives

- Understand key vocabulary for the psychology of first impressions – *speculate, cue, approachable*
- Understand phrases that speakers use to signal generalizations and summaries
- Listen, identify and take notes on generalizations and summaries in a conversation about research into the psychology of first impressions
- Listen and understand detail
- Differentiate between main ideas and details
- Understand the use of stress to emphasize main ideas in thought groups
- Understand and explain the ideas and implications of psychological research findings about first impressions

Lead-in

Write *first impression* on the board and ask students if they understand the meaning of this phrase (the event when one person first meets another person and forms a mental image of that person). Note that first impressions are not always accurate. Elicit examples from students if possible. Explain that the speakers in the audio discuss the psychology of first impressions as the topic of their presentation.

Exercises 1–2 page 106

Answers will vary.

Exercise 3 page 107

a competent   **b** exposure   **c** speculate
d approachable   **e** applications   **f** dominance
g relate to   **h** cue

Exercise 4 page 107

a, c, d

Exercise 5 page 108

Answers will vary. Possible answers:

1 people respond to a variety of cues and form first impressions very fast

2 physical appearance is the most important cue in first impressions

3 during early human evolution, deciding quickly if you could trust somebody must have been a really important ability

4 the judgements they made in a few milliseconds held true in real life

5 our first response is to go for somebody who is generally attractive

6 he was able to get consistent judgements for particular features of the faces on three traits

Optional activity

Ask students to review the final one or two paragraphs of a few scripts from previous units. Do they contain some of the phrases listed in the Skills box on page 108? If not, how do the speakers sum up the content of their presentation? Do they always do so? What are other ways the speakers summarize or conclude their presentations?

Exercise 6 page 109

1 a, b, c, d, f, g, j   **2** trustworthiness; attractiveness, dominance; approachability

Exercise 7 page 109

1 MI   **2** MI   **3** D   **4** D   **5** MI   **6** D

Exercise 8 page 109

Answers will vary.

Exercise 9 page 110

1 **Eva:** So, cues; **Ramzi:** nutshell, physical appearance, important cue, first impressions

2 **Ramzi:** Basically, quickly, trust, most important, early; **Eva:** probably, is, really, another, similar, specific

3 **Sara:** photos, attractive, all, agreed, fours, some, few

4 **Sara:** first, generally, call, good catch

5 **Sara:** different, also, who, good catch, me

Exercise 10 page 110

Answers will vary.

LANGUAGE DEVELOPMENT

Learning objectives

- Use noun clauses with *wh- words* and *if/whether* to talk about first impressions – *When I meet people for the first time, I watch how they act in the first few minutes very carefully.*
- Understand the relationship between adjectives and nouns in academic word families and use them in sentences: *dominant* (adj) *dominance* (n); *attractive* (adj) *attractiveness* (n); *aggressive* (adj) *aggression* (n)

Exercise 1 page 111

1 This quiz can tell you who would make a good life partner.

2 It's difficult to say what people react to in first impressions.

3 It's surprising which facial features are particularly significant in first impressions.

4 Researchers wanted to find out if / whether initial judgements are accurate.

5 One recent study looked at how fast people make decisions about traits such as reliability and intelligence.

Exercise 2 page 111

Answers will vary.

Optional activity

👥 Select a volunteer for a conversation. Ask a question such as *What did you do last weekend?* or *Did the football team play a good game last night?* Then ask the rest of the class, *What did I ask?*. Students should report back: *You asked about… .* Repeat with one more learner. Then divide the class into small groups. Two people in each group have a conversation (e.g. one student asks the other a question), and then the rest of the group asks about what was asked and either of the two report back using *if / whether* or *wh-* noun clauses. You may wish to specify the topic of their conversations, such as ways to revise for an exam or talking about an activity they did recently.

Exercise 3 page 112

1 thoughtful   **2** dominant   **3** competence
4 approachable   **5** attractiveness

Exercise 4 page 112

Answers will vary.

LISTENING 2

Learning objectives

- Understand key vocabulary for the psychology of memory and spatial awareness – *navigate, reconstruct, impair*
- Listen and identify main ideas in a lecture about memory and spatial navigation research
- Listen and take detailed notes
- Use detailed notes to summarize the most important ideas in a presentation
- Gain an awareness of words and phrases which signal dependency relationships
- Listen and identify words and phrases which signal dependency relationships and note the relationships they describe
- Use your notes to summarize the information in a presentation
- Make inferences about the details and implications of research
- Synthesize information from a conversation about research into the psychology of first impressions and a lecture about memory and spatial navigation research

---

Lead-in

Give students a multiple choice quiz about the brain. This should give them an idea of the brain's importance.

1 The brain accounts for ___ percent of the body's weight.

   a 2 ✓   **b** 5   **c** 10

2 The brain uses ___ percent of the body's oxygen.

   a 10   **b** 20 ✓   **c** 40

3 The brain uses ___ percent of the body's energy.

   a 10   **b** 20 ✓   **c** 40

Exercise 1 page 113

1 frontal lobe   **2** parietal lobe   **3** occipital lobe
4 temporal lobe   **5** hippocampus

Exercise 2 page 113

f

Exercise 3 page 114

1 b   **2** a   **3** b   **4** b   **5** b   **6** a   **7** c   **8** a

Exercise 4 page 115

Answers will vary.

Exercise 5 page 115

a, d

Exercise 6 page 115

1 plays a key role in spatial memory and navigation
2 spatial or landmark; response   **3** spatial or landmark
4 an increase in the size of the hippocampus

Exercise 7 page 116

1 spatial memory and navigation
2 the hippocampus
3 repeated trips along the same route
4 the drivers' brains
5 the creation of mental maps and the increased size of the hippocampus

---

Be flexible

👥 Ask students to review the script for Listening 1 and summarize dependency relationships in the studies described there.

Challenge **stronger students** to describe other dependency relationships in science. If needed, suggest that students review the relationships they read about in Unit 1 Conservation.

Exercise 8 page 116

Answers will vary.

Exercise 9 page 117

1 b   2 c   3 b

Exercise 10 page 117

Answers will vary.

CRITICAL THINKING

Learning objectives

- Understand three descriptions of psychological phenomena and choose a topic for your presentation
- Read research papers related to psychological studies and analyze the methods used by researchers
- Evaluate the reliability of research studies and internet sources
- Analyze the similarities and difference in content and implications of two research studies
- Synthesize information from two research studies and draw conclusions

UNL🔒CK TEACHER DEVELOPMENT

BE INFORMED

→ **Synthesizing information from multiple sources** is an important skill for students because: (1) It is a skill required in every academic subject; (2) Students coming from academic, social or cultural backgrounds which place emphasis on 'authority' find it particularly difficult to do this; (3) Students frequently lack the knowledge or tools to make decisions about what constitutes a good source, e.g. who wrote it, when it was written, who published it and where it is found.

BE CONFIDENT

→ Develop this skill for yourself by doing the following activity:

Imagine that you want to find out more about critical thinking, and you do an internet search. Look at the five results below. Rank them from most useful to least useful. What criteria are you using to make your decision?

1 Hong Kong University description of critical thinking: It includes the ability to engage in reflective and independent thinking. Somebody with critical thinking skills is able to ...

2 *Think Think Think* **(online subscription service):** Your first stop for critical thinking materials. One-month free membership if you join today.

3 *Critical Thinking* **second edition, by Alec Fisher (Cambridge University Press, 2011):** This engaging coursebook aims to teach critical thinking skills – the ability to interpret, analyze and evaluate ideas and arguments. Alec Fisher's approach is based on a widely shared conception of critical thinking.

4 Book review: *Taking critical thinking to the MAX* (New Modern Publishing House) ★★★☆☆

'If you have ever felt confused about critical thinking, DON'T PANIC. This book contains EVERYTHING you need to know.'

5 Book review: *Critical Thinking: an analytical summary*

'Published nearly three decades ago, this book continues to have a considerable influence over the critical thinking landscape.'

Lead-in

Give students a minute to read the speaking task they will do at the end of the unit. Then give them a few minutes to brainstorm sources of research. Tell them to keep their brainstorming notes for later, when they begin to develop their presentations.

UNL🔒CK TEACHER DEVELOPMENT

BE READY

Look at the Critical Thinking section in the Student's Book on pages 118–120.

→Which elements of the lesson do you think your students will find easiest / most difficult / most useful? Why?

→ Are your answers true for all students in your class?

→ How can you adapt your teaching or the material to meet your students' needs?

BE FLEXIBLE

A useful strategy for this lesson is to ask students to share their own experiences of searching the internet (and elsewhere) for information. They could also analyze what they could have done differently in order to get better search results.

Exercises 1–5 pages 119–120

Answers will vary.

UNLOCK TEACHER DEVELOPMENT

BE REFLECTIVE

Think about the following points:

→ Ask colleagues if they have any useful sources for critical thinking. Ask them to say why they think these sources are especially useful.

→ Evaluate how successful your teaching of critical thinking was. Which part was most successful? Which part was least successful? Why?

BE COLLABORATIVE

Your development is more meaningful when it is shared. See page 14 for ideas on how to peer-collaborate. Why not share any texts you sourced from the *Be reflective* section, and their impact on the lesson?

PREPARATION FOR SPEAKING

Learning objectives

- Prepare talking points which organize information about research studies for a presentation
- Prepare effective slides to accompany talking points in a presentation

Optional activity

Tell students to analyze Maguire's study in terms of the elements listed in the Skills box on Talking about research on page 121. This is the fifth paragraph in the script on page 254.

Exercises 1–2 page 121
Answers will vary.

SPEAKING TASK

Learning objectives

- Prepare for a group presentation on an aspect of human behaviour by assigning roles
- Present and respond to feedback on the content of your presentation, presentation style and slides
- Give feedback on the content of other students' presentations, presentation styles and slides
- Give a group presentation on an aspect of human behaviour

Exercises 1–5 pages 122–123
Answers will vary

RESEARCH PROJECT

Create a blog post on internet research sources.

Ask students to write a blog post describing internet research sources, specifically *unreliable* academic sources. Students research different kinds of unreliable sources (e.g., blogs, personal websites). If students are working in groups, each group can look at one type of source. They should collect typical or egregious examples and present evidence for their lack of reliability. As a class, they should compile their findings to create the final blog post. The post should end with practical recommendations for readers (e.g. to check for when an online document was created or last updated).

CLASSROOM APP

Exercises 1–2
Answers will vary

Exercise 3

1 how people respond
2 why some people in the study misinterpreted
3 if other studies; whether other studies
4 how subjects learned; how subjects learnt
5 if you want to participate; whether you want to participate
6 what we concluded

Exercise 4

1 attractiveness 2 dominance 3 aggression
4 likeability 5 approachability 6 thoughtfulness
7 competence

Exercise 5

1 cues 2 speculate 3 applications 4 reconstruct
5 impaired 6 exposure 7 landmark 8 deteriorated

Exercise 6

1 results 2 method (what happened) 3 research question 4 introduction 5 conclusion 6 results
7 method (what happened) 8 research question
9 participants

UNIT OBJECTIVES	
Watch and listen	Watch and understand a video about a job fair.
Listening skill	Make inferences.
Critical thinking	Understand job descriptions.
Grammar	Use degree expressions with *so ... that*; *such a ... that*.
Speaking skill	Prepare for a job interview.
Speaking task	Participate in a mock job interview.
⟳ **Teacher development**	Help your students become better at **understanding job descriptions**.

UNL⟳CK YOUR KNOWLEDGE

Background note

The photo shows an engineer and a group of trainees using an industrial machine. Career experts recommend on-the-job training for young people who want to get employment early and prefer practical learning. As well as academic learning and training, you can prepare for a career by developing an online profile, seeing a careers adviser, organizing work placements and networking. According to HR experts, there are many new job opportunities in areas such as: apps and computer programming; online communications and social media; marketing and advertising; environmental management; robotics and engineering; and data analysis.

Lead-in

Ask students to work in teams to brainstorm career and job training vocabulary for the following categories:

- looking for a job
- changing jobs
- job training
- career development
- qualifications

You could add your own categories to make the exercise more challenging. The first team to think of four words in each category wins.

page 125
Answers will vary.

WATCH AND LISTEN

Learning objectives

- Listen and identify the main ideas in a video about jobs for young people in the USA
- Listen, take notes and summarize detailed information
- Make inferences about the event in the video
- Practise talking about jobs fairs and equal opportunities in education

Exercises 1–2 page 126
Answers will vary.

Exercise 3 page 127

6, 1, 7, 5, 4, 3, 2

Exercise 4 page 127
Answers will vary. Possible answers:

1 Violent crime is high in areas of Chicago with high unemployment.
2 Opportunity youth are the disadvantaged young people whom the job fair will help.
3 These are the qualities young people learn from work and which lead to success at university, according to the politician.
4 These factors should not affect opportunities for the young, according to the politician.
5 These are the personal qualities the young woman believes will get her a job at the job fair.
6 This is the reason Nordstrom's recruiter gives for offering Everett Young a job.

Exercise 5 page 127
Answers will vary. Possible answers:

1 careers advice; apprenticeships; training; help writing a CV; interview practice

2 to offer hope to young people; to show young people from disadvantaged backgrounds that large employers are interested in them; to find talented young people from disadvantaged backgrounds who want to work

3 violent crime; other types of street crime, e.g. vandalism, drugs, gangs, etc.; mental health problems; people not having enough food to eat, etc.

4 helps them pay for education; helps them learn about better jobs they could do if they had more qualifications; helps them prove their personal qualities and get character references

5 he is articulate and charming; he seems intelligent; he presents himself well

Exercise 6 page 127
Answers will vary.

LISTENING 1

Learning objectives

- Understand key vocabulary for employment and workplaces – *probationary period, daunting, discrimination*
- Listen and take notes on the main ideas in a presentation about careers in IT
- Listen and take detailed notes
- Make inferences about a speaker's implications
- Gain an awareness of the reduced sounds of unstressed auxiliary verbs
- Listen and identify particular auxiliary verbs in fast speech
- Explain the information communicated in infographics about start-up businesses and entrepreneurs
- Discuss information from a presentation and infographics, and advise qualified jobseekers in IT on their best strategies

Exercise 1 page 128
Answers will vary.

Exercise 2 page 128
1 the proportion of people in the UK who are self-employed   **2** *Possible answers:* small shopkeepers; writers; musicians; plumbers   **3–4** *Answers will vary.*

Lead-in

Ask students to think about the ways they can find jobs after they complete their studies. Elicit ideas from the class. Some ideas may be e.g. through a careers adviser at a university, on social media websites, through shared connections (networking), etc. Write the ideas on the board. Then ask students to rank the different methods from most useful to least useful and give reasons for their choices.

Exercise 3 page 129
a probationary period   **b** daunting   **c** discrimination
d cap   **e** vision   **f** distinct   **g** start out   **h** be landed with

Exercise 4 page 129

1 to address the pros and cons of three distinct ways Computer Science students can enter the job market in the United Kingdom

2 Computer Science students

3 take a position as an employee; become a consultant / an independent contractor / a freelance worker; establish your own business

Exercise 5 page 130
Possible answers:

	pros	cons
work for a company	immediately start using the skills and knowledge you've gained in your studies; good bet if you lack experience; job security; regular pay cheque; no business expenses; safe workplace – protected against discrimination and harassment	probationary period (can be asked to leave); maybe wardrobe and travel expenses
work as a consultant / independent contractor / freelancer	earn more money; control over work and income; no limit to growth	no workplace protection; unpredictable; have to find your work; no sickness / pension benefits; start-up costs; insurance; business taxes; unpaid bills
establish your own start-up company	you are your own boss; independence; decide what work you want to do; your vision; rewarding	risky; can be stressful to start; needs discipline; impact on personal relationships

Exercise 6 page 130
Answers will vary.

Exercise 7 pages 130–131
1 a   **2** a   **3** c   **4** b   **5** a   **6** c

Optional activity

👤👥 Give students other examples of information that they can infer. Start with some informal ones (see examples below) and then use the listening. Once they understand the activity, ask them to work in pairs to go through the rest of the text and find inferable ideas. (See support following each sentence for explanation of underlining.)

- *You should really study this section of the textbook.* → They infer that it may be in the test.
- *I was going to discuss the reading today but perhaps some of you need a little extra time.* → You think a lot of them haven't read it yet.
- *This job for is for people who have difficulty finding jobs because of their backgrounds.* → These people are poor and have not had a good education.
- *If you're considering taking a position abroad, keep in mind that some of the legal issues and government regulations that we're going to discuss may not apply to you.* → Employment laws differ across countries.
- *For those of you getting an undergraduate degree and who haven't had a lot of work experience, this option may be your best bet.* → You need more work experience for the other options.

Exercise 8 page 131

1 going to **2** could **3** would **4** want to **5** should **6** can; can **7** want to; can

Exercise 9 page 131

Answers will vary.

Exercises 10–11 page 132

Answers will vary.

LANGUAGE DEVELOPMENT

Learning objectives

- Use appropriate structures to show the consequences of extreme conditions or behaviour – *You shouldn't prepare so much (that) your answers sound rehearsed or mechanical. This is such an important point (that) I'll repeat it.*
- Use phrases to emphasize belief and certainty in sentences about businesses – *Make no mistake, not every computer science graduate is going to become a millionaire. It goes without saying that not every IT graduate will become a millionaire.*

Exercise 1 page 133

1 The current market is so strong that most businesses can make a profit.
2 She has so little energy that she cannot get to work most days.
3 Her company has been so successful / such a success that everyone asks her for business advice.
4 We bought so much / such a lot of equipment that we can't find anywhere to put it.
5 The volume is so low that nobody can hear the sound.
6 I had so little time that I had to make a very quick decision.

Exercise 2 page 133

Answers will vary.

Exercise 3 page 134

Answers will vary.

LISTENING 2

Learning objectives

- Understand key vocabulary for discussing job interviews – *dreaded, accomplishment, ramble on*
- Listen and take detailed notes on a workshop about job interviews
- Use your notes to answer questions about the main ideas and details in a workshop about job interviews
- Listen and improve a set of detailed notes
- Make inferences about a speaker's implications
- Synthesize information from a presentation about careers in IT and a workshop about job interviews in a discussion

Lead-in

In this activity, let students imagine the worst. What could go wrong at a job interview? What are their biggest fears? What do they dread the most about interviews? Have them work in small groups to brainstorm and discuss the questions.

Exercise 1 pages 134–135

1 a **2** c **3** c **4** b **5** a **6** b **7** c **8** a

Exercises 2–3 pages 135–136

Answers will vary.

Be flexible

👤👥 Tell students to write answers to the questions they wrote in Exercise 3, then ask and answer their questions with a partner. Remind students to use the language structures they have learnt thus far in the unit.

Exercise 4 page 136

Answers will vary.

Exercise 5 page 136

1 an overview of the job interview process
2 Prepare for your interview.

Exercise 6 page 136

Possible answers:

1 do research on the company; prepare for questions you think you might be asked / develop talking points; find out the format of the interview; do a practice interview; prepare questions to ask the interviewers
2 accomplishments; goals; work style; weaknesses
3 explain something you have struggled with and how you are working to improve it
4 answer the question that is being asked; be concise in your answers; give concrete examples; be honest
5 follow up with a brief message thanking the person for his or her time

Exercise 7 page 137

1 a 2 a 3 c 4 b 5 c

Exercise 8 page 137

Answers will vary.

CRITICAL THINKING

Learning objectives

- Remember information that is included in job descriptions
- Analyze common elements and language in job descriptions
- Evaluate your attributes and skills in relation to a job description
- Evaluate and create links between personal experiences and criteria in job description
- Evaluate another student's suitability for a particular job

UNL⌀CK TEACHER DEVELOPMENT

BE INFORMED

→ **Understanding job descriptions** is an important skill for students because: (1) students need all the support possible to get the kind of work they want in competitive job markets; (2) Writing a good job application is time-consuming, so students need to be selective in which jobs they apply for. Understanding a job description (and your suitability for the position) is therefore key; (3) Sometimes you need to 'read between the lines' – the more knowledge you have about how job descriptions are written, the better equipped you will be to understand what kind of person is sought.

BE CONFIDENT

→ Develop this skill for yourself by doing the following activity:

Imagine that you have been asked to write a job description for your own job. What would you include? Think about specific headings such as 'Responsibilities', 'Skills required' and 'Education and experience'.

Lead-in

Give students a minute to read the Speaking task they will do at the end of the unit. Then give them a few minutes to brainstorm their experience of interviews of any sort. Tell them to keep their brainstorming notes for later, when they begin to prepare for their interviews.

UNL⌀CK TEACHER DEVELOPMENT

BE READY

Look at the Critical Thinking section in the Student's Book on pages 138–140.

→ Which elements of the lesson do you think your students will find easiest / most difficult / most useful? Why?

→ Are your answers true for all students in your class?

→ How can you adapt your teaching or the material to meet your students' needs?

BE FLEXIBLE

With older students, sharing experiences (including your own) of reading job descriptions and applying for jobs will help link the theoretical with the real. You could also bring in a variety of real-life job descriptions for groups of mixed ability to discuss.

Exercise 1 page 138

Answers will vary.

Exercise 2 page 138

Possible answers:

1 job responsibilities; skills; qualifications

2 duties and responsibilities: verbs; skills and qualifications; nouns

3 age, gender, family status and other personal information

Exercises 3–6 page 140

Answers will vary.

UNL⌔CK TEACHER DEVELOPMENT

BE REFLECTIVE

Think about the following questions:

→ Look back at the job description which you wrote for your own job in the *Be confident* section. Are there any of your responsibilities which you find particularly difficult or challenging? If so, is there anything you could do to improve this situation?

→ Did you talk about your own personal experiences in this lesson? If so, how did the students respond? Would you do it again?

BE COLLABORATIVE

Your development is more meaningful when it is shared. See page 14 for ideas on how to peer-collaborate. Why not share the ideas you generated in the *Be ready* section, and their outcome?

PREPARATION FOR SPEAKING

Learning objectives

- Understand and evaluate different kinds of body language
- Understand and use appropriate phrases to present yourself as a good fit in a job interview

Exercise 1 page 141

Possible answers:

A negative: nail biting, slouched posture

B positive: firm handshake, good posture, eye contact, smile

C positive: leaning slightly forward, good posture, smile

D negative: arms crossed, unfriendly facial expression, slouched posture

Exercise 2 pages 142–143

Possible answers: **1** I work well   **2** am good at
3 three years' experience   **4** sales assistant
5 a large department store   **6** a BA in Management
7 City University   **8** make me a good fit for the position
9 to develop my skills

Exercise 3 page 143

Answers will vary.

Optional activity

Tell students to incorporate what they have learnt about body language into their presentation. Their partner's feedback should include feedback on appropriate body language.

SPEAKING TASK

Learning objectives

- Prepare questions, introductions and a way to sign off for a mock job interview
- Prepare talking points for a job interview
- Anticipate and prepare for questions in a job interview
- Practise using and responding to feedback on positive body language for a job interview
- Take part in a mock interview as an interviewer
- Take part in a mock interview as an interviewee

Exercises 1–6 pages 143–145

Answers will vary.

RESEARCH PROJECT

Develop a podcast or video series on careers.

Students do research individually or in pairs on careers or positions that interest them. They should find out what skills, education and qualifications are required, and describe the duties and responsibilities for an entry level (or higher if appropriate) position. If possible, they should interview somebody who holds such a position. The interview could be part of the podcast or serve as background information that the students present. Each student or pair presents their findings in a brief (about three minutes) podcast or video.

CLASSROOM APP

Exercises 1–2
Answers will vary.

Exercise 3
1 most of the shops have sold out
2 he should really consider the offer
3 he almost fell asleep at work
4 her hands were shaking
5 she got a promotion in her first year
6 she rarely had to study

Exercise 4
1 without saying   **2** all means   **3** believe me
4 no mistake   **5** a doubt   **6** beyond question

Exercise 5
1 analytical   **2** vision   **3** rehearsed   **4** accomplishments
5 discrimination   **6** distinct   **7** rambles on   **8** format

Exercise 6
1 I've always been good at, my degree is in
2 I studied at
3 I've had three years of experience; I hope to develop my skills
4 is exactly the kind of place
5 I'd be a great fit for this position

UNIT OBJECTIVES	
Watch and listen	Watch and understand a video about the impact of a chemical leak on the water supply.
Listening skills	Make unstructured notes as you listen; identify persuasive appeals.
Critical thinking	Understand motivation.
Grammar	Establish cohesion with *so* and *such*.
Speaking skill	Use inclusive language.
Speaking task	Participate in a community meeting about a local health controversy.
↻ **Teacher development**	Help your students become better at **understanding motivation**.

UNLOCK YOUR KNOWLEDGE

Background note

The photo shows dandelions blowing in the wind. Dandelions produce pollen that can cause allergies. Some of the symptoms of dandelion allergies include painful and itchy eyes, sneezing and a sore throat. They can also cause asthma symptoms, headaches and sinusitis.

Other environmental factors that can cause danger to human health are biological factors, such as bacteria, fungi and viruses. There are also chemical hazards, such as exposure to heavy metals like mercury and lead, and physical problems, such as water and waste management, housing and transportation. Unlike other health problems, conditions caused by environmental factors have an external cause and can be prevented.

Lead-in

When students answer the second question, press them further on environmental health hazards specifically, to develop a list of those that emanate directly from nature (e.g. pollen) and those that are created by human activity (e.g. toxic chemicals). Make a list on the board. Ask students to evaluate the seriousness of the threats.

page 147
Answers will vary.

WATCH AND LISTEN

Learning objectives

- Listen and understand the main ideas in a video about water pollution
- Listen and complete a detailed summary of a video about water pollution
- Make inferences about the implications of the ideas in a video about water pollution
- Practise talking about the relationship between the public and business in environmental scandals

Exercises 1–2 page 148
Answers will vary.

Exercise 3 page 149
1 T   **2** F; The effects of the chemical MCHM are unknown.   **3** F; The former governor supports legislation that requires regular inspections of chemical facilities.
4 T

Exercise 4 page 149
1 leak   **2** contaminated   **3** safe   **4** industry   **5** supports
6 inspections

Exercise 5 page 149
3, 4, 5

Exercise 6 page 149
Answers will vary.

LISTENING 1

Learning objectives

- Understand key vocabulary for the science of allergies – *correlation, hygiene, obesity*
- Listen and take unstructured notes on a lecture about the causes of allergies
- Use an ideas map to organize unstructured notes
- Summarize hypotheses presented in a lecture about the causes of allergies
- Understand the use of contrastive stress to signal comparisons and contrasts
- Listen, identify, understand and summarize contrasted information
- Describe personal experiences of allergies and evaluate the hypotheses from a lecture about their causes in a discussion

Lead-in

Ask students to consider the consequences of health threats in the environment. Make a list on the board (e.g. respiratory problems from air pollution, gastro-intestinal problems from poor sanitation, developmental problems from toxins, crop failures, etc.).

Exercise 1 page 150

Answers will vary.

Exercise 2 page 150

All of them show asthma triggers.

Exercise 3 page 151

1 obesity **2** guidelines **3** severity **4** disparity **5** incidence **6** allergy **7** correlation **8** hygiene

Exercises 4–5 page 152

Answers will vary.

Exercise 6 page 152

Possible answers:

Pollution Hypothesis: An increase in pollutants in the air that accompanies the increase in cars and factories has led to a rise in the incidence of asthma.

Hygiene Hypothesis: Children are kept in a very clean environment, so they are not exposed to microbes that could stimulate their immune systems. As a result, their immune systems do not develop adequately and when they are exposed to these triggers later in life, it has a negative effect on their health.

Optional activity

Ask students to repeat the process with the other environmental hypothesis. If you include this exercise, you should delay the peer feedback until both summaries are complete.

Exercise 7 page 152

1 indoor pollution (dust, mould, tobacco smoke, pet hair) **2** outdoor pollution (particulate matter, ground level ozone) **3** children **4** people living in urban areas **5** allergies **6** coughing **7** difficulty breathing **8** numbers soaring (up 25% since 2000) **9** 'modern life' (obesity, diet, sedentary lifestyle) **10** pollution **11** hygiene

Exercise 8 page 152

The blue line indicates a connection between pollution as a possible cause and pollution as a trigger. Some other possible connections: children (affected population) and 'modern life' (possible cause); allergies (symptoms) and hygiene (possible cause)

Exercise 9 page 152

Answers will vary.

Exercise 10 page 153

1 symptoms appear when exposed to triggers; symptoms present all the time

2 more common in urban settings like LA or Chicago; less common in rural Africa

3 don't know causes of asthma or how to cure; do know triggers and ways to manage symptoms

Exercise 11 page 153

1 how pollution correlates to incidence of asthma: East Germany – more pollution but less asthma; West Germany – less pollution but more asthma

2 immune response to microbes: early exposure = prepared in later life; no or later exposure = not prepared when encountered later in life

3 hypotheses: both pollution and hygiene explain some of the mystery; neither gives complete explanation

Exercise 12 page 153

Answers will vary.

LANGUAGE DEVELOPMENT

Learning objectives

- Use expressions with *so* and *such* to establish cohesion – *The city thought the water was safe and so did I. Such measures are critical to public health.*
- Use adjectives of strong disapproval to evoke emotional responses in sentences about news stories – *The inspectors were appalled at what they found. I was outraged by their lack of concern.*

Exercise 1 page 154

1 Asthma rates have risen dramatically, and so have allergy rates.

2 Early remedies for asthma included warm milk and cool baths. Unfortunately, such treatments do little to relieve the symptoms.

3 My aunt recently quit smoking. Such a major change in behaviour may have reduced her chances of getting asthma, cancer and other diseases.

4 Vigorous exercise contributes to asthma attacks; ironically, so does a sedentary lifestyle.

5 Some cities require monthly reports on water and air pollution; unfortunately, my city has / makes no such requirement.

Optional activity

👥 Ask students to complete the following sentences, using *so* to create cohesion. Say that *so* is the easier of the two structures.

- *I left my country when I was 18 and ….*
- *A balanced diet is an important part of a healthy lifestyle and ….*

Students then create their own sentence using *so*, working in pairs and taking turns. One student creates the stem and the other student completes it.

Exercise 2 page 154
Answers will vary.

Exercise 3 page 155
1 shocked   2 atrocious   3 appalled   4 outrageous
5 dismayed   6 dreadful   7 aghast

Exercise 4 page 155
Answers will vary.

LISTENING 2

Learning objectives

- Understand key vocabulary for describing water safety – *compromise, concentration, minimal*
- Listen and complete cause-and-effect chains in a moderated discussion about water safety
- Listen and take detailed notes on the types of evidence used by speakers
- Listen and identify persuasive appeals by type: trust, emotion and logic
- Understand, identify and evaluate the features of persuasive appeals
- Synthesize information from a lecture about the causes of allergies and a moderated discussion about water safety and use in a discussion

Lead-in

Show the statements below about water. Ask students say which ones they think are true. Let them discuss any areas of disagreement. (All are true.)

- More than 700 million people around the world do not have access to clean, safe water.
- More than 400 million school days are lost each year due to water-related diseases.
- About 675 children died today as a result of a water-related disease.
- More than 250 million people have to travel more than 30 minutes to collect water.

Exercise 1 page 156
Possible answers:
1 a rusty water pipe; dirty tap water
2 *Answers will vary.*
3 stomach and other health problems; death; birth defects

Exercise 2 page 156
1 a   2 b   3 a   4 b   5 a   6 c

Exercise 3 page 157
Answers will vary.

Exercise 4 page 157
Refer back to Exercise 3 on page 157: a, c, e
a damaged pipes   b contaminated water
c lead poisoning   d behavioural and cognitive problems

Exercise 5 page 157
a damaged pipes: city changed water supplier; new water was more acidic
b contaminated water: city tested water in people's homes and found high lead levels
c lead poisoning: doctor did blood tests; studies cited about effects of lead poisoning

d behavioural and cognitive problems: mother noticed changes in her own children's development

Exercise 6 page 159

appeal for trust	Dr Khan: 'I have spent my career studying lead toxicity' Dr Hardwick: 'Numerous studies that I've been involved with have demonstrated that children with high levels of lead in their systems often end up with cognitive impairments, learning disabilities, behavioural problems' Kirk: 'The people Mrs Johnson spoke to at the council really did believe the water was safe. Since then, we've updated the procedures for testing water quality.'
appeal to emotion	Dr Khan: 'the council was at fault' / 'It was an appalling lapse in judgement' Dr Hardwick: 'the most heartbreaking part is that the damage is irreversible' / 'Their futures are deeply compromised' / 'I was appalled by what I found' / 'What I found was shocking, I would say, even criminal.' Kirk: 'The council is deeply sorry for the problems this has caused your family.' Johnson: 'My kids got terrible rashes and severe stomach pains. The situation was unbearable. I was outraged at their lack of concern.'
appeal to logic	Dr Hardwick: 'You need to understand that no level of lead in the blood is considered safe' Johnson: 'So, what do you think? What kind of life do they have to look forward to?'

Exercise 7 page 159

Possible answers:

1 The doctors (Hardwick and Khan) tended to appeal for trust and appeal to logic as well as appeal to emotion. The politician (Kirk) and city resident (Johnson) tended to appeal to emotion.

2 The technical experts had experience and facts and figures to rely on. The townsperson wanted to be heard and taken seriously. The politician wanted to assure everyone of the town's commitment to its residents.

3 deplorable, appalling, incredibly, heartbreaking, deeply, terrible, panicked, outraged, appalled, highly, serious, dramatic, shocking, criminal

4 *Answers will vary.*

Exercise 8 page 159

Answers will vary.

Learning objectives

- Analyze regional issues related to health caused by the fast-food industry
- Understand regional prospects for businesses in the fast-food industry
- Apply your understanding of regional issues to identify the effects and concerns of stakeholders
- Evaluate who should take each role in a role play
- Create a position statement for a stakeholder in a decision-making process related to a local fast-food business
- Create appeals which will strengthen the argument of your stakeholder

UNLOCK TEACHER DEVELOPMENT

BE INFORMED

➔ **Understanding motivation** is an important skill for students because: (1) Sometimes it is hard to understand the reason why people say certain things – appreciating their motivation can help clarify this; (2) Motivation can impact the way in which people see something, making their response more emotional than rational; (3) Understanding somebody's perspective can help you challenge their viewpoints more effectively and authoritatively.

BE CONFIDENT

➔ Develop this skill for yourself by doing the following activity:

1 *Imagine that your teaching institution decides that there will be an extra hour of critical thinking lessons per week. How do you think these different groups would react? What factors might affect their viewpoint?*

- Students
- Teachers
- Parents
- School marketing team

2 *If you were responsible for ensuring the success of these lessons, what would you say to / do with these groups to improve the situation?*

Lead-in

Give students a minute to read the speaking task that they will do at the end of the unit. Then give them a few minutes to brainstorm the possible issues around this topic. Tell them to keep their brainstorming notes for later, when they begin to prepare for the meeting.

UNLOCK TEACHER DEVELOPMENT

BE READY

Look at the Critical Thinking section in the Student's Book on pages 160–163.

→ Which elements of the lesson do you think your students will find easiest / most difficult / most useful? Why?

→ Are your answers true for all students in your class?

→ How can you adapt your teaching or the material to meet your students' needs?

BE FLEXIBLE

This is a long critical thinking section, so you may need to think about how you use all the material in the time available. Consider: (1) setting some exercises as homework (which students can report back on in class). It might be helpful for them to talk to parents and friends, for example; (2) dividing the work up (e.g. students work in pairs – one doing Exercise 1, the other Exercise 2, and then comparing notes).

Exercise 1 page 160

Possible answers:

1 The market is very favourable. The growth rate in fast-food locations has been around 75% in 15 years. It is a good business opportunity.

2 The country might have become more prosperous and open to Western culture and businesses. People may have higher incomes and now be able to afford to spend more on takeaway food.

3 Fast food is replacing parts of the traditional, healthier diet and this may be leading to obesity, resulting in increases in the health problems seen in Figure 2, and therefore may actually be killing people.

4 They are all 'lifestyle' diseases, associated with a less healthy diet and sedentary habits.

5 The rate of obesity rose for adults and children. This suggests that the increase in obesity is accelerating. This means that more and more deaths due to the health problems caused by obesity are likely to be seen in the future.

Exercise 2 page 160

Answers will vary.

Exercise 3 page 162

Possible answers:

	What concerns might they have?	**What do they want the outcome to be?**
manager / owner of the complex	It could lift business overall, but if there is a backlash from the public, it will have a negative impact.	An increase in business throughout the complex. There won't be any trouble.
business owners near the location	There could be some bad smells, but they hope that more customers will come.	They would like FryKing to come to the complex. More people will come to the complex and perhaps bring new business to their stores.
owner of FryKing	They hope to make a big profit, and that there is no negative publicity.	They hope to come into the complex without problems.
children	They are likely to eat more fast food. It could have a negative effect on their health. However, if they like fast food, they may not be too worried about their health, as they are children.	They hope FryKing will come.
students	They will be able to go there with their friends. They are likely to eat more fast food. It could have a negative effect on their health.	They hope FryKing will come.
local parents	They may be concerned about their children's health. Their children will hang out there and eat more fast food.	Opinion will probably be divided. Some may be against FryKing.

Exercises 4–6 pages 162–163

Answers will vary.

UNLOCK TEACHER DEVELOPMENT

BE REFLECTIVE

Think about the following points:

→ Reflect on a topic about which you have a particularly strong view. What are your motivations for your position? How might this affect your own judgement or viewpoint?

→ If you feel able to, share this insight with a colleague, either in person or electronically. Encourage others to do the same. This can be quite an empowering and educational process.

BE COLLABORATIVE

Your development is more meaningful when it is shared. See page 14 for ideas on how to peer-collaborate. Why not share the ideas you generated in the *Be ready* section, and their outcome?

PREPARATION FOR SPEAKING

Learning objectives

- Use inclusive language to persuade others in arguments about local health concerns – *Like all of you, I want to know why …*, *If we want to prevent this from happening in the future …*
- Emphasize words which carry strong emotion or important messages when making persuasive appeals

Exercise 1 page 164

Possible answers:

1 I'm sure we all agree that the factory is a threat to public health and should close down.
2 Do you want to know why there has not been any public discussion of these important issues? I do.
3 We are all aware that the food at fast food restaurants is not part of a healthy diet, so we should stop going to them so often.
4 We shouldn't allow these kinds of businesses near our children's schools.
5 The testing procedures are flawed. What can we do to get the laboratory to improve them?

Exercise 2 page 164

Answers will vary.

Exercise 3 page 165

1 incredibly; brain   2 heartbreaking; irreversible
3 terrible; severe   4 deeply   5 no   6 shocking; criminal

Exercise 4 page 165

Answers will vary.

SPEAKING TASK

Learning objectives

- Prepare for a group presentation on an aspect of human behaviour by assigning roles
- Practise presenting position statements and responding to feedback on these
- Take part in a group meeting by stating your position and making appropriate persuasive appeals

Exercises 1–5 pages 166–167

Answers will vary.

RESEARCH PROJECT

Do a group presentation on an environmental health issue.

Ask students to work in groups. What is the issue? Is it local or global? How many people does it affect? They should include statistics to support their ideas, such as the ones in the Lead-in activity to the unit. Data could be used to create an infographic or slide to accompany the presentation. Provide questions for students to consider, such as:

- Who are the stakeholders in the situation? What public positions have they taken?
- What is being done to manage, reduce, or eliminate this problem? Have these efforts been successful?

CLASSROOM APP

Exercises 1–2

Answers will vary.

Exercise 3

1 and so did   2 such an attitude; such attitudes
3 that doing so; doing so   4 such increases
5 and so do   6 such ideas

Exercise 4

1 deplorable   2 outraged   3 both   4 appalled   5 both
6 shocked   7 dreadful   8 outrageous

Exercise 5

1 properties   2 disparity   3 severity   4 compromised
5 intervene   6 guidelines   7 contaminated   8 incidence

Exercise 6

1 us; our   2 don't you   3 We   4 of you   5 Everyone
6 Let's

UNIT OBJECTIVES	
Watch and listen	Watch and understand a video about a cooperation deal between two airlines.
Listening skill	Understand anecdotes and proverbs to illustrate larger ideas.
Critical thinking	Evaluate opinions.
Grammar	Use *wh-* clefts.
Speaking skill	Use collaborative language to make suggestions and concessions.
Speaking task	Participate in a consensus-building, decision-making task.
⊘ Teacher development	Help your students become better at **evaluating opinions**.

UNLOCK YOUR KNOWLEDGE

Background note

The photograph shows a United Nations (UN) meeting. The UN is an international organization founded in 1945. It comprises of 193 Member States. It was created to deal with issues of peace and security in the world, sustainable development, human rights, health and education, and other social challenges. Most UN decisions are made during the General Assembly; a consensus is reached when all Member States agree to adopt a resolution, even if they don't agree with every part of it.

Different governments and business have different decision-making processes, for example, debate, negotiation, voting, reaching a consensus and allocating decisions to different bodies or individuals.

Lead-in

Write these sets of words on the board: *collaboration/collaborative* and *cooperation/cooperate*. Ask students the difference between the two. Elicit that although both involve working together, *collaboration* means working toward a shared goal and *cooperation* simply suggests assistance. Ask for some examples of each.

page 169
Answers will vary.

WATCH AND LISTEN

Learning objectives

- Listen and understand the main ideas in a video about a business deal
- Listen and complete detailed notes on a video about a business deal
- Listen and identify the meaning of unfamiliar words and phrases from their context in the video
- Practise talking about international collaborations between different kinds of organization

Exercises 1–2 page 170
Answers will vary.

Exercise 3 page 170
1 B   **2** E   **3** L   **4** B

Exercise 4 page 171
1 contract   **2** global   **3** improvement   **4** strategy
5 European   **6** biggest   **7** 16   **8** four   **9** services
10 opportunities to collaborate   **11** freight   **12** passenger

Exercise 5 page 171
1 d   **2** c   **3** b   **4** e   **5** a

Exercise 6 page 171
Answers will vary.

LISTENING 1

Learning objectives

- Understand key vocabulary for group dynamics – *bully, constructive, defuse*
- Listen and summarize the main ideas in a presentation
- Listen and take notes on studies used as evidence to support claims
- Understand the use of anecdotes and proverbs to illustrate larger ideas in a presentation about group dynamics
- Understand some common proverbs
- Listen and identify linking sounds /j/ and /w/ in fast connected speech
- Suggest solutions to problems highlighted in a lecture on group dynamics
- Explain a problem and discuss the implications of the ideas in a lecture on group dynamics

Lead-in

Introduce the topic by noting that classwork often involves working in groups. Ask students to discuss the following questions in small groups then report back or discuss as a whole class:

- *Do you like working in groups? Why? / Why not?*
- *When is group work most effective?*
- *When is it least effective?*

Exercises 1–2 page 172

Answers will vary.

Exercise 3 page 174

1 dynamics   **2** perception   **3** Constructive   **4** defuse
5 prevail   **6** resentment   **7** bully   **8** counteract

Exercise 4 page 174

Possible answer: The behaviour of one 'bad apple' can negatively affect the dynamics of an entire group, and there are only a few ways to counteract this phenomenon.

Exercise 5 page 175

Possible answers:

Participants: groups consisting of regular people and one hired actor to play the 'bad apple'

Methods: The regular members of the groups didn't know the bad apple was an actor playing a part. The actor engaged in negative behaviour that ran counter to the group.

Results: Groups performed 30–40% worse. Others started to mirror bad behaviour. Others did not oppose the bad apple's behaviour. The bad apple's behaviour resulted in perceptions of unfairness among members.

Conclusion: The group's worst member was the best predictor of the whole group's performance. The behaviour of one bad apple can spread to the whole group.

Exercise 6 page 175

Possible answers:

1 A diseased or rotten apple spoils all the other apples around it. The bad behaviour of one person can also negatively affect, or spoil, the dynamics of a group and the behaviour of all the individuals in the group.

2 **Slacker:** exhibits a lack of interest; refuses to participate or contribute to the group's efforts.
Naysayer: expresses generally negative feelings and attitude; rejects or criticizes the ideas and opinions of others without offering anything constructive as an alternative.
Bully: insists on doing things his or her own way with no alternative; exhibits typical bullying behaviour to group members.

Exercise 7 page 176

Answers will vary, but the generally held meaning of these proverbs is as follows:

1 You can offer people something that is good for them, but you cannot force them to take it. You can only help somebody who wants to be helped.

2 If unpleasant things are said about somebody or something, there is probably a good reason for it.

3 Something is always expected of you in return for a favour or gift. Every gift has an expectation from the giver attached to it.

4 Sometimes, combining the talents of too many people does not make something better.

5 You always want or are tempted by what you do not have, even if there is no real reason to believe it is better than what you have.

Optional activity

Ask students to offer a situation in which a speaker might use each of the proverbs in Exercise 7. For example, somebody who does not like his job and thinks his friend has a much better job, even though the friend's job has just as many challenges, might use proverb 5.

Exercise 8 page 176

1 way- / j / -and   **2** may- / j / -also; may- / j / -or
3 the- / j / -other; to- / w / -adopt   **4** to- / w / -express
5 the- / j / -entire

Exercise 9 page 176

Answers will vary.

Learning objectives

- Use *wh-* clefts to focus on particular information in a sentence – *What these researchers found was that the behaviour of one bad apple can spread to the whole group.*
- Use *wh-* clefts to express a perspective on a particular piece of information – *What I didn't agree with were the study's conclusions.*
- Use correct dependent prepositions in phrases to describe group behaviour – *interfere with, depend on, disagree with, succeed in*

Exercise 1 page 177

2 What the participants said was (that) their group didn't have a good leader.

3 What the researchers saw was an increase in negative behaviour.

4 What the study showed was (that) one member can have a disproportionate effect.

5 What we found was (that) people are easily influenced by others to behave badly, which really surprised me. / What really surprised me was (that) we found that people are easily influenced by others to behave badly.

Exercise 2 page 177

2 What you mean is (that) nobody was aware of the effect his behaviour had on them. / Is what you mean that nobody was aware of the effect his behaviour had on them?

3 What you're saying is (that) the results were the same for children, teens and adults. / Is what you're saying that the results were the same for children, teens and adults?

4 What I mean is (that) studies like this are hard to replicate because every group of people is different.

Exercise 3 page 178

Answers will vary.

Optional activity

Ask students to create their own sentences about collaboration, groupwork or group dynamics, using *wh-* clefts.

Exercise 4 page 178

1 participate; in   **2** provide / present; with
3 agree / concentrate; on   **4** interfere; with
5 insisted; on   **6** compared; with

Exercise 5 page 178

Answers will vary.

Learning objectives

- Understand key vocabulary for decision-making – *outcome, reservations, consensus*
- Listen and take notes on main ideas and details in a discussion of two approaches to group decision-making
- Make inferences about the responses and motivations of participants in a discussion
- Make inferences about the real world from the information in a discussion about group decision-making
- Synthesize information from a presentation about group dynamics and a discussion of two approaches to group decision-making and use in a discussion

Lead-in

Give students the following scenario: *Eight classmates want to go out for dinner to celebrate the end of their term. Six of them want to go to an expensive French restaurant. After all, it's a special day. Two of the students are from families that don't have much money. It would be difficult for them to pay. They suggest a popular, but less expensive kebab restaurant.*

Check that students understand the situation and then have them consider the following questions in small groups:

- *Where should the group have dinner?*
- *Should the majority decide?*

Exercise 1 page 179

Possible answers: **1** legislative bodies (parliament, the UN, etc.), juries, boards of directors, etc.   **2–4** *Answers will vary.*

Exercise 2 page 179

Answers will vary.

Exercise 3 page 180

a outcome   **b** consensus   **c** legacy   **d** ownership
e resolve   **f** hybrid   **g** stake   **h** reservations

Exercise 4 page 180

Possible answers:

Voting: reps from both sides presented their cases; the group had a discussion, took a vote; majority rules; losing side was not happy; process is relatively quick

Consensus-building: longer process; uses a facilitator who stays objective and focuses on process; first step – all must agree to work together; all participants can talk and present ideas, concerns; issue broken down into component pieces and discussed; proposals altered until everyone can accept them; no final vote, just agreement

Exercise 5 page 180

Possible answers:

1 whether a waterfront space should be used as a museum which is a businessman's legacy, or a park
2 Citizens for Open Spaces (the uses of the space as a park) won, 18–8; losers were not happy
3 hybrid proposal to build a museum on the space with a lower environmental impact agreed upon by all

Exercises 6–7 page 181

Answers will vary.

Be flexible

Identify the segment of the script that outlines the process students summarized in Exercise 7. Assign students roles and ask them to read their parts aloud, making sure they link words with vowels according to rules in the box on page 176. Support **lower-level students** by asking them to mark the linkages before they read.

Exercises 8–10 page 181

Answers will vary.

CRITICAL THINKING

Learning objectives

- Remember real-world experience of dining facilities and relate this to the type of facility that will be discussed in the speaking task
- Understand the dining options proposed for a university campus
- Evaluate the dining options proposed for a university campus by conducting a cost-benefit analysis
- Create a position statement for a stakeholder in a decision-making process related to the dining options proposed for a university campus

UNLOCK TEACHER DEVELOPMENT

BE INFORMED

➔ **Evaluating options** is an important skill for students because: (1) This is a very common practice in the business world (where it is often known as 'cost-benefit analysis'); (2) It is a complex skill to be able to 'weigh' the various advantages and disadvantages of certain actions; (3) Evaluating options can improve students' day-to-day lives by enabling them to make an optimal decision based on the available information.

BE CONFIDENT

➔ Develop this skill for yourself by doing the following activity:

1 *Put the following stages of doing a cost-benefit analysis in the order that you do them (1–4):*

- Think about the major consequences of all these actions
- Choose the action which has the best (or least bad) impact
- Identify all the available actions
- Decide on the positive/negative impact of each of these actions

2 *Use this model to do a cost-benefit analysis for solutions to offset global warming. Think about three options only, namely: (a) increase use of clean energy; (b) reduce consumption of meat; (c) ban fossil fuels.*

Lead-in

Give students a minute to read the speaking task they will do at the end of the unit. Then give them a few minutes to brainstorm their experiences of consensus-building decision-making. Tell them to keep their brainstorming notes for later, when they begin to prepare for the task.

UNLOCK TEACHER DEVELOPMENT

BE READY

Look at the Critical Thinking section in the Student's Book on pages 182–183.

➔ Which elements of the lesson do you think your students will find easiest / most difficult / most useful? Why?

➔ Are your answers true for all students in your class?

➔ How can you adapt your teaching or the material to meet your students' needs?

BE FLEXIBLE

If you have time, Exercise 1 offers an interesting opportunity for students to conduct a genuine piece of research. They could interview customers in dining options near your institution about their views on price, distance, healthy options, etc.

Exercise 1 page 182

Answers will vary.

Exercise 2 page 183

1 **DINESCO:** current provider; serves hot meals, salads, sandwiches, snacks, desserts; open 7 am – 11 pm; university pays annual fee; part of dining contract for on-campus students – no limit for them, but others must pay; prices good for some but not others; quality and choice not good

2 **Sharzad:** fast food; serves breakfast, pita sandwiches, kebabs, salad, snacks; moderate prices; would be open 24 hours; part of dining contract but with limits on amount; quality – popular, but not much variety; Sharzad pays university to rent space – 10% would go to support student activities

3 **Unihub:** student-run café; doesn't already exist; would be run by students studying hospitality and catering; students get experience and it would be part of their degree; would serve sandwiches, salads, pasta, informal food; lunch/dinner only with some late-night takeaway options; part of dining contract but no breakfast; prices for non-students higher than DINESCO; university would help with costs (from students' activity fund)

Exercise 3 page 183

Possible answers:

	DINESCO	**Sharzad**	**Unihub**
costs	university pays annual fee; non-contract prices high for students; not good quality choice for students	expansion into whole university system; not a lot of variety; not unlimited	must be created, which will cost money; university would subsidize operation; prices high; no breakfasts for students on campus
benefits	already on campus so no additional costs; part of dining contract; no limits on food for contract students	already has one location on campus, so knows how to do it; popular with students; part of dining contract (with limits); open 24/7; would pay university – 10% to go to support students activities	Students get credit for working there; part of dining contract (lunch / dinner only); late-night takeaway food

| **winners** | food staff (no changes); students on contract (unlimited food); university (nothing to change) | students who like Sharzad; students' activity fund and university | students studying hospitality and catering |
| **losers** | university (annual fee); students and visitors (quality, lack of choice) | students (lack of variety and limits on amount) | students who want breakfast; students' activity fund; food staff |

Exercise 4 page 183

Answers will vary.

UNL⊘CK TEACHER DEVELOPMENT

BE REFLECTIVE

Consider the following points:

→ Think about two things which went well in your lesson, and two things which went less well than you had hoped. If you were to teach this lesson again, what would you do differently?

→ Share these ideas with a colleague. Whilst reflection by yourself is very important after a lesson, telling somebody what you would do differently is even more effective.

BE COLLABORATIVE

Your development is more meaningful when it is shared. See page 14 for ideas on how to peer-collaborate. Why not share the research methods you encouraged in the *Be flexible* section, and their impact on the lesson?

PREPARATION FOR SPEAKING

Learning objectives

- Understand and identify the steps used and positions that are possible in a consensus-building process
- Use collaborative language to express positions in a consensus-building process

Exercises 1–2 pages 184–185

Answers will vary.

Optional activity

Ask students to analyze the statements in Exercise 2 for the use of inclusive language (see Unit 7). Ask them to describe the relationship between inclusive language and collaborative language. For example, collaborative language such as *What do you suggest we do?* includes inclusive language such as *we*.

Exercise 3 page 186

1 b block   **c** reservation   **d** agreement   **e** agreement
f reservation   **g** stand aside

2 collaborative language: a, c, d, f

Exercises 4–5 page 187

Answers will vary.

SPEAKING TASK

Learning objectives

- Prepare for a consensus-building decision-making task by anticipating the arguments of others and considering concessions you could offer or accept
- Practise presenting arguments and responding to feedback on these
- Give feedback to other students on their arguments
- Participate in a consensus-building decision-making task
- Evaluate the success of a consensus-building decision-making task

Exercises 1–6 pages 187–188

Answers will vary.

RESEARCH PROJECT

Do group presentations on famous negotiation cases.

Students work in groups to conduct research on famous negotiation cases from business, politics, sport, labour, law, etc. They should investigate what the issues were, the costs and benefits of various outcomes, and who the eventual winners and losers were. If possible, they should find out about the process by which the final agreement was made. They should support their presentations with visuals (e.g. a chart) that show costs and benefits and winners and losers.

CLASSROOM APP

Exercises 1–2

Answers will vary.

Exercise 3

1 What made me angry was that
2 What the results suggested was that
3 What I concluded from my recent experience
4 What you're telling me is that
5 What you need to understand is that
6 What I think you mean is that

Exercise 4

1 on   **2** in   **3** with   **4** in   **5** on   **6** with   **7** on   **8** on

Exercise 5

1 reservations   **2** stake   **3** perception   **4** defuse
5 outcome   **6** prevailed   **7** resentment   **8** consensus

Exercise 6

1 I would be willing   **2** Why don't   **3** don't we
4 Would you be open   **5** What do you   **6** Let's try

Exercise 7

Answers will vary.

UNIT OBJECTIVES	
Watch and listen	Watch and understand a video about an anthropomimetic robot.
Listening skills	Listen for examples; supporting speculation.
Critical thinking	Provide supporting detail.
Grammar	Use hypothetical future.
Speaking skills	Leave and return to the topic; ask for clarification and confirmation.
Speaking task	Take part in an informal discussion.
⟳ **Teacher development**	Help your students become better at **providing supporting detail**.

UNLOCK YOUR KNOWLEDGE

Background note

The photo shows robot arms being used on a car production line. A robot is a physical machine that is controlled by a computer and can perform certain tasks independently or automatically. Industrial robots used in factories and on production lines are automatic and able to move on two or more fixed points. They are often used for metalwork, painting, assembly and packaging. In the last two decades, a variety of robots have been developed that can be used in different environments, like robotic vacuum cleaners, robot drones and self-driving cars. Robots are currently used in space exploration, by the military, during surgery and in search and rescue missions.

Lead-in

Write the following list of technological innovations on the board. Ask students to vote on the three they think have had the greatest impact on humans. Then ask for volunteers to defend their choices.

- printing press
- electric lightbulb
- the wheel
- mobile phone
- guns
- the compass
- magnifying lenses (telescopes, microscopes, glasses)
- personal computer
- steel
- antibiotics
- the internet
- engine (steam, combustion)
- spinning wheel

page 191
Answers will vary.

WATCH AND LISTEN

Learning objectives

- Listen and understand the main ideas in a video about a type of robot
- Identify the main idea in a video about a robot
- Listen and answer detailed questions on a video about a robot
- Listen and identify the meaning of unfamiliar words and phrases from their context in the video
- Make inferences about the implications in a video about robots
- Practise talking about human-like machines

Exercises 1–2 page 192
Answers will vary.

Exercise 3 page 192

b

Refer back to Exercise 2 on page 192, questions 1 and 2: The robot is human-like in that it mimics humans, it has a body, and it is able to have human-like interactions with its world.

Refer back to Exercise 2 on page 192, question 3: Scientists are trying to replicate movement, rather than sensation.

Exercise 4 page 193

1 Our physical form shapes the way we think.
2 It has bones, muscles, joints and tendons.
3 It tells them about the particular kind of intelligence that comes from the body interacting with the physical environment.
4 The first robots were controlled by AI and computers. They were just boxes.
5 touching objects and moving objects; because they require a lot of unconscious (mental) computation

Exercise 5 page 193

1 a 2 b 3 b 4 c

Exercise 6 page 193

1 Scientists originally focused on imitating only the human mind, but now they are focusing on mimicking the human body as the key to AI. 2 *Answers will vary.*

Exercise 7 page 193

Answers will vary.

LISTENING 1

Learning objectives

- Understand key vocabulary for technology adoption – *disposable income, peer, reluctant*
- Listen and use a table to take structured notes on main ideas and details in a lecture about the technology adoption life cycle
- Use your notes to identify and understand main ideas, details and examples
- Gain awareness of phrases and strategies which signal when a speaker is presenting an example
- Understand a speaker's bias towards different groups when talking about technology adoption
- Listen and identify the omitted sounds in fast speech
- Listen and understand words with omitted sounds in fast speech

Lead-in

Make a line on the board. On the far-left side, write *I always want to buy the newest technology as soon as it appears.* On the far-right side, write *I usually wait until I am absolutely sure that this technology is useful and effective before I buy it.* Then give each student a sticky note to place themselves on the line. Ask volunteers to explain their placement.

Exercise 1 page 194

1 verify 2 reluctant 3 constitutes 4 rational 5 peers
6 related 7 confronted with 8 disposable income

Exercise 2 pages 194–195

1 It shows the pattern that populations follow when they adopt new technologies, divided into different groups according to when they adopt the new technology.

2 first: innovators; last: laggards 3 laggards; innovators; late majority 4 *Answers will vary.*

Exercise 3 page 195

Answers will vary.

Exercise 4 page 195

a, c, e, g, h

Exercise 5 page 196

Answers will vary.

Exercise 6 page 196

1 People can have irrational responses to new technology.
2 They lost their jobs to machines.
3 The British government made damaging machines a capital offence (punishable by death).
4 a rational fear
5 They feared that travelling at the incredible speed of 30 miles an hour could kill you; that peoples' organs would melt or explode while travelling on the train at this velocity; that people might not be able to breathe; that passing trains would harm crops and livestock, and so on.
6 an irrational fear of technology – one that is not based on scientific facts
7 In the late 1990s, large sections of the population were convinced that using mobile phones caused brain tumours.
8 Yes, we do need to distinguish between a rational fear of technology (for instance, when machines threaten to take over our jobs) and an irrational fear (which is often unfounded and based on hearsay and speculation).
9 Both innovators and early adopters are distinguished from the other groups by two factors: they are able to take financial risks, and they perform leadership roles in their social networks.
10 Once the early majority starts to buy into the new technology, the late majority has no choice but to adopt it – this is the tipping point in its adoption.

Exercise 7 page 197

1 She is biased towards innovators and early adopters. She is biased against laggards.
2 against laggards: irrational to fear every piece of new technology, scaremongering, refuse to learn, choose to ignore scientific facts; for early adopters and innovators: fortunately for our civilization, more likely to make an informed decision
3 *Answers will vary.*

Be flexible

👥 Ask students to work in pairs, taking turns to summarize diffusion theory as it relates to the spread of technology, using at least three of the target words from Exercise 1. Encourage them to give each other feedback on their summaries.

Provide **lower-level students** with more structure by telling them to base their summary on the graph on page 195 of the Student's Book and to include the terms *innovators, early adopters* and *laggards*.

Exercise 8 page 197

1 An irrational fear which is often unfounded and based on hearsay.
2 Many people refused to get on the train.
3 Scientists have refuted these claims.
4 Any new technology will be accompanied with a great deal of anxiety.

Exercise 9 page 198

1 resentment; towards   2 crafts; lost   3 grounds   4 have
5 last; to   6 reluctant; to; adopt   7 informed; decision

Exercise 10 page 198

Answers will vary.

LANGUAGE DEVELOPMENT

Learning objectives

- Use words with negative prefixes to express ideas more concisely – *These examples demonstrate irrational feelings. Skilled workers were replaced by unskilled labourers.*
- Use hypothetical future forms to describe a possible future scenario – *It would be difficult to live in a world where there were no prospects for gainful employment. Without expert knowledge of how the robots worked, we could not shut them down.*

Exercise 1 page 199

Answers will vary.

Exercise 2 page 199

1 immoral/unscrupulous   2 implausible   3 inefficient/unproductive   4 irreplaceable   5 undesirable
6 indispensable   7 irrational/illogical   8 irreversible damage/damage that is irreversible/irrevocable damage/damage that is irrevocable   9 impersonal
10 undesirable/unsustainable

Exercise 3 page 199

Answers will vary.

Exercise 4 page 200

Answers will vary. Possible answers:

1 People whose jobs were given to robots would struggle to find a place in society.
2 Even if they looked human, they wouldn't be able to think like us.
3 Once robots took over the AI industry, they would create super-intelligent robots.
4 While robots kept evolving, human cognitive skills would / could / might gradually diminish.
5 It would / could / might be difficult for young people to find part-time jobs because they would / could / might have been filled by robots.

6 How people spent the free time created by the widespread use of AI would be determined by how much disposable income they had.

Exercise 5 page 201

Answers will vary.

Be flexible

Tell students to write three hypothetical statements about their own future, using the structures from the Skills box on page 200. They then share their sentences with a partner.

Provide **lower-level students** with more support. Do this as a paired activity and limit the examples to *if... were.* One student begins the activity: *If travel to other planets were to become common...* and the second student completes the sentence.

LISTENING 2

Learning objectives

- Understand key vocabulary for robotics and artificial intelligence – *mimic, intuition, dexterity*
- Listen and identify the main ideas of different speakers in a seminar about artificial intelligence
- Listen and take detailed notes
- Use your notes to identify and understand details and examples
- Listen and identify a speaker's speculations and understand whether or not, and if so, how, they support their views with facts
- Synthesize information from a lecture about the technology adoption life cycle and a seminar about artificial intelligence in a discussion

Lead-in

Bring in or show images of robots from popular culture, such as from *Star Wars*, *Transformers* and *Star Trek*. Ask students what qualities of robots these figures embody. In what ways do they think these are different from real robots? What do we want and fear from robots?

Exercise 1 page 202

a elaborate   b at stake   c dexterity   d mundane
e pervasive   f intuition   g mimic   h compassion

Exercise 2 page 203

Answers will vary.

Exercise 3 page 203

1 robots working in hotels, restaurants or hospitals; military robots rescuing injured soldiers, assisting in search-and-rescue missions; AI in driverless taxis

2 *Answers will vary.*

Exercise 4 page 204

1 Faiz c; f   2 Enrique e; d   3 Ayşe a; b

Exercise 5 page 204

Answers will vary.

Exercise 6 page 204

1 mundane, repetitive jobs

2 Robots are limited in their physical movements; they have sensors and actuators; they do simple, repetitive tasks and move within fixed parameters. AI involves complex algorithms and machine learning; programs are trained on large sets of data and can then begin to behave in ways that mimic human cognition.

3 They are robots that use AI. Their high costs prevent widespread use at present.

4 jobs that involve processing large amounts of data in order to make decisions: accountants, legal and financial analysts

5 jobs that involve creativity and compassion: teachers, doctors, nurses; unskilled manual jobs – because the intelligent robots required to do these jobs would be too expensive

Exercise 7 page 205

1 Algorithms in AI can mimic the human cognition required for these jobs.

2 These robots are too expensive.

3 The article said that 95% of accounting jobs would disappear.

4 Historically, when cars replaced horses, horse-related jobs were lost but new jobs were created.

5 This claim was published in an article.

6 AI does not yet have the capacity to read emotions, use intuition or show empathy.

Exercise 8 page 205

1 facts   2 facts   3 expert opinion; examples
4 facts; examples   5 expert opinion   6 facts

Optional activity

👥 Ask the students to speculate about the future of their own profession or the one they hope to enter. They should support their speculation with known facts and examples.

Exercise 9 page 205

Answers will vary.

CRITICAL THINKING

Learning objectives

- Analyze opinions related to droids and robots and add support to the arguments.
- Apply ideas about supporting detail to arguments
- Research and evaluate evidence related to whether a profession can be automated.
- Evaluate statements regarding whether a profession can be automated and add supporting details.

UNLOCK TEACHER DEVELOPMENT

BE INFORMED

➔ **Providing supporting detail** is an important skill for students because: (1) One of the main criticisms of university essays is that students' arguments are not well-supported; (2) If what you say is not supported, it is no more than an opinion. Adding supporting detail can transform it into an argument; (3) Students are sometimes unclear as to what constitutes good evidence, and need to know that it can include facts, statistics, data, results, etc.

BE CONFIDENT

➔ Develop this skill for yourself by doing the following activity:

Exercise 3 asks about the future outlook of several jobs, and whether some aspects of the job are likely to be replaced by AI. It is almost inevitable that some aspects of teaching will be affected in this way.

You should think about: (a) which aspects of teaching will be replaced, and (b) what impact this will have on students' experience of education.

Lead-in

Give students a minute to read the Speaking task they will do at the end of the unit. Then give them a few minutes to brainstorm their own experience of AI. Tell them to keep their brainstorming notes for later, when they begin to prepare for the discussion.

UNLOCK TEACHER DEVELOPMENT

BE READY

Look at the Critical Thinking section in the Student's Book on pages 206–207.

→ Which elements of the lesson do you think your students will find easiest / most difficult / most useful? Why?

→ Are your answers true for all students in your class?

→ How can you adapt your teaching or the material to meet your students' needs?

BE FLEXIBLE

An interesting additional exercise to do (after Exercise 1 or Exercise 3) would be for students to create a role-play set in the future. They would be able to bring out some of the main points discussed in a fun and interactive way.

Exercises 1–5 pages 206–207

Answers will vary.

UNLOCK TEACHER DEVELOPMENT

BE REFLECTIVE

Think about these follow-ups:

→ Ask your colleagues, either in person or electronically, whether different subject areas have different viewpoints regarding AI, and whether there are specific areas which people are convinced will *not* be replaced by AI.

→ Based on this, think about whether there is any way you can make yourself 'AI-proof' for the future. If you can, tell your colleagues!

BE COLLABORATIVE

Your development is more meaningful when it is shared. See page 14 for ideas on how to peer-collaborate. Why not share the ideas you generated in the *Be ready* section, and their outcome?

PREPARATION FOR SPEAKING

Learning objectives

- Use words and phrases to signal going off-topic and returning to a topic: *Incidentally, ..., Anyway, returning to my point, ...*
- Use appropriate questions, phrases and paraphrasing to clarify your own points and the points of others: *Could you be more specific/ explicit? Are you saying that* (paraphrase)*...? Anyway, returning to my point, ..., What I'm trying to say is ...*
- Use assimilation in connected speech when asking questions.

Exercises 1–2 page 208

1 I just want to clarify something (D)
2 let's get to our discussion (R)
3 Before I answer the question (D)
4 let me take a minute to make sure everyone understands (D)
5 Everybody got that? So, unless there are other questions, let's return to our topic. (R)
6 it brings us back to my original question about the future of skilled and unskilled labour (R)

Exercise 3 page 209

Answers will vary.

Exercise 4 page 209

1 Coul<u>d</u> <u>y</u>ou be more specific?
2 What <u>d</u>o <u>y</u>ou mea<u>n b</u>y saying that?
3 Don'<u>t</u> you think that robots will soo<u>n b</u>e in every workplace?
4 Woul<u>d y</u>ou elaborate, please?
5 Wouldn'<u>t</u> <u>y</u>ou see a robot doctor, if you needed medical attention?

SPEAKING TASK

Learning objectives

- Prepare for a discussion about the future of a specific profession by practising presenting your ideas and responding to requests for clarification
- Anticipate opposing points of view and prepare counter-arguments for a discussion
- Take part in a class discussion and evaluate the future of different professions

Exercises 1–5 pages 209–210

Answers will vary.

RESEARCH PROJECT

Create a podcast on emerging but controversial technology.

Students work in small groups on a shared topic. Their podcasts should: (1) describe the technology; (2) explain its benefits; (3) explain why it is controversial, in other words, what do people fear from it; and finally (4) make a prediction about the future of this technology. Possible topics include:

- drones
- recognition of facial features or other biological markers
- stem cell research
- wearable technology
- genetic engineering
- satellite imaging
- identity chips

CLASSROOM APP

Exercises 1–2
Answers will vary.

Exercise 3
1 impersonal   **2** irrational   **3** inefficient   **4** indispensable
5 inconsiderate   **6** irrevocable   **7** unbelievable

Exercise 4
1 would require   **2** could relax   **3** continued
4 would work   **5** happened   **6** would be

Exercise 5
1 intuition   **2** reluctant   **3** mimic   **4** dexterity
5 mundane   **6** elaborate   **7** pervasive
8 disposable income

Exercise 6
1 let's take a moment
2 That reminds me; Before I forget; Incidentally
3 Changing the topic for a moment; Before I forget
4 I just want to clarify something
5 That brings us back

Exercise 7
1 confirming the meaning of others
2 clarifying your own meaning
3 asking for clarification
4 asking for clarification
5 clarifying your own meaning
6 confirming the meaning of others

UNIT OBJECTIVES	
Watch and listen	Watch and understand a video about language diversity.
Listening skill	Note down follow-up questions while listening.
Critical thinking	Ask appropriate and productive questions.
Grammar	Use complex gerunds and infinitives.
Speaking skill	Interrupt and handle questions.
Speaking task	Conduct an in-depth semi-structured interview.
⌀ **Teacher development**	Help your students become better at **asking appropriate and productive questions**.

UNLOCK YOUR KNOWLEDGE

Background note

The photo shows a Japanese man teaching his daughter calligraphy. Classical Japanese calligraphy is considered to be a form of art and is practised by around 20 million people worldwide. Writing systems are one way that languages differ from one another. The sounds of a language, the grammar system and the way we construct words also make a language unique. Many linguists agree that language reflects our culture and the way we think about the world. This is often evident by studying words and expressions specific to a certain culture. Another aspect of language is that it changes over time. These changes often reflect developments in culture, social relations, historical events and the innovation of new technologies.

Lead-in

Find a map of language families online and show it to the class. Ask what they can learn from the map (e.g. how languages spread). Ask how the map might look different in 50 years, 100 years and 200 years. Why?

page 213
Answers will vary.

WATCH AND LISTEN

Learning objectives

- Predict, then listen and understand ideas in a video about the history of languages
- Listen, take notes and summarize main ideas
- Listen and complete a detailed summary of the information in a video

- Make inferences about the information presented in the video
- Practise talking about languages and their role in human culture

Exercises 1–3 page 214
Answers will vary.

Exercise 4 page 215

Refer back to Exercise 2 on page 214: The words on the diagrams are the names of languages, such as Sanskrit, Slavic, etc. The diagrams show the ways in which languages evolved and diverged from one another.

Refer back to Exercise 3 on page 214: Sanskrit is an ancient language. English is a Germanic language.

Exercise 5 page 215

1 It implies that many European and Asian languages are derived from the same common language.   **2** Proto-Indo-European   **3** Everything that people do and achieve is based on language – it's what makes us human.

Exercise 6 page 215

1 huge   **2** accidental   **3** p   **4** f   **5** migrated   **6** dialects   **7** evidence   **8** ancestor

Exercise 7 page 215

Possible answers:

1 Evidence of PIE only comes from its descendent languages – statistical evidence. We might think there were earlier languages if PIE seems to be formed from more than one root language, for example, with multiple words having the same meaning.

2 He means that language is central to everything humans do – without language there would be no shared knowledge, no history, no law, no wars, no empires, etc.

Exercise 8 page 215
Answers will vary.

LISTENING 1

Lead-in

If you have a linguistically homogeneous class, do a live version of something similar to the example in Exercise 2. Prepare your example before so you know it will work. Type a short passage into an online translator in the students' first language and show the output in English, or vice versa. Discuss what the translator got wrong. This assumes you have internet access in the classroom. If you do not, just prepare it before and show the two versions. If your class is not homogeneous, you can just show them an example of the output of an automatic translation from another language you know into English and then discuss its shortcomings. This can help them see why you (the teacher) can always tell if they are using one of these tools in their work.

Exercise 1 page 216

a complexities   **b** determine   **c** vague   **d** statistical
e frowned upon   **f** remotely   **g** incomprehensible
h radically

Exercise 2 page 216
Answers will vary.

Exercise 3 page 218
a, c, d, e, g

Exercise 4 page 218

1 *get* or *have* are notoriously difficult to translate; expressions like 'Did you get it?' which can have a literal or idiomatic meaning, depending on the context
2 a literal or idiomatic meaning, depending on the context
3 Her guests were confused and could not understand the directions – the word *drive* was translated as a noun, as *hard drive*. Also, the name of her street got translated into Russian.
4 since the 1950s

5 To translate a small section of text required more programming than it took to simulate the flight of a guided missile.
6 The scientists have to create an enormous database of grammar, language rules and vocabulary sets; the machine then translates from one language to another by searching for equivalents.
7 The machine utilizes databases made up of parallel bilingual texts – texts that have already been translated by humans – and uses data-mining techniques to detect patterns across hundreds of millions of documents and then make intelligent guesses as to their meaning; a final, grammatical translation is then created.
8 As a starting point – then he revises the translation and corrects any lexical inaccuracies.
9 In Spanish, nouns have gender and so the English pronoun *it* has to be translated according to whether it's referring to a female noun or a masculine noun. English word order usually follows the subject-verb-object pattern. However, there are many languages, like Arabic, that follow a different word order.
10 the use of logographic characters, which represent concepts rather than sounds; the sentence structure, which is radically different from English sentence structure

Exercises 5–7 page 219
Answers will vary.

Optional activity

Tell students that, as they listen to their classmate telling his or her anecdote about using an automatic translator in Exercise 7, they should write down one or two follow-up questions to ask them.

Exercise 8 page 219
Answers will vary.

LANGUAGE DEVELOPMENT

Exercise 1 page 220

1 pick; up; on   **2** come; out; with   **3** get; across   **4** talk; through   **5** come; across   **6** talk; into   **7** getting; at

Exercise 2 page 221

Answers will vary.

Exercise 3 page 222

1 Not doing / Not having done any speaking activities had an obvious impact on our fluency.

2 Despite not studying / not having studied any grammar, we were remarkably competent communicators.

3 Not being exposed to native speakers at school didn't really affect me.

4 Travelling to different countries taught him the usefulness of online translation devices.

Exercise 4 page 222

1 not to have spent / not to spend   2 to be living
3 to have been given   4 to have finished   5 to be used

Be flexible

Ask students to write three sentences of their own about their language education experience or about language education more generally, using complex gerund or infinitive forms.

Give **lower-level students** extra support. Concentrate on the active forms. Provide sentence stems to help students start their sentences, such as *I'm sorry to..., We hope to..., They are likely to...*. Challenge **stronger students** by asking them to do this activity using passive forms.

LISTENING 2

Learning objectives

- Understand key vocabulary for discussing English as a Foreign Language – *aptitude, coherent, grasp*
- Listen and take notes on main ideas and details in a research interview schedule
- Listen and understand detailed information in a research interview with a student language teacher
- Make inferences about a speaker's implications
- Listen and understand meaning in fast, connected speech
- Synthesize information from a seminar about machine translation and a research interview with a student language teacher in a discussion

Lead-in

Ask students to work in small groups to create and execute a poll of their peers. Do they like to work out language rules from the input on their own, or do they prefer to be told the rules before they see it or hear it in the input? Then ask, beyond what they *like*, which method do they think is more likely to facilitate learning?

Exercise 1 page 223

1 frustrating   2 discrepancy   3 coherent   4 excelled
5 grasp   6 lacking in   7 explicit   8 aptitude

Exercise 2 page 223

Answers will vary.

Exercise 3 page 224

1 **Experience of learning English: a** I think we started to study English in Grade 3; I would have been about nine years old   **b** native speakers   **c** not highly qualified; they were fun, young and enthusiastic   **d** lessons were well-structured; practised all four skills and did a lot of grammar   **e** no, more to do with their training; a teacher who trained at a British institute had a similar style to native speakers; most local teachers studied English at university – knowledgeable but lessons not always interesting

2 **Beliefs about teaching English: a** she prefers to work out rules; they appeal to her logical–mathematical intelligence; however, not having explicit input from the teacher may be frustrating for some students – they may feel short-changed if the teacher asks them to guess the language rules. Another issue: asking students to work out the language rules on their own may not be feasible with complete beginners or small children – use different methods with younger learners and beginners   **b** two crucial factors determine whether a student is successful or not: aptitude and motivation

Optional activity

As they listen to the interview, have students write down three follow-up questions they would like to ask.

Exercise 4 page 225

1 They didn't have teaching qualifications; they came across as lacking teaching experience; their classes did not seem to have much structure; she feels they were fresh from university.

2 In order to be able to guess or discuss language rules, you may need to have terms to talk about language. For example, you need to understand what nouns and verbs are, or what a subject and object are in a sentence.

3 Learners with motivation – a genuine interest in the language and culture – are more likely to excel. This kind of motivation is what makes you read English in your free time, or speak English outside the classroom.

Exercise 5 page 225

1 b   2 a   3 c   4 b   5 a

Exercise 6 page 226

1 I'd just like to pick up on what you were saying.

2 I'd like to ask you if it's OK for me to record this interview, so I can use it in my research.

Exercise 7 page 226

1 work; out **2** appeals; to **3** part; of **4** verbs; are
5 move; on **6** excel; at; it

Exercise 8 page 226

Answers will vary.

CRITICAL THINKING

Learning objectives

- Evaluate the effectiveness of interview questions against a set of criteria
- Create a list of questions for a research interview
- Evaluate and refine your questions for a research interview

UNLOCK TEACHER DEVELOPMENT

BE INFORMED

→ **Asking appropriate and productive questions** is an important skill for students because: (1) Mastering this will help them avoid unintentionally asking inappropriate questions and accidentally causing offence; (2) It is an especially important skill for conducting original qualitative research at university; (3) Even for students who do not need this skill for their degree, it is a very necessary skill for the workplace.

BE CONFIDENT

→ Develop this skill for yourself by doing the following activity:

In a critical thinking survey undertaken by Cambridge University Press, respondents were asked to say whether they agreed or disagreed with the following statements. In your opinion, were these good questions? Why / Why not?

- It is important to me that I develop my students' critical thinking skills.
- I believe my students want to develop their critical thinking skills.
- I struggle to find the time to develop effective means to teach critical thinking skills.
- My current materials offer adequate practice in analyzing data, evaluating opinions and planning and composing texts.

Lead-in

Give students a minute to read the speaking task they will do at the end of the unit. Then give them a few minutes to brainstorm their own practices of learning English outside the classroom. Tell them to keep their brainstorming notes for later, when they begin to prepare for their interview.

UNLOCK TEACHER DEVELOPMENT

BE READY

Look at the Critical Thinking section in the Student's Book on pages 227–229.

→ Which elements of the lesson do you think your students will find easiest / most difficult / most useful? Why?

→ Are your answers true for all students in your class?

→ How can you adapt your teaching or the material to meet your students' needs?

BE FLEXIBLE

To clearly show students why the interview questions on page 227 are bad, get them to close their books, and ask them these questions. You can then elicit their reasons as to why they were bad.

Exercise 1 page 228

1 x; leading **2** x; technical **3** x; Y/N **4** x; multiple
5 ✓; Y/N and follow-up question **6** ✓; *Wh-* question
7 x; personal **8** x; leading

Exercises 2–6 pages 228–229

Answers will vary.

UNLOCK TEACHER DEVELOPMENT

BE REFLECTIVE

Think about these follow-ups:

→ Write your own short survey and share it with your colleagues. You should focus on an aspect of teaching which (a) interests you or (b) challenges you, in the hope that you will be given some ideas about how to teach this aspect effectively.

→ Think about any survey, questionnaire or research which you have created or done in the past. From what you have learnt in this unit, what changes would you make? If you were to create or do any of these in the future, what would you do?

BE COLLABORATIVE

Your development is more meaningful when it is shared. See page 14 for ideas on how to peer-collaborate. Why not share the approach you adopted in the *Be flexible* section, and its impact on the lesson?

PREPARATION FOR SPEAKING

Learning objectives

- Use appropriate questions and phrases to interrupt a speaker: *Could I just stop you there? If I could just come in here, ..., I'm sorry to interrupt, but are you saying that...?*
- Use appropriate questions and phrases to handle interruptions: *As I was saying ... If I could just return to ... To get back to the point I was making about ...*
- Use appropriate intonation when interrupting.

Exercise 1 page 230

Possible answers:

1 I just wanted to clarify one thing. You said you are Korean, but your father is a native English speaker?
2 Could I just stop you there? What language do you speak with your mother?
3 If I could just return to talking about when you use English.
4 If I could just come in here, do you watch any English language films or television?

Exercise 2 page 230

Answers will vary.

Exercise 3 page 231

1 Could I just stop you there and ask about your high school experience?

2 I'd just like to pick up on what you were saying about using the internet to learn English.

3 If I could just come in here and ask about your family background.

4 I'm sorry to interrupt. I just wanted to clarify one thing.

5 Let me stop you there. When did you say you started learning English?

Be flexible

Tell students to practise the interruptions in Exercise 3, using correct intonation. Then they practise correct intonation with the interrupting expressions and follow-up questions they added to Exercise 1.

Challenge **stronger students** by asking another volunteer to talk about his or her interview plans. This time the other students should use some of the more sophisticated interrupting expressions they have learnt, again using appropriate intonation.

SPEAKING TASK

Learning objectives

- Review an interview schedule and prepare follow-up questions
- Take part in a research interview as an interviewer
- Take part in a research interview as an interviewee

Exercises 1–5 pages 232–233

Answers will vary.

RESEARCH PROJECT

Do a group presentation on a language.

Students choose a language that they would like to find out about, preferably one that they are not familiar with. If they wish, they could choose an artificial language such as Esperanto. They should find the answers to the following questions, and add at least two of their own:

- Where is it spoken?
- How many speakers are there – as a first language and as a second language?
- Has this number changed in recent years? If so, what might be the reason for this?
- Is it used in education?
- Is it an official language?
- Is it a language of wider communication?
- What are its prospects for the future?

Ethnologue (www.ethnologue.com/) is a good source to find answers to some of these questions (although it will not include Esperanto). Groups may wish to include a map in their presentation. One interesting approach to mapping can be found at *Worldmapper* (https://worldmapper.org/).

CLASSROOM APP

Exercise 1

Answers will vary.

Exercise 2

1 talk; out   **2** getting; across   **3** come; across
4 getting; at   **5** came; out

Exercise 3

1 not having prepared for the maths test.
2 Having been; Being exposed to English at an early age
3 being caught with the answers to the test; having been caught
4 never having visited a French-speaking country
5 for not having written

Exercise 4

1 to have been left out of the negotiation
2 to have completed their safety training
3 to have been informed
4 to have been keeping

Exercise 5

1 complexities   **2** frowned upon   **3** incomprehensible
4 explicit   **5** aptitude   **6** frustrating   **7** grasp   **8** vague

Exercise 6

Answers will vary.

Exercise 7

1 could just return to
2 sorry to interrupt
3 Could I just stop
4 to clarify; to pick up on
5 was trying to say; was saying
6 to pick up on; to return to

Exercise 8

Answers will vary

READING, WRITING & CRITICAL THINKING 1

UNIT OBJECTIVES	
Watch and listen	Watch and understand a video about people who catch fish in different countries.
Reading skill	Preview a text.
Critical thinking	Collect information.
Grammar	Use nouns and verbs; use subject pronouns; use the verb *be*; use possessive adjectives.
Academic writing skill	Write simple sentences.
Writing task	Write a profile.
⌀ **Teacher development**	Help your students become better at **collecting information**.

UNLOCK YOUR KNOWLEDGE

Background note

The photo shows a bird's-eye view of the Old Town Square in Prague, the Czech Republic. The medieval square continues to attract tourists and local people alike. Millions of tourists visit it every year to admire the famous Astronomical Clock, its historical buildings and the markets that are often held in the square. Important sporting events are shown on big screens in the centre of the square.

Lead-in

Show students a photo of a family. Write the words *mother, father, brother* and *sister* on the board. After you briefly describe the family members in the photo (e.g. their ages, interests, jobs, etc.), pair students to talk about their family members. Provide sentence frames if needed: *My brother is … years old. His name is …. He is a …. He likes ….*

page 15
Answers will vary.

WATCH AND LISTEN

Learning objectives

- Listen and identify main ideas in a video about fishermen
- Listen and identify details about fishing around the world
- Make inferences about the ideas in the video
- Practise talking about fishing and the sea

Exercise 1 page 16
Answers will vary.

Exercise 2 page 16
1 fourth photo   **2** second photo   **3** first photo
4 third photo

Exercise 3 page 16
1, 4, 5, 6

Exercise 4 page 17
1 tonnes   **2** small   **3** nets   **4** 10,000

Exercise 5 page 17
1, 3, 4, 5

Exercise 6 page 17
Answers will vary.

READING 1

Learning objectives

- Preview a text
- Understand key vocabulary for profiles – *languages, city, date of birth*
- Skim a profile and identify missing headings
- Scan the profile for facts
- Read and identify details
- Describe facts about yourself

Lead-in

Our personal lives have become public in the age of the internet. Students will read the online profile of a famous cricket player. Before reading, invite students to discuss what information people share online and where they find it. Briefly poll students to ask what social networking sites they use. Then make a list of the typical information they find on these sites: name, age, interests, family, friends, job, etc.

Exercise 1 page 18

1 information about a person and their life

2 A profile is a short description about somebody's life. You can find these on social networking websites like Facebook.

3 a cricket player

Exercise 2 page 18

1 city   2 languages   3 country   4 date of birth   5 job
6 hobbies

Exercise 3 page 20

1 Contact information   2 My family   3 My hobbies and interests   4 My life

Exercise 4 page 20

1 the United Kingdom   2 cricket
3 watching cricket and reading   4 English   5 brother
6 info@Mofans.cup.org   7 father

Optional activity

👤 👥 You could encourage students to scan the text quickly by turning this activity into a race. Make sure students start at the same time and ask them to close their books as soon as they have found all the correct options. Make a note of the first three or four finishers. Check the first finishers' answers. The first finisher with all the correct answers is the winner.

Exercise 5 page 20

1 cricket   2 Birmingham   3 1987   4 brothers
5 Munir Ali

Exercise 6 page 20
Answers will vary.

READING 2

Learning objectives

- Understand key vocabulary for people – *unusual, live, interested in*
- Scan the text to identify facts and complete a profile
- Read and understand detail
- Synthesize information from a profile and a text about an unusual man in a discussion

Lead-in

The text is about an unusually tall man, but the details show he has a lot in common with everybody else. Invite students to look at the picture of Sultan Kösen on page 22, and name ways Sultan's life may be different from others' (e.g. buying clothing, fitting in cars and through doorways, being looked at / paid attention to, etc.) and ways it may be the same (e.g. has a job/family, likes to travel, etc.).

Exercise 1 page 21

1 a   2 c   3 a

Exercise 2 page 21

a family   b normal   c live   d interested in   e music
f unusual   g work   h watch

Be flexible

👤 Ask **more advanced students** to write sentences using the new vocabulary. Fast finishers could write a couple of gap-fill sentences for a partner to complete with the missing new words.

Help **lower-level students** acquire this vocabulary. Point out the collocations *live in, work in* and *is interested in* in the sentences on page 21. Then ask students to generate additional phrases using these forms, e.g. *lives in Jordan, works in an office, is interested in music*, etc.

Exercise 3 page 23

1 Sultan   2 Kösen   3 Turkey   4 Mardin   5 one sister and three brothers   6 watching TV

Exercise 4 page 23

1 is   2 lives   3 family   4 is   5 watching   6 speaks

Exercise 5 page 23

1 People look at him in the street. Normal clothes and shoes are too small.

2 Moeen is interested in cricket, reading and playing with his son. Sultan is interested in music.

3 You learn the name, job and hobbies of a person. You learn about their family and where the person lives.

4 *Answers will vary.*

LANGUAGE DEVELOPMENT

Learning objectives

- Identify male and female family vocabulary – *grandmother, father, son*
- Differentiate between nouns and verbs – *cricket, farmer, live*
- Complete sentences with singular and plural nouns – *Ray has one brother. His brother is a farmer. Fernando has two brothers. His brothers are farmers.*

Exercise 1 page 24

1 grandfather   **2** brother   **3** uncle   **4** mother
5 daughter

Exercise 2 pages 24–25

nouns: Pakistan; cricket; languages
verbs: lives; works; is; plays

Be flexible

👥 Divide the class into teams. Say a word (i.e. either a verb or a noun) from the unit (e.g. *is, has, farmer*). The first team to correctly identify the form by calling out 'noun' or 'verb' wins a point. Meet the needs of **more advanced students** by challenging the class to use the word in a sentence. Students say the sentence and then the class evaluates if the word has been used correctly.

Exercise 3 page 25

1 sisters   **2** aunt   **3** grandfather   **4** sons   **5** brothers

Exercise 4 page 25

1 reads   **2** sister   **3** languages   **4** brothers   **5** lives
6 city

CRITICAL THINKING

Learning objectives

- Understand the kind of information needed for a profile
- Collect information for a profile in a table
- Compare information you collected with that of another student

UNLOCK TEACHER DEVELOPMENT

BE INFORMED

➜ **Collecting information** is an important skill for students because: (1) It is a key stage of the research and writing process; (2) Students need to be aware of how different sources of information can be used to collect data; (3) Students need to develop systems for recording information.

BE CONFIDENT

➜ Develop this skill for yourself by doing the following activity:

Think about an aspect of teaching the English language, or an academic subject which you are interested in. Imagine that you are going to write about this topic. Identify four or five sources of information which you could use.

Were there any sources you found which you would not use? Why?

Lead-in

Go through the instruction and the writing task carefully with the class. Explain that the following sections of the unit will help them to prepare to write descriptive sentences about somebody in their family.

UNLOCK TEACHER DEVELOPMENT

BE READY

Look at the Critical Thinking section in the Student's Book on page 26.

➜ Which elements of the lesson do you think your students will find easiest / most difficult / most useful? Why?

➜ Are your answers true for all students in your class?

➜ How can you adapt your teaching or the material to meet your students' needs?

BE FLEXIBLE

You can add an Exercise 4 if you have time, where students have to report back to larger groups (or the whole class) about their partner.

Exercise 1 page 26

1 Kösen   **2** Mardin (in Turkey)   **3** his wife, his mother, his three brothers and his sister   **4** farmer
5 watching TV / interested in music   **6** Turkish and English

Exercises 2–3 page 26

Answers will vary.

UNLOCK TEACHER DEVELOPMENT

BE REFLECTIVE

Think about the following points:

→ Since this may be your first Critical Thinking lesson with this class, think about their attitude towards critical thinking. Did they enjoy it? Were they confused? Did they understand why they were doing this? Knowing this can help you plan better for future critical thinking lessons.

→ Share your thoughts on the questions above with your colleagues. Compare and contrast your experiences.

BE COLLABORATIVE

Your development is more meaningful when it's shared. See page 14 for ideas on how to peer-collaborate. Why not share your reflections from the *Be ready* section?

GRAMMAR FOR WRITING

Learning objectives

- Understand which words are replaced by different subject pronouns – *aunts = they, grandfather = he, mother = she*, etc.
- Use subject pronouns to complete sentences – *Busan is a city in South Korea. It is a big city. Sarah is a student. She is 18 years old.*
- Use the correct form of the verb *be* to complete sentences describing people – *I am from Busan. Busan is in South Korea. My mother and father are not from Seoul.*
- Correct errors with the verb *be*
- Use contractions with the verb *be* in sentences about people – *I'm from Tokyo. We're students. She's not a student.*
- Use possessive adjectives in sentences describing people – *You are from Egypt. Your school is in Alexandria. Marta and Luis have a sister. Their sister is a teacher.*

Exercise 1 page 27

she: daughter; mother; grandmother
he: brother; father; grandfather
they: sons; aunts; uncles; sisters

Exercise 2 page 27

1 She **2** They **3** He **4** It

Exercise 3 page 29

A 1 is **2** am **3** am **4** is **5** is **6** is **7** is **8** is
B 1 am **2** am **3** is **4** are **5** is **6** is **7** is **8** are

Exercise 4 page 30

1 am not **2** are not **3** is not **4** is not **5** are not
6 are not

Exercise 5 page 30

My name **is** Ibrihim. My sisters **are** in school in Tunis. He **is** a teacher in Spain. We **are** in Madrid. I **am** at university.

Exercise 6 page 30

1 I'm from Tokyo.   **2** We're students in London.
3 It's a big city.   **4** You're not tall. / You aren't tall.
5 She's not a student. / She isn't a student.
6 He's a teacher.   **7** You're students in my class.
8 It's not a big school. / It isn't a big school.
9 We're not in Mexico. / We aren't in Mexico.
10 I'm not at university.

Exercise 7 page 31

1 Their **2** Her **3** Our **4** My **5** His **6** Its

ACADEMIC WRITING SKILLS

Learning objectives

- Write simple sentences with correct word order (subject + verb) – *Sultan is from Turkey. His life is not easy. He watches TV.*
- Punctuate simple sentences correctly with capital letters and full stops.

Exercise 1 page 32

1 My grandfather's name is Zhong Shan.
2 He is 59.   **3** He is a doctor.
4 He is from Hong Kong.   **5** He has two daughters.
6 He lives with my mother and father.

Exercise 2 page 33

1 My name is Gustavo. *(capital M)*
2 I am from Ecuador. *(capital I; full stop)*
3 I am 19. *(capital I; verb; full stop)*
4 My father's name **is** Marcus. *(capital M; verb)*
5 She **is** a teacher. *(capital S; verb; full stop)*
6 He has two sons. *(capital H)*
7 My brother's name is Paulo. *(capital M)*
8 He / She is a doctor. *(subject; full stop)*

9 She **is** in Canada. / She **lives/works** in Canada.
(capital S; verb; full stop)

10 Paulo's hobbies **are** playing with his son and watching TV. *(verb; full stop)*

Optional activity

👥 👥👥 Ask students to identify the subjects and verbs in simple sentences from Section 4 of the reading text on page 19. Students make a list of the subjects and verbs for each of the sentences in the paragraph. Make it into a competition to see which pairs complete the activity first and correctly.

Answers:

Subjects: I (x6), My brothers, names, My father, He, His father

Verbs: 'm, am (x2), speak, play, are, is (x3), like

WRITING TASK

Learning objectives

- Plan the information you will use in a profile about your family
- Draft your profile
- Review and revise the content and structure of your profile
- Review and revise the use of language in your profile

Exercises 1–5 pages 33–34

Answers will vary.

RESEARCH PROJECT

Create a profile or article on an interesting person.

Ask partners to pick a famous sportsperson or other person they are interested in. Monitor so students don't choose the same person. They should research the person and create a profile. Encourage students to use the categories from Moeen Ali's profile on page 19. Alternatively, students could create a text, like the one about Sultan Kösen, about a fascinating person. The main purpose is for students to focus on somebody they are interested in and can learn about while practising the grammar and vocabulary from the unit. Allow students to use pictures to create the profile. Share with the class on a blog or other online tool.

CLASSROOM APP

Exercise 1
Answers will vary.

Exercise 2
1 job, hobbies   **2** city, languages   **3** live, work
4 watch, music

Exercise 3
Answers will vary.

Exercise 4
1 nouns   **2** verbs   **3** nouns   **4** nouns   **5** verbs

Exercise 5
1 brothers / sisters   **2** people / women   **3** uncle / aunt
4 grandmother / brother   **5** job / hobby

Exercise 6
1 Moeen Ali is a cricket player.
2 She lives in Jordan.
3 My brother works on a farm.
4 I speak Urdu.
5 My father is from India.
6 He plays cricket.
7 It's an unusual day!
8 My daughter is interested in music.

UNIT OBJECTIVES	
Watch and listen	Watch and understand a video about the Taiga forest.
Reading skill	Scan to find information.
Critical thinking	Categorize information.
Grammar	Use nouns and adjectives; use noun phrases; use prepositional phrases.
Academic writing skills	Use correct word order; use correct punctuation.
Writing task	Write about the weather.
⟁ **Teacher development**	Help your students become better at **categorizing information**.

UNLⓄCK YOUR KNOWLEDGE

Background note

The photo shows cherry blossoms in Japan. The cherry trees blossom in the spring from late March until late April or even early May, depending on the area and the weather. Japan is known all over the world for its cherry blossoms, and they are an important part of Japanese culture. International and local tourists visit Japan in the spring to admire the pink blossoms in the parks and gardens.

Lead-in

Ask: *What's the weather today? Is it hot/cold/ sunny/rainy?* Show the class newspaper or internet weather forecasts and look at the weather symbols for your city and other cities. Elicit what the symbols mean. Pre-teach the following vocabulary: *hot, warm, cold, sunny, windy, rainy, cloudy* (and any other words that are useful for your teaching context).

page 37
Answers will vary.

WATCH AND LISTEN

Learning objectives

* Listen and identify the main ideas in a video about the weather in a forest
* Listen and understand details
* Complete a set of inferences about the ideas in the video
* Practise talking about cold places

Exercise 1 page 38
Answers will vary.

Exercise 2 page 38
1 F; This part of the Earth is cold.
2 T   **3** T   **4** F; The trees can live in cold temperatures.

Exercise 3 page 39
1, 2, 3, 5

Exercise 4 page 39
1 south   **2** cold   **3** 30%   **4** snow

Exercise 5 page 39
1 winter   **2** near   **3** difficult   **4** flowers

Exercise 6 page 39
Answers will vary.

READING 1

Learning objectives

* Understand key vocabulary for weather and seasons – *warm, spring, winter*
* Preview photos, title and subtitles to predict the detail in an article about a cold place
* Scan and identify figures about the people and weather described in the article
* Read and complete a summary of the article
* Describe your feelings about the place in the article
* Describe what you do in cold weather

Lead-in

Tell students they are going to read a travel article about a very cold city. Invite them to look at the pictures and say what they think the article will discuss. Make a list of questions students want to know about this place. Encourage them to think like the writer and traveller, i.e. *You are in Yakutsk to learn about the city and people there. What questions do you ask? What do you want to know about life in a cold place?*

Exercise 1 page 40

1 b **2** a **3** c

Exercise 2 page 40

1 f **2** b **3** e **4** d **5** g **6** a **7** c

Exercise 3 page 40

Answers will vary.

Exercise 4 page 40

1 T **2** T **3** F; Summer is warm in Yakutsk.
4 F; Svetlana has a café in Yakutsk.

Exercise 5 page 42

1 f **2** b **3** a **4** c **5** e **6** d

Exercise 6 page 42

1 Svetlana **2** Yakutsk **3** cold **4** spring **5** warm

Exercise 7 page 42

Answers will vary.

Optional activity

To extend the discussion, give students time to prepare their responses to the questions in Exercise 7. You could also put them into new pairs or small groups. Suggest further questions and discussion points, e.g.:

What is the average summer temperature in your country?
What is the average winter temperature in your country?
Is life easier in the winter or the summer? Why?
Is a change in weather good? Why / Why not?

Circulate and provide follow-up questions as needed to provoke further discussion (e.g. *What do people enjoy doing in the summer/winter in your country?*). At the end, give feedback on students' ideas and language (consider both range and accuracy).

READING 2

Learning objectives

- Preview three texts about Cuban weather
- Understand key vocabulary for weather – *dry, rainfall, season*
- Scan and identify figures about the weather described in the article
- Read and make notes on weather in different seasons
- Identify and predict the original context of the text
- Synthesize information from an article about a cold place and three texts about weather in Cuba in a discussion

Lead-in

Ask students how they find out about the weather in places they want to visit. Then share a variety of travel websites and books with descriptions of the climate. Students can note the type of information included (e.g. temperature, rainfall). Point out that these resources are often used for planning trips and deciding when to go. Then look at weather websites that give forecasts for upcoming days. Emphasize the difference in how these resources are used. Give students a variety of scenarios and get them to determine which resource they would use for each (e.g. *you want to plan a trip to Fiji; you want to know the best season to visit Fiji; your trip to Fiji is next week and you want to check the weather; you are in Fiji and you want to know tomorrow's weather*).

Exercise 1 page 43
Answers will vary.

Exercise 2 page 43

1 c **2** a **3** b

Exercise 3 page 43

1 rainfall **2** season **3** dry **4** climate

Exercise 4 page 44

1 cloudy **2** rainy **3** sunny **4** windy

Exercise 5 page 45

1 e **2** c **3** f **4** d **5** a **6** b

Exercise 6 page 45

dry season: November to April; average temperatures between +22 °C and +25 °C; average rainfall 62 mm; windy and sunny

rainy season: May to October; average temperatures between +26 °C and +28 °C; average rainfall 146 mm; cloudy

Exercise 7 page 45

Answers will vary. Possible answers:

1 April or May; dry weather and warm temperatures
2 the dry season and the rainy season
3 the internet; guide books; tourist information brochures
4 *Answers will vary but may include:* so they can plan activities, what to wear, etc.

Be flexible

👥 👥👥 To extend the discussion, give students time to prepare their responses to the questions in Exercise 7. You could also put them into new pairs or small groups. For **fast finishers / stronger students**, you can suggest further questions and discussion points, e.g.:
Is the weather in Cuba good for farmers? Why? / Why not?
Would you like to go to Cuba? Why? / Why not?
Is the weather in your country good or bad for tourists? Why? / Why not?
Is the weather in your country good or bad for farmers? Why? / Why not?

LANGUAGE DEVELOPMENT

Learning objectives

- Identify opposite adjectives – *difficult > easy; cold > hot; sunny > cloudy*
- Identify nouns and adjectives in sentences
- Complete sentences with correct adjectives – *In Yakutsk, life is difficult in winter.*
- Form adjective + noun phrases – *warm summers, high rainfall, cold winters*
- Correct mistakes with noun phrases

Exercise 1 page 46

1 f   2 c   3 d   4 a   5 b   6 e   7 g

Exercise 2 page 46

1 **noun:** café; **adjective:** warm
2 **noun:** October; **adjective:** rainy
3 **noun:** climate; **adjective:** good
4 **noun:** Summers; **adjective:** hot
5 **noun:** Winters; **adjective:** cold

Exercise 3 page 46

1 difficult   2 happy   3 sunny   4 cold   5 cloudy

Exercise 4 page 47

1 cold winters   2 dry season   3 high rainfall
4 warm summers

Exercise 5 page 47

1 Cuba has a rainy season.
2 Yakutsk has a cold autumn.
3 In summer, we have sunny weather.
4 The dry season is windy.
5 In spring, the rainfall is high.

CRITICAL THINKING

Learning objectives

- Categorize information about seasons in Yakutsk in a table
- Analyze the seasons in your city or town
- Add information about the seasons in your city or town to a table

UNL⟲CK TEACHER DEVELOPMENT

BE INFORMED

→ **Categorizing information** is an important skill for students because: (1) It is the next logical stage of the research and writing process (after collecting information); (2) Developing this skill can help students with learning English, e.g. learning vocabulary; (3) The use of tables in this way is common across many academic subjects.

BE CONFIDENT

→ Develop this skill for yourself by doing the following activity:
Below is a list of words. How many groups of three can you make? For example, 'medicine', 'doctor' and 'hospital' are all connected to health; 'ball', 'mall' and 'small' all rhyme. You can use a word in more than one group.

aircraft	ball	bird	bus	car	deer	doctor
fish	hospital	mall	medicine	nurse		
office	rain	school	small	student	sun	
teacher	train	wind				

Lead-in

Go through the instruction and the writing task carefully with the class. Explain that the following sections of the unit will help them to prepare and write factual sentences about the weather in their city or town.

UNLOCK TEACHER DEVELOPMENT

BE READY

Look at the Critical Thinking section in the Student's Book on pages 48–49.

→ Which elements of the lesson do you think your students will find easiest / most difficult / most useful? Why?

→ Are your answers true for all students in your class?

→ How can you adapt your teaching or the material to meet your students' needs?

BE FLEXIBLE

You could also ask students to think about weather in other places. This would also extend their world knowledge. This could be done in the lesson, or as a piece of home/project work.

Exercise 1 page 48

season	months	average temperature
winter	December, January, February	–42 °C
spring	March, April, May	–21 °C
summer	June, July, August	+20 °C
autumn	September, October, November	–21 °C

Exercise 2 page 49

1 yes **2** yes **3** cold **4** September, October, November **5** cold but warmer than winter

Exercises 3–5 page 49

Answers will vary.

UNLOCK TEACHER DEVELOPMENT

BE REFLECTIVE

Think about the following points:

→ With your colleagues, share three groups which you created in the *Be confident* that you think are particularly interesting. Ask them to do the same.

→ How did your students feel when you asked them to do the critical thinking exercises? Were they confident, or were they nervous about doing it? Why?

BE COLLABORATIVE

Your development is more meaningful when it's shared. See page 14 for ideas on how to peer-collaborate. Why not share the ideas you generated in the *Be flexible* section, and their outcome?

GRAMMAR FOR WRITING

Learning objectives

- Complete prepositional phrases in sentences – *Svetlana is from Yakutsk. Yakutsk is in Russia. It is warm in summer.*
- Answer questions using prepositional phrases – *Where are you from? I'm from England. How long is the winter in your country? Winter lasts six months in my country.*
- Add missing commas after prepositional phrases to a paragraph
- Use correct word order in sentences with prepositional phrases

Exercise 1 page 50

1 in **2** in **3** between **4** in; about **5** for

Exercise 2 page 50

Answers will vary. Possible ways to form the sentences are:

1 I am from …. **2** It is warmest in … (months).

3 The winter in my country is from … (month) to … (month).

4 The average temperature in May is …. **5** The weather is nice in … (month).

Exercise 3 page 51

1 In the dry season **2** in the dry season

Exercise 4 page 51

1 sentence 1 **2** between

Exercise 5 page 51

1 in July **2** In the rainy season, **3** in the dry season

Exercise 6 page 51

Dubai is a great place to visit. From November to March, many people go to the beach. The weather is good. In these months, the temperatures are between +24 °C and +35 °C. From January to March, Dubai has a rainy season, but it does not rain a lot. Summer is from April to October. In summer, Dubai is very hot. People do not go outside. In this season, the temperatures are too high.

Exercise 7 page 52

1 In October, it is windy.

2 The weather is good in summer.

3 In Cuba, the climate is good.

4 In autumn, the average rainfall is 34 mm.

5 The winters are cold in Yakutsk.

6 The average temperature in summer is +20 °C.

7 In the dry season, the average rainfall is 62 mm.

Be flexible

👥 Help **lower-level students** by making this activity interactive and visual. Before the lesson, write each word in the first one or two sentences in Exercise 6 on separate large pieces of paper and ask a matching number of students to stand in front of the class. Give each student one word (or comma) to hold up and ask the rest of the class to tell their classmates to move into the right positions to show the correct sentence order. As the class thinks through this process, reiterate their decisions or provide guidance as needed (e.g. *OK, so I see the first word begins with a capital letter, and the comma follows a noun, the object of the preposition*).

ACADEMIC WRITING SKILLS

Learning objectives

- Use correct word order in sentences with adjectives or nouns after *be* – *Tuesday is sunny in Cuba. There are two seasons in Cuba.*
- Use capital letters for proper nouns – *June, New York City, Rodrigo*
- Use commas after prepositional phrases and in lists – *In summer, we go swimming. It is going to be windy on Monday, Wednesday, Thursday and Saturday.*

Exercise 1 page 53

Answers will vary.

Exercise 2 page 53

1 Ice skating is popular in Russia.

2 There are two seasons in Cuba.

3 It is rainy in April.

4 It is hot in Cuba.

5 The summers are warm.

6 It is dry in August.

7 In winter, it is windy.

Optional activity

👤👥 List or display nouns, noun phrases and adjectives from the first two units on the board. Ask students to pick a subject, and then tell them to link it with a noun (e.g. *Moeen Ali is a cricket player.*). Share examples. Repeat so students choose a different subject, and then link it with a noun phrase

---

(e.g. *Summer is a dry season.*). Lastly, ask students to link a subject with an adjective (e.g. *Spring is warm.*). Students can write sentences on a shared document or share out loud. Correct verb forms and parts of speech as needed. Repeat for additional practice.

Exercise 3 page 54

1 It is spring in March, April and May.

2 It rains in spring, summer and autumn.

3 The coldest months are December, January and February.

4 The warmest months are June, July and August.

Exercise 4 page 54

1 In January, the weather is cold in Russia.

2 The average temperature is +21 °C in July.

3 In the rainy season, the average rainfall is 146 mm in Cuba.

4 The weather is sunny in summer.

5 In Dubai, August is a hot month.

WRITING TASK

Learning objectives

- Draft sentences about your city or town
- Review and revise the content and structure of your sentences
- Review and revise the use of language in your sentences

Exercises 1–6 pages 55–56

Answers will vary.

RESEARCH PROJECT

Research the weather in a place to visit.

Divide the class into small group. Ask students to use the internet to access weather information for a place they would like to visit. Students will collect information to give a general overview of the climate and seasons, including average temperature/rainfall or number of days of rain per month. The group must select the best time of year to visit. The groups then present their information to the class. As a class, vote on the best place to visit.

CLASSROOM APP

Exercises 1-2

Answers will vary.

Exercise 3

1

2

3

4

5

6

7

8

Exercise 4

1 Adjective – hot, Noun – month

2 Adjective – nice, Noun – night

3 Adjective – fun, Noun – day

4 Adjective – interesting, Noun – weather

5 Adjective – average, Noun – temperature

6 Adjective – beautiful, Noun – flowers

Exercise 5

1 June is a warm month.

2 September has rainy days.

3 Spring is a beautiful season.

4 The Mediterranean has nice winters.

5 Winter is an unpopular season.

6 Sunny days are fun.

Exercise 6

1 It is dry in September.

2 In Cuba, the weather is nice.

3 Children are happy in the summer.

4 July is sunny in my country.

5 Life is fun in the summer.

6 Children are sad on a rainy day.

UNIT OBJECTIVES

Watch and listen	Watch and understand a video about visiting Toronto on holiday.
Reading skill	Annotate a text.
Critical thinking	Choose relevant information.
Grammar	Use time expressions; recognize parts of a sentence; use the present simple.
Academic writing skill	Write about main ideas and details.
Writing task	Write about the life of a student in your class.
↺ Teacher development	Help your students become better at **choosing relevant information**.

UNLOCK YOUR KNOWLEDGE

Background note

The photo shows two people sitting at a table in the courtyard of the Green Tangerine Restaurant and Café in Hanoi, Vietnam. The café is located in the Old Quarter of Hanoi and is famous for its unique atmosphere. The couple in the photo seem to be having lunch followed by coffee. The woman is reading a book or looking for information in a book.

Lead-in

Ask students about a typical working day in their country:
What time do people usually get up?
What time do they start/finish work?
When do they have breakfast/lunch/dinner?

Put students in pairs and get them to ask and answer similar questions for a typical student in their country. Monitor, then ask one pair to report back to the class. You could pre-teach *lecture* /ˈlektʃə/ (a formal talk on a serious or specialist subject given to a group of people, especially students), *seminar* /ˈsemɪnɑː/ (an occasion when a teacher or expert and a group of people meet to study and discuss something) and *timetable* /ˈtaɪmˌteɪbl/ (a list of the times when lessons in school happen).

page 59

1 In a café   **2** They are looking at a book and eating.
3–4 *Answers will vary.*

WATCH AND LISTEN

Learning objectives

- Listen and identify main ideas in a video about the CN Tower in Toronto
- Listen and identify numbers
- Complete a set of inferences about the video
- Practise talking about towers and holidays

Exercise 1 page 60
Answers will vary.

Exercise 2 page 60
1 You can see the city from the top of the CN Tower.
2 Toronto is on the shore of Lake Ontario.
3 This is the main pod of the tower that people visit.
4 Five people are walking on the outside of the CN Tower.

Exercise 3 page 61
2, 4, 5, 6

Exercise 4 page 61
1 1976   **2** 360   **3** 160   **4** 116

Exercise 5 page 61
1 c   **2** a   **3** d   **4** b

Exercise 6 page 61
Answers will vary.

READING 1

Learning objectives

- Use images to preview the topic of a book review about a tribe
- Understand key vocabulary for lifestyle – *get up, cook, breakfast*
- Read and identify main ideas
- Scan and identify detailed information
- Discuss the lifestyle of the Kombai people

Lead-in

Preview the quotes about the book on page 63 and discuss the purpose of them in getting the reader interested in the book. Point out the large print at the beginning of the text and discuss how those questions engage the reader. You may want to discuss the format of book reviews (that they summarize a book and give interesting details, so readers will want to buy the book). If possible, look at simple reviews of books that students are familiar with for more examples.

Exercise 1 page 62
Answers will vary.

Exercise 2 page 62
a hunter; a jungle; a tree house

Exercise 3 page 62
a dinner **b** get up **c** meet **d** breakfast **e** swim **f** cook **g** lunch **h** travel

Exercises 4–5 page 64
1 b **2** a **3** d **4** c

Exercise 6 page 64
2 Rebecca Moore
3 Kombai women
4 Kombai men; Kombai women; Kombai children
5 Kombai men; Kombai women; Kombai children
6 Kombai men; Kombai women
7 Kombai men; Kombai women; Kombai children
8 Rebecca Moore

Exercise 7 page 64
1 *Possible answer:* Maybe it is safer to live in the trees. Maybe it floods and they need to live in the trees.
2 They teach their children to cook, hunt and swim.
3 *Answers will vary.*

READING 2

Learning objectives

- Understand key vocabulary for routine – *afternoon, busy, timetable*
- Preview a student's timetable
- Annotate key words and phrases in a description of a student's routine
- Scan for key information in a text about a student
- Synthesize information from a book review about a tribe and a description of a student's routine in a discussion

Lead-in

To lead in to Reading 2, about the daily routine of a university student, you could discuss the following questions with individual students / the whole class:

How is your day/week going? Are you busy? Do students work too hard in your country? Do students need more holidays?

Exercise 1 page 65
1 a **2** b **3** b **4** a **5** a **6** b **7** a **8** a

Optional activity

👥 👥👥 Preview vocabulary *morning, afternoon* and *evening* from Reading 2 with students. Ask partners to assign times to each part of the day (e.g. morning 6 am to 12 pm) Review *am* and *pm*. Then ask students to use vocabulary from Reading 1 (*get up, breakfast, lunch, dinner*) in sentences with the parts of the day. Ask students to compare when they get up, have breakfast, lunch and dinner, using the vocabulary in complete sentences. For example, *I get up at 8 am in the morning.* You may want to plan ahead for this activity and get information from students, so you can make it into a scavenger hunt activity, e.g. *Find somebody who gets up at 7 am in the morning. Find somebody who has lunch at 1 pm in the afternoon,* etc.

Exercise 2 page 65
Answers will vary.

Exercise 3 page 66
noun: timetable; **verb:** relax; **adjective:** busy
part of the day: morning, afternoon, evening
part of the week: weekday, weekend

Exercise 4 page 66
1 T   **2** F; The timetable and text are from a diary.
3 T   **4** F; Abdullah's weekend is on Friday and Saturday.

Exercise 5 page 68

Possible answers:

Paragraph 1: student; busy timetable; five courses

Paragraph 2: gets up at 6 am; studies every evening

Paragraph 3: three classes every morning

Paragraph 4: afternoon; study group; English class; Arab history

Paragraph 5: evening; studies in the library; relaxes with friends; Camera Club

Paragraph 6: weekend; time to relax

Exercise 6 page 68

1 on Thursday evening **2** Cairo **3** busy **4** three **5** gym
6 morning **7** early **8** five **9** Thursday **10** Engineering

Exercise 7 page 68

1 Thursday evenings and weekends; goes to the cinema and to Camera Club; takes photographs; relaxes with friends and family

2–4 *Answers will vary.*

LANGUAGE DEVELOPMENT

Learning objectives

- Recognize verb + noun collocations for free-time activities – *play video games, study English, have breakfast.*
- Complete verb + preposition collocations in sentences about free time – *You go to the gym every day. My sister cooks dinner for my family. Abdullah studies in the library.*
- Understand vocabulary for study by area – *Physics > Science; English > Languages; History > Arts and Humanities*
- Spell the names of subjects correctly
- Use time expressions to describe routine – *I do my homework every week. She has an English class on Sunday night. They swim at 3 pm in the afternoon.*

Exercise 1 page 69

1 b **2** c **3** e **4** a **5** d

Exercise 2 page 69

1 meets **2** take **3** go **4** have **5** eats **6** relax
7 cooks **8** do

Be flexible

Write the words of the collocations from the Vocabulary box or Exercise 2 on page 69 on separate index cards. Hand out the cards to students and ask them to find the person with the matching word to complete the collocation. Then collect the cards. Ask each set of partners to take a card from the set; the class then competes to list as many collocations as possible for their word. Check the collocations students create. Provide additional challenge for **more advanced students**. Ask them to identify the form of the collocation, e.g. *verb + noun or noun phrase* or *verb + preposition.*

Exercise 3 page 70

Arts and Humanities: Literature; History; Art and Design
Business: Economics; Management
Science: Maths; Physics; Biology; Geography; Chemistry
Languages: English; Arabic

Exercise 4 page 70

Answers will vary.

Exercise 5 page 71

1 Geography **2** English **3** Physics **4** Chemistry
5 History **6** Biology **7** Economics

Exercise 6 page 71

1 on; at **2** In **3** On; at **4** in **5** On; at **6** on **7** in
8 at **9** At

Exercise 7 page 71

Answers will vary.

CRITICAL THINKING

Learning objectives

- Answer questions about a student's routine
- Ask questions about another student's routine and complete a timetable
- Evaluate and choose the most important information about a person

UNLOCK TEACHER DEVELOPMENT

BE INFORMED

→ **Choosing relevant information** is an important skill for students because: (1) It is the next logical stage of the research and writing process (after categorizing information); (2) They might think that all research information has the same value and importance, which is clearly not true; (3) A problem area when writing essays is including irrelevant information which does not answer the question.

BE CONFIDENT

→ Develop this skill for yourself by doing the following activity:

Look at the website for your educational institution. Think about whether there is any information there which is not relevant. Why is it not relevant?

Lead-in

Go through the instruction and the writing task carefully with the class. Explain that the following sections of the unit will help them to prepare to write factual sentences about the life of a student in their class.

UNLOCK TEACHER DEVELOPMENT

BE READY

Look at the Critical Thinking section in the Student's Book on pages 72–73.

→ Which elements of the lesson do you think your students will find easiest / most difficult / most useful? Why?

→ Are your answers true for all students in your class?

→ How can you adapt your teaching or the material to meet your students' needs?

BE FLEXIBLE

Exercise 4 can be done with the whole class. Students leave their books open. Everybody circulates and looks at the timetables. They should tick what they think are the most important facts. Finally, each student looks at the facts which have the most ticks, and says whether they agree.

Exercise 1 page 72

1 Taha   2 Cairo University

3 Physics, Maths, English, Engineering, Arab History

4 6 am   5 Every weekday morning: Physics, Maths, Engineering; Monday and Wednesday afternoon: English; Thursday afternoon: Arab History

6 On Sunday afternoon

7 In the evenings, from Sunday to Wednesday

8 On Thursday evenings, and at the weekends

Exercises 2–4 pages 72–73

Answers will vary.

UNLOCK TEACHER DEVELOPMENT

BE REFLECTIVE

Think about the following questions:

→ Were you able to teach this lesson more effectively by thinking about your own weekly timetable beforehand?

→ How well did your students understand Bloom's taxonomy? If they are still unclear about how it works, you might want to clarify their understanding in subsequent lessons. You can do this by specifically referencing Bloom's six areas when they do an activity of that type in the Critical Thinking section.

BE COLLABORATIVE

Your development is more meaningful when it's shared. See page 14 for ideas on how to peer-collaborate. If you did the activity in *Be flexible*, tell a colleague how it went and whether it was successful.

GRAMMAR FOR WRITING

Learning objectives

- Identify different types of simple sentence structures – subject + verb + object; subject + verb + prepositional phrase; subject + verb + object + prepositional phrase
- Form the third person singular of verbs – *travels, goes, studies*
- Choose the correct present simple verb forms to complete a paragraph about a student.
- Ask and answer questions in the third person singular – *What does your partner do on Saturdays? She goes to the zoo. What does your partner study? She studies Animal Biology.*

Exercise 1 page 73

1 b   2 a   3 d   4 c

Exercise 2 page 74

1 b   2 a   3 d   4 c

Exercise 3 page 75

2 travels **3** goes **4** studies **5** stays **6** has

Exercise 4 page 75

1 is **2** is **3** studies **4** gets up **5** eats **6** meets **7** has **8** studies **9** goes **10** is

Exercise 5 page 75

Answers will vary but should use third person singular verb forms.

ACADEMIC WRITING SKILLS

Learning objectives

- Identify main ideas and details in paragraphs
- Add details to paragraphs

Exercise 1 page 76

Main idea: Abdullah has three classes every weekday morning.
Details: He gets up at 6 am every day. Then he has Physics from 8 am to 9 am, Maths from 9:15 am to 10:15 am and Engineering from 10:30 am to 11:30 am.

1 a **2** b

Exercise 2 page 76

Main idea: At the weekends, Abdullah relaxes with friends.
Details: Sometimes, he goes to the cinema. He enjoys his busy life.
Answers will vary. Possible answer: He also likes taking photographs.

Be flexible

Provide guided support for **lower-level students**. Ask small groups to write a detail sentence for one of the paragraphs from the text on page 67. For example, give them the main idea from Paragraph 2: *Abdullah is a busy student.* Then project their sentences on a shared document or get students to read them out loud, and as a class evaluate if they add more detail to the main idea. Give feedback and guidance as you relate each sentence back to the main idea to determine if it fits.

WRITING TASK

Learning objectives

- Draft sentences about your partner's timetable and lifestyle
- Review and revise the content and structure of your sentences
- Review and revise the use of language in your sentences

Exercises 1–6 pages 77–78
Answers will vary.

RESEARCH PROJECT

Create a short magazine article.

Explain to your students that they are going to research and write about a culture or people they are interested in. Encourage them to think of their writing as a short magazine article. Divide the project into three parts: (1) First, students should research and gather information about the culture, on how people spend their free time or time at the weekend, and how they spend time on weekdays at work or school. Include other relevant topics from the unit, such as family, friends, food, meals, education and sport; (2) Second, students should choose two or three topics to write about. Ask them to write main idea sentences and identify the details to include. Encourage students to find pictures to illustrate the ideas; (3) Lastly, Ask students to draft their paragraphs and present their information. You may want to let students review each other's work and give feedback. They can create a poster, a web page or other document to share their research.

CLASSROOM APP

Exercises 1–2
Answers will vary.

Exercise 3

1 morning **2** relaxing **3** evening **4** breakfast **5** swim **6** travelling **7** cook **8** during the week

Exercise 4

1 with **2** to **3** in **4** plays **5** takes **6** get **7** have **8** with

Exercise 5

1 C, in **2** on **3** on **4** C **5** in **6** at **7** C

Exercise 6

1 detail **2** main idea **3** main idea **4** detail **5** detail **6** main idea

PLACES UNIT 4

UNIT OBJECTIVES	
Watch and listen	Watch and understand a video about *cenotes* in Mexico.
Reading skill	Read for main ideas.
Critical thinking	Classify topics and key words.
Grammar	Use noun phrases with *of*; use *there is / there are*; use articles.
Academic writing skills	Use capital letters for cities, country names and nationalities; write topic sentences.
Writing task	Write facts about your country.
⟳ **Teacher development**	Help your students become better at **classifying topics and key words**.

UNLOCK YOUR KNOWLEDGE

Background note

The photo shows Pamukkale, in southwest Turkey. Pamukkale is the most visited tourist attraction in Turkey. The terraces are made of limestone, a type of stone left behind by the natural hot springs. The limestone steps contain warm pools of water where visitors can bathe. The pools are naturally heated and reach a temperature of 36 °C. Pamukkale used to be a Greco-Roman spa city, called Hierapolis. Today, Hierapolis-Pamukkale is a UNESCO World Heritage site.

Lead-in

Play a matching game. Write the two columns below on the board. (Take this opportunity to pre-teach *capital* and *country*.) In pairs, students match the capitals to the correct countries. Ask pairs to raise their hands as soon as they have finished. The first pair to match them all correctly wins.

Country /ˈkʌntri/	Capital /ˈkapɪtl/
France	Ottawa
Morocco	Jakarta
Turkey	Tokyo
Indonesia	Canberra
India	Rabat
Japan	Paris
China	New Delhi
Canada	Beijing
Australia	Ankara

Answers

France, Paris; Morocco, Rabat; Turkey, Ankara; Indonesia, Jakarta; India, New Delhi; Japan, Tokyo; China, Beijing; Canada, Ottawa; Australia, Canberra

page 81
1 Pamukkale in Turkey   **2–4** *Answers will vary.*

WATCH AND LISTEN

Learning objectives

* Listen and identify the main ideas in a video about a place in a Mexican forest
* Listen and understand details
* Complete a set of inferences about the place in the video
* Practise talking about special places

Exercise 1 page 82
Answers will vary.

Exercise 2 page 82
1 There is a monkey in the forest.   **2** There is a space in the trees.   **3** Plants are growing in the water.   **4** A man is swimming in the water.

Exercise 3 page 83
2, 5, 6

Exercise 4 page 83
1 trees   **2** special   **3** Water   **4** animals   **5** cold

Exercise 5 page 83
1 very   **2** need   **3** is   **4** dangerous

Exercise 6 page 83
Answers will vary.

READING 1

Learning objectives

- Preview the texts and identify topics
- Understand key vocabulary for places – *lake, mountain, forest*
- Scan and annotate ideas in a text about an old map
- Scan and identify countries and continents
- Read and understand details
- Talk about maps

Lead-in

List the names of the texts that students have read so far from each unit and get them to match them to the type of text (an online profile, a short biography, a travel article, weather websites, a book review and a short report on a student). Preview Reading 1 on page 86 with students and ask them to identify the text type (a history book). Notice with students the name of Figure 4.3 on page 86. Preview the language, calling attention to the past tense verbs and the proper nouns which are used to discuss and give factual information on this topic.

Exercise 1 page 84

1 b   2 b   3 a   4 b   5 a   6 a   7 a

Exercise 2 page 85

1 c   2 b

Exercise 3 page 85

1 Muhammad al-Idrisi / King Roger II of Sicily   2 Tabula Rogeriana   3 Norway, Spain, Italy, India and China
4 the Mediterranean Sea; the Indian Ocean; the river Nile

Exercise 4 page 85

continents: Asia, Europe, Africa

countries: Spain, Norway, Morocco, China, France, England, Italy and India

Exercise 5 page 85

1 F; he was Moroccan / from Morocco.
2 F; it is written in Arabic.   3 T   4 T   5 T

Exercise 6 page 87

1 He used information from earlier Arab and Greek maps, and from explorers.

2 *Possible answer:* Where people at that time thought mountains, rivers, lakes, seas and countries were.

3 *Answers will vary.*

READING 2

Learning objectives

- Understand key vocabulary for places – *island, capital, beach*
- Read and identify topics and main ideas in a text about the Maldives
- Give opinions on tourism in the Maldives
- Synthesize information from a text about an old map and the Maldives in a discussion

Lead-in

Compare and contrast this text with that in Reading 1. Point out to students that it is also a factual text. Review the information on the right side and again notice the proper nouns the text uses to give factual information. You may want to say a detail and have students identify what it is, e.g. *rufiyaa = currency, Malé = capital*, etc. Point out the layout of the text and discuss the purpose of the different side bars, photos and map.

Exercise 1 page 87

Answers will vary.

Exercise 2 page 87

a tourist   **b** modern   **c** island   **d** beach   **e** capital
f famous   **g** popular   **h** international

Exercise 3 page 89

1 **topic:** where the Maldives are; **information:** in the Indian Ocean, near Sri Lanka

2 **topic:** the population; **information:** 440,000 people

3 **topic:** the capital city; **information:** Malé, airport, harbour

4 **topic:** languages; **information:** English and Dhivehi

6 **topic:** a young Maldivian's home; **information:** island south of Malé, simple life

7 **topic:** traditional food; **information:** delicious fish soup called *garudiya*

8 **topic** hobbies and sport; **information:** swimming and diving

Exercise 4 page 90

1 for their good climate, beautiful beaches and warm seas

2–3 *Answers will vary.*

Be flexible

👤👥 Extend the discussion for **more advanced students** to include research and analysis. Invite students to research additional information they would like to know before answering Question 2

Do you want to visit the Maldives? Why / Why not?. Use this information to justify their answers. Encourage them to incorporate information from Unit 2 on weather and do related research on the climate of the Maldives. You may want to assign questions for partners or small groups to research and report back on. Then build on Question 3 *Why do people travel to different countries? What's important to know about a country?*. Have students generate a list of questions they think are important to answer before travelling.

LANGUAGE DEVELOPMENT

Learning objectives

- Identify noun phrases with *of – the history of Japan, a world history of maps, the currency of the United States*
- Use noun phrases with *of* to answer questions – *What country is Lisbon the capital of? Lisbon is the capital of Portugal.*
- Use vocabulary for places to label a landscape – *hill, mountain, sea, valley*

Exercise 1 page 90

1 d **2** a **3** c **4** b

Exercise 2 page 90

1 Lisbon is the capital of Portugal.

2–4 *Answers will vary. Possible answers:*

2 … is the capital of my country. / The capital of my country is ….

3 … is the currency of my country. / The currency of my country is ….

4 … and … are the main languages of my country. / The main languages of my country are … and ….

Be flexible

👥👥👥 Provide **lower-level students** with oral practice using noun phrases with *of* and questions on familiar topics. Invite partners to ask and answer the following questions:

Who is the author of your favourite book?
What is the name of your favourite song?
What kinds of food do you like?
What type of work do people in your country do?

Encourage students to think of additional questions that use noun phrases with *of*. List them on the board for students to ask and answer.

Exercise 3 page 91

1 sea **2** mountain **3** desert **4** hill **5** cliff **6** beach
7 field **8** forest **9** farm **10** valley

CRITICAL THINKING

Learning objectives

- Identify key words relating to different topics in a text about the Maldives
- Classify words about topics relating to your country
- Review your lists and amend as necessary

UNLOCK TEACHER DEVELOPMENT

BE INFORMED

→ **Classifying topics and key words** is an important skill for students because: (1) They often find English word order challenging; (2) Students' writing will become more coherent if they follow these patterns; (3) This knowledge can also help with students' reading, as they can understand text structure better.

BE CONFIDENT

→ Develop this skill for yourself by doing the following activity:

The six components of Bloom's taxonomy all have specific 'active verbs' associated with them. Two examples for each topic are given in the table. Write three more from the list for each topic.

appraise   calculate   classify   combine   compare
demonstrate   judge   memorize   observe
paraphrase   prioritize   quote   rank
role play   solve   summarize   use   write

Topic	Key words
Remember	examine, name
Understand	explain, predict
Apply	discover, produce
Analyze	contrast, select
Evaluate	decide, recommend
Create	construct, plan

Lead-in

Go through the instruction and the writing task carefully with the class. Explain that the following sections of the unit will help them to prepare to write facts about their country.

UNLOCK TEACHER DEVELOPMENT

BE READY

Look at the Critical Thinking section in the Student's Book on pages 92–93.

→ Which elements of the lesson do you think your students will find easiest / most difficult / most useful? Why?

→ Are your answers true for all students in your class?

→ How can you adapt your teaching or the material to meet your students' needs?

BE FLEXIBLE

You can extend Exercise 1 by asking students to add more words to the three topics. Sharing words they already know with their classmates is empowering and helps build vocabulary in an effective way.

Exercise 1 page 92

geography: islands; climate; Indian Ocean, near Sri Lanka

language: English; Dhivehi

industry: tourism; fishing; currency

Exercise 2 page 92

capital: Malé; modern city; international airport; big harbour

population: 440,000; small islands

Exercises 3–5 page 93

Answers will vary.

UNLOCK TEACHER DEVELOPMENT

BE REFLECTIVE

Think about the following points:

→ Compare your answers to the *Be confident* section with a colleague who also did the task. Did you have the same answers?

→ How easily were your students able to understand this critical thinking point? Is there anything you could have done more effectively?

BE COLLABORATIVE

Your development is more meaningful when it's shared. See page 14 for ideas on how to peer-collaborate. Why not tell a colleague how you adapted your teaching of the material to meet your students' needs?

GRAMMAR FOR WRITING

Learning objectives

- Write the correct form of *there is* or *there are* in sentences – *There is a beautiful park in my city. There are many tourist resorts in the Maldives.*
- Correct errors with *there is* and *there are* in sentences about places – *There are many languages in London. In Thailand, there are many islands. There is a big river in my city.*
- Use *a, an, the* and zero article appropriately in sentences about places – *a lake, an ocean, the United Kingdom, Chile*
- Correct mistakes with *a, an, the* and zero article in sentences about places.

Exercise 1 page 94

1 There are **2** There are **3** There are **4** There is **5** There is

Exercise 2 page 94

Correct sentences: 1, 4, 6 **Incorrect sentences:** 2, 3, 5, 7, 8

Exercise 3 page 94

2 There **are** mountains in Switzerland.

3 There **are** many parks in Tokyo.

5 There **are** many people in Buenos Aires.

7 **There** are many lakes in Italy.

8 There **is** a big river in my city.

Optional activity

👤 Practise *there is / there are* by saying a noun phrase and asking students to put it in a sentence with the correct form. For example: *an airport in Malé = There is an airport in Malé. 440,000 people in the Maldives = There are 440,000 people in the Maldives.*

Exercise 4 page 95

1 a **2** an; the **3** ∅ **4** ∅; ∅ **5** the **6** The **7** the **8** ∅; a

Exercise 5 page 96

1 I come from India. *(zero article: country)*

2 Paris is **a** popular city with tourists.

3 There is **a** very tall building in Abu Dhabi.

4 I go to **a** university in Dublin.

5 **The** United Kingdom is in Europe. *(zero article: continent)*

6 I live by **a** big lake.

7 **The** Ural mountains are in Russia.

8 He studies in **the** United Kingdom.

9 Turkey is a beautiful country. *(zero article: country)*

10 There is **a** big mountain near my city.

Exercise 6 page 96
Answers will vary.

ACADEMIC WRITING SKILLS

Learning objectives
- Spell adjectives of nationality correctly – *Chinese, Indian, Egyptian*
- Punctuate sentences about countries and nationality
- Identify topic sentences in two paragraphs
- Choose topic sentences for paragraphs
- Write a topic sentence for a paragraph

Exercise 1 page 97
nationality: Chinese, Indian, Egyptian, Saudi, Emirati, Algerian, Japanese, Thai, Turkish, French, British, Canadian

Exercise 2 page 97
1 I am from **C**airo.
2 There are many beautiful beaches in **P**ortugal.
3 The climate is good in the **M**aldives.
4 There are four main islands in **J**apan.
5 Chicken is very popular in **M**alaysia.

Exercise 3 page 98
1 The Maldives are islands in the Indian Ocean.
2 Tourism and fishing are very important businesses in the Maldives.

Exercise 4 page 99
1 b   **2** a

Exercise 5 page 99
Answers will vary.

WRITING TASK

Learning objectives
- Draft three paragraphs about your country
- Review and revise the content and structure of your paragraphs
- Review and revise the use of language in your paragraphs

Exercises 1–5 pages 99–100
Answers will vary.

RESEARCH PROJECT

Write and post an online travel review.

Ask your class which places they have visited on holiday. They can be either national or international destinations. Place students in pairs or small groups based on their travel destinations. Working in pairs or groups, students will write an entry for a travel review blog. They can comment on and rate places to eat and stay and write about the climate, nearby nature spots, beaches, parks and entertainment. Each pair or group will post to a site. Use travel review sites that you or your students are familiar with. Based on your students, determine the number of paragraphs to include. Ask students to focus on paragraph organization in their reviews. Students should submit their written reviews to you before posting so they can be revised as needed. Encourage students to later check the sites to see any comments their reviews get.

CLASSROOM APP

Exercises 1–2
Answers will vary.

Exercise 3
1 tourists, beach   **2** map, river   **3** island, ocean
4 famous, seas

Exercise 4
1 Niigata is a city on the coast of Japan.
2 Zadie Smith is the author of my favourite book.
3 Nelson Mandela was the president of South Africa.
4 Polish is the main language of my country.
5 The map shows parts of Australia.
6 Spring is a nice time of year.

Exercise 5
1 cliff   **2** field   **3** sea   **4** forest   **5** hill   **6** farm

Exercise 6
1 is   **2** are   **3** are   **4** is   **5** is   **6** are   **7** is   **8** are

UNIT OBJECTIVES	
Watch and listen	Watch and understand a video about a mine.
Reading skill	Read for detail.
Critical thinking	Analyze and evaluate opinions.
Grammar	Use adjective phrases; use *must* and *have to*; use the pronoun *you*.
Academic writing skills	Join sentences with *and*; write emails.
Writing task	Write an email about a job.
⊘ **Teacher development**	Help your students become better at **analyzing and evaluating opinions**.

UNLOCK YOUR KNOWLEDGE

Background note

The photo shows two builders, high up on some scaffolding. The men in the photograph could be builders or scaffolding engineers. Working at height is extremely dangerous and requires special training for all the workers and engineers involved. The men in the photo are wearing safety clothing and equipment, such as hard hats, gloves, and harnesses that protect them from falls.

Lead-in

Ask: *How many jobs do you know in English?* Give students one minute to write down as many jobs as they can (see jobs vocabulary in the wordlist for this unit on page 123). For feedback, ask how many they wrote down, and ask one or two pairs to share their lists with the class. Ask if anybody has a job that nobody has mentioned yet. Invite students to define jobs that others are unfamiliar with.

page 103

1 The men are building a skyscraper. They are builders.
2–4 *Answers will vary.*

WATCH AND LISTEN

Learning objectives

- Listen and identify the main ideas in a video about a mine
- Listen and understand details
- Identify correct inferences about work in the Bingham mine
- Practise talking about mining and dangerous jobs

Exercise 1 page 104
Answers will vary.

Exercise 2 page 104
1 c **2** d **3** a **4** b

Exercise 3 page 104
1 T **2** F; The mine produces enough copper wires for all the homes in the USA and Mexico.
3 T **4** F; The trucks work 24 hours a day.

Exercise 4 page 105
1 largest **2** one mile **3** small **4** stronger

Exercise 5 page 105
1, 2, 4, 5

Exercise 6 page 105
Answers will vary.

READING 1

Learning objectives

- Preview the texts to identify the source
- Understand key vocabulary for job adverts – *fit, pay, friendly*
- Scan job advertisements to identify key information
- Read and understand detailed information
- Give personal opinions on the jobs in the texts

Lead-in

Share some job ads with the class; print them out to bring in or find them online. Look at several examples and notice the types of information they include. With students, make a list of this information (i.e. job title, pay, hours, location and skills needed). Then categorize the job ads into areas, such as medicine, education, etc. Invite students to brainstorm other jobs that fit into these categories.

Background note

The Chinese Yuan Renminbi (CNY) is the currency of China.
The Indian Rupee (INR) is the currency of India.
The Japanese Yen (JPY) is the currency of Japan.

Exercise 1 page 106

1–3 *Answers will vary.*

Exercise 2 page 106

b

Exercise 3 page 106

1 a **2** a **3** b **4** b **5** a **6** a **7** a **8** b

Exercise 4 page 107

1 nurse **2** teacher **3** China **4** India
5 FlyHigh (Air Transport Company) **6** INR 200,000 per journey **7** JPY 320,000 per month **8** full time

Exercise 5 page 107

1 T **2** F; The teacher has to teach grades 1–3. **3** T **4** T
5 F; They are paid per journey. **6** T

Exercise 6 page 109

1 The pilot and nurse; The people they work with speak different languages. It's necessary for them to talk with their customers.
2 *Answers will vary.*

READING 2

Learning objectives

- Understand key vocabulary for jobs – *interesting, company, gym*
- Scan three emails to find key information about jobs
- Read and identify main ideas
- Read and identify details
- Synthesize ideas from job advertisements and emails about jobs in a discussion

Lead-in

Ask students to make a short list of people they routinely email. Then ask them to share greetings and closings they use when they email. You may want to ask students to look through their emails for ideas. Contrast the appropriate ways to greet and close a more formal email to a teacher or manager with those used with friends. Point out other differences in register in informal emails, such as the use of contractions, all capitals and exclamation marks for emphasis. Give examples as needed and elicit additional examples from students.

Exercise 1 page 109

Answers will vary.

Optional activity

Use a Venn diagram for students to sort email greetings and closings into the correct category: *Formal, Informal/Friendly* and *Both*. In addition, invite students to evaluate some sentences you have given them for their level of formality. You may want to preview sentences from the reading and point out the use of contractions, exclamation marks and other language features discussed in the Lead-in that are used in friendly or informal emails. Include some more formal sentences that do not use contractions and would be appropriate for a formal email to a teacher, manager or another person. Students can determine if sentences are appropriate for *Formal, Informal/Friendly* or *Both* situations.

Exercise 2 page 109

Answers will vary.

Exercise 3 page 109

a engineer **b** company **c** high school **d** good at
e gym **f** great **g** interesting

Exercise 4 page 111

1 fitness instructor **2** 12 **3** software engineer **4** £4,150
5 Suncheon, South Korea **6** 10; 12

Exercise 5 page 111

c

Exercise 6 page 111

1 A **2** D **3** E **4** A **5** D

Exercise 7 page 111

1–2 *Answers will vary.*

3 *Possible answer:*
type of job; employer; where the job is situated; hours; pay; experience required; languages required; qualifications required; responsibilities in job

LANGUAGE DEVELOPMENT

Learning objectives

- Write sentences about different jobs using vocabulary for related activities and places – *A farmer grows food and looks after animals on a farm. A manager manages people in a company.*
- Choose correct adjective phrases to complete sentences about jobs – *Nurses have to be kind and helpful.*
- Choose correct prepositions to complete adjective phrases in sentences about jobs – *Nurses must be good with people.*

Exercises 1–2 pages 112–113

A jobs	B activities	C locations
1 A farmer	grows food and looks after animals	on a farm.
2 A manager	manages people	in an office. in a company.
3 A doctor	gives people medicine	in a hospital.
4 A journalist	writes news stories	in an office.
5 A software engineer	makes software for computers	in a company. in an office.
6 A football player	plays sport in a team	in big cities.
7 A school teacher	teaches children	in a school.
8 A fitness instructor	teaches people to do exercises	in a gym.
9 A nurse	takes care of sick people	in a hospital.
10 A language teacher	teaches languages	in a school.

Exercise 3 page 113

1 healthy and strong   **2** very intelligent   **3** friendly
4 strong

Exercise 4 page 113

1 with   **2** with   **3** with   **4** at   **5** at

Be flexible

👥 👥👥 Challenge **more advanced students** by asking them to analyze the language used in job ads. Ask partners to pick one or two jobs and use the internet to search for job ads for that job. Students note adjective and adjective phrases that are used in the ad. Encourage students to use a dictionary as needed to understand these words. Then ask students to share their findings with another pair. As a class, discuss which adjectives and adjective phrases were used most often. Which skills are most desirable?

CRITICAL THINKING

Learning objectives

- Use Likert scales to evaluate yourself
- Analyze jobs and match them with characteristics
- Evaluate your partner's questionnaire results and choose a job for them

UNLOCK TEACHER DEVELOPMENT

BE INFORMED

➔ **Analyzing and evaluating opinions** is an important skill for students because: (1) They may already be familiar with this concept (e.g. through surveys they have done), but may not have a good understanding of it; (2) Analyzing and evaluating tools, such as Likert scales, are used for research in many academic subjects, especially sciences; (3) Such scales are also commonly used in the business world (e.g. for marketing or customer feedback).

BE CONFIDENT

➔ Develop this skill for yourself by doing the following activity:

When Cambridge University Press recently conducted a critical thinking survey among English teachers, they used Likert scales to gather data. Below are some of the survey statements which teachers had to respond to. They used the same scale as on page 114. Give your response to these statements.

'It is important to me that I develop my students' critical thinking skills.'

'I believe my students want to develop their critical thinking skills.'

'I feel confident in my ability to develop my students' critical thinking skills.'

Lead-in

Go through the instruction and the writing task carefully with the class. Explain that the following sections of the unit will help them to prepare to write an email describing a job for another student.

UNLOCK TEACHER DEVELOPMENT

BE READY

Look at the Critical Thinking section in the Student's Book on pages 114–115.

→ Which elements of the lesson do you think your students will find easiest / most difficult / most useful? Why?

→ Are your answers true for all students in your class?

→ How can you adapt your teaching or the material to meet your students' needs?

BE FLEXIBLE

A potential extension to Exercise 4 is that students should give evidence and reasons for their answers to Exercise 1, and to explain why they gave the score they did.

Exercise 1 page 114

Answers will vary.

Exercise 2 page 115

1 very healthy   **2** fit and strong   **3** good with people   **4** very intelligent   **5** kind and helpful   **6** good with children   **7** very good at football   **8** good at Maths   **9** good at writing   **10** good with computers   **11** good with animals   **12** good at languages

Exercise 3 page 115

Answers may vary. Possible answers:

2 manager = good with people

3 doctor = very intelligent

4 journalist = good at writing

5 software engineer = good with computers

6 football player = very good at football

7 school teacher = good with children

8 fitness instructor = fit and strong

9 nurse = kind and helpful, good with people /children

10 language teacher = good at languages

Exercise 4 page 115

Answers will vary.

Optional activity

Guide students in interpreting the results from the Likert scale. Ask the class for their thoughts on the best ways to analyze the information from their partner's answers to Exercise 1. One way to approach the activity is for students to note which statements their partners answered *agree* (4) or *strongly agree* (5) for. Then students can find the job descriptions from Exercise 3 that best match those preferences. Share with students that there is more than one way to approach this task. Discuss different ways to best match their partner to a job based on their responses. Then point out that while the Likert scale is useful, it gathers information in numerical data, which does not allow for details and additional information to be collected. As a result, students may need to ask their partner follow-up questions to the Likert scale.

UNLOCK TEACHER DEVELOPMENT

BE REFLECTIVE

Think about the following points:

→ Share your results from the *Be confident* section and explain why you gave the scores that you did.

→ If you answered any of those questions with a low score (i.e. a *1* or a *2*), think about how you could improve this score.

BE COLLABORATIVE

Your development is more meaningful when it's shared. See page 14 for ideas on how to peer-collaborate. Why not share something which you learnt from the *Be ready* section?

GRAMMAR FOR WRITING

Learning objectives

- Use the pronoun *you* to rewrite sentences
- Correct mistakes with the form of *must + verb* and *have to + verb* in sentences about jobs – *Teachers must be good with people. Farmers have to be good with animals.*
- Use correct word order in sentences with *not have to – Farmers do not have to be good with computers. A language teacher does not have to be good at Maths.*

Exercise 1 page 116

1 A football player **must** be strong and healthy. *(delete 's' from 'must')*

2 Pilots have **to** work at night.

3 A manager **has to** be helpful.

4 Teachers must **be** good with people.

5 A software engineer **must be** good at Maths. *(delete 'to' after 'must')*

6 Farmers have **to** be good with animals.

7 Journalists **must be** good at writing. *(delete 'to' after 'must')*

8 A language teacher must **be** good at speaking and writing.

Exercise 2 page 117

1 A farmer does not have to be good with people.

2 A software engineer does not have to be patient and kind.

3 Nurses do not have to be good with animals.

4 You do not have to be strong.

5 A French teacher does not have to be good at Maths.

6 You do not have to be good at French.

Exercise 3 page 117

1 You must have three years' experience.

2 You are kind and good with people.

3 You have a university education.

4 You speak Chinese.   **5** You speak Turkish.

Exercise 4 page 117

Email A: *You have to get up early in the morning. You have to be very friendly and good at sport. You don't have to work on Fridays.*

Email B: *You must have studied Computer Science at university, and you have to have two years' experience.*

… you must know some Norwegian.

You don't have to speak Norwegian a lot …

Email C: *You have to teach English and French to grades 10 to 12.*

You don't have to speak Korean …

You have to work many hours every day.

ACADEMIC WRITING SKILLS

Learning objectives

- Use *and* to join information in sentences about characteristics and skills – *You are friendly and good with people. The pay is good and the job is interesting.*
- Rewrite emails, adding key features: greeting, contractions and a closing

Exercise 1 page 118

1 You must be intelligent and good with people.

2 You have to be healthy and strong.

3 Football players have to be fit, and you are fit.

4 The job is to teach English, and you are an English and French teacher.

5 You have to be good at Maths and friendly.

Exercise 2 pages 119–120

Answers will vary.

WRITING TASK

Learning objectives

- Use a planner to create a list of details for an email about a job
- Draft an email recommending a job to your partner
- Review and revise the content and structure of your email
- Review and revise the use of language in your email

Exercises 1–6 pages 120–122

Answers will vary.

RESEARCH PROJECT

Create your own CV.

Tell students that if they want a good job, then it is important to write a good Curriculum Vitae, or CV – a description of your education, qualifications and previous work experience you send to an employer when you are trying to get a job. (In American English it is known as a *résumé*.). Inform the students that CVs are often in document form but in order to make their CV different, they are going to make a video or audio file to practise speaking about themselves. Tell the students to think about their skills, hobbies, educational history, qualifications and adjectives to describe themselves. They could also write their CV using a CV template or writing software as an alternative. This project is completed individually, but consider asking students to post their work online for their classmates to review and comment on.

Exercises 1–2

Answers will vary.

Exercise 3

1 friendly **2** pay **3** medicine **4** healthy **5** interesting
6 company **7** great

Exercise 4

1

2

3

4

5

6

7

8

Exercise 5

1 very good **2** great at **3** very good **4** very strong
5 fit and healthy **6** good with

Exercise 6

1 compound **2** simple **3** compound **4** simple
5 simple **6** compound **7** simple

UNIT OBJECTIVES	
Watch and listen	Watch and understand a video about homes and buildings in Singapore.
Reading skill	Predict content using visuals.
Critical thinking	Analyze data.
Grammar	Use pronouns; use adjectives; compare quantities; use comparative adjectives.
Academic writing skills	Write compound sentences with *but*; spell words with double consonants correctly; write supporting sentences and details.
Writing task	Write a comparison of two buildings.
⟳ **Teacher development**	Help your students become better at **analyzing data**.

UNLOCK YOUR KNOWLEDGE

Background note

The photo shows the skyline of Singapore. The city has often been named as one of the fastest-developing cities in the world. Its development is often compared to that of Dubai and Hong Kong, with skyscrapers and modern architecture taking over the skyline. Architecturally, Singapore is a mixture of old and new styles. Modern hotels and shopping centres have been built next to colonial buildings and *shophouses* – a traditional type of building in Southeast Asia.

Lead-in

Ask: *Where are we now?* (in a college/school/university building). Ask students to describe it (a/an old/modern/new/big/small building). *What do you think of this building?* Then ask: *How many different buildings were you in / did you go into yesterday?* Give students one minute to write down as many buildings as they can. For feedback, ask them how many they wrote down and get one or two pairs to share their lists with the class. These could include: *house, apartment (US)* or *flat (UK), bus/train station, shopping mall/centre, school, shop, restaurant, leisure centre, library, post office,* etc.

page 125
Answers will vary.

WATCH AND LISTEN

Learning objectives

- Listen and understand main ideas in a video about Singapore
- Listen and identify details about Singapore
- Complete a set of inferences about Singapore
- Practise talking about places to visit and homes

Exercise 1 page 126
Answers will vary.

Exercise 2 page 126
1 2   2 1   3 4   4 3

Exercise 3 page 127
1 T   2 F; it's the second busiest
3 F; they live in apartments   4 T   5 T

Exercise 4 page 127
1 technology   2 Space   3 above shops   4 80%
5 modern

Exercise 5 page 127
1 close   2 shopping   3 plane   4 home

Exercise 6 page 127
Answers will vary.

READING 1

Learning objectives

- Understand key vocabulary for buildings – *garden, plastic, tall*
- Use visuals to make predictions about the content of a text about buildings
- Scan the text to identify key information about different buildings
- Identify the main ideas
- Read and understand details
- Give opinions on buildings and homes

Lead-in

Show students the word *expert* in the subtitle and elicit the meaning. If students do not know the word, then define *expert*. Ask: *What kind of expert do you think will be in the interview?*

Exercise 1 page 128
Answers will vary.

Exercise 2 page 128
a window **b** roof **c** plastic **d** garden **e** wall
f tall **g** glass **h** wood

Exercise 3 page 129
Answers will vary. Most common answers will be a and c.

Exercise 4 page 130
Japanese roof house: windows are different sizes; rooms are narrow
Vietnamese 'garden home': has glass walls; has a small garden on the roof

Exercise 5 page 130
1 c **2** b **3** a

Exercise 6 page 130
1 F; Professor Chan's favourite home designs are Japanese.
2 T
3 F; Professor Chan says it is important to build houses that are good for the Earth.
4 T **5** T **6** F; In Amsterdam, one architect put mirrors on the walls.

Exercise 7 page 131
1 *Answers will vary.* **2** *Answers will vary, but may include:* building with gardens; energy saving designs

Optional activity

👥 Give students the following questions to answer in pairs:
Which house design from the magazine on page 129 do you prefer? Why?
What are popular building materials in your country? (You may want to show pictures of additional building materials for this if necessary, e.g. *concrete, brick, steel,* etc.)
What types of homes, e.g. apartments, houses, etc. are popular in your country?

Ask one or two pairs to report back to the class.

READING 2

Learning objectives

- Understand key vocabulary for buildings – *buildings, expensive, apartment*
- Scan the text to identify key information about different buildings
- Read and understand details
- Describe skyscrapers
- Synthesize ideas from two texts about different kinds of buildings in a discussion

Lead-in

Contrast this text type with the printed interview from Reading 1. Ask students to identify the questions in this text, but point out how these are used as headings to organize the information, rather than as actual questions asked to a person. Preview some of the content from the text with students. Read a sentence and ask students to identify which heading they think it falls under.

Exercise 1 page 131
Answers will vary.

Exercise 2 page 131
a expensive **b** buildings **c** cheap **d** apartment
e cost **f** lift

Be flexible

👥 Engage **lower-level students** by activating prior knowledge and using visuals to support the vocabulary and content students will see in Reading 2. Invite students to share experiences and information on skyscrapers they have visited. Make a list of the buildings they are familiar with and preview pictures of them. With students, notice the design and comment on the look. You may want to include The Shard in London, Federation Tower in Moscow and others from around the world (see page 137 for additional buildings). Then, list unit vocabulary for students to use to describe the skyscrapers (*garden, wall, roof, glass, window, expensive, lift, building*, etc.). Pair students and ask each student to describe a skyscraper for the other to guess, based on the description.

Exercise 3 page 133

1 Dubai **2** 492 **3** 546 **4** 101 **5** 31 **6** 3,900,000,000

Exercise 4 page 133

1 What are skyscrapers?; What are some famous skyscrapers?; How much money do skyscrapers cost?; What is inside a skyscraper?

2 Paragraph 1: very tall buildings, usually more than 300 metres

Paragraph 2: the Empire State Building, Shanghai World Financial Center, One World Trade Center, Burj Khalifa

Paragraph 3: very expensive, cost more than other buildings

Paragraph 4: floors, lifts, shopping centres / malls

Exercise 5 page 133

1 One World Trade Center. *Answers will vary.*

2–3 *Answers will vary.*

LANGUAGE DEVELOPMENT

Learning objectives

- Understand referencing across sentences with pronouns *it* and *they* in sentences from a text about skyscrapers
- Complete sentences with vocabulary for buildings – *car park, roof, shopping centre*
- Identify opposite adjectives – *big > small; traditional > modern; expensive > cheap*
- Complete sentences with correct adjectives – *It is expensive to build skyscrapers. Buildings with glass look ugly. It is hard to find a traditional apartment in the city.*

Exercise 1 page 134

1 The Burj Khalifa **2** One World Trade Center
3 Skyscrapers **4** The Shanghai World Financial Center

Optional activity

👤👥 Ask students to make a list of the pronouns from each reading and identify the noun they refer to. Point out that in some sentences *it* does not refer to an object but is used to make a point: *It is very important to build houses which are good for the Earth.* Pronouns and antecedents (the noun the pronoun refers to) from Reading 1 include: *I really like Japanese designs (I = Michael Chan); It is simple and very small inside (It = roof house); It is a garden home (It = house); But, in fact, it is a house (it = garden); It keeps your house warm in winter (It = wood); They also use metal and glass (They = architects).*

If needed, give students additional examples to review *he/she*.

Exercise 2 pages 134–135

1 shopping centre **2** apartments **3** garden; roof
4 stairs **5** entrance; exit **6** windows **7** ceiling
8 car park **9** walls **10** lifts

Exercise 3 page 135

1 car park **2** lift **3** entrance **4** stairs **5** exit
6 an apartment **7** walls **8** windows

Exercise 4 page 135

1 d **2** c **3** e **4** f **5** b **6** a

Exercise 5 page 135

1 expensive **2** beautiful/modern
3 modern/beautiful **4** traditional **5** cheap **6** ugly

CRITICAL THINKING

Learning objectives

- Identify data described by a paragraph in a table
- Research and analyze information about two buildings you are interested in
- Answer questions to compare two buildings

UNLOCK TEACHER DEVELOPMENT

BE INFORMED

→ **Analyzing data** is an important skill for students because: (1) In the modern world, 'big data' is an increasingly common phenomenon which students need to be aware of; (2) The analysis of data (whether quantitative or qualitative) is common in all academic subjects; (3) Students often find it difficult to look at data deeply.

BE CONFIDENT

→ Develop this skill for yourself by doing the following activity:

These charts contain the results of the Cambridge University Press critical thinking survey of 1,019 English teachers. They relate to the three statements looked at previously in the Be confident section in Unit 5.

Analyze the data and identify (a) what are the main findings, and (b) what your recommendations would be, based on these findings.

Figure 1: Responses to the statement, 'It is important to me that I develop my students' Critical Thinking skills'.

1 = strongly disagree; 5 = strongly agree

1	7/1%
2	10/1%
3	51/5%
4	224/22%
5	727/71%

Figure 2: Responses to the statement, 'I believe my students want to develop their Critical Thinking skills'.

1 = strongly disagree; 5 = strongly agree

1	15/2%
2	87/9%
3	369/36%
4	309/30%
5	239/23%

Figure 3: Responses to the statement, 'I feel confident in my ability to develop my students' Critical Thinking skills'.

1 = strongly disagree; 5 = strongly agree

1	19/2%
2	71/7%
3	268/26%
4	395/39%
5	266/26%

Lead-in

Go through the instruction and the writing task carefully with the class. Explain that the following sections of the unit will help them to prepare to write a comparison of two buildings.

UNLOCK TEACHER DEVELOPMENT

BE READY

Look at the Critical Thinking section in the Student's Book on pages 136–137.

→ Which elements of the lesson do you think your students will find easiest / most difficult / most useful? Why?

→ Are your answers true for all students in your class?

→ How can you adapt your teaching or the material to meet your students' needs?

BE FLEXIBLE

Exercise 1 could be done as a jigsaw activity. In pairs, Student A looks at page 136 only, and Student B looks at page 133 only. Student A must complete the exercise only by asking Student B questions.

Exercise 1 page 136

1 F   **2** D   **3** E   **4** B   **5** C

Exercises 2–4 pages 136–137

Answers will vary.

UNLOCK TEACHER DEVELOPMENT

BE REFLECTIVE

Think about the following questions:

→ If you did the *Be flexible* exercise, how did it work? Was it effective? Could you do it again in a different situation?

→ How much 'world knowledge' did students have? Did they know about the other buildings mentioned in Exercise 3, or did you have to direct them towards this information?

BE COLLABORATIVE

Your development is more meaningful when it's shared. See page 14 for ideas on how to peer-collaborate. Why not share the ideas you generated in the *Be flexible* section, and their outcome?

GRAMMAR FOR WRITING

Learning objectives

- Use correct word order in sentences comparing quantities – *Skyscrapers cost more money than other buildings. The garden home in Saigon has more rooms than the roof house. The Shanghai World Financial Center has fewer lifts than One World Trade Center.*
- Correct errors with comparative adjectives in sentences about buildings – *The roof house is smaller than the garden home. One World Trade Center was more expensive than the Burj Khalifa. The Burj Khalifa was less expensive than One World Trade Center.*

Exercise 1 page 138

1 The Burj Khalifa has more floors than Taipei 101.
2 The Burj Khalifa has more visitors than the Shanghai World Financial Center.
3 The Shard has more stairs than the British Museum.
4 The Louvre Museum has more lifts than the British Museum.
5 One World Trade Center cost more money than the Burj Khalifa.
6 The Burj Khalifa cost less money than One World Trade Center.
7 The Shanghai World Financial Center has fewer lifts than One World Trade Center.

Exercise 2 page 139

1 The Louvre museum is more popular **than** the British Museum.
2 The SM Mall of Asia is more modern **than** the Istanbul Cevahir. *(delete 'of')*
3 The Country Club Plaza is **smaller than** the Istanbul Cevahir.
4 Modern buildings are **more beautiful** than traditional buildings. *('beautiful' has more than two syllables)*
5 The Burj Khalifa **is taller than** One World Trade Center.
6 Wood is more expensive **than** plastic.
7 This street is **busier** than the main road. *(delete 'many')*
8 Many buildings in London are **older** than buildings in New York. *('old' has one syllable)*
9 The traffic in the city is **worse** than the traffic in the village. *('bad' is irregular)*

Be flexible

👥 Ask **more advanced students** to write an adjective on a slip of paper and the name of two (local) places on two other separate slips. They then give the slips to a partner and ask him/her to make a comparative sentence using the words. Encourage students to think about meaning as well as grammatical accuracy.

ACADEMIC WRITING SKILLS

Learning objectives

- Use *but* to connect ideas in compound sentences about buildings – *One World Trade Center is tall, but the Burj Khalifa is taller. The Istanbul Cevahir has more cinemas than the SM Mall of Asia, but the SM Mall of Asia has more shops.*
- Correct spelling mistakes in words with double consonants – *shopping, bigger, running*
- Choose supporting sentences to add detail and examples after topic sentences about buildings
- Write supporting sentences for topic sentences about buildings

Exercise 1 page 140

1 The Metro Centre has more floors than the Country Club Plaza, but the Country Club Plaza has more restaurants.
2 The Istanbul Cevahir has more cinemas than the SM Mall of Asia, but the SM Mall of Asia has more shops.
3 The Metro Centre is more modern than the Country Club Plaza, but the Country Club Plaza is bigger.
4 The SM Mall of Asia is bigger than the Country Club Plaza, but the Country Club Plaza is older.

Exercise 2 page 141

What are <u>malls</u>?

Malls are big buildings for <u>shopping</u>. They are near big cities. Sometimes they are inside skyscrapers. Many cities have more than one mall. Malls have <u>restaurants</u> and <u>cinemas</u>. The <u>restaurants</u> are <u>bigger</u> than <u>restaurants</u> in the city. Some malls also have gyms and <u>swimming</u> pools.

The <u>Southdale Center</u> in <u>Minnesota</u> in the <u>United States</u> was the first mall in the world. It is popular today but there are <u>bigger</u> malls in <u>America</u>, <u>Europe</u>, the <u>Gulf</u> and <u>Asia</u>.

Exercise 3 page 142

1

- ✓ They are usually more than 300 metres tall.
- ✓ Many countries build skyscrapers so tourists go there.
- ✓ There are many skyscrapers in Asia, the Gulf, the Americas and Europe.

2

- ✓ The Burj Khalifa has more lifts than One World Trade Center or the Shanghai World Financial Center.
- ✓ It has 57 lifts.
- ✓ One World Trade Center has 54 lifts, but the Shanghai World Financial Center has fewer.

Exercises 4–5 page 143

Answers will vary. Possible answers:

1 They are usually more than 300 metres tall.
2 My favourite example is a house in Saigon, Vietnam. It is a 'garden home'.

WRITING TASK

Learning objectives

- Review your ideas about buildings and research additional details
- Draft your paragraph
- Review and revise the content and structure of your paragraph
- Review and revise the use of language in your paragraph

Exercises 1–5 pages 143–144

Answers will vary.

RESEARCH PROJECT

Propose a new building for the campus.

Divide the class into teams and ask students to identify one building on campus they think needs a better design. Invite students to discuss how people use the building, its location, the best design for the location, 'green' designs, materials, cost and other information from the unit. Invite students to create a concept board with pictures of buildings that they like. From that, ask them to create a short description about their proposed building. Students should include adjectives for buildings, number of floors, lifts and the materials the building will be made out of. Ask students to present their concept boards and proposed buildings to the class. Vote on which idea the students like best.

CLASSROOM APP

Exercise 1

Answers will vary.

Exercise 2

1 cost **2** expensive **3** cheap **4** window **5** wood
6 glass

Exercise 3

Answers will vary.

Exercise 4

1 She **2** They **3** They **4** He **5** It

Exercise 5

1

2

3

4

5

6

Exercise 6

1 No **2** Yes **3** Yes **4** No **5** No **6** No **7** Yes **8** Yes

UNIT OBJECTIVES	
Watch and listen	Watch and understand a video about goat's cheese.
Reading skills	Skim a text; take notes.
Critical thinking	Generate ideas.
Grammar	Use countable and uncountable nouns; use *can* and *cannot*; use subject—verb agreement; use determiners *a*, *an* and *some*.
Academic writing skills	Understand error correction marks; write concluding sentences.
Writing task	Write about popular food in your country.
⟲ **Teacher development**	Help your students become better at **generating ideas**.

UNLOCK YOUR KNOWLEDGE

Background note

The photo shows a fruit and vegetable market in Yangon, Myanmar. The woman in the photo is selling fruit and vegetables, including limes, different types of tomatoes, ginger, carrots and chilli peppers. It's a typical temporary street stall where sellers sell local fruit and vegetables. Yangon – the largest city in Myanmar – is famous for its busy and colourful markets, which attract local people and tourists alike.

Lead-in

Tell the class what you had for breakfast today, e.g. *I had a cup of tea, toast with jam and a banana.* Ask: *What did you have for breakfast today?*. Give students one minute to tell their partners. For feedback, ask one or two pairs to tell the class.

page 147

1 selling fruit and vegetables at a market   **2** tomatoes, beans, limes, carrots, ginger, chillies   **3** *Answers will vary.*

WATCH AND LISTEN

Learning objectives

- Listen and identify the main ideas in a video about a goat's cheese
- Listen and understand details
- Complete a set of inferences about the ideas in the video
- Practise talking about traditional foods

Exercise 1 page 148
Answers will vary.

Exercise 2 page 148
1 village   **2** fruit   **3** farm   **4** cheese

Exercise 3 page 149
1, 3, 4, 6

Exercise 4 page 149
1 fruit, vegetables, bread, meat and cheese   **2** goat's cheese   **3** at the door   **4** more than two quarts
5 in another room   **6** one to three weeks

Exercise 5 page 149
1 c   **2** d   **3** a   **4** b

Exercise 6 page 149
Answers will vary.

READING 1

Learning objectives

- Understand key vocabulary for food and drink – *honey, prepare, type*
- Skim a text to identify the main topics
- Read and identify the main ideas in each paragraph in a text about tea
- Read and make a set of detailed notes about tea in different countries
- Scan the text for key information
- Discuss tea in your country and around the world

Lead-in

Create or project a KWL chart (see below) for students to complete about what they *know* about tea or what they *want* to know. Then revisit it after the reading to list what they *learnt*. Ask guiding questions to help facilitate completing the chart: *What is tea? What kinds of tea are there? How do you drink your tea? Why do people drink tea? When do people usually drink tea?*

K (know)	W (want to know)	L (learnt)

Exercise 1 page 150

Answers will vary.

Exercise 2 page 150

a bread   **b** same   **c** different   **d** types   **e** honey
f drinks   **g** prepares

Exercise 3 page 151

1 F; The text compares how people from different places drink tea.   **2** T
3 F; There are many/four kinds of tea   **4** T

Exercise 4 page 151

5 a   **3** b   **2** c   **4** d   **1** e

Exercise 5 page 153

Russia: Use a special kettle called a samovar; like drinking tea with lemon; sometimes drink with some sugar or jam

Turkey: Use two kettles: one for the water and one for the tea; drink with some sugar; drink with some sugar

Arab countries: Make with cardamom, ginger, milk and sugar

United Kingdom: Add some milk and sugar; usually eat biscuits with their tea

Exercise 6 page 153

1 Malaysia (Kuala Lumpur is the capital city)   **2** Russia
3 Turkey   **4** Kuala Lumpur / Malaysia

Exercise 7 page 153

Answers will vary.

Optional activity

👥 Conduct a quick class survey on students' favourite drinks, e.g. *Do you prefer hot or cold drinks? What is your favourite cold drink?* Record the results on the board and ask students to analyze the results. Elicit sentences such as: *Coffee is more popular than tea.*, etc.

READING 2

Learning objectives

- Understand key vocabulary for food – *meat, vegetables, fish*
- Preview a text and identify the source and topic
- Scan the text for key information
- Read and understand details about different cuisines
- Describe your food preferences
- Synthesize information from a text about tea and a guide to international cuisines in a discussion

Lead-in

Ask students how they choose a restaurant. List different apps, websites or other tools available to students for finding local restaurants. Then take a look at a website or guidebook that describes the food and cuisines available in the city or region you are located. Invite students to share additional information about the types of food and cuisines available in the area.

Background note

- The Arab world is made up of the Arabic-speaking countries of North Africa and western Asia.
- Australia, officially the Commonwealth of Australia, is the sixth largest country in the world by area, with 7.7 million square kilometres (2.9 million square miles). Its capital is Canberra; its largest city is Sydney and its population is approximately 24.7 million.
- Cambodia, officially known as the Kingdom of Cambodia, is in Southeast Asia. The capital city is Phnom Penh, the official language is Khmer and the population is approximately 16.3 million.

Exercise 1 page 154
Answers will vary.

Be flexible

👥 Use a two-column chart. Ask pairs to create a list of cuisines they are familiar with (from your local area or their home countries), and then list typical foods and their ingredients from the cuisine. Use a cuisine from the list on page 156 as an example. Use one that the students are familiar with.

Cuisine	Food
Mexican	Tamales (fried tortillas, tomatoes, chicken, cheese)
	Guacamole (avocado, lime, onions, tomatoes)

Support **lower-level students** with this activity by having them find pictures online of the different foods. Circulate to give guidance with vocabulary. To help students acquire food names, you may want them to label pictures or sort new words into a chart according to food group, e.g. *bread, meat, fruits and vegetables*, etc.

Exercise 2 page 153

1 students   **2** types of food

Exercise 3 page 154

1 d   **2** c   **3** b   **4** a   **5** e

Exercise 4 page 155

1 b   **2** a

Exercise 5 page 155

1 F; American should come before Arab.

2 F; *Shawarma* is a savoury meat dish.

3 F; *Amok trey* is a Cambodian dish.

4 F; You can get kangaroo meat in Australian restaurants.

5 T   **6** T   **7** F; Kangaroo burgers are served on a type of bread.

Exercise 6 page 155

1 in many Arab countries   **2** *shawarma* and kangaroo burgers   **3** crocodile and kangaroo   **4** Arab and Cambodian   **5** Australian and Cambodian

Exercise 7 page 157

Answers will vary.

LANGUAGE DEVELOPMENT

Learning objectives

- Name types of food and drink – *rice, dates, milk*
- Identify and evaluate different qualities of food and drink
- Correct mistakes with countable and uncountable nouns – *honey, vegetables, bread*
- Correct mistakes with *can* and *cannot* in sentences about food – *You can get many delicious vegetable dishes. I cannot eat spicy food.*

Exercise 1 page 157

1 milk   **2** dates   **3** jam   **4** chillies   **5** rice   **6** honey
7 spices   **8** almonds   **9** water   **10** onion   **11** yoghurt
12 coconuts

Exercises 2–3 page 158

Answers will vary.

Exercise 4 page 159

1 Honey **is** sweet.   **2** correct   **3** Milk **is** good for children.
4 Fish **is** tasty.   **5** correct   **6** Water **is** served in a glass.

Optional activity

👤 👥 First, ask students to correct the incorrect sentences from the exercise (1. *Honey is sweet.*) Then challenge students to replace the noun in each sentence with another countable or uncountable noun to match the correct verb and create a new sentence (1. *Cake is sweet.*) Alternatively, or for additional practice, ask students to write a sentence about the food and drinks pictured on page 157. Exchange with a partner and correct any mistakes.

Exercise 5 page 159

1 U   **2** C   **3** C   **4** C   **5** U   **6** U   **7** C   **8** C   **9** U   **10** C
11 C   **12** C

Exercise 6 page 159

1 can have   **2** cannot smell   **3** can come   **4** cannot eat
5 can be

CRITICAL THINKING

Learning objectives

- Complete an ideas map about *shawarma*
- Develop ideas maps for two popular foods from your country

UNL⭕CK TEACHER DEVELOPMENT

BE INFORMED

➜ **Generating ideas** is an important skill for students because: (1) This is the basis for all academic creation; (2) Students often find it very difficult to start this process and need advice on how to do this; (3) The skill of brainstorming or using an ideas map, as a way of generating ideas, is also very useful in the workplace.

BE CONFIDENT

➜ Develop this skill for yourself by doing the following activity:

Think about your class, using the ideas map below. You can add other circles which may be relevant for your situation.

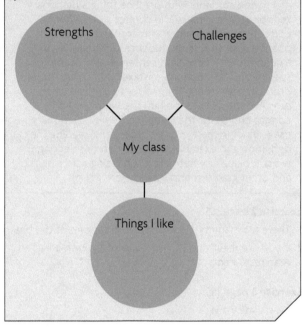

Lead-in

Go through the instruction and the writing task carefully with the class. Explain that the following sections of the unit will help them to prepare to write descriptive sentences about popular food in their country.

UNL⭕CK TEACHER DEVELOPMENT

BE READY

Look at the Critical Thinking section in the Student's Book on pages 160–161.

➜ Which elements of the lesson do you think your students will find easiest / most difficult / most useful? Why?

➜ Are your answers true for all students in your class?

➜ How can you adapt your teaching or the material to meet your students' needs?

BE FLEXIBLE

If your students come from the same country, an alternative way of doing Exercise 2 would be to ask them to think about dishes from their specific region.

Exercise 1 page 160
made of meat; **served with** vegetables in a pita; **tastes** savoury

Exercises 2–3 page 161
Answers will vary.

Be flexible

👤 👥 Extend the activity to provide additional practice and visual support for **lower-level students**. Invite them to create a poster or magazine spread for each dish. Encourage them to go online to find a picture of the dish, and then a separate picture for each ingredient to explain what the dish is made of. Ask students to share their work in small groups. Students listen and record any new names of food or ingredients they hear. Challenge them to identify if the ingredient is countable or uncountable. Consider categorizing ingredients students share in a two-column chart for the class showing countable and uncountable nouns.

UNL⭕CK TEACHER DEVELOPMENT

BE REFLECTIVE

Think about the following questions:

➜ Did colleagues who also completed the ideas map in *Be confident* come up with the same ideas as you?

➜ What can you do about the challenges which you identified in your ideas map?

BE COLLABORATIVE

Your development is more meaningful when it's shared. See page 14 for ideas on how to peer-collaborate. Why not share something which you learnt from the *Be ready* section?

GRAMMAR FOR WRITING

Learning objectives

- Use the correct form of present simple verbs to complete sentences about foods – *They are popular dishes. This yoghurt is tasty. It is a popular dish.*
- Identify and correct mistakes with verb forms in sentences about food
- Correct mistakes with *a, an,* and *some* in sentences about food – *Add some honey to the dish. A famous dish from Italy is risotto. Jambalaya is an American dish.*

Exercise 1 page 162
1 prepare   **2** uses   **3** is   **4** is   **5** is   **6** are

Exercise 2 page 163
Correct: 2, 5 **Incorrect:** 1, 3, 4, 6

Exercise 3 page 163
1 Korean restaurants **serve** rice with meat and vegetables.
3 Latin American chefs **use** many different kinds of vegetables in their dishes.
4 Kangaroo burgers **are** served on a type of bread.
6 French vegetable soup **is** delicious.

Optional activity
👥 Ask students to write gapped sentences and give them to a partner to complete with the correct verb forms, e.g. *A kangaroo burger ... (is) good for you. Vegetables ... (are) healthy.*

Exercise 4 page 164
1 At **(some)** Arab restaurant**s**, you can find delicious meat dishes.
2 The curry is served with **(some)** rice. *(delete 'a')*
3 Some famous **dishes** in New Orleans **are** jambalaya and gumbo.
4 French chefs add **an apple/apples** to this dish.
5 Korean chefs prepare many dishes with meat. *(delete 'a')*
6 Australian**s** like eating crocodile meat. *(delete 'a')*
7 There are **(some)** vegetable**s** in Korean kimchi.
8 **A** popular dish in Latin America is chicken soup.

ACADEMIC WRITING SKILLS

Learning objectives

- Understand error correction codes and correct errors in a student paragraph
- Relate topic sentences to concluding sentences
- Write concluding sentences for paragraphs about food and restaurants

Exercise 1 page 164
2 [MW] are   **3** [WP] with   **4** [G] be   **5** [CL] Mexican
6 [P] it

Optional activity
👤 Provide students with practice using a dictionary to look up and choose the correct word when correcting spelling and grammar usage mistakes. If possible, use an English student's dictionary as an example. Write or project sentences with common spelling and homophone mistakes using *then/than, are/our, their/there/they're, to/two/too* and *by/buy*. Ask students to look up the words to verify the correct choice for the sentence. Review dictionary usage (finding the words alphabetically; reading the definition and example sentence before selecting the word; looking at whether a noun is singular or plural; and other grammar and usage information).

Exercise 2 page 165
1 There are many tasty dishes, but this is one of the best.
2 If you like meat dishes, you will enjoy your meal at an Arab restaurant.

Exercise 3 page 165
Answers will vary.

WRITING TASK

Learning objectives

- Draft two paragraphs about popular foods from your country
- Review and revise the content and structure of your paragraph
- Review and revise the use of language in your paragraph

Exercises 1–6 page 166
Answers will vary.

RESEARCH PROJECT

Write your own menu.

After dividing the class into teams, tell the students that they are going to write a menu of popular dishes. These can be ones from the unit, and/or other ones from their own country. The menu should be divided into starters, main courses and desserts (you might need to explain these terms), with several options for each course. Students can design the menu and add pictures of the dishes. They can also add details such as what the dish is made of or served with. They should then share their menus and choose what they would most like to eat from them.

CLASSROOM APP

Exercise 1

Answers will vary.

Exercise 2

1 bring   **2** kinds of   **3** make   **4** not the same   **5** food
6 food that you eat at one time

Exercise 3

Answers will vary.

Exercise 4

1 Uncountable – meat; **Countable** – eggs
2 Uncountable – chicken; **Countable** – dishes
3 Uncountable – sugar; **Countable** – apple
4 Uncountable – pasta; **Countable** – cookies
5 Uncountable – bread; **Countable** – chillis

Exercise 5

1 can get   **2** cannot order   **3** cannot eat   **4** can be
5 can sit   **6** cannot give

Exercise 6

1 SP   **2** CL   **3** WP   **4** P   **5** MW   **6** G

UNIT OBJECTIVES

Watch and listen	Watch and understand a video about metros.
Reading skill	Work out meaning from context.
Critical thinking	Collect and analyze data.
Grammar	Use superlative adjectives; use quantifiers; use subject–verb–object sentence order; link sentences with pronouns.
Academic writing skill	Give reasons with *because* and results with *so*.
Writing task	Write a paragraph explaining the results of a survey.
⟳ Teacher development	Help your students become better at **collecting and analyzing data**.

UNL⟳CK YOUR KNOWLEDGE

Background note

The photo shows a bird's-eye view of the Taksin bridge in Bangkok, Thailand, and the surrounding areas. The bridge crosses the Chao Phraya River. It is used by the Bangkok SkyTrain, which is one of the fastest ways to travel around the city. There are also buses, cars, mopeds and taxis crossing the bridge. There is a lot of traffic. The taxis in Bangkok are painted in bright colours, including pink, yellow and blue. On the river, we can see water taxis, ferries and boats.

Lead-in

Elicit the meaning of *public transport* and ask: *What kinds of public transport are there in your town / city?* Give students one minute to write down as many types of transport as they can. For feedback, ask one or two pairs to share their lists with the class, e.g. *buses, taxis, trains, coaches, trams, ferries, cable cars, rickshaws,* etc. Give a point for every correct item and give an extra point to a student who has a correct item nobody else has listed.

page 169
1 by boat; by car; by train; by motorbike; on foot
2 and **3** *Answers will vary.*

WATCH AND LISTEN

Learning objectives

- Listen and identify the main ideas in a video about underground railways
- Listen and identify numbers and details
- Complete a set of inferences about underground travel
- Practise talking about transport in cities

Exercise 1 page 170
Answers will vary.

Exercise 2 page 170
1 underground **2** on **3** busy **4** metro station

Exercise 3 page 170
1 T **2** F; The oldest underground system is in London. **3** T
4 F; Tokyo has the busiest underground system. **5** T

Exercise 4 page 171
1 c **2** a **3** b **4** b

Exercise 5 page 171
1 traffic **2** faster **3** usually **4** helpful

Exercise 6 page 171
Answers will vary.

READING 1

Learning objectives

- Preview a text to identify type and purpose
- Understand key vocabulary for transport – *traffic, train, metro*
- Skim the survey to identify the main topics
- Scan the survey to find key information
- Read and understand details about the survey and responses
- Read and identify synonymous words from their context in the survey
- Describe and evaluate different forms of transport in your town

Lead-in

Bring in or show online examples of surveys. Then write the name of the survey and next to it write the information the survey is created to get. For example, *census = information about the people in a country, size of family, employment, education,* etc. List other surveys that students may be more familiar with, such as *a campus survey, customer service follow-up,* etc. Then make a list of the typical information that surveys collect: *age, gender, job,* etc.

Background note

The SkyTrain, officially known as the Bangkok Mass Transit System, is an elevated railway system. It has 35 stations and two lines that run for a total of 38.7 kilometres (24 miles).

Exercise 1 page 172

1 a questionnaire / a survey
2 to get information from people

Exercise 2 page 172

1 a 2 a 3 a 4 b 5 a 6 b 7 a 8 a

Exercise 3 page 174

Topics: 2, 4 and 6

Exercise 4 page 174

1 32–53 2 15–45 minutes 3 metro 4 motorbike 5 Yes

Exercise 5 page 174

1 F; There is a place for people to write their suggestions.
2 T 3 F; The purpose is to see how people in Bangkok travel and how they feel about transport in Bangkok.
4 F; She sometimes takes the bus. 5 F; She thinks more metro lines should be added.

Exercise 6 page 175

1 occupation 2 survey 3 walk 4 kind(s) 5 gender

Exercise 7 page 175

Answers will vary.

READING 2

Learning objectives

- Use your knowledge to complete a table showing the type of information that would appear in different reports
- Preview a text to identify type, topic and author
- Understand key vocabulary for transport – *drive, prefer, ride*
- Scan a report for figures and add to a pie chart
- Read and complete a summary of a report
- Read and understand details
- Synthesize information from a survey and a report about transport in Bangkok in a discussion

Lead-in

Revisit the list you created of surveys and the information students collected from Reading 1. For each survey you listed, discuss the purpose of the survey and how the information may be used. For example, *A census gathers information so the government knows the population for planning. Customer service surveys are for improving the business.,* etc. Discuss also what kind of text is used for presenting information from a survey, and what kind of graph could be used.

Exercise 1 page 176

weather report: information about the weather
news report: information about the news
Possible answers: school report: information about your grades; traffic report: information about traffic

Exercise 2 page 176

1 b 2 c 3 a

Exercise 3 page 177

1 prefer 2 takes 3 spends 4 report 5 results
6 drives 7 ride

Exercise 4 page 178

bicycle 2%, car 23%, tuk-tuk 8%, motorbike 14%, bus 18%, SkyTrain 21%

Exercise 5 page 179

1 transport **2** takes **3** take **4** drive **5** traffic
6 motorbikes

Exercise 6 page 179

1 over 8 million **2** a public form of transport **3** 23%
4 more than 1 hour every day **5** almost 35%

Exercise 7 page 179

1 car; *Answers will vary.* **2–3** *Answers will vary.*

Be flexible

👤👥👥 Point out that the report is a formal text
and its purpose is to share the results of the survey.
Challenge **more advanced students** to do a quick
online search of 'transport survey results' and compare
the text on page 178 to the language and features
used in other reports. Ask students to list examples
of collocations and other features from reports that
show the purpose and formal nature of the text
(percentages, facts, figures, graphics, examples from
the study, and collocations to explain results, such as
results of, prefer x to x, spend more than, etc.).

LANGUAGE DEVELOPMENT

Learning objectives

- Use superlative adjectives to complete sentences
  about transport in Bangkok.
- Identify quantifiers and nouns in sentences
  about transport – *Most people in Bangkok drive
  their own cars. Not many people cycle to work
  or school. Many people take the SkyTrain.*
- Describe people's use of transport in London
  using quantifiers
- Use correct word order in sentences with
  transport collocations – *Many students take
  the metro to work. I cycle to school. People
  travel to work by bus.*
- Use the correct verb in sentences with transport
  collocations – *ride a motorbike, take a taxi, take
  the bus*

Exercise 1 page 180

2 the longest **3** the hottest **4** the busiest **5** the most
important **6** the shortest **7** the worst **8** the prettiest
9 the best **10** the biggest

Exercise 2 page 181

1 quantifier: Most; **noun:** people
2 quantifier: Some; **noun:** people
3 quantifier: Not many; **noun:** people
4 quantifier: A few; **noun:** people

5 quantifier: Many; **noun:** people
6 quantifier: Not many; **noun:** people
7 quantifier: Most; **noun:** people

Exercise 3 page 181

1 Many / Most / A lot of **2** Not many / A few
3 Some **4** Not many / A few **5** Not many / A few
6 Many / A lot of / Most **7** No **8** All

Optional activity

👥👥👥 Draw a pie chart divided into sections of
different sizes on the board and write sentences
using *some, not many*, etc. in a list beside it. Ask
students to match each sentence to the correct
slice of the pie chart. Draw another pie chart
with different-sized sections and label these with
different kinds of drink, e.g. *tea, coffee, cola, water,
juice, milk*. Then ask students to write sentences
using the quantifiers to describe it, e.g. *A few people
like water. Not many people like milk.*, etc.

Exercise 4 page 182

1 We take a bus to school.
2 Malai travels to work by train.
3 Sunan takes the metro to the city.
4 Many people get to work by motorbike.
5 My children get to school by bike.
6 Suni takes a taxi to the shop.

Exercise 5 page 182

1 rides **2** take **3** ride **4** takes **5** drives

CRITICAL THINKING

Learning objectives

- Analyze the questions from a survey and match
  them to the responses
- Identify information that can be represented in a
  pie chart
- Label a pie chart with information from a survey

UNL♡CK TEACHER DEVELOPMENT

BE INFORMED

➜ **Collecting and analyzing data** is an important
skill for students because: (1) Students are not likely to
have had experience of collecting data before, but it
is an important skill for academic and work life; (2) As
such, students may be unfamiliar with the different
ways that data can be collected and presented;
(3) Students may also not know how to discuss
and analyze their data in essays.

BE CONFIDENT

➜ Develop this skill for yourself by doing the following activity:

The two pie charts below were generated from a survey done by Cambridge University Press among English teachers. Over 1,000 respondents were asked to give their response to the two statements. Look at the pie charts, and write one short paragraph which summarizes the main findings.

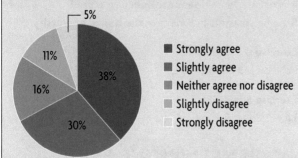

- ■ Strongly agree
- ■ Slightly agree
- ■ Neither agree nor disagree
- ■ Slightly disagree
- ■ Strongly disagree

Figure 1: Responses to the statement, 'I have all the material I need to develop my students' critical thinking skills'.

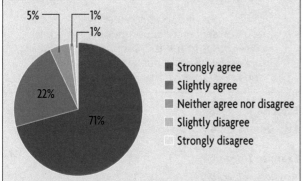

- ■ Strongly agree
- ■ Slightly agree
- ■ Neither agree nor disagree
- ■ Slightly disagree
- ■ Strongly disagree

Figure 2: Responses to the statement, 'It is important to me that I develop my students' critical thinking skills'.

Lead-in

Go through the instruction and the writing task carefully with the class. Explain that the following sections of the unit will help them to prepare to write a paragraph explaining the results of a survey about transport.

UNLOCK TEACHER DEVELOPMENT

BE READY

Look at the Critical Thinking section in the Student's Book on pages 183–184.

➜ Which elements of the lesson do you think your students will find easiest / most difficult / most useful? Why?

➜ Are your answers true for all students in your class?
➜ How can you adapt your teaching or the material to meet your students' needs?

BE FLEXIBLE

As an extension task, students could create a pie chart for what they think the results would be in their own country or home town. Alternatively, they could do this for their school or class. As a longer project task, they could do a survey to gather actual data.

Exercise 1 page 183
paragraphs 2 and 3

Exercise 2 page 183
1 b　**2** c　**3** a

Exercise 3 page 183
Seventeen percent take the train.
Eight percent take the bus.
Two percent take a water taxi.
One percent cycle to work.
Seven percent walk to work.
Three percent take a taxi to work.
Sixty-two percent drive to work.

Exercise 4 page 183
train 17%, bus 8%, water taxi 2%, cycle 1%, walk 7%, taxi 3%, car 62%

Optional activity

👤 Provide support for students to complete these critical thinking tasks and analyze data. First, ask students to create a two-column chart to list the seven types of transport and their corresponding percentages. They should then rank the transport in order from least popular to most popular. Point out that when working with data, before analyzing it, it is best to organize it. Next, ask students to rank the sections of the pie chart from smallest to biggest, 1–7. Ask students to compare their information with a partner before they complete the exercise and record the information on the pie chart.

Be flexible

For **more advanced students** who are ready for a challenge, ask them to represent the same data from the pie chart in a bar graph. They can then present the information to the class. As a class, discuss which is the best way to represent the information.

Exercise 5 page 184

1 by car / They drive.

2 by bus / by train / on foot; They take the train / take the bus / walk.

3 They cycle / take a taxi / take a water taxi.

Exercise 6 page 184

Answers will vary.

GRAMMAR FOR WRITING

Learning objectives

- Differentiate between objects and prepositional phrases
- Correct mistakes with word order and prepositions in sentences about travel
- Link sentences using pronouns to avoid repeating nouns – *Many students ride motorbikes. They are not expensive. The pie chart shows the most popular types of transport in Bangkok. It shows the percentage of people who use each type of transport to get to work or school.*

Exercise 1 page 184

2, 4

Exercise 2 page 185

2 Juan drives a car to university.

4 Many people ride bikes to work in London.

5 People in Bangkok often take the SkyTrain.

Exercise 3 page 185

1 In Abu Dhabi, **people drive cars** to work.

2 Not many people in Ankara take **taxis to work**.

3 Workers in Seoul take the train **to** work.

4 Most students **ride motorbikes to school**.

5 Some students in Paris take **the bus to university**.

Exercise 4 page 185

1 d **2** a **3** e **4** c **5** b

Exercise 5 page 186

1 It **2** She **3** They **4** They **5** It

ACADEMIC WRITING SKILLS

Learning objectives

- Use *because* and *so* to connect reasons and results in sentences about transport – *People prefer buses to tuk-tuks because buses cost less money. People take public transport so they don't have to drive themselves.*

Exercise 1 page 187

1 b **2** e **3** c **4** a **5** d

Exercise 2 page 187

Answers will vary.

WRITING TASK

Learning objectives

- Prepare sentences for a paragraph explaining the results of a survey about transport
- Draft your paragraph
- Review and revise the content and structure of your paragraph
- Review and revise the use of language in your paragraph

Exercises 1–7 pages 187–188

Answers will vary.

RESEARCH PROJECT

> ## Plan an exhibition on types of transport used in different parts of the world.
>
> Explain that students will be setting up an exhibition on transport to showcase different types of transport used throughout the world. Groups will pick a city or an area of the world to focus on and will be responsible for a poster or video presentation on popular types of transport there.
>
> Students should include pictures, a description of the types of transport and a discussion on the positives and the negatives of each type. As a class, determine how long the presentations should be, other content to include and if others outside of the class will be invited to the exhibition. Consider inviting specialists, city planners or others to attend and share information.

CLASSROOM APP

Exercises 1–2
Answers will vary.

Exercise 3
1 I like to bike to work.
2 It takes a long time to drive in the morning.
3 I wrote a paper about popular jobs in the UK.
4 I pay someone to drive me to the airport.
5 In my small city, there are not a lot of ways to travel.
6 I'm late because the underground is not on time today.
7 The information from my survey is very interesting.

Exercise 4
1 a lot of   **2** A few   **3** Some   **4** Many   **5** Most

Exercise 5
1 bus / metro   **2** car   **3** bike / motorbike
4 by bus / by bike   **5** metro   **6** bike   **7** taxi / bus

Exercise 6
1 because   **2** so   **3** Because of   **4** because
5 so   **6** because of

PLACES UNIT 1

UNIT OBJECTIVES

Watch and listen	Watch and understand a video about Jakarta.
Reading skill	Scan for numbers.
Critical thinking	Evaluate positives and negatives.
Grammar	Use nouns and adjectives; use countable and uncountable nouns; use quantifiers; write simple sentences; use *there is / there are*.
Academic writing skill	Use capital letters and punctuation.
Writing task	Write descriptive sentences.
⟳ **Teacher development**	Help your students become better at **evaluating positives and negatives**.

UNLOCK YOUR KNOWLEDGE

Background note

The photo shows the Seattle skyline at sunset. Seattle is in the state of Washington, the USA, and is the largest city in the northwest. It is surrounded by water and mountains. In the photo, there are tall, modern skyscrapers, and smaller buildings and houses. At the front of the photo, we can see Seattle's most famous landmark, called the Space Needle. The Space Needle was built for the 1962 World Fair and has since become an icon of the city. In the background, we can see lots of trees and the snow-covered Mount Rainier, the highest mountain in the Cascades Range.

Lead-in

Print out some world maps from the internet (search for images of 'world map outline', and choose a map with national boundaries marked). Divide the class into teams and give each team a map. Then read out the list of place names (see Answers), pausing for about 30 seconds between each place to allow the teams time to discuss where on the map the place might be. They draw a cross (for cities) or shade in a country/region, and mark them with the number of that place (see Answers). You could also write the place names on the board. At the end, they swap maps with another team to check their answers. Explain where each place really is. (**Important:** You will need to check that you know all the answers before the lesson!) Award one point for a correct cross / shading in the right country. At the end, the team with the most points is the winner. Note that all the places are mentioned in this unit.

Answers

1 Delhi (city)   2 Dubai (city)   3 Egypt (country)
4 Istanbul (city)   5 Jakarta (city)   6 Moscow (city)
7 Nepal (country)   8 Siberia (region)   9 Tarragona (city)   10 Oman (country)   11 Tokyo (city)

page 15

1 The photo is of Seattle, Washington, in the USA.

2–3 *Answers will vary.*

WATCH AND LISTEN

Learning objectives

*   Use visuals to predict information in a video about a city
*   Listen and identify main ideas and details about the city
*   Make inferences about the city and the audience for the video
*   Practise talking about life in the city and features of your own country or city

Exercises 1–2 page 16
Answers will vary.

Exercise 3 page 17
1 Asia   **2** megacity / popular destination / capital city
3 an old town / a harbour

Exercise 4 page 17
1 a   **2** b   **3** b   **4** b   **5** a   **6** b

Exercise 5 page 17

Answers will vary. Possible answers:

1 Because two million people travel into the city to work there every day.

2 Because it had an important international harbour.

3 Because Europeans (the Dutch) used to work in the harbour.

4 Probably 1.5 million years. You can learn about this at the National Museum.

5 Tourists, because it shows things that tourists are interested in, such as old buildings, street food and firework displays.

Exercises 6–7 page 17

Answers will vary.

READING 1

Learning objectives

- Understand key vocabulary for cities – *population, opportunity, traffic*
- Predict the meaning of the title of an article about megacities
- Read and understand main ideas
- Read and identify the features of different megacities
- Scan an article for numbers and complete a set of detailed notes
- Read and identify the meaning of a word from context
- Give opinions on megacities and city life

Lead-in

👥 Write the following city names on the board: Tokyo, Moscow, Manila, Tianjin, Mumbai. Ask students to discuss in pairs what they know about each city and what the cities have in common. Tell students the cities are in the top ten most populous cities in the world (nos 6–10). Ask students to complete the list by guessing the top five most populous cities in the world. When they're finished, have them write their list on the board to see who had the most correct answers.

Answers

1 Shanghai 2 Beijing 3 Karachi 4 Istanbul 5 Dhaka
6 Tokyo 7 Moscow 8 Manila 9 Tianjin 10 Mumbai

Exercise 1 page 18

a traffic **b** countryside **c** modern **d** population
e pollution **f** capital **g** expert **h** opportunity

Exercises 2–3 page 18

c

Be flexible

👤 While reading the article, students could find and underline words and phrases related to the size of megacities, as well as good and bad things about them. They compare their answers in pairs before feeding back to the class.

Increase the challenge for **stronger students** by asking them to review their list of good and bad things. They name which cities share these qualities (e.g. *good places to study; housing shortage*).

Exercise 4 page 20

1 T **2** T **3** T

4 F; More than 35 cities in the world are megacities.

5 F; Most megacities are in Asia, South America and Africa.

6 F; Finding a nice place to live is difficult in megacities.

Exercise 5 page 20

Tokyo	lots of jobs, bad traffic, busy trains, good place to study
Delhi	interesting places to visit, mix of different people, housing problems
Cairo	important industries, good place to study

Exercise 6 page 21

Paragraph 1: 1950 **Paragraph 2:** 12; eight billion; 2025; 40
Paragraph 3: 35; 75 **Paragraph 6:** 37.8 million; 20; 8.7 million
Paragraph 7: 25 million; four **Paragraph 8:** 18.3 million; 1,200

Exercise 7 page 21

1 two **2** 40 **3** 12 **4** eight **5** 8.7 **6** 20 **7** 25 **8** four
9 1,200

Exercise 8 page 21

a

Optional activity

👥 Elicit from the class some more difficult words from the text (e.g. *opportunities, industries*) and write them on the board. Students then work in pairs to use clues to work out the meaning of these words then feed back to the class. You could elicit some examples of industries from the class (see Suggested answers).

Suggested answers

Opportunities: the text suggests these are positive (*better*) and gives examples of some opportunities. Another clue is that the word expands on why people are leaving the countryside and moving to the city.

Industries: The text gives examples (*car* and *film*) which show that industries are not always industrial (i.e. connected with factories).

Exercise 9 page 21
Answers will vary.

READING 2

Learning objectives

- Understand key vocabulary for holiday accommodation – *area, cheap, city centre*
- Scan the title and introduction to predict the content of an article about holiday accommodation
- Read and identify the main ideas of the paragraphs in the article
- Read and understand detail to correct a summary of the text
- Make inferences about the places and people in the article
- Synthesize information from an article about megacities and an article about holiday accommodation in a discussion

Lead-in

Ask students to write the name of a city or town they have recently visited. Then get them to write three words only that describe the city or town (*quiet, expensive*, etc.) Ask the students to read out their words and write them on the board as they do so. Check that everybody knows the meaning of the words. To make it more challenging, don't allow the same word on the board twice.

Exercise 1 page 22

1 quiet **2** area **3** local **4** cheap **5** city centre **6** expensive **7** noisy

Exercises 2–3 page 22

b

Exercise 4 page 22

Answers will vary. Possible answers:

homestays, hotels, places to stay, guests, another country

Exercise 5 page 24

a A mountain village **b** A house near the forest **c** A big city

Exercise 6 page 24

1 The Atal family live in a village. It is a friendly place. The mountains are very beautiful.

2 Kate and Julian Foxton live in the southwest of England. The area is great for sport. The houses are quite expensive.

3 Chafic and Aline Halwany live in a large city. People learn Arabic and French in the city centre. There is a lot of traffic during the day.

Be flexible

👥 Discuss any remaining vocabulary problems with the class. Encourage students to work out the meaning of difficult words (e.g. *run homestays, kayaking, get around*) from context.

If students are having trouble doing this, you can **support** them by pointing out clues and strategies for guessing (*run homestays [inference], kayaking [sport examples], get around [buses, trains, without a car].*)

Exercise 7 page 24

1 The Atal family and the Foxton family

2 Chafic and Aline Halwany's homestay, because it is noisy at night and there is a lot of traffic during the day.

Exercise 8 page 24

Answers will vary.

LANGUAGE DEVELOPMENT

Learning objectives

- Identify nouns and adjectives in a text
- Use adjectives in sentences (adjective + noun / noun + *be* + adjective)
- Differentiate between countable and uncountable nouns – *transport, beach, building*
- Use *a, an* and *zero article* appropriately in sentences with countable and uncountable nouns – *a house, an area, buildings, pollution*
- Use quantifiers in sentences to describe the amount or number of something

Exercise 1 page 25

noun – 1, adjective – 2

Exercise 2 page 25

1 b **2** a **3** c **4** e **5** d

Optional activity

👥 Elicit from the class examples of suffixes (= endings) from the ten adjectives in Exercise 1. For each ending, elicit more adjectives with the same endings. You could elicit from the class a sentence for each adjective, to check everybody understands how to use them.

Exercise 3 page 25

1 polluted **2** expensive **3** quiet **4** interesting **5** ugly

Exercise 4 page 26

countable: beach, building, hotel, museum, village

uncountable: air, food, rain, traffic, transport, water, work

Exercise 5 page 26

1 X   2 a   3 X   4 a   5 an   6 a   7 X

Exercise 6 page 27

a a lot of; lots of; many   **b** a few; a little; not much; not many

Exercise 7 page 27

1 a lot of   2 a few   3 A lot of   4 Many   5 Some
6 Much

Exercise 8 page 27

Answers will vary.

CRITICAL THINKING

Learning objectives

- Evaluate whether features of a place are positive or negative
- Use a T-chart to list positive and negative features of places described in texts
- Create a T-chart listing positive and negative features of the place you come from

UNL⌀CK TEACHER DEVELOPMENT

BE INFORMED

→ **Evaluating positives and negatives** is an important skill for students because: (1) In real life, as well as academic life, it is important not to see things as absolutely right or absolutely wrong; (2) If they can evaluate positives and negatives in a situation, they will be able to better understand arguments and decide their own position and opinion; (3) Students often do not know about strategies which can help them do this more effectively, such as T-charts.

BE CONFIDENT

→ Develop this skill for yourself by doing the following activity:

What are the positives and negatives of where you live? Complete the T-chart below.

positive (+)	negative (−)

Lead-in

Go through the instruction and the writing task carefully with the class. Check that everybody understands the meaning of descriptive sentences by showing some examples. Make sure they understand that such sentences should be more than simple opinions (e.g. *It is boring*) or facts (e.g. *It is big*). See Exercise 3 on page 25 in the Student's Book for some examples of better descriptive sentences.

UNL⌀CK TEACHER DEVELOPMENT

BE READY

Look at the Critical Thinking section in the Student's Book on pages 28–29.
→ Which elements of the lesson do you think your students will find easiest / most difficult / most useful? Why?
→ Are your answers true for all students in your class?
→ How can you adapt your teaching or the material to meet your students' needs?

BE FLEXIBLE

When doing Exercise 7, it could be interesting to explore during feedback whether different students have identified the same aspects as a positive or a negative and what opinions they share. Doing this can help students develop empathy.

Exercise 1 page 28

Reading 1 is about megacities. Reading 2 is about smaller parts of cities, towns and villages.

Exercise 2 page 28

1 +   2 +   3 −   4 −   5 +

Exercise 3 page 28

Positive: lots of cafés and restaurants; places stay open late at night; lots of jobs and businesses
Negative: a lot of traffic; it can be noisy

Exercise 4 page 29

Answers will vary. Possible answers:

Positive: good public transport; museums and art galleries; good schools and universities
Negative: more expensive; crime; possibly unfriendly

Exercise 5 page 29

Answers will vary. Possible answers:

Positive: quiet; friendly **Negative:** boring; no jobs

Exercises 6–7 page 29

Answers will vary.

UNLOCK TEACHER DEVELOPMENT

BE REFLECTIVE

Think about the following questions:

➔ Compare the T-chart you created in *Be ready* with a colleague who lives in the same location. Did you identify the same positives and negatives? Evaluate whether your views are similar or different.

➔ It is important that students evaluate the strength of each of the positives and negatives they identify in a situation, and not just think that if more negatives are identified, this means it is worse (and vice-versa). Did they do this? If not, is it something you could address in a future lesson?

BE COLLABORATIVE

Your development is more meaningful when it's shared. See page 14 for ideas on how to peer-collaborate. Why not share the thoughts generated in the *Be flexible* section, and their outcome?

GRAMMAR FOR WRITING

Learning objectives

- Identify subjects and verbs in simple sentences
- Write simple sentences containing subjects and verbs from prompts
- Choose the correct form of the verb *be* in sentences with *there is* or *there are* – *There is a bank. There are a lot of houses.*
- Rewrite and write sentences with *there is* and *there are* to describe places – *There are not many people in my town. There is not a lake in my town. There are three sport stadiums in Abu Dhabi.*

Exercise 1 page 30

1 **subject** – Paris; **verb** – is
2 **subject** – The town; **verb** – does not have
3 **subject** – I; **verb** – live
4 **subject** – Istanbul; **verb** – has
5 **subject** – Many students; **verb** – live
6 **subject** – The village; **verb** – is not
7 **subject** – The shops; **verb** – are
8 **subject** – The houses (in the town); **verb** – are not

Exercise 2 page 30

1 I (S) am (V) Mexican.   2 He (S) is (V) an engineer.
3 The people (S) are (V) nice.   4 We (S) are (V) happy.
5 Kyoto (S) is (V) beautiful.   6 It (S) is (V) a small town.

Exercise 3 page 31

1 aren't   2 is   3 aren't   4 are   5 is   6 aren't

Exercise 4 page 3

2 There is a famous museum in my city.
3 There is not / isn't a lake in my town.
4 There are a lot of cars in my city.
5 There are many expensive shops in my city.
6 There are a few big hotels in my town.
7 There are not / aren't many people in my town.

Exercise 5 page 31

Answers will vary.

Exercise 6 page 32

2 There are lots of / a lot of museums.
3 There are many universities.
4 There are 11 ports.
5 There is one airport. / There are not / aren't many airports.
6 There are lots of / a lot of five-star hotels.
7 There is a palace.

ACADEMIC WRITING SKILLS

Learning objective

- Correct punctuation errors with commas, full stops and capital letters in a paragraph about Montreal

Exercise 1 page 33

I live in **M**ontreal. **I**t is a city in **C**anada. **I**t is a beautiful city. **T**here are many shops and restaurants. **T**he people are friendly. **T**here is an art festival in **J**une. **P**eople in **M**ontreal speak both **F**rench and **E**nglish. **I**t is very crowded with tourists in the summer. **I**n the winter, people like to ice skate, cross-country ski and play ice hockey.

WRITING TASK

Learning objectives

- Choose six features to write about
- Draft six sentences about the place where you live
- Review and revise the content and structure of your writing
- Review and revise the use of language in your writing

Exercises 1–7 pages 33–34
Answers will vary.

RESEARCH PROJECT

Help other students understand how your country has changed.

Ask students to brainstorm what their country is like now compared to the past. This can include the physical appearance of cities, the lifestyles of the people and what jobs they do. They may also want to look at reasons for these changes. If you have students from the same country, they can work in groups and/or choose only one aspect to focus on. Students can use blogs, leaflets, presentations and social media to convey information and share it with the rest of the class.

CLASSROOM APP

Exercises 1-2
Answers will vary.

Exercise 3

1 capital **2** area **3** local **4** opportunity
5 quiet **6** modern **7** traffic **8** population

Exercise 4

1 The children were very noisy during the long car ride.

2 The seafood in this restaurant is always cheap.

3 The National Museum has a lot of interesting paintings.

4 The sunset over the mountains is beautiful.

5 There are many expensive restaurants in Athens.

6 I eft the cinema because the film was boring.

7 The city is polluted so I stayed inside my hotel.

8 The countryside is quiet in the morning.

Exercise 5

1 a hotel **2** two rings **3** a bicycle **4** traffic
5 an island **6** information **7** food **8** a car

Exercise 6

1 South America **2** spaghetti, salad and bread
3 tomorrow. We **4** mother and I **5** May or June
6 a horror, a comedy and a romance **7** week. She

FESTIVALS AND CELEBRATIONS

UNIT OBJECTIVES

Watch and listen	Watch and understand a video about New Year celebrations in England and Scotland.
Reading skill	Preview a text.
Critical thinking	Identify important information.
Grammar	Use prepositions of time and place; use adverbs of frequency; write simple sentences.
Academic writing skill	Organize sentences into a paragraph.
Writing task	Write a descriptive paragraph.
⟳ **Teacher development**	Help your students become better at **identifying important information**.

UNLOCK YOUR KNOWLEDGE

Background note

The large photo shows fireworks near the Rainbow Bridge in Tokyo Bay, Japan. The bridge is lit with colourful rainbow lights. There are skyscrapers in the background, and in the foreground there are boats with multi-coloured lights on the river. The lights and fireworks are reflected in the water. The Tokyo Bay area between the Rainbow Bridge and Odaiba Island is a common site for firework displays during festivals, such as New Year celebrations. The small photos show a Korean wedding, a celebratory meal in Saudi Arabia and a graduation ceremony in the USA.

Lead-in

Divide the class into teams. The teams race to write out the names of the twelve months of the year and the seven days of the week. The first team with the correct answer is the winner. When you check with the class, elicit the spelling of each day/month from the class and write it on the board. You could also award points for each correct spelling, with a bonus of five points for the correct total. As a follow-up, you could elicit some examples of famous festivals in each month.

page 37

1 The photo is in Tokyo, Japan. There is a fireworks display.

2 Two people are getting married; People are enjoying a special meal; Students are graduating.

3 (left to right) South Korea, Saudi Arabia, the USA

WATCH AND LISTEN

Learning objectives

- Listen and identify the main ideas in a video about New Year celebrations in the UK
- Listen and identify facts and figures
- Listen and understand details
- Understand the meaning of unfamiliar words and phrases from their context in the video
- Practise talking about celebrations

Exercises 1–2 page 38
Answers will vary.

Exercise 3 page 39
1 B   **2** L   **3** E   **4** L   **5** E

Exercise 4 page 39
1 d   **2** c   **3** e   **4** b   **5** f   **6** a

Exercise 5 page 39
1 F; It was a clear night in London.   **2** T   **3** T
4 F; In Edinburgh, people carried torches in the streets.
5 T

Exercise 6 page 39
Possible answers:
1 thinking about what has happened in the past year
2 thinking about what you want to do in the year ahead
3 watching the fireworks

Exercise 7 page 39
Answers will vary.

320   READING, WRITING & CRITICAL THINKING 2

READING 1

Learning objectives

- Understand key vocabulary for festivals and celebrations – *celebrate, culture, fireworks*
- Preview photos, title and subtitles to predict the topic of an article
- Read and identify which main ideas relate to which country in the article
- Read and understand detail
- Identify the purpose of an article
- Describe personal experiences of festivals and celebrations

Lead-in

Find Somebody Who... make copies of the questionnaire below to give one out to each student. They should convert each statement into a question and find a classmate who can answer 'Yes' to one question. Encourage them to find a different classmate to say yes to each category to find out more information about each question (e.g. *what sweets do you eat on holidays?*) and to interview at least five different students.

Find somebody who...	Classmate's name	More information
...wears traditional clothes on special days		
...eats sweets on holidays		
...celebrates Mother's Day		
...watches fireworks		
...eats traditional food on special days		

Exercise 1 page 40

1 celebrate   **2** gift   **3** culture   **4** traditional   **5** lucky
6 fireworks

Exercises 2–3 page 40

a

Exercise 4 page 42

1 Mexico   **2** China   **3** the UK   **4** Japan   **5** the UK

Exercise 5 page 42

1 F; Piñatas have sweets inside them.
2 F; Long noodles are lucky in Chinese culture.
3 F; Mother's Day in the UK is in March or April.
4 T   **5** T

Optional activity

Students discuss which special events from Reading 1 they celebrate. Then, they discuss which special events from Reading 1 they would like to celebrate and explain why.

Exercise 6 page 42

a

Exercise 7 page 42

Possible answers:
colour and design of the article, length of paragraphs, photos, title

Exercise 8 page 42

Answers will vary.

READING 2

Learning objectives

- Understand key vocabulary for festivals – *activities, history, highlight*
- Scan a text to identify proper nouns
- Read and identify the main ideas of each paragraph in a text about a festival
- Read and understand details
- Identify and predict the original context of the text
- Synthesize information from an article about celebrations around the world and a text about a festival in a discussion

Lead-in

Elicit what students expect to see when they attend a cultural festival and write their ideas on the board. When they can't come up with any more answers, ask them to scan Reading 2 to see what is mentioned that they didn't think of (*local businesses showing their products, sport competitions, traditional food, music and plays, visitors from other countries*). Discuss whether they would expect to see those activities mentioned in Reading 2 at a cultural festival.

Exercise 1 page 43

1 a   **2** b   **3** a   **4** b   **5** a   **6** b

Exercise 2 page 43

Oman; Muscat Festival; February

Exercise 3 page 44

a 5; Brazil, Cuba, Italy, India, Russia, South Korea, Spain, Tunisia, Turkey and many other countries

b 1; about one month

c 4; Other highlights of the Muscat Festival include

d 2; and international history and traditions

e 3; six-day Tour of Oman cycle race

Exercise 4 page 45

1 February   **2** visit / attend / enjoy
3 Green Mountain **4** Muscat Art Festival   **5** popular
6 *Possible answers:* food, music, the mix of different cultures

Exercise 5 page 45

a

Exercise 6 page 45

Answers will vary. Possible answers:

language, family, art, literature, film, sport, TV

Exercise 7 page 45

Answers will vary.

Be flexible

👥 For Question 2, students swap partners and ask and answer the four questions about each other's chosen festivals.

If **lower-level students** need more support for the final question (d), tell them to use *there is / there are* in their responses (e.g. *there are fireworks, there is a parade*).

LANGUAGE DEVELOPMENT

Learning objectives

- Use the correct prepositions with nouns to show time and place – *in Thailand, on Tuesday, at school*
- Use *in, on* and *at* to complete phrases showing time and place in sentences about celebrations – *The holiday is on 1 May. We eat a special dinner in the evening. We have a party at school.*
- Use adverbs of frequency to complete sentences about yourself – *I sometimes go to weddings. I never celebrate New Year. I usually visit my mother on Mother's Day.*
- Use correct word order to write sentences with adverbs of frequency

Exercise 1 page 46

	on	*in*	*at*
places		a town Istanbul my country Thailand	school home work
times	1 January Sunday Tuesday	June the evening the morning	night eight o'clock

---

Be flexible

👥 Students test each other in pairs by saying one of the phrases from the box (or their own ideas) to elicit the correct preposition from their partner.

Stronger students can ask each other questions that require a time or place answer (e.g. *When is your birthday? Where is Rome? When do you eat dinner?*).

Exercise 2 page 46

1 at   **2** on   **3** in   **4** on   **5** at   **6** in   **7** at   **8** at   **9** at

Exercises 3–4 page 47

Answers will vary.

Exercise 5 page 47

1 The dinner usually starts at eight o'clock in the evening.

2 I always eat chocolates at festivals.

3 She never forgets to call her family.

4 The children sometimes get money instead of toys.

5 We often go skiing for our winter holiday.

CRITICAL THINKING

Learning objectives

- Complete an ideas map with information about a festival you have read about
- Analyze details about a festival or celebration you know
- Create an ideas map for a festival or celebration you know
- Evaluate your ideas map and decide if you need more information

UNLOCK TEACHER DEVELOPMENT

BE INFORMED

➔ **Identifying important information** is an important skill for students because: (1) It is very important in academic writing to include information which is relevant; (2) Often, students do not do this for one of two main reasons – they have not read the title properly, or they are just trying to meet the word count without considering the relevance of what they write; (3) The process of selecting/ categorizing information by using an ideas map is a way of getting students to focus on the specific question they have been asked.

BE CONFIDENT

➔ Develop this skill for yourself by doing the following activity:

Look at the ideas map below. Think about why each of the components of Bloom's Taxonomy are important for students in their academic writing. Make brief notes under each heading.

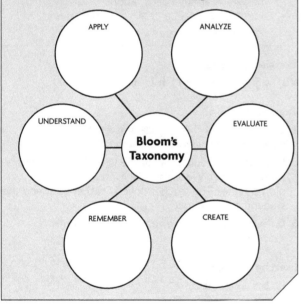

Lead-in

Tell students that Reading 1 is a good model for the writing task. Students should look at Reading 1 and underline any words that describe *who*, *what*, *where* and *why*. (*Suggested answers:* children, piñatas, Mexico, China, weddings, noodles, lucky, etc).

UNLOCK TEACHER DEVELOPMENT

BE READY

Look at the Critical Thinking section in the Student's Book on pages 48–49.

➔ Which elements of the lesson do you think your students will find easiest / most difficult / most useful? Why?

➔ Are your answers true for all students in your class?

➔ How can you adapt your teaching or the material to meet your students' needs?

BE FLEXIBLE

When doing Exercise 1, as a test of the students' ability to remember information they have read, get them to complete as much of the ideas map as they can before looking back at page 44. Students could also swap information which they can remember with a partner, and then verify this information by looking in the book.

Exercise 1 page 48
Possible answers:
Name: Muscat Festival
When: February, every year
Where: Oman
Food & drinks: different types of food
Activities: look at new products, watch the cycle race, go to the Muscat Art Festival
Clothes: traditional clothes (inferred from photos; no information in text)

Exercises 2–5 page 49
Answers will vary.

UNLOCK TEACHER DEVELOPMENT

BE REFLECTIVE

Think about the following points:

➔ Consider asking your students to do the same task as you did in *Be confident*. Doing this would help show them the importance and relevance of critical thinking. You could also compare your answers with theirs and see if you have a shared understanding.

➔ Were students able to be creative in Exercise 3? Some groups find it difficult when they are given so much freedom. If they found this hard, next time there is a similar type of activity, could you provide more guidance and support?

GRAMMAR FOR WRITING

Learning objectives

- Identify subjects and verbs in simple sentences
- Identify whether objects, adjectives or prepositional phrases follow verbs in simple sentences – *The festival is in May. I visit my family. The people are happy.*
- Use correct word order in simple sentences with objects, adjectives or prepositional phrases following verbs
- Discriminate between objects and prepositional phrases in sentences with both – *Children have parties at school. On Saturday, we watch the parades.*

Exercise 1 page 50

1 **subject** – The children; **verb** – wear
2 **subject** – My family and I; **verb** – watch
3 **subject** – I; **verb** – visit
4 **subject** – People in the UK; **verb** – celebrate
5 **subject** – My parents and I; **verb** – go

Exercise 2 page 50

1 at home; P　2 beautiful; A　3 presents; N
4 in the evening; P　5 traditional; A

Exercise 3 page 51

1 People in Wales celebrate New Year.
2 My parents and I cook together at the weekend.
3 Everybody in my town is excited about the festival.
4 My family eat in the morning.
5 We do not visit my grandparents.

Exercise 4 page 51

1 **P** – at night; **O** – films
2 **P** – In India; **O** – the Magh Bihu festival
3 **P** – in the morning; **O** – their homes
4 **P** – at school; **O** – parties
5 **P** – On Saturday; **O** – the parade

Optional activity

Students work in pairs (orally) to rearrange the sentences by moving the prepositional object.

Answers:

1 At night, we film concerts.
2 People celebrate the Magh Bihu festival in India.
3 In the morning, people clean their homes.
4 At school, children have parties.
5 We watch the parades on Saturday.

ACADEMIC WRITING SKILLS

Learning objectives

- Organize topic sentences, supporting sentences and concluding sentences into paragraphs
- Identify the topic sentence, supporting sentences and the concluding sentence in a paragraph about a celebration
- Identify supporting details and examples in sentences

Exercise 1 page 52

c 2　d 1　e 2　f 1　g 1　h 2　i 1

Exercise 2 page 52

1 **T:** When I was a child, my classmates and I always celebrated International Teacher's Day.
2 **S:** It was my favourite day of the year. We brought gifts for our teacher. We ate special food and we usually played games. The teachers loved Teacher's Day and the students loved it, too.
3 **C:** To summarize, I have very special memories of Teacher's Day.

Exercise 3 page 53

a S　b S　c T　d C　e S

Exercise 4 page 53

Students should circle the following:

a lasts two days; people laugh, have fun, forget their troubles.
b ancient; celebrates the beginning of spring
e friends and family get together and throw coloured water and powder at each other; celebrates the beautiful colours that come with spring

Exercise 5 page 53

India celebrates the Festival of Colours, also known as Holi. Holi is an ancient festival that celebrates the beginning of spring. During this festival, friends and family get together and throw coloured water and powder at each other – this activity celebrates the beautiful colours that come with spring. Holi usually lasts for two days, and people laugh, have fun and forget their troubles. In conclusion, this festival is an interesting Indian celebration.

WRITING TASK

Learning objectives

- Use an ideas map to complete a paragraph about a festival in Spain
- Use your ideas map to prepare sentences for a paragraph about a festival or special event
- Draft a paragraph about a festival or special event
- Review and revise the content and structure of your paragraph
- Review and revise the use of language in your paragraph

Exercise 1 page 54

1 March **2** 17th **3** parade **4** beach **5** paella
6 rice **7** red **8** clothes

Exercises 2–10 pages 55–56

Answers will vary.

RESEARCH PROJECT

Recreate celebrations from different countries.

Divide the class into groups and assign each group a foreign country (yours or the students' choice). Explain that they are going to research and plan a one-day festival that celebrates that country's culture. Celebrations could include crafts, food, dance, sport, clothing and/or traditions.

Students could put photos on a poster board or on paper to create an advert for their event. Classes could convert an area of their learning environment to set up a display of these different countries' cultures and advertise their event.

CLASSROOM APP

Exercise 1

Answers will vary.

Exercise 2

1 fireworks **2** celebrate **3** activity **4** visitors
5 popular **6** culture **7** take part **8** Traditional

Exercise 3

Answers will vary.

Exercise 4

1 on **2** at **3** in **4** at **5** on **6** in

Exercise 5

1 The Mardi Gras festival always happens in February.

2 People usually celebrate the end of Ramadan with a special meal.

3 During Chuseok in Korea, women often wear traditional clothing called *hanbok*.

4 We sometimes travel to another country during the holidays.

5 I never buy expensive gifts.

Exercise 6

1 supporting sentence 1 **2** concluding sentence
3 topic sentence **4** supporting sentence 2
5 supporting sentence 3

UNIT OBJECTIVES

Watch and listen	Watch and understand a video about advertising.
Reading skills	Read for main ideas; make inferences.
Critical thinking	Identify appropriate answers.
Grammar	Give opinions; connect ideas.
Academic writing skill	Write topic sentences.
Writing task	Write a one-sided opinion paragraph.
⊘ Teacher development	Help your students become better at **identifying appropriate answers**.

UNL⊘CK YOUR KNOWLEDGE

Background note

The photo shows a rice farmer in Asia. The farmer is standing in the middle of a rice paddy, inspecting the plants and looking at a tablet. The farmer may be using an agricultural app on her tablet. There are many smartphone and tablet apps that are designed to help farmers. There are apps that give information about fertilizers, pests and diseases and crop management.

Lead-in

Students work in small groups to come up with a list of their top ten websites. The list could include well-known sites (e.g. Google, Facebook), but also encourage them to include at least five less well–known sites which they would recommend to other members of the class. After a few minutes, collect their ideas on the board. You could hold a class vote to choose the class's favourite sites.

page 59

1 A farmer   **2** Checking the weather or checking the crop   **3–4** *Answers will vary.*

WATCH AND LISTEN

Learning objectives

- Listen and describe behaviours in a video about predictive advertising
- Listen and understand detailed information and main ideas
- Make an inference about a speaker's meaning
- Practise talking about advertising

Exercises 1–2 page 60
Answers will vary.

Exercise 3 page 61
1 texting   **2** talking   **3** walking; looking   **4** taking   **5** showing

Exercise 4 page 61
1 billion   **2** money   **3** advertising   **4** buy   **5** quickly   **6** customers

Exercise 5 page 61
1 c   **2** b   **3** a   **4** d

Exercises 6–7 page 61
Answers will vary.

READING 1

Learning objectives

- Understand key vocabulary for IT – *software, security, record*
- Scan the title and subtitles and identify the topic of the website
- Read and understand the main ideas in a website about data collection
- Read and identify details about the actions of internet companies
- Make inferences about the target audience for this website
- Make inferences about the implications of the information on the website
- Explain your opinions on the actions of internet companies

Lead-in

Make a handout with a list of internet dangers and their definitions. Cut up the list so that each 'danger' and 'definition' is on its own strip of paper. Distribute the strips evenly. For larger classes, make two or more sets. Students walk around the classroom, trying to match their 'danger' with the correct 'definition', finding each other by only saying the words on their strip of paper. Students should not show their strips to each other. Once all students have found their partners, write the dangers on the board. Students discuss possible solutions with their partners. Note: The first four terms are discussed in Reading 1; 'cyberbullying' and 'internet addiction' are not, but can create a more thorough discussion about internet dangers.

secret software: software that collects information about you and sends it to internet companies

data brokers: companies that collect and sell your personal information

social media: a place online where your pictures and videos can be shared for free. People can learn a lot of information about you

identity theft: when somebody uses your name and personal information to buy things online

cyberbullying: using the internet to harm or frighten another person, especially by sending them unpleasant messages

internet addiction: the need or strong desire to use the internet often

Exercise 1 page 62

a advert b interest c collect d free e security
f record g software h secret

Exercise 2 page 62

Title: Someone's always watching you online …

Subtitle: How companies buy and sell your personal information

Exercises 3–4 page 62

b

Optional activity

👥 Students work in groups to brainstorm ideas for each of the three topics: a, b and c. After a few minutes, elicit lists of ideas from the class and make notes on the board.

Exercise 5 page 64

1 take information without asking you
2 different adverts to different people

Exercise 6 page 64

A your address, your online habits, the websites you visit
B your address, your online habits, the websites you visit
C other websites you might like
D your social media page, a data broker

Exercise 7 page 65

Answers will vary. Possible answers:

1 The users are probably in their early-to-mid 20s.
2 The users are probably interested in finding information on technology and careers after university.

Exercise 8 page 65

a, c, d

Exercises 9–11 page 65

Answers will vary.

READING 2

Learning objectives

- Understand key vocabulary for video games – *affect, creative, download*
- Read an essay about video games and identify the main ideas of two paragraphs
- Read and identify details
- Evaluate the advantages and disadvantages described in the essay
- Read and identify the text type and author
- Synthesize information from a website about data collection and an essay about video games in a discussion

Lead-in

Ask students to think about the positive and negative aspects of video games. Are they helpful or harmful? Do they affect society? Elicit answers and discuss as a class.

Exercise 1 page 66

1 download 2 educational 3 improve 4 imagination
5 creative 6 affect

Exercise 2 page 66

+ advantage, benefit, positive – disadvantage, negative

Exercise 3 page 66

Answers will vary. Possible answers:

+ plus, strength, good (for) – difficulty, weakness, bad (for)

Exercise 4 page 66

Answers will vary.

Exercise 5 page 68

1 3; However, a recent study suggests that video games can also be bad for children.
2 2; For many people, video games are fun and educational.

Optional activity

👤 👥 Ask students to choose one of the video game advantages in Exercise 6 on page 68. They should think of a real video game they know about that shows that advantage (a game that is creative, improves the way children think, etc.). If they don't know of a video game, they can find one online or think of their own idea for a new game. They then discuss their ideas with a partner.

Exercise 6 page 68

(+) cross outs: 3 teach children about money; **5** can help children exercise.

(−) cross outs: 7 are boring; **10** can cause problems between parents and children.

Exercise 7 page 68

Answers will vary.

Exercise 8 page 68

1 a   2 c

Exercise 9 page 68

Answers will vary.

LANGUAGE DEVELOPMENT

Learning objectives

- Understand the meaning of IT compound nouns – *video game, computer program, email address*
- Use IT compound nouns to complete sentences – *I can play this video game on my smartphone. I downloaded a computer program. What's your email address?*
- Use phrases to introduce your opinions about different types of technology – *It seems to me that video games are bad for children. I think that video games are bad for children. I believe that video games are bad for children.*
- Use a variety of words and phrases to make suggestions about improvements to transport systems – *Cities should encourage commuters to use public transport. It is important to encourage commuters to use public transport. Encouraging commuters to use public transport is a good idea.*

Exercise 1 page 69

1 d   2 e   3 b   4 f   5 a   6 c

Be flexible

👥 Students work in pairs to test their partners on the words. One student reads a definition; the partner has to say the compound noun without looking at his/her book. They could also test each other the other way, by saying a compound noun to elicit a definition. To increase the challenge for **more advanced students**, ask them to notice where the stress falls on all of these words. (Stress is on the first element in compound nouns.)

Exercise 2 page 69

1 keyboard   2 smartphone   3 email address   4 website
5 video game   6 computer program

Exercise 3 page 70

d

Exercises 4–6 page 70

Answers will vary.

CRITICAL THINKING

- Identify relevant content to include when answering essay questions
- Understand, evaluate and analyze other people's opinions of using the internet
- Make lists of advantages and disadvantages of using the internet
- Evaluate and select the most convincing arguments for or against using the internet

UNLOCK TEACHER DEVELOPMENT

BE INFORMED

→ **Identifying appropriate answers** is an important skill for students because: (1) Students often misinterpret what an essay question is actually asking them to do; (2) If they do this, the quality of their essay would be significantly impacted, since they may be answering a different question to the one they have actually been set; (3) As such, it is important for students to take time to accurately interpret the question, and to then identify what information should be included in the answer.

BE CONFIDENT

→ Develop this skill for yourself by doing the following activity:

Match each question (1–3) to the correct way to answer it (a–c).

1 Why is critical thinking important for today's students?

2 Outline the advantages and disadvantages of integrating critical thinking with ELT, and state what your position is.

3 'Critical thinking is the most important twenty-first-century skill which students should try to develop.' Discuss.

a You should present both sides of the argument and then give your own position.

b You should summarize the argument presented and state whether you agree or disagree with it.

c You should present a well-developed, evidence-based argument.

Lead-in

Tell students to read the writing task. Discuss with the class which paragraphs of the two Reading sections, Reading 1 or Reading 2, could serve as a model for this writing. (*Suggested answer*: The second and third paragraphs of Reading 2. Note that Reading 2 as a whole is not suitable as a model, as it presents both sides of an argument. The Writing task requires a one-sided opinion paragraph.)

UNL⌀CK TEACHER DEVELOPMENT

BE READY

Look at the Critical Thinking section in the Student's Book on pages 71–72.

→ Which elements of the lesson do you think your students will find easiest / most difficult / most useful? Why?

→ Are your answers true for all students in your class?

→ How can you adapt your teaching or the material to meet your students' needs?

BE FLEXIBLE

Exercise 3 could also be done as a role play. Students work in groups of three, playing Chen, Adalaide and Yasir. They should have a conversation using the information provided, agreeing and disagreeing as appropriate.

Exercise 1 page 71

1 b   2 a

Exercise 2 page 71

Advantages: read newspapers from all over the world; read news from home; learn new words; have fun with video games; helps with homework; email; connect with people; watching educational videos; learning about new cultures and traditions

Disadvantages: can get addicted; can lose a lot of information if computer breaks down

Exercise 3 page 71

Answers will vary.

Exercise 4 page 72

Answers will vary. Suggested answers:

The internet helps us do work	The internet wastes our time
You can get help from different websites.	You could lose valuable information if your computer breaks down.
You can read newspapers from around the world.	You can visit social networking sites.
You can work or do your homework at home sometimes.	You can play video games.
You can read your email.	You could get addicted to it
You can watch educational videos.	
You can learn new words in a different language.	
You can learn a lot about other cultures and traditions.	

Exercises 5–6 page 72

Answers will vary. Possible answers:

Help: Lots of information from different sources is available. You can check facts with different sources. Information is available quickly.

Waste time: You can be distracted by irrelevant but interesting information. You get interrupted by emails and social messages.

UNLOCK TEACHER DEVELOPMENT

BE REFLECTIVE

Think about the following points:

→ Having checked your answers to *Be confident* (1c, 2a, 3b), try to find previous questions from exams (either internal or external) in your institution, and analyze the questions there. You could even share and analyze these questions with your students.

→ This section offers an opportunity for students to be reflective about their own practice, given the nature of the topic. Students should think about their findings in Exercise 3 and decide whether they need to make any changes to how they manage their time.

BE COLLABORATIVE

Your development is more meaningful when it's shared. See page 14 for ideas on how to peer-collaborate. Why not share your reflections from the *Be ready* section, and their outcome?

GRAMMAR FOR WRITING

Learning objectives

- Use *and* to join information in sentences about using technology – *My sister has a computer and a smartphone. Jessica texts her friends and shares photos. Video games are boring and bad for children.*
- Use *also* or *too* to connect ideas across two sentences about using technology – *My sister uses her computer a lot. She also has a smartphone. My sister uses her computer a lot. She has a smartphone, too.*
- Use *and* or *but* to connect ideas in compound sentences about using technology – *Lina doesn't have a smartphone and she doesn't want one. Martin reads books on a tablet, but José likes to read printed books.*
- Use *however* to connect contrasting ideas across sentences about technology – *Smartphones are very popular. However, they are very expensive. The internet is very useful. However, it can be dangerous.*

Exercise 1 page 73

2 You can share photos and talk to your friends.

3 I use online banking and check my email.

4 She does homework and watches films on her computer.

5 I often shop for clothes on the internet and pay with my credit card.

Exercise 2 page 73

Second sentences:

1 They also download videos. 2 I read a lot of travel blogs, too. 3 I also check social media. 4 I also look at photos on my phone.

Exercise 3 page 74

2 I sent an email to Alan, but he did not write back to me.

3 I like to shop online, but my father thinks it's not safe.

4 I call my mother every Saturday, and I visit her every Sunday.

5 I bought a new phone, but it doesn't work.

6 You can check the weather, and you can find a good restaurant.

7 Some games are educational, but other games are just for fun.

8 I want to learn about the new company, but I can't find their website.

9 The class went to the library, and they learnt how to use the new computers.

10 The home page gives the company's address, but it is the wrong address.

Be flexible

In pairs, students look again at Exercise 3 on page 74. Student A reads the first sentence in each item and Student B forms a compound sentence using *and* or *but* with information that is true for him/her, or that the student makes up. Both students can substitute the sentences with their own information.

Give **lower-level students** more support by asking them to return to Exercise 1 on page 73 and create a new sentence to add to the first one, but this time, they connect the two sentences with *but*.

Exercise 4 page 75

2 a Many apps are educational, but some apps are a waste of time.

  b Many apps are educational. However, some apps are a waste of time.

3 a I use online banking, but I sometimes forget my password.

  b I use online banking. However, I sometimes forget my password.

4 a I use the internet on my smartphone, but sometimes it is very slow.

  b I use the internet on my smartphone. However, sometimes it is very slow.

Exercise 5 page 75

Answers will vary.

ACADEMIC WRITING SKILLS

Learning objectives

- Identify topic sentences in two paragraphs
- Identify the key features of topic sentences
- Write topic sentences for paragraphs about the internet and technology

Exercise 1 page 76

Paragraph 2: For many people, video games are fun and educational.

Paragraph 3: However, a recent study suggests that video games can also be bad for children.

Exercise 2 page 76

1 topic: social media sites; **controlling idea:** make it easy to keep in touch with your friends

2 topic: smartphones; **controlling idea:** can be expensive

3 topic: information on the internet; **controlling idea:** is not reliable

4 topic: information online; **controlling idea:** You can access [it] from all over the world.

Exercise 3 page 76

a Smartphones can be expensive.

b You can access information online from all over the world.

c Social media sites make it easy to keep in touch with your friends.

d Information on the internet is not reliable.

WRITING TASK

Learning objectives

- Use a paragraph planner to create an outline of a paragraph about whether the internet is a waste of time or not
- Draft a paragraph
- Review and revise the content and structure of your paragraph
- Review and revise the use of language in your paragraph

Exercises 1–9 pages 77–78

Answers will vary.

RESEARCH PROJECT

Create a short documentary about the impact of social media on our lives.

Explain to your class that they are going to create an audio or video documentary on the positive and negative effects of social media on their lives. Divide the class into groups and ask them to brainstorm questions to be used for interviews. Ask them to allocate responsibilities in their groups for graphics, sound, editing, narration, etc. Students could collaborate outside the class to create a short film or online podcast festival where they screen or play the results of their projects.

CLASSROOM APP

Exercise 1

Answers will vary.

Exercise 2

1 security **2** download **3** interest **4** advert
5 improve **6** creative **7** affect **8** record

Exercise 3

Answers will vary.

Exercise 4

1 video **2** paper **3** screen **4** smart **5** shopping
6 pass **7** media **8** computer

Exercise 5

1 In my opinion, smartphones are too expensive.

2 I believe that websites collect too much information about people.

3 It seems to me that video games are very popular.

4 I don't think that social media is a good way to make friends.

5 In my opinion, people should change their passwords every month.

6 It seems to me that people waste too much time on the internet.

Exercise 6

1 Smartphones are useful in many ways.

2 Social media is very popular in the European Union.

3 New technology played an important role at the 2018 Winter Olympics.

UNIT OBJECTIVES	
Watch and listen	Watch and understand a video about tornadoes.
Reading skills	Read for detail; use your knowledge to predict content.
Critical thinking	Analyze graphs.
Grammar	Use comparative and superlative adjectives.
Academic writing skills	Write topic sentences for descriptive paragraphs about a graph; write supporting sentences; give examples with *like*, *such as* and *for example*.
Writing task	Write a paragraph describing data from graphs.
⟳ **Teacher development**	Help your students become better at **analyzing graphs**.

UNLOCK YOUR KNOWLEDGE

Background note

The photo shows a sandstorm approaching the Merzouga settlement in Erg Chebbi, Morocco. Merzouga is a small village in southeastern Morocco. It is in a desert region and the climate is very hot and dry. Merzouga is a popular destination for tourists who want to explore the sand dunes of Erg Chebbi in the Sahara Desert. Some of the dunes there are 150 metres high.

Lead-in

Preview the meaning of the words *weather* /ˈweð.ə/ (the conditions in the air above the Earth such as wind, rain or temperature) and *climate* /ˈklaɪ.mət/ (the general weather conditions usually found in a particular place). Ask students to give examples of weather v climate, e.g. weather = *It's raining today and it will be sunny tomorrow.*; climate = *The temperature in Antarctica is very cold all year.*

page 81
1 a sun **b** wind **c** rain **d** snow   **2–3** *Answers will vary.*
4 a sandstorm

WATCH AND LISTEN

Learning objectives

* Listen and understand details in a video about tornadoes
* Identify the main idea in a video about tornadoes
* Make inferences about the feelings of the people in the video
* Practise talking about extreme weather

Exercises 1–2 page 82
Answers will vary.

Exercise 3 page 82
1 Alley   **2** 2011   **3** 160   **4** cannot   **5** weather
6 twenty-five   **7** difficult

Exercise 4 page 83
1 b   **2** c   **3** a   **4** e   **5** d

Exercise 5 page 83
b

Exercise 6 page 83
Yes, they enjoy their work. They sound very excited when they find the right tornado.

Exercises 7–8 page 83
Answers will vary.

READING 1

Learning objectives

* Understand key vocabulary for extreme weather – *dangerous, lightning, last*
* Read and identify the main ideas in each paragraph in a text about extreme weather
* Read and identify details
* Read and identify the text type and possible audience
* Make inferences about the reasons for specific customs around the world
* Describe your experiences of extreme weather

Lead-in

Explain that in the reading, students will find out about different types of *extreme* weather. Preview the meaning of the word *extreme* /ɪkˈstriːm/ in this context (very severe or strong, not normal). Ask students to brainstorm examples of extreme weather and write them on the board. Which types are common in their countries? Which ones are not?

Exercise 1 page 84

1 cover **2** lightning **3** Almost **4** last **5** thunder
6 huge **7** dangerous

Exercise 2 page 84

1 *Answers will vary.*

2 *Extreme* means the worst or the most serious possible.

3 *Possible answers:* tornado, hurricane, drought, sandstorm, flood

Exercise 3 page 86

1 a **2** b **3** a **4** b **5** a

Exercise 4 page 86

1 b **2** a **3** a **4** b

Exercise 5 page 86

1 b **2** b **3** a

Exercise 6 page 87

Answers will vary.

Be flexible

Take students beyond the text and ask them to discuss instances of extreme weather not mentioned, what the results of that weather could be, and where in the world experiences each type of weather, e.g. snowstorms, ice storms, tornadoes, hailstorms. You could also elicit natural disasters as a result of extreme weather, such as wildfires and mudslides, and where those might take place.

Some of these phenomena may be unfamiliar to students. You can **lower the challenge** level by bringing in photos, or, if your classroom is equipped, showing short video clips.

READING 2

Learning objectives

- Use your knowledge to predict details in a text about the Sahara
- Understand key vocabulary – *shock, rise, decide*
- Read and identify the main ideas in each paragraph of the text
- Read and identify facts and figures
- Identify the text type
- Evaluate and prioritize items needed to survive in the desert
- Synthesize information from a text about extreme weather and a text about the Sahara in a discussion

Lead-in

Give students one minute to brainstorm words associated with the word *desert*. You can stop there and write their words on the board, or continue to brainstorm more specific lists, such as *things you need in the desert* or *Sahara Desert*. Once all the words are on the board, read the article to see if students' ideas match ideas in the reading.

Background note

The text mentions that the desert covers 11 countries. Of course, it doesn't completely cover them – there are large parts of each country which are not desert. The countries are: Algeria, Chad, Egypt, Libya, Mali, Mauritania, Morocco, Niger, Western Sahara, Sudan and Tunisia. (Note: the status of Western Sahara as a separate country is disputed it was annexed by Morocco in 1975, so some people would argue that there are only ten Saharan countries.)

Exercises 1 and 3 page 87

1 b **2** a

Exercise 2 page 87

a careful **b** drop **c** decide **d** shock **e** rise
f precipitation

Exercise 4 page 88

a 8 **b** 6 **c** 4 **d** 7 **e** 5

Exercise 5 page 88

1 d **2** c **3** a **4** b

Exercise 6 page 88

b

Exercises 7–9 page 88

Answers will vary.

LANGUAGE DEVELOPMENT

Learning objectives

- Select the correct collocations with temperature to describe graphs – *In July, there are high/low temperatures. The maximum/minimum temperature is 1°C in December.*
- Select the correct verbs and nouns to describe temperature changes over time in graphs – *The graph shows an increase / a decrease in temperature. In December, the temperature rises/falls to 7°C.*

Exercise 1 page 90

1 high   **2** low   **3** maximum   **4** minimum

Exercise 2 page 90

1 A   **2** B   **3** A   **4** B   **5** B   **6** A

Exercise 3 page 91

1 rise(s), reach(es)   **2** fall(s), drop(s)

Exercise 4 page 91

1a an increase   **1b** reaches   **2a** a decrease   **2b** drops
3a a decrease   **3b** falls to   **4a** an increase   **4b** rises

Be flexible

👥 Students cover the sentences and look only at the graphs. They work in pairs to try to remember the correct sentence for each graph. If necessary, they can look at the first few words of each sentence to remind them.

You can **reduce the challenge** by writing the relevant words (e.g. *increase, falls to*) on the board so students can refer to them as they say their sentences. This may have the added advantage of encouraging them to use any appropriate verb rather than simply memorizing what was in the textbook.

CRITICAL THINKING

Learning objectives

- Explain the key features of a graph in an article about the Sahara Desert
- Analyze graphs and choose the correct words to complete sentences about the data
- Use data from a graph to complete a table
- Evaluate the implications for the places in the graphs and the people who live there

UNL⟳CK TEACHER DEVELOPMENT

BE INFORMED

→ **Analyzing graphs** is an important skill for students because: (1) Graphs are commonly used in scientific subjects, such as physics, economics and mathematics; (2) Students often don't know how to interpret graphs properly – whilst they might include them in their written work, they do not say much about them; (3) Not analyzing graphs properly represents a wasted opportunity, since they are rich in data.

BE CONFIDENT

→ Develop this skill for yourself by doing the following activity:

The graphs below show the results of a critical thinking survey of 1,019 English teachers by Cambridge University Press, using Likert scales. Look at the graphs and answer the questions which follow.

Figure 1: Responses to the statement, 'It is important to me that I develop my students' critical thinking skills.'

1 = strongly disagree; 5 = strongly agree

1	7/1%
2	10/1%
3	51/5%
4	224/22%
5	727/71%

Figure 2: Responses to the statement, 'I believe my students want to develop their critical thinking skills.'

1 = strongly disagree; 5 = strongly agree

1	15/2%
2	87/9%
3	369/36%
4	309/30%
5	239/23%

1 What are the main findings of Figure 1?

2 What are the main findings of Figure 2?

3 What are the implications of the combined findings of Figure 1 and Figure 2?

Lead-in

Tell students to read the writing task. Explain that they will compare the weather in two places, using four graphs. Each set of graphs is about a different place, showing different aspects of the weather (precipitation and temperature).

UNLOCK TEACHER DEVELOPMENT

BE READY

Look at the Critical Thinking section in the Student's Book on pages 92–94.

→ Which elements of the lesson do you think your students will find easiest / most difficult / most useful? Why?

→ Are your answers true for all students in your class?

→ How can you adapt your teaching or the material to meet your students' needs?

BE FLEXIBLE

Exercise 4 could be done as a spoken activity. In pairs, Student A looks only at the table (and not at the graphs) while Student B looks only at the graphs. Student A must ask for the information required, and Student B responds accordingly. They then swap roles for the second table and set of graphs.

Exercise 1 page 92

1 temperatures   2 times   3 maximum temperature in the day   4 minimum temperature at night

Exercise 2 page 92

Answers will vary. Possible answers:

The graphs show information on temperature and precipitation in Svalbard and Amman throughout the year.

Exercise 3 page 93

1 precipitation in millimetres   2 temperature in Celsius
3 Amman   4 average temperatures   5 bar charts
6 line graphs

Exercise 4 page 93

Note: a small margin of error either way is acceptable.

Svalbard, Norway

	Jan	Feb	Mar	Apr	May	Jun
precipitation	20 mm	30 mm	30 mm	15 mm	15 mm	20 mm
average high temperature	−13°C	−13°C	−13°C	−9°C	−3°C	3°C
average low temperature	−20°C	−21°C	−20°C	−16°C	−7°C	−1°C

	Jul	Aug	Sept	Oct	Nov	Dec
precipitation	25 mm	30 mm	25 mm	20 mm	20 mm	25 mm
average high temperature	7°C	6°C	1°C	−4°C	−8°C	−11°C
average low temperature	3°C	2°C	−3°C	−9°C	−14°C	−18°C

Amman, Jordan

	Jan	Feb	Mar	Apr	May	Jun
precipitation	63 mm	61 mm	43 mm	14 mm	3 mm	0 mm
average high temperature	13°C	14°C	18°C	23°C	28°C	31°C
average low temperature	4°C	5°C	7°C	10°C	14°C	18°C

	Jul	Aug	Sept	Oct	Nov	Dec
precipitation	0 mm	0 mm	0 mm	7 mm	28 mm	49 mm
average high temperature	32°C	32°C	31°C	27°C	20°C	14°C
average low temperature	20°C	20°C	18°C	15°C	9°C	5°C

Exercise 5 page 94

1 **Svalbard:** July; **Amman:** July and August
2 **Svalbard:** February; **Amman:** January
3 **Svalbard:** February, March and August; **Amman:** January
4 **Svalbard:** April and May; **Amman:** June–September
5 *Possible answers:*
Svalbard: heavy snow; **Amman:** drought
6 *Possible answers:*
Svalbard: problems with travel and transportation; **Amman:** limited growing of food
7 *Answers will vary.*

UNLOCK TEACHER DEVELOPMENT

BE REFLECTIVE

Think about the following questions:

→ Do the findings of the critical thinking survey (in *Be confident*) surprise you at all? Would you get the same results in your educational institution? Why / Why not?

→ How confident were your students in the mathematical aspects of this section? Depending on your class and their academic background, they might have found it straightforward or difficult. This could be useful to know for the next time you do something similar.

BE COLLABORATIVE

Your development is more meaningful when it's shared. See page 14 for ideas on how to peer-collaborate. Why not share your reflections on the survey results from the *Be confident* section, and the impact it had on the class?

GRAMMAR FOR WRITING

Learning objectives

- Complete a table with the correct forms of comparative and superlative adjectives – *cold, colder, coldest*
- Choose between comparative and superlative adjective forms to complete sentences about the weather
- Use comparative and superlative adjectives to complete sentences about weather in Cuba and Iceland – *Iceland is colder than Cuba. Cuba is the rainiest country.*

Exercise 1 page 95

adjective	comparative	superlative
cold	colder	the coldest
low	lower	the lowest
extreme	more extreme	the most extreme
dry	drier	the driest
big	bigger	the biggest
easy	easier	the easiest

Exercise 2 page 95

1 the driest   **2** colder   **3** the most extreme   **4** lower
5 the biggest

Be flexible

Students test each other in pairs. One student reads the names of the countries from a sentence and the adjective (e.g. *Cuba, high; Iceland, low*) and the other student has to make a complete sentence (without looking at the book).

Stronger students could create new sentences comparing the weather in two or three cities that they know well.

Exercise 3 page 96

1 higher   **2** colder   **3** lowest   **4** wetter   **5** drier
6 rainiest   **7** sunny

ACADEMIC WRITING SKILLS

Learning objectives

- Complete topic sentences for descriptive paragraphs about a graph – *The graph shows the temperature in Degrees Celsius over 24 hours in the Sahara Desert*
- Choose supporting information for a topic sentence about the climate in Costa Rica
- Use words and phrases to introduce supporting examples in sentences about the weather – *Wildfires have many different causes, like lightning. Hurricanes are usually given names, such as Hurricane Sandy. Some cities are very wet and rainy, for example, Hong Kong and Mumbai.*

Exercise 1 page 96

1 precipitation; year; Svalbard, Norway
2 temperature; year; Svalbard, Norway

Exercise 2 page 97

1 Main idea: The hottest time is between 2 pm and 4 pm.
Data: Temperatures rise to 33 °C.
2 Main idea: The coldest time is at 4 am.
Data: Temperatures fall to –1°C.

Exercise 3 page 97

1 a   **2** b

Exercise 4 page 97

1 c   **2** b   **3** a   **4** d

Exercise 5 page 97

a, b, d, f

Exercise 6 page 98

Answers will vary. Possible answers:

2 It is too hot to snow in some Central American cities, like Managua and Guadalajara.

It is too hot to snow in some Central American cities, such as Managua and Guadalajara.

It is too hot to snow in some Central American cities, for example Managua and Guadalajara.

3 There are a lot of tornadoes in certain US states, like Oklahoma and Texas.

There are a lot of tornadoes in certain US states, such as Oklahoma and Texas.

There are a lot of tornadoes in certain US states, for example Oklahoma and Texas.

4 When you go camping, bring important items, like water and sunscreen.

When you go camping, bring important items, such as water and sunscreen.

When you go camping, bring important items, for example water and sunscreen.

5 You can do a lot of outdoor activities in warm weather, like swimming and walking.

You can do a lot of outdoor activities in warm weather, such as swimming and walking.

You can do a lot of outdoor activities in warm weather, for example swimming and walking.

6 Some cities are very wet and rainy, like Hong Kong and Mumbai.

Some cities are very wet and rainy, such as Hong Kong and Mumbai.

Some cities are very wet and rainy, for example Hong Kong and Mumbai.

WRITING TASK

Learning objectives

- Prepare sentences for a paragraph comparing the climate in two places
- Draft a paragraph
- Review and revise the content and structure of your paragraph
- Review and revise the use of language in your paragraph

Exercises 1–9 pages 99–100

Answers will vary.

RESEARCH PROJECT

Improve your local environment.

Students should collect data on the amount of waste produced by their class or school and identify improvements. For example, they could monitor the waste they produce during each lesson and/or ask a school official how much waste is produced each day or each week by the school. They can also interview classmates and other students in the school about their recycling habits. They should brainstorm a plan to educate and encourage other students to recycle and reduce waste material. Then, the students should try to implement their plan.

Explain to the class that they should measure how successful their solutions were and report back with any lessons learnt.

CLASSROOM APP

Exercise 1

Answers will vary.

Exercise 2

1 precipitation **2** rises **3** dangerous **4** shock
5 covered **6** decide **7** lasted **8** almost

Exercise 3

Answers will vary.

Exercise 4

1 maximum **2** minimum **3** high **4** low

Exercise 5

1 In March, the temperature reaches 10°C.

2 At about 1.30, the temperature drops to -1°C.

3 On Sunday, the temperature decreases to 40°C.

4 In November, the temperature rises to 4°C.

5 The temperature falls every hour.

6 The temperature increases every month.

Exercise 6

1 The graph shows precipitation in millimetres (mm) over a year in Svalbard, Norway.

2 From January to February, precipitation increases from 20 mm to 30 mm.

3 Between August and September, the amount of precipitation decreases by about 5 mm.

4 Some months have around the same amount of precipitation, for example, February and March.

UNIT OBJECTIVES

Watch and listen	Watch and understand a video about a 96-year-old bungee jumper.
Reading skill	Scan to predict content.
Critical thinking	Analyze a diagram.
Grammar	Use prepositions of movement; use correct subject and verb agreement.
Academic writing skills	Order events in a process; remove unrelated information.
Writing task	Write a process paragraph.
⟳ **Teacher development**	Help your students become better at **analyzing a diagram**.

UNLOCK YOUR KNOWLEDGE

Background note

The photo shows people snowboarding in St. Moritz, Switzerland. St. Moritz is a famous Alpine resort situated 1,800 metres above sea level. It has many natural hills and open countryside which attracts freeriders. Freeriding is a type of snowboarding practised across natural landscapes and without a set course. It is also sometimes called backcountry riding and requires a great deal of skill and attention to safety.

Lead-in

Students work in teams to brainstorm a list of English names for types of sport. Set a time limit (e.g. five minutes). Go round the class eliciting one sport from each team and write it on the board. They may not repeat a sport that has already been mentioned. Keep going until teams run out of ideas. The last team still offering names is the winner.

Use the list of sports on the board to elicit a list of nouns for sport equipment (e.g. *ball, bat, racquet, club, net, goal*), places (e.g. *football pitch, golf course, tennis court, boxing ring*) and sport verbs (e.g. *run, jump, kick, throw, catch, hit, miss, ride, fight*).

page 103
1 snowboarding **2–5** *Answers will vary.*

WATCH AND LISTEN

Learning objectives

*   Listen and identify the main ideas in a video about a bungee-jumper
*   Listen and understand details
*   Practise talking about dangerous sport

Exercises 1–2 page 104
Answers will vary.

Exercise 3 page 105
1 oldest **2** dangerous **3** three **4** windy **5** was not

Exercise 4 page 105
1 216 **2** back; neck (in any order) **3** 88 **4** likes
5 experience **6** 96

Exercise 5 page 105
1 F; The Bloukrans Bridge is one of the highest bungee jumps.
2 F; Bungee ropes don't often break. **3** T
4 F; Mohr didn't know about the world record when he jumped. / He did not know he was going to break the world record. **5** T
6 F; Mohr didn't think (about anything) before he jumped.

Exercise 6 page 105
Answers will vary.

READING 1

Learning objectives

*   Understand key vocabulary for sport – *swimming, compete, competition*
*   Scan an article about sport for key words to identify the topic and other key ideas
*   Read and identify the main ideas in each paragraph
*   Read and understand detailed information
*   Identify the target audience for this text and possible source
*   Describe and give personal opinions on unusual sport

9 The Ephesus camel wrestling competition happens once a year.

10 In camel wrestling, two male camels fight each other.

Lead-in

Tell students they will read about sport from five different countries. Give them the names (the United States, Singapore, Scotland, Indonesia, Turkey) and elicit what types of sport they think are popular in each country.

Exercise 1 page 106

1 take place   **2** compete   **3** ancient   **4** strange
5 throw   **6** competition   **7** swimming

Exercises 2–3 page 107

1 b   **2** b   **3** b d

Optional activity

Students work in pairs to find and underline at least one noun, verb and adjective in the other five paragraphs (2–6). You could do this as a race, or set a time limit (e.g. one minute). When you check with the class, tell students to cover the text, and get them to predict what each paragraph will be about based only on the words they found.

Possible answers:

2: nouns – *Atlantic Ocean, snow*; verbs – *swim, believe*; adjectives – *cold, good*

3: nouns – *dragon, boat*; verbs – *watch, race*; adjectives – *traditional, popular*

4: nouns – *wood, tree*; verbs – *compete, throw*; adjectives – *large, official*

5: nouns – *coconut shells, fire*; verbs – *pour, play*; adjectives – *similar, bare*

6: nouns – *camel, competition*; verbs – *fight, run*; adjectives – *old, dangerous*

Exercise 4 page 109

a Paragraph 5   **b** Paragraph 3   **c** Paragraph 6
d Paragraph 4   **e** Paragraph 2

Exercise 5 page 109

1 Indonesia   **2** Singapore, China, Malaysia, Indonesia
3 Turkey   **4** Scotland   **5** the USA

Exercise 6 page 109

1 The Coney Island Polar Bear Plunge takes place every Sunday from October to April and on New Year's Day.

2 The Coney Island Polar Bear Plunge began in 1903.

3 A dragon boat has a dragon's head painted on it.

4 There are 22 people in each dragon boat team.

5 A caber is a large piece of wood.

6 A caber is usually the size of a small tree.

7 In fireball football, the ball is made from coconut shells.

8 The ball is on fire throughout a game of fireball football.

Exercises 7–8 page 110

1 a   **2** b   **3** b

Exercise 9 page 110

Answers will vary.

READING 2

Learning objectives

- Understand key vocabulary for competitions – *participant, course, accident*
- Preview the text to identify type and topic
- Read and identify main ideas in an article about a competition
- Use a diagram to understand the ideas in the text
- Read and understand facts and figures
- Identify how specific words are used in discourse in the article
- Read and identify the meaning of words from the context
- Synthesize ideas from an article about unusual sport and an article about a competition in a discussion

Lead-in

In groups, students brainstorm a list of extreme sports and discuss which ones they have participated in or would like to try. (*Possible answers:* hang gliding, ice climbing, kite surfing, mountain biking, rafting, sandboarding.)

Exercise 1 page 110–111

1 a   **2** a   **3** b   **4** a   **5** b   **6** b

Exercise 2 page 111

a magazine article

Exercises 3–4 page 111

Answers will vary. Possible answers: a competition, a difficult race

Exercise 5 page 111

1 difficult   **2** cold   **3** countries   **4** get hurt   **5** strong
6 different

Exercise 6 page 111

1 d   **2** f   **3** e   **4** b   **5** a   **6** c

Exercise 7 page 113

1 the UK   **2** January   **3** 15 kilometres   **4** all year
5 Because it is exciting and challenging, and it is a different course every year.

Exercise 8 page 113

1 c; e **2** b; d **3** a; f

Exercise 9 page 113

1 a **2** a

Be flexible

👥 👥👥 Write the following words and phrases on the board. Students close their books and work in pairs to try to work out what the words and phrases mean (using a dictionary if necessary) and to remember what was said in the text about each: *a race to the limit*; *freezing*; *accidents*; *injuries*; *broken bones*; *cuts*; *fit and healthy*; *prepare for something*; *exciting*; *challenging*; *reach the finish line*. When they are ready, discuss the answers with the class.

For a **less challenging task**, allow students to work out meaning using context; that is, with their books open.

Exercise 10 page 113

Answers will vary.

Optional activity

👥 Students close their books. Write the following phrases from Exercise 6 on page 111 on the board in the form of a table. Students work in pairs to make sentences. Encourage them to be creative, and not just to use the sentences from the book. They can then compare their sentences with the ones in the book. Note that the prepositions will be analyzed in the next section, so treat this as a way of introducing that language rather than testing it.

Participants The runners They	run jump crawl	through across over along off under into	a Ø (no article)	wet dirty low small	road. bonfires. platform. field. lake. ground.

LANGUAGE DEVELOPMENT

Learning objectives

- Work out the meaning of prepositions of movement in context – *around the track, through the tunnel, over the bridge*
- Complete a set of directions with prepositions of movement

Exercise 1 page 114

1 f **2** g **3** c **4** b **5** e **6** d **7** a

Be flexible

👥 Students take turns to test each other in pairs by pointing to a picture to elicit the correct description from their partner, whose book is closed. For **a more challenging task**, ask students to give each other step-by-step directions to a place nearby, using prepositions of movement.

Exercise 2 page 115

1 along **2** past **3** over / across **4** through / across
5 under **6** through **7** across **8** around / along

CRITICAL THINKING

Learning objectives

- Understand and label a diagram relating to a sporting event
- Use a diagram to understand information about a sporting event

---

UNLOCK TEACHER DEVELOPMENT

BE INFORMED

→ **Analyzing a diagram** is an important skill for students because: (1) Diagrams are common both in real life and in academic study; (2) Diagrams can convey a lot of information in a reasonably straightforward way, and so are very valuable; (3) Analyzing diagrams contributes greatly to students' understanding of how to effectively create their own diagrams.

BE CONFIDENT

→ Develop this skill for yourself by doing the following activity:

Find a diagram. It might be printed in a book, available online or a physical object in your educational institution. Look at this diagram and ask yourself the following questions:

1 Is the diagram easy to understand? Why / Why not?

2 Is the diagram clearly labelled?

3 Are there any improvements you could make to this diagram?

Lead-in

Tell students to read the writing task. Elicit from the class where in this unit they can find a good model for this task (*Answer:* The last paragraph of Reading 2).

Ask students to look back at the diagram in Reading 2 on page 112. Tell them to imagine they have to write about the diagram. Elicit (a) in what order they would describe the parts of the diagram and (b) whether they would describe every detail.

Possible answers: The best order is the order of the events; it is not necessary to describe every detail, only the most important parts.

Finally, tell them to read the information in the Skills box to compare it with their ideas.

UNLOCK TEACHER DEVELOPMENT

BE READY

Look at the Critical Thinking section in the Student's Book on pages 116–117.
→ Which elements of the lesson do you think your students will find easiest / most difficult / most useful? Why?
→ Are your answers true for all students in your class?
→ How can you adapt your teaching or the material to meet your students' needs?

BE FLEXIBLE

To make this whole critical thinking section 'come to life', ask students to find examples/diagrams of other triathlon routes, or similar types of events. Alternatively, students could invent a triathlon route in their local area.

Exercise 1 page 116

1 bridge   **2** swimming route   **3** tunnel   **4** cycle route
5 central library   **6** running route

Exercise 2 page 117

1 10 kilometres   **2** 1,500 metres   **3** 40 kilometres

Exercise 3 page 117

a over / across   **b** through   **c** along   **d** across   **e** past

Exercise 4 page 117

a 4   **b** 3   **c** 5   **d** 1   **e** 2

Optional activity

Students work in pairs. They take turns to describe the parts of the race (using phrases from Exercise 3), but looking only at the map.

UNLOCK TEACHER DEVELOPMENT

BE REFLECTIVE

Think about the following questions:
→ How confident were your students in interpreting the diagram? Some students find it difficult to analyze visuals, whereas others find it straightforward.
→ If you followed the advice in *Be flexible*, was it successful? Did the students enjoy it? Think about why / why not, and if you think there might be other opportunities to do something similar in future lessons.

BE COLLABORATIVE

Your development is more meaningful when it's shared. See page 14 for ideas on how to peer-collaborate. Why not share some of your experiences from the *Be ready* section, and their outcome?

GRAMMAR FOR WRITING

Learning objectives

- Identify singular and plural subjects, and verbs in sentences – *The footballers play three times a week. Football and tennis are popular sports.*
- Use the correct form of present simple verbs to complete sentences about sport – *The coach swims every day. The race begins at 3 pm. The teams and the referee run onto the field.*

Exercise 1 page 117

1 **subject** – The boys and girls; **verb** – play
2 **subject** – We; **verb** – watch
3 **subject** – Aisha; **verb** – runs
4 **subject** – Football; **verb** – is
5 **subject** – You; **verb** – run
6 **subject** – Hanh and I; **verb** – love

Exercise 2 page 118

1 is   **2** swims   **3** cycle   **4** wins   **5** practise   **6** is

Exercise 3 page 118

1 try   **2** carries   **3** is   **4** watch   **5** miss   **6** wants   **7** run
8 are   **9** catch

Be flexible

ACADEMIC WRITING SKILLS

Learning objectives

- Use transition words to connect sentences about sequences of actions – *First, the participants run ten kilometres. Next, they swim across the river.; Participants run ten kilometres. Then, they swim across the river.*
- Review a paragraph and delete unrelated (irrelevant) information.

Exercise 1 page 119

1 b   **2** d   **3** c   **4** a

Exercise 2 page 119

1 First, the weightlifter lifts the weight onto his shoulders.

2 Next / Then / After that, the weightlifter lifts the weight above his head.

3 Then / Next / After that, the weightlifter holds the weight above his head for as long as he can.

4 Finally, the weightlifter drops the weight to the ground.

Exercises 3–4 page 120

Answers will vary. Possible answer:

First, the tennis players walk onto the court. Next, they pick up their racquets. Then, one player hits the ball over the net. After that, the other player hits the ball back.

Exercises 5–6 page 120

The high jump is an Olympic sport that is practised in many countries. ~~Athletes competed in over 30 venues during the 2012 London Olympic Games.~~ First, the high jumper runs towards the bar. It is important to run very fast. ~~The high jump is the most popular sport in Russia.~~ Next, the high jumper jumps. ~~I was on the track and field team at school.~~ The high jumper must jump from the right foot and keep their arms close to their sides. Then, the high jumper twists their body so their back is to the bar. They must lift their head and feet and keep them high above the bar. ~~The high jump is a really interesting sport.~~ After that, the high jumper lands. They must be careful to land safely on the mat. ~~Derek Drouin from Canada won the gold medal in the men's high jump at the 2016 Rio Olympic Games, and Ruth Beitia from Spain won the gold for the women's high jump.~~ Finally, the high jumper stands up, takes a bow and leaves the mat.

WRITING TASK

Learning objectives

- Use a paragraph planner to create an outline of a paragraph about the Sydney Triathlon
- Draft a paragraph
- Review and revise the content and structure of your paragraph
- Review and revise the use of language in your paragraph

Exercise 1 page 121

A *Answers will vary.*

B 1 swim across the bay   **2** cycle a bike past the library   **3** cycle a bike through the tunnel   **4** cycle a bike over / across the bridge   **5** run along the road

Exercises 2–8 pages 121–122

Answers will vary.

RESEARCH PROJECT

Design a competition where students increase their weekly sport activity.

Divide the class into groups and make each group responsible for things like rules, goals, rewards and levels of difficulty. Tell them that the idea is for them to make physical activity more interesting by turning it into a game, with the aim of increasing how much physical activity they do, as well as how much other students and teachers do. They should design a competition that contains rewards, progress levels, points, a virtual currency or leader boards, just as in other games.

You may also want to look at and adapt information on 'gamification' (improving user engagement by turning educational materials into a game) to help students with their designs.

CLASSROOM APP

Exercise 1

Answers will vary.

Exercise 2

1 ancient **2** competition **3** course **4** throw
5 take place **6** challenging **7** strange **8** fit

Exercise 3

Answers will vary.

Exercise 4

1 past **2** through **3** across **4** under
5 around **6** over **7** along

Exercise 5

1 a bridge **2** a city **3** a lake **4** a tree **5** a tunnel

Exercise 6

[1] Underwater hockey is a popular but strange sport.
[2] First, two teams of six players get into a swimming
pool. **[3]** Next, the puck must be dropped in the middle
of the pool. **[4]** Then, all the players can swim around
and try to put the puck in the correct goal. **[5]** Finally,
the game ends and the winner is the team with the most
goals.
[X] The first underwater hockey game took place in 1954
in England.

UNIT OBJECTIVES	
Watch and listen	Watch and understand a video about Amazon's fulfilment centre.
Reading skills	Work out meaning from context; annotate a text.
Critical thinking	Organize events in time order.
Grammar	Use the present simple and the past simple; use time clauses with *when* to describe past events.
Academic writing skill	Add details to main facts.
Writing task	Write a narrative paragraph.
⟳ **Teacher development**	Help your students become better at **organizing events in time order**.

UNLOCK YOUR KNOWLEDGE

Background note

The large photo shows a tall, glass skyscraper. Through the windows we can see offices and people working. The small photos show two famous entrepreneurs: Bill Gates and Oprah Winfrey. Bill Gates started Microsoft, the world's largest software company. The company was launched in 1975 and Gates remained its CEO until 2000. Oprah Winfrey is best known for her television talk show, which she hosted from 1986 to 2011. The show earnt her millions and she soon started her own production company. Winfrey became the richest African American woman of the twentieth century. Both Winfrey and Gates are also famous for their charity work.

Lead-in

Students work in teams to brainstorm a list of famous companies. They are allowed only one company per country, so they will need to identify the country in each case. After about five minutes, go round the class, eliciting a country and company from each team, and write them on the board. Teams can only name a country or company that has not yet been given. The last team to give a country, after the others have run out of ideas, is the winner.

Possible answers

Brazil (Embraer, …), Finland (Nokia, …), France (Citroën, Carrefour, …), Germany (Siemens, Volkswagen, …), India (Tata Group, …), Italy (Fiat, Ferrari, …), Japan (Toyota, Sony, …), South Korea (Samsung, LG, …), Russia (Gazprom, …), Sweden (Ikea, Volvo, …), Switzerland (Nestlé, …), UAE (Emirates Airways, …), UK (Tesco, BP, …), USA (Apple, Disney, …), etc.

page 125

1 a top: Bill Gates; bottom: Oprah Winfrey **b** Bill Gates – Microsoft; Oprah Winfrey – The Oprah Winfrey Show, O Magazine, OWN: The Oprah Winfrey Network **c** *Answers will vary.*

2–3 *Answers will vary.*

WATCH AND LISTEN

Learning objectives

- Use your knowledge to predict details about the company, Amazon
- Listen and identify details in a video about the Amazon fulfilment centre
- Listen and complete a summary with facts and figures from the video
- Identify main ideas and sequence main events in the video
- Identify an inference that can be made from a speaker's statement in the video
- Practise talking about the future of different jobs

Exercises 1–2 page 126

Answers will vary.

Exercise 3 page 126

1 T **2** F; An Amazon worker walks through the warehouse to find the item you ordered.

3 F; Amazon does sell kitchen items.

Exercise 4 page 126

1, 2, 3, 4, 5, 6, 7, 8, 9, 10

Exercise 5 page 127

1 Seattle **2** 100 **3** website **4** large **5** fulfilment

Exercise 6 page 127

1 T   **2** F; The first warehouse was a basement.   **3** F; Only the central computer knows where everything is. **4** F; An Amazon worker finds your item after you pay for it.   **5** T

Exercise 7 page 127

a 5 **b** 3 **c** 2 **d** 1 **e** 4

Exercise 8 page 127

b

Exercise 9 page 127

Answers will vary.

READING 1

Learning objectives

- Understand key vocabulary for work – *organize, apply, occupation*
- Skim the text for text type and topic
- Read a quiz about work and correct the description
- Follow detailed instructions in a quiz
- Describe your response to the result of a quiz
- Identify the meaning of new words from their context in the quiz
- Identify the target reader for the quiz
- Give personal opinions on jobs

Lead-in

Students work in pairs. Look at the four main types of jobs in Reading 1. Write the types of jobs on the board, one at a time. For each job type, give the students one minute to brainstorm jobs. At the end of each minute, ask pairs how many jobs they thought of. At the end of the fourth minute, the pair with the most jobs wins. Volunteers can then write their jobs on the board and students decide if they are all in the correct category.

Exercise 1 page 128

1 a **2** b **3** a **4** b **5** b **6** a

Exercises 2–3 page 128

1 b **2** a

Exercise 4 page 130

There are ~~three~~ four main kinds of jobs – jobs with ~~animals~~ people, jobs with information, jobs with ~~machines~~ things and jobs with ideas. The quiz helps you to find out about the kind of ~~people~~ jobs you might like. After doing the quiz, read the advice to find ~~universities~~ jobs you might like.

Exercises 5–6 page 130

Answers will vary.

Be flexible

With **stronger classes**, tell students to repeat the quiz in pairs, this time giving their own honest answers (i.e. not restricting themselves to the four options provided). Afterwards, they discuss in pairs what these new answers say about the sort of job they would be good at.

Exercise 7 page 130

advice: Q2; hobby: Q1; neat: *Mostly 'b' answers* description; sections: Q2

Exercise 8 page 130

1 b **2** a **3** a **4** b

Exercise 9 page 131

b; c

Exercise 10 page 131

Answers will vary.

READING 2

Learning objectives

- Understand key vocabulary for businesses – *goal, employ, partner*
- Scan a text for key words to predict the topic
- Read and annotate the important words, dates, numbers and ideas in a text about Google
- Read and identify main ideas
- Read and understand details
- Read and sequence main events in Google's history
- Identify an inference about the attitude of the creators of Google
- Synthesize ideas from a quiz about work and an article about Google in a discussion

Lead-in

Talk about Google with the class. What do students already know about the company? What kinds of things does Google do?

Exercise 1 page 131

a set up **b** office **c** run **d** partner **e** goal **f** employ **g** introduce **h** advertise

Exercise 2 page 132

Possible answers:

Google; online; business; entrepreneurs

Optional activity

👥 For Exercise 3, students can work in small groups, comparing their annotations with each other. Check if they noted any of the same words, numbers or ideas, and what they wrote in the margins. Discuss why they annotated the way they did.

Exercise 4 page 132

a 3   b 1   c 2

Exercise 5 page 132

1 b   2 a   3 a   4 a

Exercise 6 page 134

1 F; Google has three main focuses: to make its search engine fast and smart; to develop products that can work on different devices and in different places; and to help new businesses advertise and find new customers.

2 T   3 T

4 F; Google released a program which enabled people to see famous works of art.

Exercise 7 page 134

	A year	**B event**
a Google searches could be done in 15 languages.	2000	2
b Google started an art contest for students.	2008	4
c The partners registered the domain name Google.com.	1997	1
d Google introduced a map service.	2005	3

Exercise 8 page 134

a

Exercise 9 page 134

3

Exercise 10 page 134

Answers will vary.

LANGUAGE DEVELOPMENT

Learning objectives

- Identify the meanings of collocations with *business – business plan, business contact, set up a business, expand a business*
- Identify the meaning of business vocabulary – *employee, product, colleague*
- Use business vocabulary to complete an email

Exercise 1 page 135

a N   b N   c V   d N   e V   f V

Exercise 2 page 135

1 plan   2 Expand   3 partner   4 Run   5 Set up
6 contact

Exercise 3 page 135

1 before   2 after

Be flexible

👥 Put collocations with *business* on pieces of paper in a basket. Divide students into teams. A member from each team comes to the board at the same time. They choose a collocation from the basket and write a sentence on the board using the collocation, with a gap for their team member to complete, for example: *My business _____ and I own a coffee shop together.* The team who guesses the word correctly first wins a point.

Give **lower-level students** more support by asking them instead to each create a new -fill gap exercise with half of the *business +_____* collocations, for an other student to complete.

Exercise 4 page 136

1 c   2 g   3 f   4 h   5 e   6 d   7 b   8 a

Exercise 5 page 136

1 employees   2 office   3 software   4 employ
5 products   6 department   7 colleagues   8 manager

CRITICAL THINKING

Learning objectives

- Identify important events in the history of Google
- Complete a timeline of Google's history
- Research and create a timeline for a business which you are interested in
- Create a table of supporting information

UNLOCK TEACHER DEVELOPMENT

BE INFORMED

→ **Organizing events in time order** is an important skill for students because: (1) It is very common in spoken and written texts for events to be described in chronological order; (2) Organizing the order is an important first step to evaluating the relative importance of events in a time sequence, something students may find it difficult; (3) Organizing events in time order can help students decide whether they are also linked causally (i.e. does one thing happen *because of* something else, or just *after* it).

BE CONFIDENT

→ Develop this skill for yourself by doing the following activity:

Think about six important events in your teaching career. Complete a timeline like the one below, writing the year above the line and the event below the line. Use a maximum of eight words to describe each event.

Lead-in

Students read the writing task. Elicit from the class where in this unit they can find a good model for this task (*Possible answer:* Paragraph 2 of Reading 2, although this is much longer than the paragraph students are expected to write). Ask students what other information in the text might be useful (*Possible answers:* Paragraph 1: the year Page and Brin met each other; Paragraph 3: Google's most recent project).

UNLOCK TEACHER DEVELOPMENT

BE READY

Look at the Critical Thinking section in the Student's Book on pages 137–138.

→ Which elements of the lesson do you think your students will find easiest / most difficult / most useful? Why?

→ Are your answers true for all students in your class?

→ How can you adapt your teaching or the material to meet your students' needs?

BE FLEXIBLE

An interesting alternative for Exercise 5 is to get students to work in pairs. Student A writes out the eight events on separate pieces of paper and gives them to Student B.

Student B must then put them in what they think is the correct order. Student A then checks whether they are correct. They then swap roles.

Exercises 1–2 page 137

Answers will vary.

Optional activity

Students close their books. In pairs, they recall the events in Google's history that were the most important. They should consider which events made the strongest impression on them while they were reading, then decide if those events were actually the most important events for Google in developing its business.

Exercise 3 page 137

c 1997   **b** 1998   **g** 2000   **a** 2005   **f** 2006   **e** 2008   **h** 2011

Background note

The left–right alignment of the timeline reflects the way we write European languages. Speakers of other languages (e.g. Arabic) may find a right-left timeline more logical. *Chronological* /krɒnəˈlɒdʒkəl/ order simply means in the order of real time. We sometimes describe events out of chronological order (e.g. *The company closed* [3] *because it had lost money* [2] *as a result of poor planning* [1]), but it is simpler and often clearer to use chronological order (e.g. *It didn't plan well* [1], *so it lost money* [2] *and in the end the company closed* [3]).

Exercises 4–6 page 138

Answers will vary.

UNLOCK TEACHER DEVELOPMENT

BE REFLECTIVE

Think about the following points:

→ If you feel comfortable doing so, share your timeline with colleagues, and invite them to ask questions about why these events are so important to your teaching career. You could also reflect on what other events might be included, if you created this same timeline again in ten years' time?

→ Which aspects of the lesson did students find most interesting? Why do you think this was the case?

BE COLLABORATIVE

Your development is more meaningful when it's shared. See page 14 for ideas on how to peer-collaborate. Why not share some of your experiences from the *Be ready* section, and their outcome?

GRAMMAR FOR WRITING

Learning objectives

- Differentiate between present simple and past simple verbs
- Choose the correct form of verbs to complete a paragraph about a company and its history
- Complete sentences about companies with past simple and present simple verbs – *Lego sells toys. In 1995, Amazon sold its first book on Amazon. com.*
- Use time clauses with *when* to link events in sequence in the past – *When she was 30, she became the CEO. The shop closed when the economy crashed.*

Exercise 1 page 139

1 is; present **2** joined; past **3** is; present **4** became; past **5** bought; past **6** celebrated; past

Exercise 2 page 139

1 sells **2** set up **3** did **4** employed **5** expanded **6** opened **7** is

Exercise 3 page 140

1 is **2** opened **3** sells **4** is **5** started **6** sold **7** makes **8** designed

Exercise 4 page 140

1 became **2** graduated **3** began **4** voted **5** was

Lead-in

Students close their books. Write the two sentences from the Grammar box on page 140 on the board. Elicit the word that shows the date or time that something happened (*when*). Then elicit in which sentence the time is more important (the second sentence: *When he was sixteen.*).

Exercise 5 page 141

1 She became the CEO when she was 30. / When she was 30, she became the CEO.
2 They employed six new workers when the business expanded. / When the business expanded, they employed six new workers.
3 He left his job when he was 65. / When he was 65, he left his job.
4 The shop closed when the economy crashed. / When the economy crashed, the shop closed.
5 They expanded the company when it was still successful. / When it was still successful, they expanded the company.

Exercise 6 page 141

1 When Lei finished her master's degree, she started a company.
2 The owners opened a second café when the first one was one year old.
3 When Samir wanted to get more customers, he advertised his business online.
4 Anika loved to learn about computers when she was a child.
5 When Yoko became CEO, she moved to a bigger office.

Optional activity

Students work in small groups. Give them information about entrepreneurs, so they can write sentences with *when*. When they finish, students can write more sentences about entrepreneurs they know about, or about the companies they brainstormed in the lead-in to the Unlock your knowledge section. Students must decide if the time clause should go first or last in the sentence.

Information to give students and possible answers:

Bill Gates – 26 – millionaire (Bill Gates was 26 when he became a millionaire.)

Elon Musk – 27 – sold a web-software company for $300 million. (When Elon Musk was 27, he sold a web-software company for $300 million.)

Oprah Winfrey – started a talk show on television – became famous. (Oprah Winfrey became famous when she started a talk show on television.)

Coco Chanel – a child – learnt how to make clothes. (When Coco Chanel was a child, she learnt how to make clothes.)

Enzo Ferrari – young man – competed in car races. (Enzo Ferrari competed in car races when he was a young man.)

ACADEMIC WRITING SKILLS

Learning objectives

- Make a paragraph about YouTube more interesting by adding details in appropriate places
- Link details about Google with important events in its history

Exercise 1 page 142

1 a 2 d 3 b 4 c

Exercise 2 page 142

1 a 2 d 3 b 4 e 5 c 6 g 7 h 8 f

Optional activity

👥 Tell students to look back at the paragraph about JLX (*Grammar for Writing*, Exercise 2, page 139). In pairs, they invent details to make the text more interesting. After a few minutes, ask volunteers to present their ideas.

WRITING TASK

Learning objectives

- Plan the events and details you will use in a paragraph about the history of a business
- Prepare a topic sentence for your paragraph
- Draft your paragraph
- Review and revise the content and structure of your paragraph
- Review and revise the use of language in your paragraph

Exercises 1–9 pages 143–144

Answers will vary.

RESEARCH PROJECT

Create a small business.

After dividing the class into groups, explain that they are going to create a new small business. They should write a business plan that includes a description of the product or service they plan to sell, ideas on target customers, and an advertising plan. They will also have to think about the source of the capital to start the business.

Students can present their business idea to the class and vote on the best one to launch.

CLASSROOM APP

Exercise 1

Answers will vary.

Exercise 2

1 customers 2 set up 3 goal 4 introduce
5 occupation 6 applied 7 organize 8 results

Exercise 3

Answers will vary.

Exercise 4

1 expand the business 2 be your business partner
3 make business contacts 4 write a business plan
5 develop both skills

Exercise 5

1 office 2 software 3 departments 4 colleague
5 products

Exercise 6

1 Her new business was a food truck.

2 She didn't want people to have to wait in traffic to get to a restaurant.

3 She believes in giving women the opportunity to be independent by earning their own money.

UNIT OBJECTIVES	
Watch and listen	Watch and understand a video about a professional gold prospector.
Reading skill	Skim a text.
Critical thinking	Categorize ideas.
Grammar	Use noun phrases with *of*; use modals of necessity.
Academic writing skill	Write concluding sentences.
Writing task	Write an explanatory paragraph.
⌀ **Teacher development**	Help your students become better at **categorizing ideas**.

UNL⌀CK YOUR KNOWLEDGE

Background note

The large photo shows the Shibuya Crossing in Tokyo, Japan. The Shibuya Crossing is one of the biggest and the busiest pedestrian crossings in the world. At rush hour, up to 2,500 people cross the street at the same time. The small photos show Barack Obama, Princess Diana and Mahatma Gandhi. Barack Obama was the first African American President of the USA. He was President from 2009 until 2017. Princess Diana was married to Prince Charles and was one of the most popular members of the British royal family. She was also famous for her charity work. Mahatma Gandhi was known for his anti-war activism and his role in the Indian independence movement. He's recognized across the world for his philosophy of non-violence.

Lead-in

Ask students to look at the large photo on pages 146–147, and to discuss in small groups what the people in the photo are doing. Encourage students to be as creative as possible (for example, somebody in the photo might be going to an important meeting about a product she created, and is going to sell it to a big company). Elicit ideas from the class.

page 147

1 Barack Obama; Diana, Princess of Wales; Mahatma Gandhi

2 Barack Obama (1961–) was the first African American President of the USA. He was the President from January 2009 to January 2017. He attended Harvard Law School and he won the Nobel Peace Prize in 2009.

Diana, Princess of Wales (1961–1997) was married to Prince Charles. She was known for her work for various charities. She divorced Prince Charles in 1996 and died in a car crash in Paris the following year.

Mahatma Gandhi (1869–1948) was a leader of the Indian independence movement. He led protests against British rule, using non-violent methods of civil disobedience (i.e. breaking rules without hurting people). He is known in India as the Father of the Nation. He was assassinated in 1948, shortly after India declared independence.

WATCH AND LISTEN

Learning objectives

- Listen and understand the main ideas in a video about a treasure hunter
- Listen and understand details and figures
- Make inferences about the treasure hunter's life and feelings
- Practise talking about dreams

Exercises 1–2 page 148

Answers will vary.

Exercise 3 page 149

1 F; Vince's job is finding gold. 2 T 3 T 4 F; Looking for gold is not easy. 5 T 6 F; Vince doesn't earn a lot of money from finding gold. 7 T

Exercise 4 page 149

1 another prospector / a man he met 2 in an office
3 a plastic or metal dish 4 12 5 about £200 worth
6 £50,000 a year 7 about £12,000 a year

Exercise 5 page 149

Possible answers:

1 he was bored with it; he was excited about finding gold.

2 gold is very heavy, and rivers can't move it far.

3 the pieces are very small.

4 happy, because he is doing his dream job.

Exercise 6 page 149

Answers will vary.

READING 1

Learning objectives

- Understand key vocabulary for describing people – *blind, incredible, inspire*
- Skim a blog to identify the topic
- Read and understand main ideas and details in a blog about an unusual boy
- Read and sequence events in somebody's life story on a timeline
- Read and identify the meaning of a word from context
- Identify the possible author and their purpose in writing the blog
- Describe a famous young person and evaluate how their life differs from others'

Lead-in

Model the following activities and ask students to repeat them: tap your pencil, lightly stamp your foot, make clicking sounds with your mouth. Ask students how those sounds might help a person who is blind. If necessary, you can explain 'echolocation' – sounds can travel from their original source, bounce off a surface and then enter a person's ears. This helps blind people 'see' the things that are around them.

Exercise 1 page 150

1 operation **2** incredible **3** blind **4** talent **5** respect
6 inspire

Exercise 2 page 150

c

Exercise 3 page 152

a 3 **b** 1 **c** 4 **d** 2

Exercise 4 page 152

1 T **2** F; He was different from most other teenagers.
3 F; He learnt to 'see' with his ears.
4 F; Ben loved cycling his bike. **5** T **6** T

Exercise 5 page 152

1 b **2** e **3** a **4** c **5** g **6** d **7** f

Optional activity

👥 Write the following words and phrases on the board: *healthy, incredible, to bounce off something, to click, a dolphin, a bat, anything is possible.* Students work in pairs to remember what was said in the text about each word or phrase. They then look back at the text to check.

Exercise 6 page 153

b

Exercises 7–8 page 153

1 b **2** b

Exercise 9 page 153

Answers will vary.

READING 2

Learning objectives

- Understand key vocabulary for describing people – *look after, honest, intelligent*
- Read and understand main ideas in blog posts about special people
- Read and understand detail
- Make inferences about the possible authors of the blogs
- Synthesize information from blog posts about special people in a discussion

Lead-in

Take a poll on the most important things a person can achieve in his/her life. Students should rank the following 1–4, with 1 being the most important. Students then compare their answers with a partner and explain why they answered as they did.

Win the Nobel Peace Prize
Climb Mount Everest
Invent a new kind of technology
Bring up five children

Exercise 1 page 154

a dream **b** look after **c** brave **d** former **e** intelligent
f train **g** honest **h** achieve

Be flexible

👤 For a greater challenge, **more advanced students** could write their own sentences with the key vocabulary words and then check sentences with a partner.

Exercise 2 page 156

1 c **2** a **3** d **4** b

Exercise 3 page 156

1 In 2009, the Singapore Women's Everest team climbed Everest after seven years of training.
2 Malala Yousafzai donated $1.1 million to build a school in Pakistan.

3 Steve Jobs died in October 2011.

4 Mark's mother looks after Mark's nephew in hospital.

Exercise 4 page 156

Answers will vary. Suggested answers:

Explorer – most likely Li Chan

Teacher – most likely Jane Kloster

IT technician – most likely Ahmed Aziz

University student – most likely Mark Evans

Exercise 5 page 156

Answers will vary.

LANGUAGE DEVELOPMENT

Learning objectives

- Use correct word order in noun phrases with *of – the President of the country, a type of technology, the end of an essay*
- Differentiate between adjectives describing positive and negative characteristics – *reliable, confident, lazy*
- Use adjectives to complete sentences describing people's characters – *Luka is very honest. He always tells the truth. She always chats with students in other classes. She's so friendly.*

Exercise 1 page 157

1 c **2** d **3** g **4** e **5** f **6** a **7** b

Exercise 2 page 157

1 She is the new leader of the country.

2 I met a friend of my brother's.

3 My mother gave me a piece of cake.

4 A dentist is a kind of doctor.

5 He is the former director of technology.

6 Jules is one of my best friends.

7 I always feel tired in the middle of the day.

8 Our son has a good group of friends at his school.

Exercise 3 page 158

Positive: calm, clever, confident, friendly, honest, intelligent, kind, patient, reliable, sensible, shy, talented

Negative: difficult, lazy, selfish, shy, stupid

Note: *Shy* can be both positive and negative, depending on the context.

Exercise 4 page 158

1 honest **2** calm **3** friendly **4** shy **5** lazy **6** reliable
7 sensible **8** talented **9** selfish **10** clever; intelligent

Be flexible

Students choose five adjectives from the list that best describe them. They then work in pairs to explain why each adjective applies to them, giving specific examples where they have demonstrated each characteristic. They could also choose one or two of the adjectives which least apply to them, again supporting their arguments with specific examples. After a few minutes, ask volunteers to report back on what their partners said.

Ask **stronger students** to give a sentence describing their own behaviour, and other students guess which adjective best fits this behaviour. For example: *I don't like to go to parties because I am uncomfortable around people I don't know -> shy.*

CRITICAL THINKING

Learning objectives

- Organize characteristics of two people in a Venn diagram to identify similarities and differences
- Identify the characteristics of role models
- Evaluate a role model and add evidence to support your ideas

UNLOCK TEACHER DEVELOPMENT

BE INFORMED

→ **Categorizing ideas** is an important skill for students because: (1) It is an important stage of the research and writing process – once students have collected ideas, they need to categorize them in order to use them in the most effective way possible in their writing; (2) If students do not categorize information, their essays may be difficult to follow and lack coherence and cohesion; (3) Venn diagrams are one of the most useful visual tools that students can use to categorize information.

BE CONFIDENT

→ Develop this skill for yourself by doing the following activity:

Think of two people working in the field of education whom you admire. Complete the Venn diagram with adjectives which describe them. Write any adjectives which they share in the overlap.

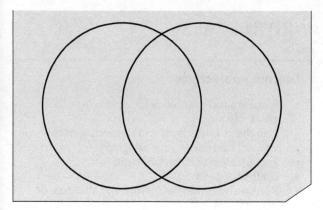

Lead-in

Tell students to read through the writing task. Elicit from the class where they can find a model for this task. (*Answer:* Any of the paragraphs in Reading 2).

UNLOCK TEACHER DEVELOPMENT

BE READY

Look at the Critical Thinking section in the Student's Book on pages 159–160.
➔ Which elements of the lesson do you think your students will find easiest / most difficult / most useful? Why?
➔ Are your answers true for all students in your class?
➔ How can you adapt your teaching or the material to meet your students' needs?

BE FLEXIBLE

A challenging, but interesting, variation of Exercise 1 is to get students to work together in larger groups (three or four) and to have a Venn diagram with three overlapping circles. They should choose three people out of Reading 2 and identify adjectives which describe all three of them (which would be placed in the middle) as well as characteristics which are shared by only two of the three people, and characteristics which only one person has.

Exercise 1 page 159
Answers will vary.

Exercise 2 page 160
a Singapore Women's Everest Team   **b** Mary Evans, Malala Yousafzai   **c** Steve Jobs, Malala Yousafzai
d Steve Jobs

Exercises 3–7 page 160
Answers will vary.

UNLOCK TEACHER DEVELOPMENT

BE REFLECTIVE

Think about the following points:
➔ Share your Venn diagram with a colleague. Explain to them why these people are role models to you. This can be a useful process for identifying the kind of characteristics you would like to incorporate into your own teaching.
➔ Think about the role models which your students chose in Exercise 3. This is a very useful source of information to get to know your students better. Knowing the kinds of people whom they find inspirational can help you better plan future lessons.

BE COLLABORATIVE

Your development is more meaningful when it's shared. See page 14 for ideas on how to peer-collaborate. Why not share the ideas you generated in the *Be ready* section, and their outcomes?

GRAMMAR FOR WRITING

Learning objectives

- Use modals and other phrases to describe the required characteristics of role models – *Good role models must work hard. Good role models must not be selfish. It is important for role models to be patient.*
- Use modals and other phrases to describe how people can accomplish their goals – *Jun should read a lot of literature. Hanif must work hard and save a lot of money. It is important to learn the language.*

Exercise 1 page 161
Answers will vary. Suggested answers:
1 Good role models should / must / have to work hard.
2 Good role models don't have to be / should be / must be famous.
3 Good role models should / must / have to ask others what they need.
4 Good role models should / must / have to be patient.
5 Good role models should not / must not be unfriendly to others.
6 Good role models don't have to be / should be / must be clever.

Exercise 2 page 162
1 It is important to be patient.
2 It is important to spend time with your family.
3 It is important to learn about other people.

4 It is important to get a good education.

5 It is important to be reliable.

Exercise 3 page 162

Answers will vary.

Exercise 4 page 162

Answers will vary. Possible answers:

2 Maria has to study hard and go to medical school.

3 Jun should read lots of different authors' books.

4 Thomas should not spend money on clothes or games.

5 Jamila must not spend too much time with her friends.

6 It is important for Helen to learn different languages.

ACADEMIC WRITING SKILLS

Learning objectives

- Evaluate concluding sentences for the end of a paragraph
- Relate topic sentences to concluding sentences
- Write concluding sentences for paragraphs about famous people and achievements

Exercise 1 page 163

a

Exercise 2 page 163

In summary

Exercise 3 page 163

b

Exercise 4 page 163

1 d   **2** c   **3** b   **4** a

Optional activity

Students look at the concluding sentences in Reading 2. Elicit what they have in common and how they know they are concluding sentences (*Possible answer:* the sentences give an opinion and repeat the main idea of the paragraph using different words).

Exercise 5 page 164

b

Exercise 6 page 164

Answers will vary. Possible answers:

1 In conclusion, Chan worked hard and invented something that could help a lot of people.

2 In summary, da Vinci was very talented and had a lot of different interests during his life.

3 In short, it takes a lot of hard work and patience to get the job that you want.

WRITING TASK

Learning objectives

- Prepare a topic sentence for a paragraph about a good role model
- Plan the characteristics and supporting details you will describe in your paragraph
- Prepare a concluding statement
- Draft your paragraph
- Review and revise the content and structure of your paragraph
- Review and revise the use of language in your paragraph

Exercises 1–9 pages 165–166

Answers will vary.

RESEARCH PROJECT

Do something amazing for people who are less fortunate than you in your community.

Explain to the class that they are going to think of something to help people who are less fortunate than them live better lives. They should form groups and brainstorm a list of charitable organizations in their area. The students can find out ways that people can help the charitable organization. Each group should then put a plan into action. They can decide to collect money, food or clothing and donate it to the organization. They can also decide to volunteer for a day. The students should report back to the class about their project.

Note: To help the students, you may want to bring in a list of charitable organizations in the area. You can then brainstorm with the class ways that people often help other people in need. You may need to preteach *volunteer*, and *donate*.

CLASSROOM APP

Exercises 1–2

Answers will vary.

Exercise 3

1 incredible   **2** talent   **3** honest   **4** look after   **5** former
6 inspired   **7** trains   **8** intelligent

Exercise 4

1 I saw a photo of your sister.

2 We hiked to the top of the mountain.

3 The history of my country is very interesting.

4 The education of children is necessary in every country.

5 Experts agree that there are many benefits of exercise.

Exercise 5

1 patient   **2** lazy   **3** clever   **4** reliable
5 intelligent   **6** selfish

Exercise 6

1 In short, he is one of the smartest kids in the world.

2 In summary, Olivia has many different interests.

3 In short, yoga has helped her remain active all her life.

4 In short, Curie achieved great things in her life.

UNIT OBJECTIVES

Watch and listen	Watch and understand a video about going to the International Space Station.
Reading skill	Identify the author's purpose.
Critical thinking	Evaluate arguments.
Grammar	Use *that* clauses in complex sentences; use infinitives of purpose; use *because* and *so*.
Academic writing skill	Organize an essay.
Writing task	Complete an opinion essay.
⟳ **Teacher development**	Help your students become better at **evaluating arguments**.

UNLOCK YOUR KNOWLEDGE

Background note

The photo shows the American astronaut Stephen K. Robinson in space. In the background, we can see the Earth. The astronaut's feet are attached to a robotic arm, which is part of the International Space Station. He is doing a spacewalk, also referred to as an extravehicular activity (EVA). During spacewalks, astronauts do science experiments, test new equipment and repair satellites or spacecraft. Most spacewalks last between five and eight hours.

Lead-in

Give the following situation for students to discuss in groups. Make sure you check or explain the key words (underlined) while you are setting up the discussions.

Tell students to imagine that they are going to spend a year in a spacecraft travelling through space. The spacecraft has everything they need (e.g. food, medicine), but nothing to make the journey less boring. They make a list of ten things to take with them. Afterwards, they present their lists to the class, and decide which team will have the most fun.

page 169

1 The person is doing a spacewalk / repairing a space station.

2–3 *Answers will vary.*

WATCH AND LISTEN

Learning objectives

- Listen and understand the main ideas in a video about visiting a space station
- Listen and understand numbers
- Listen and understand details
- Practise talking about space

Exercise 1 page 170
Answers will vary.

Exercise 2 page 170
Possible answers: **Adjectives:** weightless, exciting, dangerous, amazing, difficult
Nouns: space suit, space shuttle, gravity, astronaut, rocket

Exercise 3 page 171
1 She is an astronaut.   **2** The International Space Station
3 She got there in a rocket.   **4** Traffic
5 Her drive to work

Exercise 4 page 171
1 15–20   **2** two   **3** four   **4** 250   **5** nine

Exercise 5 page 171
1 The rocket is ~~American~~ Russian.
2 The trip took ~~double~~ half the time it takes her to drive to work.
3 She travelled in a ~~big~~ tiny capsule.
4 She went with a Russian cosmonaut and a ~~Korean~~ Japanese astronaut.
5 They rode the lift to the ~~bottom~~ top.

Exercise 6 page 171
Answers will vary.

READING 1

Learning objectives

- Understand key vocabulary for space travel – *explore, advances, beyond*
- Discuss questions about space travel to activate your knowledge
- Read and understand the main ideas in a text about space travel
- Read and understand detail
- Identify the author's purpose and the context of the article
- Express opinions on space travel

Lead-in

Students work in small groups. Tell them they are going to read about the past, present and future of space travel. Give each group an index card with a key word/phrase from the reading. They should note on the index card what, if anything, they know about their assigned key word/phrase, and then pass the index card to another group to do the same. Once all groups have seen all index cards, write the key words/phrases on the board. Students can then scan the reading to add more information to the notes on the board.

Suggested key words/phrases: Sputnik I, NASA, men walked on the moon, SpaceX, Elon Musk, Sir Richard Branson, Virgin Galactic

Exercise 1 page 172

a entrepreneur **b** advance **c** private **d** explore **e** beyond **f** crash **g** public

Exercise 2 page 172

Answers will vary.

Exercise 3 page 174

1 The era when governments began sending spacecraft into space. It continues, as several countries still send astronauts, cosmonauts and spacecraft into space.
2 To make new discoveries in space, especially on Mars.
3 To take people to the moon and back; to take people to Mars.
4 Private companies don't need money from the government.

Exercise 4 page 174

1 F; The Soviet Union sent *Sputnik I* into space, and it was the first successful spacecraft to orbit the Earth.
2 F; Entrepreneurs like Elon Musk and Sir Richard Branson don't have to wait for government money in order to build new spacecraft.

3 F; In 2014, a SpaceX spacecraft crashed in the Mojave Desert and killed its pilot.
4 T 5 T

Exercise 5 page 174

1 b 2 a 3 b

Exercise 6 page 175

Answers will vary.

READING 2

Learning objectives

- Understand key vocabulary for hypothetical science – *wonder, support, evidence*
- Skim a text to identify text type
- Read and identify the main ideas in each paragraph of an essay about life on other planets
- Read and understand details
- Make an inference about an idea in the article
- Differentiate between facts and opinions expressed by the essay writer
- Identify the purpose and beliefs of the essay writer
- Rank inventions in order of importance
- Synthesize information from an article about space travel and an essay about life on other planets in a discussion

Lead-in

Ask: *When scientists say they are searching for life on other planets, what kind of "life" could they mean?* (trees, animals, people). Ask: *What conditions are necessary to support life on other planets?* (air, water, animals, trees). Ask: *How can scientists learn more about conditions on other planets?* (send cameras, use telescopes).

Exercise 1 page 175

1 a 2 b 3 b 4 a 5 a 6 b 7 b 8 a

Exercise 2 page 176

b

Optional activity

👥 👥 Students work in pairs to think of arguments for and against the statement in the title. After a few minutes, elicit a range of arguments from the class. When students read the text in Exercise 3, they can check which of the ideas from the board are mentioned.

Exercise 3 page 176

a 2 **b** 4 **c** 1 **d** 3

Exercise 4 page 176

1 Thousands **2** The Kepler telescope **3** A planet (that is similar to Earth) **4** Princeton University **5** Scientific evidence

Exercise 5 page 178

Answers will vary.

Possible answers: because the telescope that discovered it is called Kepler; because it is the 22nd system that was discovered; because it orbits a star that is called 22a.

Exercise 6 page 178

1 O **2** F **3** O **4** F

Exercise 7 page 178

1 b **2** b **3** a

Exercises 8–9 page 178

Answers will vary.

LANGUAGE DEVELOPMENT

Learning objectives

- Identify the meaning of nouns to describe the existence of scientific support for your arguments – *report, study, research, expert*
- Use verbs to complete sentences giving scientific support for an argument – *Experts believe that the moon is too cold for people to live there. Reports show that parts of Mars were once covered in ice.*

Exercise 1 page 179

1 expert **2** report / study **3** research

Exercise 2 page 179

1 think / believe **2** show / suggest **3** think / believe **4** show / suggest **5** shows / suggests

Be flexible

👤 Ask **stronger students** to look at the last paragraph in Reading 2. Do the verbs *think* and *believe* have the same function here as in the rest of the reading? (*Answer:* No, here they do not introduce the views of experts or the scientific observations. Instead, they report the author's conclusions, based on his or her review of research.)

CRITICAL THINKING

Learning objectives

- Analyze an essay's introductory paragraph and identify the main argument
- Identify supporting reasons for the main argument in an essay
- Identify opinions about funding for space travel in different sources
- Organize arguments, reasons and evidence in a T-chart
- Evaluate the arguments and add further support
- Explain your views on funding space travel

UNLOCK TEACHER DEVELOPMENT

BE INFORMED

→ **Evaluating arguments** is an important skill for students because: (1) Different people/organizations can interpret the same thing in very different ways; (2) Sometimes people can sound very convincing (e.g. by using good language) when the actual content of their argument is weak; (3) When writing essays, you are assessed not on how many arguments you make, but on the quality of your arguments.

BE CONFIDENT

→ Develop these skills for yourself by doing the following activity:

Imagine that a group of teachers were asked: 'Are your students good at critical thinking?'. These are some of the responses.

'My students are poor critical thinkers because they don't enjoy it.'

'My students are really good at critical thinking, so I must be a good teacher.'

'My students don't have any opportunity to practise critical thinking, so they don't improve.'

'My students work hard to improve their critical thinking skills because they see its relevance to their studies and lives.'

1 Which of these arguments is the strongest? Which is the weakest?

2 What is the problem with the arguments which are poorly supported? How could they be improved?

Lead-in

Tell students to read the writing task to decide where in Unit 8 they can find a good model (*Possible answer:* Reading 2, which is also an opinion essay, although it is rather longer than the essay that students will need to write). Another good model would be the opinion paragraphs on page 181.

UNL⊘CK TEACHER DEVELOPMENT

BE READY

Look at the Critical Thinking section in the Student's Book on pages 180–182.

→ Which elements of the lesson do you think your students will find easiest / most difficult / most useful? Why?

→ Are your answers true for all students in your class?

→ How can you adapt your teaching or the material to meet your students' needs?

BE FLEXIBLE

Think of a recent event (e.g. in the news, or in your school/college) where different people have different opinions about the same thing. This could be a good introduction to the topic – or offer a good opportunity to apply this knowledge.

Exercise 1 page 180

The author does not believe that there is life on other planets.

Exercise 2 page 180

Paragraph 2: Although it has the right conditions, experts with the best technology can see no signs of life on Kepler 22B. Until there is hard evidence, we cannot use Kepler 22b to support the idea of life on other planets.

Paragraph 3: Earth has the perfect conditions for life, and it is highly unlikely that another planet has exactly the same environment as Earth. In addition, although scientists believe that life might exist on other planets, they have never found evidence to prove it.

Exercise 3 page 180

a Governments around the world should spend more money on space programmes.

b More money should be spent on people who need clean water and food, on access to education and on medical research. Governments should spend more money on ocean exploration than on space exploration.

c Uncovering the mysteries of space is a huge task that should continue to be funded. Governments should absolutely spend more money on space programmes.

Exercise 4 page 182

For: brings many countries together (a); astronauts take part in important experiments (a); is necessary for long-term space journeys (to Mars) (a); proves countries can work together (a); makes technological advances (c); encourages young people to study Science and Engineering (c); results in medical advances (c); improves life on Earth by doing research in space (c)

Against: expensive (b); dangerous (b); wastes natural resources (b); spends money that should be used on other things that people need (clean water and food, access to education, medical research) (b).

Exercises 5–7 page 182

Answers will vary.

UNL⊘CK TEACHER DEVELOPMENT

BE REFLECTIVE

Think about the following questions:

→ Evaluate how successful your teaching of critical thinking was. Which part was most successful? Which part was least successful? Why?

→ If you heard one of your teaching colleagues making one of the weak arguments (or similar) in the *Be confident* section, what could you say to them?

BE COLLABORATIVE

Your development is more meaningful when it's shared. See page 14 for ideas on how to peer-collaborate. Why not share what you did in the *Be flexible* section, and its outcome?

GRAMMAR FOR WRITING

Learning objectives

- Use correct word order in sentences with *that* clauses – *NASA scientists learnt that human bones can become weaker in space. Many people are sure that they will travel to Mars someday.*
- Rewrite quotations with reporting verbs followed by *that* clauses – *Elon Musk said that SpaceX built Dragon in order to deliver supplies to the International Space Station.*
- Give reasons for exploring space using infinitives of purpose with or without *in order* – *We explore space (in order) to discover new life.*
- Use *because* and *so* to express cause and effect relationships – *I'm studying Maths and Physics because I want to be an engineer. I want to be an engineer, so I'm studying Maths and Physics.*

Exercise 1 page 184

1 Scientists believe that we could live on the moon by 2050.

2 Reports show that Pluto is not a planet.

3 Some people think that TV programmes are a good way to learn about science.

4 Studies suggest that life could exist on other planets.

Exercise 2 page 184

Answers will vary. Possible answers:

2 Sir Richard Branson thinks that regular people should have the opportunity to travel in space.

3 Researchers at Princeton University doubt that alien life exists.

4 NASA stated that the Kepler telescope looks for liveable planets beyond Earth.

Exercise 3 page 184

1 b   **2** c   **3** a

Exercise 4 page 184

Answers will vary.

Exercise 5 page 185

2 d   **3** a   **4** b   **5** c

Exercise 6 page 185

A results   **B** reasons

Exercise 7 page 185

1 Result: I'm studying Maths and Physics; **Reason:** because I want to be an engineer.   **2 Reason:** I want to be an engineer; **Result:** so I'm studying Maths and Physics.

Exercise 8 page 185

2 I'm studying Mars because I want to explore new places.
I want to explore new places, so I'm studying Mars.

3 I want to design spaceships, so I study Engineering.
I study Engineering because I want to design spaceships.

4 I bought a telescope because I like to look at the stars and planets.
I like to look at the stars and planets, so I bought a telescope.

5 I want to be an entrepreneur, so I study Business.
I study Business because I want to be an entrepreneur.

Optional activity

👥 Students work in pairs. Tell them to think of two to three actions they are doing in their life. They should write the reasons and the results of their actions on pieces of paper, along with their name. Mix up the pieces of paper and hand them out to pairs in random order. The pairs write sentences about their classmates, based on the information they received. Volunteers can read their sentences aloud.

ACADEMIC WRITING SKILLS

Learning objectives

- Understand the sections of an academic essay
- Identify the key features of each section of an academic essay

Exercise 1 page 186

1 first   **2** middle   **3** one   **4** last

Exercise 2 page 186

1 Background information: For many years, people have wondered whether we are the only living things in the universe. Some scientists believe that there must be life on other planets because the universe is so big. However, it is unlikely that there is life on other planets because planets need a very specific environment for life to start.

Thesis statement: In the end, there are no facts that support the idea of life on other planets.

2 Facts, reasons and examples: one of these planets, named Kepler 22b, has the right conditions – the right atmosphere and temperature – to support life; a planet needs very particular conditions to have life; it is very unlikely that another planet has exactly the same environment as Earth; although scientists believe that life might exist on other planets, they have never found evidence to prove it; a recent report from Princeton University suggests that it is very unlikely that there is life on other planets; we don't have enough scientific evidence to decide if there is life on other planets; just because similar conditions to Earth exist on other planets, it doesn't mean that life could exist.

3 Phrases that retell the main points in the essay: Although the universe is very big, a planet with life needs very special conditions; I do not think that any other planets could have exactly the same conditions as Earth.

The writer's opinion: In conclusion, I do not believe that there is life on other planets. / Therefore, I do not think that there could be life on other planets.

WRITING TASK

Learning objectives

- Understand the sections of an essay planner
- Use an essay planner to draft an opinion essay about funding space exploration
- Review and revise the content and structure of your essay
- Review and revise the use of language in your essay

Exercise 1 page 187

a 2 and 3   **b** 4   **c** 1 and 4   **d** *Answers will vary.*

Answers will vary.

RESEARCH PROJECT

Plan a lesson to teach local school children about the solar system.

Divide the class into teams and explain that they will be producing teaching materials for a lesson on the solar system. They should brainstorm the material's objectives, discuss the age of their prospective audience and the types of activities they will use. They should produce a comprehensive plan including aims, methodology and challenges and write self-reflection pieces afterwards.

CLASSROOM APP

Exercise 1
Answers will vary.

Exercise 2
1 crashed **2** wonder **3** beyond **4** unlikely **5** explore
6 conditions **7** proved **8** support

Exercise 3
Answers will vary.

Exercise 4
1 Research shows that water exists on the moon's surface.
2 Experts believe that vegetables can successfully grow in space.
3 Studies suggest that astronauts may grow taller or shorter in space.
4 Scientists think that there are more than 100 billion galaxies in our universe.
5 Reports show that the body temperature of astronauts rises in space.

Exercise 5
1 that they are **2** she loves **3** that you didn't
4 that they must **5** he was

Exercise 6
1 main body **2** introductory **3** main body
4 concluding **5** introductory **6** introductory

UNIT OBJECTIVES

Watch and listen	Watch and understand a video about great egret and dolphin fishing teamwork.
Reading skill	Read for main ideas in academic texts.
Critical thinking	Compare and contrast facts.
Grammar	Use comparative adjectives; use correct word order; combine sentences with *and, or, but, whereas, both, neither*.
Academic writing skill	Write topic sentences.
Writing task	Complete a comparison-and-contrast essay.
⟳ **Teacher development**	Help your students become better at **comparing and contrasting facts**.

UNLOCK YOUR KNOWLEDGE

Background note

The photo shows a majestic male lion in its natural habitat, standing in tall grass and bathed in a warm evening light. The photo was taken in the Maasai Mara National Reserve in Kenya. The reserve was created to protect the local animal population, as well as the environment. It is well known for its remarkable population of wild cats, as well as the annual migration of wildebeest, during which more than 1.5 million animals travel to new territories. At Maasai Mara, visitors can go on car or balloon safaris and see the wild animals in their natural environment.

Lead-in

Ask students for examples of typical weekend activities for families with small children. Elicit *a trip to the zoo* (or similar) and ask one or two of the students for their early memories of such trips.

page 15

1 *Possible answer:* Many people think it is better to see animals in the wild because they can then be appreciated in their natural habitat. However, seeing animals in a zoo means that people who cannot travel can still see animals from other parts of the world.

2 *Answers will vary.*

3 *Possible answer:* Many regions rely on animals for heavy work, such as pulling ploughs or transporting goods or people. Animals can provide materials such as wool and leather. Animals also provide meat and dairy produce such as milk and cheese.

4 *Answers will vary.*

WATCH AND LISTEN

Learning objectives

- Listen and identify the main ideas in a video about the relationship between two animal species
- Listen and understand details about animal behaviour
- Practise talking about animals working together

Exercise 1 page 16
Answers will vary.

Exercise 2 page 16
Possible answers:
1 to get food   2 They help/protect each other.
3 They both eat fish so live in similar places.

Exercise 3 page 17
a 4   b 1   c 5   d 2   e 3

Exercise 4 page 17
1 T
2 F; The dolphins push the fish onto the shore.
3 F; When the fish are out of the water, the dolphins start eating.
4 F; The dolphins always use their right sides to push the fish.
5 DNS

Exercise 5 page 17
Answers will vary.

READING 1

Learning objectives

- Understand key vocabulary for endangered animals – *species, protect, endangered*
- Categorize details in an essay about endangered species
- Read and identify the main idea in each paragraph in an essay about endangered species
- Read and understand details
- Read and identify academic synonyms from their context in the article
- Discuss the use of animal products and give opinions on protecting animal habitats

Exercise 1 page 18

1 endangered   2 species   3 chemicals   4 pollute
5 destroys   6 due to   7 natural   8 protect

Exercise 2 page 18

An endangered species is a species that may soon not exist because there are very few left alive. An extinct species is one that no longer exists.

Possible answers:

endangered species: giant panda, Chinese alligator, Indian elephant, white rhinoceros, sea turtle

extinct species: Tyrannosaurus rex, woolly mammoth, dodo, Caspian tiger, sabre tooth tiger, woolly rhinoceros

Lead-in

Students consider the animals they listed in the table and think of reasons why those particular animals are endangered or extinct. For example, if students say elephants are endangered, the reason why is because their ivory tusks are sold illegally for very high prices.

Exercise 3 page 19

Added to endangered species column: Arabian oryx, some seal species, tigers, crocodiles, whales, tuna, sharks

Exercise 4 page 20

a 3   b 1   c 4   d 2

Exercise 5 page 20

1 humans / human activities   2 Their habitats are destroyed.   3 for food; for fur to make coats and skin to make bags and shoes; for sport; to make medicines and teas from their bones   4 whales, tuna and sharks
5 We can try not to pollute natural areas and refuse to buy products made from animals.   6 Governments can make it against the law to hunt, fish, or trade in endangered species.   7 animal sanctuaries and zoos

Exercise 6 page 20

1 face a financial penalty   2 refusing to buy   3 against the law   4 provide funding for   5 cooperate by taking these steps

Exercise 7 page 21

1 *Possible answers:* perfume, fur coats, leather gloves, bags, some glues and fabric softeners

2 *Answers will vary.*

Optional activity

Ask the students to find out what their own local or national governments are doing to conserve animal habitats. Is this seen as a controversial issue?

READING 2

Learning objectives

- Understand key vocabulary for animal protection – *common, cruel, disease*
- Read and understand main ideas in an article about invasive species
- Read and identify the correct words to complete a summary of the text
- Make inferences about invasive species from the information in the article
- Synthesize information from an essay about endangered species and an article about invasive species in a discussion

Lead-in

Show the students a blank outline map of the United Kingdom, with the borders between England, Scotland, Wales and Northern Ireland on it, but not the countries' names. Elicit the names of the countries. Finally, point out the Isle of Wight in the very south of England.

Exercise 1 page 21

1 common   2 fatal   3 disease   4 cruel   5 major
6 survive   7 native   8 introduce

Exercise 2 page 21

1 (red and grey) squirrels   2 *Answers will vary.*

Exercise 3 page 22

1 An invasive species is a plant or animal that arrives in an area where it is not native.

2 Grey squirrels were introduced from North America by people who wanted them as a fashionable addition to the grounds of their homes.

3 Red and grey squirrels both have long tails, large eyes, small ears and powerful back legs.

4 Red squirrels are smaller and lighter than grey squirrels.

5 The reasons stated for the success of the grey squirrel in the UK are:

They are better able to store fat, which helps them survive hard winters.

They spend more time on the ground, so are not as badly affected by the loss of woodland habits as red squirrels.

They are more intelligent and better able to adapt to new situations, e.g. they can use food provided by humans.

They carry parapoxvirus but are not affected by it, while it is fatal to red squirrels.

Exercise 4 page 22

1 grey **2** fewer **3** fatter **4** able **5** kills **6** pest
7 few **8** aren't

Exercise 5 page 22

Possible answers:

1 in ships; in wood products; in garden plants or food produce; via the pet trade; by illegal animal trading

2 Because they damage trees, they eat humans' food and they carry a virus that kills red squirrels.

3 Perhaps because they are the only native squirrel species in the UK and people don't want to lose it.

4 Because it is an island, and the sea acts as a natural defence against invasive species.

Exercise 6 page 24

1 *Possible answers:* habitat destruction, disease, climate
2–4 *Answers will vary.*

Be flexible

With **more advanced students**, you might want to introduce other terms similar to *introduced animal species* such as *non-indigenous species* (though these do not only refer to those that have been deliberately introduced). Such plants and animals can threaten native wildlife by competing with them for the same food and habitat. Encourage students to make a list and add other collocations with the word *species* that they come across in their reading and research.

LANGUAGE DEVELOPMENT

Learning objectives

- Read and identify the meaning of academic verbs from their context – *survive, affect, release*
- Use the correct form of comparative adjectives to complete sentences about animals – *The grey squirrel is larger than the red squirrel. The red squirrel is less common than the grey squirrel.*

Exercise 1 page 24

a cooperate **b** affect **c** release **d** survive **e** contrast
f attach

Exercise 2 page 25

1 weaker than **2** healthier than **3** more successful than
4 more endangered than

Optional activity

Give students several small strips of paper. They write one type of animal on each strip. Collect the strips and put the students into small teams. Randomly select two strips of paper and read the animals to the class (or ask a volunteer to do it). Each team should write as many sentences using comparative adjectives as they can. Give each team one point for each correct sentence. Repeat the process. The team with the most points at the end wins. Provide **lower-level students** with a sentence frame to complete the task (e.g. _____ *are more* _____ *than* _____.). Then ask students to read back their sentences to check the forms and pronunciation. Saying words aloud not only helps students connect the written word to the oral, it also helps them commit words and grammatical forms to memory. After students have had an opportunity to use the sentence frame, erase it so students now recall and generate sentences on their own.

CRITICAL THINKING

Learning objectives

- Use a Venn diagram to compare and contrast two animal species
- Understand diagrams and write sentences comparing two shark species
- Understand and compare information about two shark species
- Complete a Venn diagram comparing and contrasting two shark species

UNLOCK TEACHER DEVELOPMENT

BE INFORMED

➔ **Comparing and contrasting facts** is an important skill for students because: (1) The ability to compare and contrast facts is essential in every single academic subject; (2) Students often do not know how to identify similarities and differences, and so need to develop techniques such as using Venn diagrams to do this; (3) Whilst students are often able to be descriptive when comparing and contrasting, they are often not analytical enough.

BE CONFIDENT

→ Develop this skill for yourself by doing the following activity:

Think about your own teaching practice, specifically the way in which you teach now, and the way in which you taught at the beginning of your career. Then, complete the Venn diagram below.

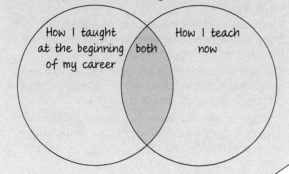

Lead-in

At this point in each unit students are asked to begin to think about the writing task they will do at the end of the unit. Give them a minute to read the box and to look at the diagram below it.

UNLOCK TEACHER DEVELOPMENT

BE READY

Look at the Critical Thinking section in the Student's Book on pages 26–28.

→ Which elements of the lesson do you think your students will find easiest / most difficult / most useful? Why?

→ Are your answers true for all students in your class?

→ How can you adapt your teaching or the material to meet your students' needs?

BE FLEXIBLE

After Exercise 4, an interesting area to explore with students is that animals which are larger and heavier are not necessarily more dangerous – small animals can also be very dangerous (e.g. mosquitoes). Discuss with students whether any other facts about the animals surprised them.

Exercise 1 page 26

Possible answers:

red squirrels: red in colour; only 140,000 left; not seen as pests, protected; smaller and lighter; shorter tail; store less fat, so more likely to die in winter; live high up in trees; less intelligent, so can't survive as well; in an urban environment, can't eat human food; can die from parapoxvirus

both: live in Britain; long tail, large eyes, small ears, powerful back legs; can carry parapoxvirus

grey squirrels: grey in colour; very common; seen as pests, can be trapped and destroyed; larger and heavier; longer tail; store more fat, so survive winter more easily; spend most of their time on the ground; more intelligent, so can survive better; in an urban environment, can eat human food; don't die from parapoxvirus

Exercise 2 page 26

Answers will vary.

Exercise 3 page 27

Possible answers:

1 The whale shark is larger/longer than the tiger shark.
2 The sharks have a different colour on their backs and sides, but they both have a white stomach.
3 The tiger shark has stripes on its back, but the whale shark has spots.
4 The whale shark has a larger mouth than the tiger shark.
5 Both sharks have the same number of fins, but the whale shark has a longer tail and larger fins.

Exercise 4 page 27

1 T 2 W 3 T 4 W 5 W 6 T

Exercise 5 page 28

Possible answers:

whale shark: grey-blue in colour with white stomach and white spots; longer (5.5–10 m); longer tail and wider fins; heavier (18 tonnes); eats plankton, krill and other small animals; currently endangered; no recorded attacks on humans

both: chondrichthyes (fish); live in the ocean

tiger shark: grey-brown in colour with white stomach and darker grey-brown stripes; shorter (3–4.2 m); shorter tail and fins; lighter (0.86 tonnes); eats tuna, dolphins and turtles; not at risk of extinction; many reports of attacks on humans

UNLOCK TEACHER DEVELOPMENT

BE REFLECTIVE

Think about the following questions:

→ Compare your answers from the *Be confident* section with a colleague. What similarities and differences are there in your responses to this question? You can do this electronically or face-to-face.

→ Did your students already know about Venn diagrams and how they work? If so, was this knowledge universal, or did some know and some not know? Understanding their levels of background knowledge can help you plan more effectively throughout the course.

BE COLLABORATIVE

Your development is more meaningful when it is shared. See page 14 for ideas on how to peer-collaborate. Why not share the ideas you generated in the *Be flexible* section, and their outcome?

GRAMMAR FOR WRITING

Learning objectives

- Use correct word order in sentences.
- Use *and* and *or* to avoid repetition in sentences about the same subject – *The tiger shark has sharp teeth and a powerful bite. The tiger shark is not an endangered or a protected species.*
- Use *but* and *whereas* to link contrasting ideas in sentences – *The tiger shark has sharp teeth and a powerful bite, whereas the whale shark does not have sharp teeth or a powerful bite.*
- Use *both* and *neither* to write sentences describing similarities between types of squirrels – *Both the grey and red squirrel carry squirrel parapoxvirus. Neither the grey nor the red squirrel has large ears.*

Exercise 1 page 29

1 The tiger shark lives in tropical oceans.
2 However, the whale shark isn't dangerous.
3 The tiger shark has markings on its skin.
4 The whale shark has a large mouth and eats plankton.

Be flexible

👤 👥 Provide **lower-level students** with additional practice. Tell them to choose sentences from the reading texts (or create them themselves) to match the grammatical forms in the chart on page 28 (subject, verb and object; subject, verb, adjective, prepositional phrase; and linker, subject, verb, prepositional phrase). Ask students to read the sentences aloud and as a class decide if they match the forms given.

Exercise 2 page 29

1 The whale shark is grey-blue and has light spots on its body.
2 The tiger shark is grey-brown and has a striped pattern on its body.

3 The tiger shark eats large sea creatures and can be dangerous to humans.
4 The whale shark is not aggressive or dangerous to swim with.
5 The whale shark is an endangered and (a) protected species.

Exercise 3 page 30

Possible answers:

1 The whale shark is grey-blue and has light spots on its body, but/whereas the tiger shark is grey-brown and has a striped pattern on its body.
2 The tiger shark eats large sea creatures and can be dangerous to humans, but/whereas the whale shark is not aggressive or dangerous to swim with.
3 The tiger shark is not an endangered or protected species, but/whereas the whale shark is (an endangered and protected species).

Exercise 4 page 30

Possible answers:

1 Both the red (squirrel) and the grey squirrel have long tails. / Both red (squirrels) and grey squirrels have long tails.
2 Neither the red (squirrel) nor the grey squirrel live on the Isle of Man. / Neither red (squirrels) nor grey squirrels live on the Isle of Man.
3 Neither the grey nor the red squirrel is an endangered species.
4 Both red (squirrels) and grey squirrels live in forests.

Optional activity

👤 👥 Ask students to each write down two sentences, one using *neither* and one using *both*. Elicit examples and lead a discussion on the differences between the two. Then ask students to check their ideas against the *both* and *neither* Grammar box.

ACADEMIC WRITING SKILLS

Learning objectives

- Understand the different types of topic sentence used in body paragraphs in academic essays
- Identify appropriate topic sentences for body paragraphs about animals

Exercise 1 page 31

1 b, c 2 a 3 Each paragraph has between one and seven supporting sentences, which differ in length. This suggests that there is no 'correct' number of sentences in a paragraph.

Exercise 2 page 32

1 b, c   **2** a, b

WRITING TASK

Learning objectives

- Draft two body paragraphs for an essay comparing and contrasting two sharks
- Review and revise the content and structure of the essay
- Review and edit the use of language in the essay

Exercises 1–6 pages 33–34

Answers will vary.

RESEARCH PROJECT

Educate people about endangered species in your region.

Divide the class into groups and ask them to research these questions:

What endangered animals are there in your part of the world?
Why are they endangered? How can we help them?
Why are animals important to us?

Students should create a blog to answer the questions. Each group should write a blog post on their assigned topic and think of a headline for their post. The whole class should think of a name for the blog. Students can publish their blog online.

CLASSROOM APP

Exercise 1

Answers will vary.

Exercise 2

1 common   **2** destroy   **3** disease   **4** cruel   **5** fatal
6 native   **7** polluted   **8** protect

Exercise 3

Answers will vary.

Exercise 4

1 cooperate   **2** attached   **3** affects   **4** contrast
5 release   **6** survive

Exercise 5

1 On average, donkeys are shorter than horses.
2 Because they are bigger, horses are heavier than donkeys.
3 Donkeys are usually less nervous than horses.
4 Horses are less curious than donkeys.
5 As sport animals, horses are more popular than donkeys.

Exercise 6

1 and   **2** neither   **3** but   **4** but   **5** both
6 or   **7** Both   **8** nor

UNIT OBJECTIVES

Watch and listen	Watch and understand a video about the natural environment.
Reading skills	Read for detail; identify purpose and audience.
Critical thinking	Analyze cause and effect.
Grammar	Use verbs of cause and effect; use *because* and *because of*.
Academic writing skills	Understand paragraph unity; write supporting sentences and details; give examples.
Writing task	Complete a cause-and-effect essay.
⟳ **Teacher development**	Help your students become better at **analyzing cause and effect**.

UNLOCK YOUR KNOWLEDGE

Background note

The photo shows old, rusty ships lying on sand at the bottom of the Aral Sea, between Kazakhstan and Uzbekistan. The Aral Sea used to be one of the world's largest lakes, with an area of 68,000 km². However, since the 1960s, the rivers that flowed into the lake have been used to provide water for crops instead. This has caused the lake to shrink – by 2007, the lake was only 10% of its original size. The remaining water is very salty, which has destroyed most of its fish, animals and plants. The boats shown in the photo belong to the old fishing communities that used to surround the lake. These villages are now more than 150 km from the water and are a symbol of the disastrous effects on the local environment.

Lead-in

Ask the students to discuss in pairs the small steps that people can take in their daily lives to protect the environment. They can also discuss whether they personally take any of those steps. Give the students two minutes to discuss their answers and then put pairs together to discuss their ideas. Allow three to five minutes for discussion. Then go on to Exercise 1.

page 37

1 This is the Aral Sea in Central Asia. It was once one of the world's four largest freshwater lakes. Its size has declined significantly since the 1960s. Diverting the rivers which feed it for irrigation projects has been stated as the main cause.

2–4 *Answers will vary.*

WATCH AND LISTEN

Learning objectives

- Listen and identify the main ideas in a video about the natural environment
- Listen and identify details
- Practise talking about the future of the natural environment

Exercise 1 page 38

1 Aurora Borealis (the Northern Lights), Grand Canyon, Great Barrier Reef, Harbour of Rio de Janeiro, Mount Everest, Paricutín; Victoria Falls   **2–3** *Answers will vary.*

Exercise 2 page 38

Possible answers:

1 They are all in the United States.

2 Millions of years old (the rocks are almost two billion years old).

3 The landscapes were all formed by water, sometimes in the form of glaciers.

Exercise 3 page 39

a 3   **b** 4   **c** 5   **d** 1   **e** 2   **f** 6

Exercise 4 page 39

1 b   **2** b   **3** c   **4** b   **5** a

Exercise 5 page 39

Answers will vary.

READING 1

Learning objectives

- Understand key vocabulary for climate change – *ecosystem, climate, threaten*
- Read and identify the main ideas in an article about a glacier which is shrinking
- Scan an article to find specific details
- Use topic sentences to find supporting details in an article
- Identify the purpose and audience of an article
- Explain the advantages and disadvantages of environmental change and renewable energy

Lead-in

Students work in small groups. Write three issues on the board: *Rise in global temperature; Rise in global sea levels; Increase in human population*. Assign one issue to each group. They brainstorm the damage that may be caused to the environment as a result of their assigned issue. After a few minutes, the groups can come to the board and write their ideas under their assigned issue. When everybody is finished, the groups can read each other's ideas and add more ideas to them. For a large class, students can write their ideas on paper, and then pass it to another group. Students then compare their answers with the reading.

Exercise 1 page 40

a greenhouse gas   **b** cause   **c** atmosphere   **d** climate
e global warming   **f** threaten   **g** ecosystem
h fossil fuels

Exercise 2 page 40

1 It has melted.   2 It is likely to be global warming.
3 The Arctic, the Alps, Alaska and other mountain areas around the world.
4 Sea levels will rise and many coastal areas will be underwater.

Exercise 3 page 42

solution to the problem 4; changing ecosystems 2; melting glaciers 1; causes of climate change 3

Exercise 4 page 42

1 global temperatures   2 extinction   3 Sea levels
4 mangrove forests   5 coral reefs   6 farming
7 CO$_2$ levels

Exercise 5 page 43

1 Argentina   2 Northwest Passage   3 to provide land for growing food   4 asthma   5 greenhouse gases (such as methane and carbon dioxide)   6 cutting down trees
7 stop burning fossil fuels, start using renewable energy

Be flexible

👥 Challenge **more advanced students** to determine what types of information supporting details might add. Students refer to the types of supporting details that are listed in the Skills box on page 42. Then for each supporting detail they write in Exercise 5, they discuss with a partner what type of supporting detail it is (fact, statistic, example, etc.). Ask students to present their ideas to another pair or share with the class and explain their choices. Encourage them to refer to language within the sentence or text to justify their answers.

Exercise 6 page 43

1 a   2 b

Exercise 7 page 43

Answers will vary.

Exercise 8 page 43

Possible answers:

1 An increase in land for farming; new transport routes; increased fresh water; melt water can be used for hydroelectric power.
2 The start-up costs can be expensive; some people say that things like solar panels and wind turbines are ugly; some renewable energy sources aren't suitable for certain countries.

READING 2

Learning objectives

- Understand key vocabulary for deforestation – *rainforest, destruction, logging*
- Read and complete a summary of an essay about deforestation
- Read and understand details
- Make inferences about the meaning of phrases in the essay
- Make inferences about the implication for the future of the ideas in the essay
- Synthesize information from an article about a glacier and an essay about deforestation in a discussion

Exercise 1 page 44

Possible answers:

1 They release oxygen into the atmosphere, provide shade and are home to many species of animals.
2 People cut down trees to clear land for farming or to provide wood for building.
3 The Earth's temperature will rise, erosion will cause dust storms and floods, animals will lose their habitats.

Exercise 2 page 44

1 absorb   2 Farming   3 Logging   4 rainforest
5 construction   6 effects   7 destruction

Exercise 3 page 46

1 deforestation   2 effects   3 animals   4 crops
5 decade   6 erosion   7 warming   8 habitats
9 protected   10 environment

Exercise 4 page 46

1 ~~olive~~ palm   2 ~~ten years~~ two or three years   3 ~~2.5~~ 25
times   4 ~~protects~~ destroys   5 ~~oxygen~~ carbon dioxide
6 ~~Small-scale~~ Large-scale

Exercise 5 page 46

Possible answers:

1 logging and farming that are done on a large scale by
giant corporations
2 The Earth's climate will become much warmer and
thousands of plants and animals will become extinct.
3 Many of the foods we eat and medicines we use come
from forests.

Exercise 6 page 47

Possible answers:

1 Low-lying islands, cities near coastlines and places with
more rain and storms will have too much water. Places
that are normally dry, such as Australia and certain
African countries will become even drier.
2 As the glaciers and forests disappear, the animals that
live there lose their habitat and/or food sources and
they die out.

LANGUAGE DEVELOPMENT

Learning objectives

- Use academic synonyms in sentences about
  environmental issues – *issue, predict, trend*
- Use environment collocations to complete
  sentences about the environment – *climate
  change, natural resource, greenhouse gas*

Exercise 1 page 47

1 issue   2 predict   3 consequences   4 trend   5 areas
6 annual   7 challenge   8 contributes to

Exercise 2 page 48

*Possible alternatives in brackets (Note: these will not be
appropriate for Exercise 3):*

carbon dioxide; climate change; environmental group
(environmental change); greenhouse gas; natural resource
(natural gas); power plant; tropical rainforest

Be flexible

👥 Provide practice and feedback to **lower-
level students** who are using the environment
collocations. Using all the words from the boxes in
Exercise 2, give each student an index card with one

word written on it. Students move around the room,
saying their words aloud until they find a partner
who they can make a collocation with. When they
find each other, each pair should think of a sentence
containing their collocation and write it on the board
or a shared document to display to the class. Repeat
this several times until there are several sentences for
each collocation. As a class, check to make sure the
collocations are used correctly in the sentences, and
correct as needed.

Exercise 3 page 48

1 power plant   2 greenhouse gases   3 climate change
4 carbon dioxide   5 environmental groups   6 natural
resource   7 tropical rainforests

CRITICAL THINKING

Learning objectives

- Understand the causes and effects of deforestation
- Complete a cause-and-effect chain about
  deforestation
- List causes and effects of global warming
- Create a cause-and-effect chain for global warming

UNL◯CK TEACHER DEVELOPMENT

BE INFORMED

➜ **Analyzing cause and effect** is an important skill for
students because: (1) This is a crucial skill in all academic
disciplines, especially in the sciences; (2) Many essay
types are based on a cause-and-effect structure
– this might be talking about one cause which has
several effects, or alternatively, one effect which has
several causes; (3) Since students often confuse 'time
relationships' (where one thing simply happens *after*
another) and 'causal relationships' (where one things
happens *because of* another), they need to develop as
much knowledge as possible in this area.

BE CONFIDENT

➜ Develop this skill for yourself by doing the
following activity:
*Look at the following comments by teachers
about the effects of using critical thinking in their
classrooms. What might be some of the causes?*

> My students do not enjoy
> critical thinking.

> My students do not see the
> purpose of critical thinking.

Lead-in

At this point in each unit, students are asked to begin to think about the writing task they will do at the end of the unit. Give them a minute to read the box and to look at the table below it.

UNL⌀CK TEACHER DEVELOPMENT

BE READY

Look at the Critical Thinking section in the Student's Book on pages 49–50.

→ Which elements of the lesson do you think your students will find easiest / most difficult / most useful? Why?

→ Are your answers true for all students in your class?

→ How can you adapt your teaching or the material to meet your students' needs?

BE FLEXIBLE

Exercise 4 could be done as a more challenging activity, for example with stronger groups. Rather than students showing each other their diagrams, Student A should keep theirs hidden and read out the component parts in a random order. Student B must then reconstruct this in what they think is the correct order. They can then check. Repeat this process with the students changing roles.

Exercise 1 page 49

CAUSES	EFFECTS
commercial farming by big business	climate change
industrial logging	damage to animal habitats
farming by local people	land can't recover and becomes eroded; heavy erosion, flooding

Exercise 2 page 50

4 global warming **1** less rain **5** forests dry out **3** fires
2 more CO_2 emissions

Exercise 3 page 50
Possible answers:

CAUSES	EFFECTS
greenhouse gases	melting glaciers
growing world population	rising sea levels
burning fossil fuels	the amount of CO_2 in the atmosphere increases
cutting down trees	habitat loss

CAUSES	EFFECTS
commercial farming	species extinction
industrial logging	health problems, e.g. asthma
clear cutting by local farmers	heavy erosion of land, flooding
destruction of rainforests	less CO_2 consumed and less oxygen produced by trees; the greenhouse effect

Exercise 4 page 50
Answers will vary.

UNL⌀CK TEACHER DEVELOPMENT

BE REFLECTIVE

Think about the following questions:

→ What advice would you give the teachers who identified the problems mentioned in the *Be confident* section? What would be the best way of giving this advice?

→ Did your students confuse 'time relationships' with 'casual relationships' at any point? As mentioned in the *Be informed* section, trying to predict common mistakes by students before the lesson can be a useful strategy.

BE COLLABORATIVE

Your development is more meaningful when it is shared. See page 14 for ideas on how to peer-collaborate. Why not share the ideas you generated in the *Be flexible* section, and their outcome?

GRAMMAR FOR WRITING

Learning objectives

- Use verbs to describe cause-and-effect relationships in sentences – *Deforestation leads to habitat destruction. Habitat destruction is caused by deforestation.*
- Use *because* and *because of* to describe cause-and-effect relationships in sentences – *The environment is changing because humans are burning fossil fuels. The climate is changing because of human activity.*

Exercise 1 page 51

2 causes / results in **3** caused by / due to / the result of
4 caused by / due to / the result of

Be flexible

👤 👥 Provide **lower-level students** with additional practice using the language of cause and effect. Refer them back to the environmental issues they discussed in the Lead-in to Reading 1 and ask them to write cause-and-effect sentences for each, using the structures outlined in the Verbs of cause and effect box on page 51. Consider using a shared document to display the sentences and as a class evaluate the structure and discuss the meaning of each sentence.

Exercise 2 page 51

1 results   **2** due   **3** leads to / causes / results in   **4** caused   **5** result   **6** result

Exercise 3 page 52

1 because of   **2** because   **3** because of   **4** because

ACADEMIC WRITING SKILLS

Learning objectives

- Evaluate paragraph unity in a paragraph about bottled water
- Identify different types of support for an argument in a paragraph about bottled water
- Add supporting examples to a paragraph about desertification

Exercise 1 page 52

Main idea: Plastic water bottles hurt both people and the environment.

Cross out: In the 1970s, the United States was the world's biggest exporter of fossil fuels.

Exercise 2 page 53

1 Supporting sentences: Plastic bottles contain two harmful chemicals: BPA and phthalates.; Plastic bottles hurt the environment.

2 Both types of chemicals cause serious health problems for adults and children. This is a fact.

3 Transporting bottles requires an enormous amount of polluting fossil fuels. (Fact)

Most plastic bottles are not recycled, and end up in our landfills. (Fact)

Plastic bottles take many decades to break down. (Fact)

Exercise 3 page 54

1 lakes   **2** trees   **3** climate change   **4** Africa, Asia and the Middle East   **5** the Gobi Desert   **6** northern Lebanon   **7** peas and beans   **8** placing stones

Optional activity

👤 👥 Write the beginning of a sentence on the board that's general enough for students to think of examples, e.g. *Deforestation can lead to a lot of problems.* Ask one student to choose one of the expressions from the Skills box on page 54. Write the expression they choose next to the sentence and tell students to complete the sentence. (*Possible answer: Deforestation can lead to a lot of problems, such as damage to an animal's food source.*). Continue the process. Tell students they can't use the same expression from the Skills box more than once. (Other examples to write on the board: *Humans can take steps to prevent climate change; There are a lot of negative consequences to climate change*)

WRITING TASK

Learning objectives

- Plan which human causes of climate change you will include in an essay
- Draft two body paragraphs for an essay describing the human causes of climate change and the effects that climate change will have on the planet
- Review and revise the content and structure of your essay
- Review and revise the use of language in your essay

Exercises 1–9, pages 55–56

Answers will vary.

RESEARCH PROJECT

Help stop global warming by reducing your use of fossil fuels.

Divide the class into small groups and ask them to find out:

- what all the types of fossil fuels are
- why fossil fuels cause global warming
- how fossil fuels are used by the students in their homes and school
- what the alternatives are for fossil fuels in their environment.

Explain that the students are responsible for recording the class consumption of fossil fuels. They will create data and analyze the data. They can then research and write about how to reduce their consumption as a way to educate others.

CLASSROOM APP

Exercise 1

Answers will vary.

Exercise 2

1 climate   **2** construction   **3** absorb   **4** destruction
5 atmosphere   **6** cause   **7** threaten   **8** farming

Exercise 3

Answers will vary.

Exercise 4

1 issue   **2** annual   **3** contribute to   **4** trend
5 challenge   **6** consequences

Exercise 5

1 dioxide   **2** resources   **3** plant   **4** gases
5 rainforest   **6** change

Exercise 6

1 The pyramid stands approximately 147 metres tall and is the only one of the Seven Wonders which hasn't been destroyed.; Archeologists believe it was completed around 2,560 BCE.

2 Traditional Indian cooking includes flowers such as hibiscus, roses and jasmine, as well as the flowers of banana trees, cucumber and pumpkin plants.; Dried lily flowers are used in Chinese cooking to increase the flavour of vegetarian dishes, soups and stews.

3 A number of words of Arabic origin relate to mathematics, including *algorithm* and *algebra*.; The 15th-century Arabic word *qahwa* is pronounced *coffee* in English-speaking countries today.

UNIT OBJECTIVES

Watch and listen	Watch and understand a video about the jumbo jet.
Reading skill	Predict content using visuals.
Critical thinking	Evaluate solutions to a problem.
Grammar	Make suggestions; use the first conditional; use *if ... not* and *unless*.
Academic writing skill	Write a concluding sentence.
Writing task	Complete a problem–solution essay.
⊘ **Teacher development**	Help your students become better at **evaluating solutions to a problem**.

UNLOCK YOUR KNOWLEDGE

Background note

The photo shows busy traffic during the rush hour in Jaipur, India. Some of the forms of transport in the photo are: walking, cars, vans, motorbikes, carts pulled by oxen and rickshaws. There are two types of rickshaw in the photo: cycle rickshaws, which are pulled by a bicycle, and auto rickshaws, which use a motor engine. The rickshaw is a form of transport used, predominantly, in Asia.

Lead-in

Ask the class how they usually get to school / the class. Write the different forms of transport mentioned on the board, e.g. *on foot (walking), by bike, by bus, by car.*

page 59

1 *Possible answers:* car, bicycle, motorcycle, scooter, moped, bus, rickshaw, auto-rickshaw (tuktuk), truck, cart

2 *Answers will vary.*

WATCH AND LISTEN

Learning objectives

- Listen and complete a summary of the ideas in a video about the jumbo jet aeroplane
- Listen and identify facts and figures
- Evaluate the advantages and disadvantages of different types of transport

Exercise 1 page 60
Answers will vary.

Exercise 2 page 60
Possible answers:

1 The plane could be from the 1960s or 1970s, when the first jumbo jets flew. In fact, this is the first jumbo jet, from 1969.

2 First-class passengers would have used the lounge in the third photo.

3 First class has more leg room, bigger seats, better food and personalized service.

Exercise 3 page 60
1 flew 2 helped 3 worked 4 had 5 changed

Exercise 4 page 61
1 b 2 c 3 a 4 a 5 a

Exercise 5 page 61
Answers will vary.

Exercise 6 page 61
Possible answers:

1 **advantage:** convenient; **disadvantage:** contributes to pollution

2 **advantage:** environmentally friendly; **disadvantage:** high ticket prices in some countries, e.g. the UK

3 **advantage:** cheap; **disadvantage:** slow

4 **advantage:** good exercise; **disadvantage:** can be dangerous

5 **advantage:** fun; **disadvantage:** only useful for sea crossings, nothing else

READING 1

Learning objectives

- Understand key vocabulary for city transport – *commuter, connect, outskirts*
- Read and understand the main ideas in a news article about Masdar City in the UAE
- Read and understand facts and figures
- Make inferences about the future of Abu Dhabi and Masdar City
- Explain and justify personal opinions on life in Masdar City and its modern transport system

Lead-in

Tell students to imagine they are going to plan the development of a new city. It should be a 'city of the future' which limits traffic congestion and is friendly to the environment. In pairs, students should think of at least three ways their new city can accomplish this (*Possible answers: underground metro system, electric cars, make a city that's easy to walk and cycle bicycles in*).

Exercise 1 page 62

1 The problem is that there is too much traffic on the road, which causes noise and air pollution and leads to delays.
2 The vehicle in the second photo is a kind of electric car. It could be a solution because it would be quieter and cause less pollution than cars now. The photo was taken in a modern, technologically advanced city, in this case Masdar City in Abu Dhabi.
3 In photo 1 there is a lot of noise and air pollution as well as long delays, whereas in photo 2 the transport is quiet and clean, while delays might also be less of a problem.

Exercise 2 page 63

1 public transport   2 outskirts   3 rail   4 Traffic congestion   5 destination   6 commuter   7 connect

Exercise 3 page 63

1 a wall around the city and narrow streets
2 A transport system called Personal Rapid Transit. It involves using driverless vehicles called 'podcars', which run on solar energy and carry commuter passengers to stations around the city.
3 an underground rail system; a light rail transit system; and electric cars and buses
4 It reduced the money available for the project.

Exercise 4 page 65

1 traffic congestion   2 45 minutes   3 solar power
4 not allowed   5 24 billion   6 50,000; 40,000

Exercise 5 page 65

Possible answers:

1 An expanding economy means more people have more money for healthcare, education, travel and other lifestyle improvements.

A rising population means there are more people to work and help build the economy.

2 As it is a brand new city, there may not be much sense of community. At first, it may also lack facilities which you would expect in a normal city, e.g. schools, hospitals, etc., so people will have to travel to Abu Dhabi. With all the technology and the convenience of getting into Abu Dhabi, property prices may be very high, meaning ordinary people cannot live there. If it doesn't prove a popular place to live, it may turn into the 'green ghost town' people fear.

3 Perhaps not, because changes in technology have made it easier and cheaper for residents to use their own electric vehicles.

Exercise 6 page 65

Answers will vary.

READING 2

Learning objectives

- Understand key vocabulary for urban travel – *cycle, fuel, vehicle*
- Read an essay about traffic congestion and choose the best title
- Read and complete a table with details about solutions to traffic congestion problems
- Make inferences about the impact on people of the problems surrounding traffic congestion
- Synthesize information from a news article about Masdar City in the UAE and an essay about traffic congestion in a discussion

Lead-in

Write on the board *drivers, cities* and *the environment*. Tell students they are going to read about the negative effects that traffic jams can have on these three things. In pairs, students brainstorm these negative effects. Either you or they can write their ideas on the board. Tell students to read Paragraph 2 to see what negative effects they thought of that are the same, and ones they missed.

Exercise 1 page 66

1 cycle   2 practical   3 fuel   4 government
5 engineering   6 vehicles   7 emergency

Exercise 2 page 66

1 public transport – ferry, city bicycle hire, underground train   2 *Answers will vary.*

Exercise 3 page 68

b

Exercise 4 page 68

stress on drivers (and wasted time); economic losses; blocked access for emergency services; and negative effects on the environment – fuel waste and pollution

Exercise 5 page 68

1 tunnels **2** travel **3** result **4** fuel **5** jobs **6** health **7** traffic **8** bus **9** congestion / traffic **10** night

Exercise 6 page 68

Answers will vary.

Exercise 7 page 68

Possible answers:

1 high blood pressure, insomnia, trouble concentrating

2 People might not re-elect the politicians who approved the tax.

3 The bus stop might not be close to their home or work. They might have to wait a long time for the bus to arrive.

Exercise 8 page 69

1 *Possible answer:* Yes, lots of cities have problems with long commute times, traffic congestion, pollution, etc.

2 *Possible answer:* The solutions probably wouldn't work in other, bigger cities because those big cities are already built, whereas Masdar City is a new city.

3 *Answers will vary.*

> **Optional activity**
>
> Ask students to discuss in small groups whether they think the solutions in Reading 2 could help solve traffic problems in their town or city. Why / Why not?

LANGUAGE DEVELOPMENT

Learning objectives

- Use collocations to complete sentences about transport – *traffic congestion, rush hour, parking restrictions*
- Use academic verbs to replace less formal synonymous verbs and phrases in sentences about transport – *try > attempt; think about > consider; get > convince*
- Use a variety of words and phrases to make suggestions about improvements to transport systems – *Cities should encourage commuters to use public transport. It is important to encourage commuters to use public transport. Encouraging commuters to use public transport is a good idea.*

Exercise 1 page 69

1 c **2** a **3** d **4** g **5** e **6** f **7** b

Exercise 2 page 69

1 Rush hour **2** public transport **3** road rage **4** parking restrictions **5** Traffic congestion **6** car share **7** cycle lane

Exercise 3 page 70

1 require **2** attempt **3** produce **4** reduce **5** waste **6** consider **7** convince

Exercise 4 page 71

1 use bicycles to travel short distances

2 Using bicycles to travel short distances

3 build more high-speed railways between cities

4 Building more high-speed railways between cities

5 consider new ways of reducing traffic congestion

6 Considering new ways of reducing traffic congestion

Exercise 5 page 71

1 we should **2** is a good idea **3** we should **4** It is important **5** we should **6** is a good idea

CRITICAL THINKING

Learning objectives

- Use a table to organize ideas about transport solutions and their advantages and disadvantages
- Analyze a map of a city and describe its possible transport problems
- Evaluate potential solutions to a city's transport problems and their advantages and disadvantages
- Choose the best solutions to a city's transport problems and justify your choices

UNLⒸCK TEACHER DEVELOPMENT

BE INFORMED

→ **Evaluating solutions to a problem** is an important skill for students because: (1) Students may sometimes think that there is only one possible solution to a problem, when in fact there may be multiple solutions; (2) It can take time to develop this awareness for a whole range of different reasons (e.g. social, cultural), and even when students have the critical awareness that more than one solution may be possible, they may find it difficult to evaluate which solution is best; (3) To achieve this, developing specific criteria (e.g. determining how fast, cheap or reliable something is) can be useful to have as a framework.

BE CONFIDENT

→ Develop this skill for yourself by doing the following activity:

Think of a recent problem or challenge faced by your educational institution and answer these questions:

1 What possible solutions were there to this problem/challenge?

2 Which one was chosen?

3 Did you agree with this decision? Why / Why not?

4 Why do you think this solution was chosen rather than another one?

Lead-in

At this point in each unit students are asked to begin to think about the writing task they will do at the end of the unit. Give them a minute to read the box and to look at the table below it.

UNLØCK TEACHER DEVELOPMENT

BE READY

Look at the Critical Thinking section in the Student's Book on pages 72–74.

→ Which elements of the lesson do you think your students will find easiest / most difficult / most useful? Why?

→ Are your answers true for all students in your class?

→ How can you adapt your teaching or the material to meet your students' needs?

BE FLEXIBLE

When doing Exercise 1, ask students to decide beforehand what criteria they will use to decide on their three solutions – e.g. the three cheapest / most effective / healthiest. This is an opportunity for them to apply their critical thinking skills to their own practice, rather than just make a random choice.

Exercise 1 page 72

Possible answers:

problem	goal(s)
Traffic congestion, resulting in wasted time, stress, road rage, economic losses, problems for emergency services and the environment	To reduce traffic congestion and its effects

solutions	advantages/disadvantages
engineering – building new roads with wider lanes, and tunnels and bridges	+ more people can travel at the same time + tunnels and bridges direct drivers away from congested areas
	– extremely high cost; – more roads may result in more traffic
tax on fuel or travel on a motorway or into a city centre motorway	+ people think more carefully about using their cars
	– some people cannot afford to drive their cars and they may have to give up their jobs – may be unpopular with voters
promote cycling	+ health benefits + does not pollute the air
	– not practical in every climate – dangerous in heavy traffic
persuade people to use buses more	+ allows flexibility for drivers + reduces congestion in the centre of the city
	– no buses at night for people who work late shifts

decision(s)	reason(s)
encourage alternative forms of transport, e.g. cycling, buses	reduces the amount of traffic on the roads and has a positive effect on the environment

Exercise 2 page 73

Possible answers: Only one road connecting people's homes to their schools or places of work; morning rush hour will be very busy because schools are also starting; no train service – only buses, which use the same road; traffic lights may cause congestion; high-temperatures in the desert may lead to road rage; fuel is expensive.

Exercise 3 page 73

Possible answers:

problem: There is only a single two-lane motorway joining the residential area to the area of schools and offices. This means there is traffic congestion, especially at rush hour.

goal(s): To stop traffic congestion in the city

Exercise 4 page 74

Possible answers:

solutions	advantages/disadvantages
build a tunnel	+ people would be happy as they could still drive
	− expensive to build; would take a long time to build; would eventually fill with traffic
encourage people to cycle	+ cheap and quick
	− too hot to cycle over a desert; it can be dangerous; not many people would want to change to cycling
park-and-ride bus system	+ fairly quick; people would like it more than cycling; could have a dedicated bus lane to get to the schools and offices
	− designed to keep people from driving in the centre, but the problem is getting to the centre; people don't like buses; the bus might get stuck in other traffic congestion
move the residential area to the other side of the river	+ long-term solution that completely solves the congestion problem
	− very expensive; people won't want to move
road tax	+ cheap and quick to implement; makes money for the government
	− it may not stop people from using their cars, they'll just pay more money to drive; will make people dislike the government
ferry	+ people could drive their cars on to the ferry, which would reduce road traffic
	− there will be a queue for cars to board, might not be very frequent; may be expensive to run; fairly expensive to build; would take a while to build a port and a new road to reach the ferry

Exercises 5–6 page 74

Answers will vary.

UNLOCK TEACHER DEVELOPMENT

BE REFLECTIVE

Think about the following questions:

→ Are problems generally solved in a good and effective manner in your educational institution? Is there a way the process could be improved? If so, are you able in any way to improve or influence this process?

→ Did the students' own social or cultural backgrounds affect the way they were able to do the exercises in this section? For example, the idea of there being more than one solution to a problem may have been new for some of them. If this was the case, consider how you might address this in future lessons.

BE COLLABORATIVE

Your development is more meaningful when it is shared. See page 14 for ideas on how to peer-collaborate. Why not share how problems and challenges are addressed in your educational institution with a colleague?

GRAMMAR FOR WRITING

Learning objectives

- Use the first conditional to describe the consequences of actions – *If the council creates a park-and-ride scheme, traffic congestion will decrease.*
- Use the first conditional with *if ... not* or *unless* to describe the consequences of not doing a certain action – *If the council doesn't create a park-and-ride scheme, the city won't be able to reduce pollution. The city won't be able to reduce pollution unless the council creates a park-and-ride scheme.*

Exercise 1 page 75

1 If we move the offices and schools next to the houses, we will have fewer traffic problems. / We will have fewer traffic problems if we move the offices and schools next to the houses.

2 If we have a ferry over the river, fewer people will use the bridge. / Fewer people will use the bridge if we have a ferry over the river.

3 Fewer cars will use the roads if we increase the price of fuel. / If we increase the price of fuel, fewer cars will use the roads.

4 If we change the office hours, cars won't all use the road at the same time. / Cars won't all use the road at the same time if we change the office hours.

5 If we build a railway line, people will be able to use the train instead of their cars. / People will be able to use the train instead of their cars if we build a railway line.

Exercise 2 page 75
Possible answers:

2 Pollution won't be reduced unless we use cleaner transport.

3 If we don't provide a solution, people won't get to work on time.

4 We won't solve the traffic problem unless we build houses closer to the business areas.

5 If the city doesn't invest in public transport, there won't be less congestion.

ACADEMIC WRITING SKILLS

Learning objective
- Evaluate concluding sentences for paragraphs about transport issues

Exercise 1 page 76
Paragraph 1: b; **Paragraph 2:** a

Optional activity

Remind students that a concluding sentence can restate the main idea with different words, summarize the main points of a paragraph, or add an opinion or prediction. Tell students to look again at the topic and concluding sentences in Paragraph 2, Reading 2, in the Skills box, and in the paragraphs in Exercise 1. Ask *What function does each of these concluding sentences serve?*

Possible answers:

Paragraph 2, Reading 2: restates the main idea with different words.

In the Skills box: summarizes the main points of a paragraph, adds a prediction.

In Exercise 1: Paragraph 1: it adds an opinion. Paragraph 2: it restates the main idea with different words.

WRITING TASK

Learning objectives
- Create an outline of your body paragraphs for an essay about solutions to a city's traffic congestion problems
- Draft two body paragraphs for your essay which each include a concluding statement

- Review and revise the content and structure of your essay
- Review and revise the use of language in your essay

Exercises 1–7 pages 77–78
Answers will vary.

RESEARCH PROJECT

Improve the transport in your area.

Explain to your class that they are going to write a proposal to the local council, explaining ways they could improve transport in the area. They should focus on two areas: road safety and the improvement and promotion of public transport. The proposal needs to discuss the current situation and state where any problems exist. It should also contain a description of improvements to the transport network and the advantages of these improvements.

Students could extend this activity by developing a public transport promotion focusing on awareness of the issues through promotional products, leaflets, logos, slogans and videos.

CLASSROOM APP

Exercise 1
Answers will vary.

Exercise 2
1 destination **2** outskirts **3** cycle **4** fuel
5 emergency **6** practical **7** public transport
8 connects

Exercise 3
Answers will vary.

Exercise 4
1 congestion **2** transport **3** lane **4** hour **5** share
6 rage **7** restrictions

Exercise 5
1 prevent **2** convince **3** waste **4** attempt
5 consider **6** requires

Exercise 6
1 go, will find **2** don't close, will escape; is going to escape **3** will continue, decides **4** will meet, finish, don't feel **5** finds, will be, will move; move **6** will buy, don't save

UNIT OBJECTIVES	
Watch and listen	Watch and understand a video about the Coming of Age Day in South Korea.
Reading skills	Annotate a text; preview a text.
Critical thinking	Respond to an author's ideas.
Grammar	Avoid generalizations; use adverbs of frequency to avoid generalizations; paraphrase.
Academic writing skill	Write a summary and a personal response.
Writing task	Write a summary paragraph and a response paragraph.
⚙ Teacher development	Help your students become better at **responding to an author's ideas**.

UNLOCK YOUR KNOWLEDGE

Background note

The photo shows a floating market in Thailand. The traditional boats are full of colourful local fruits, flowers and vegetables, as well as prepared snacks and sweets to sell. The tradition of floating markets comes from the time when water transport was the cheapest and the fastest way to transport goods. Floating markets are common in Thailand, Indonesia, Vietnam, Sri Lanka, Bangladesh and India.

Lead-in

Find out from the class what the most recent holiday they celebrated was. What did they do to celebrate? Elicit ideas. Are they different or similar? Repeat for the next holiday they will celebrate.

page 81

1 This photo was taken in a Southeast Asian country, in this case Thailand. It is a floating market where people buy and sell daily goods, such as fruit and vegetables, from their boats.

2–3 *Answers will vary.*

WATCH AND LISTEN

Learning objectives

- Listen and understand the main ideas in a video about changing traditions in South Korea
- Listen and understand details about traditions and ceremonies
- Understand the meaning of unfamiliar words and phrases from their context in the video
- Practise talking about traditional celebrations in your country

Exercise 1 page 82
Answers will vary.

Exercise 2 page 82
The activities which appear in the video are giving presents, wearing traditional clothes, taking photos and taking part in a ceremony.

Exercise 3 page 83
The modern celebration involves giving gifts (of flowers and perfume). The traditional celebration involved the young people arranging their hair in a special way (for women, wearing a hair pin and a wooden crown; for men, wearing a special hat), wearing traditional clothes and taking part in a ceremony with their parents.

Exercise 4 page 83
1 day   **2** 20   **3** meaning   **4** 1,000   **5** (Young) women
6 net   **7** hat   **8** brightly-coloured / formal   **9** parents
10 proud

Exercise 5 page 83
1 ornament   **2** bow   **3** bamboo   **4** crown   **5** jade
6 topknot

Exercise 6 page 83
Answers will vary.

READING 1

Learning objectives

- Understand key vocabulary for customs and traditions – *appearance, exchange, formal*
- Read and annotate main ideas, key words, supporting examples and arguments in an article about customs around the world
- Read and identify main ideas
- Read and complete a set of detailed notes on different aspects of culture around the world

- Make inferences about the reasons for specific customs around the world
- Discuss your personal response to the customs described in the article

Lead-in

Tell the class to imagine that a foreign student is coming to spend several months in their country. The student wants to avoid making any cultural gaffes (= embarrassing mistakes) when meeting new people. What should the student know that would help them make a good impression?

Exercise 1 page 84

1 cultures   **2** exchange   **3** expect   **4** greet   **5** formal
6 appearance   **7** relationship

Exercises 2–3 page 85

Answers will vary.

Optional activity

Divide the class into small groups and assign each group a country from the reading (Brazil, Japan or Saudi Arabia). Ask them to discuss differences and similarities between their own cultures and what they have read about the target culture. Give them three to five minutes and then ask each group to report back. Finish by asking the class if they know anything else about the three cultures represented in the text, e.g. *What else do you know about Brazilians?*

Exercise 4 page 85

Answers will vary.

Exercise 5 page 85

e

Exercise 6 page 87

1 kiss   **2** shake hands with   **3** shake hands   **4** bowing
5 the oldest   **6** women   **7** men   **8** house / home
9 refuse   **10** token of your appreciation   **11** necessary
12 chocolate, coffee or dates   **13** gift   **14** both hands
15 immediately read it carefully   **16** start   **17** family
18 health   **19** well   **20** formally   **21** formal   **22** at least
thirty minutes late   **23** early   **24** on time

Exercise 7 page 87

Possible answers:

1 They might think you are trying to bribe them or 'buy' a favour.

2 Brazilians are accustomed to touching, so they might be offended if you move away.

3 Hierarchy is important in Japanese culture.

4 Hierarchy is important to Saudis.

5 People become offended and relationships could suffer or possibly end.

Exercise 8 page 88

Answers will vary.

READING 2

Learning objectives

- Understand key vocabulary for cultural heritage – *belief, ceremony, generation*
- Use the title, subtitles and photos to preview the topic and content of an article about cultural heritage
- Read and annotate main ideas, key words, supporting examples and arguments in an article
- Choose the best summary of an article
- Read and understand the details in supporting examples
- Make inferences about the idea of intangible cultural heritage
- Synthesize information from an article about customs around the world and an article about cultural heritage in a discussion

Lead-in

Ask students for some examples of things very specific to their culture (e.g. Turkish coffee, luxury fruit in Japan, Almezmar in Saudi Arabia, classic red post boxes in the UK, etc.). What makes these things special? Is it important to preserve or protect these parts of a culture?

Exercise 1 page 88

1 ceremony   **2** generations   **3** beliefs   **4** preserve
5 tradition   **6** endangered   **7** protection

Exercise 2 page 89

1 *Answers will vary.*   **2** In the first photo, the women are dressed in diving suits. They are from South Korea and have been fishing. In the second photo a Middle Eastern man has a falcon sitting on his arm. Perhaps he has trained the bird to hunt.

Exercise 3 page 89

Answers will vary.

Exercise 4 page 89

a 2   **b** 5   **c** 4   **d** 1   **e** 3

Exercise 5 page 89

a

Exercise 6 page 89

1 ~~2003~~ 2008   **2** ~~intangible~~ tangible   **3** ~~all year round~~ 90 days of the year   **4** ~~Many~~ Fewer   **5** ~~only in the United Arab Emirates~~ around the world

Exercise 7 page 91

Possible answers:

1 Tangible culture refers to actual places, buildings, objects, etc., for example, the Great Barrier Reef off the coast of Australia or the Pyramids of Giza in Egypt. Intangible culture relates to living customs and traditional practice, for example the culture of the women divers of Jeju Island in South Korea.

2 Because fewer young people are interested in continuing them; because growth of cities and loss of natural habitats affects their practice.

3 To save or preserve customs and traditions that may otherwise die out.

4 Yes; she says its efforts are valuable, and that at the end we 'must never stop trying' to preserve our intangible cultural heritage.

Exercise 8 page 91

Possible answers:

1 Yes, although this will might be difficult with increasing globalization happening.

2 Those which younger people want to continue may be the ones which will survive.

3 Countries need to promote their cultural practices, especially to the younger generation.

Be flexible

For homework, challenge **more advanced students** to research a tradition that's currently on the Intangible Cultural Heritage list. They should note what the tradition is, its country of heritage and why it's in danger of dying out. In the next lesson, students can share what they learnt in small groups.

Note: Searching for 'UNESCO Intangible Cultural Heritage list' on the internet should yield enough sources for students to complete the assignment.

LANGUAGE DEVELOPMENT

Learning objectives

- Use *many, can* and *tend to* to avoid generalizations in statements about customs around the world – *Many cultural traditions change. Cultural traditions tend to change. Cultural traditions can change.*
- Use adverbs of frequency to avoid generalizations in statements about customs around the world – *In Tokyo, people usually go to work by train or bus. Formal dinner parties are often difficult to organize.*
- Replace common words with synonyms in sentences – *short > brief; bad > serious; clear > obvious*

Exercise 1 page 92

1 We tend to tip the waiter in restaurants.

2 Brazilian culture tends to be informal.

3 Expensive gifts can look suspicious.

4 Common hand gestures like waving can be misunderstood in a different culture.

5 In the Middle East, many old people live with their children.

Exercise 2 page 93

1 Brazilian men usually shake hands, though it is not unusual for men to kiss each other on the cheek.

2 Saudi men often wear traditional clothing, even to business meetings.

3 Professionals sometimes get upset if you don't use their correct title.

4 Cultural knowledge is frequently helpful in business situations.

5 In Japan, you should always arrive on time for an appointment.

Exercise 3 page 93

1 brief   2 serious   3 separate   4 certain   5 important
6 obvious   7 common

CRITICAL THINKING

Learning objectives

- Organize notes about the ideas from an essay about cultural heritage in a table
- Evaluate each idea in an outline of an essay about cultural heritage and add personal responses

UNLOCK TEACHER DEVELOPMENT

BE INFORMED

→ **Responding to an author's ideas** is an important skill for students because: (1) One key writing skill is the ability to summarize what other writers have argued; (2) Another key writing skill is the ability to present a response to what other writers have argued; (3) The ability to combine these skills – e.g. agreeing and disagreeing, presenting an example, connecting ideas or evaluating – is indicative of a sophisticated writer, and something which students should be aiming to do.

BE CONFIDENT

→ Develop this skill for yourself by doing the following activity:

Read the paragraph. What is your opinion of what is said? Plan, or write, a response paragraph to it.

Critical thinking has become an extremely popular concept in the modern education system. Everywhere you look, textbooks and courses talk about twenty-first-century skills' and 'getting your students to think more critically'. However, it seems as if this has gone too far, and that education establishments are not focusing enough on core subjects – English, Maths, Science, and so on. There should be more of a focus on these basics again – twenty-first-century skills can wait.

Lead-in

At this point in each unit students are asked to begin to think about the writing task they will do at the end of the unit. Give them a minute to read the box and to look at the table below it.

UNL⌀CK TEACHER DEVELOPMENT

BE READY

Look at the Critical Thinking section in the Student's Book on pages 94–95.

→ Which elements of the lesson do you think your students will find easiest / most difficult / most useful? Why?

→ Are your answers true for all students in your class?

→ How can you adapt your teaching or the material to meet your students' needs?

BE FLEXIBLE

After Exercise 2, get students to compare and share their responses with a partner, in a group or a whole-class situation. Students should listen and, if appropriate, be willing to change their response if they hear a superior argument from another student.

Exercises 1–2 pages 94–95

'My response' column will vary. Possible answers:

	main idea	details
1	Should we be preserving our intangible culture for future generations?	Already protecting heritage sites Intangible aspects – songs, stories, traditional practices.
2	ICH list was established to protect living customs and practices.	List includes languages, spoken traditions, performing arts, craftsmanship, knowledge and beliefs.

	main idea	details
3	First example	The culture of the Jeju Haenyeo – under threat as young women are not stepping in to carry on the tradition.
4	Second example	Falcony – practised in different countries around the world but is threatened by the growth of cities.
5	Trying to answer the question in the introduction and concluding we must never stop trying for the sake of future generations.	Both examples illustrate the diversity of practices on the list. Is the list fair? Will it make a difference? Is it too late?

Exercise 2 page 95

Answers will vary.

UNL⌀CK TEACHER DEVELOPMENT

BE REFLECTIVE

Think about the following questions:

→ With colleagues, discuss the paragraph in the *Be confident* section. Do they have the same response to you? Can you reach a consensus about your response to the writer's opinion?

→ How confident were your students in responding to a written text? Some students find it difficult to challenge, or even just comment on, what 'expert' writers have written. How can you help them develop this skill of critiquing/responding to what others have written?

BE COLLABORATIVE

Your development is more meaningful when it is shared. See page 14 for ideas on how to peer-collaborate. Perhaps you could share strategies for encouraging your students to challenge / comment on what other people have written.

GRAMMAR FOR WRITING

Learning objectives

- Identify different techniques for paraphrasing ideas: synonyms, word order changes, using indirect speech
- Use synonyms, word order changes and indirect speech to paraphrase ideas about cultural heritage
- Evaluate and improve your paraphrases

Exercise 1 page 96

1 c **2** a **3** b

Exercise 2 page 96

Possible answers:

1 In today's rapidly-developing world, many of us see the importance of saving our diverse cultural heritage.

2 Due to our cities expanding and our loss of natural environments, falconry is unfortunately now under threat.

3 According to Barker (2018), it may be too late to save our unique and varied cultural heritage, because not as many young people want to learn about ancient customs and practices.

Exercise 3 page 96

Answers will vary.

Optional activity

After comparing paraphrases with a partner in Exercise 3, each pair should select one paraphrase and write it on a separate piece of paper. The pair should give that paraphrase to the pair next to them, who will write a 'paraphrase of the paraphrase'. Each paraphrase should continue circulating to different pairs. This will give students practice paraphrasing one sentence using different strategies. When the sentences reach the original pair who wrote the first paraphrase, the pair should check their paraphrase and be sure it has maintained the original author's meaning.

ACADEMIC WRITING SKILLS

Learning objectives

- Identify the key features of an essay summarizing and responding to another author's ideas

Exercise 1 pages 97–98

Possible answers:

1 In the article 'Customs around the world,' author Andy Schmidt (2018) says it is important for travellers to learn about the customs of other countries, in order to prevent cultural misunderstandings in the places they are visiting.

2 indirect speech, synonyms, change the order of words or phrases.

3 important details about each of the three countries in the article

4 Brazil: touching, punctuality; Japan: touching, business cards, dress, gifts, punctuality; Saudi Arabia: formality, men and women not touching in public, the importance of personal relationships. This gives a few details from each country, so is about the right amount of information.

5 Four references: 'Andy Schmidt (2018) says ...', 'Schmidt focuses on ...', 'According to the author, ...', 'The author stresses ...'

6 It's the topic sentence at the beginning of the second paragraph: 'I definitely agree with Schmidt's main point'.

7 with examples from her own experience

8 She restates the main idea: 'In short, ...'

Exercise 2 page 98

Answers will vary.

Optional activity

Tell students to think of something they've seen/heard/read recently. They should describe it to a partner, and then give their opinion on whether they liked it or not. If the summary isn't clear or complete, the partner should ask clarifying questions. Rotate partners several times so students can give their summary more than once.

WRITING TASK

Learning objectives

- Prepare an outline of two paragraphs, summarizing and responding to efforts to preserve the world's intangible cultural heritage
- Draft two paragraphs
- Review and revise the content and structure of your paragraphs
- Review and revise the use of language in your paragraphs

Exercises 1–7 pages 99–100

Answers will vary.

RESEARCH PROJECT

Compare two countries' cultural traditions

Divide the class into groups and ask them to think of two different countries; each group should choose two different ones. Ask them to research, compare and contrast the cultural traditions of those two countries. This should include both tangible and intangible cultures. The groups can create a slideshow presentation about the countries they have researched.

CLASSROOM APP

Exercise 1

Answers will vary.

Exercise 2

1 greet **2** generations **3** exchanging **4** protection
5 appearance **6** ceremony **7** beliefs **8** formal

Exercise 3

Answers will vary.

Exercise 4

1 it usually rains **2** seldom played **3** are almost never
4 is not always **5** often have **6** hardly ever tastes
7 rarely have **8** is often

Exercise 5

1 brief **2** obvious **3** common; usual **4** certain; some
5 serious; bad **6** powerful; important
7 separate; different

Exercise 6

1 use synonyms; change order of words or phrases

2 use synonyms; change order of words or phrases

3 use synonyms; change order of words or phrases; use
indirect speech

UNIT OBJECTIVES	
Watch and listen	Watch and understand a video about the amount of sugar in food and drinks.
Reading skill	Make inferences.
Critical thinking	Support an argument.
Grammar	Use verb and noun forms; state opinions; state a purpose; link contrasting sentences.
Academic writing skill	Structure an essay (introductory, body and concluding paragraphs).
Writing task	Write a balanced opinion essay.
⟳ **Teacher development**	Help your students become better at **supporting an argument**.

UNL⟳CK YOUR KNOWLEDGE

Background note

The photo shows a woman mountain biking in Val Gardenia, which is a valley in the Dolomites in Northern Italy. Mountain biking increases fitness levels by building leg muscle, exercising your heart and burning fat. Exercising outdoors also has many health benefits. You can also go mountain biking with family or friends, which can help you build relationships and have fun. However, some extreme forms of mountain biking can be dangerous, especially when riders go down very steep slopes. Mountain biking can also be very tiring and is not suitable for everybody.

Lead-in

To engage students in the topic, you could write the following questions on the board and ask them to work in pairs and discuss: *What does being healthy mean to you? How do people develop a healthy or unhealthy lifestyle? What foods should people eat daily? What foods should people try to avoid?* Get feedback from the class but don't give feedback or go into much detail, as these and other issues to do with health and fitness will be dealt with in this unit.

page 103

1 *Answers will vary.*

2 *Possible answers:* Healthy people eat a balanced diet, exercise regularly, get enough sleep, have a positive mental attitude.

3 *Possible answers:* They avoid overeating or eating the wrong things. They avoid smoking, drugs and alcohol.

4 *Possible answers:* walking, jogging, swimming, cycling, yoga, tennis, and all kinds of team sport.

WATCH AND LISTEN

Learning objectives

- Listen and identify the main idea in a video about sugar content in food
- Listen and complete a set of student notes with numbers from the video
- Identify the meaning of unfamiliar words and phrases from their context in the video
- Listen and make inferences about the ideas in the video and their wider implications
- Practise talking about food labelling and public eating habits

Exercises 1–2 page 104
Answers will vary.

Exercise 3 page 104
2

Exercise 4 page 105
1 6½ / 6.5 / six and a half   2 4   3 ⅓ / one-third   4 3
5 ⅔ / two-thirds   6 4½ / 4.5 / four and a half
7 less than 5%

Exercise 5 page 105
deliver – add; bring
component – ingredient
natural – not made or done by people
gradually – slowly over a period of time
differentiate – to show the difference between things
palate – the ability you use to decide if you like a taste
disclose – to give information that was secret

Exercise 6 page 105
Answers will vary. Possible answers:

1 Because they wanted to do a report on the amount of sugar manufacturers add to food, but this information is not available on the product labels.

2 Because they may add a lot of sugar to their products and not want the customer to know this, in case it affects their sales.

3 Because laws are made after reading scientific reports, or because people decide what food to eat because of scientific opinions.

Exercise 7 page 105

Answers will vary.

READING 1

Learning objectives

- Understand key vocabulary for health and fitness – *self-esteem, active, calories*
- Skim an article about physical exercise to identify the best title
- Read and identify the main idea of each paragraph and choose the best heading for each one
- Read and find examples and detailed information
- Make inferences about the article and its audience
- Give personal opinions on issues relating to health and exercise

Lead-in

Ask the class what they do to stay healthy. Do they do any special activities? Elicit ideas from the class and write them on the board. Ask students which ideas are most common.

Exercise 1 page 106

a active **b** reduce **c** serious **d** self-esteem
e calories **f** recognize **g** moderate

Exercise 2 page 106

a basketball **b** squash **c** housework / cleaning
d football **e** gardening **f** jogging / running
g swimming **h** cycling

Exercise 3 page 108

c

Exercise 4 page 108

a 3 **b** 1 **c** 5 **d** 2 **e** 4

Exercise 5 page 108

1 heart disease; type 2 diabetes; stroke; some cancers
2 mood; self-esteem; sleep quality **3** seven hours or more **4** the field or court **5** at off-peak times
6 running shoes / trainers **7** the park

Exercise 6 page 109

Possible answers:

1 It helps improve their self-esteem by helping them to stay fit, making them strong and giving them a sense of achievement.

2 It is written for adults. The word 'adult' appears several times in the text. There are also references in the text to adult activities such as having a job, and to playing games you haven't played since you were a child.

Exercise 7 page 109

1 *Answers will vary.*

2 *Possible answers:* It is a good way, but only one way of keeping fit. You can keep fit by gardening or doing other physical jobs.

3 *Possible answers:* People can become dehydrated or get injured. Some people exercise too hard and damage their bodies.

READING 2

Learning objectives

- Understand key vocabulary for health and diet – *balanced diet, junk food, nutritional*
- Scan an essay to check your ideas about nutrition and obesity
- Read and identify the writer's main ideas about who is responsible for problem obesity
- Complete a table with detailed information from the essay
- Identify the type of support the writer uses in an essay
- Read and find examples of different food types mentioned by the writer
- Make inferences about the writer's opinions on issues related to obesity
- Synthesize information from an article about physical exercise and an essay about nutrition and obesity in a discussion

Lead-in

Ask students to define *obesity*. They may use their dictionaries for help. Elicit answers. Then ask if obesity is a problem in their country. Why / Why not?

Exercise 1 page 109

1 balanced diet **2** junk food **3** Obesity **4** portions
5 campaign **6** nutritional

Exercise 2 page 110

Answers will vary.

Exercise 3 page 110

1 a 50% **b** 30% **c** 5% **d** 15%

2 have laws for showing nutritional information on packaging; require restaurants to inform customers of calories; tax high-fat/high-sugar foods; support educational campaigns for healthy eating

3 Control portion size; eat a balanced diet; read nutritional information on food packaging; exercise regularly.

Exercise 4 page 110

a G **b** I **c** I **d** I **e** G **f** I **g** G **h** I

Exercise 5 page 110

1 d – read nutritional information on food packaging
2 c – eat a balanced diet **3** g – put a tax on foods which are high in sugar and fat **4** b – control portion size
5 h – do exercise

Exercise 6 page 110

1 R **2** E **3** R **4** F **5** R

Exercise 7 page 112

1 rice; potatoes; pasta **2** milk; cheese **3** meat; fish; eggs; beans **4** pizza; crisps **5** chocolate; sweets

Exercise 8 page 112

Possible answers:

1 D: Obesity has become a major problem in many parts of the world. According to the World Health Organization (WHO), in 2016 about 13% of adults worldwide, both male and female, were obese.

2 A: In many Western countries, for example, a typical healthy diet might include approximately 50% fruit and vegetables; 30% carbohydrates, such as bread, rice, potatoes and pasta; 15% proteins, for example, meat, fish, eggs and beans; and around 5% dairy products (e.g. milk and cheese).

3 A: Such campaigns would be similar to the anti-smoking campaigns that have helped reduce the number of smokers all over the world.

4 D: And finally, each of us should make time to exercise because, as we all know, exercise burns calories.

5 D: If we really wish to see an end to the problem of obesity in the future, individuals and governments must both take action.

Exercise 9 page 112

Answers will vary.

LANGUAGE DEVELOPMENT

Learning objectives

- Identify noun forms of verbs in a text – *advertise > advertisement; ban > ban; encourage > encouragement*
- Identify health and fitness collocations in a text – *life expectancy; heart disease; balanced diet*
- Read and identify the meaning of health and fitness collocations from context

Exercise 1 page 113

We need to see a <u>reduction</u> in the rate of obesity among children and teenagers. The first step is <u>recognition</u> that fat is a real problem for young people. One solution is for schools to offer children the opportunity to participate in sport. This would require the involvement and <u>encouragement</u> of parents, who are our main weapon against increasing obesity. Parents can also support the <u>promotion</u> of educational campaigns to teach children about healthy eating.

All of us should be responsible for the <u>protection</u> of our own health, but governments can also help fight the obesity epidemic. For example, they can impose a <u>ban</u> on junk food <u>adverts</u> aimed at children.

Exercise 2 page 114

Obesity can reduce <u>life expectancy</u> and lead to <u>serious illness</u> such as <u>heart disease</u> and diabetes. To address this problem, some governments run <u>educational programmes</u> and <u>advertising campaigns</u>. These educate people about the dangers of <u>junk food</u> and the importance of a <u>balanced diet</u>. They also show people how to find out about the <u>nutritional value</u> of food. Another important way to tackle obesity is <u>regular exercise</u>, because the more <u>physical activity</u> we have, the better we feel.

Exercise 3 page 114

2 nutritional value **3** educational programmes **4** heart disease **5** physical activity **6** advertising campaigns
7 serious illness **8** balanced diet **9** regular exercise
10 junk food

Be flexible

Provide **lower-level students** with additional practice with collocations. Use this activity to encourage fast recall of the collocations in this unit. This can work for both Verb and noun forms and Health and fitness collocations. You'll need a small ball that students can throw to each other. Ask students to stand in a circle. For verb and noun forms, start by saying *encourage*. Tell the students you'll throw the ball to somebody and that student has to say *encouragement*. That same student says another word (*recognition*, for example) and throws the ball to another student, who must say *recognize*. If the student holding the ball doesn't know the answer, he/she has to sit down. The last student standing is the winner. For *fitness collocations*, students say the first word in the collocation and the person they throw the ball to says the second word.

CRITICAL THINKING

Learning objectives

- Use a table to understand the content of a paragraph
- List arguments for and against compulsory physical education in universities
- Use a table to evaluate and support your arguments

UNL⊘CK TEACHER DEVELOPMENT

BE INFORMED

→ **Supporting an argument** is an important skill for students because: (1) Students may be too quick to decide what they think about a particular subject, and may not think through all the possible options; (2) A key academic skill is to show that you can understand an issue from all sides, with supporting arguments, and represent this in a piece of writing; (3) Whichever students decide, the argument they make should be presented with good supporting evidence, e.g. facts, examples and reasons.

BE CONFIDENT

→ Develop this skill for yourself by doing the following activity:

Rank the following supporting details 1–5 (1 = strongest, 5 = weakest) that you would use for this statement: 'It is important that students study critical thinking at school to prepare them for university and the workplace.'

1 Several articles clearly demonstrate how developing critical thinking skills at school prepares you well for college and university studies. _____

2 My daughter studied critical thinking and now she is at university. _____

3 Critical thinking skills, I argue, can help you pass university entrance tests. _____

4 Developing critical thinking fosters a better, deeper understanding of important ideas (Miletzki and Broten, 2017). _____

5 Some students at my school have gone on to university, and I think they took some critical thinking lessons. _____

If you wanted to oppose this position, what supporting details would you give?

Lead-in

At this point in each unit students are asked to begin to think about the writing task they will do at the end of the unit. Give them a minute to read the box and to look at the table below it.

UNL⊘CK TEACHER DEVELOPMENT

BE READY

Look at the Critical Thinking section in the Student's Book on pages 115–116.

→ Which elements of the lesson do you think your students will find easiest / most difficult / most useful? Why?

→ Are your answers true for all students in your class?

→ How can you adapt your teaching or the material to meet your students' needs?

BE FLEXIBLE

An optional 'Exercise 6' which you could do, to develop students' general critical thinking skills, is to ask the class whether anybody changed their opinion based on the discussions they had in Exercise 5. Students should understand that it is perfectly acceptable for them to change their minds if they think they have heard better arguments or more compelling evidence.

Exercise 1 page 115
Possible answers:

position: Governments must take the leading role in fighting obesity.	
argument 1: Large restaurant groups should be made to give nutritional information on their menus to customers.	**supporting details:** This information would then help people choose low-calorie, nutritious food when they eat out.
argument 2: There should be a tax on foods high in fat and sugar.	**supporting details:** People will not be able to buy as much junk food, so will eat less of it.
argument 3: Governments should support education programmes helping people to eat balanced diets.	**supporting details:** An example where this idea has already worked is the 'stop smoking' campaigns all over the world.

Exercises 2–5 pages 115–116
Answers will vary.

UNLOCK TEACHER DEVELOPMENT

BE REFLECTIVE

Think about the following questions:

→ Compare your answers in the *Be confident* section with a colleague, either in person or electronically. Did you have the same opinion? If not, discuss and try and reach a consensus. The suggested order of answers, from strongest to weakest, is 4, 1, 3, 2, 5.

→ Were students able to link the critical thinking focus in this section to their own writing? Trying to link the learning to their actual experience is a useful strategy and deepens the education value.

BE COLLABORATIVE

Your development is more meaningful when it is shared. See page 14 for ideas on how to peer-collaborate. Why not share the ideas you generated in the *Be flexible* section, and their outcome?

GRAMMAR FOR WRITING

Learning objectives

- Use phrases to express opinions on issues related to health and fitness – *In my opinion, both parties have a role to play in dealing with this global problem.*
- Use modal verbs to express opinions on issues related to health and fitness – *Individuals ought to make better food choices.*
- Use language to state the purpose of an idea or recommendation – *Governments should promote healthy eating in order to increase life expectancy.*
- Identify the grammar and punctuation used to link contrasting sentences.
- Use linking words to connect contrasting ideas in sentences about diet and exercise – *Although meat and fish are healthy foods, they are expensive in most countries.*

Exercise 1 page 117

Possible answers:

1 I believe junk food adverts should be illegal.
2 In my view, running is not the best exercise for keeping fit.
3 In my opinion, it's not necessary to sleep eight hours a night in order to stay healthy.

Exercise 2 page 118

Answers will vary.

Exercise 3 page 118

Possible answers:

1 shouldn't   2 ought to   3 need to   4 don't need to
5 must

Optional activity

👥 In pairs, students look back at Exercise 3. Ask students to add language to express a purpose to their opinions (e.g. *Governments should control advertising on television in order to...*).

Exercise 4 page 118

1 to / in order to   2 so / so that   3 so / so that
4 to / in order to   5 so / so that

Exercise 5 page 119

1 but; C   2 although; C   3 However; F   4 On the other hand; F

Exercise 6 page 119

2 Although some forms of exercise, such as running, are free, many people never exercise. / Many people never exercise, although some forms of exercise, such as running, are free.
3 Although junk food advertising on TV is exciting for children, it can have a negative influence on their eating habits. / Junk food advertising on TV is exciting for children, although it can have a negative influence on their eating habits.
4 Although most adults should exercise for at least two hours a week, they don't have to do it all at once. / Most adults should exercise for at least two hours a week, although they don't have to do it all at once.

ACADEMIC WRITING SKILLS

Learning objective

- Complete an outline of a balanced opinion essay with notes from an essay about responsibility for obesity

Exercise 1 page 120

Possible answers:

introductory paragraph

background information:

– obesity big problem in the world today

– the WHO says 13% of all adults obese

– can cause serious health problems

– who is responsible? Individual or governments?

thesis statement:

Some people believe governments should introduce laws to help improve the obesity problem, but others believe it is up to the individual.

body paragraph 1

position 1 with supporting arguments and details:

Individuals should take responsibility for controlling their own weight.

– control portion size – calorie intake for adults

– learn to eat a balanced diet – proportions of different food types

– read nutritional information on packaging – to eat less of the unhealthy things like sugar and fat

body paragraph 2

position 2 with supporting arguments and details:

Governments should be responsible for the problem.

– restaurant groups should give information to customers – help people choose a healthy meal

– should be a tax on foods high in fat and sugar – junk food expensive so people buy less

– governments should support healthy eating campaigns – helping people to eat a low-calorie, balanced diet

concluding paragraph

summary of both arguments:

Government should pass new laws, but individuals still need to take responsibility.

your opinion with reasons:

I believe governments can encourage people but ultimately it is up to the individual.

prediction or recommendation:

Individuals and governments need to take action to solve the obesity problem.

WRITING TASK

Learning objectives

- Create an outline for a balanced opinion essay about whether universities should require students to take physical education classes
- Draft your essay
- Review and revise the content and structure of your essay
- Review and revise the use of language in your essay

Exercises 1–6 pages 121–122

Answers will vary.

RESEARCH PROJECT

Help people to eat healthily.

Divide the class into groups and ask them to research different ways of eating healthily. Tell them about different areas of the topic they could research, such as:

vegetarian lifestyles
extreme diets
healthy eating
superfoods

Ask the students to design an informative guide, posters, websites and dietary schemes to explore their findings. Students could also create journals to record what foods they have eaten and activities they have taken part in, and analyze this data to present to the class.

CLASSROOM APP

Exercise 1

Answers will vary.

Exercise 2

1 calories **2** campaign **3** portion **4** reduce **5** serious **6** moderate **7** recognize **8** self-esteem

Exercise 3

Answers will vary.

Exercise 4

1 advertise **2** ban **3** encouragement **4** promotion **5** protect **6** recognition **7** reduce

Exercise 5

1 expectancy **2** programme **3** diet **4** disease **5** campaign **6** food **7** value **8** exercise

Exercise 6

1 in order to **2** so that **3** so **4** to **5** so that **6** to

UNIT OBJECTIVES	
Watch and listen	Watch and understand a video about China's artificial river.
Reading skill	Scan to find information.
Critical thinking	Analyze advantages and disadvantages.
Grammar	Make predictions with modals and adverbs of certainty; use relative clauses; use prepositional phrases with advantages and disadvantages.
Academic writing skill	Write an introductory paragraph (hook, background information, thesis statement).
Writing task	Write an explanatory essay.
⌀ **Teacher development**	Help your students become better at **analyzing advantages and disadvantages**.

UNL⌀CK YOUR KNOWLEDGE

Background note

The photo shows a development workshop at SoftBank Robotics in Tokyo, Japan. The children are learning about the robots and how to interact with them. The humanoid robot in the photo is called Pepper. Pepper was designed to understand human emotions and adapt his behaviour according to the person he is interacting with. The robot was initially used to welcome and help customers in shops in Japan. Subsequently, Pepper has been used in offices, banks, medical facilities and restaurants, and is now available in several countries across the world. He has even been adopted by families in Japan to use at home. Pepper is also used as a research robot for schools, colleges and universities to teach students about programming and robotics.

Lead-in

Ask the students to each write down the first five words that come to mind when thinking about science and technology. Then put them in small groups. Each group chooses one of the words from each group member's list as the basis of their discussion. For example, if a student writes *smartphones*, then that group could discuss how smartphones will evolve in the next ten years. This might lead to a more focused discussion than simply asking the students to discuss the world of science and technology in general.

page 125

1 *Answers will vary.* The photo shows a workshop for students and robot enthusiasts to interact with a new human-like robot.

2–3 *Answers will vary.*

WATCH AND LISTEN

Learning objectives

- Listen and understand the main ideas in a video about a Chinese river
- Listen and correct a set of notes with facts and figures from the video
- Discuss how large-scale engineering has solved problems and evaluate how engineering could help solve a problem in your country

Exercise 1 page 126
Possible answers:
1 Dams are built to hold back and store water.
2 Water comes into my home through pipes from the water main.
3 The water is cleaned at the water treatment plant.

Exercise 2 page 126
Answers will vary.

Exercise 3 page 127
Possible answers:
1 They live in cities in the north.
2 Most people live in the north, but most of the water is in the south.
3 Each section is built separately.
4 Because each section has to be in the perfect position.
5 2030
6 It will help millions of people in the north.

Exercise 4 page 127
1 food water **2** lake river / canal / aqueduct **3** 715 750
4 12 1200 **5** higher lower **6** 2020 2030

Exercise 5 page 127
Answers will vary.

READING 1

Learning objectives

- Understand key vocabulary for inventions – *essential, harmful, helpful*
- Read an article about biomimicry and select the best summary
- Scan the article for examples of biomimicry
- Annotate the text with summary notes
- Make inferences about the ideas in the article
- Give opinions on the use and future of biomimicry

Exercise 1 page 128

1 harmful   2 helpful   3 prevent   4 pattern   5 unlimited
6 essential   7 illustrate

Exercise 2 page 128

Possible answers:

1 biology / biological, biography / biographical, biopic, biomedicine / biomedical, bioengineering, biodata, biometrics   2 the act of copying (mimicry), the act of copying from nature (biomimicry)   3 *Answers will vary.*

Lead-in

Show photos of the things in nature that are mentioned in the reading (burdock seeds, a shark, an eagle and a falcon, a tropical boxfish). Tell students to discuss in pairs possible inventions that were based on these things from nature. They then read the article to find out.

Exercise 3 page 130

c

Exercise 4 page 130

1 Velcro®; Speedo Fastskin® swimsuit; Eagle Eyes® sunglasses; Bionic Car   2 burdock seeds; shark skin; eagle and falcon eyes; boxfish

Exercise 5 page 130

1 hooks and loops   2 children's clothing; lunch bags, shoes   3 Fastskin® fabric   4 swim faster
5 astronauts' eyes   6 the yellow oil which filters out harmful radiation   7 the shape of the boxfish

Exercise 6 page 130

Possible answers:

1 It replaces buttons, zips and shoelaces, so it's easier for children to get dressed by themselves.

2 It was argued that suits made of Fastskin® gave some swimmers an unfair advantage.

3 Some people might think that it is ugly. Others might find it cute.

Exercise 7 page 131

Answers will vary.

Optional activity

With the whole class, brainstorm different items from nature that might be inspirations for inventions. Put students into small groups and tell them to choose one item and invent a new technology based on it. Tell them they'll present their findings to the class, and that they should use as many of the new vocabulary words from Reading 1 as they can. Give them 10–15 minutes to prepare. When giving their presentations, each student in the group should speak and each should try to use new vocabulary.

Examples of items from nature: spider web, octopus, sea sponge, hummingbird.

READING 2

Learning objectives

- Understand key vocabulary for technology – *artificial, break down, three-dimensional*
- Scan an article about future technologies to identify the technologies discussed
- Read and understand the main ideas in an article on future technologies
- Read and identify detailed information
- Make inferences about the implications of the inventions in the article for society
- Synthesize information from an article about biomimicry and an article about future technologies in a discussion

Lead-in

Give students an unnumbered list of the top ten innovations that changed history. Tell them to put the list in order, with number 1 being the innovation that they think has been most important in changing history. Then show them the numbered list, and they can discuss whether they agree or disagree with it, and whether any of the innovations have disadvantages. You may need to explain or show photos of some of the innovations.

Top ten list: 1. Printing Press 2. Compass
3. Paper currency 4. Steel 5. The electric light
6. Domestication of the horse 7. Transistors
8. Magnifying lenses 9. The telegraph 10. Antibiotics

Exercise 1 page 131

1 equipment   2 personal   3 electronic   4 Three-dimensional   5 movement   6 breaks down   7 objects
8 Artificial

Exercise 2 page 132

Possible answers:

1 They could become a reality – a Slovakian company is reportedly planning to start selling flying cars from 2020. However, drivers of such a car would need a pilot's licence to fly it, while commercial production would be very expensive. Therefore, these cars are unlikely to be an everyday reality any time soon.

2 A 3-D printer is a printer attached to a computer that can make solid objects from a digital model by printing many separate layers of the object. It is used in manufacturing to print models, novelty food, low cost artificial limbs, etc.

3 Robots can help people who are missing arms or legs by providing artificial limbs that help people to have normal function, such as picking things up with their artificial hand.

Exercise 3 page 132

1 4   **2** 2   **3** 3

Exercise 4 page 132

1 advantages: b; **disadvantages:** d   **2 advantages:** f; **disadvantages:** a   **3 advantages:** c; **disadvantages:** e

Exercise 5 page 134

1 T   **2** F; Mechanical failure will be a problem for flying cars.   **3** DNS   **4** DNS   **5** T   **6** T   **7** F; The battery life of a robot suit is short at the moment.

Exercise 6 page 134

Possible answers:

1 All machines have the potential to break down and a breakdown in the air might cause falling objects that would be a serious danger below.

2 If everybody has a personal flying car and uses it like people use the roads today, then there will be air congestion.

3 These medical benefits might include: enabling people who are unable to walk, or who have missing limbs or some kind of paralysis, to regain some movement; increasing mobility in partially sighted or blind people; doing dangerous work in place of people, so that they avoid injury.

4 Because they have taken a long time to develop; the materials used to make the exoskeleton might be very specialized.

Exercise 7 page 134

Answers will vary.

Be flexible

👤 Provide **advanced students** with a related creative writing opportunity. Tell students to imagine they are living in a future where the three inventions mentioned in Reading 2 are widely available. Students should choose one of the inventions and

imagine they use it in their daily life or their job. They should write a letter to a friend that describes their experience of using the invention.

LANGUAGE DEVELOPMENT

Learning objectives

- Use modals and adverbs of certainty to complete predictions with varying degrees of certainty – *Cars will definitely become more efficient in the future. We could possibly see humans walking on Mars soon. We probably won't have flying cars.*
- Record words by prefix and prefix meaning in a table – *decrease, disagree, enable, prevent, rebuild, transport, unlikely*
- Use the meanings of prefixes to identify the meaning of new vocabulary

Exercise 1 page 135

1 will definitely   **2** probably won't   **3** will probably   **4** will probably   **5** will definitely   **6** definitely won't   **7** could possibly

Exercise 2 page 135

1 In years to come   **2** before the end of the decade   **3** In the near future   **4** before too long   **5** within the next ten years   **6** within the next few years   **7** By 2035

Exercise 3 page 136

Possible answers:

de-	deactivate, defrost, degenerate
dis-	disengage, disobey, disappear
en-	enrage, endanger, enrich
pre-	prepare, predict
re-	reread, rewrite, replay
trans-	transfer, translate, transcribe
un-	uncertain, unbelievable, unfair

Exercise 4 page 136

1 same   **2** same   **3** opposite   **4** same   **5** opposite   **6** opposite   **7** same

Exercise 5 page 136

Answers will vary.

CRITICAL THINKING

Learning objectives

- Use a T-chart to organize a list of advantages and disadvantages
- Brainstorm a list of recent inventions by their area of use
- Analyze the advantages and disadvantages of an invention using a T-chart

UNL*O*CK TEACHER DEVELOPMENT

BE INFORMED

→ **Analyzing advantages and disadvantages** is an important skill for students because: (1) Doing this can be a relatively quick and straightforward way into exploring a topic, which can be particularly useful if students are showing reluctance or lack of interest; (2) A T-chart is a very useful tool which can be used in a wide range of different situations, and should become a familiar part of students' academic education; (3) Going through the process of analyzing advantages and disadvantages will result in the development of a stronger argument.

BE CONFIDENT

→ Develop this skill for yourself by doing the following activity:

Think about one of the classroom activities listed below. Then complete the T-chart with its advantages and disadvantages.

debating   flipped classroom   group work pair work   project work

advantages	disadvantages

Lead-in

At this point in each unit students are asked to begin to think about the writing task they will do at the end of the unit. Give them a minute to read the box and to look at the T-chart.

UNL*O*CK TEACHER DEVELOPMENT

BE READY

Look at the Critical Thinking section in the Student's Book on pages 137–138.

→ Which elements of the lesson do you think your students will find easiest / most difficult / most useful? Why?

→ Are your answers true for all students in your class?

→ How can you adapt your teaching or the material to meet your students' needs?

BE FLEXIBLE

If you think your students will struggle with Exercise 2 (or you cannot access the internet in class), ask them to just focus on the areas of technology which they know about. They can ignore the others. All they need are a few items from which they can make their selection in Exercise 3.

Exercise 1 page 137
Possible answers:

flying car: advantages: 3-D freedom of movement, avoid traffic lights, busy roads and speeding tickets; **disadvantages:** traffic control, mechanical failure, air traffic congestion

3-D printer: advantages: make life-size models, print body parts; **disadvantages:** equipment is extremely expensive

Ironman suit: advantages: lift heavy objects, walk long distances, punch through walls, military uses, help people with disabilities; **disadvantages:** expensive, short battery life, heavy

Exercise 2 page 138
Possible answers:

medicine: advances in 3-D imaging

home: solar roof, low-flush toilet, stand-up desk

space: SpaceX, Mars Rover, International Space Station

transport: microcars, e-bikes, boosted skateboards, driverless cars

entertainment: HD TV, Bluetooth, smart watch, 3-D glasses

computers: tablet computers, the Cloud

agriculture: hydroponics, genetically engineered seeds

Exercises 3–4 page 138
Answers will vary.

GRAMMAR FOR WRITING

Learning objectives

- Use a relative pronoun to complete the relative clause in sentences – *People who are unable to walk may be able to walk with the help of a robotic suit.*
- Differentiate between defining and non-defining relative clauses
- Join pairs of sentences using a relative clause
- Differentiate between prepositional phrases presenting advantages and disadvantages – *The main advantage of ... is ..., The main argument in favour of ... is ..., The problem with ... is ...*
- Use prepositional phrases to complete sentences about the advantages and disadvantages of inventions – *One good thing about robots is that they can do dangerous or boring jobs instead of humans. Perhaps the biggest concern with flying cars is that they could crash, causing terrible accidents.*

Exercise 1 page 139

1 which/that, D; relative clause: *which is based on the rough patterns on a shark's skin*

2 which, ND; relative clause: *which filters out harmful radiation*

3 who, ND; relative clause: *who often have to lift people out of burning buildings or cars*

4 who, D; relative clause: *who are unable to walk*

5 which, ND; relative clause: *which makes it possible to build objects using layers of liquid plastic*

Exercise 2 page 140

Possible answers:

1 Scientists have already developed new robots which/that are able to do dangerous work.

2 There is a great deal of technology to help elderly people who may have trouble doing some tasks by themselves.

3 There is a huge amount of new investment in biofuels, which are cleaner and more sustainable than fossil fuels.

4 The Bionic Car has a special design which/that makes it more fuel efficient.

5 Important research is being done by scientists at the University of Cambridge, who hope to publish it next year.

Exercise 3 page 141

Positive arguments: 1, 5, 7, 8; **Negative arguments:** 2, 3, 4, 6, 9, 10

Exercise 4 page 141

Possible answers:

1 The main advantage of   2 The main worry about
3 A real benefit of   4 The main disadvantage of
5 One bad thing about

ACADEMIC WRITING SKILLS

Learning objectives

- Identify the key features of the introductory paragraph to an academic essay in the article on biomimicry and the article on future technologies
- Evaluate the two introductions to the texts in the unit and decide which has more impact on the reader

Exercise 1 page 142

1 The hook is that ideas from nature are used in a huge range of everyday products. It is not a very strong hook and does not really grab the reader's attention.

2 The background information consists of definitions of the terms *mimic* and *biomimicry*.

3 The topic is the influence of biomimicry. The point of view is that it can be seen in many everyday products. We don't know how many paragraphs there will be, but each paragraph will probably discuss a different product.

Exercise 2 page 143

1 The hook is a question: 'What will the world of the next generation look like?' It gets your attention by making you start thinking about the topic.

2 The background information consists of two opposing views about the role of technology.

3 The topic is predictions about the uses of innovations in technology. The point of view is that there are advantages and disadvantages to innovation. We know there will be three body paragraphs and each one will discuss the advantages and disadvantages of a different prediction.

4 *Possible answer:* The second introduction is probably more interesting, as it has a stronger hook and a thesis statement which clearly shows what the following paragraphs will discuss.

WRITING TASK

Learning objectives

- Prepare an introductory paragraph for an essay on a new technology
- Create an outline for the body of your essay
- Plan a conclusion
- Draft your essay
- Review and revise the content and structure of your essay
- Review and revise the use of language in your essay

Exercises 1–10 pages 143–144

Answers will vary.

RESEARCH PROJECT

Invent a robot concept.

Divide the class into groups and ask them to think about how they could use robots in these areas:

food production
the household
care of elderly people
companionship
construction
helping in dangerous places

Tell them that they have to produce a brochure and presentation which sells a robot concept to a particular group of people. They have to think about design, the target audience, specifications, features, marketing and the user experience.

Students should present their projects to the rest of the class and decide on the best idea.

CLASSROOM APP

Exercise 1
Answers will vary.

Exercise 2
1 essential **2** artificial **3** equipment **4** movement
5 illustrate **6** prevent **7** object **8** unlimited

Exercise 3
Answers will vary.

Exercise 4
1 100% **2** 20% **3** 90% **4** 50% **5** 0%

Exercise 5
1 trans **2** un **3** en **4** pre **5** dis **6** de **7** re

Exercise 6
1 Sentence 1 **2** Sentence 3 **3** historical information.
4 the Lego brand. **5** reasons for the popularity of Lego.

UNIT OBJECTIVES

Watch and listen	Watch and understand a video about Savile Row's first female Master Tailor.
Reading skill	Distinguish fact from opinion.
Critical thinking	Identify strong arguments.
Grammar	Use multi-word prepositions to combine information.
Academic writing skills	Use body paragraphs in point–counterpoint essays; use counter-arguments; use cohesion.
Writing task	Write a point–counterpoint essay.
⟲ **Teacher development**	Help your students become better at **identifying strong arguments**.

UNLOCK YOUR KNOWLEDGE

Background note

The photo shows fashion design students in class. The student pictured is looking at drawings of clothing designs, and there are other students and a mannequin in the background. Fashion designers design and make clothes that are sold in shops or online. They may be sold in small boutiques by designer fashion labels or by large chains.

Lead-in

Write the names of two or three well-known brands of clothing on the board. Then ask the students individually to write down as many other brands as they can think of in two minutes, on the left-hand side of a piece of paper. After two minutes, tell them to stop, then give them another two minutes to go around the class and find as many people wearing the brands on their list as possible. They should do this as a fast-paced mingling activity, asking their fellow classmates which of the brands on their own list they are wearing. They should write the name of a student wearing that brand on the right-hand side of the paper, next to the brand name. When time is up, tell the students to stop and count up the number of brands found. The winner is the student with the most brands found in the class.

page 147
1 The photo shows a man working as a fashion designer.
2–4 *Answers will vary.*

WATCH AND LISTEN

Learning objectives

- Listen and understand the main ideas in a video about a female Master Tailor in a male-dominated industry
- Listen and understand facts and figures
- Understand the meaning of unfamiliar words and phrases from their context in the video
- Practise talking about jobs in the clothing industry

Exercises 1–2 page 148
Answers will vary.

Exercise 3 page 149
Answers will vary. Possible answers:
1 It is famous for selling high-quality, handmade men's suits.
2 She is a tailor. She is the first female Master Tailor on Savile Row. / She is the first woman to have her name above the door on Savile Row.
3 More women are becoming tailors; more women are getting more important jobs.

Exercise 4 page 149
1 T   **2** F; Women have always worked on Savile Row.   **3** T
4 F; Last year, more than 65% of new tailors were female.
5 T   **6** F; Kathryn has the same values and principles as the other Savile Row tailors.

Exercise 5 page 149
1 become a Master Tailor   **2** women in the industry
3 rising to more prominent positions   **4** we all know each other

make it to the top: to become the head of a business / very successful in your work

a sign of the times: something that has changed because society has changed

behind the scenes: in a business, where the customers cannot see

network: a group of people who work together or cooperate for professional purposes

Exercise 6 page 149

Answers will vary.

READING 1

Learning objectives

- Understand key vocabulary for fashion – *brand, volume, season*
- Use your knowledge to predict ideas in an article about fast fashion
- Read and understand main ideas and details about fast fashion
- Make inferences about people's opinions based on their comments about the article
- Give opinions on fashion culture

Exercise 1 page 150

a season   **b** manufacture   **c** volume   **d** collection
e cotton   **f** invest   **g** brand

Exercises 2–3 page 150

Possible answers:

1 Inexpensive clothing that is sold briefly for a short period in stores and then replaced with other styles.
2 In some shops they change frequently, while luxury brands usually only have a new collection each season.
3 Frequent style changes make shoppers want to buy more. This can have a positive effect on the economy.

Lead-in

After students have discussed the term 'fast fashion' in Exercise 2, tell them that fast fashion may be a result of consumers wanting things to happen quickly. In order to put fast fashion in the context of modern society, ask: *What are some other indications that life today is fast-paced?* (fast food, the internet, smartphones) Then ask: *Who are the winners and the losers in each of these situations?* Put students in small groups for this discussion. Hold a follow-up discussion with the whole class, focusing mainly on the idea of fast fashion.

Exercise 4 page 152

a 4   **b** 2   **c** not mentioned   **e** 3

Exercise 5 page 153

2 ~~High-end fashion~~ Fast-fashion designs that are unpopular are withdrawn in less than a week.
3 ~~Traditional~~ Fast fashion is good for the manufacturer because of the greater volume of sales.

4 The biggest problem with fast fashion is ~~the theft of ideas~~ the impact of wasted clothes on the environment.
5 Cotton growers need to produce more, so they have to use ~~fewer~~ more chemicals.
6 Designer clothing is popular with ~~poorer~~ wealthy shoppers.

Be flexible

You could encourage a little competition here by asking students to do the task as quickly as possible and to raise their hands as soon as they have all the answers. The person with their hand up first should be called on to provide the answers. Encourage feedback from the rest of the class. If the answering student got any of the questions wrong, try to elicit the correct answer(s) from the class.

Exercise 6 page 153

1 Ahmet   2 Carmen   3 Sara   4 Fatima; Many people agree with her opinion about protecting the Earth.
5 Jasmine; People dislike her wasteful attitude.

Exercise 7 page 153

Answers will vary.

READING 2

Learning objectives

- Understand key vocabulary for the fashion industry – *conditions, import, multinational*
- Skim the title and introductory paragraph of an essay to understand the topic and writer's point of view
- Read and understand main arguments in an essay about offshore production in the fashion industry
- Scan the essay for facts and figures
- Distinguish facts about overseas production from the writer's opinions
- Synthesize information from an article about fast fashion and an essay about offshore production in a discussion

Lead-in

Tell students that production of clothing can be controversial because the work is often outsourced to developing countries, where working conditions may be poor. Ask students what they think *poor working conditions* means. Write their answers on the board and then read the article to see if they missed anything.

Exercise 1 page 154

1 multinational   2 wages   3 conditions   4 textiles
5 outsource   6 offshore   7 import

Exercise 2 page 154

Possible answers:

1 Because labour costs are lower and sometimes environmental regulations aren't as strict.

2 Multinational companies bring more jobs to local workers. Workers pay taxes, and this enriches the country.

3 Sometimes, working conditions are bad and workers are paid low wages.

Exercise 3 page 155

1 It is about using offshore production to keep costs down in the textile industry.

2 Supporters claim it helps local economies. The writer is against it. In the thesis statement, the writer says that she thinks outsourcing is harmful.

Exercise 4 page 156

Arguments for outsourcing:

Provides jobs at higher wages than local workers can make in agriculture.

People in developing countries often line up to take jobs in multinational factories.

Overseas factories have become safer and more ethical in recent years.

Arguments against outsourcing:

Most workers are paid by the piece.

Working conditions in many offshore factories remain uncomfortable and unsafe.

Workers often work 14 hours a day and earn less than €100 a month.

Worker protection laws, like those in developed nations, often don't exist or are not followed.

Exercise 5 page 156

1 €29 billion   2 Multinational   3 40   4 don't exist or are not followed   5 117   6 economist

Exercise 6 page 157

1 fact   2 writer's opinion   3 fact   4 fact   5 fact
6 writer's opinion

Exercise 7 page 157

Answers will vary.

Be flexible

👤 If internet access is available, you could ask the students to follow up Question 2 by researching what multinationals are currently doing to support the local communities in which they invest. Provide guidance in conducting the research for **lower-level students**. Ask students to brainstorm what keywords they would need to use to conduct a search, and what websites they could use to find information. Point out that simply going to a search engine and typing in some keywords is not always the best option when trying to find specific information; they could start by going to a multinational's website and seeing if they can find any information on local initiatives.

LANGUAGE DEVELOPMENT

Learning objective

- Understand vocabulary for the fashion business – *advertising, consumer, designer label*

Exercise 1 page 158

a supplier   b designer label   c overseas   d consumer
e advertising   f competitor   g labour   h manufacturing

Optional activity

👥 Write the vocabulary words on the board, spreading them out in random order. Divide the class into teams. One student from the first team comes to the board and chooses a word. The student must say the word correctly, give the definition and use it in a sentence. If everything is correct, the team gets a point and the student erases the word. If not everything is correct, the word remains in play on the board. The game is over when all the words are erased from the board. The team with the most points wins.

CRITICAL THINKING

Learning objectives

- Organize arguments from an essay about outsourcing fashion production in a table
- Identify the types of support used by the writer
- Evaluate the types of support used by the writer
- Categorize a list of arguments relating to the writing task for Unit 7
- Evaluate the strength of the arguments and justify your opinion
- Support the three strongest arguments with additional evidence

UNLOCK TEACHER DEVELOPMENT

BE INFORMED

→ **Identifying strong arguments** is an important skill for students because: (1) When students read, they need to be able to identify what is a strong argument and what is a weak argument; (2) This is also a skill they need when they write, so that they can ensure their writing is as persuasive as possible; (3) Whilst arguments by 'experts' can be very strong evidence, students should also not be afraid to challenge these arguments if they have different evidence which they think is stronger.

BE CONFIDENT

→ Develop this skill for yourself by doing the following activity:

Writing which contains strong arguments may use some or all of the following types of evidence: facts, statistics, expert opinions, reasons, quotations, examples, personal experience. Which of these can you identify in the paragraph below?

Teacher development, in my experience, is extremely valuable. Participating in teacher training sessions at my school has definitely made me a better teacher in the classroom. Over the past few years, my results have improved by 10%, and my students' enjoyment of my lesson by 20%. My students are now more focused and attentive in class, mainly because my lessons are more structured. For example, they work together in pairs much more effectively. This view is supported by the academic literature, which shows that when teachers are effective classroom managers, their students achieve more (Stronge et al., 2008, 2011) and are more interested in what is being taught (Kunter et al., 2007).

Key: Sentences 1/2 Personal experience; 3 Statistics; 4 Reason; 5 Example; 6 Expert opinions / quotations

Lead-in

At this point in each unit students are asked to begin to think about the writing task they will do at the end of the unit. Give them a minute to read the box and to look at the table below it.

UNLOCK TEACHER DEVELOPMENT

BE READY

Look at the Critical Thinking section in the Student's Book on pages 159–160.

→ Which elements of the lesson do you think your students will find easiest / most difficult / most useful? Why?

→ Are your answers true for all students in your class?
→ How can you adapt your teaching or the material to meet your students' needs?

BE FLEXIBLE

Some students may find Exercise 5 difficult to do, so it might be useful to take class feedback at this point. Let different students say whether they think the arguments *for* or *against* are stronger, and give reasons. This may help some students decide what they think, which will make it easier to do Exercise 6.

Exercise 1 page 159
Possible answers:
4 earn less than €100 per month
5 textiles workers
6 most workers are paid by the piece
supporting argument 2: Overseas factories have become safer and more ethical in recent years.
8 now provide day-care centres
9 work conditions remain uncomfortable and unsafe
10 worker protection laws often don't exist
11 workers are exposed to chemicals, dust and unsafe noise levels
author's conclusion: The arguments for offshore production do not justify the low wages and dangerous conditions seen. The author believes the multinational companies should use a much higher share of their profits to correct these problems.

Exercise 2 page 160
facts: 2, 6, 9, 10; **statistics:** 3, 4, 5
expert opinions: 1; **quotations:** 7
examples: 8, 12; **personal experience:** 11

Exercise 3 page 160
1 Facts were used the most in Reading 2. Facts present a more convincing argument.
2–3 *Answers will vary.*

Exercise 4 page 160
1 F **2** A **3** A **4** A **5** F **6** F **7** A **8** A **9** A **10** F

Exercise 5 page 160
Against: The arguments *against* far outweigh the arguments *for*.

Exercise 6 page 160
Answers will vary.

UNLOCK TEACHER DEVELOPMENT

BE REFLECTIVE

Think about the following questions:

→ How well were your students able to answer Questions 2 and 3 in Exercise 3? Some classes may find it very difficult to answer these types of question, having never been asked them before, or not knowing how to answer them. If this is the case, think of how you can help them develop this knowledge.

→ Think about the writing (or speaking) which you do. When you are trying to persuade people, do you use the types of evidence presented in the *Be confident* section? Are there any types you think you should use more than you already do? Why / Why not?

BE COLLABORATIVE

Your development is more meaningful when it is shared. See page 14 for ideas on how to peer-collaborate. Why not share the ideas you generated in the *Be flexible* section, and their outcome?

GRAMMAR FOR WRITING

Learning objectives

- Identify multi-word prepositions in sentences about fashion – *Due to their longer lifespan, expensive designer clothes are more environmentally friendly than cheap clothes.*
- Identify the meanings of multi-word prepositions in sentences
- Use prepositional phrases to complete sentences about the fashion industry – *The company closed its offshore production facilities in addition to its overseas retail stores. Instead of buying disposable fashion, it is better for the environment if people choose clothes that last longer.*

Exercise 1 page 161

1 instead of; preference   **2** due to; reason   **3** because of; reason   **4** in spite of; contrast   **5** along with; addition

Exercise 2 page 161

1 in addition to / along with   **2** instead of / rather than   **3** Other than / Apart from / Except for   **4** Due to / As a result of / Because of   **5** rather than / instead of

Exercise 3 page 162

1 Instead of   **2** In addition to   **3** In spite of   **4** except for   **5** along with

Optional activity

Divide the students into small groups. Tell them to imagine they are the new management team for a clothing factory and they are going to write new rules for a safe, comfortable work environment. The students should refer to Reading 2 for poor working conditions that need to change. They have to use a multi-word preposition in each sentence. For example: *Because of the rising cost of living, all employees will get an increase in wages.*

ACADEMIC WRITING SKILLS

Learning objectives

- Evaluate opening statements for the first body paragraph of an essay about the fashion industry and body-image
- Identify the types of support used in a body paragraph from an essay on the fashion industry and body-image
- Evaluate the writer's arguments and evidence
- Use words and phrases to express counter-arguments – *Supporters of moving production overseas are in favour of foreign investment. They insist that this investment plays a central role in improving the economy in developing countries.*
- Identify different ways of creating cohesion in writing in paragraphs about fashion
- Complete a paragraph with a range of words and phrases to create cohesion

Exercise 1 page 162

b

Exercise 2 page 163

Some magazines and designers have recently begun promoting a more positive and realistic body-image in their products.

Exercise 3 page 163

Possible answers:

Leading fashion magazines encourage a healthier approach to body image; some fashion companies use realistic models; there is a quote from Pierre Dupont about representing all body shapes.

Exercise 4 page 163

Answers will vary.

Exercise 5 page 164

Possible answers:

1 in favour; claim/argue; has a positive impact on
2 Critics/Opponents; argue   **3** point out; is an important factor in; because

Exercise 6 page 164

Possible answers:

1 it is important to the economy
2 it creates new jobs
3 it brings investment to developing countries
4 it pays overseas workers badly; encourages child labour
5 it causes too much waste

Be flexible

👆 For homework, ask students to find an article in a newspaper about a controversial topic. They should read the article and then write five or six sentences in their own words, stating what supporters and critics say about the issue. In the lesson, they can read their sentences to each other in small groups.

👥 For **lower-level students**, adapt this into an in-class activity. Find an article from the news for students to read. Assign some small groups to focus on arguments for the topic and others against it. Ask both sides to state their arguments and then invite students to reorganize themselves into groups based on the argument they agree with. Ask students from each side to explain their choice.

Exercise 7 page 164

1 Traditionally (example) – transition between ideas; fashion retailers – synonym for fashion industry; one – pronoun referring to clothing collections; Nowadays – transition between sentences or ideas; in contrast – transition between ideas; they – fashion industry

2 the same outfits – synonym for sets of clothes; This – refers to earlier idea; clothing – repetition of noun; Furthermore, transition between ideas; so quickly – refers to earlier idea; and – transition between ideas; that – refers to earlier idea

Exercise 8 page 165

1 this   **2** change   **3** them   **4** ones   **5** they   **6** This
7 that   **8** In addition   **9** these   **10** Meanwhile

WRITING TASK

Learning objectives

- Prepare an outline of a point–counterpoint essay about whether the fashion industry is harmful to society and the environment
- Draft your essay
- Review and revise the content and structure of your paragraphs
- Review and revise the use of language in your paragraphs

Exercises 1–7 pages 165–166

Answers will vary.

RESEARCH PROJECT

Find out how ethical your brands are.

After dividing the class into groups, ask students to list as many different clothing brands as they know. Tell them that they have to pick five from their list and find out how ethical they are. They must look at:

- how each company affects the environment
- how sustainable the clothing is
- where the clothing is made and the conditions of the workers
- the company's ethical and environmental policies

Students can create an awareness campaign to educate people on the most ethical brands. They should write about how different fabrics are made and the lives of people who make their clothes.

CLASSROOM APP

Exercise 1

Answers will vary.

Exercise 2

1 imports   **2** textiles   **3** season   **4** brands **5** offshore
6 volume   **7** invest   **8** conditions

Exercise 3

Answers will vary.

Exercise 4

1 overseas   **2** manufacturing   **3** supplier   **4** designer
labels   **5** advertising   **6** labour   **7** competitor
8 consumer

Exercise 5

1 a. transitions between sentences or between ideas;
  b. repetition of nouns or use of synonyms;
  c. pronouns that refer back to nouns in earlier sentences
2 a. transitions between sentences or between ideas;
  b. repetition of nouns or use of synonyms;
  c. pronouns that refer back to nouns in earlier sentences
3 a. transitions between sentences or between ideas;
  b. repetition of nouns or use of synonyms;
  d. *this / that / these / those* to refer to earlier nouns or ideas.

UNIT OBJECTIVES

Watch and listen	Watch and understand a video about the stock market crash of 1929.
Reading skill	Skim for general ideas.
Critical thinking	Understand and interpret line graphs.
Grammar	Describe graphs using noun and verb phrases; use prepositions and conjunctions to add data; use approximations.
Academic writing skills	Write a description of a graph; write a concluding paragraph.
Writing task	Write an analysis essay.
⦿ **Teacher development**	Help your students become better at **understanding line graphs**.

UNL⦿CK YOUR KNOWLEDGE

Background note

The photo shows investors watching the stock market at an exchange hall in Beijing, China. Beijing is one of the major economic centres in China. The country is rich in natural resources such as coal and metals, and has the world's largest manufacturing industry, which exports goods around the world. In general, factors that may affect a country's economy are geographical factors, the country's debt level, environmental factors, social and political factors and the availability of natural resources.

Lead-in

In this unit, students will be exposed to the academic subject area of Economics. Elicit from the class the meaning of *Economics* (the study of the way in which trade, industry and money are organized). Ask what sorts of jobs people with an Economics degree might have.

page 169
Answers will vary.

WATCH AND LISTEN

Learning objectives

- Listen and identify main ideas in a video about a bad day for the world economy
- Listen and understand details
- Make inferences about the ideas in the video
- Practise talking about the world economy

Exercise 1 page 170
Possible answers:

1 New York, London, Hong Kong, Tokyo, Singapore
2 *Possible answers:* People lose their jobs. / People don't have money. / Banks and businesses fail.
3 *Answers will vary.*

Exercise 2 page 170

1 There was a financial disaster / stock market crash.
2 in the US / New York / on Wall Street
3 a long time ago

Exercise 3 page 170
Answers will vary.

Exercise 4 page 171
1 c   **2** e   **3** d   **4** a   **5** b

Exercise 5 page 171
Possible answers:

1 (Tuesday) October 29, 1929   **2** They fell by 90%
3 They failed   **4** Wall Street, New York   **5** Computers and electronic boards

Exercise 6 page 171
Possible answers:

1 Yes

2 Because the economies of countries are connected. The US lent money to Europe after World War I and when the US economy collapsed, money stopped being sent to Europe and economies in European countries collapsed as well, resulting in job losses.

3 Computers let people get information quickly. More people can get stock information with computers.

Exercise 7 page 171
Answers will vary.

READING 1

Learning objectives

- Understand key vocabulary for the economy – *recession, interest rate, stocks and shares*
- Skim an article about investments to identify the main topics
- Identify the main ideas in the text and write them in the order they appear
- Read and understand facts and figures
- Make inferences about investments according to the article
- Express opinions on investments

Exercise 1 page 172

a interest rate   **b** return   **c** stocks and shares
d investor   **e** value   **f** recession   **g** investment

Exercise 2 page 172

1 *Possible answers:* stocks, bonds, real estate, gold, jewels, coins, art
2–3 *Answers will vary.*

Lead-in

After deciding whether collecting gold or classic cars is the better investment, students should look at the graphs in the reading. They should discuss the graphs and then decide whether they want to change their answer or keep it the same.

Exercise 3 page 174

two popular investments; the price of gold over time; classic cars as an investment; the risks of investing

Exercise 4 page 174

Paragraph 1: two popular investments
Paragraph 2: the price of gold over time
Paragraph 3: classic cars as an investment
Paragraph 4: the risks of investing

Exercise 5 page 174

1 $1,087 an ounce   **2** In 2012. It cost $1,664 an ounce.
3 The price will remain in the same range.   **4** $13,000
5 about $1 million   **6** $4.1 million

Exercise 6 page 174

Possible answers:

1 The stock market, because historically it has brought in higher returns than gold.
2 Probably yes, because it costs money to keep them in excellent condition, and because investors have to guess which car is going to become valuable. The Aston Martin's high value was mainly due to its connection to the James Bond films.

3 *Answers will vary.*

Optional activity

👥👥👥 You could ask half the class to research sources that disagree with the advice given in the article, and half the class to find sources that agree. The students could then compare their ideas in small groups ('agree' groups and 'disagree' groups) and report back to the class. This would be useful reading practice and would help students see that it is important to check sources before relying on them. For example, good journalists often check a 'fact' against at least two authoritative sources before relying on it in an article. The same is true of other professional writers, as their reputations rest on both the accuracy of their work and the way in which they interpret the facts about which they write.

Exercise 7 page 175
Answers will vary.

READING 2

Learning objectives

- Understand key vocabulary for personal finances – *standard of living, income, expenditure*
- Read and annotate main ideas, key words, supporting examples and arguments in an article about the standard of living in countries around the world
- Read and identify facts and figures
- Make inferences about the issues described in the article
- Synthesize information from an article about investments and an article about the standard of living in countries around the world in a discussion

Lead-in

Put students into pairs. Tell them to make two columns on a piece of paper: one for basic needs and one for luxuries. They should brainstorm items and decide under which category each item falls. They may disagree on certain items, such as new clothes and mobile phones, so encourage them to come to an agreement on each item. Students can then come to the board and make a whole-class table of basic needs v luxuries. Then you can discuss which items are rising in cost the fastest.

Exercise 1 page 175

a savings   **b** standard of living   **c** factor   **d** expenditure
e income   **f** percentage

Exercise 2 page 176
Answers will vary.

Exercise 3 page 176

1 Many people are actually poorer than they were 10 or 20 years ago. **2** income, number of people in family, costs for housing, utilities, food, medical bills, education, etc.

Exercise 4 page 176

Answers will vary.

Exercise 5 page 176

b

Exercise 6 page 176

1 b **2** a **3** b **4** b **5** a

Exercise 7 page 178

Possible answers:

1 Japan, the United States, (West) Germany, France, Italy

2 rising populations in cities as more people move to cities; lack of investment in building new houses and apartments by businesses and governments

3 $14,750 (25% of income)

Exercise 8 page 178

Possible answers:

1 less, because wages have decreased or stayed the same and expenditure has increased **2** probably not, because the stock market is risky **3** *Answers will vary.*

Optional activity

Put students into small groups and ask them to research the cost of living around the world. Each group should research a different country (Japan, United States, United Kingdom, China, United Arab Emirates). Areas they research can be, e.g. median income, cost of housing, seeing a film, a cup of coffee, public transport, etc. Each group should put their information in a table then explain their findings to the class. This can be given as homework.

LANGUAGE DEVELOPMENT

Learning objectives

- Use related nouns and adjectives for economics to complete sentences about the economy – *employment/employed; profession/professional; expense/expensive*
- Use nouns for economic trends to complete sentences about the economy – *demand, market, purchase*

Exercise 1 page 178

Possible answers:

1 economy (n) the system by which a country produces and uses goods and money
economic (adj) relating to money, industry or trade

2 finance (n) the control of how large amounts of money should be spent
financial (adj) relating to money or how money is managed

3 wealth (n) a large amount of money or valuable possessions that somebody has
wealthy (adj) having lots of money or possessions; rich

4 poverty (n) the condition of being extremely poor
poor (adj) having very little money or few possessions

5 value (n) how much money something could be sold for
valuable (adj) worth a lot of money

6 employment (n) the fact of somebody being paid to work for a company or organization
employed (adj) working for a company that pays you a wage

7 profession (n) a type of work that needs special training or education
professional (adj) relating to work that needs special training or education

8 expense (n) the money that you spend on something
expensive (adj) costing a lot of money

Exercise 2 page 179

1 economy **2** financial **3** wealthy **4** poverty
5 valuable **6** employment **7** Professional **8** expensive

Be flexible

Provide **lower-level students** with additional practice using the correct word form. Select words from Exercise 1 that students need more practice with. In pairs, students will have to supply the correct form of the words and write sentences. For example, say *Write a sentence with the noun form of* financial. Students have to write a sentence with *finance*. Review the sentences and check for correct usage.

Exercise 3 page 179

1 markets **2** purchase **3** consumers **4** trend
5 demand **6** Revenue **7** supply

CRITICAL THINKING

Learning objectives

- Understand the organization of information presented in a line graph about income and expenditure
- Analyze the trends shown in a line graph about income and expenditure
- Analyze the information and trends in a line graph about revenue from DVDs and video streaming

UNLOCK TEACHER DEVELOPMENT

BE INFORMED

→ **Understanding line graphs** is an important skill for students because: (1) Line graphs, as a way of showing data, are very commonly used in many academic subjects, especially the natural and social sciences; (2) Students can find it difficult to understand the different components of a graph (e.g. axis, legend) and what they mean; (3) When using line graphs in their writing, students often do not use them as effectively as they could to support their arguments – they need to say why they are important.

BE CONFIDENT

→ Develop this skill for yourself by doing the following activity:

The line graph below shows an imaginary set of survey results about critical thinking exams at the primary, secondary and tertiary level in a particular country. Look at it and answer these questions:

1 What are the main findings?
2 How would you report these findings in an academic text?
3 How do you think you could explain these findings?

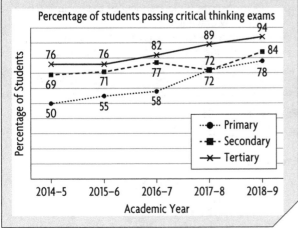

Lead-in

At this point in each unit students are asked to begin to think about the writing task they will do at the end of the unit. Give them a minute to read about line graphs and ask questions.

UNLOCK TEACHER DEVELOPMENT

BE READY

Look at the Critical Thinking section in the Student's Book on pages 180–182.

→ Which elements of the lesson do you think your students will find easiest / most difficult / most useful? Why?

→ Are your answers true for all students in your class?

→ How can you adapt your teaching or the material to meet your students' needs?

BE FLEXIBLE

Before doing Exercise 3, get students to predict what they think the graph might look like. You can give them the background information, and ask what they think the trend for the graph would be. They can then open their books and check their predictions.

Exercise 1 page 180

1 expenditure in five key categories as a percentage of income   **2** the numbers represent percentages of income   **3** 1998–2016   **4** There are five categories of expenditure: housing (dark red); food (pink); transport (green); entertainment (blue); and health (orange)   **5** 12.5% **6** decrease   **7** There was a slight upward trend, which was shared by most of the types of expenditure. However, entertainment remained relatively stable.

Exercise 2 page 181

Possible answers:

1 Between 2000 and 2006, expenditure as a percentage of income generally went down for housing, food and transport. From about 2006, these same categories started to increase in general. There are many possible reasons for this change. Housing prices go up when there aren't enough affordable houses and apartments. Transport costs go up when the price of oil increases or people live farther from their places of employment. Food prices are affected by the weather, for example, in years when there is not enough rain, crop yields are lower and food becomes more expensive.

2 Housing. Housing costs are affected by availability, bank interest rates, changes in the stock market and global events. Housing prices are very sensitive to changes in any of these factors.

3 Entertainment. This is a non-essential and a small part of most people's budget. Health costs were also fairly stable.

4 The percentage that Americans spent on all categories went up. This trend is probably part of the normal rise and fall in prices.

5 It is lower than it was in 1998.

Exercise 3 page 182

Possible answers:

1 The red line = total money made from the sale or rental of physical DVDs. The blue line = total money made from films and TV shows that can be downloaded or streamed. **2** 2010 to 2019   **3** The numbers represent millions of dollars. The highest dollar amounts are at the top.   **4** 2014

Exercise 4 page 182

1 16,000   **2** 5,000   **3** 2019

Exercise 5 page 182

1 (1) video streaming (2) DVDs   **2** *Possible answer:* Reasons could include the loss of physical stores as customers have increasingly moved online. Also, improved computer processing speeds have enabled higher quality streaming, so people are more motivated to use a streaming service as opposed to an actual DVD. There is also an element of convenience to streaming services, where all the content is in one place.   **3** Because video streaming sales matched DVD sales, then overtook them into 2015 and beyond.

UNLOCK TEACHER DEVELOPMENT

BE REFLECTIVE

Think about the following questions:

→ How much background knowledge / understanding did your students have about line graphs? Was there a noticeable difference between students with a background in sciences and those without?

→ Since this is the final critical thinking section of the course, think about how well your students have progressed overall. Is there anything you could/should do differently if you teach the course again?

BE COLLABORATIVE

Your development is more meaningful when it is shared. See page 14 for ideas on how to peer-collaborate. Why not share the ideas you generated in the *Be confident* section, and their outcome?

GRAMMAR FOR WRITING

Learning objectives

- Match graphs to their descriptions – *Sales of DVDs rose sharply and then fell dramatically.*
- Write equivalent noun phrases for verb phrases describing trends in graphs
- Complete sentences describing change with the correct prepositions and conjunctions – *Prices fluctuated considerably between 2010 and 2018.*
- Understand synonymous words and phrases used to express figures approximately – *almost a hundred euros = €99.99, roughly half a million euros = €485,134, over ten thousand euros = €10,237*

Exercise 1 page 183

1 a   **2** f   **3** d   **4** c   **5** b   **6** e

Exercise 2 page 183

2 a dramatic fall   **3** a slight decrease   **4** a gradual increase   **5** a considerable fluctuation

Exercise 3 page 184

1 from; to; of   **2** from; to; of   **3** From; to / Between; and; from; to   **4** between; and   **5** from; to

Exercise 4 page 184

1 nearly   **2** over   **3** around; about; approximately   **4** under

Be flexible

👥 Students should interview each other to find out how much they spend per week on clothing, eating in restaurants, coffee or tea, seeing films, concerts, etc. The students answering the questions can give approximations using the words and phrases in Exercises 4 and 5. Consider comparing answers and evaluating spending patterns across the group. Guide **lower-level students** in generating questions, and encourage them to use the internet for pictures to support their discussion as needed.

Exercise 5 page 184

1 g   **2** d   **3** e   **4** a   **5** c   **6** b   **7** f

ACADEMIC WRITING SKILLS

Learning objectives

- Understand the key features of a paragraph describing a graph
- Demonstrate understanding of a description of a graph by drawing it
- Describe the trends shown in the graph you drew
- Identify the relationship between a thesis statement and a conclusion
- Identify the key features of concluding paragraphs

Exercise 1 page 185

a 2   **b** 1   **c** 2   **d** 2   **e** 3   **f** 2

Exercise 2 page 185

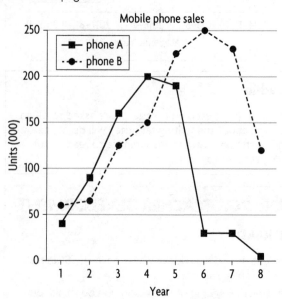

Mobile phone sales

Exercise 3 page 185

Possible answers:

1 The graph shows that sales of both phones increased over a period of time, but then decreased over a number of years and look set to decline further.

2 Both phones showed an initial increase in sales before declining. Sales of phone A started to decrease earlier than phone B. Sales of phone B reached a peak of 250,000, whereas sales of phone A only reached 200,000. In the first few years, phone A sales increased more sharply than phone B sales.

Exercise 4 page 186

1 In conclusion, the combination of rising prices and falling incomes has left many people with less spending power than they had in previous decades.   2 In conclusion   3 a; d

WRITING TASK

Learning objectives

- Plan and draft an essay describing a multiple-line graph comparing revenue from DVD sales and video streaming and explain the data
- Review and revise the content and structure of your essay
- Review and revise the use of language in your essay

Exercises 1–10 pages 187–188

Answers will vary.

RESEARCH PROJECT

Advise your government on how to grow a sustainable economy.

Explain to your class that they are going to research different ways to make their country's economy more sustainable. Explain that in order to be sustainable, the country's natural resources should not be in danger. Ask them to look at these different areas of the economy: manufacturing, fishing (if relevant), small businesses, technology, farming. Ask them to research how to make these areas more sustainable. Some direction you could offer may be to look at areas like local produce, minimizing environmental impact from manufacturing, local economies, technology and health, and overfishing. Doing an internet search with phrases such as 'sustainable farming', 'sustainable fishing' or 'benefits of local businesses' should produce enough information to get them started with their research.

They could produce a report to present to local government representatives.

CLASSROOM APP

Exercise 1

Answers will vary.

Exercise 2

1 expenditure   2 percentage   3 interest rate
4 standard of living   5 recession   6 factor
7 investment   8 value

Exercise 3

Answers will vary.

Exercise 4

1 economic   2 financial   3 wealth   4 poverty
5 valuable   6 employed   7 professional   8 expense

Exercise 5

1 supply   2 consumer   3 trend   4 market
5 revenue   6 demand   7 purchase

Exercise 6

1 a sharp decrease   2 rose sharply
3 a gradual decrease   4 fell slightly
5 fell dramatically   6 fluctuated considerably

UNIT OBJECTIVES	
Watch and listen	Watch and understand a video about China's plans to revive the Silk Road trade routes.
Reading skills	Make predictions from a text type; recognize topic sentences.
Critical thinking	Evaluate supporting examples; use tables and diagrams.
Grammar	Use noun phrases; use time phrases.
Academic writing skills	Use correct essay structure; write an effective thesis statement.
Writing task	Write an explanatory essay.
♻ **Teacher development**	Help your students become better at **evaluating supporting examples** and **using tables and diagrams**.

UNLOCK YOUR KNOWLEDGE

Background note

The photo shows a container ship and a tugboat in the Port of Tacoma, Washington, the USA. It is one of the biggest container ports in North America. Its main trading partner is China. Free trade and increased exchange of goods between different nations is one of the benefits of globalization. Other advantages of globalization include improved access to technology, media, education and consumer goods. Some of the disadvantages of globalization include the exploitation of developing countries, homogenization of culture and the destruction of the natural environment.

Lead-in

Give students one minute to consider the clothes they are wearing and the possessions they are carrying. In what country was each of them made? Students note this down. Tell them that they are going to spell the names of these countries. Give them a few minutes to check the spelling of each country in a dictionary. Everybody starts with three points. One person says the first letter of a country on their list and the next person says another letter that together with the first makes the beginning of the word. The next student adds another letter and so on. If at any time somebody doubts that the student who says a letter has a real (correctly spelt) country in mind, they can challenge that person. If the challenged student can't give an appropriate answer, they lose a point and a new word is started. If they can give a word, the challenger loses a point. If somebody can't continue a word, they also lose a point. The winner is the last student with points remaining at the end of the game.

When the game is complete, ask students to reveal their entire lists. What country appeared most frequently? Why do they think this is the case?

page 15
Answers will vary.

WATCH AND LISTEN

Learning objectives

- Listen and identify the main idea in a video about trade routes
- Listen and understand details about a future project
- Listen and identify the meaning of unfamiliar words and phrases from their context in the video
- Practise talking about international trade and infrastructure

Exercises 1–2 page 16
Answers will vary.

Exercise 3 page 17
Main idea: Sentence 2

Exercise 4 page 17
1 F; Korgas is at the heart of the trading route.   **2** F; Five years ago, there was no infrastructure in the area.   **3** T
4 T   **5** F; The project has economic and political goals.

Exercise 5 page 17
1. If something is built **from scratch,** it is built from the very beginning without using anything that already exists.
2. The phrase **so the theory goes** means that something is still only a theory, and it may not happen this way.
3. If you **project** a particular quality, that quality is what most people notice about you.

Exercise 6 page 17
Answers will vary.

READING 1

Learning objectives

- Understand key vocabulary for global companies – *dominant, reputation, multinational*
- Use the text type to predict style and content in a blog post about IKEA's global success
- Read and understand detail
- Read and identify formal equivalents of informal language from the context of the blog
- Make inferences about the writer's implications and attitude
- Describe personal experiences of blogs and online reviews

Lead-in

Ask students to look at the logo in the first reading. Ask if anybody knows the company and what kind of products it sells. Ask if anybody has shopped there and if so, to describe the experience and the store more generally. How is this store different from other stores?

Exercise 1 page 18

a domestic **b** dominant **c** discount **d** reputation
e supplier **f** inflation **g** multinational **h** selling point

Exercises 2–3 page 19

1 use of informal language: use of phrasal verbs, 'check out'; informal vocabulary, 'a lot of', 'super-low'; contractions, 'I'll look at' **3** use of first person, such as 'I will check out', 'it seems to me,' 'I'll look at'

Exercise 4 page 20

1 Because he/she is writing a blog series about successful multinational companies, one of which is IKEA. **2** A UK store might feature a bedroom display with a British flag bedspread, while a Tokyo store might have a bedroom display with a traditional mat on the floor. **3** Because it sells its furniture in flat boxes which use less space and paper and are easier to transport. **4** Multinational companies which specialize in household goods and automobile production.

Exercise 5 page 20

1 T **2** T **3** F; They have long understood the need to research other markets. **4** T **5** DNS
6 F; It will only be in some markets.

Exercise 6 page 20

1 b **2** c **3** a

Optional activity

Write the words and phrases in the table randomly on the board. Ask students to find pairs of words with similar meanings and decide which is more likely to be used in a blog (informal) and which in an academic article (formal).

Answers:

informal	formal
a lot	a great deal
ask for	request
get	receive
stuff	possessions
pretty	rather
get better	recover

Exercise 7 page 20

Answers will vary. Possible answers:

1 As an example of what they learnt about what customers in different markets want, based on their research. **2** Because if customers feel strongly about protecting the environment, it might make them more likely to shop at stores that follow eco-friendly policies. **3** He/She does not explicitly say.

Exercise 8 page 21

Answers will vary.

READING 2

Learning objectives

- Understand key vocabulary for global eating habits – *consumption, convenience, experiment*
- Use topic sentences to predict the content of an essay about eating habits in Italy
- Read and identify the main changes over time in Italian eating habits
- Read and identify the target readers and author's purpose in writing the essay
- Synthesize information from two texts about globalization in a discussion

Lead-in

Ask students if they like Italian food. Why do they think it is so popular worldwide? Elicit some Italian dishes and any restaurants where they are served in the town where the class is studying. Ask if they think this food is similar to the food in Italy, or if it has been adapted to local taste. Elicit some examples of local adaptations.

Exercise 1 page 21

1 convenience **2** ensure **3** consumption **4** increase **5** relatively **6** specialty **7** influence **8** experiment

Exercises 2–3 page 22

Answers will vary. Possible answers:

1 more ready-made food, frozen food and take-away food **2** greater variety of food available in shops and restaurants **3** positive and negative impact of fast-food restaurant chains

---

Optional activity

👤 Get students to predict the content of a paragraph (not in the text), based on each of the topic sentences below, for four paragraphs of an essay about globalization. They should be able to infer that the paragraphs will discuss some of the pros and cons of globalization. Ask them to justify their answers. (For example, the first two topic sentences suggest those paragraphs will be about advantages and the third and fourth topic sentences suggest those paragraphs will be about disadvantages. Together, they would probably be from an essay about both.)

1 Supporters of globalization argue that it is good for the country's economy.

2 Globalization helps us learn about other countries and their cultures.

3 Globalization generally helps rich countries more than poor countries.

4 Globalization gives a lot of power to large, multinational companies.

Exercise 4 page 22

2 both **3** present **4** past **5** present **6** both

Exercise 5 page 22

Answers will vary. Possible answers:

1 all over the world **2** eat Asian food **3** foreign food **4** less common

Exercise 6 page 24

1 a **2** b

Exercise 7 page 24

Answers will vary.

LANGUAGE DEVELOPMENT

Learning objectives

- Rewrite sentences using academic alternatives to phrasal verbs – *The amount of migrant labour is expected to go up (increase). Academics have been looking into (investigating) the implications of globalization for many years.*
- Use globalization vocabulary to complete a text about businesses – *monopoly, multinational outlets*

Exercise 1 page 24

1 b **2** a **3** f **4** c **5** h **6** d **7** g **8** e

Optional activity

👤 👥 Ask students to write their own sentences that might appear in a blog about changing eating habits, using the phrasal verbs in Exercise 1. Students should then exchange papers with a partner and rewrite the sentences in a more academic form, substituting academic synonyms for the phrasal verbs.

Exercise 2 page 25

1 increase **2** continue **3** studying **4** confused **5** excluded **6** refused **7** exhausted **8** removed

Exercise 3 page 25

1 domestic **2** consumption **3** outlets **4** multinational **5** monopoly **6** discounts **7** inflation

---

CRITICAL THINKING

Learning objectives

- Use examples from a text to support arguments
- Choose and analyze a globalization topic, using an ideas map
- Create a plan for a body paragraph of your essay in a table

---

UNLOCK TEACHER DEVELOPMENT

BE INFORMED

→ **Evaluating supporting examples** and **using tables and diagrams** are important skills for students because: (1) Whilst students are often aware that they need to use supporting examples in their writing, these examples are not always directly relevant; (2) Students need to develop skills in evaluating those examples which are relevant, and those which are not;

(3) Tables and diagrams can help in organizing appropriate information to support ideas and plan content in students' writing.

BE CONFIDENT

→ Develop these skills for yourself by doing the following activity:

Imagine that you have been asked to write a short article on the following topic: 'Why all young people must develop their critical thinking skills'. Which three points below would you focus on? Why?

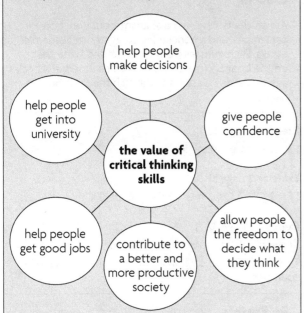

How would you develop each point you chose in detail? What supporting examples would you give?

Lead-in

Give students a minute to read the writing task. Ask them to brainstorm in groups for a few minutes if the changes have been mostly positive or negative. Tell them to keep their brainstorming notes for later, when they begin to write their essay.

UNL◯CK TEACHER DEVELOPMENT

BE READY

Look at the Critical Thinking section in the Student's Book on pages 26–27.
→ Which elements of the lesson do you think your students will find easiest / most difficult / most useful? Why?

→ Are your answers true for all students in your class?
→ How can you adapt your teaching or the material to meet your students' needs?

BE FLEXIBLE

With weaker groups, restrict your class to three to four topics from the list in Exercise 2. Students first create an ideas map by themselves, and then compare with a partner who has created the same ideas map. Students can then add any useful and relevant ideas to their own map.

Exercise 1 page 26
Answers will vary. Possible answers:

1 Until recently, pasta would have been made by people in their local area. Families would also have made the sauces to eat with the pasta at home.
2 Only pizza and pasta were available in the local town square.
3 Frozen or take-out meals, mass-produced dried pasta, and ready-made pasta sauces have become very popular. Fast food chains are seen as more convenient.
4 People worry about the destruction of local and national specialties. The 'Slow Food' movement was started in Italy to encourage people to eat locally sourced food.
5 The popularity of foreign food, international chain restaurants and convenient food are results of globalization, and this has changed the way Italians eat.

Exercises 2–3 pages 26–27
Answers will vary.

UNL◯CK TEACHER DEVELOPMENT

BE REFLECTIVE

Think about the following questions:
→ Did you choose the same three points as your colleague(s) who also did the activity in the *Be confident* section? Why? / Why not?
→ How much are your students already using tables and diagrams to plan their writing? If they are not doing this on a regular basis, they should begin to incorporate it into their academic practice as soon as possible.

BE COLLABORATIVE

Your development is more meaningful when it is shared. See page 14 for ideas on how to peer-collaborate. Why not share the ideas you generated in the *Be ready* section, and their outcome?

GRAMMAR FOR WRITING

Learning objectives

- Use correct word order in academic noun phrases – *a chain which is growing globally, a fact of modern life, a contribution that benefits us the most*
- Use time phrases to refer to general and specific past times – *around ten years ago, historically, in the 1990s*
- Use time phrases to refer to present time – *currently, presently, these days*
- Complete sentences with time phrases about food in your country – *Nowadays, you can buy many different kinds of noodles. Until the 1990s, it was impossible to find sushi in a supermarket.*

Exercise 1 page 27

1 d **2** b **3** a **4** c

Exercise 2 page 28

2 a range of exports **3** a change in environmental standards **4** the exchange of technological ideas **5** the impact of multinational chains **6** a group of international entrepreneurs **7** the mixture of different cultures **8** an increase in worldwide consumption

Optional activity

👤 Ask students to write three new sentences, each with two noun phrases containing one of the following features: adjectives, prepositions, relative clauses, N+N compounds.

Exercise 3 page 28

general past time: before the war, formerly, historically, in recent years, in the past

specific past time: around ten years ago, in the 1990s, in the eighteenth century

present: at the present time, currently, nowadays, presently, these days

Exercise 4 page 29

Answers will vary. Possible answers:

1 food from all over the world **2** foreign chains **3** Thai food in my country **4** cooking programmes on television **5** Asian spices in the markets here **6** things they got from their farms

ACADEMIC WRITING SKILLS

Learning objectives

- Understand the structure of academic essays
- Identify effective thesis statements
- Write an effective thesis statement for an essay about globalization and the developing world

Lead-in

Ask students why we have an introduction, body paragraphs, and a concluding paragraph in academic essays. Elicit guesses from students and write them on the board. What purpose does each serve? Check answers as the class reads through the Skills box on page 29.

Exercise 1 page 30

1 a **2** d **3** e **4** c **5** b

Exercise 2 page 31

1 F **2** Q **3** OK **4** G **5** OK **6** G **7** D

Exercise 3 page 32

Answers will vary. Suggested answer:

The phenomenon of globalization has harmed certain countries.

Be flexible

👥 Look at the example thesis statements in the Skills box on page 30 again. In small groups, ask students to predict the content of the body paragraphs that would appear in these essays. If this is easy for **more advanced students**, ask them to write topic sentences for at least two of the body paragraphs.

WRITING TASK

Learning objectives

- Use a table to plan the content of an essay on how globalization has changed your country
- Write a thesis statement for your essay
- Draft an essay on how globalization has changed your country
- Review and revise the content and structure of your essay
- Review and revise the use of language in your essay

Exercise 1 page 32

a 2   **b** 1   **c** 5   **d** 3   **e** 4

Exercises 2–11 pages 32–34

Answers will vary.

RESEARCH PROJECT

Investigate and give a presentation on how globalization has increased awareness of your country and culture in other parts of the world.

Divide the class into groups and ask them to think about the impact of globalization. In what ways has the world become more aware of their country and culture? They should research the following 'exports' from their country: culture (e.g. entertainment, music), food, technology, sport, people (workforce), or another topic of their own choice. These points should be divided between the groups so that each one can investigate a different theme.

Each group of students should then present their findings to the class.

CLASSROOM APP

Exercise 1

Answers will vary.

Exercise 2

1 selling point   **2** supplier   **3** increase
4 consumption   **5** dominant   **6** reputation
7 experiment   **8** influence

Exercise 3

Answers will vary.

Exercise 4

1 refused   **2** confuse   **3** studying   **4** increased
5 excluded   **6** continue   **7** exhausting   **8** remove

Exercise 5

1 multinational   **2** consumption   **3** domestic
4 inflation   **5** outlet   **6** monopoly   **7** discount

Exercise 6

1 Introduction, Body, Conclusion

2 A hook; Background information; A thesis statement

3 develop your main ideas; provide evidence or information to support your ideas

4 state the thesis statement again; give your conclusions / recommendations / predictions

5 give an opinion; give an overview of the essay

6 Although there are certain benefits to globalization, there are arguably a greater number of disadvantages.

UNIT OBJECTIVES	
Watch and listen	Watch and understand a video about an app that helps children catch up outside the classroom.
Reading skill	Make inferences.
Critical thinking	Analyze similarities and differences; use a Venn diagram to plan a comparison-contrast essay.
Grammar	Use transitions to show comparison and contrast; use adverb clauses of contrast.
Academic writing skills	Avoid run-on sentences and comma splices; write a comparison and contrast essay.
Writing task	Write a comparison and contrast essay.
⟳ **Teacher development**	Help your students become better at **analyzing similarities and differences**.

UNL⌾CK YOUR KNOWLEDGE

Background note

The photo shows pupils at a school in Kawangware, Nairobi, Kenya using tablets. These tablets were designed by a specialist technology company in Nairobi, and are tailor-made to fit the needs of African classrooms. They can be used even in very remote areas. Using technology in the classroom can give students access to additional online resources. It also teaches them how to collaborate with other students and teachers online, how to use online resources and how to search for information online.

Lead-in

Show students the following simile (or use a different one of your own if you prefer):

A good lesson is like a meal, because it satisfies you and gives you the fuel to live your life.

Check students understand that in this sentence 'meal' is a simile /ˈsɪm.ɪ.li/ because we are comparing it to a good lesson, using the structure *is like*. Now replace the sentence with the following:

A good education is like _____, *because* _____.

Ask if students can think of a simile to complete the sentence. If they cannot, give prompts *(light, food, a key, a ship, a tree, money)* and ask them to complete the sentence. Students share their ideas with the class, justifying their similes.

page 37
Answers will vary.

WATCH AND LISTEN

Learning objectives

- Listen and understand the main ideas in a video about an app
- Listen and complete a summary of the ideas in the video
- Make inferences about the views held by different speakers in the video
- Practise talking about learning techniques

Exercises 1–2 page 38
Answers will vary.

Exercise 3 pages 38–39

1 F; Many students cannot afford private tuition.   **2** T
3 F; This is a new programme that is helping a small number of students.   **4** F; The teachers are very enthusiastic about the idea.   **5** T   **6** T

Exercise 4 page 39

1 extra   **2** expensive   **3** afford   **4** fall behind   **5** access
6 available

Exercise 5 page 39

1 c, e   **2** a   **3** b, d

Exercise 6 page 39
Answers will vary.

READING 1

Learning objectives

- Understand key vocabulary for university education – *discipline, oriented, pursue*
- Read and identify the main ideas about two subjects in an essay about university courses
- Read and understand detail
- Use your knowledge to make inferences about ideas implied in the text
- Explain your views on university subjects

Lead-in

Write the acronym STEM on the board and ask students what subject each letter stands for (Science, Technology, Engineering, Mathematics). Ask how many of them study these fields and which ones. If you have a mixed gender class, take note of the gender breakdown – are there more male or female students studying these subjects? Is it equal? Ask students why they think there is this difference. If your class is all male or all female, ask who typically studies these subjects and why.

Exercise 1 page 40

a pursue **b** concrete **c** launch **d** oriented **e** under-represented **f** evolve **g** discipline **h** gender gap

Exercise 2 page 41

2 discipline **3** gender gap **4** launch **5** oriented **6** under-represented **7** concrete **8** evolve

Exercise 3 page 41

Answers will vary.

Exercise 4 page 43

1 both **2** Engineering **3** Business **4** both **5** both

Exercise 5 page 43

1 F; about 40% **2** T **3** T **4** F; Science, Technology, Engineering, Mathematics **5** F; 16% of Engineering and Technology students are female.

Optional activity

👥 In small groups, ask students to make a list of university subjects. They should write down any concrete skills each subject offers (i.e. ones that students could use in the working world). Then, ask students to rank the subjects as *more* or *less* career-oriented. Finally, they explain their list and rankings to another group.

Exercise 6 page 43

Answers will vary. Possible answers:

1 easier to find a job **2 Engineering:** very specific and possibly not as transferable to different types of careers **Business:** not as academic as other subjects

Exercise 7 page 43

Answers will vary.

READING 2

Learning objectives

- Understand key vocabulary for styles of learning delivery – *distance learning, technological advances, modern phenomenon*
- Use your knowledge to predict the main ideas in an essay about distance and face-to-face learning
- Read and identify the main ideas in each paragraph of an essay
- Read and identify the features of distance and face-to-face learning
- Make inferences about the language, ideas and attitude of the essay writer
- Synthesize information from an essay about university courses and an essay about distance and face-to-face learning in a discussion

Lead-in

Ask students to think of something they have wanted to learn recently, but not as part of their formal education; for example, how to repair something, background information about a news item, or how to use a piece of technology or software. How did they learn it? Did they use books, other people or the internet? Students discuss their experiences and try to identify what is best studied face-to-face and what is better learnt online.

Exercise 1 page 44

Answers will vary. Possible answers:

1 the trend toward more online learning **2** mechanical engineering **3** you can interact with the teacher and other students **4** you can study for it from your home **5** rechargeable batteries **6** communicate with people around the world **7** high standards of academic behaviour is important **8** the cost of tuition

Be flexible

👥 For more practice of the key vocabulary, ask students to discuss these questions in pairs.

1 Do you think vocational training is a **credible alternative** to university education for most people? Explain your answer.

2 What has been the most important **technological advance** in education? Why do you think this?

3 Do you think **online degrees** will ever widely accepted? Why / Why not?

Challenge **more advanced students** to write questions using three of the remaining target vocabulary items (in the box on page 44). Students take turns asking and answering.

Exercises 2–3 page 44

Answers will vary.

Exercise 4 page 46

1 3 **2** 4 **3** 2 **4** 1

Exercise 5 page 46

1 face-to-face **2** distance **3** distance **4** both
5 distance **6** distance **7** both

Exercise 6 page 46

Suggested answers:

1 Because regardless of possible differences like curriculum, syllabus, instructor or other things that may or may not differ, we know for sure that the systems differ in this basic way.

2 Because the teacher and student rarely meet, it may be more difficult for the teacher to understand the student's learning needs. Students are more responsible for staying focused, doing the work and keeping up.

3 Mentioned in the text: helping students understand the key course sections; deciding how to present and sequence the material and topics; creating assignments; helping with resources; providing feedback. *Other possible answers:* answering questions, evaluating/ grading student work.

4 The author does not appear to take a side on this. He/ She states that 'it is difficult to state whether one form of learning is better than the other'.

Exercise 7 page 47

Answers will vary.

LANGUAGE DEVELOPMENT

Learning objectives

- Identify the definitions of educational vocabulary – *assignment*, *degree*, *journal*
- Identify the definitions of academic vocabulary – *alternative*, *virtual*, *motivation*
- Use academic words to complete sentences about university courses

Exercise 1 page 47

1 assignment **2** term **3** semester **4** Plagiarism
5 journal **6** lecturer **7** seminar **8** tutor **9** degree
10 dissertation **11** examination

Exercise 2 page 48

1 d **2** a **3** f **4** g **5** h **6** i **7** e **8** c **9** b

Exercise 3 page 48

1 alternative **2** significant **3** aspect **4** principles
5 motivation **6** specific **7** core **8** virtual

Be flexible

👤 👥 Ask students to write three new sentences of their own. Each sentence should use one item from the Education vocabulary list (in Exercise 1 on page 47) and one item from the Academic words list (in Exercise 2 on page 48). Students then share their sentences with a partner, who can give feedback on appropriateness.

If this exercise is too easy for **more advanced students**, ask students to do it as a gap-fill activity. Students exchange and complete their partner's exercise. Emphasize that their sentences should make the meaning of the missing words as clear as possible.

CRITICAL THINKING

Learning objectives

- Use ideas maps to generate ideas about key features of subjects
- Use Venn diagrams to analyze similarities and differences between two subjects

UNLOCK TEACHER DEVELOPMENT

BE INFORMED

→ **Analyzing similarities and differences** is an important skill for students because: (1) Doing this is crucial in any form of academic writing (notes, essays, lab reports, etc.) in all academic disciplines; (2) Writing which does not examine similarities and differences is unlikely to include a strong argument; (3) A Venn diagram is one of the most common tools for analyzing similarities and differences, and is both easy and highly effective.

BE CONFIDENT

→ Develop this skill for yourself by doing the following activity:

Think about the similarities and differences between teaching your strongest class and your weakest class. Complete the Venn diagram below. The things which you do similarly with both classes should be included in the middle section.

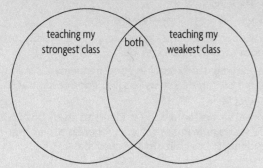

When you have done this, reflect on the following questions:

1 Did anything about this analysis surprise you?
2 Did you find more similarities than differences?

Lead-in

Give students a minute to read the writing task and to ask you any questions they might have.

UNLOCK TEACHER DEVELOPMENT

BE READY

Look at the Critical Thinking section in the Student's Book on page 49.

→ Which elements of the lesson do you think your students will find easiest / most difficult / most useful? Why?

→ Are your answers true for all students in your class?

→ How can you adapt your teaching or the material to meet your students' needs?

BE FLEXIBLE

One option to consider, especially if not all students have managed to generate enough ideas in Exercise 3, is to draw the Venn diagram on the whiteboard and ask the whole class to contribute ideas. This is a quick and easy way to share ideas as a whole class. Note: It is not essential for students to do this activity for 'language' and 'Mathematics'. They can choose subjects they are more interested in, or which are more relevant to their studies.

Exercise 1 page 49

Answers will vary. Suggested answers:

Studying a language:

access to authentic material in the new language is beneficial

learners will benefit from visiting the country where the language is spoken

plenty of practice required

students must be highly motivated, well organized and self-disciplined, especially if they are not living in the country where the language is spoken

learners need core vocabulary and grammar to build on

Studying Mathematics:

completely objective, meaning there is only one right answer

all learners will have done some Mathematics at school

plenty of practice required

learners need to understand key concepts before moving on

can use Mathematics to solve real-world problems

Exercises 2–3 page 49

Answers will vary.

UNLOCK TEACHER DEVELOPMENT

BE REFLECTIVE

Think about the following questions:

→ Look at the differences in your Venn diagram, i.e. the things which you only do with your strongest or weakest class. Are there any things which you only do with your strongest class which you think you could/should also do with your weakest class? And vice versa?

→ How frequently are your students using Venn diagrams in their planning and analyzing? As they become more independent, they need to develop their academic practice through using tools such as this.

BE COLLABORATIVE

Your development is more meaningful when it is shared. See page 14 for ideas on how to peer-collaborate. Why not share the ideas you generated in the *Be ready* section, and their outcome?

GRAMMAR FOR WRITING

Learning objectives

- Use transition words and phrases to show comparison and contrast across sentences – *Similarly, … In the same way, … Conversely, …*
- Use adverb clauses with *while* and *whereas* to show contrast within sentences – *The main difference between them is that teachers are paid, whereas parents are not. While a distance-learning teacher may need to provide written feedback, a classroom teacher may be able to correct a student directly.*
- Punctuate sentences showing contrast with *while* and *whereas* correctly

Exercise 1 page 50

1 Conversely; In contrast   **2** In the same way; Similarly
3 In contrast; Conversely   **4** Similarly; In the same way

Exercise 2 page 50

Answers will vary.

Exercise 3 page 51

1 Academic courses focus on subjects like Maths, Science and Literature, while/whereas vocational courses focus on practical skills.

While/Whereas vocational courses focus on practical skills, academic courses focus on subjects like Maths, Science and Literature.

2 A university is a very large institution which offers undergraduate and graduate degrees, while/whereas a college is a smaller institution which typically offers only undergraduate degrees.

While/Whereas a university is a very large institution which offers undergraduate and graduate degrees, a college is a smaller institution which typically offers only undergraduate degrees.

3 Academic courses are theoretical, while/whereas vocational subjects are not.

While/Whereas academic courses are theoretical, vocational subjects are not.

4 More men tend to graduate with degrees in Maths or Science, while/whereas more women tend to graduate with degrees in language or Literature.

While/Whereas more men tend to graduate with degrees in Maths or Science, more women tend to graduate with degrees in languages or Literature.

Exercise 4 page 52

1 b   **2** b   **3** a

Exercise 5 page 52

1 Some professions only require a bachelor's degree, while others require a graduate degree.

2 Whereas Japanese students can get a bachelor's degree in Law, Canadian students cannot.

3 While Business is considered a university subject that will lead to job offers, Philosophy is usually not.

Exercise 6 page 52

Answers will vary. Suggested answers:

1 While some students choose to go to university, others choose to get a full-time job.

2 Engineering study requires good mathematics skills, whereas Literature study requires good reading and writing skills.

3 Some universities require students to study both STEM and humanities subjects, whereas others require students to specialize in just one area.

ACADEMIC WRITING SKILLS

Learning objectives

- Identify run-on sentences and comma splices
- Use *and*, semicolons or new sentences to correct run-on sentences and comma splices – *Engineering and Business are both popular subjects; they both use mathematics. Business is a more popular subject than Engineering, and it also has a smaller gender gap. Business is a more popular subject than Engineering. It also has a smaller gender gap.*
- Understand the key features of comparison and contrast essays.

Exercise 1 page 54

2 C; *Possible answer:* … university course. It is not as popular …   **3** R; *Possible answer:* … focuses on numbers, but language learning …   **4** C; *Possible answer:* … very popular; you can even …   **5** R; *Possible answer:* … academic subjects; other students …   **6** R; *Possible answer:* … charge tuition, but some are …

Exercise 2 page 54

1 run-on; *Suggested answer:* Not everybody needs to go to university; there are some rewarding careers that do not require university degrees.

2 comma splice; *Suggested answer:* The two oldest universities in the UK are Oxford and Cambridge. They were both founded in the Middle Ages.

3 run-on; *Suggested answer:* Students getting PhD degrees work as research assistants. It is part of their arrangement with the university.

4 comma splice; *Suggested answers:* The experience of going to university is not just an academic one. Students also make valuable lifelong friendships there. / The experience of going to university is not just an academic one; students also make valuable lifelong friendships there.

Optional activity

👤 Ask students to look back at Exercise 1 and correct the sentences in a different way. Suggest that they use adverbs as transitions to mark any contrasts. For example:

Some students prefer to study academic subjects, whereas other students prefer vocational courses.

While all universities charge tuition fees, some are more expensive than others.

Exercise 3 page 55

1 differences **2** both (but differences are more significant) **3** Reading 2

WRITING TASK

Learning objectives

- Use a table to plan the content of an essay discussing similarities and differences between studying a language and studying Mathematics
- Write a thesis statement for your essay
- Draft an essay comparing studying a language and studying Mathematics
- Review and revise the content and structure of your essay
- Review and revise the use of language in your essay

Exercises 1–7 pages 55–56

Answers will vary.

RESEARCH PROJECT

Design a test to assess your knowledge of English from this unit.

Divide the class into groups. Explain that the students will need to identify the language and skills that they most need to test from the unit. Point out the different question types available to test vocabulary, such as the following: multiple choice, matching, ordering tasks, short-answer questions, gap-fill tasks, sentence writing and extended writing. Ask them to think of the number of questions and write the answer key, instructions and criteria by which the exam should be graded. Students can use paper, a word processor or an online quiz website. Each group produces a test.

When the tests are submitted, they should be copied and distributed to the groups. Each group then takes the test and the scores are analyzed. The class then rates which test was the most effective. If there is time, ask students to give reasons for their decision.

CLASSROOM APP

Exercises 1–2

Answers will vary.

Exercise 3

1 pursue **2** gender gap **3** Distance learning **4** discipline **5** underrepresented **6** Technological advances **7** significant difference **8** launch

Exercise 4

1 dissertation, assignments, plagiarism **2** semesters, terms **3** degree, journals **4** lecturer, seminars, tutor

Exercise 5

1 virtual **2** motivation **3** significant **4** alternative **5** core **6** specific **7** principles **8** aspects

Exercise 6

1 ; they found ; , and they found
2 , so there will be; . There will be
3 , whereas other people; , but other people
4 . You should ; , so you should
5 , but in the winter, there are ; . In the winter, there are

UNIT OBJECTIVES	
Watch and listen	Watch and understand a video about robots used in surgery.
Reading skill	Annotate a text.
Critical thinking	Evaluate ideas.
Grammar	Use articles; use transitions to show concession.
Academic writing skill	Use sentence variety.
Writing task	Write an opinion essay.
⟳ **Teacher development**	Help your students become better at **evaluating ideas**.

UNL⟳CK YOUR KNOWLEDGE

Background note

The photo shows employees inside a Traditional Chinese Medicine (TCM) pharmacy in Beijing, China. TCM refers to various treatments, such as herbal medicine, acupuncture, massage therapies (called *tui na*) and exercise and diet regimes. Outside of China, acupuncture and herbal medicine are often seen as alternative medicine. Other forms of alternative medicine include Ayurveda, homeopathy and naturopathy. These therapies have been practised in different parts of the world for centuries. Chiropractic massage, t'ai chi, yoga, reiki and meditation are also used as alternative or complementary treatments.

Lead-in

Mime an illness or symptom, such as a headache or backache, and ask students to say what it is. Students then work in small groups. One person in the group mimes a health problem and the others have to say what it is. The person who guesses the problem correctly mimes a different problem. Give them two minutes to do as many as possible. They should keep count and cannot repeat any that have already been mimed. The person with the most correct answers in the group is the winner. Monitor to help with language.

page 59

Answers will vary. Possible answers to Question 1:

a cold: take some cold medicine, have some hot tea with honey, eat raw garlic

a headache: take some painkillers, drink lots of water

a cut on your hand: bandage it and raise it, go to a hospital if it is serious

toothache: go to the dentist, take painkillers

obesity: eat less, exercise more

depression: talk to a therapist, take anti-depressants

stress: work less, exercise more

WATCH AND LISTEN

Learning objectives

- Listen and understand the main ideas in a video about robotic surgery
- Listen and note supporting details
- Make inferences about the ideas in the video and their wider implications
- Practise talking about technology

Exercise 1 page 60

Answers will vary.

Exercise 2 page 60

Possible answers:

1 They involve robots. **2** They show medical procedures / surgery. **3** His arm is artificial/red. **4** It is printing the artificial arm.

Exercise 3 page 60

1 T **2** DNS **3** T **4** F; It is not possible yet. **5** T **6** T

Exercise 4 page 61

Possible answers:

1 Robots can perform surgery in places that are too small or delicate for human surgeons. **2** Some robots are the width of a human hair. **3** Robots can create new body parts. **4** 3-D printers are much cheaper than earlier technology.

Exercise 5 page 61

Answers will vary. Possible answers:

1 Surgeries that take a very long time. **2** This would reduce the risk of infection. **3** People who can pay the high cost; in other words, rich people.   **4** Once a program for the limb is developed, the process is automatic. The material is also inexpensive.

Exercise 6 page 61
Answers will vary.

READING 1

Learning objectives

* Understand key vocabulary for alternative medicines – *proponent, conventional, substance*
* Skim the headings and introduction of an article about homeopathy and identify the topic
* Read an article and identify and annotate opinions
* Understand details in an article about a controversial form of health treatment
* Identify which perspectives on homeopathy match the author's in the article
* Make inferences to evaluate statements about homeopathy
* Explain and justify personal opinions on alternative treatments

Background information

The reading text in this section refers to the NHS, the British National Health Service. This provides free or very cheap healthcare for all UK citizens and is paid for by the government through taxation. The text features a general practitioner, or GP. This is a doctor who provides general medical treatment for people who live in a particular area. In the UK, if you are ill, you first visit the GP. You only go to hospital in an emergency or if your GP has made an appointment for you to see a specialist there.

Exercise 1 page 62
1 b **2** b **3** a **4** a **5** b **6** b **7** a **8** a

Exercise 2 page 63
3

Exercise 3 page 63
Answers will vary.

Exercise 4 page 63
1 F; Most health systems use conventional medicine.
2 T **3** T **4** DNS **5** F; Abigail Hayes thinks that homeopathic remedies have much more than just a placebo effect. **6** T **7** DNS **8** T

Optional activity

👥👥 This activity is particularly applicable to L1 speakers of Arabic.

To help students remember which words are spelt with *p* and which ones with *b*, display the following words from the text:

belief	benefit	homeopathy	patient
placebo	popular	powerful	practitioner
proof	proponent	spend	supporter
therapy			

Alternatively, you could say the words and students find them in the text. Students look at the words and count how many examples of *p* (14) there are in the words and how many examples of *b* (3). Remove the displayed words and ask students to close their books. Show them the following gapped words and ask them to complete them adding *p* or *b*:

homeo_athy	thera_y	_lace_o
_atient	_ractitioner	_owerful
_ro_onent	_roof	_elief
_o_ular	_enefit	s_end
su_ _ orter		

Say the words or give clues to the meanings, if necessary.

Alternatively, you could ask students to learn the words and do this at the beginning of the next lesson. Students read the text to check their answers.

Exercise 5 page 65
1 Piers Wehner   **2** Abigail Hayes   **3** Piers Wehner
4 Abigail Hayes   **5** Abigail Hayes   **6** Abigail Hayes
7 Piers Wehner   **8** Piers Wehner

Exercise 6 page 65
Possible answers:

1 Conventional medicine is very expensive because it needs a great deal of testing and the pharmaceutical companies want to make a large profit.

2 There is a great deal of evidence to show that if people believe they are being cured, they get better. This is called the 'placebo effect'. People are less stressed if they believe that they are well.

3 People may be less worried if they have shared their medical problems and know that somebody is looking after them. They may also be more motivated to look after themselves.

4 Most mainstream doctors will say this, and this opinion is widespread and can be found everywhere.

5 Conventional medicine is based on science. Doctors also have to prove that they are not wasting money when using homeopathy.

Exercise 7 page 65
Answers will vary.

READING 2

Learning objectives

- Understand key vocabulary for healthcare systems – *burden, consultation, contribution*
- Skim the headings and introduction of an article about healthcare funding and identify the topic
- Read and use your knowledge to analyze main ideas about healthcare systems
- Read and relate details of healthcare models to specific healthcare systems
- Scan the article for synonyms for *people, money* and *healthcare*
- Make inferences about the appeal of different healthcare models to different people
- Synthesize information from an article about homeopathy and an article about healthcare funding in a discussion

Lead-in

Ask students to describe the healthcare system in their country. What happens when they go to the doctor? The hospital? Do they have to pay for each visit? If not, who pays for the treatment? Do they know of other places around the world with different healthcare systems?

Exercise 1 page 66

1 burden **2** treatment **3** regardless **4** safety net
5 consultation **6** contribution **7** labour

Exercise 2 page 66

Answers will vary.

Exercise 3 page 67

1

Exercise 4 page 68

1 *Answers will vary.* **2** *Possible answers:* public; private

Exercise 5 page 68

1 public **2** private **3** public **4** mixed **5** private

Be flexible

👥👥👥 Ask students to work in small groups to discuss (1) which system (of those described in Exercise 5) they think works best and why, and (2) to reconsider the same question for a country that has limited resources (in other words, in a country in which it would be difficult for the government to provide free healthcare to all citizens).

If this exercise is too challenging for **lower-level students**, they can simply discuss their own healthcare system, specifying the system (from those in Exercise 5) it most closely resembles, and stating the aspects of the system they like (or consider successful) and those they don't like (or consider less successful).

Exercise 6 page 68

synonyms of *people*: residents, citizens, workers, patients, individuals

synonyms of *money*: taxes, income, contribution, costs, funding, salaries, profit

related to *healthcare*: healthcare, consultations, treatments, medicines, hospitals, medical services, health insurance, medical costs, preventative medicine, infectious diseases

Exercise 7 page 68

Answers will vary. Possible answers:

1 A person with a long-term illness might prefer free or public healthcare because of the continuing costs of treatment.

2 A person with a high income might prefer a private system because they could afford high-quality care.

Exercise 8 page 69

Answers will vary.

LANGUAGE DEVELOPMENT

Learning objectives

- Use medical vocabulary to complete sentences about healthcare – *sedentary lifestyle, patient, underfunding*
- Use academic adjectives and nouns to describe medical issues – *Hospitals can suffer adverse conditions such as underfunding. Conventional medicine involves the use of drugs. Several surgeons may be needed in complex medical operations.*

Exercise 1 page 69

1 epidemic **2** underfunding **3** Drug dependency
4 sedentary lifestyle **5** preventable illness **6** patents

Exercise 2 page 70

1 adverse **2** professional **3** illegal **4** physical
5 complex **6** adequate **7** conventional **8** precise
9 medical

Optional activity

👤 Ask students what adjectives 2, 3, 4, 7 and 9 have in common. They all end in the sound /l/ and all end in the letters -al. Point out that academic adjectives that end with this sound usually end with the letters -al. Ask students to think of more or look through a text related to their field of study and find more -al words. Students record them.

Exercise 3 page 70

1 illegal **2** professional **3** adequate **4** Conventional
5 complex **6** physical **7** adverse **8** medical **9** precise

CRITICAL THINKING

Learning objectives

- Understand the variety of ways in which diseases can be prevented
- Use a Likert scale to evaluate your opinion on responsibility for disease prevention
- Analyze different ways to prevent diseases in relation to a set of questions
- Rank a list of preventative actions that people can take against disease and justify your ranking
- Describe ways that individuals and families or governments can encourage or take preventative actions
- Analyze statements which support different positions on responsibility for healthcare

UNL⌂CK TEACHER DEVELOPMENT

BE INFORMED

→ **Evaluating ideas** is an important skill for students because: (1) Not all ideas which students have are strong, and the weaker ones need to be identified; however, the brainstorming process is still very valuable for ensuring all ideas are collected as a starting point; (2) One way of doing this is to use a Likert scale, which can help you identify what you think about a particular issue; (3) By evaluating ideas, students can identify both the arguments which support and do not support their position.

BE CONFIDENT

→ Develop this skill for yourself by doing the following activity:
Circle the number on the Likert scale according to how you think critical thinking is best taught.

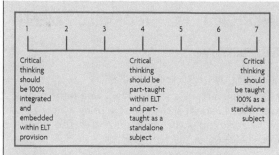

| 1 | 2 | 3 | 4 | 5 | 6 | 7 |

Critical thinking should be 100% integrated and embedded within ELT provision

Critical thinking should be part-taught within ELT and part-taught as a standalone subject

Critical thinking should be taught 100% as a standalone subject

After you have circled a number, reflect on the reasons why you think this. What evidence would you use to defend your position?

Lead-in

Give students a minute to read the writing task. Ask them to brainstorm what they do individually to prevent disease. Tell them to keep their brainstorming notes for later, when they begin to write their essay.

UNL⌂CK TEACHER DEVELOPMENT

BE READY

Look at the Critical Thinking section in the Student's Book on pages 71–72.

→ Which elements of the lesson do you think your students will find easiest / most difficult / most useful? Why?

→ Are your answers true for all students in your class?

→ How can you adapt your teaching or the material to meet your students' needs?

BE FLEXIBLE

Exercise 4 could be done as a whole-class activity. Write the numbers one to seven on separate pieces of paper and put them in a line on a wall. Students should stand next to the number which represents their view. You can then ask each group why they think that, and encourage discussion between the students. Students can then move to a new number if they change their opinion.

Exercises 1–7 pages 71–72
Answers will vary.

Exercise 8 page 72

1 in favour **2** in favour **3** in favour **4** against
5 against **6** against **7** against **8** against **9** in favour

BE REFLECTIVE

Think about the following questions:

→ Did the Likert scale activity work well with your students? Did you feel comfortable using it? It is a very versatile tool – you could potentially use it more extensively in your teaching practice.

→ How well were your students able to cope with this critical thinking section? There were eight exercises, which is more than usual. Did you have to do anything differently within (or outside) the class for this section?

BE COLLABORATIVE

Your development is more meaningful when it is shared. See page 14 for ideas on how to peer-collaborate. Why not share the ideas you generated in the *Be confident* section, and their outcome?

GRAMMAR FOR WRITING

Learning objectives

- Understand rules relating to the use of articles in English and identify examples
- Complete sentences about healthcare with the correct article (*a, an, the* or zero article)
- Use simple and complex transition words and phrases to introduce opposing arguments – *Homeopathy seems to be ineffective. However, people claim that it works. In spite of the fact that homeopathy seems to be ineffective, people still use it. Despite its ineffectiveness, people still use it.*

Exercise 1 page 74

1 f **2** d **3** h **4** b **5** g, g **6** c **7** e, e
8 c **9** i **10** e, e **11** j

Exercise 2 page 74

1 Ø; a **2** Ø; Ø **3** The **4** The; the **5** Ø **6** Ø; an
7 Ø; an **8** Ø; an; Ø **9** the **10** Ø; Ø

Optional activity

👥 Ask students to return to the first paragraph of Reading 2, this time looking at examples of zero article. Ask them to explain why no article is needed for: *healthcare, residents, health insurance, citizens.*

Exercise 3 page 75

Answers will vary. Suggested answers:

1 in spite of **2** Even though **3** other people claim that
4 However **5** Even though

ACADEMIC WRITING SKILLS

Learning objective

- Produce sentences of different lengths on the topic of healthcare

Exercise 1 page 77

2 Although my country's healthcare system is not perfect, it is better than many others.

3 This is the medication that I need to take for my illness.

4 All (of the) people in our society should have access to affordable healthcare. It is their right.

5 On this subject, doctors agree the most.

6 A good healthcare system can save money, and it can also save lives.

Be flexible

Challenge **more advanced students** to review a piece of writing they did in the past. Is there enough sentence variety? They should revise a paragraph to increase sentence variety, using at least three of the five techniques from the Skills box on page 76.

WRITING TASK

Learning objectives

- Use a table to plan the content of an essay discussing responsibility for disease prevention.
- Draft an essay discussing responsibility for disease prevention.
- Review and revise the content and structure of your essay
- Review and revise the use of language in your essay

Exercises 1–7 pages 77–78

Answers will vary.

RESEARCH PROJECT

Create a website describing how medicine has changed over time.

Explain to the class that they are going to research how medicine has changed over time, which could include nutrition, surgery, the diagnosis and treatment of diseases, preventive medicine, or another field of the students' choice. They will use this information to create a website on the topic.

Students should be encouraged to find out about traditional remedies as well as modern medicine. They could find science journals and websites for information or interview elderly family members. Alternatively, they could make videos, pictures and recordings to populate their website.

CLASSROOM APP

Exercises 1–2

Answers will vary.

Exercise 3

1 surgery   **2** safety net   **3** consultation   **4** funded
5 controversial   **6** burden   **7** contribution   **8** chief

Exercise 4

1 epidemic   **2** sedentary lifestyle   **3** patent
4 drug dependency   **5** Preventable illnesses
6 underfunding

Exercise 5

1 profession, profession   **2** complex, complexity
3 adequacy, adequate   **4** medicine, medical
5 precise, precision   **6** illegality, illegal

Exercise 6

1 In the past   **2** If medicine causes sickness
3 which employs over 2,000   **4** and
5 which has angered passengers

UNIT OBJECTIVES	
Watch and listen	Watch and understand a video about population and water.
Reading skill	Identify cohesive devices.
Critical thinking	Analyze a case study; evaluate arguments.
Grammar	Express solutions using *it*.
Academic writing skills	Develop ideas; use parallel structure.
Writing task	Write a problem–solution essay.
⊘ **Teacher development**	Help your students become better at **analyzing a case study** and **evaluating arguments**.

UNLOCK YOUR KNOWLEDGE

Background note

The photo shows floods in central Phetchaburi, Thailand. The floods were caused by a tropical storm, Kirogi, which caused the local river to overflow. As a result of the flood, people had to be evacuated from their homes, many roads and highways were cut off, and local businesses and schools had to close. Heavy rains are the usual causes of floods, especially when there is no appropriate water draining system. Droughts are periods of time when there is less rain than normal, which can cause water shortages. Apart from floods and droughts, other natural disasters include hurricanes, tornadoes, volcanic eruptions, earthquakes and tsunamis. Natural disasters can destroy and damage buildings and important infrastructure, like roads and power stations, force people to leave their homes and can cause disease and death.

Lead-in

Show the students the word *weather* written vertically top to bottom in capitals. They have to write words related to weather going across that include those letters. Show as an example that the letters *sno* could be written before *W* to make the word *snow* and that the capital letter can be anywhere in the word. Students work in pairs to try to complete the other six words.

Possible answers:

snoW	hurricanE	rAin	
droughT	Hail	tEmperature	thundeR

page 81

1 Floods can occur when a lot of rain falls in a short period of time, especially after a long period of dry weather; they can also occur when rivers get too full after prolonged rainfall.

Droughts can be the result of unusual weather patterns, e.g. changes in the prevailing wind direction or jet stream.

Both weather conditions can affect the economy because people cannot travel to work or damage is caused to roads, bridges and buildings. They can also severely affect agriculture, damaging crops and making it difficult to feed animals, causing food prices to increase.

2–3 *Answers will vary.*

WATCH AND LISTEN

Learning objectives

- Listen and understand facts and figures about water around the world
- Make inferences about implications for society from the information in a video about water use
- Practise describing issues related to water use

Exercises 1–2 page 82
Answers will vary.

Exercise 3 page 82

1 F; Only 1% of the fresh water is available for human use. **2** T **3** T **4** F; Water shortages are the result of increasing population, poor infrastructure, politics, poverty or living in a dry part of the world.
5 F; The Aral Sea once covered more than 25,000 square miles. It is now 10% of its original size.

Exercise 4 page 83

1 70% **2** distribution **3** population **4** infrastructure
5 common **6** space **7** drought

Exercises 5–6 page 83
Answers will vary.

READING 1

Learning objectives

- Understand key vocabulary for natural disasters – *identify*, *devastating*, *measures*
- Skim an article to identify the topic
- Read and understand detailed information in an article about disaster mitigation
- Understand referencing with cohesive devices in an article about disaster mitigation
- Make inferences about the opinions of an interviewee in an article about disaster mitigation
- Explain the impacts of rainfall and flooding in a discussion

Lead-in

Ask students to name different kinds of extreme weather and describe where they typically occur. Let students know that similar weather phenomena may have different names in different parts of the world (e.g. *typhoon/cyclone/hurricane*). Write the words on the board.

Exercise 1 page 84

1 measures   **2** identify   **3** crucial   **4** devastating
5 community   **6** maintenance   **7** reduction   **8** criticize

Exercise 2 page 85

1 levee   **2** tsunami   **3** dam   **4** hurricane   **5** flood barrier
6 sandbagging

Exercise 3 page 86

1 'Controlling the flow' is the best title because the interview is about ways to control the flow of water in a flood.

2 'What to do about risk' is not as good because it is too general and does not mention water or flooding.

3 'A way to protect people from flooding' is not as good because the interviewer says there are several ways, and people also have to help themselves in a flood situation.

4 'Protect your house against flooding' is not as good because the text is not just about protecting houses.

Exercise 4 page 87

1 F; Dan Smith works for a government agency.
2 T   **3** DNS   **4** T   **5** DNS   **6** T

Exercise 5 page 87

1 attempting to minimize the impact of natural disasters both before and after they happen   **2** earth-wall defences   **3** because of their environmental impact
4 both the government and individuals

Exercise 6 page 87

1 risk reduction and risk analysis   **2** risk reduction
3 the construction and maintenance of levees
4 a tsunami   **5** new flood prevention solutions
6 construction of seas walls and bulkheads; the redesign of power stations and subway tunnels; the Thames Barrier
7 expensive early-warning systems

Be flexible

👤 Students can do a similar activity with any text. Encourage them to take a text from their own field of study, highlight the pronouns and general nouns (such as *case*, *measures*, *areas*) and work out what they refer to.

👥 It may be useful for **lower-level students** to work together on the same text (for example, Reading 2 in Unit 2 would work well). They can work in pairs or on their own. Be sure to point out examples when the pronoun *this* refers to an entire idea.

Exercise 7 page 88

Dan Smith would probably only agree with statement 5.

Exercise 8 page 88

1–2 *Answers may vary.*   **3** *Possible answers:* Bangladesh, China, India, Pakistan. Heavy monsoon rains and global warming means snow and ice on the Himalayas is melting into rivers and increasing the risk of flooding in these countries.

READING 2

Learning objectives

- Understand key vocabulary for natural disasters – *casualty*, *disrupt*, *infrastructure*
- Understand the function of each paragraph in an essay about disaster mitigation
- Read and understand detailed information in an essay about disaster mitigation
- Understand referencing with cohesive devices in an essay about disaster mitigation
- Make inferences about key considerations and background information in an essay about disaster mitigation
- Synthesize information from two texts about disaster mitigation in a discussion

Lead-in

There are several country names in this unit, so it is worth spending some time on the spelling of these. Ask students to work in groups of three or four. In one minute, they should think of as many countries as they can ending in a letter or group of letters you give them. One person writes down the countries that the others suggest. They should not look up the answers at this stage. Ask questions such as the following (possible answers are given, although there are many more):

1 Which countries end with -*land*? (*England, Ireland, Thailand, Poland, Switzerland, Finland, Iceland, New Zealand*)

2 Which countries end with the letter *a*? (*China, Kenya, Saudi Arabia, Algeria, Argentina, Canada, Botswana, Indonesia, India, Romania*)

3 Which countries end with the letter *n*? (*Jordan, Afghanistan, Oman, Sudan, Japan, Spain, Pakistan, Kazakhstan*)

Exercise 1 pages 88–89

1 disrupted   **2** casualties   **3** strategies   **4** issue
5 monitor   **6** rely on   **7** infrastructure   **8** policy

Exercise 2 page 89

Droughts are most common in countries that have little rain. These are predominantly found in sub-Saharan Africa. Australia also suffers badly, but as a richer country, it is better able to mitigate the problems arising from little or no rain. On the map, the areas with the highest temperatures (in red) and little rainfall are the ones most likely to suffer from drought: Africa and Australia.

Exercise 3 page 89

Possible answers:

1 Drought kills animals and crops and causes starvation. **2** Bottles of drinking water can be brought into the drought area.   **3** Drought monitoring, rainwater harvesting and water recycling.   **4** Many long-term drought solutions are expensive and need technical knowledge that may not be available.

Exercise 4 page 91

a 6   **b** 5   **c** 1   **d** 4   **e** 3   **f** 2

Exercise 5 page 91

Possible answers:

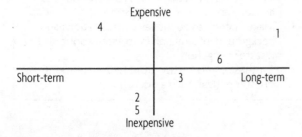

Exercise 6 page 91

1 b   **2** b   **3** a

Exercise 7 page 92

Answers will vary.

LANGUAGE DEVELOPMENT

Learning objectives

- Form and use academic noun phrases in sentences about natural disasters – *risk analysis, disaster mitigation, flood protection*
- Use adjective-noun collocations to describe natural disasters – *minor problem, major disaster, seasonal drought*

Exercise 1 pages 92–93

2 Risk reduction   **3** water-management system
4 government report   **5** flood protection
6 Community-based projects

Exercise 2 page 93

2 natural   **3** controlled   **4** long-term   **5** seasonal

Exercise 3 page 93

2 natural disasters   **3** Controlled floods   **4** Large-scale/Wide-reaching disaster mitigation projects   **5** devastating/severe flood   **6** extreme/serious drought   **7** seasonal drought   **8** terrible/major disaster

Optional activity

Ask students to find collocations for the following nouns, related to solutions to water-related disasters in Reading 2. Ask them to identify the N+N noun phrase in the list.

___ strategies (long-term)   ___ solutions (long-term)
___ waterways (seasonal)   ___ systems (irrigation)
___ measures (preventative)

CRITICAL THINKING

Learning objectives

- Identify the strategies used in two case studies of environmental disaster prevention
- Evaluate the cost and timeframe of disaster prevention strategies simultaneously
- Evaluate how easy different disaster prevention strategies are to implement for a developing country which experiences wildfires or dust storms and choose the three best strategies
- Suggest new disaster prevention strategies for a developing country which experiences wildfires or dust storms

UNLOCK TEACHER DEVELOPMENT

BE INFORMED

➜ **Analyzing a case study** and **evaluating arguments** are important skills for students because: (1) Case studies are often a rich, interesting and empirical source of information, and therefore extremely useful for students; (2) Evaluating arguments using different criteria is sometimes challenging for students, so they need both more practice and specific techniques; (3) The diagram presented in this unit is a useful graphic way of analyzing and evaluating arguments.

BE CONFIDENT

➜ Develop these skills for yourself by doing the following activity:

Write the following verbs in the correct place on the diagram below. As you do this, think about what the verb means, and why you are putting it at that particular point.

calculate	list	paraphrase
demonstrate	listen	recognize
design	measure	role play
evaluate	modify	translate

higher-order critical
thinking skill

common in daily life   not common in daily life

lower-order critical
thinking skill

Lead-in

Give students a minute to read the writing task. Ask students to brainstorm environmental problems that interest them. They should keep any notes they make for later, when they begin to write their essay.

UNLOCK TEACHER DEVELOPMENT

BE READY

Look at the Critical Thinking section in the Student's Book on pages 94–96.

➜ Which elements of the lesson do you think your students will find easiest / most difficult / most useful? Why?

➜ Are your answers true for all students in your class?

➜ How can you adapt your teaching or the material to meet your students' needs?

BE FLEXIBLE

Some classes may find Exercise 2 challenging. If they are unable to do it by themselves, or you think they will struggle, you could do it either as a whole-class activity or in pairs. Alternatively, whilst some students may not find the content difficult, they may not understand some of the terminology (e.g. *x/y* axis), and so you may need to explain this.

Exercise 1 pages 94–95

1 B   **2** A, B   **3** B   **4** A   **5** A   **6** B   **7** A   **8** B   **9** A

Exercise 2 page 95
Answers will vary. Suggested answers:
expensive, short-term: 1, 9
inexpensive, short-term: 2, 4, 5, 8
expensive, long-term: 3, 6
inexpensive, long-term: 7

Exercises 3–4 page 96
Answers will vary.

UNLOCK TEACHER DEVELOPMENT

BE REFLECTIVE

Think about the following questions:

➜ Have you considered talking to teachers of other subjects in your educational institutions about case studies? It may be useful to talk to business studies teachers, since case studies are commonly used in this subject.

➜ How well did students understand how to use the diagram? As it is a very useful academic tool, it may be beneficial to ask students over the next few weeks whether they are using it for their studies. If they are not, encourage them to do so.

GRAMMAR FOR WRITING

Learning objective

- Use *it* as an empty subject in sentences with particular structures – *It is important to prepare for natural disasters. It is worth preparing for natural disasters. It is a sad fact that many lives were lost.*

Exercise 1 page 97

Answers will vary. Possible answers:

1 b **2** f **3** c **4** a **5** h **6** e **7** d **8** g

Exercise 2 page 97

Answers will vary. Possible answers:

1 using sandbags to stop water **2** in a flood zone **3** harvesting and storing rainwater **4** to get people to agree on a strategy **5** that they are expensive **6** rebuild communities

Exercises 3–4 page 97

Answers will vary.

Be flexible

Students look at a report from their own field of study and find examples of these types of *it* phrases. They share examples with a partner.

Challenge **stronger students** to write some of their own *it* phrases, based on information in a report they have chosen from their own field. They should write one of each type of *it* clause (infinitive, gerund, *that* + clause).

ACADEMIC WRITING SKILLS

Learning objectives

- Organize ideas in a logical sequence in a body paragraph of an essay
- Correct non-parallel structures in sentences with ideas linked with conjunctions
- Use parallel structure for ideas linked with conjunctions in sentences about natural disasters

Exercise 1 page 98

1 b **2** c **3** a **4** e **5** d **6** f

Exercise 2 page 99

1 'talk to their friends and neighbours' needs to be a noun phrase: 'their friends and neighbours'

2 'they should establish desalination plants' needs to be a gerund phrase: 'establishing desalination plants'

3 'he analyzes risk' should be a noun phrase: 'risk analysis'

4 'the expense is surprising' should be an adjective phrase: 'surprisingly expensive'

5 'typhoons can also occur' needs to be a noun with no verb: 'typhoons'

Exercise 3 page 99

Answers will vary. Possible answers:

1 an emergency kit and a torch (answer should be a noun or a noun phrase) **2** roads (answer should be a noun or noun phrase) **3** using satellite images and following fires (answer should be a gerund phrase)

Be flexible

Have students compare their answers. Ask them what part of speech each example requires (1 noun phrase, 2 verb phrase [a noun phrase is also possible], 3 gerund). Challenge **stronger students** to expand the first sentence of Exercise 3 into a paragraph. They should write three additional sentences with parallel structure.

WRITING TASK

Learning objectives

- Prepare an outline of an essay suggesting solutions to an environmental problem in a developing country
- Draft an essay suggesting solutions to an environmental problem in a developing country
- Review and revise the content and structure of your essay
- Review and revise the use of language in your essay

Exercises 1–7 pages 99–100

Answers will vary.

RESEARCH PROJECT

Calculate your environmental impact and take measures to reduce it.

This is initially an individual project. Tell the class that they will calculate their environmental impact. Students should think about how much and how they travel, flights they have taken, the size of their home and how much energy it uses, whether they recycle or not and their diet. They could use an online calculator to help them.

They can then compare their impact, in groups, and make a graphical representation of this compared to the country as a whole, and other countries. They can then formulate their own class pledge to reduce their impact, sign this and then try and promote this idea to others.

CLASSROOM APP

Exercise 1

Answers will vary.

Exercise 2

1 community **2** crucial **3** casualties **4** issue
5 criticized **6** rely on **7** maintenance **8** policy

Exercise 3

Answers will vary.

Exercise 4

1 train's late arrival / late arrival of the train
2 difficulty of the exercise / difficult exercise
3 Climate change **4** dangerous driving
5 job losses **6** the safety **7** waste management plan

Exercise 5

1 seasonal drought **2** natural disasters **3** severe floods
4 minor problem **5** long-term disaster

Exercise 6

1 more environmentally friendly
2 thoroughly
3 go out in the evenings
4 that they would deliver them on time
5 to improve air quality
6 a large amount of cash

UNIT OBJECTIVES	
Watch and listen	Watch and understand a video about government grants for energy-efficient homes.
Reading skill	Skim a text.
Critical thinking	Create a persuasive argument.
Grammar	Use correct register in academic writing.
Academic writing skills	Order information; prioritize arguments.
Writing task	Write a persuasive essay.
⟳ **Teacher development**	Help your students become better at **creating a persuasive argument**.

UNL⟳CK YOUR KNOWLEDGE

Background note

The photo shows the Tokyo Tower in Tokyo, Japan. The design resembles the Eiffel Tower in Paris, but the Tokyo Tower is painted white and orange to meet air safety regulations. The tower was built in 1958 and it is 333 metres high. In the background, we can see the modern skyscrapers and apartment blocks of the Tokyo skyline. In Tokyo, around 62% of people live in apartments. To the right of the Tokyo tower, we can see low, traditional Japanese buildings. This is the Zojoji temple, built in 1393.

Lead-in

Students look the photo of the Tokyo skyline and in pairs say in what ways it is similar to and different from the skyline of their own town or city. If your class is in Tokyo, ask students to look at a photo from another city, like London or Dubai. Monitor to help with language and guide students to talk about any architectural features. Check answers with the class.

page 103
Answers will vary.

WATCH AND LISTEN

Learning objectives

* Listen and understand the main ideas in a video about housing
* Listen and complete a detailed summary of the ideas in the video
* Make inferences about the ideas in the video and their wider implications
* Practise talking about energy-efficient housing

Exercises 1–2 page 104
Answers will vary.

Exercise 3 pages 104–105

1 T **2** T **3** F; It will take much longer – 100 years
4 F; Builders already know how to construct energy-efficient homes. **5** T **6** T

Exercise 4 page 105

1 Twenty-five percent / A quarter **2** insulation
3 reduction/decrease **4** energy-efficient / zero carbon
5 temperature **6** rising/increasing **7** 'zero-carbon home standard' **8** scrapped/dropped **9** confused/uncertain

Exercises 5–6 page 105
Answers will vary.

READING 1

Learning objectives

* Understand key vocabulary for architecture – *conservation, durable, efficiency*
* Skim the images, title, introduction and conclusion of an article to identify the topic
* Evaluate what was the most useful indicator of topic when skimming
* Skim the text of an article about green buildings to identify the topic of paragraphs
* Read and identify detailed information about different types of green building
* Read and understand detailed information
* Make inferences about the ideas and implications of the article
* Give opinions on issues relating to green buildings

Lead-in

Ask students what the word *green* has come to mean. Then ask them how the word applies to buildings: in other words, what is a 'green' building? Expect answers about conservation of resources such as water and energy and the use of recycled or low-impact materials. Introduce the term *sustainability* if it is not already familiar to students.

Exercise 1 page 106

Answers will vary.

Exercise 2 page 106

1 durable   **2** compromise   **3** efficiency   **4** conservation   **5** second-hand   **6** sector   **7** relevant

Exercise 3 page 107

d

Exercise 4 page 107

Answers will vary.

Exercise 5 page 107

a 2   **b** 4   **c** 1   **d** 6   **e** 5   **f** 3

Be flexible

👤 Ask students to locate the thesis statement in Reading 1 (the last sentence of the first paragraph). Then ask them to look for both the examples of sustainable practices and some of the barriers to green building.

Challenge **more advanced students** to create an outline of Reading 1. This will encourage them to find the main idea and supporting details in each paragraph.

Exercise 6 page 109

1 HH   **2** HH   **3** RC   **4** N   **5** HH   **6** HH   **7** RC   **8** HH

Exercise 7 page 109

1 T   **2** DNS   **3** F; Environmentally friendly practices become less practical / too costly for large-volume construction.   **4** DNS   **5** F; Fossil fuels are non-renewable.   **6** T   **7** T

Exercise 8 page 109

Answers will vary. Suggested answers:

1 the benefits will be for the environment   **2** because they needed to know about and plan for them before construction began, to make sure they could be most easily and efficiently implemented   **3** to teach students about the importance of recycling

Exercise 9 page 109

Answers will vary.

READING 2

Learning objectives

- Understand key vocabulary – *function, civilized, reputation*
- Skim an essay about form v function in building design for the writer's opinion
- Read and complete a summary of the essay
- Identify paraphrases of ideas and opinions from the essay
- Apply real-world knowledge to make inferences about the design ideas in the essay
- Synthesize information from an article about green buildings and an essay about form v function in building design in a discussion

Lead-in

Ask students to consider a building they know well that they consider beautiful. What makes it beautiful? Then get them to think of a building that they use that does not work very well for them (e.g. the bathrooms are too far away, there is not enough light, the rooms get wet during rainstorms, etc). Introduce the terms *form* and *function*.

Exercise 1 page 110

1 b   **2** a   **3** a   **4** a   **5** b   **6** a   **7** b

Exercise 2 page 110

Answers will vary.

Exercise 3 page 110

The writer thinks that both are equally important.

Exercise 4 page 112

Possible answers:

1 function   **2** beauty   **3** architects   **4** reflect   **5** mood/happiness   **6** building   **7** users   **8** celebrated

Exercise 5 page 112

1 b   **2** a   **3** f   **4** c   **5** e   **6** d

Optional activity

👤 Ask students to paraphrase (1) the definition of functionality in the first paragraph of the reading and (2) the first sentence of the second paragraph.

Possible answers:

(1) an approach to architecture in which the design of the building is shaped by its purpose.

(2) Addressing a building's purpose is a basic first step in its design.

Exercise 6 page 113

Possible answers:

1 They can create a more positive and inspired workforce. They allow the users of the building to function well. They can give a positive impression of the owner to other people.

2 It maximizes the number of planes that can fit in the airport terminal and makes it easier and quicker for passengers to access the planes.

3 The buildings might reflect badly on them.

4 Poor lighting, lack of or poor view from windows, the temperature inside the building (either too cold or too hot), decoration

5 If workers have been provided with a comfortable and pleasant working environment, they may feel more appreciated and want to work harder for the employer.

Exercise 7 page 113

Answers will vary.

LANGUAGE DEVELOPMENT

Learning objectives

- Record word families by part of speech in a table – *function, functionalism, functional, functionally*
- Use the correct word form to complete sentences about buildings
- Use architecture and planning vocabulary to describe opinions about buildings – *Green belt land is important because it is the lungs of a city. When building skyscrapers, it is important to consider wind factors. Urban sprawl has a negative effect on the environment because it impacts on animals' habitats.*

Exercise 1 page 114

1 environmental   **2** environmentally   **3** depression
4 depress   **5** depressingly   **6** responsible   **7** responsibly
8 architecture   **9** architectural   **10** architecturally
11 efficiency   **12** efficient

Exercise 2 page 114

1 environmental   **2** Functionalism   **3** efficiently
4 responsibly   **5** depress   **6** architecture   **7** environment
8 responsible   **9** depression   **10** architectural

Exercise 3 page 115

1 structural engineer   **2** Skyscrapers   **3** urban sprawl
4 green belt   **5** Suburban, outskirts   **6** amenities

Exercise 4 page 115

Possible answers:

1 … to design environmentally friendly, cost-effective buildings.   **2** … consider their environmental impact.
3 … it is important to protect the Earth.

4 … it protects the countryside from urban sprawl.   **5** … municipal buildings and sport facilities.   **6** … it increases people's dependence on cars.

CRITICAL THINKING

Learning objectives

- Analyze the advantages of different focuses in architecture
- Evaluate your arguments
- Support arguments with evidence and reasons

UNL⦾CK TEACHER DEVELOPMENT

BE INFORMED

→ **Creating a persuasive argument** is an important skill for students because: (1) One of the key underlying factors of all academic writing is that you are trying to persuade the reader; (2) Students sometimes think that all evidence / supporting information is the same; that what is important is just to add evidence, regardless of how relevant it actually is; (3) Students must focus on information and evidence which is relevant, looking at quality, not just quantity. They need to understand why and how they can do this.

BE CONFIDENT

→ Develop this skill for yourself by doing the following activity:

Prescriptive grammar is a set of rules about language based on how people think language should be used – there is correct and incorrect language. Descriptive grammar is a set of rules based on how people actually use language.

Complete the T-chart below.

advantages of teaching prescriptive grammar	advantages of teaching descriptive grammar

Look at your chart. Highlight the points which you think are the most persuasive in each column. Put an X next to the ideas which you think are the least persuasive.

Lead-in

Give students a minute to read the writing task. Ask students to brainstorm to what they think is the most positive quality of the building they live in now. Tell them to keep their brainstorming notes for later, when they begin to write their essay.

UNLOCK TEACHER DEVELOPMENT

BE READY

Look at the Critical Thinking section in the Student's Book on pages 116–117.

→ Which elements of the lesson do you think your students will find easiest / most difficult / most useful? Why?

→ Are your answers true for all students in your class?

→ How can you adapt your teaching or the material to meet your students' needs?

BE FLEXIBLE

After doing Exercise 4, you could ask students to look at the arguments which they wrote an X next to, and think of whether there is any way they could make them more persuasive; for example, by changing the emphasis or adding new evidence.

Exercise 1 page 116

Answers will vary. Possible answers:

Advantages of focusing on beauty (in addition to students' own ideas):

beautiful buildings are a symbol of a civilized society; they can create a more positive and motivated workforce; they give a good impression; they are 'warmer' than strictly functional buildings; they can be more interesting

Advantages of focusing on function (in addition to students' own ideas):

ease of use; possible greater ease of movement within the building, more practical

Exercises 2–4 pages 116–117

Answers will vary.

UNLOCK TEACHER DEVELOPMENT

BE REFLECTIVE

Think about the following questions:

→ Do your English teaching colleagues share the same view as you about prescriptive and descriptive grammar? Discuss your views with them. If you are teaching the same students, this may be confusing for them if the way you and your colleagues approach the subject is very different.

→ When you assess your students' work, do you give specific feedback about how persuasive their argument is? Doing so could help them develop this ability.

BE COLLABORATIVE

Your development is more meaningful when it is shared. See page 14 for ideas on how to peer-collaborate. If you followed the suggestion in the *Be flexible* section, tell a colleague whether or not it was successful.

GRAMMAR FOR WRITING

Learning objectives

- Identify informal language in a text
- Rewrite a text using equivalents with a more formal register
- Complete sentences using a consistent register

Exercise 1 page 117

1 fundamentally   **2** Undoubtedly   **3** critical   **4** considerable investment   **5** calculate   **6** can be justified   **7** there is no real benefit   **8** has a positive impact on   **9** and desire to work effectively   **10** approximately   **11** This supports the accuracy of this notion.

Exercise 2 page 118

Possible answers:

1 provide the space and facilities that are needed   **2** how much money an eco-friendly building will save in the long term   **3** the well-being of the local community   **4** there is plenty of sunlight   **5** the people who use the buildings   **6** constructing ugly buildings

Optional activity

👤 Ask students to review Reading 2 and to find formal equivalents of the following:

mostly (primarily); mix x2 (combine, blend); make x2 (create, produce); build (construct); often (repeatedly)

ACADEMIC WRITING SKILLS

Learning objectives

- Use paraphrases to reference previous ideas in academic writing – *When choosing a new house, the most important consideration may be location. Areas near good schools are often popular.*
- Use pronouns and other phrases to reference previous ideas – *Some families prefer to expand their existing houses. This allows all family members to live together.*
- Complete texts with appropriate words, phrases and paraphrases to refer to previous ideas
- Evaluate and prioritize supporting arguments

Exercise 1 page 118

1 In spite of this   **2** this profession / it   **3** This combination   **4** it / this profession   **5** For this reason

Exercise 2 page 119

1 This style   **2** the columns   **3** They   **4** these Greek architects   **5** These structures

Exercise 3 page 120

1 a   **2** a   **3** a   **4** b   **5** a

Optional activity

👤 Ask students to write persuasive examples to support the following statements:

1 The most important thing to do after a natural disaster is to build shelters quickly. Their quality is less important.
2 Most people don't really notice the buildings that they work in.
3 Great buildings endure long after their style has gone out of fashion.
4 A building's design affects the interaction of the people who work or live in it.

Exercise 4 page 120

1 b   **2** a   **3** c   **4** b   **5** a   **6** c

WRITING TASK

Learning objectives

- Prioritize your arguments for an essay evaluating the importance of size against location when building or buying a home
- Draft your essay
- Review and revise the content and structure of your essay

Exercises 1–7 pages 121–122

Answers will vary.

RESEARCH PROJECT

Create an online architectural tour of a famous building in your country.

Divide the class into groups and ask them to think about an online guide or documentary for tourists to their country, or the country they are in. Ask them to take pictures or make videos of an interesting architectural building. If it isn't possible for students to take pictures or make videos, they can use pictures they have researched online.

Using presentation software or an online tool, they can create an interactive tour of the building with descriptions and photos of architectural features and historical facts. Alternatively, they can use a movie app to make their own documentary.

CLASSROOM APP

Exercises 1–2

Answers will vary.

Exercise 3

1 depressing   **2** demonstrated   **3** durable   **4** reflect   **5** Second-hand   **6** civilized   **7** compromise   **8** relevant

Exercise 4

1 environmental   **2** responsibility   **3** efficient   **4** architect   **5** depressingly   **6** functional

Exercise 5

1 Suburban   **2** skyscrapers   **3** Urban sprawl   **4** amenities   **5** outskirts   **6** green belts

Exercise 6

1 Despite this, hunting them is permitted in certain countries.

2 This demonstrates the importance of not using your phone before sleeping.

3 A higher salary would allow her to buy a house.

4 These items can be seen at the national museum.

5 For this reason, passengers are advised to book early.

UNIT OBJECTIVES

Watch and listen	Watch and understand a video about wind power.
Reading skill	Work out meaning from context.
Critical thinking	Evaluate benefits and drawbacks; organize ideas for an essay.
Grammar	Use defining and non-defining relative clauses.
Academic writing skills	Introduce advantages and disadvantages; make academic writing coherent.
Writing task	Write an advantages and disadvantages essay.
⟳ **Teacher development**	Help your students become better at **evaluating benefits and drawbacks**.

UNLOCK YOUR KNOWLEDGE

Background note

The photo shows an engineer cycling next to solar panels, in a solar power station in Ain Beni Mathar, Morocco. The purpose of this power station is to increase people's access to renewable energy and to reduce the country's dependency on oil. Using renewable sources of energy, like solar, wind and hydro energy, can reduce the use of fossil fuels. Fossil fuels such as coal, oil and natural gas are formed from plants and animals that lived millions of years ago. The main disadvantages of using fossil fuels are that they are non-renewable, and they release carbon dioxide when they burn, which, in turn, pollutes the Earth's atmosphere and contributes to climate change.

Lead-in

Students work in groups. They imagine that they have got lost in the desert. It is mid-afternoon and very hot and sunny, but it will be very cold when the sun goes down so they need to make a fire. They have no matches, lighter or glass with them. However, they do have a can of cola and a bar of chocolate. Around them there are some small pieces of wood. Students discuss how they can light a fire with only these objects. Allow five minutes for discussion. Students share their ideas with the rest of the class. If nobody gives the correct answer, explain it using the answer below.

Suggested answer:
It is claimed that you can start a fire by rubbing the bottom of a drinks can with chocolate to make it smooth and shiny. You alternate rubbing with chocolate and rubbing with the chocolate wrapper (it does not matter what this is made of). You may

have to do this for up to an hour! Once the bottom of the can is very shiny, you point it at the sun with a piece of the chocolate wrapper held to it. The sun will soon reflect strongly enough to set the paper on fire. You use that to light a small piece of wood and then bigger ones. **Warning:** should your students ever try to do this, they should not eat the chocolate as it will be full of aluminium!

page 125

1 solar power **2** Fossil fuels like coal and oil are formed underground from plant and animal remains millions of years ago. Renewable energy like solar and hydropower is produced using the sun, water, etc. **3–4** *Answers will vary.*

WATCH AND LISTEN

Learning objectives

- Listen and understand the main ideas in a video about wind power
- Listen and note supporting details
- Make inferences about the ideas in the video and their wider implications
- Practise talking about wind power

Exercise 1 page 126
Answers will vary.

Exercise 2 page 126
Possible answers:
1 onshore versus offshore wind farms **2** how a wind turbine works **3** the advantages of wind power

Exercise 3 page 127
1 F; five percent **2** T **3** T **4** F; more expensive **5** DNS **6** T

Exercise 4 page 127

Possible answers:

1 The energy is renewable and the wind itself is free.
2 It is very windy. **3** People are less likely to object to the appearance and noise of turbines that are offshore or far from their homes. **4** The turbines are noisy and unattractive.

Exercise 5 page 127

Possible answers:

1 There is widespread support because: the UK is windy, people want to reduce CO_2 emissions. There is also opposition because: people think the turbines spoil the landscape, they are noisy. **2** Experts know that fossil fuels will run out and we will need to switch to renewable sources of energy.

Exercise 6 page 127

Answers will vary.

READING 1

Learning objectives

- Understand key vocabulary for energy – *offshore, inexhaustible, generate*
- Read an article about energy and select the best title
- Read and identify detailed information about different sources of energy
- Read and understand the meaning of unfamiliar words and phrases from their context in the article
- Give opinions and make predictions on energy sources

Lead-in

Ask students the difference between renewable and non-renewable energy. Ask them for examples of each. You may need to provide translations or explanations of terms such as *coal* and *hydropower*.

Exercise 1 page 128

1 wind power **2** geothermal energy **3** solar power
4 hydropower

Exercise 2 page 128

a initial **b** generate **c** aquatic **d** offshore **e** universal
f utilize **g** inexhaustible

Exercise 3 page 130

C

Be flexible

In pairs, ask students to explain their choice of answers to Exercise 3, including why they rejected the alternatives (e.g. It can't be (e) because the discussion is limited to energy consumption/conservation, not <u>all</u> types of conservation). Then ask them to point to passages in the text that support their choice (i.e. subheads and paragraphs that provide both pros and cons).

If **lower-level students** have difficulty with this activity, help them break down each choice. For example, (a) is about fossil fuels. Skim the subheads. Are all of them about fossil fuels? No? Then this is not a good choice. Continue with the other choices.

Exercise 4 page 130

1 solar **2** biomass **3** geothermal **4** hydropower
5 solar **6** geothermal

Exercise 5 page 130

1 hydropower **2** wind **3** biomass **4** solar
5 geothermal **6** hydropower **7** biomass

Exercise 6 page 131

1 of or from the sun **2** easily damaged, broken or harmed **3** when something is put or kept somewhere for use in the future **4** involving or produced by the heat that is inside the Earth **5** animals that live independently of people in natural conditions **6** to put into the ground **7** to have a border with

Exercise 7 page 131

Answers will vary.

READING 2

Learning objectives

- Understand key vocabulary for natural resources – *alarming, diminish, vital*
- Use your knowledge to make predictions about the future of natural resources and their conservation in an article about maintaining natural resources
- Read and understand the writer's opinions on strategies for maintaining natural resources
- Complete a set of detailed notes about the article
- Make inferences about the implications of the ideas in the article
- Synthesize information from an article about renewable energy and an article about maintaining natural resources in a discussion

Lead-in

Introduce the topic by reminding students that they have read about *energy* conservation and renewable *energy* sources. Ask them what other natural resources they use on a daily basis (e.g. water) and if they are renewable. Ask them what happens when these resources become scarce. What can be done to make sure they don't run out?

Exercise 1 page 132

1 urgent   **2** alarming   **3** adopt   **4** address   **5** diminish
6 vital   **7** resistant   **8** instigated

Exercise 2 page 132

Possible answers:

2 droughts, problems with growing crops, the death of livestock and other animals   **3** less food and fewer habitats for animals; flooding due to excess water run-off   **4** food prices would rise and there could be riots, starvation and death   **5** prices of metals would rise sharply; consumer goods would be more expensive

Exercise 3 page 133

Possible answers:

2 build water storage facilities (dams, irrigation channels, etc.)   **3** protect forests; create national parks; plant new trees; build dams to stop serious flooding   **4** reduce food waste through education; encourage people to eat produce that needs less land, enforce fishing quotas   **5** find new sources of metal; ensure that metal is recycled from old items

Exercises 4–5 page 133

Possible answers:

Reduce means to consume and use less. We can reduce our use of electricity, gas, oil and chemicals for example.

Re-use means to use things again, for example plastic bags from the supermarket or plastic containers.

Recycle means to collect and treat rubbish in order to produce useful materials. Paper, glass and some metals and plastics can be recycled.

Optional activity

👤 Point out that all three verbs start with the prefix *re-*. Ask students what this often means (*again*). Ask students for some more words that begin with the prefix *re-*: *rewrite, repaint, reconsider, redevelop, refill, refresh,* etc. Students record any useful words.

Exercise 6 page 133

1 He implies that reducing is the easiest to do, but does not say that one is better than the other.

2 They may not be available to people in certain places because of environmental limitations; they can be expensive; they can be time-consuming to install the required elements.

3 It is crucial for the future of the planet to follow the 'reduce, re-use, recycle strategy'.

Exercise 7 page 133

2 motorized   **3** medical; food storage   **4** metals
5 fossil fuels   **6** solar; geothermal   **7** the planet

Exercise 8 page 135

1 because people will be more careful about how they use or waste energy if it gets more expensive   **2** because it uses so much energy   **3** because it may not be safe or clean, and handling it could cause illness   **4** because following these laws could force them to raise their costs or reduce their profits

Exercise 9 page 135

Answers will vary.

LANGUAGE DEVELOPMENT

Learning objectives

- Recognize common compound nouns and adjective-noun collocations related to the topic of energy – *fossil fuel, power source, environmental problem*
- Complete sentences with the correct collocations of nouns or adjectives
- Use formal academic verbs in sentences – *Resources are beginning to diminish; soon they will run out. If people consult the documents on our website, they can see how biofuel is made. Advocates of biofuels sometimes omit key details.*

Exercise 1 page 135

1 fuel   **2** energy   **3** pollution   **4** source   **5** production
6 problem

Exercise 2 page 136

1 nuclear   **2** health/medical   **3** source   **4** Fossil
5 Alternative/Renewable   **6** water

Exercise 3 page 136

1 d   **2** h   **3** g   **4** f   **5** c   **6** b   **7** a   **8** e

Exercise 4 page 136

1 diminish   **2** deliver   **3** contested   **4** consult
5 instigate   **6** utilizes   **7** omit   **8** secure

CRITICAL THINKING

Learning objectives

- List the benefits and drawbacks of renewable energy sources and evaluate them
- Choose the three best renewable power sources for your country
- Provide support for your choices of renewable power sources

UNLOCK TEACHER DEVELOPMENT

BE INFORMED

→ **Evaluating benefits and drawbacks** is an important skill for students because: (1) Going through the process of evaluating benefits and drawbacks is a useful strategy for students to work out what their specific opinion on a topic is; (2) Evaluating benefits and drawbacks is a common type of essay question, so they will need a good understanding of this skill to answer these questions successfully; (3) Students many not have mechanisms and techniques for doing this effectively, so developing these skills – through a table, for example – is very helpful for them.

BE CONFIDENT

→ Develop this skill for yourself by doing the following activity:

Choose one of the topics below. Then, complete the table accordingly.

- All classes should be mixed ability
- All classes should be optional for students
- Smartphone use should be encouraged in class

What are the benefits?	What are the drawbacks?	Is it effective for your educational institution? What would be the impact?

What did you learn by doing this activity? Are there any practical implications for you or your educational institution?

Lead-in

Give students a minute to read the writing task. Ask student to brainstorm what types of energy sources (renewable and non-renewable) are already used in their country. Tell them to keep their brainstorming notes for later, when they begin to write their essay.

UNLOCK TEACHER DEVELOPMENT

BE READY

Look at the Critical Thinking section in the Student's Book on pages 137–138.

→ Which elements of the lesson do you think your students will find easiest / most difficult / most useful? Why?

→ Are your answers true for all students in your class?

→ How can you adapt your teaching or the material to meet your students' needs?

BE FLEXIBLE

An interesting extension to Exercise 4, probably for more advanced groups, would be to compare what they have written with the actual government energy policy in their country. This would obviously require some research. If the class were collectively able to research this information, it would be interesting to note the similarities and differences.

Exercise 1 page 137

*In the last column, '**Is it effective for your country? What is the impact of producing it?**', answers will vary.*

	What are the benefits?	What are the drawbacks?
hydropower	inexhaustible amount of energy	negative impact on aquatic wildlife; endangers boats; dams can flood land; expensive
wind power	Can be large- or small-scale; relatively cheap; no pollution	ugly; noisy; rely on wind; threat to wildlife
solar energy	inexhaustible resource; no pollution; adaptable	large area of land needed to produce a large amount; requires sunlight; photovoltaic cells are fragile

	What are the benefits?	**What are the drawbacks?**
biomass energy	can re-grow; universal; reduces the need for burying rubbish	produces greenhouse gases; can be expensive
geothermal energy	simple technology; no pollution; inexhaustible	regionally limited; high initial costs

Exercises 2–4 pages 137–138

Answers will vary.

UNL🔒CK TEACHER DEVELOPMENT

BE REFLECTIVE

→ Think about what you did in the *Be confident* section. Is there another question more relevant to your educational institution which would have been more interesting to ask?

→ How successful were your students in integrating information from the two readings into the table in Exercise 1? Synthesizing data from more than one text is often a challenge for students. If so, it may mean that they require more practice in doing this.

BE COLLABORATIVE

Your development is more meaningful when it is shared. See page 14 for ideas on how to peer-collaborate. Why not share the ideas you generated in the *Be ready* section, and their outcome?

GRAMMAR FOR WRITING

Learning objectives

- Use the correct relative pronoun or adverb in defining relative clauses – *Rachel Carson was the environmentalist who wrote the book* Silent Spring. *This was the book which instigated the modern environmental movement. The UK is the country where the first clean air law was passed.*
- Use commas around non-defining relative clauses – *Wind turbines, which may be offshore, provide clean, renewable energy. Rachel Carson, who wrote* Silent Spring, *began her career as a biologist. Nuclear energy, which is primarily generated by splitting atoms, provides 11% of the world's energy supplies.*

Exercise 1 page 139

1 who first split the atom (Enrico Fermi)　**2** whose houses are near nuclear power stations (people)　**3** where the electricity is located (cupboard)　**4** when fewer people are using it (at night)　**5** which is made from sugar found in certain crops (ethanol)

Optional activity

👥👥 Tell students they are going to play a game. Divide the class into two teams. Give each team slips of paper with different words that are related to energy and energy production/innovation (e.g. *coal, Saudi Arabia, Thomas Edison,* etc.). Each team must make up a sentence with a relative clause to define or describe it by saying the word followed by a relative clause (e.g. *This is a kind of fuel that is renewable but results in carbon emissions. This is the country that produces the second largest amount of oil per year.*). The other team has to guess what it is within a specific amount of time (e.g. 30 seconds). If they guess correctly in time, the asking team gets a point – in other words, it is in the team's interest to make their definitions clear and easy to guess.

Exercise 2 page 140

1 that/which (no commas required)　**2** Solar power, which is a form of renewable energy, is very popular in southern Spain.　**3** that/which (no commas required)　**4** that/which (no commas required)　**5** who/that (no commas required)　**6** Al Gore, who is a key supporter of alternative energy, won the Nobel Prize in 2007.

Exercise 3 page 140

1 which　**2** who　**3** which　**4** that　**5** which　**6** which

ACADEMIC WRITING SKILLS

Learning objectives

- Use phrases to describe advantages or disadvantages in sentences about renewable energy – *One advantage of wind power is that it is inexhaustible, so it will never run out. One other apparent advantage of wind power is that it produces no harmful emissions. Another potential drawback of biofuels is the amount of methane generated by their production.*
- Use a variety of techniques for creating coherence in a paragraph about alternative energy sources.

Exercise 1 page 141

Answers will vary. Suggested answers:

2 A serious disadvantage of biomass is that it produces greenhouse gases.　**3** One major drawback of biomass is that large areas of land are needed.　**4** The most obvious benefit of hydropower is that energy can be stored and used as needed. **5** One other inherent disadvantage of geothermal energy is that it is only available in certain places.

Exercise 2 page 142

1 For example **2** however **3** they **4** this **5** In the same way **6** they

Exercise 3 page 142

Answers will vary. Suggested answer:

Turbines and hydropower plants both change the landscape of an area. Even though some people think they alter the natural landscape in an unattractive way, others think that they are important sources of alternative energy. It is important to use alternative energy sources so that we are less dependent on fossil fuels, which have been linked to global warming. There is resistance to this idea, however. Some people are more concerned about using fossil fuels than other people are. Also, some think it is more important to save money than to reduce global warming, and alternative energy production facilities can be expensive to construct.

WRITING TASK

Learning objectives

- Prepare an outline of an essay describing the advantages and disadvantages of three types of renewable energy and which would work best in your country
- Draft your essay
- Review and revise the content and structure of your essay

Exercises 1–7 pages 143–144

Answers will vary.

RESEARCH PROJECT

Transform an area of your learning environment so that it is more energy efficient.

Ask the class to find ways to reduce their energy usage in their learning environment. They may want to look at areas such as air conditioning / heating alternatives, lighting, insulation, energy efficiency guides, electrical equipment, etc.

Tell students that they have to start a campaign to change an area of their learning environment and encourage others to do the same. They need to think of marketing, branding, issuing information and presentations, etc.

CLASSROOM APP

Exercises 1–2

Answers will vary.

Exercise 3

1 generated **2** initial **3** resistant **4** utilize
5 alarming **6** universal **7** urgent

Exercise 4

1 renewable; green **2** industrial; Air **3** serious; major
4 clean; alternative **5** energy; power

Exercise 5

1 consult **2** secure **3** omitted **4** delivered
5 contest **6** utilize **7** instigate **8** diminish

Exercise 6

1 They claim **2** These factors **3** For example
4 Although **5** but

UNIT OBJECTIVES	
Watch and listen	Watch and understand a video about an art district in Beijing.
Reading skill	Scan to find information.
Critical thinking	Understand and evaluate analogies.
Grammar	Paraphrase quotations; use substitution; use ellipsis.
Academic writing skill	Write arguments, counter-arguments and refutations.
Writing task	Write an argumentative essay.
⟳ Teacher development	Help your students become better at **understanding and evaluating analogies**.

UNLOCK YOUR KNOWLEDGE

Background note

The photo shows a sculpture called *The Accident* by the Spanish artist Julio Lafuente (1921–2013). The sculpture is situated in Jeddah, Saudi Arabia, on the coast of the Red Sea. The artwork shows five cars which have crashed into a huge concrete cube. The artist worked as an architect in Jeddah in the 1970s, and it was his idea to create large monuments at important junctions in the city in order to help people find their way around. Jeddah is famous for its street art, where many roundabouts are used to display works of art.

Lead-in

Students choose an object from the classroom or from their personal possessions that they have with them. They show their group and discuss which features of it are purely functional (they exist because they do a job), which are non-functional (only included for decorative purposes), and which are a combination. For example, on a pair of trainers a blue stripe may only be decorative whereas a yellow one may help the wearer be seen better. The treads on the bottom of the shoe are functional, but the design of the treads may be decorative.

page 147
Answers will vary.

WATCH AND LISTEN

Learning objectives

- Listen and identify the main ideas in a video about art in Beijing
- Listen and complete a detailed summary of the ideas in the video
- Identify inferences which can be made from the ideas in the video
- Practise talking about places where artists are encouraged

Exercises 1–2 page 148
Answers will vary.

Exercise 3 page 149
3

Exercise 4 page 149
1 military factory   **2** artists   **3** large works of art
4 painters, sculptors   **5** popular   **6** gift shops and cafés
7 afford to work   **8** new locations

Exercise 5 page 149
2, 3

Exercise 6 page 149
Answers will vary.

READING 1

Learning objectives

- Understand key vocabulary for art – *aesthetic, conceptual, contemporary*
- Scan an essay about art to locate information about four artists

- Read and understand details about the writer's definition of art
- Make inferences about artists' views on the nature of art
- Give opinions on the nature of art

- Identify paraphrases of ideas and opinions from the essay
- Make inferences about photographers' views on the nature of photography
- Evaluate statements about photography and express your opinions
- Synthesize information from an essay about art and an essay about photography as art in a discussion

Lead-in

Ask students how they would define art. What criteria would they use to decide if something is or is not art? Ask if they have seen pieces that are presented as art, but they think are not. They should explain their reasoning.

Exercise 1 page 150

1 conceptual **2** aesthetic **3** contemporary
4 distinction **5** established **6** significance **7** notion

Exercise 2 page 151

1 c **2** d **3** a **4** b

Exercise 3 page 151

a 3 **b** 4 **c** 2 **d** 1

Optional activity

👤 Give students another short text about an artist or several artists and ask them to scan for key information, such as their names, dates or names of works.

Exercise 4 page 153

1 T **2** F; Metalworking is an example of applied art.
3 T **4** DNS **5** DNS
6 F; 'Art for art's sake' refers to fine art. **7** DNS
8 F; Damien Hirst's assistants produce his art, although the ideas are his own.

Exercise 5 page 153

1 Hirst **2** Warhol **3** Duchamp **4** Banksy **5** Hirst
6 Kusama

Exercise 6 page 153

Answers will vary.

READING 2

Learning objectives

- Understand key vocabulary for photography – *perceive, mechanical, medium*
- Scan an essay about photography as art to find the main idea of each paragraph
- Make inferences about the writer's arguments about photography as art

Lead-in

Ask students to think back to their definition of art before Reading 1 and to apply it to photography. Ask them to consider which kinds of photographs might qualify as art and why. Would they include smartphone photos? All of them or only certain ones? Why?

Exercise 1 page 154

Answers will vary.

Exercise 2 page 154

1 a **2** b **3** a **4** b **5** a **6** a **7** b **8** a

Exercise 3 page 154

1 paragraph 1 **2** paragraph 3 **3** paragraph 2 **4** paragraph 4

Exercise 4 page 156

1 b **2** a **3** a

Exercise 5 page 156

1 d **2** c **3** a **4** e **5** b

Exercise 6 page 157

1 c **2** d **3** a **4** e **5** b

Be flexible

👤 Ask students to write paraphrases for the opinions expressed in Exercise 6.

👥 Provide more support for **lower-level students**. Students exchange and compare paraphrases. What elements of the original text have they changed? What elements have they kept? Are their versions sufficiently different to be considered a paraphrase? Why / Why not? This will help provide a foundation for the Language development section.

Exercise 7 page 157

Answers will vary.

LANGUAGE DEVELOPMENT

Learning objectives

- Paraphrase famous quotations about art and creativity
- Use adjectives related to art and design to complete sentences describing artworks — *abstract, avant-garde, decorative*

Exercise 1 pages 158–159

Possible answers:

1 Horace pointed out that a picture is like a work of literature without words.　**2** Henri Matisse felt that being creative required overcoming cowardice.　**3** Leonardo da Vinci stated that a painter uses his or her mind and hands to paint unlimited subjects.

Exercise 2 page 159

Answers will vary. Possible answers:

1 Creativity involves making connections between things or ideas that do not seem to be connected at first.
2 Creating art helps me feel better when I am feeling bad.
3 When we create art, we can understand ourselves better and we can also escape from our usual identity.

Exercise 3 page 159

1 monumental　**2** moving　**3** decorative　**4** lifelike
5 avant-garde　**6** Abstract　**7** figurative　**8** expressive

Optional activity

👤 Focus students on the adjectives *decorative, figurative* and *expressive*. Ask the following questions:

1　What do these adjectives have in common in terms of spelling and pronunciation? (*They all end in -ive and are pronounced* /ɪv/. Check that students are pronouncing this ending with a short /ɪ/ sound.)
2　Do you know any other adjectives ending in *-ive*? (*descriptive, native, comparative, active, administrative, attractive, creative, effective, expensive* and many more)

Suggest students keep a list of these adjectives and add to it when they find more.

CRITICAL THINKING

Learning objectives

- Analyze the presentation of opposing views (counter-arguments) and ways to argue against them (refutations) in an essay about photography

- Understand whether opinions on fashion, cooking or video games support or challenge the idea of these genres as fine art
- Evaluate opinions on fashion, cooking or video games and express your opinions
- Create analogies between fashion, cooking or video games and fine art

UNL🔗CK TEACHER DEVELOPMENT

BE INFORMED

→ **Understanding and evaluating analogies** is an important skill for students because: (1) Students may be unfamiliar with analogies in English, and the concept may not be common in their native language; (2) Although analogies can be useful in academic writing, students must be careful not to overuse them, or to use analogies which are considered too informal; they need to understand what kind of analogies are acceptable; (3) Analogies are very common in day-to-day English, and therefore have a wider relevance for students.

BE CONFIDENT

→ Develop these skills for yourself by doing the following activity:

Read through the analogies below. Can you explain what they mean? Do you have similar analogies in your own language?

1　Your memory is like a computer, in that it saves things differently for the short and long term.
2　Writing an essay is like climbing a mountain.
3　A doctor diagnoses diseases in the same way a detective investigates crimes.
4　Learning a language is mostly walking through water, but sometimes you get to swim.

Lead-in

Give students a minute to read the writing task. Ask students to work in small groups and discuss which one of the three they might want to write about and why. Tell them to keep any notes they make for later, when they begin to write their essay.

UNL🔗CK TEACHER DEVELOPMENT

BE READY

Look at the Critical Thinking section in the Student's Book on pages 160–161.

→ Which elements of the lesson do you think your students will find easiest / most difficult / most useful? Why?

➜ Are your answers true for all students in your class?

➜ How can you adapt your teaching or the material to meet your students' needs?

BE FLEXIBLE

A useful addition to Exercise 4 would be to ask pairs to present their analogies to the rest of the class. The class then evaluates whether they think they are good analogies, and also whether they would be appropriate in a piece of academic writing.

Exercise 1 page 160

paragraph 2 argument:	argument against author's opinion:	why the other side is wrong:
Photography has similarities to other art, but artists can sell their pieces in the higher-priced, fine-art markets, whereas photographers usually cannot.	A photograph can be a deliberately created image with its own artistic features. As Ansel Adams said, we don't 'take' a photograph, we 'make it'.	It is rare for a photographer to get a high price for his/her 'art', unlike other artists.
paragraph 3 argument:	**argument against author's opinion:**	**why the other side is wrong:**
Photography cannot really be 'abstract' in the way that other art can.	Sometimes it can, but not as easily.	Beauty that is perceived in a photograph comes from the time and place where it was taken, the equipment used, and luck.

Exercise 2 page 161

1 challenge   **2** support   **3** support   **4** challenge
5 challenge   **6** support

Exercises 3–4 page 161

Answers will vary.

UNLOCK TEACHER DEVELOPMENT

BE REFLECTIVE

Think about the following questions:

➜ Did you refer to analogies in your own language during the class? If you did, did it help students understand how they could be used? If you did not, do you think it would have helped? If your class is multilingual, did students talk about the use of analogies in their own languages?

➜ Do you think your students now feel confident to use analogies in their academic writing? Monitor their writing over the next few weeks to see if they use any – and if so, how effective they are.

BE COLLABORATIVE

Your development is more meaningful when it is shared. See page 14 for ideas on how to peer-collaborate. Why not share the ideas you generated in the *Be ready* section, and their outcome?

GRAMMAR FOR WRITING

Learning objectives

- Identify synonyms and substitutions used to avoid repetition in a text about a car
- Use ellipsis and substitution to avoid repetition in a text about a famous painting

Exercise 1 page 162

The two-seater roadster; the fastest sports car; the car; the E-type; the machine's; the car's; the most beautiful car in the world

Exercise 2 page 163

The Scream is the popular name given to each of four paintings ~~of The Scream~~ by the artist Edvard Munch**,** who painted **them** ~~The Scream~~ between 1893 and 1910. The National Gallery in Oslo holds one painting ~~of The Scream~~, the Munch Museum holds two more paintings ~~of The Scream~~, and the fourth version ~~of The Scream~~ sold for $119 million at Sotheby's on 2 May, 2012. To explain the picture ~~of The Scream~~, the artist ~~Edvard Munch~~ wrote in his diary, 'One evening I felt tired and ill. I stopped and looked out over the sea – the sun was setting, and the clouds were turning blood red. I sensed a scream passing through nature; it seemed to me that I heard the scream.'

Optional activity

👤 Ask students to continue to practise the skills used in Exercise 2 in the following paragraph:

Robert Rauschenberg was one of the first artists to create 'Combines'. Combines are works that are made of odd bits of old things – tyres, furniture or pieces of wood that artists find on the street. Rauschenberg used this approach and many others started to use this approach too. One of his most famous works is called *Bed*. Rauschenberg made *Bed* in 1955. Rauschenberg took a pillow, a sheet and a quilt. He scribbled with pencil and splashed paint all over the pillow, the sheet and the quilt. Then he put a frame around his work of art. He said his work of art was a form of personal expression. Many critics think this is an important work of personal expression that relates to both art and life.

ACADEMIC WRITING SKILLS

Learning objectives

- Compare the strength of arguments and identify the stronger
- Evaluate the weaknesses in arguments about art
- Refute counter-arguments in sentences about art

Exercise 1 page 164

1 a stronger **b** weaker; the statement does not support the idea that photography has the properties of other art as convincingly.   **2 a** stronger **b** weaker; no details are provided to persuade the reader.   **3 a** weaker; It is too subjective and not evidence-based like the other statement. **b** stronger

Exercise 2 page 165

Answers will vary. Suggested answers:

1 Critics of mandatory art education say that art is not as important as academic subjects. Even though that might be true, art education is still important since it encourages students to use their creativity.

2 Some people believe that art is only for the rich. However, all people should be able to see great art.

3 Opponents of public funding for art think that it is not a good use of public money. Nevertheless, public art beautifies our town and enriches our community culture.

Exercise 3 page 165

1 Refutation: However, it does take creativity to choose an image to photograph and to frame it in a certain way.   **2 Refutation:** Just because something violates the law, this does not mean that creativity and artistry have not gone into the work.

Be flexible

👥 Tell students to return to the (strong) arguments on page 164. One student comes up with a counter-argument and the other student offers a refutation. Then pairs can compare their work with what other pairs have written.

Challenge **more advanced students** to consider other issues they have studied in this book (e.g. the depletion of natural resources, green buildings, the cost of healthcare). Ask them to create an argument/counter-argument/refutation sequence (as in Exercise 3) for one of these issues.

Exercise 4 page 165

Answers will vary.

WRITING TASK

Learning objectives

- Plan the body paragraphs of an essay which argues whether either fashion, cooking or video games is fine art
- Draft your essay
- Review and revise the content and structure of your essay
- Review and revise the use of language in your essay

Exercises 1–7 page 166

Answers will vary.

RESEARCH PROJECT

Plan an arts and crafts exhibition.

Explain to the class that they are going to plan an art exhibition of local artists and crafts. Crafts could include weaving, jewellery-making, costumes, leatherwork, metalwork, pottery, etc. Tell them to research local artists and craftspeople, by visiting galleries and searching online. They should look at the artists and their work or the history of the craft. Students could also interview local artists or craftspeople.

Ask students to present this information and images of the artists' work or examples of local crafts as part of an exhibition.

CLASSROOM APP

Exercises 1–2

Answers will vary.

Exercise 3

1 objective   **2** acknowledged   **3** contemporary
4 notion   **5** distinction   **6** deliberately   **7** sophisticated
8 significance

Exercise 4

1 use synonyms, use reported speech   **2** use synonyms, sequence the ideas differently   **3** change part of the speech, sequence the ideas differently   **4** use synonyms, change part of the speech   **5** use antonyms, sequence the ideas differently

Exercise 5

1 abstract   **2** expressive   **3** monumental   **4** lifelike
5 moving   **6** avant-garde   **7** decorative   **8** figurative

Exercise 6

1 are not   **2** will   **3** was too   **4** there are only two
5 It   **6** refused   **7** didn't

UNIT OBJECTIVES	
Watch and listen	Watch and understand a video about a walking group for retired people.
Reading skill	Identify evidence in a text.
Critical thinking	Draw appropriate conclusions from graphical data.
Grammar	Use verb phrases to show cause and effect; use language of prediction; use the first conditional.
Academic writing skills	Use numerical words and phrases; interpret graphs and charts.
Writing task	Write an analysis essay.
⟳ **Teacher development**	Help your students become better at **drawing appropriate conclusions from graphical data**.

UNL⟳CK YOUR KNOWLEDGE

Background note

The photo shows an older woman hiking in the mountains. In many cultures, there are some common stereotypes associated with the elderly. Older people are often considered to be ill or weak. They are often stereotyped as physically unattractive and not as mentally quick as younger people. However, as the world's population ages and life expectancies become longer than ever, our ideas of old age are changing. Many people who are now in their 60s and 70s are healthier and more active than people who were that age only a few decades ago.

Lead-in

Students think about the oldest person in their extended family, perhaps a grandparent or great aunt or uncle. In small groups, they describe this person, mentioning their relationship to the person, their age, their character, their role in their family, etc. They also discuss how the world has changed in that person's lifetime. Ask some students to share their stories with the class.

page 169
Answers will vary.

WATCH AND LISTEN

Learning objectives

- Listen and identify the main idea in a video about retired people
- Listen and note details
- Make inferences about the ideas in the video
- Practise talking about exercise and the elderly

Exercises 1–2 page 170
Answers will vary.

Exercise 3 page 171
3

Exercise 4 page 171

1 It can prevent cancer, heart disease and poor mental health.   **2** You don't need special equipment or a gym membership to walk.   **3** People in the UK are 20% less active than they were in the 1960s.   **4** They may be alone most of the time. Walking may be one of the few times they see other people.

Exercises 5–6 page 171
Answers will vary.

READING 1

Learning objectives

- Understand key vocabulary for society – *demographic, adapt, voluntary*
- Use your knowledge to predict the main ideas in an article about ageing populations
- Read and understand detailed information about ageing populations
- Identify supporting evidence and evaluate its effect in the article
- Describe and make suggestions for the population where you live

Lead-in

Ask students how they envision their lives when they are older (65+). Will they continue to work? If they retire, how will they support themselves? Do they plan to travel? Spend time on a hobby? Ask students to discuss their plans in pairs or small groups.

Exercise 1 page 172

a capacity **b** demographic **c** leisure **d** voluntary
e adapt **f** undertake

Exercise 2 page 172

Answers will vary.

Exercise 3 page 172

Possible answers:

1 A great deal in many countries. People are able to live far longer due to improved healthcare and the prevention/cure of many diseases.

2 People are living longer in most regions.

3 Old people may be unable to care for themselves for health reasons.

4 If old people are retired and not paying taxes but still need healthcare, this could put a strain on social systems.

5 The benefits could be that less money is needed for education. Older people may have saved money to spend on themselves and their families and may give time to voluntary organizations or be able to help care for younger family members.

Exercise 4 page 173

Answers will vary.

Exercise 5 page 174

1 DNS **2** T **3** F; In many countries, an increasing number of older people are living by themselves, often without any relatives living nearby. **4** T **5** F; Supermarkets have responded by providing more home-delivery services, and there has been a significant growth in companies providing services that would have traditionally been undertaken by family members. **6** F; In countries where the percentage of children and young people is lower, there are lower costs in the education system. **7** DNS **8** T

Exercise 6 page 174

1 look after **2** social activities **3** private nursing care
4 economic impact **5** savings, leisure time **6** voluntary

---

Optional activity

👥👥 Ask students to think about other possible changes that may come with an ageing population. Specifically, ask them to brainstorm about new products and services that could serve this population. Point them to the references to grocery delivery services in the reading as a starting point. Discuss as a class.

Exercise 7 page 175

1 Italy has Europe's oldest population; people in Italy are now living 30 to 40 years beyond retirement; the number of needy pensioners there is rising. **2** It is evidence that older people in Japan tend to have more savings and more leisure time. **3** They are authoritative, credible sources which provide convincing support for the writer's main ideas.

Exercise 8 page 175

Answers will vary.

READING 2

Learning objectives

- Understand key vocabulary for society – *documented, median, proportion*
- Use your knowledge and read and understand the main ideas in an essay about Saudi Arabia's young population
- Read and complete sentences about facts and figures
- Read and understand the meaning of fixed expressions using context clues
- Synthesize information from an article about ageing populations and an essay about Saudi Arabia's young population in a discussion

---

Lead-in

Remind students that they have just read an article about the problems a country faces when a large percentage of the population is older. Ask them to brainstorm about the kind of challenges a country might face with the opposite problem – a bulge in the population of young people in their 20s and younger.

Exercise 1 page 175

Answers will vary.

Exercise 2 page 176

1 a **2** b **3** a **4** b **5** c **6** a **7** c

Exercise 3 page 176

Possible answer:

High education costs, risk of increasing unemployment and increased demand for housing.

Exercise 4 page 178

1 young **2** 27 **3** 19 **4** 27; Japan **5** education
6 sectors **7** expansion

Exercise 5 page 178

1 if you consider the facts carefully **2** spending
3 very specific problems that require specific solutions
4 as a result or effect of something

Exercise 6 page 178

1 It does not have to cope with the demands of an ageing population. Because the country has relatively fewer old people, the costs of healthcare and pensions are lower. This allows more funds to be allocated to improving the lives of young people. **2** Because the government can collect more taxes and has more resources to provide for its citizens. **3** *Answers will vary.*

LANGUAGE DEVELOPMENT

Learning objectives

- Use academic collocations with prepositions in sentences about age and society – *There is a tendency to identify with the problems of the elderly. To sum up, the main recommendation is that more should be saved toward pensions. Young people, in contrast, have too little time.*
- Use simple verb phrases to show cause and effect between ideas – *Ageing results in greater life experience and wisdom. Ageing leads to greater life experience and wisdom.*
- Use more complex linkers to show cause and effect between ideas – *As a result of ageing, the elderly have greater life experience and wisdom. Ageing leads to greater life experience. As a consequence the elderly have the benefit of wisdom.*

Exercise 1 page 179

1 in   **2** of   **3** on   **4** up   **5** with   **6** in   **7** on   **8** in

Be flexible

👤 Ask students to review the two readings and find markers of cause and effect. They should underline the marker and label the cause (C) and effect (E).

Challenge **stronger students** to write three more sentences expressing cause and effect, using information from either of the two readings. Encourage them to try using more complex linkers.

Exercise 2 page 179

1 rely on   **2** In contrast   **3** range of   **4** focus on   **5** In brief   **6** in theory   **7** identify with   **8** sum up

Exercise 3 page 180

1 b; An ageing population leads to / results in lower education costs.   **2** b; Encouraging immigration leads to / results in more young people.   **3** b; An increasingly older population leads to / results in economic problems.

Exercise 4 page 180

Possible answers:

1 Some people never have children. Consequently, they have no family to care for them when they get old. **2** In some cultures, elderly people commonly live with their adult children. As a result of this, the grandchildren have somebody to care for them while the parents are at work. **3** It is not always easy for a country to predict how its population will change. Because of this, it's a good idea to encourage immigration.

CRITICAL THINKING

Learning objectives

- Analyze the information presented in a graph about Saudi Arabia's demographics
- Analyze the information presented in a graph about Japan's demographics
- Work out the meaning of expressions to describe demographics
- Identify which topics could be a problem for a society with an ageing population
- Connect topics to different contexts in a society
- Evaluate and rank the advantages of older populations

UNL⊘CK TEACHER DEVELOPMENT

BE INFORMED

➔ **Drawing appropriate conclusions from graphical data** is an important skill for students because: (1) Graphs and charts are commonly used in many academic subjects, especially the sciences; (2) Students often find it challenging to interpret graphs and charts; they either insert them into essays without comment, or focus on less relevant issues; (3) This kind of knowledge is very important in day-to-day life, especially in the business world.

BE CONFIDENT

➔ Develop this skill for yourself by doing the following activity:

Look at the graphs on page 177 and page 181 of the Student's Book, but do not look at Reading 2. Answer the following questions:

1 What are the main points shown in these graphs?
2 What are the main implications of these graphs?
3 How do the graphs differ in terms of how the data is presented?

Lead-in

Give students a minute to read the writing task and to ask you any questions they might have about it.

UNL⊘CK TEACHER DEVELOPMENT

BE READY

Look at the Critical Thinking section in the Student's Book on pages 181–182.

➔ Which elements of the lesson do you think your students will find easiest / most difficult / most useful? Why?

→ Are your answers true for all students in your class?

→ How can you adapt your teaching or the material to meet your students' needs?

BE FLEXIBLE

For Exercise 3, especially with smaller classes, it might be useful to divide the items between pairs/groups to ensure that all ten items are covered. It is important for students to understand all these terms.

Exercise 1 page 181

1 2016 **2** 28,160,273 **3** under 65 **4** more men

Exercise 2 page 181

1 January 2012 **2** approximately 125 million **3** over 65 **4** The graph shows that Saudi Arabia has a much younger overall population than Japan does. Saudis have been having more children and larger families than Japanese people in recent years.

Exercise 3 page 182

1 youth unemployment: when young people in a society do not have jobs **2 housing shortages:** when there are not enough homes for the people in a society to live in **3 higher pension costs:** when the government has to spend more of its budget on retired people because the population is ageing **4 increased healthcare costs:** when the government or health insurers have to spend more money to provide healthcare for people **5 stress on the education system:** when the resources for educating young people (money, teachers, schools) are no longer enough **6 lower consumer spending:** when people in a society spend less money to buy things **7 declining birth rate:** when women in a society have fewer children than before **8 higher taxes:** when the government collects more money from citizens than before **9 increased emigration:** when more people move out of their home country to another country **10 increased immigration:** when more people move into a new country from their home country

Exercise 4 page 182

Answers will vary. Suggested answers:

3, 4, 6, 7

Exercise 5 page 182

1 Increased healthcare costs **2** youth unemployment **3** Higher taxes **4** higher pension costs **5** declining birth rate **6** increased immigration

Exercise 6 page 182

Answers will vary.

UNLOCK TEACHER DEVELOPMENT

BE REFLECTIVE

Think about the following questions:

→ How many of the terms in Exercise 3 did your class already know? Depending on their background or area of study, students may have a very good (or very poor) understanding of these terms. Knowing this may help you plan better in the future.

→ To what extent has your students' understanding of critical thinking developed across this course? Is there anything you would do differently if (or when) you teach it again?

BE COLLABORATIVE

Your development is more meaningful when it is shared. See page 14 for ideas on how to peer-collaborate. Why not share the ideas you generated in the *Be ready* section, and their outcome?

GRAMMAR FOR WRITING

Learning objectives

- Use phrases to make stronger and weaker predictions – *be predicted to, may be, be unlikely to*
- Write sentences expressing strong and weak predictions about the future
- Use the first conditional with *provided that, as long as* and *on the condition that* in sentences about ageing populations

Exercise 1 page 183

1 b **2** a **3** e **4** d **5** g **6** c **7** f

Exercise 2 page 183

Answers will vary. Possible answers:

1 The population is likely to increase in the future. **2** Oil prices may come down this year. **3** Unemployment is predicted to remain at the same level in the coming months. **4** The cost of living is set to rise over the decade. **5** A reduction in the number of schools is unlikely.

Exercise 3 page 184

1 will face; ages **2** continues; will live **3** will move in; agrees **4** does not create; will face

Exercise 4 page 184

Answers will vary. Possible answers:

1 If a country has an ageing population, the result will be fewer children. **2** Fewer people will pay income taxes if more people retire. **3** Provided that a country provides better education, its young people will find good jobs in other countries. **4** As long as the population continues to get younger, the government should prioritize public funds for the young over the ageing.

ACADEMIC WRITING SKILLS

Learning objectives

- Use numerical words and phrases to describe data in a pie chart about Japan – *minority proportion*, *quarter*
- Follow guidelines on writing about information in graphs and write sentences about the demographics shown in a graph
- Evaluate descriptions of data in terms of their usefulness in a topical essay

Exercise 1 page 185

1 majority   **2** minority   **3** times   **4** proportion
5 double   **6** triple   **7** half   **8** quarter

Exercise 2 page 186

Answers will vary. Possible answers:

1 By 2050 the global population will be 9 billion if the projected figures are correct.   **2** If the ageing population continues to grow, 16% of the population will be 65 or over.   **3** The world will have fewer young people in the future if birth rates continue to decline.

Exercise 3 page 186

1 not good; very specific data, not necessary to mention.
2 not good; not relevant to the data   **3** good; explains a trend   **4** good; mentions the main topic of the data
5 good; a prediction

WRITING TASK

Learning objectives

- Plan and draft an essay using graphical support about population trends in Japan including implications for the future
- Review and revise the content and structure of your essay
- Review and revise the use of language in your essay

Exercise 1 page 187

2 Presentation and description of the data from the graphs   **4** Second related challenge   **3** First related challenge   **6** Summary of the challenges but also a mention of an advantage   **5** Third related challenge
1 Introduction

Exercise 2 page 187

Answers will vary. Possible answer:

The graph shows the proportion of three age ranges of the population of Japan since 1950 and predicts what those ranges will be through to the year 2050.

Exercises 3–11 pages 187–188
Answers will vary.

RESEARCH PROJECT

Produce a podcast which explores the concerns of the elderly for the future.

Divide the class into groups. Explain that they will be producing a podcast on the elderly. Ask them to interview elderly relatives about their concerns for the future. They could ask them how things have changed, where the world is heading, health, the home and travel. The group thinks of the questions for the interview and each student asks their relatives, before bringing together their answers as a group to create and broadcast the podcast.

CLASSROOM APP

Exercise 1
Answers will vary.

Exercise 2

1 voluntary   **2** cope with   **3** pension   **4** adapt
5 undertake   **6** range   **7** allocate   **8** leisure

Exercise 3
Answers will vary.

Exercise 4

1 In theory   **2** focus on   **3** In brief   **4** rely on   **5** sum up
6 In contrast   **7** range of   **8** identify with

Exercise 5

1 Exercising regularly leads to better health.
2 As a result of the growing population, food demand has increased.
3 Meditation can result in a decrease in stress levels.
4 As a consequence, they stay more active.
5 Because of this, elderly people are being advised to stay indoors.
6 As a result of this, many young people are moving abroad.

Exercise 6

1 half   **2** half   **3** triple   **4** times   **5** majority   **6** minority
7 double   **8** proportion

READING, WRITING & CRITICAL THINKING 5

CONSERVATION   UNIT 1

UNIT OBJECTIVES	
Watch and listen	Watch and understand a video about preserving digital records.
Reading skill	Identify an argument.
Critical thinking	Evaluate facts to build support for an argument.
Grammar	Use first and second conditionals.
Academic writing skills	Write structured and unified paragraphs; write impersonal statements.
Writing task	Write an argumentative essay.
⟳ **Teacher development**	Help your students become better at **evaluating facts**.

UNLOCK YOUR KNOWLEDGE

Background note

The photo was taken at the centrally-located neighbourhoods of Fener and Balat in Istanbul, Turkey. Despite their central location and rich history, the buildings in these areas fell into bad condition during the second half of the twentieth century. In recent decades, the local authorities have started to rebuild the old buildings in these historical areas. However, not everybody sees this as positive development. Many argue that modernizing the area has negative effects on local residents, who can't afford to live there any longer and find it difficult to adjust.

Lead-in

Ask students to list ways they can learn about the past other than from books. You may wish to specify the history of their own country/city/community. Ask how they can learn about history first-hand. Once they have offered suggestions, ask them to describe what they can learn from a place or person. If they cannot come up with anything, you might start them off with an example. Possibilities include museums, old buildings, excavations, artefacts (items people once used), old documents (newspapers, letters) and older members of the community.

page 15

Answers will vary.

WATCH AND LISTEN

Learning objectives

- Use visuals to predict the main ideas in a video about the Library of Congress
- Listen and identify the main ideas in a video about the Library of Congress
- Listen and understand detailed information
- Make inferences about wider implications of the information in a video
- Practise talking about the importance of preservation

Exercises 1–2 page 16

Answers will vary.

Exercise 3 page 17

3

Exercise 4 page 17

Answers will vary. Possible answers:

1 This will help them better understand how to keep them safe for posterity.

2 CDs are cooked in chambers by manipulating the humidity and the temperature.

3 Do not put fancy labels on them, do not use permanent marker and write only in the small centre region.

Exercises 5–6 page 17

Answers will vary.

READING 1

Learning objectives

- Understand key vocabulary for preserving records – *retrieve, longevity, compatible*
- Read and identify the main ideas in an article about preserving digital records
- Read and identify the types of support the writer offers for their central claim
- Read and understand detailed information
- Make inferences about the writer's implications and the meaning of terminology
- Describe personal responses to the scenarios in the article in a discussion

Lead-in

Show students pictures of old forms of digital storage such as a VHS tape, a cassette tape, a floppy disk (3½ inches and 5¼ inches), a zip drive, a laser disc, a Betamax tape, and/or a CD. Ask what they know about them. They will probably recognize CDs, but the others may be a mystery to them. Ask them to think about what sort of information might be stored on each of them, and whether or not the information can be accessed today.

Exercises 1–2 pages 18–19

Answers will vary.

Exercise 3 page 19

a vulnerable   **b** common practice   **c** prompt
d longevity   **e** scenario   **f** retrieve   **g** memorabilia
h compatible

Exercise 4 page 21

1 c   **2** If current practices continue, future generations may not have access to the digital record of our lives and our world.

Exercise 5 page 21

1 A box of memorabilia, including floppy disks and VHS tapes, is found in the attic of an old house with a label that says, 'Records and early videos of Bill Gates (1975–1985).'

[A]n envelope labelled 'bank records' in your grandmother's desk. Inside the envelope, there is an old CD marked with the date 1998, your great-grandfather's name, and the words 'all overseas bank accounts.'

2 a EA   **b** E   **c** F   **d** E   **e** EA

Be flexible

👤 Ask students where they might read a text like Reading 1 (a magazine). Then ask them to decide how an argument is likely to be supported (*Emotional appeal* [EA], *expertise* [E], or *facts* [F]) in each of the following:

- an academic article
- a textbook
- a blog
- a newspaper editorial
- a news report
- a personal conversation

Answers will vary, but they should report that emotional appeals are uncommon in academic genres and hard news, but more common in personal genres or soft news.

Challenge **stronger students** by reversing the order of the activity: ask students in what kind of texts they might find arguments supported in each way (*EA, E* and *F*).

Exercise 6 page 22

2, 3

Exercise 7 page 22

1 F; The text describes a scenario of finding Bill Gates' records.   **2** T   **3** T   **4** DNS   **5** F; Satyanarayanan has been able to solve the problem.   **6** DNS

Exercise 8 page 22

Answers will vary. Possible answers:

1 They would be excited to have discovered things which might be worth a lot of money.

2 We don't have a lot of information about the Dark Ages (a period in European history from AD 476 to around AD 1000), so we don't fully understand what happened during that time. Our time could become like that to the people of the future.

3 A *bit* is the smallest unit of data on a computer. *Rot* means to decay. So *bit rot* might mean the permanent loss of digitally held information.

4 Interactive apps and websites go out of date very quickly.

Exercise 9 page 22

Answers will vary.

READING 2

Learning objectives

- Understand key vocabulary for preserving cultural heritage – *anonymous, renovation, demolition*
- Read and identify main and detailed arguments in an article about preserving cultural heritage
- Read and identify the types of support the writer offers for their arguments
- Read and distinguish facts from the writer's own opinions
- Make inferences about the writer's implications
- Synthesize information from two texts about preservation in a discussion

Lead-in

Ask students to name the oldest building or structure in their community. If the building is very old, ask them to explain how it has managed to survive for so long. If there are no old buildings in their community, ask them to reflect on the reasons for this. This should help them to articulate the value their community places on preserving the built environment as part of its heritage.

Exercise 1 page 23

Answers will vary.

Exercise 2 page 23

1 a   2 c   3 a   4 a   5 b   6 c   7 a   8 c

Exercise 3 page 25

1 b   **2** What is left of the city's traditional buildings and neighbourhoods must be preserved and it is imperative that this process begins now.

3 The author says the consequence of not accepting his argument is losing our past.

4 Once these treasures are lost, they are lost for ever, an important link in our heritage that can never be recovered.

Exercise 4 page 25

1 renovation of an existing structure for adaptive re-use can cost about £40 per square metre less than even the most basic new construction (fact); New construction almost always has a more serious environmental impact because it requires the use of all-new materials that must be transported, often over long distances, instead of recycled materials that are already on site (fact).; architects and environmental experts maintain that the greenest building is the one that is already built (support with expertise).

2 *Possible answer*: He says that children will lose their connection to the past and to their culture.

3 These are physical symbols of the cultural past.

4 a, c, e, f, h

5 a There are also good economic arguments in favour of preservation.

c New construction almost always has a more serious environmental impact because it requires the use of all new materials that must be transported, often over long distances, instead of recycled materials that are already on site.

e International visitors are not interested only in shopping centres; they also want to learn about our culture and traditions like these.

f How can our children understand and maintain their cultural identity if we erase so much of the physical evidence of it?

h [R]enovation of an existing structure for adaptive re-use can cost about £40 per square metre less than even the most basic new construction.

Exercise 5 page 26

1 a facts   **c** facts   **e** facts   **f** opinion   **h** facts
2 a, b, d

Optional activity

Ask students to return to Reading 1 and review the text with the following question in mind: *Does the author of the article have an opinion about bit rot? What is it?* (Answer = yes, the author thinks this is a problem). How can they tell? Are there any examples of signals of opinion listed in Exercise 5.2? (In fact, modal verbs are the only type of device used in this article. For the most part, the author does not overtly express an opinion.) This should help students understand the distinction between a well-supported claim and a simple statement of opinion.

Exercise 6 page 26

Answers will vary. Possible answers:

1 Because they are replacing buildings the author recognizes.

2 They were renovated as cultural attractions.

3 The adaptive re-use, because the author says it is important that locals still live and work in the district.

4 Renovation has a lower environmental impact than building a new one.

5 They are closely linked – the culture is remembered through the features of the buildings.

Exercise 7 page 26

Answers will vary.

LANGUAGE DEVELOPMENT

Learning objectives

- Use appropriate time phrases in sentences about change – *at the turn of the century, slowly but surely, up to date*
- Use correct hyphenation in compound adjectives in sentences – *The out-of-date computer systems will be replaced next month. Those technologies are out of date.*
- Use a range of compound adjectives in sentences about urban development – *The new development will be wind powered. It's a million-dollar development.*

Exercise 1 page 27

1 out of date   **2** It's about time for   **3** slowly but surely
4 at the turn of the century   **5** At one time / At the turn of the century   **6** in a flash / in the blink of an eye
7 for the time being   **8** Over the past / Over the last
9 up to date

Exercise 2 page 28

Answers will vary.

> ### Be flexible
>
> 👤 Ask students to find time expressions in Reading 1 and decide what kind of information they provide. (It is possible to do this with Reading 2 as well, but Reading 1 has more obvious examples.)
>
> You can make this task less challenging for **lower-level students** by setting a fixed number of expressions that students need to find; say, three examples of *when* and three examples of *in relation to a time frame*. There are only two examples of *how* in the text.

Exercise 3 pages 28–29

1 long-term   **2** sixty-page   **3** turn of the century
4 one-way   **5** well known   **6** one-bedroom
7 energy efficient   **8** fast-growing

Exercise 4 page 29

Answers will vary. Possible answers:

1 A multinational company is planning a twenty-storey office building.
2 Starting next year I would like to find a full-time job.
3 We are trying to determine which the best long-term plan is.
4 The wind-powered construction in the new development will reduce energy costs.
5 The demolition will take place in a four-square-kilometre area.

Exercise 5 page 29

Answers will vary.

CRITICAL THINKING

Learning objectives

- Analyze facts about preservation and new construction and decide which position they support
- Evaluate a local area and make recommendations for its future
- Research and evaluate supporting evidence for your recommendations

UNLOCK TEACHER DEVELOPMENT

BE INFORMED

→ **Evaluating facts** is an important skill for students because: (1) Some facts are more important than others and students need to be able to prioritize and differentiate them; (2) Knowing how to evaluate facts can help students when creating written arguments in their future studies; (3) Evaluating facts is also a very useful life skill.

BE CONFIDENT

→ Develop this skill for yourself by doing the following activity:

Below are three comments made by teachers about teaching critical thinking. Read them, and then answer the questions which follow.

"A lot of teachers struggle to find the time to develop an effective means to teach critical thinking skills."

"Stronger students like critical thinking, but weaker students do not."

"Students don't want to learn about critical thinking, because they don't see the point."

1 *What do you think of the statements made above? Do you agree with them? Do you think the teachers are being 100% honest in what they are saying? Why / Why not?*

2 *Why do you think critical thinking is important for your students?*

3 *Look again at what you have written. What evidence can you give for what you have written? Make changes so it is more robust.*

Lead-in

Give students a minute to read the writing task. Ask them to brainstorm in groups for a few minutes to help them come up with a list of possible areas. Tell them to keep their brainstorming notes for later, when they begin to write their essay.

UNLOCK TEACHER DEVELOPMENT

BE READY

Look at the Critical Thinking section in the Student's Book on pages 30–31.

→ Which elements of the lesson do you think your students will find easiest / most difficult / most useful? Why?

→ Are your answers true for all students in your class?

→ How can you adapt your teaching or the material to meet your students' needs?

BE FLEXIBLE

Before the lesson, think about the specific academic subjects your students intend to study. What changes can you make to the lesson to make it more relevant to their chosen field?

Exercise 1 pages 30–31

1 P   **2** NC   **3** NC   **4** P   **5** P   **6** P   **7** P   **8** NC   **9** NC
10 NC

Exercises 2–4 page 31

Answers will vary.

UNLOCK TEACHER DEVELOPMENT

BE REFLECTIVE

Think about the following questions:

→ If you were to teach the critical thinking section again, what would you do differently? What would you do the same? Why?

→ How did you feel when teaching the critical thinking section? Is there anything you could have done to prepare more effectively?

BE COLLABORATIVE

Your development is more meaningful when it is shared. See page 14 for ideas on how to peer-collaborate. Why not share the ideas you generated in the *Be flexible* section, and their outcome?

GRAMMAR FOR WRITING

Learning objectives

- Use first conditional sentences to make proposals and describe consequences – *If we preserve our heritage, our children will grow up with a sense of cultural identity.*
- Use second conditional sentences to describe alternative proposals and their negative consequences – *If the developers were allowed to demolish the building, the city centre would lose an important part of its character. If the old building were to be kept, we would waste an opportunity to develop the local infrastructure.*

Exercise 1 page 32

1 a   **2** b   **3** a   **4** b

Exercise 2 page 32

Answers will vary.

ACADEMIC WRITING SKILLS

Learning objectives

- Evaluate paragraph unity in paragraphs about preservation
- Use impersonal statements to make arguments about preservation and development

Exercise 1 page 33

1 unified

2 not unified; Homeowners cannot make major changes that affect the appearance of their home or the surrounding gardens and trees without planning permission.

3 unified

4 not unified; Stonehenge is visited by thousands of people on the longest and shortest days of the year, which often causes significant damage to the site.

Exercise 2 page 34

Answers will vary. Possible answers:

1 Restoring the old fishing village was a huge waste of money.

2 Re-using and recycling materials is better than using up additional resources.

3 It would be foolish to pass up the opportunity of building a new convention centre, which would be beneficial for this city and its citizens as it would provide both jobs and revenue.

4 If all the old buildings are torn down and replaced with new ones, it will make the city lose its character and look like any other large city.

5 Placing this building on the register of historic places is a step in the right direction because it has the potential to draw tourists who are interested in architectural and cultural history.

Optional activity

👤 Tell students to write three impersonal statements giving their opinions about the area or neighbourhood they have researched. They can use these statements in their final writing task.

WRITING TASK

Learning objectives

- Draft an essay proposing what should be done with a historic area
- Review and revise the content and structure of your essay
- Review and revise the use of language in your essay

Exercises 1–10 pages 35–36

Answers will vary.

RESEARCH PROJECT

Give a presentation on successful historic preservation projects.

Students work in small groups to research successful historic preservation projects. What was the history of this building or area? Who lived there? How was it used? Why was it preserved? Who promoted the project? Who paid for it: the government or a private person or organization? Why was it considered important to preserve it? How is it doing now? Has it been a success? Possible candidates include those listed in the reading (*Al-Bastakiya*, *Beit al Jasra*, *Muharraq*) or others around the world (Singapore's *Chinatown*, *hutongs* in Beijing, *Xochimilco* in Mexico City). Groups present their findings to the class.

CLASSROOM APP

Exercises 1–2
Answers will vary.

Exercise 3
1 longevity **2** affluent **3** demolition **4** retrieved
5 opted for **6** renovation **7** scenarios **8** compatible

Exercise 4
1 but that has changed **2** are also being stored
3 thousands of military records were destroyed
4 With increasing concern about the possible loss of digital records **5** has saved billions of webpages

Exercise 5
1 long-term; long-term **2** brightly lit; brightly-lit
3 carefully-controlled; well managed **4** all-too-common; well meaning **5** 34-metre; two thousand years old
6 state-of-the-art; up to date

Exercise 6
People use plastic because it is convenient and because it travels well and doesn't break.

Most coastal populations consume a lot of fish.

UNIT OBJECTIVES	
Watch and listen	Watch and understand a video about the importance of fonts.
Reading skills	Take notes in outline form; challenge ideas in a text.
Critical thinking	Determine and apply criteria.
Grammar	Use non-defining relative clauses; use appositives.
Academic writing skills	Structure a summary–response essay; write a conclusion.
Writing task	Write a summary–response essay.
⟡ **Teacher development**	Help your students become better at **determining and applying criteria**.

UNLOCK YOUR KNOWLEDGE

Background note

The photo shows white trainers with minimal branding. Some of the trainers in the photograph are produced by famous brands like *Adidas*, *Puma*, *Mizuno* and *Asics*. These are easily identifiable by their logos. In the world of branding and design, some of the most iconic logos include *Starbucks*, *McDonald's*, *Pepsi*, *Coca-Cola*, *Nike* and *Apple*.

Lead-in

Students work in groups and look at all the clothing they are wearing, as well as any accessories (e.g. backpacks, watches, etc.) they have with them. Do any of them have logos? Students should make a list of them. Did these logos play a part in their decision to buy these items? Ask them to explain why or why not.

page 39

Answers will vary.

WATCH AND LISTEN

Learning objectives

- Use visuals to predict the main ideas in a video about design in advertising
- Listen and identify the main idea about design in advertising
- Listen and note examples for main ideas
- Make inferences about the information in a video
- Practise talking about the importance of design in advertising, signs and logos

Exercises 1–2 page 40

Answers will vary.

Exercise 3 page 41

2

Exercise 4 page 41

1 zany hand lettering; exclamation points; cursive wedding invitation typography

2 neutral; efficient; human; accessible; transparent; accountable

Exercise 5 page 41

Answers will vary. Possible answers:

1 Designers were experimenting.

2 He points them out as examples of visual bad habits, so he doesn't like them being overused.

3 friendly and approachable

Exercise 6 page 41

Answers will vary.

READING 1

Learning objectives

- Understand key vocabulary for marketing – *convey*, *evocative*, *retain*
- Read and identify the main ideas in a textbook chapter about logos
- Read and complete a set of notes in outline form
- Evaluate the evidence for claims made in a textbook chapter
- Apply the criteria given for evaluating logos in a textbook chapter
- Describe and evaluate logos in a discussion

Lead-in

Bring in photographs of some famous logos (e.g. cars, drinks, sportswear, fast food). Do the logos have anything in common? What makes them easy to recognize or remember? Make a list on the board of qualities they suggest. (For ideas, look ahead in the unit.)

Exercise 1 page 42

Answers will vary.

Exercise 2 page 42

a reinforce **b** evocative **c** subsequent **d** sustainable
e criteria **f** retain **g** convey **h** arouse

Exercise 3 page 43

b

Exercise 4 page 43

I. Efficient form of visual communication

  A. Simple and easy to remember

  B. Unique so it is unlikely to be confused with other logos.

  Example: **IKEA**

  C. Arouses **curiosity**

  Example: **UNIQLO**

II. Flexible and adaptable

  A. Across **time**

  Example: **Apple**

  B. Across **placement**

  1. Can shrink

  Examples: **Twitter, Facebook**

  2. Can be recognized from a distance

III. Tells a **story**

  A. Conveys company's **identity**

  1. Example: **Toys R Us**

  2. Example: **FedEx**

  B. Evokes **emotional response**

  Example: **World Wildlife Foundation**

Be flexible

Ask students to compare their outlines with a partner. They should discuss any differences they find. The differences should help illustrate that it is possible to have two different outlines that are both correct. Then tell students to review a text from the previous unit. Ask them to create an outline based on the text.

To reduce the level of challenge for **lower-level students**, use Reading 1 from Unit 1. Tell students to begin their outline with the central claim they chose in Exercise 4 on page 21.

Exercises 5–6 page 46

Answers will vary.

Exercise 7 page 46

Answers will vary.

READING 2

Learning objectives

- Understand key vocabulary for marketing – *resemble, refine, associate*
- Read and identify the main ideas in a textbook chapter about logos
- Read and identify detailed information
- Read and add details to create a set of notes in outline form
- Make inferences about implied information in textbook chapter about logos
- Synthesize information from two chapters of a marketing textbook in a discussion

Lead-in

Find an image of an old logo of a famous brand in your country. Ask students to think about how this logo is different from the current logo and to reflect on how it has changed and why. Good examples include soft drinks, petrol companies, tech companies and airlines.

Exercise 1 page 47

Answers will vary.

Exercise 2 page 47

1 b **2** a **3** b **4** c **5** a **6** c **7** b

Exercise 3 page 49

a, b, d

Exercise 4 page 49

1 f **2** c **3** d **4** b **5** a **6** e

Exercise 5 page 50

Answers will vary. Possible answers:

I. Change in focus

  A: Companies expand/change products they sell, e.g. Xerox = from photocopiers to bigger document technology

  B: Neg. associations with companies, e.g. Kentucky Fried Chicken = unhealthy fried food; British Petroleum = product bad for climate

II. Brand has matured

  Mostly tech companies; original logo reflected entrepreneurs' young age, e.g. Spotify = sound waves; Snapchat = no silly face on ghost

III. Problems with rebranding

People resistant to change; sometimes don't like new logo, e.g. Tropicana dropped orange logo, people hated it, so went back to old logo

IV. Impact of changing technology

A: Smaller devices and platforms need smaller logos, e.g. Airbnb and PayPal = drop names, simpler graphic

B: New tech offers new opportunities, e.g. Google's transforming logo

Be flexible

👥 Ask students to compare their notes with a partner. They should discuss any differences they find. It is likely that they will see more differences since this exercise is less controlled than the one for the previous reading. They can challenge each other if they think their partners' outlines are inaccurate, but again they should be able to see that there is more than one correct way to outline a reading.

👥👥 If **lower-level students** need additional support, do the first section of the outline (*Change in focus*) as a class. Elicit suggestions from students. Make sure they understand that the central claim here is that a company may start out selling one product or service and then shift to another. Perhaps give them another example: *Companies such as Xerox, which began by selling photocopiers, now offer all sorts of document storage and printing services.*

Exercise 6 page 50

a, b, c, d, e

Exercise 7 page 50

Answers will vary.

LANGUAGE DEVELOPMENT

Learning objectives

- Use common verb + noun collocations in sentences to describe emotional responses – *It aroused interest among consumers. The decision to change the logo provoked controversy.*
- Paraphrase ideas without changing the meaning, using synonyms, changing word order and varying grammatical structures

Exercise 1 page 51

2 mixed   **3** mixed   **4** negative   **5** positive   **6** negative

Exercise 2 page 51

1 aroused suspicion/curiosity/interest

2 provoked controversy / provoked outrage / stirred up opposition / aroused anger

3 aroused, interest / generated, interest / generated, excitement

4 inspires confidence / stirs up opposition / provokes outrage

5 provoked, response

6 evoke, memories

Exercise 3 page 51

Answers will vary.

Exercise 4 page 52

Answers will vary. Possible answers:

1 A logo can be defined as a symbol used to promote an organization's identity and to ensure the public recognize the brand.

2 Companies want consumers to associate the logo with their brand, so they choose logos that reflect the names, origins and products.

3 Colour is really important in a logo, because it helps consumers distinguish between similar logos by fixing them permanently in their minds.

4 Sport products are often visibly branded with the companies' logos, making them highly recognizable and encouraging loyalty among consumers to the brand.

Exercise 5 page 52

Answers will vary. Possible answers:

1 To avoid confusion, a logo must be unlike any other organization's logo.

2 A logo needs to be adaptable to anywhere it may be placed, and recognizable at any time it might be seen.

3 If a logo can communicate a brand's message and make people feel something, then it has achieved its most crucial purpose.

Be flexible

👤 Ask students to paraphrase the first three sentences of Paragraph 1 and the first two sentences of Paragraph 2 in Reading 2. Make it clear to them that they do not have to paraphrase sentence by sentence; instead, they should consider the passage as a whole. For example, they could paraphrase the first three sentences of Paragraph 1 like this:

Companies may decide to update their logo when they make a change in a product or advertising campaign. The process, called rebranding, often occurs when there is a change in the market for the product.

The sentences suggested above are relatively straightforward to paraphrase, and perhaps less typical of academic texts. Choose another, more authentic short text to give **more advanced students** a greater challenge.

CRITICAL THINKING

Learning objectives

- Remember criteria for designing a good logo
- Evaluate the importance of different criteria for designing a good logo
- Apply the criteria for designing a good logo to an existing logo
- Evaluate your process and explain any additional criteria that were part of this process

UNLOCK TEACHER DEVELOPMENT

BE INFORMED

→ **Determining and applying criteria** is an important skill for students because: (1) It is useful both in real life (e.g. deciding which film to watch at the cinema) as well as in academic studies (e.g. deciding which points are most important to include in an essay); (2) Understanding how criteria work can help students improve their working practices, e.g. prioritizing which articles/books are relevant and appropriate for a particular piece of work; (3) For students to determine and apply criteria effectively, they need to understand what they are evaluating, i.e. the components, purpose and goals.

BE CONFIDENT

→ Develop this skill for yourself by doing the following activity:

Imagine that you have been asked to create a logo to represent critical thinking in your educational institution. What would it look like? What would you include? Why? Refer to the criteria identified in Unit 2 which constitute a successful logo.

Lead-in

Give students a minute to read the writing task. Ask them to brainstorm in groups for a few minutes to help them come up with a list of possible logos. Tell them to keep their brainstorming notes for later, when they begin to write their essay.

UNLOCK TEACHER DEVELOPMENT

BE READY

Look at the Critical Thinking section in the Student's Book on pages 53–54.

→ Which elements of the lesson do you think your students will find easiest / most difficult / most useful? Why?

→ Are your answers true for all students in your class?

→ How can you adapt your teaching or the material to meet your students' needs?

BE FLEXIBLE

For Exercise 2, Question 2, you could take feedback using the 'snowball' technique. This is where: (1) Students decide what their personal view is on an issue; (2) In pairs, they must come to a consensus; (3) In groups of four, they must come to a consensus. This keeps doubling (8... 16... 32) until the whole class must reach a consensus. In doing this, they learn how to compromise and listen to others.

Exercise 1 page 53

Answers will vary. Possible answers:

simple; easy to remember; unique; arouses curiosity; flexible / adaptable across placement / over time; tells a story; conveys a company's message; evokes a response

Exercises 2–4 pages 53–54

Answers will vary.

UNLOCK TEACHER DEVELOPMENT

BE REFLECTIVE

Think about the following points:

→ Draw the logo you designed in the *Be confident* section or create it on a computer. Share it electronically or show it to a colleague. Ask them for feedback, and whether they think it accurately represents critical thinking.

→ Think about the criteria for a good lesson. What are they? Did you meet these criteria in this lesson? Why / Why not?

BE COLLABORATIVE

Your development is more meaningful when it is shared. See page 14 for ideas on how to peer-collaborate. Why not share the ideas you generated in the *Be ready* section, and their outcome?

GRAMMAR FOR WRITING

Learning objectives

- Use non-defining relative clauses to provide additional information about a noun – *IKEA, which is a multinational company, has a logo that is recognized around the world.*
- Use appositives to provide additional information about a noun – *IKEA, a multinational company, has a logo that is recognized around the world.*

Exercise 1 pages 54–55

1 Apple's logo, which was once rainbow coloured, has been redesigned several times in the past 40 years.

2 The letters in the logo for FedEx, which is a delivery service company, form an arrow moving forward.

3 Predrag Stakić, who is a Serbian designer, won an international competition for a logo that features images of a dove and a hand. / Predrag Stakić, whose design encapsulated the features of a dove and a hand, won an international competition.

4 Rebranding, which is a process that can revive interest in a company's products, is only one of many options available to the marketing department.

5 High-tech companies, which often have very young founders, have realized that they need to reconsider and revise their logos.

Exercise 2 page 56

Answers will vary. Possible answers:

1 McDonald's logo, the golden arches, has achieved international recognition as a symbol of fast food.

2 The design of logos, a company's public face, requires careful thought and preparation before release.

3 Rupert Murdoch, a media mogul, has announced he will turn over his empire to his son next year. / Media mogul Rupert Murdoch has announced he will turn over his empire to his son next year.

4 Microsoft, a software giant, has lost some of its market share to Google in the past five years. / Software giant Microsoft has lost some of its market share to Google in the past five years.

5–6 *Answers will vary.*

ACADEMIC WRITING SKILLS

Learning objectives

- Write a paragraph which includes both a short summary of the ideas in a paragraph in another text and a response to the ideas in a paragraph in one or two sentences
- Understand the key features of conclusions and identify these in two texts you have read

Exercises 1–3 page 57

Answers will vary.

Exercise 4 page 58

Answers will vary. Possible answers:

1 **'What Makes a Successful Logo' main idea:** A successful logo captures a company's identity and message in a way that is memorable and pleasing to look at.

   'Rebranding and Logos' main idea: Rebranding is a way a company can revitalize its image and message in order to appeal to today's customers.

2 **Main idea:** Making a brand stand out from the crowd is key to the survival of a business – and a logo is one powerful tool in achieving this.

   Something new to think about: [T]hose who get their logos right will reap the benefits for many years to come.

3 **Main idea:** The process can inject new energy into a brand.

   Something new to think about: New logos can be expensive. [They] can also be risky.

WRITING TASK

Learning objectives

- Draft an essay summarizing Reading 1 and evaluating a logo
- Review and revise the content and structure of your essay
- Review and revise the use of language in your essay

Exercises 1–9 pages 58–60

Answers will vary.

RESEARCH PROJECT

Give a presentation on unsuccessful or ineffective logos.

Divide students into small groups. Each group should choose a logo that they think is ineffective, or could be improved. They will analyze why the logo is not effective in terms of the criteria they have learnt, and then design an alternative logo that they think would be more effective. Finally, they will need to explain why they think their design is an improvement, again referring to the criteria they have studied. If you have talented artists in the class, let them try their hand at creating a better logo.

CLASSROOM APP

Exercises 1–2

Answers will vary.

Exercise 3

1 sustainable　**2** criteria　**3** foremost　**4** strategic
5 retain　**6** foremost　**7** subsequent　**8** opposition

Exercise 4

1 memories　**2** suspicion　**3** excitement　**4** trouble
5 controversy　**6** confidence

Exercise 5

1 There has been a drop in the sale of e-books in the last few years.

2 Print books have become more popular again recently.

3 A book can draw 50% more attention if the cover is designed well.

4 'Millennial pink' conveys youth and sophistication on the covers of many books nowadays.

5 Large fonts in bold colours have been trending recently.

Exercise 6

1 Emoji designs, which were originally created in Japan,

2 which was a response

3 which people really liked

4 which is one of the most popular emojis

5 The original emoji set, which included 176 designs, is now in the Museum of Modern Art in New York.

UNIT OBJECTIVES	
Watch and listen	Watch and understand a video about online harassment.
Reading skills	Preview a text; identify purpose and tone.
Critical thinking	Analyze problems and solutions.
Grammar	Use impersonal passive constructions; use passives for continuity.
Academic writing skills	Write about problems; write about solutions.
Writing task	Write a problem–solution essay.
⊘ **Teacher development**	Help your students become better at **analyzing problems and solutions**.

UNL⊘CK YOUR KNOWLEDGE

Background note

The photo shows a man working on a laptop. His face is hidden in the shadow of a hooded top. The texts in the unit raise issues of identity in social media and the fact that we don't always know who we are interacting with online. Because many people share their profiles and private lives with strangers, being anonymous allows identity thieves, cyber-bullies and internet trolls to thrive.

Lead-in

Ask students if they worry about the privacy of their online identity and activities. They can work in pairs or small groups to discuss their concerns, or reasons for the lack of concern. Then ask them to describe what they do, if anything, to protect their identity and privacy online.

page 63

Answers will vary.

WATCH AND LISTEN

Learning objectives

- Listen and understand the main ideas in video about cyber-bullying
- Listen and identify the main points made by different speakers
- Listen and note detailed information and examples
- Practise talking about protecting children who use the internet

Exercises 1–2 page 64

Answers will vary.

Exercise 3 page 64

1 F; Charlotte Thomas is still a victim of bullying (she has been bullied since she was 11).   **2** T   **3** F; The Safer Internet campaign has many supporters.   **4** F; Nicola Sturgeon believes everybody should be able to access the internet safely.

Exercise 4 page 65

a 2   **b** 1   **c** 4   **d** 5   **e** 3   **f** 1   **g** 2

Exercise 5 page 65

1 People can make fake accounts.   **2** record it   **3** an unflattering photograph   **4** You could offend somebody.   **5** to update their Safer Internet Action Plan   **6** Internet safety techniques need to keep up to date.

Exercise 6 page 65

Answers will vary.

READING 1

Learning objectives

- Understand key vocabulary for cyber-harassment – *hostile, humiliation, abusive*
- Use the first sentence of each paragraph to preview an article about cyber-harassment
- Read, understand and differentiate main ideas and details
- Create an outline of an article
- Read and understand the writer's perspective on cyber-harassment and purpose in writing the article
- Describe issues related to cyber harassment in your country and experience

Lead-in

Students work in small groups or pairs. Do they know anybody, or have they heard of anybody, who has had an online experience in which another internet user was hostile or nasty? They can describe a personal experience if they are comfortable doing so. What did they do in response, if anything?

Exercise 1 page 66

a abusive **b** precedent **c** hostile **d** anonymity
e humiliation **f** withdraw

Exercise 2 page 66

Answers will vary. Possible answers:

1 cyber: of or having to do with the internet

2 harassment: behaviours that annoy or upset somebody, especially repeated behaviours intended to annoy or upset

cyber-harassment: intimidating or pressuring somebody online through email and social media

Exercise 3 page 67

Answers will vary.

Exercise 4 page 67

a, b, c, e, f

Exercise 5 page 67

a D **b** M **c** D **d** M **e** M **f** M **g** D **h** M **i** D **j** D
Paragraphs: **a** 5 **b** 3 **c** 2 **d** 4 **e** 5 **f** 1 **g** 4 **h** 2
i 1 **j** 3

Exercise 6 page 67

Answers will vary.

Exercise 7 page 69

1 c **2** c **3** *Answers will vary. Possible answers:*

disturbing behaviour; In the most serious cases; offensive and threatening; the full extent of the problem; falling victim to; more serious forms; for no other reason than; all of these nasty things; the worst behaviour; disrupt internet communications; serious psychological shock and pain; suffer abusive treatment

Be flexible

👤 Ask students to repeat the activities in Exercise 7, Questions 1 and 3, with another text, either from earlier in this book (Unit 1, Reading 2 would be ideal) or another text of your choosing. If you decide to use Unit 1 Reading 2, students would need to determine the author's perspective regarding historic preservation.

To make the task more challenging for **more advanced students**, choose a text that is not designed for English-language students, but that expresses a clear point of view. Ask students to determine the author's point of view and identify words and phrases that make the author's perspective clear.

Exercise 8 page 69

Answers will vary.

READING 2

Learning objectives

- Understand key vocabulary for cyber-harassment – *accountable, prosecute, malicious*
- Read and identify main ideas
- Read and take notes on details
- Read and understand the writer's perspective on cyber-harassment and purpose in writing the article
- Synthesize information from two articles on cyber-harassment in a discussion

Lead-in

Students now know about some of the abusive practices that occur on the internet. Ask them to discuss in small groups or as a class any personal solutions for these practices they have used successfully.

Exercise 1 page 70

Answers will vary.

Exercise 2 pages 70–71

1 c **2** b **3** c **4** a **5** a **6** b **7** a **8** c

Optional activity

👤 Ask students to preview Reading 2 as they did for Reading 1 (read the title and first sentences of each paragraph). Have them check which of the ideas Exercise 1 that they came up with in (to prevent or eliminate cyber harassment) are mentioned in the text, based on the previewing activity.

Exercise 3 page 71

a 2 **b** 4 **c** 5 **d** 1 **e** 3

Exercise 4 page 71

group	actions
online gaming communities	create barriers to bad behaviours, such as removing chat function, and establish player rating system

group	actions
Twitter	add 'report abuse' button
Google	do research to identify abusers using an algorithm
the US government	update laws to cover stalking and threats on the internet

Exercise 5 page 73

1 b **2** b, e **3** *Answers will vary. Possible answers:*

prompted the public to demand; Additionally; In short; requires a two-pronged approach; yet; To try to address this problem; they discovered that; This resulted in; This study suggests that; In other words; Nevertheless, these laws still lag disturbingly behind; Although this is generally considered; is becoming increasingly important

Exercise 6 page 73

Answers will vary.

LANGUAGE DEVELOPMENT

Learning objectives

- Use common verb + noun collocations to describe behaviour – *build a reputation, suffer abuse*
- Use a range of adjectives to describe online behaviour – *hostile, malicious, offensive*
- Use common verb + noun collocations to describe problems and solutions – *run into problems, resolve an issue, pose a threat*

Exercise 1 page 74

1 take responsibility **2** built a reputation **3** experienced abuse **4** exhibit; behaviour **5** suffer pain **6** lose confidence

Exercise 2 page 74

Answers will vary.

Exercise 3 page 75

1 poses/represents; a threat / a danger **2** resolve/address/confront/face; problem/issue **3** address/confront/face; problem/issue **4** run into; problems/trouble **5** eliminate; the risk/threat/problem

Exercise 4 page 75

Answers will vary.

Optional activity

👥 Ask students to review Reading 2. They should identify and underline collocations to describe problems and solutions. Then ask them to work in pairs to describe a problem they (or somebody they know) had and how they resolved (or were unable to resolve) the problem.

CRITICAL THINKING

Learning objectives

- Explain and evaluate the challenges involved in combatting different types of negative online behaviour
- Analyze the causes and consequences of negative online behaviours for victims and internet users
- Suggest solutions to combat negative online behaviours
- Evaluate and improve suggestions for solutions to combat negative online behaviours

UNLOCK TEACHER DEVELOPMENT

BE INFORMED

➜ **Analyzing problems and solutions** is an important skill for students because: (1) This 'problem–solution' kind of structure is very commonly found in academic writing – where a problem must be identified, then analyzed from different angles. Students often find it difficult to think from many different perspectives; (2) These perspectives might include: *How did this problem begin? What is the impact of the problem? How can the problem be minimized or solved?*; (3) There may be several solutions to a problem, and it is important for students to realize this rather than struggling to find the single 'true' answer.

BE CONFIDENT

➜ Develop this skill for yourself by doing the following activity:

Think about a problem which you have experienced when teaching critical thinking. Address this problem using the three questions above, i.e. (a) How did this problem begin?; (b) What is the impact of the problem?; (c) How can the problem be minimized or solved?

Lead-in

Give students a minute to read the writing task. Ask them to rank the behaviours they have read about in terms of severity. Tell them to keep their brainstorming notes for later, when they begin to write their essay.

UNLOCK TEACHER DEVELOPMENT

BE READY

Look at the Critical Thinking section in the Student's Book on pages 76–78.

➔ Which elements of the lesson do you think your students will find easiest / most difficult / most useful? Why?

➔ Are your answers true for all students in your class?

➔ How can you adapt your teaching or the material to meet your students' needs?

BE FLEXIBLE

Exercises 4 and 5 could be done as a 'soap box' activity. Students must select what they think is the best solution and try to convince the rest of the class. You can conclude by holding a vote.

Exercises 1–5 pages 76–78

Answers will vary.

UNLOCK TEACHER DEVELOPMENT

BE REFLECTIVE

Think about the following points:

➔ Ask colleagues about times when they have faced problems in the classroom, and how they solved them.

➔ Did you feel you had a good enough understanding of the content in this lesson? If not, what could you have done differently either before the lesson, or during it?

BE COLLABORATIVE

Your development is more meaningful when it is shared. See page 14 for ideas on how to peer-collaborate. Why not share the ideas you generated in the *Be ready* section, and their outcome?

GRAMMAR FOR WRITING

Learning objectives

- Use impersonal passive constructions to write sentences where the agent is 'people' – *Cyber-harassment is said to be most common in the male-dominated online gaming world.*

- Use the passive to create continuity within and across sentences in a paragraph about a negative online behaviour – *Because the harassment takes place online, it is not always taken seriously.*

Exercise 1 page 79

1 The figures are believed to underestimate the size of the problem. / It is believed that the figures underestimate the size of the problem.

2 Trolls are claimed to be responsible for the most abusive forms of cyber-harassment. / It is claimed that trolls are responsible for the most abusive forms of cyber-harassment.

3 Victims of online harassment are expected to speak out against their abusers. / It is expected that victims of online harassment will speak out against their abusers.

4 Self-regulation is understood to be the best way to control bad behaviour. / It is understood that self-regulation is the best way to control bad behaviour.

5 'Just ignore it' is considered to be sensible advice to victims of online harassment.

6 It has been argued that these problems will require a legal solution.

Exercise 2 page 79

Answers will vary.

Optional activity

Divide students into two teams. Give them a list of nouns, for example, *the internet*. The first team to create an impersonal passive in a set amount of time (perhaps one minute) wins a point; e.g.: *The internet is often considered to be the most important technological development since the printing press.*

Exercise 3 page 79

1 Although the stalker had been harassing students for weeks, he was not caught until yesterday.

2 A full year after the attacks began, the troll's identity was discovered.

3 These cyber stalkers were not very careful. Evidence of their activity was found quite quickly.

4 The news generally includes positive stories about technology, but recently it has been dominated by stories of cybercrime.

Exercise 4 page 80

Identity theft is a growing problem. <u>It</u> occurs when somebody uses your personal information to open bank accounts, borrow money or make purchases. Almost 17 million people reported <u>identity theft</u> last year. The elderly are especially likely to become victims. Criminals targeted over 2.6 million <u>older people</u> in 2014. Stolen credit cards were the most common source of identity theft. Unfortunately, police do not usually recover <u>the stolen cards</u>.

For the rewritten paragraph, answers will vary.

Possible answer:

Identity theft is a growing problem. It occurs when somebody uses your personal information to open bank accounts, borrow money and make purchases. **Identity theft was reported by almost 17 million people last year**. The elderly are especially likely to become victims. **Over 2.6 million older people were targeted in 2014**. Stolen credit cards were the most common source of identity theft. Unfortunately, **they are not usually recovered.**

ACADEMIC WRITING SKILLS

Learning objectives

- Write sentences using a range of strategies to highlight the seriousness of the problem of cyber harassment
- Write sentences using a range of strategies to offer solutions to victims of cyber harassment

Exercise 1 pages 80–81

1 S   **2** E   **3** S   **4** F   **5** E   **6** E   **7** F   **8** F

Exercise 2 page 81

Answers will vary. Possible answers:

Example: Criado-Perez made the suggestion online that the Bank of England should put more women on its banknotes. For this idea, she received hundreds of hostile comments against her personally and against women more generally.

Statistic: Almost three quarters of all internet users have seen it happen, and 40% have experienced it personally.

Fact: Cyber-harassment is particularly common among younger internet users, and women are more likely to experience its more serious forms.

Exercise 3 page 81

Answers will vary.

Exercise 4 page 82

1 R   **2** S   **3** G   **4** G   **5** S   **6** R

Exercise 5 page 82

Answers will vary.

Be flexible

👥 Give **lower-level students** additional support by asking them, in pairs, to underline words and phrases in the text that refer to (1) problems or (2) solutions, and (3) to types of each strategy. They should use the strategy labels in the Skills boxes on pages 80 and 82.

WRITING TASK

Learning objectives

- Plan and draft a problem–solution essay about a problematic online behaviour
- Review and revise the content and structure of your essay
- Review and revise the use of language in your essay

Exercises 1–9 pages 82–84

Answers will vary.

RESEARCH PROJECT

Create a website with guidelines for victims of cyber-harassment.

Ask students to work in groups to research the topic. The website should include definitions and examples of different types of abuse and harassment. It should also list steps victims can take to combat harassment, as well as steps friends of victims can take to help. Students may also wish to include personal stories of people who have experienced and overcome online harassment.

The groups can come together as a class to collate their materials and create a website that can be uploaded to the internet.

CLASSROOM APP

Exercises 1–2

Answers will vary.

Exercise 3

1 regulate   **2** withdraw   **3** anonymity   **4** accountable
5 eliminate   **6** malicious   **7** combat   **8** precedent

Exercise 4

1 a reputation   **2** abuse   **3** pain   **4** confidence
5 behaviour   **6** responsibility

Exercise 5

1 pose   **2** resolved   **3** presents   **4** address   **5** becomes
6 represent   **7** respond to   **8** eliminate

Exercise 6

1 However, in a 2016 survey, 91% of Americans said they feel that they have lost control of their personal data.

2 For instance, with so much information, some people have a hard time staying focused at work.

3 According to cybersecurity experts, smartphone users need to secure their phones with a locked screen and regular updates.

UNIT OBJECTIVES

Watch and listen	Watch and understand a video about problems faced by small, independent businesses.
Reading skill	Work out meaning from context.
Critical thinking	Analyze advantages and disadvantages.
Grammar	Express contrast; use reductions of subordinate clauses.
Academic writing skill	Write about similarities and differences.
Writing task	Write a comparison and contrast essay.
⌀ Teacher development	Help your students become better at **analyzing advantages and disadvantages**.

UNLOCK YOUR KNOWLEDGE

Background note

The photo shows a food truck with the owner and the menu. In the unit, a food truck is presented as an alternative model for a retail business where the start-up costs and associated risks are low. Unlike traditional food trucks that used to provide food for factory and construction workers and the military, many modern food trucks specialize in high-quality food and cater for special events like weddings or festivals. A food truck is just one type of mobile business; others include florists, the sale of clothes and shoes, IT repairs, etc.

Lead-in

Divide the class in half. Ask half of the students to work in small groups to identify and discuss the biggest challenge of starting one's own business. The other half works to identify and discuss the biggest challenge of maintaining a business once it is established. The groups then compare to find areas of overlap and points of contrast.

page 87

Answers will vary.

WATCH AND LISTEN

Learning objectives

- Listen and summarize the main ideas in video about small businesses
- Listen and note facts and figures in a video about small businesses
- Listen and identify the meaning of unfamiliar words and phrases from their context in the video
- Practise talking about the issues faced by small business owners

Exercises 1–2 page 88

Answers will vary.

Exercise 3 page 88

Answers will vary. Possible answer:

There is an event, 'Small Business Saturday', which hopes to attract shoppers to small businesses. They are also discussing the ways that government taxes can help small businesses.

Exercise 4 page 89

1 specialist shops **2** 5.2 million **3** 1/3 **4** first Saturday in December **5** three quarters of a billion pounds (£750,000,000) **6** 19/20 **7** £50 **8** no deposit **9** sold the family home **10** road to be swept **11** by size / by square footage **12** £7,000–£7,500 **13** access to finance; cuts to regulatory burden (tax cuts)

Exercise 5 page 89

1 c **2** b **3** c **4** b

Exercise 6 page 89

Answers will vary.

READING 1

Learning objectives

- Understand key vocabulary for mobile business ventures – *aspiring, break even, proposition*
- Preview an article about mobile businesses
- Scan an article to identify its usefulness to different audiences
- Read and summarize the main argument in an article
- Read and identify the meaning of unfamiliar words and phrases from their context in the article
- Give opinions on mobile retail in a discussion

Lead-in

Show students the title of the reading: *Starting Out Mobile*. Ask students what kinds of mobile businesses they have used. If they have never patronized a mobile business, ask why not (e.g. they may not exist in their community). What kinds of businesses do they think would work in a mobile environment and why?

Exercise 1 page 90

Answers will vary.

Exercise 2 page 90

1 fluctuated   **2** propositions   **3** aspiring   **4** outweigh
5 component   **6** transition   **7** broke even   **8** revenue

Optional activity

Remind students about compound adjectives. Reading 1 has quite a few of them. When these appear in the pre-noun position (as in *before* the noun), they often require a hyphen, particularly if the hyphen helps make the meaning clear.

This business is two years old. v *This two-year-old business is doing very well.*

Many online businesses started in the twentieth century. v *The internet has dramatically changed twentieth-century business practices.*

Tell students to find four examples of hyphenated compound adjectives in Reading 1 (*brick-and-mortar, start-up, low-risk, high-tech, stand-alone*). Then tell them to write their own sentences with the following compound adjectives: *full-time, face-to-face, easy-to-remember*.

Exercise 3 page 91

1 £5,000–£10,000   **2** waffles and pancakes from a truck
3 flowers, shoes, clothes, hair styling, pet grooming, repair of high-tech devices

4 12%   **5** weather, fluctuating fuel prices, parking
6 $857 million

Exercise 4 page 91

1 N   **2** M   **3** Y   **4** N   **5** Y   **6** N

Exercise 5 page 91

Mobile businesses are a good first step into the retail market.

Exercise 6 page 93

1 b   **2** e   **3** g   **4** c   **5** a   **6** d   **7** h   **8** f

Exercises 7–8 pages 93–94

Answers will vary.

READING 2

Learning objectives

- Understand key vocabulary for customer loyalty schemes – *incentive, retention, attainable*
- Read and understand the main claims in an essay about customer loyalty schemes
- Read and complete a detailed summary of the essay
- Make inferences about the topics discussed in an article about customer loyalty schemes
- Synthesize information from an article about mobile businesses and an essay about customer loyalty schemes in a discussion

Lead-in

Ask students to keep their books closed. Choose a few products or services that would be familiar to your students, e.g. shoes, sportswear, airlines, fast food. Ask for volunteers who feel loyal to a brand of this product (*I always eat burgers at X. I only wear Y shoes.*) For each volunteer, create a small group. The rest of each group tries to think of strategies that would induce the volunteer to buy the product from another company. An obvious example would be lower price, but push students to develop others. For the fast food example, it could include: *A different fast-food provider opens closer to your house and it: offers a drive-through service / offers delivery / starts a more diverse menu / offers a free burger after five purchases. / You discover fast-food restaurant X: uses inappropriate ingredients / treats its workers badly / has raised its prices.* Don't offer all of these examples; let them generate a list on their own. If some overlap with Exercise 1 on page 94, so much the better. Return to the whole-class format and ask each group to report the strategies (if any) that induced the volunteer to change brands (if any).

Exercise 1 page 94

Answers will vary.

Exercise 2 pages 94–95

1 b **2** a **3** a **4** c **5** a **6** b **7** a **8** c

Exercise 3 page 95

a NC **b** C **c** C **d** NC **e** NC **f** C

Exercise 4 page 97

1 simple **2** attainable **3** valuable **4** consumers
5 airlines **6** convenience **7** desires **8** decisions **9** 100%

Be flexible

👤 Ask students to use the context to work out the meaning of the following phrases from Reading 2: *hold on to, track record, on a regular basis, tailored to.*

Track record and *tailored to* are probably the most opaque of these phrases. You can help **lower-level students** by talking about the origins of the terms. *Track record* comes from horse racing and *tailored to* is related to the occupation and activity of a *tailor,* somebody who makes clothing that fits a specific person.

Exercises 5–6 page 97

Answers will vary.

LANGUAGE DEVELOPMENT

Learning objectives

- Use a range of connectors to show contrast accurately – *nevertheless, in fact, unlike*
- Use a range of expressions to describe business ventures – *break even, brick-and-mortar, generate revenue*

Exercise 1 page 99

1 b **2** a **3** c **4** a **5** b

Optional activity

👥👥 Tell students to finish the following sentences:
In spite of the bad weather, ...
Instead of eating rice with my dinner, tonight I ...

Explain that these markers of contrast are extremely helpful because they help the reader predict what will come next.

Ask students to start their own sentences for a classmate to finish. Make sure that they cover the range of these signals, including both *syntactic* (connecting both clauses and noun phrases) and *semantic* (concession and correction as well as direct contrast) varieties. You may wish to point out the all-around utility of *however* as a connector. It can perform all three semantic functions. Although it is a good idea to use variety, using *however* is a good default strategy.

Exercise 2 page 100

1 on a small scale **2** start-up costs / utility bills **3** utility bills / start-up costs **4** breaks even **5** make a profit **6** brick-and-mortar **7** track record **8** generate revenue **9** marketing tools

CRITICAL THINKING

Learning objectives

- Analyze the advantages and disadvantages of a mobile setting for new retail business owners
- Explain the factors that contribute to success or failure of a new retail business in a mobile setting
- Evaluate and analyze the possibility of success or failure for a range of new businesses in a mobile setting

---

UNLOCK TEACHER DEVELOPMENT

BE INFORMED

➔ **Analyzing advantages and disadvantages** is an important skill for students because: (1) This process is common in many academic activities, both written and spoken; (2) It is only by looking at both sides of an issue that it is possible to identify what you genuinely think about an issue; (3) Sometimes when students analyze all sides of a subject, they come across a new idea which could change their view.

BE CONFIDENT

➔ Develop this skill for yourself by doing the following activity:

Think about a type of activity which you do regularly in your classroom which sometimes works well and sometimes does not. Consider the advantages and disadvantages of doing this activity.

Lead-in

Give students a minute to read the writing task they will do at the end of the unit. Ask them to brainstorm in groups for a few minutes to help them come up with a list of possible candidates. Tell them to keep their brainstorming notes for later, when they begin to write their essay.

UNLOCK TEACHER DEVELOPMENT

BE READY

Look at the Critical Thinking section in the Student's Book on pages 101–102.

➔ Which elements of the lesson do you think your students will find easiest / most difficult / most useful? Why?

➔ Are your answers true for all students in your class?

➔ How can you adapt your teaching or the material to meet your students' needs?

BE FLEXIBLE

Showing the relevance of what the students are learning in the classroom to their everyday lives can deepen their understanding of a particular topic. One way of doing this is to ask students to research companies mentioned in Exercise 2 which can be found locally.

Exercise 1 page 101

1

advantages of a mobile setting	disadvantages of a mobile setting
a good way to test your business idea for a lower cost	parking costs
gradual start for those who don't know much about business	petrol prices are unpredictable
	bad weather can affect sales
can take product directly to customers	small size limits activity not every kind of business can work in a van

2 *Answers will vary. Possible answers:*

factors that contribute to success of mobile operation	factors that contribute to failure of mobile operation
lower financial risk lower costs for • start-up • utilities • overheads gradual start for those who don't know much about business a van is its own advertisement not limited to operating in one location	location unpredictable for customers parking fees petrol prices are unpredictable laws that restrict mobile businesses

3 *Answers will vary.*

Exercises 2–4 page 102

Answers will vary.

UNLOCK TEACHER DEVELOPMENT

BE REFLECTIVE

Think about the following points:

➔ Think specifically about the activity you considered in *Be confident*. Will you do it again? If so, will you change it at all?

➔ If you decide to make a change in your teaching, tell somebody else about this change – either in person or electronically. Doing this will encourage you to genuinely change your practice.

BE COLLABORATIVE

Your development is more meaningful when it is shared. See page 14 for ideas on how to peer-collaborate. Why not share the ideas you generated in the *Be ready* section, and their outcome?

GRAMMAR FOR WRITING

Learning objectives

- Use reduced subordinate clauses in sentences about new business ventures – *Although concerned about the risks, the brothers decided to start a business.*

Exercise 1 page 103

Answers will vary. Possible answers:

1 <u>Although impressed by the presentation of the sales manager</u>, Nour decided not to make the initial investment.

Although Nour/she was impressed by the presentation of the sales manager,

2 <u>While working in a street food van</u>, Kwan developed enough experience to start his own business.

While Kwan/he was working in a street food van,

3 <u>While interviewing dozens of mobile phone users</u>, Isabelle got an idea for a new mobile business – a phone-charging service at the park!

While Isabelle/she was interviewing dozens of mobile phone users,

4 <u>Once discovered by the food reporter for a local food blog</u>, the Vietnamese street food van had more business than its owners could handle.

Once the Vietnamese street food van/it was discovered by the food reporter for a local food blog,

5 <u>When it is supported by good reviews and positive feedback</u>, a subscription service can become part of a successful plan.

When a subscription service/it is supported by good reviews and positive feedback,

Exercise 2 page 104

Answers will vary. Possible answers:

1 When considering the mobile option for your business, you need to be flexible in the planning phase.

2 While researching marketing tools, Ali was surprised to learn about the inconsistent track record of loyalty schemes.

3 Unless embraced by a large number of customers, loyalty schemes are not a very effective marketing tool.

4 Although worried about the risks, the Smith brothers decided to begin their business online.

5 If taken seriously, this advice can improve a company's chances of success.

Be flexible

👤 👥 In this activity, the focus is on reconstructing the subject of reduced clauses. Write this sentence from Unit 1 on the board. Ask students to reduce the subordinate clause to a participle phrase.

- *Once these treasures are lost, they are lost forever.*

Some students may write: *Once lost, they are lost forever.* Point out that when they reduce clauses, information is lost. They need to ensure that the information is retrievable, so they need to place this information in the remaining full clause. *Once lost, **these treasures** are lost forever.* You may wish to repeat Exercise 2, items 2–5, with the full noun phrase in the first clause, or you can create new ones for students to reduce. This will require them to change the position of the full noun phrase:

- *Whether **loyalty schemes** are offered on a regular basis or just once in a while, they can often boost the bottom line.*
- *When **Felipe** was designing the original loyalty scheme, he failed to account for its rising cost to the company.*

For additional challenge, **stronger students** can work in pairs. One student creates a sentence with a full clause, then a partner writes the reduction.

ACADEMIC WRITING SKILLS

Learning objectives

- Use two different essay structures – block organization and point-by-point organization – to organize ideas in a comparison of two things
- Identify the best conclusion for an essay

Exercise 1 page 105

1 block; point-by-point   2 *Answers will vary.*

Exercise 2 page 106

1 b   2 *Answers will vary.*   3 c

Optional activity

👤 Ask students to consider the two products or services they have chosen for their writing task. In what ways are they similar? In what ways are they different? Ask them to analyze how these similarities and differences relate to the advantages and disadvantages of going mobile. For example, a mobile food operation might require preparation at another location (a disadvantage) whereas an exercise studio would not (an advantage).

WRITING TASK

Learning objectives

- Draft an essay contrasting two products or services in regards to their potential as mobile businesses using either point-by-point or block organization
- Review and revise the content and structure of your essay
- Review and revise the use of language in your essay

Exercises 1–8 pages 107–108

Answers will vary.

RESEARCH PROJECT

Create a plan for a mobile business.

Students should work in small groups. Ask them to research how to start a mobile business in their community. They will need to choose a business, create a budget, decide on the equipment and employees they will need, and make a plan for their first year of business. Students should then present their business plans to an objective group of listeners (perhaps other teachers or another class) who act as potential investors. The audience will vote on the best plan.

CLASSROOM APP

Exercises 1–2

Answers will vary.

Exercise 3

1 pioneers   **2** proposition   **3** component   **4** transition
5 outweighed   **6** retention   **7** followed suit   **8** revenue

Exercise 4

1 instead of selling in shops

2 rather, they can work from home

3 unlike bricks-and-mortar shops, which are expensive

4 However, an owner needs to be active on social media too

5 On the other hand, some customers like to see products before they buy

6 despite the popularity of online retail

Exercise 5

1 Many startups generate revenue on a website like Kickstarter.

2 Businesses with a good track record will attract investors.

3 New businesses often need money for start-up costs, such as supplies.

4 Good marketing tools can attract new customers, and a lot are free.

5 It takes several years for most startups to make a profit.

6 Starting a business on a small scale is easier to manage.

Exercise 6

1 Paragraph 1 gardening service – work outdoors; gardening service – seasonal work

Paragraph 2 flower shop – work indoors; flower shop – customers all year

2 Paragraph 1 gardening service – work outdoors; flower shop – work indoors

Paragraph 2 gardening service – seasonal work; flower shop – customers all year

UNIT OBJECTIVES	
Watch and listen	Watch and understand a video about an artist who creates sculptures from plastic bricks.
Reading skills	Annotate a text; interpret quotes.
Critical thinking	Synthesize information from more than one text.
Grammar	Use complex noun phrases with *what*.
Academic writing skills	Cite quoted material; write an expository essay.
Writing task	Write an expository essay.
⟁ **Teacher development**	Help your students become better at **synthesizing information from more than one text**.

UNLOCK YOUR KNOWLEDGE

Background note

The photo shows Japanese artist Yayoi Kusama. She is sitting in her studio in Tokyo in front of some finished paintings. Kusama is one of the best-selling living female artists and one of the most respected artists in Japan. People usually consider a creative person to be somebody who is involved in art, music or literature. However, you can also be creative in fields like Business, Medicine, Maths or Science, for example, by finding new and innovative solutions to difficult problems. Creative people are often considered to have particular characteristics, such as having good problem-solving skills, thinking in different or unusual ways, challenging authority or social norms, and being independent, curious, determined and open to new ideas.

Lead-in

Students work in small groups. Ask them to write an informal definition of *creativity*. If they need a nudge, ask them if being creative is the same as being artistic (i.e. is it possible to be creative outside of the arts?). Then ask groups to share their definitions.

page 111
Answers will vary.

WATCH AND LISTEN

Learning objectives

- Listen and identify the main ideas in a video about an unusual artist
- Listen and note detailed information and examples
- Listen and identify the meaning of unfamiliar words and phrases from their context in the video
- Practise talking about art and creativity

Exercises 1–2 page 112

Answers will vary.

Exercise 3 page 113

1, 3, 4

Exercise 4 page 113

Answers will vary. Possible answers:

1 easy to get started; build from imagination; no physical skill needed; can change ideas, undo and rebuild

2 Lego artist; models shown in galleries around the world; 3-D paint-box only limited by vision and imagination

3 billboard in Hollywood (500,000 bricks); Tyrannosaurus Rex skeleton (20 feet long)

4 corporate law; New York City; 80 hours per week; negotiating contracts (in board room); needed creative release

5 straightforward process; gravity (forces him to work up); adds glue then the brick

6 several commissions; from all over the world; keeps it interesting

7 generally $10,000–$20,000; largest – one piece for six figures

Exercise 5 page 113

Answers will vary.

READING 1

Learning objectives

- Understand key vocabulary for creativity – *cognition, genius, attribute to*
- Use the first sentence of each paragraph to preview an article about creativity
- Read and annotate main ideas, supporting examples, definitions and quotes in an article
- Interpret key ideas in quotations from an article about creativity
- Explain the link between non-conformity and creativity and how you define creativity in a discussion

Lead-in

Ask students to describe how they take notes on written texts. If they have a textbook or other material they have taken notes on, ask them to share with other members of the class or in a small group. Make notes on the board about what they *choose* to take notes on and *how* they make notes, e.g. like the table below.

What	How
dates	*highlight*
names	*underline*
important facts	*notes in margins*
	notes in separate book

Exercise 1 page 114

1 attributed to   **2** norm   **3** cognition   **4** suppress
5 labelled   **6** trauma   **7** stimulation   **8** genius

Exercise 2 page 115

Answers will vary.

Exercise 3 page 115

a, c, e, f, g

Exercise 4 page 115

Answers will vary. Possible answers:

highlighting and margin note for words they need to look up the meaning of; underlining and margin note for supporting details and examples; square brackets and margin note for quotes and definitions

Exercise 5 page 115

Answers will vary.

Exercise 6 page 118

Answers will vary. Possible answers:

a Eureka moment: the point at which you suddenly understand the answer or solution to a problem

to open (up) the flood gates: if an action or a decision opens the flood gates, it allows something to happen a lot or allows many people to do something that was not previously allowed

> ### Optional activity
>
> Ask students to interpret the first quote from Nancy Andreasen in Reading 1 and include it in the discussion of quotes in Exercise 7.

Exercises 7–8 page 118

Answers will vary.

READING 2

Learning objectives

- Understand key vocabulary for creativity – *conformity, constrain, traits*
- Read and annotate main ideas, supporting examples, definitions and new vocabulary in an article about creativity
- Read, understand and differentiate main ideas and details
- Make inferences about the topics in an article about creativity
- Apply information from an article on creativity to a discussion of types of creativity
- Synthesize information from two articles about creativity in a discussion

Lead-in

Remind students of the *Unlock Your Knowledge* exercise at the beginning of the unit. They were asked if they considered themselves creative. For those who answered *yes*, have them speculate how they became creative. Were they born that way? Did they learn to be more creative? If so, how? For those who reported that they are not creative, ask if they think they can learn to become more creative. If so, how? If not, why not? Pick a few volunteers from each category to answer the questions.

Exercises 1–2 page 119

Answers will vary.

Exercise 3 page 120

1 c   **2** a   **3** c   **4** a   **5** b   **6** a   **7** a   **8** c

Exercise 4 page 122

Answers will vary.

Exercise 5 page 122

1 D 2 M 3 X 4 M 5 M 6 X 7 D 8 M

Exercise 6 page 122

Answers will vary.

Be flexible

👤 Tell students to use their notes and annotations to write a summary of the material in Reading 1: *What are the sources and requirements for creativity?* Include main ideas and key supporting details.

Provide more support for **lower-level students**. Ask them to organize their notes and annotations by creating an outline before they write their summaries.

Exercise 7 page 122

Answers will vary. Possible answers:

1 a limit which would prevent somebody developing expertise in something; he doesn't believe there is a limit

2 most experts agree that even if most people cannot hope to become creative geniuses, they can learn to become more creative through practice; yes

3 new ideas move us into unfamiliar territory – a place we haven't been before is less comfortable than one we are familiar with

Exercises 8–9 page 123

Answers will vary.

LANGUAGE DEVELOPMENT

Learning objectives

- Identify the meaning of experimental science terminology from context – *experimental group, contend, intervention*

Exercise 1 page 124

1 conduct a study **2** intervention **3** implications
4 control group **5** experimental group **6** research subjects **7** establish a causal link **8** contend

Optional activity

👥 Ask students to think about the kind of scientific research described in the two readings. Ask them to imagine they wanted to design an experiment to determine which is more effective: listening to new vocabulary in a song or listening to sentences that contain the same words. How would they design a study? They should use the vocabulary from Exercise 1.

CRITICAL THINKING

Learning objectives

- Restate the main arguments from two texts about creativity
- Analyze common topics and organize detailed notes by topic from two texts about creativity
- Evaluate the topics of two texts for use in an essay

UNL⊙CK TEACHER DEVELOPMENT

BE INFORMED

➜ **Synthesizing information from more than one text** is an important skill for students because: (1) It is required in all academic subjects; (2) Students often rely too much on just one source, or a small number of sources, when writing essays. The result of this is that their argument may be unbalanced; (3) Students often find it difficult to incorporate different ideas from different texts into a cohesive, coherent piece of writing.

BE CONFIDENT

➜ Develop this skill for yourself by doing the following activity:

Read the following comments about critical thinking in the classroom. How could you represent all the main arguments in a single piece of text which also accurately reflects your own opinion on the issue?

'It's difficult to find time to teach critical thinking well.'

'Teachers often complain about not having enough time to teach critical thinking, but you have to find time.'

'Students don't think it is a good use of time to teach critical thinking. They want to focus on language and grammar.'

'The classroom is the only place my students have to develop their ability to think critically.'

'Principals need to acknowledge the importance of classroom time for critical thinking.'

'I like critical thinking, and so do my students, but parents think we should focus more on grammar and writing.'

Lead-in

Give students a minute to read the writing task. Ask them to review the notes and summaries they have made so far. Tell them to keep them for later, when they begin to write their essay.

UNLOCK TEACHER DEVELOPMENT

BE READY

Look at the Critical Thinking section in the Student's Book on pages 125–126.

→ Which elements of the lesson do you think your students will find easiest / most difficult / most useful? Why?

→ Are your answers true for all students in your class?

→ How can you adapt your teaching or the material to meet your students' needs?

BE FLEXIBLE

Some students/classes might find Exercise 3 difficult. In order to support them you could (a) review key things to remember when searching for information online, or (b) identify some online sources which they can look at.

Exercise 1 page 125

Answers will vary.

Exercise 2 page 126

Answers will vary. Possible answers:

Topic	Reading 1	Reading 2
a	genes, intelligence, suffering emotional trauma, openness to experience (genetic?)	genes, deliberate practice, personality trait of openness to new experience, emulating creative people's openness, willingness to carry on in the face of failure
b	Andreasen: Eureka moments occur when precipitated by long periods of preparation and incubation, and strike when the mind is relaxed. Keri: individuals with artistic creativity suffered from severe traumas in life.	Ericsson: no limit on individual success in any skill Scientists checking Ericsson's findings: A 2014 study concluded that practice explains only about 25% of the difference between top performers and performers who were just 'very good'. The rest was due to natural ability.
c	make new connections, procrastination	risk-taking, convergent thinking, divergent thinking
d	Klee, MLK, Bach, Jack Dorsey	Hemingway, Edison

Topic	Reading 1	Reading 2
e	X	big C creativity, small c creativity, convergent thinking, divergent thinking
f	push limits, openness, take risks, curious	openness to new experience, toleration of contradiction
g	could be labelled as a troublemaker in school	potential for failure
h	X	train in divergent thinking, move outside comfort zone

Exercises 3–4 page 126

Answers will vary.

UNLOCK TEACHER DEVELOPMENT

BE REFLECTIVE

Think about the following questions:

→ Think about the comments in the *Be confident* section. Which of these views are held in your place of teaching? Is your own view on critical thinking shared by most of your colleagues?

→ Has your response to the question 'What is creative thinking?' changed as a result of teaching this class? It is important to remember that you should be willing to have your own views changed by listening to your students, as well as your own reflections about your classroom practice.

BE COLLABORATIVE

Your development is more meaningful when it is shared. See page 14 for ideas on how to peer-collaborate. Why not share the ideas you generated in the *Be ready* section, and their outcome?

GRAMMAR FOR WRITING

Learning objectives

- Use complex noun phrases with *what* instead of vague nouns, such as *things,* in sentences about creativity – *We tend to reproduce what we already know.*

Exercise 1 page 127

1 The articles describe what the research subjects did in order to demonstrate their creativity.

2 We are largely unaware of what goes on in our own brains to create our perception of reality.

3 We still do not know for certain what leads to creativity.

4 The researchers were looking for what singles out the most creative people in the population.

5 One of the goals of the study was to find out what creative people are doing when they come up with their best ideas.

Optional activity

👤 Ask students to analyze the three sentences from the reading with *wh-* noun clauses (two of which are in the Grammar box). They should rewrite these without the use of the *wh* clause (e.g., *the things that ...*), and say why the *wh-* clause version is superior.

- *Simple repetition is not enough.* **What Ericsson calls** *'deliberate practice' is required.*
- **What most people think of as creativity** *generally involves divergent thinking.*

We tend to reproduce **what we already know.**

Exercise 2 page 128

Answers will vary.

ACADEMIC WRITING SKILLS

Learning objectives

- Note information that you will need to supply when citing quoted material in your writing
- Use a table of notes to prepare topic sentences for an essay which synthesize information from two texts

Exercise 1 page 128

Answers will vary. Possible answers:

1 Year: 2014 **Source:** *Atlantic Magazine*

Nancy Andreasen, in an article published in *Atlantic Magazine* in 2014, explains that creative people are 'better at recognizing relationships, making associations and connections, and seeing things in an original way – seeing things that others cannot see.'

2 Year: 2016 **Source:** his 2016 book, *Peak: Secrets from the New Science of Expertise*

Anders Ericsson

In his 2016 book, *Peak: Secrets from the New Science of Expertise*, Anders Ericsson contends that he has 'yet to find limits that would actually constrain some individuals from being successful.'

Exercise 2 page 129

Answers will vary.

Exercises 3–4 page 130

Answers will vary.

WRITING TASK

Learning objectives

- Plan and draft an essay about creative thinking which synthesizes information from several sources
- Review and revise the content and structure of your essay
- Review and revise the use of language in your essay

Exercises 1–9 pages 130–132

Answers will vary.

RESEARCH PROJECT

Write a report on a creative mind.

Ask students to work in pairs or small groups. They should do research on a creative individual (an artist, inventor, scientist, etc.) and analyze their career to determine whether the factors students have read about in this unit can explain their creativity.

Students can then present their findings to the rest of the class.

CLASSROOM APP

Exercises 1–2

Answers will vary.

Exercise 3

1 trait   2 attributed   3 cognition   4 stimulation
5 conformity   6 norms   7 labelled   8 contends

Exercise 4

1 causal link   2 study   3 research subjects
4 experimental group; control group
5 interventions   6 implications

Exercise 5

1 is   2 What users want   3 What behavioural psychologists do   4 what people do online
5 What companies are starting to understand is

Exercise 6

1 Not correct   2 Not correct   3 Correct
4 Not correct   5 Not correct

UNIT OBJECTIVES	
Watch and listen	Watch and understand a video about vocational training.
Reading skills	Interpret graphical information.
Critical thinking	Analyze information in graphs and other figures.
Grammar	Use the active and passive voice to discuss figures.
Academic writing skill	Make a claim.
Writing task	Write an argumentative essay with graphical support.
☾ **Teacher development**	Help your students become better at **analyzing information in graphs and other figures**.

UNLⓄCK YOUR KNOWLEDGE

Background note

The photo shows a group of students wearing traditional graduation gowns and academic square caps, also known as mortarboards, at a graduation ceremony. In the UK, graduates often wear the gown of the degree that they are about to receive. The tradition of wearing an academic gown dates back to medieval times. In the modern era, the academic gown and mortarboard has come to represent academic education. The unit discusses the issue of a skills gap between new graduates' education and the job market's real needs. It also deals with the advantages of obtaining a university education.

Lead-in

Ask students to discuss how their careers or career goals differ from those of their parents' or even grandparents' generation. How did people a generation or two generations ago prepare for those jobs? How does that preparation differ from their own?

page 135

Answers will vary.

WATCH AND LISTEN

Learning objectives

- Listen and identify the main ideas in a video about vocational training
- Listen and note detailed information and examples
- Make inferences about the issues described in the video
- Practise talking about educational options after secondary school

Exercises 1–2 page 136

Answers will vary.

Exercise 3 page 137

1, 2, 3, 5

Exercise 4 page 137

Answers will vary. Possible answers:

1 4,000 are skilled.   **2** He hires 550 workers a year, 360 of which are technical. Some positions remain open for one year.
3 It has been cut by $140 million and may be cut by another 20%.
4 electronics experts, instrument technicians, mechanics

Exercises 5–6 page 137

Answers will vary.

READING 1

Learning objectives

- Use graphs to preview an article about recruitment and predict the main ideas in an article about recruitment
- Understand key vocabulary for recruitment – *expertise, prospective, labour*
- Read and identify the main ideas in an article about recruitment
- Read and understand detailed information
- Identify the purpose and context of the article
- Give opinions on information and ideas in an article about recruitment

Lead-in

Ask students to look at the graph on page 138. Ask them to identify the title, what the *x*- and *y*-axes show, and what the legend defines. What is the source?

Exercise 1 page 138

Answers will vary.

Exercise 2 page 139

1 Time: 2006–2015 (fig. 1); Time: 2011–2020 (fig. 2)
2 percentage of companies who had difficulty filling positions (fig. 1); raw number (number of jobs and qualified graduates) (fig. 2)   **3** Since 2006, between 30% and 40% of companies have had trouble filling positions (fig. 1).; Since 2011, the number of computing jobs has grown faster than the number of graduates in that field (fig. 2).

Exercise 3 page 139

Answers will vary. Possible answers:

1 There are not enough people able to do the kind of work that companies currently need done.   **2** There are not enough students learning the skills necessary to fill the increasing number of jobs that companies will have open.   **3** Figure 2 shows that there are significantly fewer students of computer science than there are jobs available, so this may partly explain why companies cannot fill the positions.

Be flexible

👤 Ask students what all three graphs they have seen so far have in common. What type of graph are they? What do they illustrate? Students should report that they are all line graphs that display numerical trends (e.g. percentage growth) across time. For an **extra challenge**, ask students to give a title to the *y*-axis in both graphs.

Exercise 4 page 139

1 expertise   **2** poses   **3** mismatch   **4** comprises
5 assertive   **6** labour   **7** prospective   **8** persistent

Exercise 5 page 141

a 5   **b** 2   **c** 6   **d** 1   **e** 4   **f** 3

Exercise 6 page 141

d

Exercise 7 page 142

1 DNS   **2** F; The most critical shortages are in the skilled trades.   **3** F; The positions that companies are trying to fill often do not require a university education.   **4** T
5 F; School curriculums have not adapted enough to meet the new demand for technical skills.   **6** T   **7** DNS   **8** T

Exercise 8 page 142

1 b   **2** a

Exercise 9 page 142

Answers will vary.

READING 2

Learning objectives

- Use graphs to preview an article about the value of a university education
- Understand key vocabulary – *chronic, founder, dispute*
- Read and understand main ideas
- Read figures in an article and extract detailed information
- Make inferences about the value of a university education from the ideas and information in the article
- Synthesize information from an article about recruitment and an article about the value of a university education in a discussion

Lead-in

In the *Unlock Your Knowledge* exercise, students discussed the purpose of a university education. Now, ask students to discuss the *value* of a university education. In other words, ask them why they (or others they know) need(ed) or want(ed) a university education. Most answers will probably relate to income. In small groups, students brainstorm other possible positive outcomes of a university education.

Exercise 1 page 143

Answers will vary. Possible answers:

1 The percentage of people with a university education has increased globally from 2000 to 2012.   **2** Median income is the amount of money that divides the top half of a country's earners from the lower half. University graduates are more likely to earn above the median income.   **3** The topic of the article will be about the relationship between a university education and income. The argument will likely be that a university education will improve your income.

Exercise 2 page 143

a dispute   **b** ambiguity   **c** founder   **d** multiple
e chronic   **f** asserts   **g** illustration

Exercise 3 page 144

Answers will vary.

Exercise 4 page 144

1 T **2** F; College graduates in the US make about $17,000 more per year than those with just secondary school qualifications. **3** T **4** DNS **5** F; Arts graduates have lower incomes than graduates with an engineering degree. **6** T

Exercise 5 page 144

1

Exercise 6 page 144

Figure 1: 1 Canada **2** South Korea and the United Kingdom are similar, but South Korea is correct. **3** 18%

Figure 2: 1 Chile **2** Greece **3** Around 65%

Optional activity

Ask students what the two graphs in the reading have in common. What type of graph are they? What do they illustrate? Students should report that they are both bar/column graphs that compare two things across time. Ask them to explain why this is the best choice of graph for these data.

Exercises 7–8 page 146

Answers will vary.

LANGUAGE DEVELOPMENT

Learning objectives

- Form common compound nouns and use them in sentences about education: *labour force participation rate*, *graduate training scheme*, *placement rate*

Exercise 1 page 147

1 training scheme **2** earning power **3** placement rate **4** job market **5** labour force **6** entry level **7** work–life balance

Exercise 2 page 147

a information technology professional **b** graduate training scheme **c** labour force participation rate **d** university enrolment trends **e** median household income

1 median household income **2** graduate training scheme **3** information technology professional **4** labour force participation rate **5** university enrolment trends

Optional activity

Ask students to create their own compound nouns with the following nouns as the head noun (final word in compound) and use each in a sentence about education or careers: *background, course, education, industry, leader, scheme.*

If you want to make it a game, you could award points for compounds with three or more elements.

CRITICAL THINKING

Learning objectives

- Understand the measures used to evaluate job quality
- Understand the use of different types of figure to display information
- Apply knowledge gained from the unit to data about jobs
- Analyze and collect information relating to the job market in a country or region of interest
- Evaluate different career paths and explain the reasons for choosing them

UNLOCK TEACHER DEVELOPMENT

BE INFORMED

→ **Analyzing information in graphs and other figures** is an important skill for students because: (1) They often find it challenging to identify and extract the key point(s) shown in a graph, and instead focus on less important information; (2) A common mistake made by students is to include interesting or relevant graphs in their writing, but not to say anything about them; (3) Students are often unclear about the different types of graphs and other figures which are available, and when it is appropriate to use the different types (e.g. line graphs, bar charts, pie charts, etc.).

BE CONFIDENT

→ Develop this skill for yourself by doing the following activity:

The graphs below come from a critical thinking survey of 1,019 English teachers by Cambridge University Press. What are the key findings? How would you report on them in a piece of writing?

Figure 1: Responses to the statement, 'It is important to me that I develop my students' Critical Thinking skills'.

1 = strongly disagree; 5 = strongly agree

1	7/1%
2	10/1%
3	51/5%
4	224/22%
5	727/71%

Figure 2: Responses to the statement, 'I struggle to find the time to develop effective means to teach Critical Thinking skills'.

1 = strongly disagree; 5 = strongly agree

1	75/7%
2	124/12%
3	313/31%
4	324/32%
5	183/18%

Lead-in

Give students a minute to read the writing task and ask any questions they may have.

UNLOCK TEACHER DEVELOPMENT

BE READY

Look at the Critical Thinking section in the Student's Book on pages 148–150.

➔ Which elements of the lesson do you think your students will find easiest / most difficult / most useful? Why?

➔ Are your answers true for all students in your class?

➔ How can you adapt your teaching or the material to meet your students' needs?

BE FLEXIBLE

An interesting additional/extension activity following Exercise 2 would be to research the situation in your own country. Alternatively, if the students in your class are very science-focused, you could research and create an exercise which requires students to match different types of graph or figure to specific situations.

Exercise 1 page 148

Possible answer:

1 because the diagram needs to show how different aspects of the measure are weighted in relation to one another.

2 *Answers will vary.*

Exercises 2–5 pages 149–150

Answers will vary.

UNLOCK TEACHER DEVELOPMENT

BE REFLECTIVE

Think about the following questions:

➔ Do you agree with the findings presented in the *Be confident* section? How would you have answered the questions?

➔ Ask colleagues, either face-to-face or electronically, about their own job satisfaction in teaching. Where do they think 'teacher' would be ranked in an overall list of jobs in your country?

BE COLLABORATIVE

Your development is more meaningful when it is shared. See page 14 for ideas on how to peer-collaborate. Why not share the strategies you explored in the *Be flexible* section, and their impact on the lesson?

GRAMMAR FOR WRITING

Learning objectives

- Use the active voice to introduce ideas shown in figures – *Figure 5 shows how the report's authors measured job quality.*
- Use the passive voice to use a figure as support for a point – *These are illustrated in Figure 5.*

Exercise 1 page 151

1 B   2 A   3 D   4 C

Exercise 2 page 152

1 C   2 B   3 D   4 A

Exercise 3 page 152

1 (active *Possible answer:* shows)   2 (passive *Possible answer:* are shown)   3 (active *Possible answer:* displays, active *Possible answer:* shows)   4 (active *Possible answer:* depicts)   5 (passive *Possible answer:* are listed)

Exercise 4 page 152

Answers will vary. Possible answers:

Figure 1, Reading 1: Figure 1 shows the results of an annual survey of about 42,000 companies worldwide. The percentage of companies with difficulty filling positions fell from 41% to 30% in 2009, but rose back to 38% in 2015.

Figure 2, Reading 1: Figure 2 displays the predicted job growth in computing jobs. There will be 1,000,000 more jobs than qualified applicants by 2020, presenting a $500 billion opportunity for jobseekers and the economy.

Figure 1, Reading 2: The number of people getting a university education rose in OECD countries around the world between the years 2000 and 2012. This information is illustrated in Figure 1, which shows the percentage of the population with a university education in a selection of OECD countries.

Figure 2, Reading 2: Figure 2 illustrates the impact of a degree on income in a selection of OECD countries. It shows that having a degree dramatically increases an individual's ability to earn above the median income in all countries.

Be flexible

👤 If students need additional practice, they can continue the pattern of Exercise 4, using the graphs and charts (A–D) in Exercise 1.

For more practice that is less challenging, ask **lower-level students** to match graph chart types to these specific kinds of data:

- Median income for different jobs (bar/column)
- Percentage response to a survey based on age (line)
- Average number of student visits to careers adviser since 2000 (histogram/column)
- Percentage of graduates employed in five different professions (pie)

Then tell them to write a sentence to introduce each of these charts and graphs.

ACADEMIC WRITING SKILLS

Learning objectives

- Use specific criteria to evaluate the effectiveness of thesis statements for an essay about the skills gap

Exercise 1 page 153

b

Exercise 2 page 153

Answers will vary. Possible answers:

a 1 Possibly, but not a clear one, e.g. the claim could be about the timeframe or the fact that it is an economic problem. **2** No; the claim is likely to be seen as a fact rather than an opinion that can be argued with. **3** No **4** No

b 1 Yes; the whole statement is a claim. **2** Yes **3** Yes **4** No

c 1 Yes; the whole statement is a claim. **2** Yes **3** No **4** It doesn't give readers a clear enough idea about the changes in the economy that might have led to the skills gap.

d 1 No

e 1 Yes **2** Yes **3** Yes **4** Yes; the claim is too detailed.

WRITING TASK

Learning objectives

- Plan and draft an essay describing the job market in your country and suggesting a secure career path
- Review and revise the content and structure of your essay
- Review and revise the use of language in your essay

Exercises 1–10 pages 154–156

Answers will vary.

RESEARCH PROJECT

Write a set of guidelines on occupational trends, to assist current and future students in choosing a career.

Ask students to work in groups, with each group working on an occupational area, e.g. art and design, education, transportation, sales, management, farming. They should find out:

- what jobs are available within that sector
- education, training and other qualifications needed to enter the occupation
- salary range
- job prospects and any anticipated changes in trends.

If possible, they should consult the government office (e.g. Office for National Statistics: www.ons.gov.uk) that reports on labour statistics and occupational trends. The guidelines should include graphical information. If feasible, all the groups should report the same information in a similar format so that readers can easily compare occupations and their trends.

CLASSROOM APP

Exercises 1–2

Answers will vary.

Exercise 3

1 persistent   **2** expertise   **3** prospective   **4** mismatch
5 chronic   **6** dispute   **7** ambiguity   **8** multiple

Exercise 4

1 balance   **2** power   **3** scheme   **4** level
5 market   **6** curve   **7** professional

Exercise 5

1 illustrates   **2** are demonstrated   **3** is depicted
4 shows   **5** is illustrated

Exercise 6

1 B Claim does not include opinion

2 C Claim has too much detail

3 D Claim is not specific enough

4 A Claim is correct

UNIT OBJECTIVES	
Watch and listen	Watch and understand a video about the growing concerns over antibiotics.
Reading skill	Recognize discourse organization.
Critical thinking	Analyze causes and effects.
Grammar	Use logical connectors with causes and effects.
Academic writing skill	Write about causes and effects.
Writing task	Write a cause-and-effect essay.
⟳ **Teacher development**	Help your students become better at **analyzing causes and effects**.

UNL⟳CK YOUR KNOWLEDGE

Background note

The photo shows two women standing on the street – one of them is wearing a surgical mask and the other is covering her hand with her mouth. The use of surgical masks in public has grown in popularity since the 2002–2003 SARS epidemic and the 2006 avian flu outbreak. According to the World Health Organization, two of the greatest threats to global health are influenza and resistance to antibiotics. Since the Spanish Flu pandemic that killed almost 100 million people between 1918 and 1920, health authorities around the world have improved their response to early symptoms of a flu outbreak, but nobody can predict when and where another will occur. Local and international travel increases the risk of a pandemic.

Lead-in

Ask students what they do when they get ill. Do they immediately go to the doctor? Do they try to get better on their own? Do they use over-the-counter medications?

page 159
Answers will vary.

WATCH AND LISTEN

Learning objectives

- Listen, take notes and summarize the main ideas in a video about antibiotics
- Listen and note examples of main ideas
- Listen and identify the meaning of unfamiliar words and phrases from their context in the video
- Practise talking about the future of antibiotics

Exercises 1–2 page 160
Answers will vary.

Exercise 3 page 161

1 The scientists are trying to deal with the problem of increasing antibiotic resistance in bacteria.
2 The problem has been caused by overuse of antibiotics.
3 The scientists are investigating how plants protect themselves from predators.

Exercise 4 page 161

Answers will vary. Possible answers:

1 MRSA infection; injuries from diving accident
2 medicine; agriculture
3 warnings have been ignored; lack of funding
4 stop overuse (in humans and animals); create (a sustainable supply of) new drugs; change public attitudes
5 large animals; small animals; insects; bacteria

Exercise 5 page 161

Answers will vary. Possible answers:

1 given a lot of; fight/beat
2 giving false warnings; university researchers and teachers; scientists who study very small living things such as bacteria
3 a medicine which can cure any kind of health problem
4 clear; very many

Exercise 6 page 161
Answers will vary.

READING 1

Learning objectives

- Understand key vocabulary for superbugs – *grim, thrive, phase out*
- Use the introduction to an essay about superbugs to understand discourse organization
- Read and complete cause-and-effect chains about drug resistance
- Identify the meaning of unfamiliar phrases from their context in the article
- Identify the purpose and context of the article
- Give opinions on issues related to drug-resistance

Lead-in

Write the word *antibiotic* on the board. Ask students to analyze the word. What is the prefix? What does *anti*-mean (against)? What does *bio* mean (life)? Why would a medicine be called 'against life'? If they cannot guess, let students know that antibiotics actually kill harmful microorganisms.

Exercise 1 page 162

Answers will vary.

Exercise 2 pages 162–163

1 b **2** a **3** a **4** c **5** c **6** c **7** a **8** b

Exercise 3 page 163

c

Exercise 4 page 163

describe the causes or consequences of things

Optional activity

👤 Tell students to think back to other texts they have read in the class. You may want to choose one or two specific texts. What kind of discourse organization did they have? Explain that the texts often include several types of organization. For example, in the Business unit, Reading 1 explains how mobile retail works, but it also compares advantages and disadvantages. Reading 2 is more of a straight compare and contrast (reward schemes and subscription services). The goal here is to help students understand that real texts rarely display pure rhetorical modes.

Exercise 5 page 165

2 patients do not finish their course of medication
3 non-therapeutic use of antibiotics on livestock
5 only drug-resistant bacteria reproduce / drug-resistant strains of bacteria thrive

Exercise 6 page 165

1 b **2** e **3** a **4** c **5** d

Exercises 7–8 page 165

Answers will vary.

READING 2

Lead-in

Ask students to name recent global health scares. Write the names on the board. They may mention Ebola, avian flu, MERS or Zika virus. Ask what makes these diseases special; in other words, why were those diseases in the news?

Learning objectives

- Scan an article about the globalization of infection to find key information
- Understand key vocabulary for the globalization of infection – *transmission, eradicate, detection*
- Read and understand the writer's main arguments
- Read and identify factors in the globalization of infection
- Complete cause-and-effect chains about the globalization of infection
- Make inferences about the ideas and information in the article
- Synthesize information from an article about superbugs and an article about the globalization of infection in a discussion

Exercise 1 page 166

1 a mosquito found in Africa and Asia **2** carries chikungunya **3** shows which parts of the US *Aedes aegypti* lives in **4** The US habitats of the *Aedes aegypti* and *Aedes albopictus* are similar in that both can be found in the southern part of the country. The habitat of the *Aedes albopictus*, however, extends farther north. **5** *Answers will vary.*

Exercise 2 page 166

a detection **b** proximity **c** surge **d** facilitate
e transmission **f** confined to **g** domesticated
h eradicate

Exercise 3 page 168

a

Exercise 4 page 168

Students should circle items a, b and e.

1 long-distance travel   **2** urbanization – overcrowding, no waste collection, lack of clean water supply
3 deforestation and urbanization = close proximity to both wild and domesticated animals   **4** overcrowding of domesticated animals

Exercise 5 pages 168–169

Chain 1: urbanization → **(a)** overcrowded cities → **(b)** people live in areas without running water → **(c)** people collect water → **(d)** mosquitoes breed freely → **(e)** diseases spread more easily

Chain 2: urbanization → **(a)** habitat destruction → **(b)** animals and humans live close together → **(c)** disease is transmitted across species

Exercise 6 page 169

1 *Answers will vary.*   **2 (b)** viruses travel with humans or insects **(c)** vectors transfer infected blood to new victim

---

Optional activity

Ask students to consider a less serious, but still real case – say, an outbreak of a virus in their school. In groups, they write a short chain of events. At this point, there is no need to push them to use causal connectors. That will come in the next exercise. For example:

One person at the school fell ill. He came to school when he was ill, and so the disease spread. He touched a door knob, then somebody else touched the same door knob. That person didn't wash his hands right away and then touched his nose or eyes. The virus infected this second person. Soon others became infected in the same way.

Groups share their descriptions.

Exercise 7 page 169

Answers will vary.

LANGUAGE DEVELOPMENT

Learning objectives

- Use common verb + verb phrases in sentences to describe causation – *Climate change leads to higher temperatures. The increasingly urban nature of the world's population also facilitates the transmission of disease.*
- Use the correct form of words related to global health and medicine – *The spread of infectious disease is a complex phenomenon. A bacterial infection triggers an automatic defensive response.*

Exercise 1 pages 170–171

Answers will vary. Possible answers:

1 promoted / facilitated / been a factor in   **2** contributes to / influences / causes / results in / brings about / has a role in / facilitates / promotes / encourages / enables / allows (present perfect simple is also possible for all verb forms here)   **3** allows/permits   **4** causes / leads to / results in / triggers / produces   **5** / allowing / causing / helping / enabling

Exercise 2 page 171

Answers will vary.

Exercise 3 page 171

1 access   **2** accessible   **3** bacterial   **4** infection
5 infect   **6** mutation   **7** prevent   **8** preventable
9 preventative   **10** resistance   **11** resist   **12** therapeutic
13 transmit   **14** transmittable   **15** viral

Exercise 4 page 171

1 bacterial   **2** viral   **3** transmitted   **4** mutate
5 resistant   **6** therapeutic   **7** prevent   **8** infecting

---

Optional activity

Tell students to rewrite and expand their descriptions from the Language development Lead-in, this time using words about global health from the chart in Exercise 3.

CRITICAL THINKING

Learning objectives

- Remember factors that have contributed to the globalization of infection
- Understand information relating to infectious diseases
- Analyze the reliability and relevance of sources of information relating to infectious diseases
- Research and create a case history for an infectious disease
- Evaluate which factors have played a role in the development or spread of a disease
- Evaluate and explain the consequences of catching an infectious disease for individuals and families
- Create cause-and-effect chains for an infectious disease

UNLOCK TEACHER DEVELOPMENT

BE INFORMED

→ **Analyzing causes and effects** is an important skill for students because: (1) In academic writing or speaking, the ability to show cause and effect (how one thing directly results in something else happening) is crucial; (2) The relationship between causes and effects is frequently misunderstood – events and actions which look like they have a causal relationship may actually not have such a relationship; (3) When presenting findings, in scientific subjects in particular, students have to be careful not to overstate how strong the link is between cause and effect.

BE CONFIDENT

→ Develop this skill for yourself by doing the following activity:

Look at the following sentences. Is the link between cause and effect accurate and clear? For the sentences which you think are incorrect, how could you rewrite them?

I failed my test because I saw a black cat on my way to school.

Learning about critical thinking helps you analyze the world more effectively.

Doing well in your exams will lead to a higher paid job.

When you boil water, it turns into steam.

A good way to help students develop critical thinking skills is to give them many opportunities to practise.

Lead-in

Give students a minute to read the writing task. Tell them they will see example case studies of Chikungunya, Dengue fever and Zika virus to help them. They should then brainstorm in groups other global infectious diseases, and what they know of them. Tell them to keep their brainstorming notes for later, when they begin to write their essay.

UNLOCK TEACHER DEVELOPMENT

BE READY

Look at the Critical Thinking section in the Student's Book on pages 172–175.

→ Which elements of the lesson do you think your students will find easiest / most difficult / most useful? Why?

→ Are your answers true for all students in your class?

→ How can you adapt your teaching or the material to meet your students' needs?

BE FLEXIBLE

The critical thinking section in this unit is quite long. You might consider 'flipping' some of the learning and getting students to do it at home before the lesson (e.g. Exercises 3 and 4).

Exercises 1–7 pages 172–175

Answers will vary.

UNLOCK TEACHER DEVELOPMENT

BE REFLECTIVE

Think about the following points:

→ Did you 'flip' the learning in your lesson, as suggested in *Be flexible*? If so, how did this work, and would you do it again? If not, consider trying to use this approach in a future lesson, and see how it works.

→ With your colleagues, either on paper or electronically, create a cause-and-effect chain for teaching critical thinking, showing the benefits which it can result in for your students.

BE COLLABORATIVE

Your development is more meaningful when it is shared. See page 14 for ideas on how to peer-collaborate. Why not share the ideas you generated in the *Be ready* section, and their outcome?

GRAMMAR FOR WRITING

Learning objectives

- Express cause and effect using logical connectors in sentences about factors in the globalization of infection
- Express cause and effect using logical connectors in sentences describing the consequences of infections

Exercises 1–2 page 177

Answers will vary.

ACADEMIC WRITING SKILLS

Learning objectives

- Write a paragraph which is either a causal analysis or an effect analysis about a cause-and-effect chain

Exercise 1 pages 177–178

1
- Glaciers are melting: getting weaker and smaller. 2
- There is an increase in shipping and other commercial activities. 5
- Floating ice, an important habitat for polar animals, is disappearing. X
- Arctic areas are more accessible to humans. 4
- Sea ice is melting. X
- Strong Arctic storms are more frequent. X
- Arctic animals, such as polar bears, have become endangered. X
- The ocean is getting warmer. 1
- Storms are breaking up weak areas of glaciers. 3

Exercise 2 page 178

cause: have had a dramatic impact...; fuelled by

effect: ... has weakened the glaciers, making them ...; As a consequence, ...

This is an effect analysis.

Exercise 3 page 178

Answers will vary.

WRITING TASK

Learning objectives

- Plan and draft an essay which explains the development or spread of a disease
- Review and revise the content and structure of your essay
- Review and revise the use of language in your essay

Exercises 1–8 pages 179–180

Answers will vary.

RESEARCH PROJECT

Make a poster presentation on eradication and response strategies to a disease.

Students should focus on the disease that they wrote about for their writing task. Ask them to do research on what has been / can be done (1) to eradicate this disease, and (2) to respond to an outbreak of this disease in the future, and to answer these questions:

- How can the spread be stopped?
- What is the best way to treat those who fall ill?

They should create a poster that communicates these ideas in a brief and effective manner and present it to the class.

CLASSROOM APP

Exercises 1–2

Answers will vary.

Exercise 3

1 revolutionized **2** surge **3** transmission **4** detection
5 facilitate **6** resistance **7** problematic **8** counter

Exercise 4

1 leading **2** contributes **3** is a result of
4 are the result of **5** bring **6** have an effect **7** result in

Exercise 5

1 Virus **2** therapeutic **3** transmission **4** resistance
5 transmit **6** infect

Exercise 6

1 cause analysis **2** effect analysis **3** mixed analysis
4 mixed analysis **5** effect analysis

UNIT OBJECTIVES	
Watch and listen	Watch and understand a video about an elite aerobatics display team.
Reading skill	Use context clues to understand terminology and fixed expressions.
Critical thinking	Understand audience and purpose.
Grammar	Make concessions and refute counter-arguments.
Academic writing skill	Anticipate counter-arguments.
Writing task	Write a report giving recommendations.
⟳ **Teacher development**	Help your students become better at **understanding audience and purpose**.

UNLOCK YOUR KNOWLEDGE

Background note

The photo shows a Formula One (F1) race car during a pit stop; this is when the pit crew services the car and makes any necessary repairs during a race. Pit crews are well-known for their collaboration and speed. The fastest pit crew in F1 completed their record-winning pit stop in less than two seconds. It is often observed that the time lost during the pit stop can determine the results of the race; therefore collaboration and teamwork at the pit stop are essential. In the reading passages, students learn about different aspects of successful teamwork.

Lead-in

Ask students if they have ever played or worked on a team, e.g. sport, debating. Did members of the team work well together? Ask them to brainstorm the factors that make a team successful. Write their ideas on the board.

page 183

Answers will vary.

WATCH AND LISTEN

Exercises 1–2 page 184

Answers will vary.

Exercise 3 page 185

6, 8, 2, 1, 7, 4, 5, 3

Exercise 4 page 185

Answers will vary. Possible answers:

1 pilots; engineers; support staff   **2** highly trained; highly skilled; motivated   **3** first permanent change to the design since the Red Arrows were formed in 1964   **4** windy weather conditions   **5** travel to displays in the seat behind the pilot   **6** make legs tense against them; stop blood from pooling in legs; keep blood pumping to head   **7** two pilots died (in separate incidents) **8** that it is too high

Exercise 5 page 185

Answers will vary. Possible answers:

1 to celebrate/commemorate the 50-year anniversary of the Red Arrows team   **2** The work they do is essential; without their work, the Red Arrows jets could not fly. **3** Their blood might not reach the pilots' brains, so they might lose consciousness and have an accident. **4** They do something that rest of the world admires: they show Britain's strength in an exciting and non-aggressive display.

Exercise 6 page 185

Answers will vary.

READING 1

Learning objectives

- Use the first sentence of each paragraph to preview an article about talent in teams
- Understand key vocabulary for talent in teams – *accomplish, amass, coordinate*
- Read and understand main ideas and detailed information

- Complete a summary of an article
- Read and understand the meaning of unfamiliar words and phrases using different kinds of context clues
- Describe experiences of teamwork

Lead-in

Write this sentence on the board:

I seem to have mislaid the document you signed yesterday. I've looked everywhere but I can't find it.

It is likely that students have not seen the word *mislaid* before, but they can probably guess its meaning. Have them guess, and then ask what clues they used. This exemplifies two of the clue types from the skills box on page 189 (word components and logical inference).

Exercise 1 page 186

Answers will vary.

Exercise 2 page 186

1 enhance **2** coordinate **3** peaked **4** accomplished **5** amassed **6** differentiate **7** detracted from **8** isolate

Exercise 3 page 187

Answers will vary. Possible answers:

1. Much of the work in today's world is accomplished in teams: in business, in scientific research, in government, on film sets, and of course, in sport.
2. Animal scientist William Muir wondered if he could build such an A-team – with chickens.
3. Of course, chickens are not a team, but this kind of group interaction and its effect on production piqued the interest of researchers who study teams and teamwork.
4. In looking for an explanation for the different results for different sport, the researchers isolated one important factor – the extent to which a good performance by a team requires its members to coordinate their actions.
5. Assembling the ideal team – for sport, business, science, or entertainment – is more complicated than simply hiring the best talent.

Exercise 4 page 187

1 detract **2** performance **3** basketball **4** coordinate **5** pursue

Exercise 5 page 187

Answers will vary. Possible answers:

a task interdependence: the extent to which a good performance by a team requires its members to coordinate their actions **b the Ringelmann effect:** when there is a lot of talent on a team, some players may begin to make less effort

Exercise 6 page 189

Answers will vary. Possible answers:

1 A-team refers to the best possible team or group of people you could have working together. It is not limited to sport. **2 pecking order** could relate to the fact that some members of the team are better than others and, therefore, have more power in the group. **3 tug-of-war:** There are two teams on either side of a rope. Both teams tug, or pull, on the rope with the goal of pulling the other team over a line. The team that pulls the hardest wins. The term could be used in other contexts when trying to explain how two groups or teams are fighting over the same thing.

Exercise 7 page 190

Answers will vary.

Optional activity

Ask students if they prefer to work alone, in pairs or in groups. Why? What are the benefits and drawbacks of each in an academic setting?

READING 2

Learning objectives

- Understand key vocabulary for group intelligence – *gesture, distraction, underlie*
- Read and understand main ideas and detailed information in an article about group intelligence
- Summarize an article and respond to feedback to improve your summary
- Read and understand the meaning of fixed expressions using context clues
- Synthesize information from an article about talent in teams and an article about group intelligence in a discussion

Lead-in

Students turn to page 191 and cover the definitions in Exercise 1. They should try to guess the approximate meaning of the bold words before looking at the definitions. Then they uncover the definitions, complete the exercise and check if their guesses were correct.

Exercise 1 page 190

Answers will vary.

Exercise 2 page 191

a fundamental   **b** exclusively   **c** underlie   **d** gesture
e distraction   **f** sensitivity   **g** stems from   **h** voice

Exercise 3 page 191

1 F   **2** F   **3** T   **4** T   **5** F   **6** F

Exercise 4 page 191

Answers will vary. Possible answers:

1 Early investigations suggest that group intelligence is not the sum of the intelligence of the individuals in it.

2 In fact, who was in the group apparently did not seem to make a difference; instead, the difference between more and less effective groups seemed to lie in the interaction among the members

3 Among the findings, the most consistent and significant is that, in effective groups, members spoke for a roughly equal amount of time – not at every meeting or interaction, but across the course of a project.

4 A second consistent finding was that members displayed empathy, an understanding of how it might feel to walk in somebody else's shoes.

5 All the findings underline the importance of having face-to-face meetings instead of phone calls, teleconferences or communicating by email.

6 Understanding group intelligence can help business and other organizations make fundamental changes necessary to improve group performance.

Exercises 5–6 page 191

Answers will vary.

Exercise 7 page 193

2 Members displayed empathy   **3** Face each other directly when they speak   **5** Communicate directly with one another, not just through the leader / Side conversations in meetings increased the group's productivity   **6** Positive behaviours occur primarily or exclusively in face-to-face interaction

Exercise 8 page 193

Answers will vary. Possible answers:

a group intelligence: the ability of a group to make good decisions or perform well on tasks   **b psychological safety:** the feeling of being able to express your ideas within a group without a negative response

Exercise 9 page 193

Answers will vary. Possible answers:

1 have a handle on: have a basic understanding of

2 walk in somebody else's shoes: understand how another person feels and why they feel that way before judging them   **3 needless to say:** so obvious that you don't need to say it (and usually said before you do say it)

Optional activity

👥 Students play a game in small groups. One member of the group finds a difficult word in the dictionary. It should be a word that other members of the group probably don't know. Then that student writes a sentence with context clues that help the other members of the group guess the meaning. If group members successfully guess the (approximate) meaning, that student gets a point.

Exercise 10 page 194

Answers will vary.

LANGUAGE DEVELOPMENT

Learning objectives

• Use hedging language to make claims more modest in sentences about collaboration – *Some groups seem to work well across tasks, even tasks that are not very similar. An A-team may require a balance – not just A players, but a few generous B players as well.*

Exercise 1 page 195

Answers will vary. Possible answers:

1 Human error is often the cause of traffic fatalities.
2 There is evidence that lack of sleep leads to both emotional and physical problems.   **3** If you know your personality type, you may be able to find the job that is best for you.   **4** Typically, tall people make the best basketball players.   **5** Generally, people who are obese are likely to develop diabetes.   **6** It is widely believed that we will run out of fossil fuels in about 100 years.

Exercise 2 page 195

Answers will vary.

Be flexible

👤👥 Tell students to review either of the readings in this unit to find examples of hedged language. Ask them to underline examples and then compare their work with a partner's. Challenge **stronger students** to review a text from their own field and identify examples of hedged language.

CRITICAL THINKING

Learning objectives

- Understand the purpose, audience and typical features of an executive summary
- Understand and apply the information from a text about effective work teams
- Evaluate and analyze the requirements and challenges facing a company
- Make recommendations to a company to meet its requirements and address its challenges

UNLOCK TEACHER DEVELOPMENT

BE INFORMED

→ **Understanding audience and purpose** is an important skill for students because: (1) It is important to know why a text was written – what the motivation was behind it – as this significantly impacts its contents; (2) All texts have two primary purposes – to inform or to persuade – and being aware of this will help your students become more active readers; (3) Students themselves need to know how their audience and purpose will impact their own writing in terms of language choices, structure, length, style, etc.

BE CONFIDENT

→ Develop this skill for yourself by doing the following activity:

Read the texts below. In each case decide (a) who the audience is, and (b) what the purpose is. Think in particular about the typical features of each text.

1 Smith and Jones (2017) provide clear support for this position.

2 Buy one, get one free. This deal ends Saturday, be quick!!!

3 First add the eggs to the milk and mix them together. Then cook.

4 For years this government has failed. We need change, and soon.

5 I spoke to your company on the 12th but have had no response.

6 The data show the changes made in 2015 have been successful.

Lead-in

Give students a minute to read the writing task. Tell them to brainstorm the specific issues that might affect the staff of a start-up company. Tell them to keep their brainstorming notes for later, when they begin to write their essay.

UNLOCK TEACHER DEVELOPMENT

BE READY

Look at the Critical Thinking section in the Student's Book on pages 196–199.

→ Which elements of the lesson do you think your students will find easiest / most difficult / most useful? Why?

→ Are your answers true for all students in your class?

→ How can you adapt your teaching or the material to meet your students' needs?

BE FLEXIBLE

Before the lesson, think of different text types which your students might be familiar with. These would be useful to include in the lesson as they might be a 'way in' for weaker groups.

Exercise 1 page 196

Answers will vary. Possible answers:

1 to decrease staff turnover and increase employee satisfaction

2 company management

3 Executive summary: a statement summarizing the content of the report; introduction describing specific problem and giving facts and figures; outline of methodology of report into workplace satisfaction; summary of results of each type of investigation undertaken; list of recommendations.

Exercise 2 page 198

Answers will vary.

Exercise 3 page 198

Answers will vary. Possible answers:

1 to win the bid for the job for a major international food service company

2 to decrease staff turnover, lower employee stress and increase employee satisfaction

3 *Answers will vary.*

Exercise 4 page 199

Answers will vary.

UNLOCK TEACHER DEVELOPMENT

BE REFLECTIVE

Think about the following questions:

→ Were students able to make the link between 'theory' and 'practice' in this lesson? Could they (1) understand the key information, and (2) identify examples of this in the text? Why / Why not?

→ If students found this difficult, is there anything you could have done differently?

BE COLLABORATIVE

Your development is more meaningful when it is shared. See page 14 for ideas on how to peer-collaborate. Why not share the texts you sourced in the *Be flexible* section, and their impact on the lesson?

GRAMMAR FOR WRITING

Learning objective

- Use appropriate structures to concede points and express counter-arguments in relation to commonly held misconceptions

Exercises 1–2 pages 201–202

Answers will vary.

Optional activity

👤 Tell students to review the readings to find an example of acknowledgement and concession in each. Let them know that the rebuttal and support for a claim do not always follow immediately. For example, the first reading begins with the alternative perspective (the best team consists of all the top performers) and gradually builds a case to counter it. The example in the second reading comes in the final paragraph.

ACADEMIC WRITING SKILLS

Learning objective

- Write a paragraph refuting an opposing point of view which includes concession statements and adequate support for counter-arguments

Exercises 1–2 pages 202–203

Answers will vary.

WRITING TASK

Learning objectives

- Plan and draft a report containing recommendations for assembling an effective team for a start-up company
- Review and revise the content and structure of your essay
- Review and revise the use of language in your essay

Exercises 1–10 pages 202–204

Answers will vary.

RESEARCH PROJECT

Give a group presentation on effective team-building strategies.

Students work in groups to research team-building strategies. Each group should select one activity. The first part of their project should report on the research, including a description of the activity, the rationale behind it, as well as any data/analysis on its effectiveness. The second part will be their analysis of whether they think it would be an effective strategy for a company in their country.

Students will then present their research findings to the rest of the class. The class could then decide which of the strategies they think would be the most effective.

CLASSROOM APP

Exercises 1–2

Answers will vary.

Exercise 3

1 coordinate　**2** differentiate　**3** stem from　**4** enhances
5 distractions　**6** voice　**7** sensitivity　**8** accomplished

Exercise 4

1 hedged claim　**2** bold claim　**3** bold claim
4 hedged claim　**5** hedged claim　**6** bold claim

Exercise 5

1 generally　**2** tend to　**3** typically　**4** often
5 perhaps　**6** assumed

Exercise 6

1 While　**2** Although　**3** on the other hand
4 However,　**5** Despite　**6** although

UNIT OBJECTIVES

Watch and listen	Watch and understand a video about mobile phone hacking.
Reading skill	Draw out common themes.
Critical thinking	Construct an argument using a premise.
Grammar	Use parenthetical phrases; use the semicolon.
Academic writing skill	Use formal style in academic writing.
Writing task	Write an argumentative essay.
⟳ **Teacher development**	Help your students become better at **constructing an argument using a premise**.

UNLOCK YOUR KNOWLEDGE

Background note

The photo shows a woman taking a selfie with a humanoid robot called RoboThespian. RoboThespian robots can move their arms, and can hold eye contact while answering questions in 30 languages. RoboThespians are sold to universities, museums and other companies to entertain the public at exhibitions and events. The company that built RoboThespian continues to develop the robots to improve their mobility range, such as walking and jumping. Some other technologies that are being developed at the moment are self-driving cars, solar-powered vehicles, mixed reality apps that help doctors, and real-time language translation apps and devices.

Lead-in

Find out where and when students use digital technology the most intensively. They may use it so automatically that they rarely reflect on it. In small groups, students make a list of their top five uses. They should name a general category and then a specific example, e.g. financial: payments by phone.

page 207
Answers will vary.

WATCH AND LISTEN

Learning objectives

- Use visuals to predict the main ideas in a video about phone hacking
- Listen and identify the main idea in the video
- Listen for detailed information
- Identify the meaning of unfamiliar words and phrases from their context in the video
- Practise talking about mobile phone security

Exercises 1–2 page 208
Answers will vary.

Exercise 3 page 208

2

Exercise 4 pages 208–209

1 You could only talk for 30 minutes and it was easy to eavesdrop on people's conversations.   **2** They protect the phones of the celebrities.   **3** 3G is quite secure but Wi-Fi is easy to hack.   **4** By setting up a bait network or by monitoring what networks mobile phones are looking for and duplicating them.   **5** They harvest login details for social media and email accounts.   **6** By not using free Wi-Fi networks and by having a different password for each website you use.

Exercise 5 page 209

a 5   **b** 4   **c** 2   **d** 6   **e** 1   **f** 3

Exercise 6 page 209
Answers will vary.

READING 1

Learning objectives

- Understand key vocabulary for augmented reality – *superimpose, immersive, projection*
- Read and understand main ideas and details in a popular science blog about augmented reality
- Identify common themes across a popular science blog and use them to summarize the blog
- Identify and evaluate speculations in an article about augmented reality
- Give opinions and speculate about the possibilities of AR technology

Lead-in

Find out if students have ever played augmented reality games. If so, ask a volunteer to describe the experience. If not, let a volunteer describe a virtual reality game experience. This will allow you to point to the distinction when students do the first reading.

Exercise 1 page 210

Answers will vary.

Exercise 2 page 210

1 hazards   **2** immersive   **3** simultaneous   **4** supplement
5 domain   **6** projection   **7** superimpose   **8** interpretation

Exercise 3 page 212

c

Optional activity

👤👥 Tell students to use the strategies they have learnt to work out meaning from context to find the meaning of these words and phrases in Paragraph 6:

- *uptake*
- *internal organs*
- *circulatory system*
- *failed needle insertions*

Then they share their definitions with a partner.

Exercise 4 page 212

AR involves ~~an immersive 3-D experience~~ **overlaying the world around us with digital content.** A common use of AR is visually mapping and providing procedures for complex systems, such as machines and the human body. AR technology allows technicians to view blueprints overlaid on the field and to ~~identify faults with~~ **display step-by-step instructions on how to maintain broken machines**. Medical professionals can see patients' ~~bones~~ **internal organs and circulatory system** projected onto their skin as a guide. AR also allows student doctors to practise ~~on real bodies~~ **without live patients**.
Other applications of AR technology involve providing information about the real-time environment. Travellers can use AR apps to see information about places and to translate ~~spoken~~ **written** words. Using a ~~smartphone screen~~ **dashboard-mounted set**, AR GPS apps can project directions and traffic information on the windscreen.

Exercise 5 page 212

A common use of AR is visually mapping and providing procedures for complex systems, such as machines and the human body. Other applications of AR technology involve providing information about the real-time environment.

Exercises 6–9 pages 212–213

Answers will vary.

READING 2

Learning objectives

- Understand key vocabulary for technology in education – *aid, advocate, engaging*
- Read and Identify the main ideas an essay about technology in education
- Read and make detailed notes in a table
- Read and identify the meaning of unfamiliar words and phrases from their context
- Synthesize information from two articles about AR technology in a discussion

Lead-in

Students have read about the use of AR in transportation, engineering and medicine. In what other areas do they envision AR being useful? Make a list on the board.

Exercise 1 page 213

a embrace   **b** advocate   **c** aid   **d** engaging   **e** inspect
f numerous   **g** novelty   **h** manipulate

Exercises 2–3 page 214

Answers will vary.

Exercise 4 page 214

a 6   **b** 5   **c** –   **d** 2   **e** –   **f** 4   **g** 3

Exercise 5 page 214

Answers will vary. Possible answers:

current applications: supplementing course content with 3-D projections; students can examine the anatomy of different species or models of human organs

future applications: students might be able to see natural phenomena; students could explore ancient monuments or engage with historic figures; students from remote schools may be able to visit famous places using AR

reported benefits: an increase in student motivation; understanding of the subject and enjoyment in studying; better learning performance and long-term memory retention

possible drawbacks: attention tunnelling, distracted by the technology

Exercise 6 page 216

a 3   **b** 5   **c** 2   **d** 4   **e** 1

Exercise 7 page 216

Answers will vary.

LANGUAGE DEVELOPMENT

Learning objectives

- Use appropriate verbs to report expert opinions in sentences about augmented reality research results – *Bacca et al. (2014) claim that students who used AR in their classes reported better understanding of the subject. Radu (2014) maintains that educational AR applications lead to better long-term memory retention.*
- Use *it* clefts to emphasize specific information in sentences about technology – *It is students who have benefited the most from the introduction of AR technology in science classes. It is the introduction of AR technology which students have benefited the most from in science classes.*

Exercise 1 page 217

a maintain b assert c suggest d claim e conclude
f acknowledge g state h observe

Exercise 2 page 218

1 acknowledge 2 claimed 3 suggests 4 states
5 maintain

Exercise 3 page 218

Answers will vary.

Exercise 4 page 219

1 ✗ It is the internet that/which has revolutionized education in remote areas of the world. 2 ✗ It is in development of new innovations that we invest most of our time and effort. 3 ✓ 4 ✗ It is in the classroom that the usefulness of the new technologies is really tested.
5 ✗ It is not until we have trialled new technology in the classroom that we can draw any conclusions about its usefulness.

Exercise 5 page 220

1 It is parents who have the greatest influence over a child's development.

2 It is the 3-D projections created by AR that/which allow learners to visualize complex phenomena.

3 It is rural schools that/which should be funded to incorporate AR technology into their classrooms.

4 It is only when we acknowledge its limitations that we can improve new technology.

5 It is record keeping that/which is made easier for teachers by cloud computing. / It is record keeping that cloud computing makes easier for teachers.

CRITICAL THINKING

Learning objectives

- Analyze the benefits and drawbacks of using different types of technology in education
- Analyze arguments for and against using a technology in education
- Evaluate and improve your arguments regarding the use of a technology in a classroom

UNLOCK TEACHER DEVELOPMENT

BE INFORMED

➜ **Constructing an argument using a premise** is an important skill for students because: (1) A clear and accurate understanding of an argument's premise can help you evaluate whether the overall argument is good; (2) Constructing an argument based on a premise should lead to your arguments being more solid; (3) When using a premise, it is likely that your argument will be more objective, which is desirable in most academic subjects.

BE CONFIDENT

➜ Develop this skill for yourself by doing the following activity:

Look at the following arguments. In each case decide (a) what is/are the premise(s), and (b) what is the conclusion?

- Your body benefits from you eating vegetables since they contain so many vitamins.
- Seeing that the overwhelming majority of climate experts agree that humans are causing global warming, it is highly likely that humans are causing global warming.
- Every year computers get more and more powerful, which means that computer operations are becoming much faster.
- Social media companies will not be able to expand so quickly in the future because their coverage is already very high in so many countries.

Lead-in

Give students a minute to read the writing task. Tell them to brainstorm the types of educational technology they have experienced themselves or one that they know about that would be a good candidate for this task. Tell them to keep their brainstorming notes for later, when they begin to write their essay.

UNL☾CK TEACHER DEVELOPMENT

BE READY

Look at the Critical Thinking section in the Student's Book on pages 221–222.

➔ Which elements of the lesson do you think your students will find easiest / most difficult / most useful? Why?

➔ Are your answers true for all students in your class?

➔ How can you adapt your teaching or the material to meet your students' needs?

BE FLEXIBLE

Try and anticipate potential exercises in lessons which your students might find difficult. For example, you could identify some specific technologies which students could analyze in Exercise 3. In addition, think about your students' specific areas of study, or the exams which they might take. Some of them place considerable importance on this kind of logical reasoning. It may be that you can tie this lesson to these very practical outcomes.

Exercise 1 page 221

Answers will vary. Possible answers:

cloud computing		
features	benefits	drawbacks
Students can access e-books and digital materials easily.	Saves paper No need to carry heavy books Students around the world have the same access to books	E-books could be plagiarized easily Can't make personal notes in the e-books E-books not available if the internet fails

cloud computing		
features	benefits	drawbacks
Students can take exams online.	Students in distant locations can take them More students can take the exams Exams can be shared and standardized more easily	Exams could be stolen easily Issues with monitoring adequately and cheating Technical issues Limitations of type of exam possible
Students can communicate with other students via a webcam.	Students can work on projects together from home	Students may be wasting their time by chatting online instead of working
Students can listen to lectures at home.	Students can review lectures and remember the information better	Students might not attend their classes if they can listen at home
School documents and student information are stored in the cloud.	Easy access from any device Makes teachers' record keeping more effective and standardized	Various security risks Possibility of identity theft Teachers have to learn how to use the system

Exercises 2–5 page 222

Answers will vary.

UNL☾CK TEACHER DEVELOPMENT

BE REFLECTIVE

Think about the following questions:

➔ Was there any part of this lesson which you think did not go as well as expected? Analyze the reason why this might have happened.

➔ Did you have a good overall level of understanding of the topic? Could you have done anything more to prepare?

BE COLLABORATIVE

Your development is more meaningful when it is shared. See page 14 for ideas on how to peer-collaborate. Why not share the ideas you generated in the *Be ready* section, and their outcome?

GRAMMAR FOR WRITING

Learning objectives

- Use parenthetical phrases to add information in sentences about education technology
- Use semicolons correctly to avoid run-on sentences

Exercise 1 page 223

Answers will vary. Possible answers:

1 Communication devices (smartphones, tablets, etc.) aid the learning of foreign languages.

2 Smartphones – which are an amazing piece of technology – are now affordable to many students.

3 The app industry, which is ever growing, has expanded into the domain of education.

4 In the past – before the internet – students had to rely on their school libraries to get information.

5 Mitra, an expert in the field of cloud computing and education, suggests that all future education will happen outside the classroom.

6 Opponents of the use of new technology – specifically smartphone apps – maintain that it distracts children from learning.

Exercise 2 page 224

Answers will vary. Possible answers:

1 Enabling students to manipulate 3-D objects in class, which is beneficial to subject knowledge retention, is one of the aims of educational technology developers.

2 Many students, especially those who are motivated, use mobile devices to learn English outside the classroom.

3 Technophobes – whose attitude I find difficult to understand – will never be convinced that using technology to learn is more engaging than traditional methods.

4 Attention tunnelling, the condition in which a person is too focused on one stimulus, may be a potential drawback until the novelty diminishes.

5 AR content (such as tourist information) can be viewed through a number of different devices.

Exercise 3 page 225

Answers will vary. Possible answers:

1 ✗ Scientists speculate that all future learning will happen in the cloud; **students and teachers will no longer be required** to meet in one place.

2 ✗ 3-D printers can be expensive for some schools; **thus,** the government should fund the purchase of 3-D printers in all schools.

3 ✗ With AR **apps,** students can see exotic animals in **3-D;** they can touch a 3-D puma or a jaguar projected in front of them.

4 ✓

5 ✗ The use of technology in the classroom will doubtless improve learning outcomes. However, not all students can afford to buy expensive smartphones or tablets.

ACADEMIC WRITING SKILLS

Learning objective

- Revise a variety of types of informal language in sentences, using an appropriate academic style

Exercise 1 page 226

1 things   2 I'm gonna   3 It's; wonderful; lots of; isn't   4 kids   5 It's; kind of; helps you learn   6 How come; we; don't   7 I think; it's OK; everybody; !   8 I can't imagine; !

Exercise 2 page 227

Answers will vary. Possible answers:

1 One issue with technology is that it can be difficult to use.   2 This essay outlines some of the disadvantages of using cloud computing.   3 It is an inexpensive and versatile educational aid with numerous useful applications.   4 It helps schoolchildren learn Science in a meaningful way.   5 It is a type of app that assists in the acquisition of new vocabulary.   6 What could be the reason that it is not used in all schools?   7 Its use appears to be beneficial and is recommended for schools.   8 It is difficult to imagine what life would be like without this technology.

WRITING TASK

Learning objectives

- Plan and draft an essay arguing for the use of an emerging technology in an educational context
- Review and revise the content and structure of your essay
- Review and revise the use of language in your essay

Exercises 1–9 pages 227–229

Answers will vary.

RESEARCH PROJECT

Give an oral history about technology in past generations.

Students do an oral history project, working in groups. Each group chooses a mature new technology, e.g. smartphones, ATMs. They will do a similar analysis of its features and advantages to the one they did for their writing task. This time, however, they interview older members of their community (e.g. parents, teachers) to find out how this task was accomplished prior to the technology (e.g. withdrawing cash, paying for purchases) and, if possible, their attitude to the newer technology.

CLASSROOM APP

Exercise 1

Answers will vary.

Exercise 2

1 immersive   **2** projections   **3** simultaneous
4 embraced   **5** novelty   **6** numerous   **7** advocate
8 supplement

Exercise 3

Answers will vary.

Exercise 4

1 maintain   **2** suggested   **3** acknowledge   **4** suggests
5 conclude   **6** claim

Exercise 5

1 that   **2** who   **3** when   **4** that   **5** they

Exercise 6

1 Not Academic   **2** Not Academic   **3** Academic
4 Not Academic   **5** Not Academic   **6** Academic
7 Academic

UNIT OBJECTIVES

Watch and listen	Watch and understand a video about languages in Ireland.
Reading skill	Use background knowledge to annotate a text.
Critical thinking	Evaluate and synthesize arguments.
Grammar	Hedge predictions.
Academic writing skills	Avoid overgeneralizations; refute counter-arguments.
Writing task	Write a pros and cons essay.
♻ Teacher development	Help your students become better at **evaluating and synthesizing arguments**.

UNLOCK YOUR KNOWLEDGE

Background note

The photo shows a student in front of a whiteboard, learning the grammar of a foreign language. Recent estimates show that there are over 1.5 billion speakers of English around the world. While English is currently a global language, other languages such as Mandarin Chinese and Spanish are also widely spoken. There are over a billion speakers of some form of Chinese and over 400 million speakers of Spanish. Other languages such as Hindi, Arabic and Russian have large numbers of speakers but are not as widely spread as English. Hindi is spoken as a first or second language by over 800 million people. Arabic is used by over 420 million people and Russian by 166 million people. Knowing more than one language is useful for travelling and adds a useful skill to your CV. However, it can also improve your memory, multitasking and problem-solving skills, help your decision-making and perception skills, and reduce your chances of getting Alzheimer's disease and dementia in old age.

Lead-in

Play a language game. Say a sentence in 'Pig Latin', explaining that it is a language game that children play in English:

Odaytay eway illway eadray boutay anguagelay.
(Today we will read about language.)

See if students can figure out the transformation rule. (Put the first sound of each word at the end, followed by the /eɪ/ sound.) Ask about any language games they played as children. Have them explain the rules.

page 231
Answers will vary.

WATCH AND LISTEN

Learning objectives

- Listen and identify the main ideas in a video about the Irish language
- Listen for detailed information
- Make inferences about the meaning of expressions and information presented in the video
- Practise talking about languages that are dying and endangered

Exercises 1–2 page 232
Answers will vary.

Exercise 3 page 232

1 T   2 F; They speak both English and Irish.
3 F; The children at the local school think of themselves as Irish speakers first.

Exercise 4 page 233

1 They banned the teaching of Irish in schools.
2 the Potato Famine, which killed over a million Irish people
3 They teach Irish to help revive it.
4 its remoteness
5 text each other; use Facebook and social media
6 talk to friends and other people

Exercise 5 page 233

Answers will vary. Possible answers:

1 The British government tried to destroy Irish identity, by destroying its language, literature and other cultural and linguistic artefacts.   2 Because in the past the British tried to suppress Irish language and culture, but the golfers don't show resentment towards the British presenter, and speak English to him.

Exercise 6 page 233

Answers will vary. Possible answers:

1 attempts to suppress and eventually kill a language
2 He's referring to the other parts of Ireland that also suffered both English oppression and the Potato Famine.
3 By teaching it in schools, which implies that it will survive better in remote areas.
4 He means that English is a global language and its knowledge is often essential to success in the modern world.

Exercise 7 page 233

Answers will vary.

READING 1

Learning objectives

- Understand key vocabulary for loanwords in languages – *be derived from, commonly, dialect*
- Read and complete notes in outline form with main ideas; detail examples from an essay about loanwords
- Read and annotate an article with your own background knowledge of the topics
- Make inferences about the ideas and information in an article about loanwords
- Relate personal experience of languages to the topics of vocabulary and loanwords and give opinions

Lead-in

Ask students what English words they regularly use when they are speaking their native language. Make a list on the board. Ask them to see if the words on the list have anything in common.

Exercise 1 page 234

1 it follows that **2** Commodities **3** are derived from
4 commonly **5** dialects **6** incorporated **7** conquered
8 terminology

Exercises 2–3 page 234

a espresso **b** beef **c** ketchup **d** saffron **e** tempura

Exercises 4–5 page 236

I. Loanwords def. words from one language that are incorporated into another language
- e.g. *café, kindergarten, safari*

II. Loanwords incorporated in different ways
- keep spell. and meaning, e.g. *café*
- change pron. and/or spell., e.g. *sugar*
- change meaning, e.g. *ketchup, tycoon*

III. Sources of loanwords
- **a)** geographical and political domination:
  - *liberty, justice, government* from French
  - *chimpanzee, mamba* from African languages
  - *jungle, bungalow* from Hindi
- **b)** historical events
  - *guerrilla* – during a period of struggle between the Spanish and Napoleon's troops
  - *blitzkrieg* and *kamikaze* during WWII
  - *cosmonaut* and *sputnik* during the space race
- **c)** trade and travel
  - *saffron, cotton, coffee, orange, lemon* were sold by Arab traders
  - *chocolate, tomato* from Nahuatl/Spanish
- **d)** academia lingua franca – means common language
  - scien., tech., medical and legal terminology from Latin as lingua franca
- **e)** globalization, immigration and low-cost travel
  - unprecedented level of linguistic and cultural exchange, e.g. Japanese words: *sushi, tsunami, tempura* and *anime*
  - surge of foreign food names in English, e.g. Italian *latte, espresso*. Cantonese *chow, wok, dim sum*

Optional activity

Tell students to use the strategies they have learnt to work out the meaning of the following words:

- *static* (para. 1) *condiment* (para. 2)
- *domination* (para. 3) *unprecedented* (para. 7)

If there are not enough clues, tell them to guess. For example, there are not enough clues to guess the exact meaning of *unprecedented*, but they could guess something like *very large*, which, while incorrect, is a well-reasoned guess that would not hinder comprehension.

Exercise 6 page 237

Answers will vary.

Exercise 7 page 237

Answers will vary. Possible answers:

1 There is some similarity: in Japanese it was used to refer to a powerful ruler and in modern English it is used to refer to a powerful businessperson; both uses refer to being powerful.

2 It is more important for the colonized people to learn the words of their rulers than for the rulers to learn the language of the people they have conquered.

3 A lot of people can afford to travel to exotic locations and learn about their culture.

4 The widespread popularity of anime (Japanese cartoons) around the world. The fact that Japanese cartoons are stylistically different from those of the US or the UK means a new word is needed and the original Japanese has filled that gap.

5 It may be because of the international chain coffee shops, such as Starbucks or Costa, that use the same coffee names around the world. It may be because of the fact that there are fashions in coffee and the name is very particular to that style of coffee – so the coffee and the word spread together.

Exercise 8 page 237

Answers will vary.

READING 2

Learning objectives

- Understand key vocabulary for linguistic purism – *stance, endorse, distort*
- Read and identify the main ideas an essay about linguistic purism
- Read and understand details
- Read and understand the meaning of unfamiliar phrases from their context
- Make inferences about the implications of the ideas in an essay about linguistic purism
- Synthesize ideas from an essay about loanwords and an essay about linguistic purism in a discussion

Lead-in

Show students a picture of a computer mouse. Ask what it is called in their language. Note that in many languages, it is the same or similar to the English word. Ask students to speculate about the reasons for these different strategies for borrowing words. Ask for similar words from English such as *hamburger* or *football*. Are they used in the students' first language?

Exercise 1 page 238

a enforce   **b** equivalent   **c** endorse   **d** stance   **e** futile
f distort   **g** misguided   **h** dilution

Exercise 2 page 239

Answers will vary.

Exercise 3 page 239

a 5   **b** 4   **c** –   **d** 2   **e** 1   **f** –   **g** 6   **h** 3

Optional activity

👤 Tell students to annotate Reading 2. Remind them to use their background knowledge (perhaps drawing on the discussion from the Lead-in activity).

Exercise 4 page 239

1 F; opinion is split on this issue.   **2** T   **3** DNS; The text mentions cognitive processes, but not long-term memory.
4 F; there are no accepted equivalents for these terms.
5 F; it is likely that they will continue to use the English term.
6 T   **7** F; it distorts the cultural and linguistic heritage.   **8** T

Exercise 5 page 241

1 the process of making culture less strong and pure
2 a quality that makes people feel good or right
3 trying to make something difficult or impossible
4 very desirable   **5** a time period when people are taking and using ideas, words, and practices from other cultures more quickly and freely than before

Exercises 6–7 page 241

Answers will vary.

LANGUAGE DEVELOPMENT

Learning objectives

- Understand the meaning of a range of Latin prefixes – *inter-, pre-, post-*
- Use a range of words with Latin prefixes in sentences about language learning results – *disproportionate, interpretation, presume*
- Use a range of linking expressions to introduce supporting examples in sentences about global languages – *that is, for example, as illustrated by*
- Use linking expressions with accurate punctuation to introduce supporting examples in sentences about global languages – *Romance languages, such as French, Italian and Spanish, are rooted in Latin. Language purists often oppose the use of global languages, in particular English.*

Exercise 1 page 242

1 postpone   **2** coexist   **3** displace   **4** precede
5 co-worker   **6** disproportionate   **7** intervene
8 preliminary

Exercise 2 page 242

1 interaction   **2** interface   **3** cofounder   **4** predict
5 discouraged   **6** Intercontinental

Optional activity

👤👥 Ask students to think of other words they know with these prefixes. Explain that although words may have the same prefix the stress on the word sometimes changes, depending on the sound at the beginning of the root word.

Exercise 3 page 243

1 Spanish, for example, replaced many local languages in South America. **2** Languages such as Spanish and Portuguese are used in countries that were once colonies. **3** Romance languages, such as French, Italian and Spanish, are rooted in Latin. **4** French, for instance, is used as a lingua franca in different African countries. **5** Language purists often oppose the use of global languages, in particular English.

Exercise 4 page 243

Answers will vary.

CRITICAL THINKING

Learning objectives

- Understand a range of arguments about English-medium university instruction and explain your own position in relation to each
- Analyze and evaluate the strength of different arguments for and against English-medium university instruction
- Analyze and collect information relating to the merits and drawbacks of English-medium university instruction in a country of interest
- Choose a position and evaluate and improve your arguments regarding English-medium university instruction in a country of interest

UNLOCK TEACHER DEVELOPMENT

BE INFORMED

→ **Evaluating and synthesizing arguments** is an important skill for students because: (1) Understanding different types of sources and how they can work together is necessary when constructing arguments; (2) Evaluating the arguments in a text can help you understand their weaknesses, and therefore how to argue against them; (3) A good academic argument considers every issue from a 360-degree perspective.

BE CONFIDENT

→ Develop this skill for yourself by doing the following activity:

Think about the following types of source. What do you think are the advantages / disadvantages of each?

- A blog by a student
- A blog by a professor
- Government statistics
- Data from a private company
- An expert's objective view
- A universally agreed scientific fact
- An opinion piece in a newspaper

Lead-in

Give students a minute to read the writing task. Tell them to brainstorm their own experience in English-medium classes. Have there been benefits? Major challenges? Tell them to keep their brainstorming notes for later, when they begin to write their essay.

UNLOCK TEACHER DEVELOPMENT

BE READY

Look at the Critical Thinking section in the Student's Book on pages 244–246.

→ Which elements of the lesson do you think your students will find easiest / most difficult / most useful? Why?

→ Are your answers true for all students in your class?

→ How can you adapt your teaching or the material to meet your students' needs?

BE FLEXIBLE

Exercise 6 could be done digitally, e.g. with the students themselves creating an online group, and posting their findings there. This would be a quick, easy and modern way of sharing their findings.

Exercise 1 page 245

Zhang Liu, China: For: Going to an English-medium university really gave me the edge against the competition. / My English proficiency gives me mobility in the job market that I would never have without it.

Anonymous student: Against: the problem is that most students at my university don't know English well enough to understand the material in their classes. / The professors know we are struggling so they try to make the material easier, but that really lowers the standard of our education. / [And] some of our professors – they don't speak English that well either, so they just read their lectures. It's so boring.

Anton, a postgraduate student from Moscow: For: It makes my life much easier and helps me communicate with other students. / [T]he vast majority of cutting-edge research is published in English.

Dr Uzun, President of a private Turkish university: For: we can attract the best students and professors from all over the world / up-to-date materials and cutting-edge technology / we can charge substantial tuition

Sonia, university student: Against: has created a two-tiered (unfair) educational system

Dr Khan, a lecturer in Culture and Communication:

For: I don't think it's a real issue for most of our students; it's part of a global shift. / This trend has a very positive impact on intercultural exchange and cultural relations.

Exercises 2–5 page 246

Answers will vary.

UNL⊘CK TEACHER DEVELOPMENT

BE REFLECTIVE

Think about the following points:

→ Reflect on what your own response would be on this issue. This is an opportunity to be critical about your own position, as somebody who has a vested interest in the status of English as a global language.

→ Think about your lesson. Regardless of how you answered above, think about whether any part of it would have been more effective if you had been able to use the students' first language(s). What implications does this have for language teaching?

BE COLLABORATIVE

Your development is more meaningful when it is shared. See page 14 for ideas on how to peer-collaborate. Why not share your approach in the *Be flexible* section, and its outcome?

GRAMMAR FOR WRITING

Learning objective

- Use hedging language to make predictions more cautious in sentences about the future of languages and language education – *Accepting English terminology may lead to cultural dilution. We should see a more liberal attitude towards language change in coming generations.*

Exercise 1 page 247

Answers will vary. Possible answers:

1 Chinese may well be the next global language.
2 Greek is highly unlikely to become a new lingua franca.
3 The global domination of one language could result in the disappearance of many local languages.
4 Students should learn English if it is the medium of instruction.
5 In the future, young people may not want to learn foreign languages other than English.
6 Schools might stop teaching local languages altogether and focus on English only.

Be flexible

👤👥 Ask students to write three appropriately hedged predictions about the use of English/EMI in their countries. For an **extra challenge**, tell students to work in pairs. One student makes a prediction. The second student reframes it as a more modest, hedged prediction.

ACADEMIC WRITING SKILLS

Learning objectives

- Rewrite sentences using more specific noun phrases to modify claims and avoid overgeneralizations
- Use a range of phrases to refute ideas in sentences about language learning

Exercise 1 page 248

Answers will vary. Possible answers:

1 Some French people do not like to speak English in everyday situations.   2 A proportion of English people are not very good at foreign languages.   3 Not a lot of people can learn a new language in a month.
4 A number of teachers encourage their students to study English outside the classroom.   5 In the colonial era, the English adopted some of the words the locals used for animals that were new to the colonizers.
6 Globalization may be one of the causes of language extinction.

Exercise 2 page 248

Answers will vary.

Exercise 3 page 249

Answers will vary. Possible answers:

1 It is not true that most loanwords in English come from Spanish. In fact, the majority of loanwords are from French.

2 Some people may say that studying English takes valuable time from other areas of study, but a knowledge of English is valuable in the job market and very much worth the time it takes to develop it.

3 It cannot be argued that English-medium instruction provides an equal opportunity to all. Those who already know English are the ones who benefit the most.

4 It is simply untrue that these words come from Latin. Their origin is Arabic.

5 While it may be true that the use of English words will lead to the loss of some of our own words, our culture is not so weak that a few foreign words can destroy it. We have been borrowing words for centuries and our culture remains vibrant and strong.

WRITING TASK

Learning objectives

- Plan and draft an essay describing the pros and cons of English-medium university education in a particular country
- Review and revise the content and structure of your essay
- Review and revise the use of language in your essay

Exercises 1–11 pages 250–252

Answers will vary.

RESEARCH PROJECT

Write a case study about English-medium instruction.

Do research on a country that has a considerable number of universities that use English-medium instruction. What justification has been offered by education or government offices for this trend? How successful have students been, both in their acquisition of English and in their content areas? How has success been measured? Is it likely that the EMI trend will continue in this country? Why? / Why not?

Students can write up their case study individually, or join with others, if they have chosen the same country, to prepare a group one. Either way, their findings should be shared with the rest of the class.

CLASSROOM APP

Exercise 1
Answers will vary.

Exercise 2
1 derived   **2** dialects   **3** commonly   **4** follows
5 commodity   **6** equivalent   **7** incorporates   **8** dilution

Exercise 3
Answers will vary.

Exercise 4
1 cooperation   **2** interpretations   **3** postwar
4 presumed   **5** collaborated

Exercise 5
1 many factors, such as
2 , as demonstrated by
3 Languages such as Korean and Japanese
4 languages, namely
5 group, that is, 10–12 students
6 For example,
7 learning environment, for instance, living in a country

Exercise 6
1 Overgeneralized   **2** Not overgeneralized
3 Not overgeneralized   **4** Overgeneralized
5 Not overgeneralized   **6** Not overgeneralized

ACKNOWLEDGEMENTS

The authors and publishers acknowledge the following sources of copyright material and are grateful for the permissions granted. While every effort has been made, it has not always been possible to identify the sources of all the material used, or to trace all copyright holders. If any omissions are brought to our notice, we will be happy to include the appropriate acknowledgements on reprinting and in the next update to the digital edition, as applicable.

Photos

All images are sourced from Getty Images.

pp. 8–9: mikimad/DigitalVision Vectors; p. 278: Eric Batashev/EyeEm, toxawww/iStock/Getty Images Plus, rpellicer/iStock/Getty Images Plus, Amanda siworae Pothography/Moment, Mats Silvan/Moment, Alistair Berg/DigitalVision, Kealan Biebesheimer/EyeEm, dkidpix/iStock/Getty Images; p 294: metamorworks/iStock/Getty Images Plus; InStock/Image Source; Phillip Waterman/Cultura; ABK/Corbis; scyther5/iStock/Getty Images Plus; Jose Luis Pelaez Inc/DigitalVision; Klaus Vedfelt/DigitalVision; Picavet/Photolibrary; pp. 300–301: Andrew Merry/Moment; Tom Merton/OJO Images; nonnie192/iStock/Getty Images Plus; Flashpop/Stone; Paul Felix/Photolibrary; B&M Noskowski/E+.

Front cover photography by ispyfriend/E+.

Typeset by Q2A Media Services Pvt. Ltd.

The answers below apply to the **Unlock Teacher Development activities** at the beginning of this manual:

INTRODUCTION TO CRITICAL THINKING

Be confident page 11

1 d **2** c **3** a **4** e **5** b **6** f

Be ready page 11

lower-order thinking skills:
What facts can you find?
Who?
Do you know ...?
Where?
Name ...
List ...
How many?
When?
What?

higher-order thinking skills:
Can you identify...?
Why?
Why might ...?
How would you ...?
What alternative ...?
Why do you think ...?
What criteria ...?

INTRODUCTION TO MIXED-ABILITY TEACHING

Be confident page 13

1 Age **2** Proficiency **3** Cultural background
4 Motivation **5** Aptitude **6** Cultural background

Be ready page 13

Answers will vary.